Praise for *About Face 2.0*

"By rigorously specifying the external design, Goal-Directed Design lets programmers focus their energies on what they do best—designing software internals to implement the design specification. Goal-Directed Design allows user experience designers to create external design specifications that programmers can actually use."

— Pete McBreen, author, *Software Craftsmanship*

"*About Face 2.0* builds on the strengths of Alan Cooper's venerated classic. Wide-ranging, informative, and insightful, this book defines the state of interaction design today."

— Jesse James Garrett, author, *The Elements of User Experience*

"Alan Cooper and Robert Reimann have a unique skill for crystallizing concepts we're all struggling with. *About Face 2.0* is full of these insights; this updated release will have readers saying, 'Yes, that's it!' once again."

— James Fawcette, founder Visual Studio Magazine and VSLive! Conferences

"In his masterful *The Inmates are Running the Asylum*, Alan Cooper threw down the gauntlet to the software industry. He decried the flagrant shortcomings in how today's software works and how it is designed. In *About Face 2.0*, Alan Cooper and Robert Reimann show how it can be done better. Their thorough and systematic discussion of design methods and interaction principles offers the best guide around for designers pursuing the quest for digital products that truly work for people."

— Terry Winograd, Professor of Computer Science, Stanford University and editor, *Bringing Design to Software*

"This update to *About Face* is especially timely for anyone interested in creating and using personas. Personas are the most compelling design tool I've seen for taking the abstract concept of "the user" and turning it into a concrete tool for design and business communication. In *About Face 2.0*, the developers of this powerful practice show you how it's done."

— Harley Manning, Research Director, Forrester Research

About Face 2.0

The Essentials of Interaction Design

Alan Cooper and Robert Reimann

Wiley Publishing, Inc.

About Face 2.0: The Essentials of Interaction Design

Published by
Wiley Publishing, Inc.
10475 Crosspoint Boulevard
Indianapolis, IN 46256
www.wiley.com

Published by Wiley Publishing, Inc., Indianapolis, Indiana
Published simultaneously in Canada

Library of Congress Control Number: 2002114842
ISBN: 0-7645-2641-3

Manufactured in the United States of America

10 9 8 7 6 5

1B/RQ/QT/QT/IN

For Sue, still my best friend after 22 years.

For Julie, for your love, kindness, and constant inspiration.

For Cooperistas past, present, and future;
and for those visionary practitioners who
have helped create a new design profession.

Credits

EXECUTIVE EDITOR
Chris Webb

PROJECT EDITOR
Sara Shlaer

COPY EDITOR
Mary Lagu

EDITORIAL MANAGER
Mary Beth Wakefield

VICE PRESIDENT & EXECUTIVE GROUP PUBLISHER
Richard Swadley

VICE PRESIDENT AND EXECUTIVE PUBLISHER
Bob Ipsen

VICE PRESIDENT AND PUBLISHER
Joseph B. Wikert

EXECUTIVE EDITORIAL DIRECTOR
Mary Bednarek

PROJECT COORDINATOR
Nancee Reeves

GRAPHICS AND PRODUCTION SPECIALISTS
Carrie Foster, Heather Pope

QUALITY CONTROL TECHNICIANS
Laura Albert, John Tyler Connoley,
Charles Spencer

PROOFREADING AND INDEXING
TECHBOOKS Production Services

COVER ILLUSTRATION
Anthony Bunyan

About the Authors

Alan Cooper is a pioneering software inventor, programmer, designer and theorist. He is credited with having produced "probably the first serious business software for microcomputers" and is well known as the "Father of Visual Basic". For the last ten years his software design consulting company, Cooper, has helped many companies invent new products and improve the behavior of their technology. At Cooper, Alan led the development of a new methodology for creating successful software that he calls the Goal-Directed process. Part of that effort was the invention of personas, a practice that has been widely adopted since he first published the technique in his second book, *The Inmates Are Running the Asylum*, in 1998. Cooper is also a well known writer, speaker and enthusiast for humanizing technology.

Robert Reimann has spent the past 15 years pushing the boundaries of digital products as a designer, writer, lecturer, and consultant. He has led dozens of interaction design projects in domains including e-commerce, portals, desktop productivity, authoring environments, medical and scientific instrumentation, wireless, and handheld devices for startups and Fortune 500 clients alike. Joining Cooper in 1996, Reimann led the development and refinement of many Goal-Directed Design methods described in *About Face 2.0*. He has lectured on these methods at major universities and to international industry audiences. He is a member of the advisory board of the UC Berkeley Institute of Design.

Acknowledgments

The authors express their deepest gratitude to the following individuals, without whom this new edition of *About Face* would not have been possible: Sue Cooper, CEO of Cooper, who saw the time was right for a new edition; Chris Webb at Wiley, who shared that vision; Pat Fleck, who juggled the finances to get the project underway; Sara Shlaer, our Project Editor, and Mary Lagu, our Copy Editor at Wiley, who each helped us sharpen our words and clarify our thoughts, and were each a pleasure to work with from start to finish.

We would also like to thank the following colleagues and Cooper designers for their contributions to this volume, for which the authors are greatly indebted: Kim Goodwin who over the last five years has collaborated with the authors, co-developing, and refining many of the concepts and processes detailed in Part I; Hugh Dubberly, for his help in developing the principles at the end of Chapter 7 and for his assistance in clarifying the Goal-Directed process with several beautiful diagrams found in Chapter 1; Gretchen Anderson, Elaine Brechin, and Doug LeMoine for their contributions on user and market research in Chapter 4; Ernest Kinsolving and Joerg Beringer at SAP for their contributions on the posture of Web portals in Chapter 8; Wayne Greenwood for his contributions on mapping controls in Chapter 11; Nate Fortin for his contributions on visual branding and visual interaction design in Chapter 19; Jonathan Korman for his contributions to the Afterword, which include ideas from his forthcoming book, *Best to Market*; Dave Cronin for his many thoughts on the topics of kiosk and Web design; and Chris Weeldreyer for his insights into the design of embedded systems. We would also like to thank Elizabeth Bacon, Steve Calde, John Dunning, Kim Goodwin, Wayne Greenwood, Lane Halley, Berm Lee, Ryan Olshavsky, Angela Quail, and Chris Weeldreyer for their contributions to the Cooper designs and illustrations featured in this volume.

We are also grateful to clients David West at Shared Healthcare Systems and Mike Kay and Bill Chang at Fujitsu Softek for granting us permission to use examples from the Cooper design projects featured in this book. We wish also to thank the many other clients who have had the vision and the foresight to work with us and support us in their organizations.

Finally, we would also like to acknowledge the following authors and industry colleagues who have influenced or clarified our thinking over the years: Christopher Alexander, Edward Tufte, Kevin Mullet, Victor Papanek, Donald Norman, Larry Constantine, Challis Hodge, Shelley Evenson, Clifford Nass, Byron Reeves, Stephen Pinker, and Terry Swack.

Foreword

In this book, authors Alan Cooper and Robert Reimann explore an area of design often ignored by traditional product designers and usability professionals: designing the behavior of complex systems — in particular, the behavior of increasingly pervasive, and sometimes all but invisible, software-enabled technology. Cooper and Reimann believe that understanding humans, not just technology, is the key to making these interactive systems both powerful and pleasurable to use.

Alan Cooper is not your typical designer — he's a programmer, inventor, strategist, *and* a card-carrying member of the American Institute of Graphic Arts (AIGA) and ACM SIGCHI. He's accomplished in each of these worlds and has something important to say to programmers, designers, product planners, and usability professionals alike.

Cooper has been designing software since the arrival of personal computers more than 25 years ago. Few people have thought as long and deeply about the design of software interfaces. His conclusion: Most software today is barely fit for human use — "weak and oppressive" are two of his more printable characterizations of digital products.

What is the problem?

It is this: Software does not reveal itself through external form — something mechanical devices tend to do. In software, the cost of adding one more new feature is almost nothing, whereas adding features to mechanical devices almost always increases their costs. Software lacks sufficient negative feedback to limit its complexity. The result is pure Rube Goldberg: digital products with feature piled upon feature. The trouble is that each incremental feature makes a product *more* difficult to use. That leaves us with products that are increasingly hard to use — and with growing frustration as we try to use them.

The problem grows as microprocessors become increasingly powerful, making computing less and less expensive. As a result, computers are built into more and more products. And where there are computers, there must also be software. And where there is software, very often, there is user interaction. Already, it's difficult to find new cars, appliances, or consumer electronics that do not require users to interact with software. We are slowly being suffocated by software that, at best, doesn't meet our needs and that, at worst, presents a danger to our well-being.

The authors of this book blame the problem on the technology-driven nature of the software development process. In *About Face 2.0*, Cooper and Reimann advocate exactly the opposite approach: a people-driven process in which "meeting the goals of the user comes first, last, and in between," a process of *Goal-Directed Design*.

In the traditional software development process, lots of people inside a company — and often customers as well — ask for new features. In many companies, the resulting list of features often becomes the *de facto* product plan. Programmers make this approach worse by picking or negotiating their way through the list, often trading development time for features. In such a process, it is difficult to know when a product is complete, let alone good.

The heart of the problem, Cooper and Reimann conclude, is that the people responsible for developing software products don't know precisely what constitutes a good product, or even the right product. It follows that they also do not know what processes lead to a successful product. In short, they are operating by trial and error, with outcomes like customer satisfaction achieved by little more than blind luck.

Cooper and Reimann advocate six significant changes to conventional methods of software development in the Goal-Directed Design methods they lay out in this book:

✓ **Design first; program second** (The old way: Begin programming as soon as possible — applying design at the end if at all; or, in more progressive environments, program and design concurrently.)

✓ **Separate responsibility for design from responsibility for programming** (The old way: Programmers made significant decisions about how users interact with the software — often while in the middle of programming, a clear conflict of interest.)

✓ **Focus on meeting user goals** (The old way: Analyze users' tasks without considering their goals, *why* they perform tasks.)

✓ **Define specific, archetypal users (personas) for your product based on careful observation of actual and potential users** (The old way: Managers and programmers talked about "the end user" without being specific — allowing the term *user* to stretch to fit almost any situation.)

✓ **Use personas as the main characters in scenarios: a primary tool in defining the function, behavior, and form of interactive products** (The old way: Use marketing checklists to define product function, or let programmers decide what they think should be built.)

✓ **Follow principles of design for behavior** (The old way: Rely on principles of form alone, guess the rest, and then, iterate bad interactions through user testing until most of the worst problems have been patched.)

This book is a primer for the design of digital-product behavior, written by pre-eminent authorities in the trenches of interaction design and based on 10 years experience in the design consulting world and more than 25 years in the computer industry. It is a book that no product planner, interface designer, usability professional, or programmer will want to be without — a guide for making our software and our world better. We should heed its authors' advice.

Hugh Dubberly

February, 2003

Hugh Dubberly is a principal in Dubberly Design Office, which focuses on communications systems, interaction design, and information design. At Apple Computer in the mid '80s and early '90s, Hugh managed cross-functional design teams and went on to manage creative services and corporate identity for the entire company. While at Apple, he served at Art Center College of Design in Pasadena as the first and founding chairman of the computer graphics department. He later moved to Netscape and became Vice President of Design. Hugh has also taught classes in the Graphic Design Department at San Jose State University, at the Institute of Design at IIT, and in the Computer Science Department at Stanford University.

Contents at a Glance

Chapter 19   Designing Look and Feel 225
Chapter 20   Metaphors, Idioms, and Affordances 247

Section Three   Interaction Details

Part V   Mice and Manipulation

Chapter 21   Direct Manipulation and Pointing Devices 263
Chapter 22   Selection 281
Chapter 23   Drag and Drop 289
Chapter 24   Manipulating Controls, Objects, and Connections ... 303

Part VI   Controls and Their Behaviors

Chapter 25   Window Behaviors 321
Chapter 26   Using Controls 337
Chapter 27   Menus: The Pedagogic Vector 363
Chapter 28   Using Menus 371
Chapter 29   Using Toolbars and ToolTips 381
Chapter 30   Using Dialogs 393
Chapter 31   Dialog Etiquette 409
Chapter 32   Creating Better Controls 425

Part VII   Communicating with Users

Chapter 33   Eliminating Errors 435
Chapter 34   Notifying and Confirming 445
Chapter 35   Other Communication with Users 457
Chapter 36   The Installation Process 465

Part VIII   Designing Beyond the Desktop

Chapter 37   Designing for the Web 477
Chapter 38   Designing for Embedded Systems 489

              Afterword: Dealing with the Inmates 501

              Appendix A: Axioms 507

              Appendix B: Design Tips 511

              Appendix C: Bibliography 515

              Index 519

Contents

Section One   Know Thy User

Part I   Bridging the Gap

Section Two   Designing Behavior and Form

Part II   Achieving Goals and Removing Barriers

Part IV   **Applying Visual Design Principles**

Chapter 20
Metaphors, Idioms, and Affordances 247

Section Three Interaction Details

Part V   Mice and Manipulation

Chapter 21
Direct Manipulation and Pointing Devices 263

Part VII	**Communicating with Users**

Introduction to the Second Edition

This book is intended to provide you with effective and practical tools for designing user interfaces. These tools come in two distinct varieties: tactical and strategic. Tactical tools are hints and tips about using and creating user interface idioms, like dialog boxes and pushbuttons. Strategic tools are ways to think about user interface idioms — in other words, the ways in which the user and the idiom interact.

Although books are available that deal with either strategic or tactical principles, our goal has been to create a book that weaves the two together. While helping you design more attractive and effective dialog boxes, this book will simultaneously help you understand how the user comprehends and interacts with your software.

Integrating the strategic and tactical approaches is the key to designing effective user interactions and interfaces. For example, there is no such thing as an objectively good dialog box — the quality depends on the situation: who the user is and what his background and goals are. Merely applying a set of tactical dictums makes user interface *creation* easier, but it doesn't make the end result *better*. Deep thoughts about how users *should* interact with your system won't improve the software, either. What *does* work is maintaining a strategic sensitivity for how users *actually* interact with specific software and having at your command a tactical toolbox to apply in any particular situation. This book both deepens your understanding of users and teaches you how to translate that understanding into design concepts.

Who Should Read This Book

When *About Face* was first published in August 1995, the landscape of interface design was a frontier wilderness. A small cadre of people brave enough to hold the title User Interface Designer operated under the shadow of software engineering, rather like the tiny, quick-witted mammals that scrambled under the shadows of hulking tyrannosaurs. Software design, as the first edition of *About Face* referred to it, was ill understood and ill appreciated; and, when it was practiced at all, programmers usually practiced it. A handful of uneasy documenters, trainers, and technical support people, along with a rising number of people from another nascent field — usability practitioners — realized that something needed to change.

The amazing growth and popularity of the Web drove that change, seemingly overnight. Suddenly, ease of use was a term on everyone's lips. Traditional design professionals, who had dabbled in digital product design during the short-lived popularity of multimedia in the early nineties, leapt to the Web en masse. Seemingly new design titles sprung up like weeds: information designer, information architect, user experience strategist, and interaction designer. For the first time ever, C-level corporate positions existed whose sole focus was creating user-centered products: the Chief Experience Officer. Major universities scrambled to offer programs to train designers in these disciplines. Meanwhile, usability and human factors practitioners have also risen in stature and are now recognized leaders in the push for better-designed products.

Although the Web knocked interface technology back by more than a decade, it inarguably placed user requirements on the radar of the corporate world for good. The aftermath of the dot-com bust aside, the authors firmly believe that visibility and concern about users and their needs will only become more pronounced in the future. People are tired of new technology. Consumers are sending a clear message that what they want is *good* technology: technology they can easily use to meet their needs.

Thus, the authors are happy to say, the audience for this new edition has greatly expanded: Anyone concerned about users interacting with digital technology will gain insights from reading this book. Programmers, designers of all stripes involved with digital product design, usability professionals, and project managers will all find something useful in this volume. People who have read the first edition of *About Face* or *The Inmates Are Running The Asylum* will find new and more detailed information about design methods and principles here.

Why *Interaction* Design?

The first edition of *About Face* described a discipline called software design and equated it with another discipline called user interface design. Of these two terms, user interface design has certainly had better longevity. We still use it occasionally in this book, where it seems most appropriate.

However, it seems clear to the authors that what is discussed in this book is a discipline larger than the design of user interfaces. The word *interface* denotes a surface, and much of the design issues that this book addresses go far deeper than the surface of a CRT screen: They go right to the heart of what a digital product *is* and what it *does*.

In recent years, a number of terms have been proposed for this type of design. When corporate interest in the Web had reached its peak around 2000, a discipline called information architecture (IA) seemed like it might eventually embody the kind of design discussed here. But, even as the financial prospects of the Web have waned, IA has largely retained its narrow, Web-centric view of organizing and navigating content in pages. With the apparent decline of the new economy, the fortunes of the IA community have similarly diminished.

Another term that has recently gained some popularity is experience design. The American Institute of Graphic Artists (AIGA), in particular, has advocated the use of this term as an umbrella under which different design and usability disciplines collaborate to create digital products and systems. This idea has great appeal, but it still begs the question of what *kind* of design is really at the heart of interactive systems, a kind of design that is clearly new and different from what came before.

The idea of designing *experience* is also a bit problematic. Experience, in the authors' opinion, is the result of the *interaction* between humans and artifacts (or other living things). Experience occurs in an environmental context, and is further modulated by an internal, psychological, personal environment shaped by motivations, past experiences, temperament, and various cognitive factors.

We can't, as designers, truthfully claim to be able to design a user's *experience* of an artifact or system, but we can design the mechanisms for *interacting* with an artifact to *enhance* the user's experience of it. Because we believe that experience occurs in the interaction between the human and the artifact, we have chosen the term interaction design — first coined by Bill Moggridge and Bill Verplank in the 1980s — to denote the kind of design this book describes. You cannot design experience itself, but you can design interactive behaviors that modulate or direct experience.

Defining Interaction Design

Simply put, interaction design is the *definition and design of the behavior of artifacts, environments, and systems,* as well as the formal elements that communicate that behavior. Unlike traditional design disciplines, whose focus has historically been on form and, more recently, on content and meaning, interaction design seeks first to plan and describe how things *behave* and then, as necessary, to describe the most effective form to communicate those behaviors (see Figure 1).

Interaction design borrows theory and technique from traditional design, usability, and engineering disciplines. It is a synthesis, however—more than a sum of its parts—with its own unique methods and practices. It is also very much a *design* discipline, with a different approach than that of scientific and engineering disciplines.

In particular, interaction design is a discipline concerned with:

- ✓ Defining the form of products as they relate to their behaviors and uses
- ✓ Anticipating how the use of products will affect human relationships and understanding
- ✓ Exploring the dialogue between products, people, and contexts (physical, cultural, historical) (Reimann and Forlizzi, 2001)

Interaction design approaches the design of products with a *Goal-Directed* perspective:

- ✓ From an understanding of how and why people desire to use them
- ✓ As an advocate for the users and their goals
- ✓ As gestalts, not simply as sets of features and attributes
- ✓ By looking to the future—seeing things as they might be, not necessarily as they currently are

Because the behaviors of complex systems are often not a matter of aesthetics, but rather one of cognitive factors and logical processes, interaction design is both amenable to and greatly aided by a systematic approach.

Interaction designers need, first and foremost, to understand the goals, motivations, and expectations (the mental models) of the people for whom they hope to design. These can best be understood as narratives—logical (or emotional) progressions over time.

In response to these narratives, designed artifacts must exhibit behavioral narratives of their own that mesh successfully with those of the user. Unlike most mechanical artifacts, which have only a few simple behaviors that become obvious upon inspection, software and other digital artifacts require interaction design because of the potential complexity of their behaviors. Software is opaque to inspection, yet its possible behaviors are almost limitless.

Some designers, entrenched in the design traditions of form (visual, audible, and tactile themes, patterns, styles, and idioms), argue that interactive elements should be treated as streams of *sense data* that change over time, similar to motion pictures, and may thus be fully described by traditional design methods. This argument, however, is seriously flawed: Although the form-oriented aspects of interaction design are obviously important, they are almost useless unless they are organized by effective and appropriate behaviors. Without a logical structure and a flow that facilitate solving the practical problems of users, form-oriented interactive design is, by itself, sensual titillation of questionable value.

To put it differently, sense data means nothing without the narrative that lets us make logical sense of it. Special effects alone do not make a movie; the narrative is also essential. This is even more valid for interactions with digital products because the dialogue is not between fictional creations observed by a third party. It is, instead, a first-person exchange of what Bill Buxton (1990) has called "non-verbal natural language" between the human and the designed artifact. The anticipation and design of this dialogue — this behavior — is the essence of interaction design.

Three Dimensions of Design

Interaction design focuses on an area that traditional design disciplines do not often explore: the design of behavior.

All design affects human behavior: Architecture is about how people use spaces as much as it is about form and light. And what would be the point of a poster if no one acted on the information it presented?

However, it is only with the introduction of interactive technologies – courtesy of the computer – that the design of the behavior of artifacts, and how this behavior affects and supports human goals and desires, has become a discipline worthy of attention.

One way of making sense of the difference in focus between interaction design and more traditional design is through a historical lens. In the first half of the twentieth century, designers focused primarily on form.

Later, designers became increasingly concerned with meaning, for example, product designers and architects introduced vernacular and retro forms in the 70s. The trend continues today with retro-styled automobiles such as the PT Cruiser. Today, information designers continue the focus on meaning to include the design of usable content.

Within the last fifteen years, a growing group of designers have begun to talk about behavior: the dynamic ways that software-enabled (or complex mechanical) products interact directly with users.

These concerns (form, meaning, and behavior) are not exclusive. Interactive products must have each in some measure; software applications focus more on behavior and form, with less demand on content; Web sites and kiosks focus more on content and form, with less sophisticated behaviors.

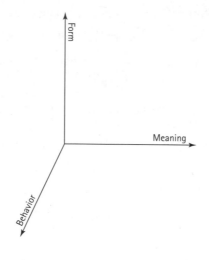

Figure 1: Three dimensions of design. Design has traditionally focused on form and, more recently, on meaning and content. The newest dimension of design is *behavior*, how complex systems interact with humans.

What This Book Is and What It Is Not

This book is a reference volume on the methods and principles of interaction design: the design of complex, user-focused behaviors of interactive systems. Section One of this book stresses design process and systematic understanding of the user. Section Two provides strategic principles and tools. Section Three delves deeper into tactical issues.

This book does *not* attempt to present a style guide or set of interface standards. In fact, you'll learn in Chapter 19 why the utility of such tools is limited and relevant only to specific circumstances. That said, the process and principles described in this book are compatible with the style guide of your choice, and it is an excellent companion volume to any of them. Style guides are good at answering *what*, but generally weak at answering *why*. This book attempts to answer those unanswered questions about the design of interactive systems.

There are four main steps when designing interactive systems: researching the domain, understanding the users and their requirements, defining the framework of a solution, and filling in the design details.

Many practitioners would include a fifth step: *validation*, the testing of the validity of that solution with users. They wouldn't be wrong. This latter step is part of a discipline widely known as *usability*.

There is a significant and ever-growing body of usability literature, but there is comparatively little in print about interaction design. This book focuses exclusively on the process and principles of interaction design, leaving instruction on the *testing* of design solutions to the many scholarly works published on the subject. This book should be a companion to any volume on usability engineering methods and practices. You will always achieve the best design results by combining the two disciplines in a harmonious relationship.

A Working Language for Interaction Design

Physical scientists develop and use terms specific to their discipline. These terms not only illuminate the specific process or object at hand, but they influence *how* we think about them. How can one scientist express to another a question, a concern, or a discovery? A technical working language is the cornerstone of every science, from the study of spiders to the behavior of printing presses.

The computer industry is no exception. We have a rich and complex language to describe the nuances of the field — words like *concurrency*, *recursion*, and *compiler*. These, however, are engineering terms. We have no such similarly rich language in the world of interaction design. This needs to change.

We've all heard discussions describing the efficiency or user-friendliness of digital artifacts and interfaces. But when someone speaks of an *efficient* user interface, is he referring to the code? To the number of controls? To the ease of programming? Ease-of-learning? Ease-of-use? Certainly, these words conjure up images in the minds of intelligent, technical people, but vague imagery is not sufficient to successfully and systematically design the interactions between humans and complex digital systems.

The lack of consistent, specific terminology in the world of interaction design frustrates the efforts of designers. Without precise terminology, we are forced to hand-wave. Without clearly differentiated terms, we accidentally put things in the wrong places, we overlook significant facts, and we inadvertently mistake the bad for the good.

To design effective digital products, we *must* have a vocabulary that accurately describes the goals we seek and the tools we use to achieve them. Interaction design will not become a true science, art, or craft until we create our own technical working language. We will not develop a *successful* practice until we develop accurate and analytical ways of thinking and talking about what we do. Not only can't we function effectively, but our credibility to the outside world—particularly to the worlds of software engineering and business—is threatened unless we can agree on terms that describe what we do, what we care about, and how to judge our relative success at achieving our goals.

Changes from the First Edition

Much in the world of interface design has changed since the first edition of About Face was published in 1995. However, much remains the same. The second edition of About Face retains what still holds true, updates those things that have changed, and provides new material reflecting not only how the industry has changed in the last seven years, but also many new concepts the authors have developed in their practice to address the changing times.

Here are some highlights of the major changes you will find in About Face 2.0:

✓ The book has been entirely reorganized to present its ideas in, what the authors hope, is a much more easy to use reference structure. The book is divided into three sections: the first deals with process and high-level ideas about users and design; the second deals with high-level interaction design principles; and the third deals with lower-level interface design principles.

✓ Building on concepts first introduced by Alan Cooper in *The Inmates Are Running the Asylum* (SAMS, 1999) several new chapters lay out in more detail the process of Goal-Directed Design, including research techniques, creation of personas, and how to use personas and scenarios to synthesize interaction design solutions.

✓ The book makes more of an effort to address issues specific to non-desktop platforms. Chapters 37 and 38 address interaction and interface design for the Web and for device platforms, respectively.

✓ Terminology and examples in the book have been updated, where possible, to reflect the current state of the art in the industry, and the text as a whole has been thoroughly edited to improve clarity and readability.

We hope that readers will find these additions and changes as rewarding to read as the authors found them to write.

Conventions Used in This Book

In this book, we've made use of several conventions that hopefully clarify some of the more important points and help provide a richer, more useful experience for the reader.

Platforms

This book is about designing digital interactive products. The majority of today's PCs run Windows and, as a result, that is where the greatest need exists for understanding how to create effective, goal-directed user interfaces.

Having said this, most of the material in this book transcends platforms. It is equally applicable to all desktop platforms — MacOS, Motif, and others — and the majority of it is relevant even for more divergent platforms such as kiosks, handhelds, embedded systems, and others.

Examples

The majority of examples in this book are from the Microsoft Office suite of Word, Excel, PowerPoint, Outlook, and Internet Explorer; Adobe Photoshop and Illustrator; and a few others. We have tried to stick with examples from these mainstream programs for two reasons. First, readers are likely to be at least slightly familiar with the examples. Second, it's important to show that the user interface design of even the most finely honed products can be significantly improved with a Goal-Directed approach. We have included a few examples from Mac OS X as well, in places where they were particularly illustrative.

A few examples in this new edition come from now moribund software or OS versions. These examples make particular design points that the authors felt were useful enough to retain in this edition. The vast majority of examples are from contemporary software and OS releases.

Design aphorisms and terms

One of the things lacking in this new field of interaction design is a set of terms and principles that designers, programmers, and usability practitioners can use to communicate together concerning the design of behavior. We have attempted in this book to provide the start of what we hope will become an evolving list of terms and principles that practitioners will use and expand upon as they see fit.

The principles, or aphorisms if you prefer, encapsulate wisdom derived from dozens of design engagements. These are divided into two categories, each identified by a unique icon, as shown here.

Buy low, sell high.

In this book, **axioms** refer to broad principles of interaction design. Pose these axioms to yourself when you find yourself stuck on tough conceptual problems. All the axioms are gathered into Appendix A.

Keep your powder dry.

Some aphorisms aren't as broad in scope; but they are, nonetheless, quite useful. When you are working with particular design elements described in the book, the **design tips** provide helpful advice. The design tips are gathered into Appendix B.

When mentioned for the first time, terms with specific meanings for the interaction design practitioner are highlighted in the text in **boldface**. Some of these terms are the authors' neologisms, but many of them were coined by others or are in common use.

Let's Design!

We hope this book informs you and intrigues you, but most of all, we hope it makes you think about the design of digital products in new ways. The practice of interaction design is constantly evolving, and it is new and varied enough to generate a wide variety of opinions on the subject. If you have an interesting opinion or just want to talk to us, we'd be happy to hear from you at acooper@cooper.com and rmreimann@aol.com.

Section One

Know Thy User

The design of interaction begins well below the surface of our systems, applications, and hardware. Imagining that we can create a good user experience for our products *after* their internals have been constructed is like saying that a good coat of paint will turn a cave into a mansion. Even as technology frees us to perform great feats of invention, it simultaneously ties us to ways of thinking that are contrary to the natural expression of human behavior. Almost all of the problems with the design of digital products originate from well-intentioned, intelligent, and capable people focusing on the wrong things. Instead of technology and tasks, we must focus on the *goals* toward which users strive and the motivations they have for doing so — even if the users themselves can't articulate them. This section provides a detailed overview of our method of bridging that gap between user goals and product design.

Part I

Bridging the Gap

Chapter 1

Goal-Directed Design

Our book has a simple premise: If achieving the user's goals is the basis of our design process, the user will be satisfied and happy. If the user is happy, he will gladly pay us money (and recommend that others do the same), and then we will be successful as a business.

On the surface, this premise sounds quite obvious and straightforward: Make the user happy, and your products will be a success. Why then are so many digital products so difficult and unpleasant to use? Why aren't we all either happy or successful — or both?

Digital Products Need Better Design Methods

Most digital products today *emerge* from the development process like a monster emerging from a bubbling tank. Developers, instead of planning and executing with their users in mind, end up creating technological solutions over which they ultimately have little control. Like mad scientists, they fail because they have not imbued their creations with humanity.

Design, according to industrial designer Victor Papanek, is *the conscious and intuitive effort to impose meaningful order*. The authors propose a somewhat more detailed definition:

- ✓ Understanding the user's wants, needs, motivations, and contexts
- ✓ Understanding business, technical, and domain requirements and constraints
- ✓ Translating this knowledge into *plans* for artifacts (or artifacts themselves) whose form, content, and behavior is useful, usable, and desirable, as well as economically viable and technically feasible

This definition applies across all design disciplines, although the precise focus on form versus content versus behavior varies by design discipline.

When performed using the appropriate methods, design can provide the missing human connection in technological products. But clearly, the current approach to the design of digital products either isn't working or isn't happening as advertised.

The design of digital products today

Most digital products are built from an engineering point of view. True, marketing departments are sometimes able to provide requirements, but these often have little to do with what users actually *need* and have more to do with following the competition, providing feature checklists to

5

IT departments, or making guesses based on user surveys or customer wish lists. None of these approaches take into account the users' *goals* in any systematic fashion. We'll soon see why goals are so important.

Developers have a different set of imperatives than users, centering on technology and engineering methodology. Meanwhile, marketing departments focus on what drives press attention, on feature lists, and on what people *say* they will buy. Users, when asked direct questions about the products they use, tend to focus on low-level tasks — contrary to what you might suspect, few users are consciously aware of or are able to clearly articulate their goals.

The result of these approaches is, unfortunately, software that irritates, reduces productivity, and fails to meet user needs. Figure 1-1 shows the evolution of the software development process, and where, if at all, design has fit in. Most of digital product development is stuck in the first, second, or third step of this evolution, where design either plays no real role or it becomes a surface-level patch on bad interactions — "lipstick on the pig," as one of the authors' clients referred to it. The design process, as we will soon discuss, needs to *precede* coding and testing to ensure that products truly meet the needs of users.

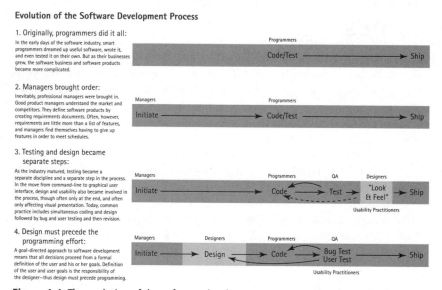

Figure 1-1: The evolution of the software development process. Today, design is often an afterthought. It should, instead, happen before any coding or testing begins.

Here are a few examples of why focusing on technology, markets, and tasks alone (instead of designing for users and their goals) results in the kind of software we've all grown to despise.

SOFTWARE IS RUDE

Software is often rude to the user. It blames the user for making mistakes that are not the user's fault, or should not be. Error message boxes like the one in Figure 1-2 pop up like weeds announcing that the user has failed yet again. These messages also demand that user acknowledge his failure by agreeing: OK.

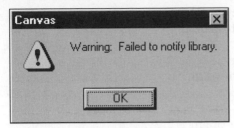

Figure 1-2: Thanks for sharing. Why didn't the program notify the library? What did it want to notify the library about? Why is it telling us? Why do we care? And what are we OKing, anyway? It is not OK that the program failed!

Software frequently interrogates the user, peppering him with a string of terse questions that he is neither inclined or prepared to answer: "Where did you hide that file?" Patronizing questions like "Are you sure?" and "Did you really want to delete that file or did you have some other reason for pressing the Delete key?" are equally irritating and demeaning.

SOFTWARE MAKES UNWARRANTED ASSUMPTIONS

Software too frequently assumes that its user is computer-literate. For example, when a user is finished editing a document, he closes it, and the program asks if he wants to save it. The technology behind this issue is not trivial. It has to do with the capability of the CPU to directly address information stored on random-access magnetic media—but how is the novice user to know that?

SOFTWARE IS OBSCURE

Software is frequently obscure, hiding meaning, intentions, and actions from the user. Programs often express themselves in incomprehensible jargon that cannot be fathomed by normal users ("How many stop bits?") and sometimes even by experts ("Please specify IRQ.").

Features are hidden behind a veil of menus and dialogs and windows. How can the user know that the answer lies in the help system if he can't find the help system? Even when the user finds the right dialog, he might find it populated with terse abbreviations, obscure commands, and inscrutable icons.

More frequently than you might think, software demands that its users answer tough questions before telling them the effects their answers might have. For example, how can a user possibly decide between a full installation, custom installation, and laptop installation if he isn't told what each of them means in terms of functionality as well as disk space?

SOFTWARE EXHIBITS INAPPROPRIATE BEHAVIOR

If a 10-year-old child behaved like some software programs, he'd be sent to his room without supper. Programs forget to shut doors behind themselves, leave shoes in the middle of the floor, and can't remember what you told them only five minutes earlier. For example, if you save a Microsoft Word document, print it, and then try to close it, the program once again asks you if you want to save it! Evidently the act of printing caused the program to think the document had changed, even though it did not. Sorry, Mom, I didn't hear you.

Programs often require us to step out of the main flow of tasks to perform functions that should fall immediately to hand. Dangerous commands, however, are often presented right up front where unsuspecting users can accidentally trigger them. The overall appearance of many programs is overly complex and confusing, making navigation and comprehension difficult.

So what, then, is the real problem here? Why does the technology industry have such a problem with design of interactive products?

We're ignorant about users

It's a sad truth that the digital technology industry doesn't have a good understanding of what it takes to make users happy. In fact, most technology products get built without much understanding of the users. We might know what *market segment* our users are in, how much money they make, how much money they like to spend on weekends, and what sort of cars they buy. Maybe we even have a vague idea what kind of jobs they have and some of the major tasks that they regularly perform. But does any of this tell us how to make them happy? Does it tell us *how* they will actually use the product we're building? Does it tell us *why* they are doing whatever it is they might need our product for, *why* they might want to choose our product over our competitors, or *how* we can make sure they do? Unfortunately, it does not.

We'll soon see how to address the issue of understanding users and their behaviors with products.

We have a conflict of interest

A second problem affects the ability of vendors and manufacturers to make users happy. There is an important conflict of interest in the world of digital product development: The people who build the products — programmers — are usually also the people who design them. Programmers are often required to choose between ease of coding and ease of use. Because programmers' performance is typically judged by their ability to code efficiently and meet incredibly tight deadlines, it isn't difficult to figure out what direction most software-enabled products take. Just as we would never permit the prosecutor in a legal trial to also adjudicate the case, we should make sure that those designing a product are not the same people building it. It simply isn't possible for a programmer to advocate for the user, the business, and the technology at the same time.

We lack a process

The third reason the digital technology industry isn't cranking out successful products is that it has no reliable *process* for doing so. Or, to be more accurate, it doesn't have a *complete* process for doing so. Engineering departments follow — or should follow — rigorous engineering methods that ensure the *feasibility* and quality of the technology. Similarly, marketing, sales, and other business units follow their own well-established methods for ensuring the commercial *viability* of new products. What's left out is a repeatable, analytical process for *transforming an understanding of users into products that both meet their needs and excite their imaginations*.

When we think about complex mechanical devices, we take for granted that they have been carefully designed for use, in addition to being engineered. Most manufactured objects are quite simple, and even complex mechanical products are quite simple when compared to most software and software-enabled products that can sport in excess of one million lines of code (compare this to a mechanical artifact of overwhelming complexity such as the space shuttle, which has 250,000 parts, only a small percentage of which are *moving* parts). Yet most software has never undergone a rigorous design process from a user-centered perspective.

The current process of determining what software will do and how it will communicate with the user is today closely intertwined with its construction. Programmers, deep in their thoughts of algorithms and code, "design" user interfaces the same way that miners "design" the landscape with their cavernous pits and enormous tailing piles. The software interface design process alternates between the accidental and the non-existent.

Many programmers today embrace the notion that integrating users directly into the programming process on a frequent basis—weekly, or sometimes even daily—can solve design problems. Although this has the salutary effect of sharing the responsibility for design with the user, it ignores a serious methodological flaw: a confusion of domain knowledge with design knowledge. Users, although they might be able to articulate the problems with an interaction, are not often capable of visualizing the solutions to those problems. Design is a specialized skill, just like programming. Programmers would never ask users to help them *code*; design problems should be treated no differently.

To understand how to create a workable process that brings user-centered design to software, we need to understand a bit more about the history of design in manufacturing and about how the challenges of interactive products have substantially changed the demands on design.

The Evolution of Design in Manufacturing

In the early days of industrial manufacturing, engineering and marketing processes alone were sufficient to produce *desirable* products: It didn't take much more than good engineering and reasonable pricing to produce a hammer, diesel engine, or tube of toothpaste that people would readily purchase. As time progressed, manufacturers of consumer products realized that they needed to differentiate their products from functionally identical products made by competitors, and so design was introduced as a means to increase user desire for a product. Graphic designers were employed to create more effective packaging and advertising, and industrial designers were engaged to create more comfortable, useful, and exciting forms.

The conscious inclusion of design heralded the ascendance of the modern triad of product development concerns identified by Larry Keeley: feasibility, viability, and desirability (see Figure 1-3). If any one of these three foundations is significantly weaker than the others in a product, it is unlikely to stand the test of time.

Now enter the computer, the first machine created by humans that is capable of almost limitless *behavior* when properly coded into software. The interesting thing about this complex behavior, or interactivity, is that it completely alters the nature of the products it touches. Interactivity is compelling to humans, so compelling that other aspects of an interactive product become marginal. Who pays attention to the black box that sits under your desk—it is the interactive screen, keyboard, and mouse to which users pay attention. Yet, the interactive behaviors of software and other digital products, which should be receiving the lion's share of design attention, all too frequently receive no attention at all.

The traditions of design that corporations have relied on to provide the critical pillar of desirability for products don't provide much guidance in the world of interactivity. Design of behavior is a different kind of problem that requires greater knowledge of *context*, not just rules of visual composition and brand. Design of behavior requires an understanding of the user's relationship with the product from prepurchase to end-of-life. Most important of all is the understanding of how the user wishes to use the product, in what ways, and to what ends.

Building Successful Products

Underlying the goal-directed approach to design is the premise that products must balance business and engineering concerns with user concerns.

You begin by asking, "What do people desire?" Then, you ask, "Of the things people desire, what will sustain a business?" And finally, you ask, "Of the things we desire that will also sustain a business, what can we build?" A common trap is to focus primarily on technology while losing sight of viability and desirability.

Understanding the importance of each dimension is only the beginning. That understanding must also be acted upon. We're familiar with this process along the business and technology dimension: you create a business model and then develop a business plan; and similarly create an engineering model and specification.

The goal-directed design process is an analog to the these planning processes. It results in a solid user model and a comprehensive user interaction plan.

The user plan determines the probability that customers will adopt a product. The business plan determines the probability that the business can sustain itself up to and through launch—and that sales will actually support growth thereafter. And the technology plan determines the probability that the product can be made to work and actually delivered.

Multiplying these three factors determines the overall probability that a product will be successful.

Larry Keeley proposed the original model (above) on which this diagram (to the right) builds. Keeley's model described the three primary qualities in a high-technology business.

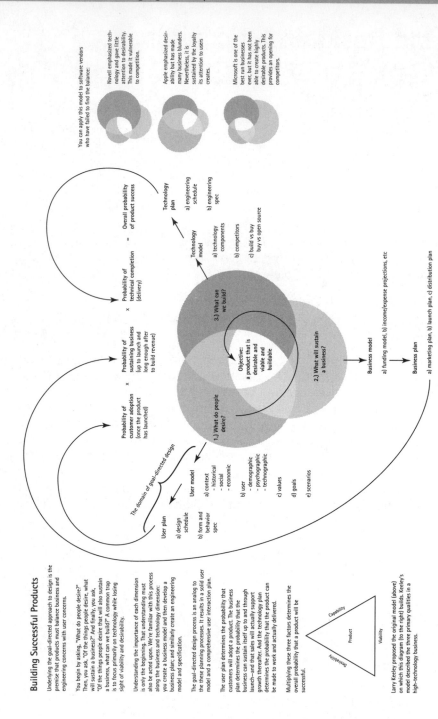

You can apply this model to software vendors who have failed to find the balance:

Novell emphasized technology and gave little attention to desirability. This made it vulnerable to competition.

Apple emphasized desirability but has made many business blunders. Nevertheless, it is sustained by the loyalty its attention to users creates.

Microsoft is one of the best run businesses ever, but it has not been able to create highly desirable products. This provides an opening for competitors.

Figure 1-3: Building successful digital products. Expanding on Keeley's triangle (left), the center diagram indicates the three major processes that need to be followed in tandem to create successful technology products. This book addresses the first and foremost issue: how to create a product people will desire.

Planning and Designing Behavior

The planning of complex digital products, especially ones that interact directly with humans, requires a significant up-front effort by professional designers, just as the planning of complex physical structures that interact with humans require a significant up-front effort by professional architects. In the case of architects, that planning involves understanding how the humans occupying the structure live and work, and designing spaces to support and facilitate those behaviors. In the case of digital products, the planning involves understanding how the humans using the product live and work, and designing product behavior and form that supports and facilitates the human behaviors. Architecture is an old, well-established field. The design of product and system behavior — **interaction design** — is quite new, and only in recent years has it begun to come of age as a discipline.

Interaction design isn't a matter of aesthetic choice, but rather it is based on an understanding of users and cognitive principles. This is good news because it makes the design of behavior quite amenable to a repeatable process of analysis and synthesis. It doesn't mean that the design of behavior can be automated, any more than the design of form or content can be automated, but it *does* mean that a systematic approach is possible. Rules of form and aesthetics mustn't be discarded, of course, but they must work in harmony with the larger concern of achieving user goals via appropriately designed behaviors.

This book presents a set of methods to address the needs of this new kind of behavior-oriented design that addresses the *goals* (Rudolf, 1998) of users: **Goal-Directed Design**. To understand Goal-Directed Design, we first need to better understand human goals and how they provide the key to designing appropriate interactive behavior.

Recognizing User Goals

So what are user goals? How can we identify them? How do we know that they are real? Are they the same for all users? Do they change over time? We'll try to answer those questions in the remainder of this chapter.

Users' goals are often quite different from what we might guess them to be. For example, we might think that an accounting clerk's goal is to process invoices efficiently. This is probably not true. Efficient invoice processing is more likely the goal of the clerk's employer. The clerk is more likely concentrating on goals like appearing competent at his job and keeping himself engaged with his work while performing routine and repetitive tasks.

Regardless of the work we do and the tasks we must accomplish, most of us share these simple, personal goals. Even if we have higher aspirations, they are still more personal than work-related: winning a promotion, learning more about our field, or setting a good example for others, for instance.

Products designed and built to achieve business goals alone will fail; personal goals of users need to be addressed. When the user's personal goals are met by the design, business goals are far more effectively achieved, for reasons we'll explore in more detail in later chapters.

If you examine most commercially available software, Web sites, and digital products today, you will find that their user interfaces fail to meet user goals with alarming frequency. They routinely:

✓ Make users feel stupid

✓ Cause users to make big mistakes

✓ Slow users down so they don't get an adequate amount of work done

✓ Prevent fun and/or bore users with navigational tedium

Most of the same software is equally poor at achieving its business purpose. Invoices don't get processed all that well. Customers don't get serviced on time. Decisions don't get properly supported. This is no coincidence.

The companies that develop these products don't have the right priorities. Most focus their attention far too narrowly on implementation issues, which distract them from the needs of users.

Even when businesses become sensitive to their users, they are often powerless to change their products because the conventional development process assumes that user interface should be addressed after coding begins—sometimes even after it ends. But just as you cannot effectively design a building after construction begins, you cannot easily make a program serve users' goals after coding has begun (and certainly not after it has ended).

Finally, when companies *do* focus on the users, they pay too much attention to the *tasks* that users engage in and not enough attention to their *goals* in performing those tasks. Software can be technologically superb and perform each business task with diligence, yet still be a critical and commercial failure. We can't ignore technology or tasks, but they play only a part in a larger schema that includes designing to meet user goals.

Goals versus tasks

Goals are not the same as tasks. A goal is an end condition, whereas a task is an intermediate step that helps to reach a goal. Goals motivate people to perform tasks. It is very important not to confuse tasks with goals, but it is easy to mix them up.

Luckily, there is an easy way to tell the difference between tasks and goals. Goals are driven by human motivations, which change very slowly, if at all, over time. Tasks are transient, based almost entirely on the technology at hand. For example, when traveling from St. Louis to San Francisco, a person's *goals* are likely to be speed, comfort, and safety. In 1850, a settler would have made the journey in a covered wagon; and, in the interest of safety, he would have brought along his trusty rifle. Traveling from St. Louis to San Francisco today, a businessman makes the journey in a jet aircraft; and, in the interest of safety, he is required to leave his firearms at home. The goals remain unchanged, but the tasks have so changed with the technology that they are, in some respects, in direct opposition.

Looking through the lens of goals allows you to leverage technology to eliminate irrelevant tasks. For example, if you want to get to work in the morning, your goal is to get there as quickly and safely as possible. With today's technology, that means executing the tasks of getting in your car and braving traffic, or perhaps waiting for a train and walking the rest of the way. In the Star Trek future, you can throw a switch and materialize in your office via transporter beam. Looking at goals can similarly help designers eliminate tasks that technology renders unnecessary for humans to perform.

Many developers and usability professionals approach the design of interfaces by asking, "What are the tasks?" Although this may get the job done, it won't produce the best solution possible, and often it won't satisfy the user. When designing an interface, task analysis is useful, but only after user goals have been analyzed. Design based solely on tasks runs the risk of trapping the design in a model imposed by an outmoded technology, or using a model that meets the goals of a corporation without meeting the goals of their users. Asking, "What are the user's goals?" lets us see through the confusion and create more appropriate and satisfactory design.

Designing to meet goals in context

Many designers assume that making interfaces easier to learn should always be a design target. Ease of learning is an important guideline, but in reality, as Brenda Laurel (1990) notes, the design target really depends on the context — who the users are, what they are doing, and what goals they have. You simply can't create good design by following rules disconnected from the goals and needs of the users of your product.

Let us illustrate: Take an automated call-distribution system. The people who use this product are paid based on how many calls they handle. Their most important concern is not ease of learning, but the efficiency with which users can route calls, and the rapidity with which those calls can be completed. Ease of learning is also important because it affects the happiness and, ultimately, the turnover rate of employees, so both ease and throughput should be considered in the design. But there is no doubt that throughput is the dominant demand placed on the system by the users and, if necessary, ease of learning should take a back seat. A program that walks the user through the call-routing process step by step each time merely frustrates him after he's learned the ropes.

On the other hand, if the product in question is a kiosk in a corporate lobby helping visitors find their way around, ease of use for first-time users is clearly the goal.

A general guideline of interaction design that seems to apply particularly well to productivity tools is that *good design makes users more effective*. This guideline takes into account the universal human goal of not looking stupid, along with more particular goals of business throughput and ease of use that are relevant in most business situations.

It is up to you as a designer to determine how you can make the users of your product more effective. Software that enables users to perform their tasks *without addressing their goals* rarely helps them be truly effective. If the task is to enter 5000 names and addresses into a database, a smoothly functioning data-entry application won't satisfy the user nearly as much as an automated system that extracts the names from the invoicing system.

Although it is the user's job to focus on her tasks, the designer's job is to look beyond the task to identify *who* the most important users are, and then to determine *what* their goals might be and *why*. The design process, which we describe in the remainder of this chapter and detail in the remaining chapters of Part I, provides a structure for determining the answers to these questions, a structure by which solutions based on this information can be systematically achieved.

The Goal-Directed Design Process

Most technology-focused companies don't have an adequate process for user-centered design, if they have a process at all. But even the more enlightened organizations, ones that can boast of an established process, come up against some critical issues that result from traditional ways of approaching the problems of research and design.

In recent years, the business community has come to recognize that user research is necessary to create good products, but the proper nature of that research is still in question in many organizations. Quantitative market research and market segmentation is quite useful for *selling* products, but falls short of providing critical information about *how people actually use products* — especially products with complex behaviors (see Chapter 5 for a more in-depth discussion of this topic). A second problem occurs after the results have been analyzed: Most traditional methods don't provide a means of *translating research results into design solutions*. A hundred pages of user survey data don't easily translate into a set of product requirements, and they say even less about how those requirements should be expressed in terms of a logical and appropriate interface structure. Design remains a black box: "A miracle happens here." This gap between research results and the ultimate design solution is the result of a process that doesn't connect the dots from user to final product. We'll soon see how to address this problem with Goal-Directed methods.

Bridging the gap

As we have briefly discussed, the role of design in the development process needs to change. We need to start thinking about design in new ways, and start thinking differently about how product decisions are made.

DESIGN AS PRODUCT DEFINITION

Design has, unfortunately, become a limiting term in the technology industry. For many developers and managers, the word has come to mean what happens in the third process diagram shown in Figure 1-1: a visual facelift on the **implementation model** (see Chapter 2). But design, when properly deployed (as in fourth process diagram shown in Figure 1-1), both identifies user requirements and defines a detailed plan for the behavior and appearance of products. In other words, design provides true **product definition**, based on goals of users, needs of business, and constraints of technology.

DESIGNERS AS RESEARCHERS

If design is to become product definition, designers need to take on broader roles than that assumed in traditional design, particularly when the object of this design is complex, interactive systems.

One of the problems with the current development process is that roles in the process are over-specialized: Researchers perform research, and designers perform design (see Figure 1-4). The results of user and market research are analyzed by the usability and market researchers and then thrown over the transom to designers or programmers. What is missing in this model is a systematic means of translating and synthesizing the research into design solutions. One of the ways to address this problem is for designers to learn to be researchers.

There is a compelling reason for involving designers in the research process. One of the most powerful tools designers bring to the table is empathy: the ability to feel what others are feeling. The direct and extensive exposure to users that proper user research entails immerses designers in the users' world, and gets them thinking about users long before they propose solutions. One of the most dangerous practices in product development is isolating designers from the users because doing so eliminates empathic knowledge.

Additionally, it is often difficult for pure researchers to know what user information is really important from a design perspective. Involving designers directly in research addresses both issues.

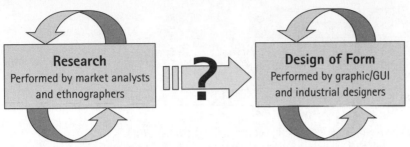

Figure 1-4: A problematic design process. Traditionally, research and design have been separated, with each activity handled by specialists. *Research* has, until recently, referred primarily to market research, and *design* is too often limited to visual design or skin-deep industrial design. More recently, **user research** has expanded to include qualitative, ethnographic data. Yet, without including designers in the research process, the connection between research data and design solutions remains tenuous at best.

In the authors' practice, designers are trained in the research techniques described in Chapter 4 and perform their research without further support or collaboration. This is a satisfactory solution, provided your team has the time and resources to train your designers fully in these techniques. If not, a cross-disciplinary team of designers and dedicated user researchers is appropriate.

Although research practiced by designers takes us part of the way to Goal-Directed Design solutions, there is still a translation gap between research results and design details. The puzzle is missing several pieces, as we will discuss next.

BETWEEN RESEARCH AND DESIGN: MODELS, REQUIREMENTS, AND FRAMEWORKS

Few design methods in common use today incorporate a means of effectively and systematically translating the knowledge gathered during research into a detailed design specification. Part of the reason for this has already been identified: Designers have historically been out of the research loop and have had to rely on third-person accounts of user behaviors and desires.

The other reason, however, is that few methods capture user behaviors in a manner that appropriately directs the definition of a product. Rather than providing information about user goals, most methods provide information at the task level. This type of information is useful for defining layout, workflow, and translation of functions into interface controls, but less useful for defining the basic framework of what a product *is*, what it *does*, and how it should meet the broad needs of the user. Instead we need explicit, systematic processes for defining user models, establishing design requirements, and translating those into a high-level interaction framework (see Figure 1-5).

Knowledge about users must be synthesized into a model that leverages user data *as a design tool*. Other models, such as workflows and environmental contexts, are also important and useful, but appropriate user models are singularly critical. After user models are created, the usage patterns, mental models, and user goals captured by them can be systematically mapped to an interaction framework that also addresses the business and technical imperatives that are captured in other models.

Goal-Directed Design seeks to bridge the gap that currently exists in the digital product development process, the gap between user research and design, through a combination of new techniques and known methods brought together in more effective ways.

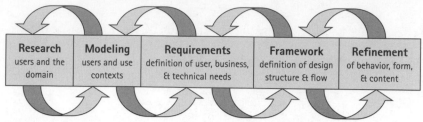

Figure 1-5: Bridging the gap between research and design. Three primary activities close the gap. A process of modeling that synthesizes research results into design tools, a process of synthesizing and defining requirements from these models, and a process of translating the knowledge captured in the models and requirements into a design framework that reflects the goals and needs of users, while also addressing business and technical imperatives.

A process overview

Goal-Directed Design combines techniques of ethnography, stakeholder interviews, market research, product/literature reviews, detailed user models, scenario-based design, and a core set of interaction principles and patterns. It provides solutions that meet the needs and goals of users, while also addressing business/organizational and technical imperatives (see Figure 1-6). This process can be roughly divided into five phases: *Research, Modeling, Requirements Definition, Framework Definition,* and *Refinement.* These phases follow the five component activities of inter-action design identified by Gillian Crampton Smith and Philip Tabor (1996) — understanding, abstracting, structuring, representing, and detailing — with a greater emphasis on modeling user behaviors and defining system behaviors.

The remainder of this chapter provides a high-level view of the five phases of Goal-Directed Design. Chapters 4, 5, and 6 provide a more process-oriented overview of the methods involved in each of these phases.

RESEARCH

The Research phase employs ethnographic field study techniques (observation and contextual interviews) to provide qualitative data about potential and/or actual users of the product. It also includes competitive product audits, reviews of market research and technology white papers, as well as one-on-one interviews with stakeholders, developers, subject matter experts (SMEs), and technology experts as suits the particular domain.

One of the principal outcomes of field observation and user interviews is an emergent set of **usage patterns** — identifiable behaviors that help categorize modes of use of a potential or existing product. These patterns suggest goals and motivations (specific and general desired outcomes of using the product). In business and technical domains, these behavior patterns tend to map to professional roles; for consumer products, they tend to correspond to lifestyle choices. Usage patterns and the goals associated with them drive the creation of **personas** in the Modeling phase. Market research helps select and filter for valid personas that fit corporate business models. Stakeholder interviews, literature reviews, and product audits deepen the designers' understanding of the domain and elucidate business goals and technical constraints that the design must support. Chapter 4 provides a more detailed discussion of Goal-Directed research techniques.

MODELING

During the Modeling phase, usage and workflow patterns discovered through analysis of the field research and interviews are synthesized into domain and user models. Domain models can include information flow and workflow diagrams. User models, or **personas**, are detailed, composite **user archetypes** that represent distinct groupings of behavior patterns, goals, and motivations observed and identified during the Research phase.

Personas serve as the main characters in a narrative, scenario-based approach to design that iteratively generates design concepts in the Framework Definition phase, provides feedback that enforces design coherence and appropriateness in the Refinement phase, and represents a powerful communication tool that helps developers and managers to understand design rationale and to prioritize features based on user needs. In the Modeling phase, designers employ a variety of methodological tools to synthesize, differentiate, and prioritize personas, exploring different *types* of goals and mapping personas across ranges of behavior to ensure there are no gaps or duplications.

Specific design targets are chosen from the cast of personas through a process of comparing goals and assigning a hierarchy of priority based on how broadly each persona's goals encompass the goals of other personas. A process of designating persona types determines the amount of influence each persona has on the eventual form and behavior of the design.

Possible user persona type designations include:

- ✓ **Primary:** the persona's needs are sufficiently unique to require a distinct interface form and behavior

- ✓ **Secondary:** a primary interface serves the needs of the persona with a minor modification or addition

- ✓ **Supplemental:** the persona's needs are fully satisfied by a primary interface

- ✓ **Served:** the persona is not an actual user of the product, but is indirectly affected by it and its use

- ✓ **Negative:** the persona is created as an explicit, rhetorical example of whom *not* to design for

A detailed discussion of persona and goal development can be found in Chapter 5.

REQUIREMENTS DEFINITION

Design methods employed by teams during the Requirements Definition phase provides the much-needed connection between user and other models and the framework of the design. This phase employs scenario-based design methods (Carroll, 1995), with the important innovation of focusing the scenarios not on user tasks in the abstract, but first and foremost on meeting the goals and needs of specific user personas. Personas provide an understanding of which tasks are truly important and why, leading to an interface that minimizes necessary tasks (effort) while maximizing return. Personas become the main characters of these scenarios, and the designers explore the design space via a form of role-playing.

For each interface/primary persona, the process of design in the Requirements Definition phase involves an analysis of persona data and functional needs (expressed in term of objects, actions, and contexts), prioritized and informed by persona goals, behaviors, and interactions with other personas in various contexts.

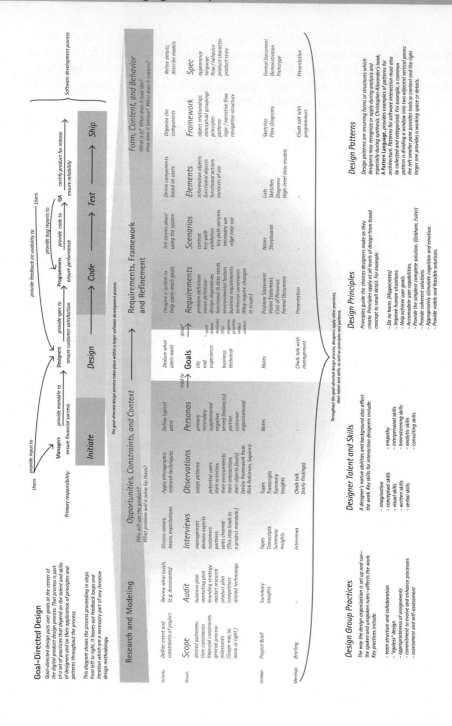

Figure 1-6: The Goal-Directed Design process

This analysis is accomplished through an iteratively refined **context scenario** that starts with a "day in the life" of the persona using the product, describing high-level product touch points, and thereafter successively defining detail at ever-deepening levels. As this iteration occurs, both business goals and technical constraints are also considered and balanced with persona goals and needs. The output of this process is a **requirements definition** that balances user, business, and technical requirements of the design to follow.

FRAMEWORK DEFINITION

In the Framework Definition phase, teams synthesize an **interaction framework** by employing two other critical methodological tools in conjunction with context scenarios. The first is a set of general **interaction design principles** that, like their visual design counterparts (see Chapter 19), provide guidance in determining appropriate system behavior in a variety of contexts. Chapters 2 and 3 and the whole of Section II are devoted to high-level interaction design principles appropriate to the Framework Definition phase.

The second critical methodological tool is a set of **interaction design patterns** that encode general solutions (with variations dependent on context) to classes of previously analyzed problems. These patterns bear close resemblance to the concept of architectural design patterns developed by Christopher Alexander (1977). Interaction design patterns are hierarchically organized and continuously evolve as new contexts arise. Rather than stifling designer creativity, they often provide needed leverage to approach difficult problems with proven design knowledge.

After data and functional needs are described at this high level, they are translated into design elements according to interaction principles and then organized using patterns and principles into design sketches and behavior descriptions. The output of this process is an **interaction framework definition**, a stable design concept that provides the logical and gross formal structure for the detail to come. Successive iterations of more narrowly focused scenarios provide this detail in the Refinement phase. The approach is often a balance of top-down (pattern-oriented) design and bottom-up (principle-oriented) design.

REFINEMENT

The **Refinement phase** proceeds similarly to the Framework Definition phase, but with greater focus on task coherence, using **key path** (walkthrough) and **validation scenarios** focused on storyboarding paths through the interface in high detail. The culmination of the Refinement phase is the detailed documentation of the design, a **form and behavior specification**, delivered in either paper or interactive media as context dictates. Chapter 6 discusses in more detail the use of personas, scenarios, principles, and patterns in the Requirements Definition, Framework Definition, and Refinement phases.

Goals, not features, are the key to product success

Programmers and engineers — people who are intrigued by technology — share a strong tendency to think about products in terms of functions and features. This is only natural, as this is how developers build software: function by function. The problem is that this isn't how users want to use it.

The decision about whether a feature should be included in a product shouldn't rest on its technological underpinnings. The driving force behind the decision should never be simply that we have the technical capability to do it. The deciding factor should be whether that feature directly, or indirectly, helps to achieve the goals of the user while still meeting the needs of the business.

The successful interaction designer must be sensitive to users' goals amid the pressures and chaos of the product-development cycle. Although we discuss many other techniques and tools of interaction in this book, we always return to users' goals. They are the bedrock upon which interaction design is practiced.

The Goal-Directed process, with its clear rationale for design decisions, makes persuading engineers easier, keeps marketing and management stakeholders in the loop, and ensures that the design in question isn't just guesswork, or a reflection of the team members' personal preferences.

AXIOM

Interaction design is not guesswork.

Goal-Directed Design is also a powerful tool for answering the most important questions that crop up during the definition and design of a digital product:

✓ How do I find out who my users are?

✓ How do I learn what my users are trying to accomplish?

✓ How should my product behave?

✓ What form should my product take?

✓ How will users interact with my product?

✓ How can my product's functions be most effectively organized?

✓ How will my product introduce itself to first-time users?

✓ How can my product put an understandable and controllable face on technology?

✓ How can my product deal with user problems?

✓ How will my product help infrequent users become more expert?

✓ How can my product provide sufficient depth for expert users?

We will help you to answer these questions in the remainder of this book. You will get tools you need to identify key users of your products, understand them and their goals, and translate this understanding into winning design solutions using Goal-Directed Design.

Chapter 2

Implementation Models and Mental Models

The computer industry makes frequent use of the term **computer literacy**. Pundits talk about how some people have it and some don't, how those who have it will succeed in the information economy, and those who lack it will inevitably fall between the socioeconomic cracks. Computer literacy, however, is nothing more than a euphemism for making the user stretch to understand an alien logic rather than having software-enabled products stretch to meet the user's way of thinking.

In this chapter, we discuss how a lack of understanding of users and the way they approach digital products has fueled the computer-literacy divide, and how software that better matches how people think and work can help solve the problem.

Implementation Models

Any machine has a mechanism for accomplishing its purpose. A motion picture projector, for example, uses a complicated sequence of intricately moving parts to create its illusion. It shines a very bright light through a translucent, miniature image for a fraction of a second. It then blocks out the light for a split second while it moves another miniature image into place. Then it unblocks the light again for another moment. It repeats this process with a new image twenty-four times per second. Software-enabled products don't have mechanisms in the sense of moving parts; these are replaced with algorithms and modules of code that communicate with each other. The representation of how a machine or a program actually works has been called the **system model** by Donald Norman (1989) and others; the authors prefer the term **implementation model** because it describes the details of the way a program is implemented in code.

User Mental Models

From the moviegoer's point-of-view, it is easy to forget the nuance of sprocket holes and light-interrupters while watching an absorbing drama. Many moviegoers, in fact, have little idea how the projector actually works, or how this differs from the way a television works. The viewer imagines that the projector merely throws a picture that moves onto the big screen. This is called the user's **mental model**, or **conceptual model**.

People don't need to know all the details of how a complex artifact actually works in order to use it, so they create a cognitive shorthand for explaining it, one that is powerful enough to cover their interactions with it, but which doesn't necessarily reflect its actual inner mechanics. For example, many people imagine that, when they plug their vacuum cleaners and blenders into outlets in the wall, the electricity flows like water from the wall to the appliances through the little black tube of the electrical cord. This mental model is perfectly adequate for using household appliances. The fact that the implementation model of household electricity involves nothing resembling a fluid actually traveling up the cord and that there is a reversal of electrical potential 120 times per second is irrelevant to the user, although the power company needs to know the details.

In the digital world, however, the differences between a user's mental model and the implementation model are often quite distinct. We tend to ignore the fact that our cellular telephone doesn't work like a landline phone; instead, it is actually a radio transceiver that might swap connections between a half-dozen different cellular base antennas in the course of a two-minute call. Knowing this doesn't help us to understand how to *use* the phone.

The discrepancy between implementation and mental models is particularly stark in the case of software applications, where the complexity of implementation can make it nearly impossible for the user to see the mechanistic connections between his actions and the program's reactions. When we use a computer to digitally edit sound or to create video special effects like morphing, we are bereft of analogy to the mechanical world, so our mental models are necessarily different from the implementation model. Even if the connections were visible, they would remain inscrutable to most people.

Represented Models

Software has a behavioral face it shows to the world that is created by the programmer or designer. This representation is not necessarily an accurate description of what is really going on inside the computer, although unfortunately, it frequently is. This ability to *represent* the computer's functioning independent of its true actions is far more pronounced in software than in any other medium. It allows a clever designer to hide some of the more unsavory facts of how the software is really getting the job done. This disconnection between what is implemented and what is offered as explanation gives rise to a *third* model in the digital world, the designer's **represented model** — the way the designer chooses to represent a program's functioning to the user. Donald Norman (1989) refers to this simply as the **designer's model**.

In the world of software, a program's represented model can (and often should) be quite different from the actual processing structure of the program. For example, an operating system can make a network file server look as though it were a local disk. The model does not represent the fact that the physical disk drive may be miles away. This concept of the represented model has no widespread counterpart in the mechanical world. The relationship between the three models is shown in Figure 2-1.

The closer the represented model comes to the user's mental model, the easier he will find the program to use and to understand. Generally, offering a represented model that follows the implementation model too closely significantly reduces the user's ability to learn and use the program, assuming (as is almost always the case) that the user's mental model of his tasks differs from the implementation model of the software.

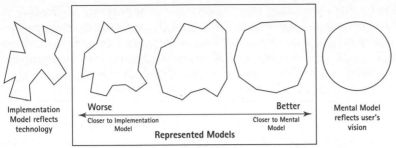

Implementation
Model reflects
technology

Worse

◄――――――――――――――――――――――――►
Closer to Implementation
Model

Better

Closer to Mental
Model

Represented Models

Mental Model
reflects user's
vision

Figure 2-1: The way engineers must build software is often a given, dictated by various technical and business constraints. The model for how the software actually works is called the implementation model. The way users perceive the jobs they need to do and how the program helps them do it is their mental model of interaction with the software. It is based on their own ideas of how they do their jobs and how computers might work. The way designers choose to represent the working of the program to the user is called the represented model, which, unlike the other two models, is an aspect of software over which designers have great control. One of the most important goals of the designer should be to make the represented model match the mental model of users as closely as possible. It is therefore critical that designers understand in detail the way their target users think about the work they do with the software.

We tend to form mental models that are simpler than reality; so if we create represented models that are simpler than the actual implementation model, we help the user achieve a better understanding. Pressing the brake pedal in your car, for example, may conjure a mental image of pushing a lever that rubs against the wheels to slow you down. The actual mechanism includes hydraulic cylinders, tubing, and metal pads that squeeze on a perforated disk, but we simplify all that out of our minds, creating a more effective, albeit less accurate, mental model. In software, we imagine that a spreadsheet scrolls new cells into view when we click on the scrollbar. Nothing of the sort actually happens. There is no sheet of cells out there, but a tightly packed data structure of values, with various pointers between them, from which the program synthesizes a new image to display in real-time.

Understanding how software actually works always helps someone to use it, but this understanding usually comes at a significant cost. The represented model allows software creators to solve the problem by simplifying the apparent way the software works. The cost is entirely internal, and the user never has to know. User interfaces that abandon implementation models to follow mental models more closely are better.

User interfaces should avoid implementation models in favor of user mental models.

In Adobe Photoshop, the user can adjust the color balance and brightness of an illustration using a feature called Variations. Instead of offering numeric fields for entering color data—the implementation model—the Variations interface shows a set of thumbnail images, each with a different color balance (see Figure 2-2). The user can click on the image that best represents the desired color setting. The interface more closely follows his mental model, because the user—likely a graphic artist—is thinking in terms of how his image looks, not in terms of abstract numbers.

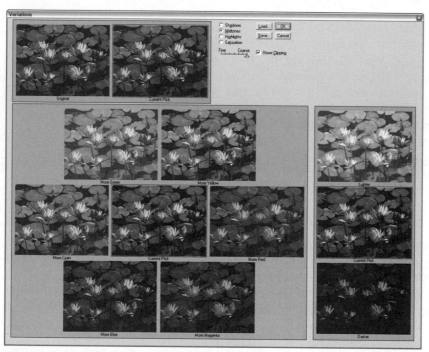

Figure 2–2: Adobe Photoshop has a great example of software design to match user mental models. The Variations interface shows a set of thumbnail images, varying color balance and brightness by adjustable increments. The user can click on the image that best represents the desired color setting. This image then becomes the new default for more varied thumbnails. The interface follows the mental model of graphic artists who are after a particular look, not a set of abstract numerical values.

If the represented model for software closely follows the user's mental model, it eliminates needless complexity from the user interface by providing a cognitive framework that makes it evident to the user how his goals and needs can be met.

Goal-directed interactions reflect user mental models.

A user's mental model doesn't necessarily have to be true or accurate, but it should enable him to work effectively. For example, most nontechnical computer users imagine that their video screen is the heart of their computer. This is only natural because the screen is what they stare at all the time and is the place where they see what the computer is doing. If you point out to a user that the computer is actually a little chip of silicon in that black box sitting under his desk, he will probably shrug and ignore this pointless (to them) bit of information. The fact that the CPU isn't the same thing as the video display doesn't help him think about how he interacts with his computer, even though it is a more technically accurate concept.

Most Software Conforms to Implementation Models

It is much easier to design software that reflects its implementation model: A button for every function, a field for every data input, a page for every transaction step, and a dialog for every code module is an all too common occurrence in the software world. But while this adequately reflects the infrastructure of the engineering effort, it does little to provide a coherent reflection of a user's goals, and the tasks he needs to perform to accomplish them. It produces an interface that affects the user rather like the ubiquitous external ductwork in Terry Gilliam's *1984*-like movie, *Brazil* (a movie full of wonderful tongue-in-cheek examples of miserable interfaces), doing little other than to alienate and confuse the user.

Software designed by engineers follows the implementation model

Software interactions designed by engineers, who know precisely how the software works, quite often lead to a represented model that is very consistent with its implementation model. To the engineers, such models are logical, truthful, and accurate; but unfortunately, they are not very helpful or effective for users. The majority of users don't much care how a program is actually implemented.

A good example of a user interface conforming to the implementation model instead of to the user's mental model can be found in a popular software-based fax product. Every step of the process is agonizingly wrought in discrete steps that the user must laboriously control, and none of which are necessary from the user's point of view. The interaction with the user is rendered in perfect conformity with the internal logic of the software. *A separate dialog box represents every possible user action.* The user is prompted for information when it is convenient for the program to receive it — not when it is natural for the user to provide it.

If we want to send a fax, we'll need to send it either to a person whose name we have previously entered into the program or to a new person whose name we haven't yet entered. But the program in question follows the implementation model: The code that performs each of these functions is located in separate modules, so the program presents each of these functions in its own separate dialog box. To select or enter names, we have to sidestep the main program *in two different ways*, even though selecting and entering names is one of the program's primary functions. Instead of imagining the steps the *user* might take to create and send a fax, the designer merely translated what the *program* has to do.

Here's a better way to manage the problem: Whenever we enter a new fax name and number, the program should automatically record it. The program's main window should display a list of the names of previous fax recipients, allowing us to quickly choose one from the list if we want.

Even the Windows interface slips into the implementation model sometimes. The Explorer attempts to show all the storage devices on the computer as a unified system, but to successfully communicate that to the user, their behavior must also be unified. Instead, their behavior depends on the physical nature of the particular storage device. If you drag a file between directories on the same hard drive, the program interprets this as a MOVE, meaning that the file is removed from the old directory and added to the new directory, closely following the mental model. However, if you drag a file from hard drive C to hard drive D, the action is interpreted as a COPY, meaning that the file is added to the new directory but *not* removed from the old directory.

This is consistent with the implementation model — the way the underlying file system actually works: When the operating system moves a file from one directory to another on the same drive, it merely relocates the file's entry in the disk's table of contents. It never actually erases and rewrites the file. But when it moves a file to another physical drive, it must physically copy the data onto the new drive. To conform to the user's mental model, it should then erase the original even though that contradicts the implementation model.

Because treating the drag of a file from one disk to another as a COPY function can be desirable behavior, especially when copying files from a hard drive to removable media such as ZIP disks, many people aren't aware that it is an inconsistent side effect of the implementation model. As computers mature and logical volumes represent more than just physical drives, the side effects stop being useful and instead become irritating because we have to memorize the idiosyncratic behavior of each volume type.

Mathematical thinking leads to implementation model interfaces

Interaction designers need to shield users from implementation models. Just because a technique is well suited to solving a problem in software construction doesn't necessarily mean that it is well suited to be a mental model for the user. Just because your car is constructed of welded metal parts doesn't mean that you should have to be skilled with a welding torch to drive it.

Most of the data structures and algorithms used to represent and manipulate information in software are logic tools based on mathematical algorithms. All programmers are fluent in these algorithms, including such things as recursion, hierarchical data structures, and multithreading. The problem arises when the user interface attempts to accurately represent the concepts of recursion, hierarchical data, or multithreading.

Mathematical thinking is an implementation model trap that is particular easy for programmers to fall into. They solve programming problems by thinking mathematically, so they naturally see these mathematical models as appropriate terms for inventing user interfaces. Nothing could be further from the truth.

DESIGN TIP

Users don't understand Boolean logic.

For example, one of the most durable and useful tools in the programmer's toolbox is Boolean algebra. It is a compact mathematical system that conveniently describes the behavior of the strictly on or off universe inside all digital computers. There are only two main operations: AND and OR. The problem is that the English language has an and and an or and they are usually interpreted—by non-programmers—as the exact opposite of the Boolean AND and OR. If the program expresses itself with Boolean notation, the user can be *expected* to misinterpret it.

For example, this problem crops up frequently when querying databases. If we want to extract from a file of employees those who live in Arizona along with those who live in Texas, we would say to a human in English, "Find all my employees in Arizona and Texas." To express this properly to a database in Boolean algebraic terms, we would say, "Find employees in Arizona OR Texas." No employee lives in two states at once, so saying, "Find employees in Arizona AND Texas" is nonsensical. In Boolean, this will almost always return the empty set as an answer.

A database query program—or any other program, for that matter—that interacts with the user in Boolean is doomed to suffer severe user-interface problems. It is unreasonable to expect users to penetrate the confusion. They are well trained in English, so why should they have to express things in an unfamiliar language that, annoyingly, redefines key words.

Mechanical-Age versus Information-Age Represented Models

We are experiencing an incredible transformation from the age of industrial, mechanical artifacts to an age of digital, information objects. The change has only begun, and the pace is accelerating rapidly. The upheaval that society underwent as a result of industrialization will likely be dwarfed by that associated with the information age.

Mechanical-age representations

It is only natural for us to try to draw the imagery and language of an earlier era that we are comfortable with into a new, less certain one. As the history of the industrial revolution shows, the fruits of new technology can often only be expressed at first with the language of an earlier technology. For example, we called railroad engines iron horses and automobiles were labeled horseless carriages. Unfortunately, this imagery and language colors our thinking more than we might admit.

Naturally, we tend to use old representations in our new environments. Sometimes, the usage is valid because the function is identical, even if the underpinning technology is different. For example, when we translate the process of typewriting with a typewriter into word processing on a computer, we are using a mechanical-age representation of a common task. Typewriters used little metal tabs to slew the carriage rapidly over several spaces until it came to rest on a particular column. The process, as a natural outgrowth of the technology, was called tabbing or setting tabs. Word processors also have tabs because their function is the same; whether you are working on paper rolled around a platen or on images on a video screen, you need to rapidly slew to a particular margin offset.

Sometimes, however, mechanical-age representations shouldn't be translated verbatim into the digital world. We don't use reins to steer our cars, or a tiller, although both of these were tried in the early days of autos. It took many years to develop a steering idiom that was appropriate for the car. In word processors, we don't need to load a new blank page after we fill the previous one; rather the document scrolls continuously, with visual markers for page breaks.

New technology demands new representations

Sometimes tasks, processes, concepts, and even goals arise solely because new technology makes them possible for the first time. With no reason to exist beforehand, they were not conceived of in advance. When the telephone was first invented, for example, it was, among other things, touted as a means to broadcast music and news, although it was personal communication that became the most popular and widely developed. Nobody at the time would ever have conceived of the telephone as being a ubiquitous personal object that people would carry in their pockets and purses and that would ring annoyingly in the midst of theater performances.

With our mechanical-age mindset, we have a hard time seeing appropriate information-age representations — at first. The real advantages of the software products that we create often remain invisible until they have a sizable population of users. For example, the real advantage of e-mail isn't simply that it's faster than postal mail — the mechanical-age view, but rather that it promotes the flattening and democratization of the modern business organization — the information-age advantage. The real advantage of the Web isn't cheaper and more-efficient communication and distribution — the mechanical age view. Instead, it is the creation of virtual communities — the information-age advantage that was revealed only after it materialized in our grasp. Because we have a hard time seeing how digital products will be used, we tend to rely too much on representations from the past, mechanical age.

Mechanical-age representations degrade user interaction

We encounter a problem when we bring our familiar mechanical-age representations over to the computer. Simply put, mechanical-age processes and representations tend to degrade user interactions in information-age products. Mechanical procedures are easier by hand than they are with computers. For example, typing an individual address on an envelope using a computer requires significant overhead compared to addressing the envelope with pen and ink (although the former might look neater). The situation improves only if the process is automated for a large number of instances in batch — 500 envelopes that you need to address.

As another example, take a contact list on a computer. If it is faithfully rendered on screen like a little bound book, it will be much more complex, inconvenient, and difficult to use than the physical address book. The physical address book, for example, stores names in alphabetical order by last name. But what if you want to find someone by her first name? The mechanical-age artifact doesn't help you: You have to scan the pages manually. So, too, does the faithfully replicated digital version: It can't search by first name either. The difference is that, on the computer screen, you lose many subtle visual cues offered by the paper-based book (bent page corners, penciled-in notes). Meanwhile, the scrollbars and dialog boxes are harder to use, harder to visualize, and harder to understand than simply flipping pages.

AXIOM

Don't replicate mechanical age artifacts in interfaces without information-age enhancements.

Real-world mechanical systems have the strengths and weaknesses of their medium, such as pen and paper. Software has a completely different set of strengths and weaknesses, yet when mechanical representations are replicated without change, they combine the weaknesses of the old with the weaknesses of the new. In our address book example, the computer could easily search for an entry by first name; but, by storing the names in exactly the same way as the mechanical artifact, we deprive ourselves of new ways of searching. We limit ourselves in terms of capabilities possible in an information medium, without reaping any of the benefits of the original mechanical medium.

When designers rely on mechanical-age representations to guide them, they are blinded to the far greater potential of the computer to provide sophisticated information management in a better, albeit different, way.

Improving on mechanical-age representations: an example

Although new technologies can bring about entirely new concepts, they can also extend and build upon old concepts, allowing designers to take advantage of the power of the new technology on behalf of users through updated representations of their interface.

For example, take the calendar. In the nondigital world, calendars are made of paper and are usually divided up into a one-month-per-page format. This is a reasonable compromise based on the size of paper, file folders, briefcases, and desk drawers.

Programs with visual representations of calendars are quite common, and they almost always display one month at a time. Even if they can show more than one month, as Outlook does, they almost always display days in discrete one-month chunks. Why?

Paper calendars showed a single month because they were limited by the size of the paper, and a month was a convenient breaking point. Computer screens are not so constrained, but most designers copy the mechanical-age artifact faithfully (see Figure 2-3). On a computer, the calendar could easily be a continuously scrolling sequence of days, weeks, or months as shown in Figure 2-4. Scheduling something from August 28th to September 4th would be simple if weeks were contiguous instead of broken up by the arbitrary monthly division.

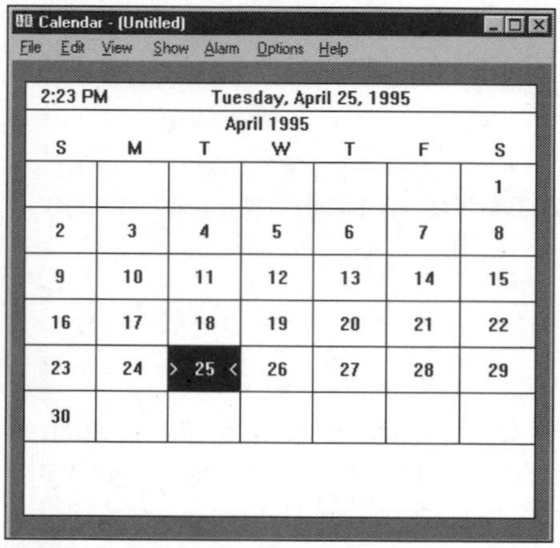
Calendar - (Untitled)
File Edit View Show Alarm Options Help
2:23 PM
Tuesday, April 25, 1995
April 1995
S M T W T F S
1
2 3 4 5 6 7 8
9 10 11 12 13 14 15
16 17 18 19 20 21 22
23 24 > 25 < 26 27 28 29
30

Figure 2-3: The ubiquitous calendar is so familiar that we rarely stop to apply information age sensibilities to its design on the screen. Calendars were originally designed to fit on stacked sheets of paper, not interactive digital displays. How would you redesign it? What aspects of the calendar are artifacts of its old, mechanical-age platform?

Similarly, the grid pattern in digital calendars is almost always of a fixed size. Why couldn't the width of columns of days or the height of rows of weeks be adjustable like a spreadsheet? Certainly you'd want to adjust the sizes of your weekends to reflect their relative importance in relation to your weekdays. If you're a businessperson, your working-week calendar would demand more space than a vacation week. The idioms are as well known as spreadsheets — that is to say, universal — but the mechanical-age representations are so firmly entrenched that we rarely see software publishers deviate from it.

The designer of the software in Figure 2-3 probably thought of calendars as canonical objects that couldn't be altered from the familiar. Surprisingly, most time-management software handles time internally — in its implementation model — as a continuum, and only renders it as discrete months in its user interface — its represented model!

96	SUN	MON	TUE	WED	THU	FRI	SAT
APRIL	21	22	23	24	25	26	27
	28	29	30	1	2	3	4
	5	6	7	8	9	10	11
	12	13	14	15	16	17	18
MAY	19	20	21	22	23	24	25
	26	27	28	29	30	31	1

Figure 2-4: Scrolling is a very familiar idiom to computer users. Why not replace the page-oriented representation of a calendar with a scrolling representation to make it better? This perpetual calendar can do everything the old one can, and it also solves the mechanical-representation problem of scheduling across monthly boundaries. Don't drag old limitations onto new platforms out of habit. What other improvements can you think of?

Some might counter that the one-month-per-page calendar is better because it is easily recognizable and familiar to users. However, the new model is not that different from the old model, except that it permits the users to easily do something they couldn't do easily before — schedule across monthly boundaries. People don't find it difficult to adapt to newer, more useful representations of familiar systems.

Significant change must be significantly better.

Paper-style calendars in personal information managers (PIMs) and schedulers are mute testimony to how our language influences our designs. If we depend on words from the mechanical age, we will build software from the mechanical age. Better software is based on information-age thinking.

Chapter 3

Beginners, Experts, and Intermediates

Most computer users know all too well that opening the shrink-wrap on a new software product augurs several days of frustration and disappointment spent learning the new interface. On the other hand, many experienced users of a program may find themselves continually frustrated because the program always treats them like rank beginners. It seems impossible to find the right balance between catering to the needs of the first-timer and the needs of the expert.

One of the eternal conundrums of interaction and interface design is deciding how to address the needs of both beginning users and expert users with a single interface. Some programmers and designers choose to abandon this idea completely, choosing instead to create software with a beginner mode and an expert mode, the former usually being an oversimplified and underpowered subset of the latter. Of course, nobody wants to be caught dead using software in beginner mode, but the leap from there to expert mode is usually off a rather tall cliff into a shark-infested moat of implementation-model design. What, then, is the answer? The solution to this predicament lies in a different understanding of the way users master new concepts and tasks.

Perpetual Intermediates

Most users are neither beginners nor experts; instead, they are *intermediates*.

The experience level of people performing an activity tends, like most population distributions, to follow the classic statistical bell curve. For any almost any activity requiring knowledge or skill, if we graph number of people against skill level, a relatively small number of beginners are on the left side, a few experts are on the right, and the majority — intermediate users — are in the center.

Statistics don't tell the whole story, however. The bell curve is a snapshot in time, and although most intermediates tend to stay in that category, the beginners do not remain beginners for very long. The difficulty of maintaining a high level of expertise also means that experts come and go rapidly, but beginners change even more rapidly. Both beginners and experts tend over time to gravitate towards intermediacy.

Although *everybody* spends some minimum time as a beginner, *nobody* remains in that state for long. People don't like to be incompetent; and beginners, by definition, are incompetent. Conversely, learning and improving is rewarding, so beginners become intermediates very quickly — or they drop out altogether. All skiers, for example, spend time as beginners, but those who find they don't rapidly progress beyond more-falling-than-skiing quickly abandon the sport. The rest soon move off of the bunny slopes onto the regular runs. Only a few ever make it onto the double-black diamond runs for experts.

Nobody wants to remain a beginner.

The occupants of the beginner end of the curve will either migrate into the center bulge of intermediates, or they will drop off of the graph altogether and find some product or activity in which they *can* migrate into intermediacy. Most users thus remain in a perpetual state of adequacy striving for fluency, with their skills ebbing and flowing like the tides depending on how frequently they use the program. Larry Constantine first identified the importance of designing for intermediates, and in his book *Software for Use* (1999), he refers to such users as **improving intermediates**. The authors prefer the term **perpetual intermediates**, because although beginners quickly improve to become intermediates, they seldom go on to become experts.

A good ski resort has a gentle slope for learning and a few expert runs to really challenge the serious skier. But if the resort wants to stay in business, it will cater to the perpetual intermediate skier, without scaring off the beginner or insulting the expert. The beginner must find it easy to matriculate into the world of intermediacy, and the expert must not find his vertical runs obstructed by aids for bewildered perpetual intermediates.

A well-balanced user interface takes the same approach. It doesn't cater to the beginner or to the expert, but rather devotes the bulk of its efforts to satisfying the perpetual intermediate. At the same time, it avoids offending either of its smaller constituencies, recognizing that they are both vital.

Most users in this middle state would like to learn more about the program but usually don't have the time. Occasionally, the opportunity to do so will surface. Sometimes these intermediates use the product extensively for weeks at a time to complete a big project. During this time, they learn new things about the program. Their knowledge grows beyond its previous boundaries.

Sometimes, however, they do not use the program for months at a time and forget significant portions of what they knew. When they return to the program, they are not beginners, but they will need reminders to jog their memory back to its former state.

If a user finds himself not satisfactorily progressing beyond the beginner stage after only a few hours, he will often abandon the program altogether and find another to take its place. No one is willing to remain incompetent at a task for long.

Optimizing for Intermediates

Now let's contrast our bell curve of intermediates with the way that software is developed. Programmers qualify as experts in the software they code because they have to explore every possible use case, no matter how obscure and unlikely, to create program code to handle it. Their natural tendency is to design implementation model software with every possible option given equal emphasis in the interaction, which they, as experts, have no problem understanding.

At the same time, sales, marketing, and management—none of whom are likely to be expert users or even intermediates—demonstrate the product to customers, reporters, partners, and investors who are themselves unfamiliar with the product. Because of their constant exposure to beginners, these professionals have a strongly biased view of the user community. Therefore, it comes as no surprise that sales and marketing folks lobby for bending the interface to serve beginners. They demand that training wheels be attached to the product to help out the struggling beginner.

Programmers create interactions suitable only for experts, while the marketers demand interactions suitable only for beginners, but—as we have seen—the largest, most stable, and most important group of users is the intermediate group.

It's amazing to think that the majority of real users are typically ignored, but more often than not that is the case. You can see it in many enterprise and commercial software-based products. The overall design biases them towards expert users, while at the same time, cumbersome tools like wizards and Clippy are grafted on to meet the marketing department's perception of new users. Experts rarely use them, and beginners soon desire to discard these embarrassing reminders of their ignorance. But the perpetual intermediate majority is perpetually stuck with them.

AXIOM

Optimize for intermediates.

Our goal should be neither to pander to beginners nor to rush intermediates into expertise. Our goal is threefold: to rapidly and painlessly get beginners into intermediacy; to avoid putting obstacles in the way of those intermediates who want to become experts; and most of all, to keep perpetual intermediates happy as they stay firmly in the middle of the skill spectrum.

We need to spend more time making our programs powerful and easy to use for perpetual intermediate users. We must accommodate beginners and experts, too, but not to the discomfort of the largest segment of users. The remainder of this chapter describes some basic strategies for doing so.

What beginners need

Beginners are undeniably sensitive, and it is easy to demoralize a first-timer; but we must keep in mind that the state of beginnerhood is *never* an objective. Nobody wants to remain a beginner. It is merely a rite of passage everyone must experience. Good software shortens that passage without bringing attention to it.

As an interaction designer, it's best to imagine that users—especially beginners—are simultaneously very intelligent and very busy. They need some instruction, but not very much, and the process has to be rapid and targeted. If a ski instructor begins lecturing on meteorology and alpine ecology, he will lose his students regardless of their aptitude for skiing. Just because a user needs to learn how to operate a program doesn't mean that he needs or wants to learn how it works inside.

Imagine users as very intelligent but very busy.

On the other hand, intelligent people always learn better when they understand cause and effect, so you must give them an understanding of why things work as they do. We use mental models to bridge the contradiction. If the represented model of the interface closely follows the user's mental model (as discussed in Chapter 2), it will provide the understanding the user needs without forcing him to figure out the implementation model.

Getting beginners on board

A new user must grasp the concepts and scope of the program quickly or he will abandon it. Thus, the first order of business of the designer is to ensure that the software adequately reflects the user's mental model of his tasks. He may not recall from use to use exactly which command is needed to act on a particular object, but he will definitely remember that the relationships between objects and actions — the important concepts — if the interface's conceptual structure is consistent with his mental model.

To get beginners to a state of intermediacy requires extra help from the program, but this extra help will get in their way as soon as they become intermediates. This means that whatever extra help you provide, it must not be fixed into the interface. It must know how to go away when its services are no longer required.

Standard online help is a poor tool for providing such beginner assistance. We'll talk more about help in Chapter 35, but its primary utility is as a reference, and beginners don't need reference information; they need overview information, such as a guided tour.

A separate guide facility — displayed within a dialog box — is a fine means for communicating overview, scope, and purpose. As the user begins the program, a dialog box can appear that states the basic goals and tools of the program, naming the main features. As long as the guide stays focused on beginner issues, like scope and goals, and avoids perpetual intermediate and expert issues (discussed below), it should be adequate for assisting beginners.

Beginners also rely heavily upon menus to learn and execute commands (see Chapter 27 for a detailed discussion about why this is true). Menus may be slow and clunky, but they are also thorough and verbose, so they offer reassurances. The dialog boxes that the menu items launch (if they do so at all) should also be (tersely) explanatory, and come with convenient Cancel buttons.

What experts need

Experts are also a vital group because they have a disproportionate influence on less-experienced users. When a prospective buyer considers your product, he will trust the expert's opinion more than an intermediate's. If the expert says, "It's not very good," she may mean "It's not very good for experts." The beginner doesn't know that, however, and will take the expert's advice, even though it may not apply.

Experts might occasionally look for esoteric features, and they might make heavy use of a few of them. However, they will definitely demand faster access to their regular working set of tools, which may be quite large. In other words, experts want shortcuts to everything.

Anyone who uses a digital product for hours a day will very quickly internalize the nuances of its interface. It isn't so much that they *want* to cram frequently used commands into their heads, as much as it is unavoidable. Their frequency of use both justifies and requires the memorization.

Expert users constantly, aggressively seek to learn more and to see more connections between their actions and the program's behavior and representation. Experts appreciate new, powerful features. Their mastery of the program insulates them from becoming disturbed by the added complexity.

What perpetual intermediates need

Perpetual intermediates need access to tools. They don't need scope and purpose explained to them because they already know these things. ToolTips (see Chapter 29) are the perfect perpetual intermediate idiom. ToolTips say nothing about scope and purpose and meaning; they only state function in the briefest of idioms, consuming the least amount of video space in the process.

Perpetual intermediates know how to use reference materials. They are motivated to dig deeper and learn, as long as they don't have to tackle too much at once. This means that online help is a perpetual intermediate tool. They use it by way of the index, so that part of help must be very comprehensive.

Perpetual intermediates will be establishing the functions that they use with regularity and those that they only use rarely. The user may experiment with obscure features, but he will soon identify — probably subconsciously — his frequently used working set. The user will demand that the tools in his working set are placed front-and-center in the user interface, easy to find and to remember.

Perpetual intermediates usually know that advanced features exist, even though they may not need them or know how to use them. But the knowledge that they are there is reassuring to the perpetual intermediate, convincing him that he made the right choice investing in this program. The average skier may find it reassuring to know that there is a really scary black diamond expert run just beyond those trees, even if she never intends to use it. It gives her something to aspire to and dream about.

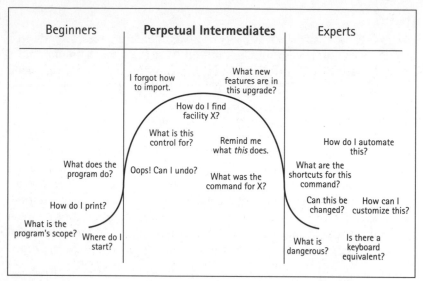

Figure 3-1: The demands that users place on software vary considerably with their experience. The tools presented to the user need to reflect this disparity. Your program won't be appreciated much if its best quality is that it is very easy for first-timers to learn, since most users will quickly become perpetual intermediates. Similarly, if only professional, full-time experts will use the product, the interface needs to cater to their unique needs.

Your program's code must provide for both rank amateurs and all the possible cases an expert might encounter. Don't let this technical requirement influence your design thinking. Yes, you must provide those features for expert users. Yes, you must provide support for beginners. But you must apply the bulk of your talents, time, and resources to designing the best interaction possible for your most representative users: the perpetual intermediates.

Chapter 4

Understanding Users: Qualitative Research

The outcome of any design effort must ultimately be judged by how successfully it meets the requirements of both the user and the organization that commissioned it. No matter how skillful and creative the designer, if she does not have a clear and detailed knowledge of the users she is designing for, what the constraints of the problem are, and what business or organizational goals the design is hoping to achieve, she will have little chance of success.

What and how questions like these are best answered by *qualitative* research, not metrics or demographics (though these also have their purpose). As we shall see in this chapter, there are many types of qualitative research, each of which plays an important role in filling in a picture of the design landscape of a product.

Qualitative versus Quantitative Research

Research is a word that most people associate with science and objectivity. This association isn't incorrect, but it biases many people towards the notion that the only valid sort of research is the kind that yields the supposed ultimate in objectivity: quantitative data. The notion that numbers don't lie is prevalent in the business and engineering communities, even though we all rationally understand that numbers — especially numbers ascribed to human activities — can be manipulated or reinterpreted at least as dramatically as words.

Data gathered by the hard sciences like physics is simply different from that gathered on human activities: electrons don't have moods that vary from minute to minute, and the tight controls physicists place on their experiments to isolate observed behaviors are next to impossible in the social sciences. Any attempt to reduce human behavior to statistics is likely to overlook important nuances, which though they might not directly affect business plans, do make an enormous difference to the design of products. Quantitative research can only answer questions about how much or how many along a few reductive axes. Qualitative research can tell you about what, how and why in rich, multivariate detail.

Social scientists have long realized that human behaviors are too complex and subject to too many variables to rely solely on quantitative data to understand them. Usability practitioners, borrowing techniques from anthropology and other social sciences, have developed many qualitative methods for gathering useful data on user behaviors to a more pragmatic end: to help create products that better serve user needs.

The remainder of this chapter will focus on qualitative research techniques that support the methods described in subsequent chapters. At the end of the chapter, we'll briefly discuss how quantitative research can, and cannot, be used to help support this effort.

The value of qualitative research

Qualitative research helps us understand the domain, context, and constraints of a product in different, more useful ways than quantitative research does. It also helps us identify patterns of behavior among users and potential users of a product much more quickly and easily than would be possible with quantitative approaches. In particular, qualitative research helps us understand:

✓ Existing products, and how they are used

✓ Potential users of new or existing products, and how they currently approach activities and problems the new product design hopes to address

✓ Technical, business, and environmental contexts — the **domain** — of the product to be designed

✓ Vocabulary and other social aspects of the domain in question

Qualitative research can also help the progress of design projects by:

✓ Providing credibility and authority to the design team, because design decisions can be traced to research results

✓ Uniting the team with a common understanding of domain issues and user concerns

✓ Empowering management to make more informed decisions about product design issues that would otherwise be based on guesswork or personal preference

It is the experience of the authors in their practice that qualitative methods, in addition to the benefits described above, tend to be faster, less expensive, more flexible, and more likely than their quantitative counterparts to provide useful answers to important questions that lead to superior design:

✓ What problems are people encountering with their current ways of doing what the product hopes to do?

✓ Into what broader contexts in people's lives does the product fit and how?

✓ What are the basic goals people have in using the product, and what basic tasks help people accomplish them?

Types of qualitative research

Social science and usability texts are full of methods and techniques for conducting qualitative research, and readers are encouraged to explore this literature. In this chapter, the authors focus specifically on techniques that have been proven in our practice over the last decade, occasionally drawing attention to similar techniques practiced in the usability field at large. Rather than bog down in theory, we try to present these techniques from a more pragmatic and less theoretical perspective. The qualitative research techniques we discuss include:

✓ Stakeholder interviews

✓ Subject matter expert (SME) interviews

✓ User and customer interviews

✓ User observation/ethnographic field studies

✓ Literature review

✓ Product/prototype and competitive audits

STAKEHOLDER INTERVIEWS

Research for any new product design, though it must end with understanding the user, should start by understanding the business and technical context in which the product will be built. This is necessary not only to ensure a viable and feasible end result, but also to provide a common language and understanding among the design team, management, and engineering teams.

Stakeholders are any key members of the organization commissioning the design work, and typically include managers and key contributors from engineering, sales, product marketing, marketing communications, customer support, and usability. They may also include similar people from other organizations in business partnership with the commissioning organization, and executives. Interviews with stakeholders should occur before any user research begins.

It is usually most effective to interview each stakeholder one-on-one, rather than in a larger, cross-departmental group. A one-on-one setting promotes candor on the part of the stakeholder, and ensures that individual views are not lost in a crowd. Interviews need not last longer than about an hour, though follow-up meetings may be called for if a particular stakeholder is identified as an exceptionally valuable source of information.

The type of information that is important to gather from stakeholders includes:

✓ **What is the preliminary vision of the product from each stakeholder perspective?** As in the fable of the blind men and the elephant, you may find that each business department has a slightly different and slightly incomplete perspective on the product to be designed. Part of the design approach must therefore involve harmonizing these perspectives with those of users and customers.

✓ **What is the budget and schedule?** The answer to this question often provides a reality check on the scope of the design effort and provides a decision point for management if user research indicates a greater (or lesser) scope is required.

✓ **What are the technical constraints?** Another important determinant of design scope is a firm understanding of what is technically feasible given budget, time, and technology constraints.

✓ **What are the business drivers?** It is important for the design team to understand what the business is trying to accomplish. This again leads to a decision point, should user research indicate a conflict between business and user needs. The design must, as much as possible, create a win-win situation for users, customers, and providers of the product.

✓ **What are the stakeholders' perceptions of the user?** Stakeholders who have relationships with users (such as customer support representatives) may have important insights on users that will help you to formulate your user research plan. You may also find that there are significant disconnects between some stakeholders' perceptions of their users and what you discover in your research. This information can become an important decision point for management later in the process.

Understanding these issues and their impact on design solutions helps you as a designer to better serve *your* customer, as well as users of the product. Building consensus internally will help you to articulate issues that the business as a whole may not have identified, build internal consensus that is critical for decision making later in the design process, and build credibility for your design team.

SUBJECT MATTER EXPERT (SME) INTERVIEWS

Some stakeholders may also be **subject matter experts** (SMEs): experts on the domain within which the product you are designing will operate. Most SMEs were users of the product or its predecessors at one time, and may now be trainers, managers, or consultants. Often they are experts hired by stakeholders, rather than stakeholders themselves. Similar to stakeholders, SMEs can provide valuable perspectives on a product and its users, but designers should be careful to recognize that SMEs represent a somewhat skewed perspective. Some points to consider about using SMEs are:

✓ **SMEs are expert users.** Their long experience with a product or its domain mean that they may have grown accustomed to current interactions. They may also lean towards expert controls rather than interactions designed for perpetual intermediates. SMEs are often not current users of the product, and may have more of a management perspective.

✓ **SMEs are knowledgeable, but they aren't designers.** They may have many ideas on how to improve a product. Some of these may be valid and valuable, but the most useful pieces of information to glean from these suggestions are the causative *problems* that lead to their proposed solutions.

✓ **SMEs are necessary in complex or specialized domains** such as medical, scientific, or financial services. If you are designing for a technical or otherwise specialized domain, you will likely need some guidance from SMEs, unless you are one yourself. Use SMEs to get information on complex regulations and industry best practices. SME knowledge of user roles and characteristics is critical for planning user research in complex domains.

✓ **You will want access to SMEs throughout the design process.** If your product domain requires use of SMEs, you should be able to bring them in at different stages of the design to help perform reality checks on design details. Make sure that you secure this access in your early interviews.

USER AND CUSTOMER INTERVIEWS

It is easy to confuse users with customers. For consumer products, customers are often the same as users, but in corporate or technical domains, users and customers rarely describe the same sets of people. Although both groups should be interviewed, each has its own perspective on the product that needs to be factored quite differently into an eventual design.

Customers of a product are those people who make the decision to purchase it. For consumer products, customers are frequently users of the product; although for products aimed at children or teens, the customers are parents or other adult supervisors of children. In the case of most enterprise or technical products, the customer is someone very different from the user — often an

IT manager—with distinct goals and needs. It's important to understand customers and their goals in order to make a product *viable*. It is also important to realize that customers seldom actually use the product themselves, and when they do, they use it quite differently than the way their users do.

When interviewing customers, you will want to understand:

- ✓ Their goals in purchasing the product

- ✓ Their frustrations with current solutions

- ✓ Their decision process for purchasing a product of the type you're designing

- ✓ Their role in installation, maintenance, and management of the product

- ✓ Domain-related issues and vocabulary

Like SMEs, customers may have many opinions about how to improve the design of the product. It is important to analyze these suggestions, as in the case of SMEs, to determine what issues or problems underlie the ideas offered, because better, more integrated solutions may become evident later in the design process.

Users of a product should be the main focus of the design effort. They are the people (not their managers or support team) who are personally trying to accomplish something with the product. **Potential users** are people who do not currently use the product, but who are good candidates for using it in the future. A good set of user interviews includes both current users (if the product already exists and is being revised) and potential users (users of competitive products and non-automated systems if appropriate). Information we are interested in learning from users includes:

- ✓ Problems and frustrations with the product (or analogous system if they are potential users)

- ✓ The context of how the product fits into their lives or workflow: when, why, and how the product is used, that is, **patterns of user behavior** with the product

- ✓ Domain knowledge from a user perspective: What do users need to know to accomplish their jobs

- ✓ A basic understanding of the users' current tasks: both those the product requires and those it doesn't support

- ✓ A clear understanding of user goals: their motivations and expectations concerning use of the product

USER OBSERVATION

Most people are incapable of accurately assessing their own behaviors (Pinker, 1999), especially outside of the context of their activities. It then follows that interviews performed outside the context of the situations the designer hopes to document will yield less complete and less accurate data. Basically, you can talk to users about how they think they behave, or you can observe it first-hand. The latter route provides superior results.

Many usability professionals make use of technological aides such as audio or video recorders to capture what users say and do. Care must be taken not to make these technologies too obtrusive; otherwise the users will be distracted and behave differently than they would off-tape.

Perhaps the most effective technique for gathering qualitative user data combines interview and observation, allowing the designer to ask clarifying questions and direct inquiries about situations and behaviors they observe in real-time.

LITERATURE REVIEW

In parallel with stakeholder interviews, the design team should review any literature pertaining to the product or its domain. This can and should include product marketing plans, market research, technology specifications and white papers, business and technical journal articles in the domain, competitive studies, Web searches for related and competing products and news, usability study results and metrics, and customer support data such as call center statistics.

The design team should collect this literature, use it as a basis for developing questions to ask stakeholders and SMEs, and later use it to supply additional domain knowledge and vocabulary, and to check against compiled user data.

PRODUCT AND COMPETITIVE AUDITS

Also in parallel to stakeholder and SME interviews, it is often quite helpful for the design team to examine any existing version or prototype of the product, as well as its chief competitors. Doing so gives the design team a sense of the state of the art, and provides fuel for questions during the interviews. The design team, ideally, should engage in an informal **heuristic** or **expert review** of both the current and competitive interfaces, comparing each against interaction and visual design principles (such as those found in later chapters of this book). This procedure both familiarizes the team with the strengths and limitations of what is currently available to users, and provides a general idea of the current functional scope of the product.

Ethnographic Interviews: Interviewing and Observing Users

Drawing on years of design research in practice, the authors believe that a combination of one-on-one interviews and work/lifestyle observation is the most effective and efficient tool in a designer's arsenal for gathering qualitative data about users and their goals. The technique of **ethnographic interviews** (Wood, 1996) is a combination of immersive observation and directed interview techniques.

Hugh Beyer and Karen Holtzblatt have pioneered an ethnographic interviewing technique that they call **contextual inquiry**. Their method has, for good reason, rapidly gained traction in the industry, and provides a sound basis for qualitative user research. It is described in detail in the first four chapters of their book, *Contextual Design* (1998). Contextual inquiry methods closely parallel the methods described here, but with some subtle and important differences.

Contextual Inquiry

Contextual inquiry, according to Beyer and Holtzblatt, is based on a **master-apprentice model** of learning: observing and asking questions of the user as if she is the master craftsman and the interviewer the new apprentice. Beyer and Holtzblatt also enumerate four basic principles for engaging in ethnographic interviews:

✓ **Context:** Rather than interviewing the user in a clean white room, it is important to interact with and observe the user in their normal work environment, or whatever physical context is appropriate for the product. Observing users as they perform activities and questioning them in their own environments, filled with the artifacts they use each day, can bring the all-important details of their behaviors to light.

✓ **Partnership:** The interview and observation should take the tone of a collaborative exploration with the user, alternating between observation of work and discussion of its structure and details.

✓ **Interpretation:** Much of the work of the designer is reading between the lines of facts gathered about users' behaviors, their environment, and what they say. These facts must be taken together as a whole, and analyzed by the designer to uncover the design implications. Interviewers must be careful, however, to avoid assumptions based on their own interpretation of the facts without verifying these assumptions with users.

✓ **Focus:** Rather than coming to interviews with a set questionnaire or letting the interview wander aimlessly, the designer needs to subtly direct the interview so as to capture data relevant to design issues.

Improving on Contextual Inquiry

Contextual inquiry forms a solid theoretical foundation for qualitative research, but as a specific method it has some limitations and inefficiencies, at least in the opinion of the authors. The following process improvements, in the authors' experience, result in a more highly leveraged research phase that better sets the stage for successful design:

✓ **Shortening the interview process:** Contextual inquiry assumes full day interviews with users. The authors have found that interviews as short as one hour in duration are sufficient to gather the necessary user data, provided that a sufficient number of interviews (about six well-selected users for each hypothesized role or type) are scheduled. It is much easier and more effective to find a diverse set of users who will consent to an hour with a designer than it is to find users who will agree to spend an entire day.

✓ **Using smaller design teams:** Contextual inquiry assumes a large design team that conducts multiple interviews in parallel, followed by debriefing sessions in which the full team participates. The authors have found that it is more effective to conduct interviews sequentially with the same designers in each interview. This allows the design team to remain small (two or three designers), but even more important, it means that the entire team interacts with all interviewed users directly, allowing the members to most effectively analyze and synthesize the user data.

✓ **Identifying goals first:** Contextual inquiry, as described by Beyer and Holtzblatt, feeds a design process that is fundamentally task-focused. We propose that ethnographic interviews first identify and prioritize user goals before determining the tasks that relate to these goals.

✓ Looking beyond business contexts: The vocabulary of contextual inquiry assumes a business product and a corporate environment. Ethnographic interviews are also possible in consumer domains, though the focus of questioning is somewhat different, as we describe later in this chapter.

The remainder of this chapter provides general methods and tips for preparing for and conducting ethnographic interviews.

Preparing for ethnographic interviews

Ethnography is a term borrowed from anthropology, meaning the systematic and immersive study of human cultures. In anthropology, ethnographic researchers spend years living immersed in the cultures they study and record. Ethnographic interviews take the spirit of this type of research and apply it on a micro level. Rather than trying to understand behaviors and social rituals of an entire culture, the goal is to understand the behaviors and rituals of people interacting with individual products.

IDENTIFYING CANDIDATES

Because the designers must capture an entire range of user behaviors regarding a product, it is critical that the designers identify an appropriately diverse sample of users and user types when planning a series of interviews. Based on information gleaned from stakeholders, SMEs, and literature reviews, designers need to create a hypothesis that serves as a starting point in determining what sorts of users and potential users to interview.

Kim Goodwin (2002a) has coined this the **persona hypothesis**, because it is the first step towards identifying and synthesizing personas, the user archetypes we will discuss in detail in the next chapter. The persona hypothesis is based on likely behavioral differences, not demographics, but takes into consideration identified target markets and demographics. The nature of a product's domain makes a significant difference in how a persona hypothesis is constructed. Business users are often quite different than consumer users in their behavior patterns and motivations, and different techniques are used to build the persona hypothesis in each case.

THE PERSONA HYPOTHESIS   The persona hypothesis is a first cut at defining the different kinds of users (and sometimes customers) for a product in a particular domain. The hypothesis serves as a basis for an initial set of interviews; as interviews proceed, new interviews may be required if the data indicates the existence of user types not originally identified.

The persona hypothesis attempts to address, at a high level, these three questions:

✓ What different sorts of people might use this product?

✓ How might their needs and behaviors vary?

✓ What ranges of behavior and types of environments need to be explored?

ROLES IN BUSINESS AND CONSUMER DOMAINS   Patterns of needs and behavior, and therefore types of users, vary significantly between business and technical, and consumer products. For business products, **roles** — common sets of tasks and information needs related to distinct classes of users — provide an important initial organizing principle. For example, in an enterprise portal, we might find these rough roles:

✓ People who search for content on the portal

✓ People who upload and update content on the portal

✓ People who technically administer the portal

In business and technical contexts, roles often map roughly to job descriptions, so it is relatively easy to get a reasonable first cut of user types to interview by understanding the kind of jobs held by users (or potential users) of the system.

Unlike business users, consumers don't have concrete job descriptions, and their use of products tends to cross multiple contexts. Their roles map more closely to *lifestyle choices*, and it is possible for consumer users to assume multiple roles even for a single product in this sense. For consumers, roles can usually better be expressed by behavioral variables.

BEHAVIORAL AND DEMOGRAPHIC VARIABLES   Beyond roles, a persona hypothesis seeks to identify variables that might distinguish users based on their needs and behaviors. The most useful, but most difficult to anticipate without research, are behavioral variables: types of behavior that vary across a spectrum. For example, for an e-commerce application, there are several ranges of behavior concerning shopping that we might identify:

✓ Frequency of shopping (frequent — infrequent)

✓ Desire to shop (loves to shop — hates to shop)

✓ Motivation to shop (bargain hunting — searching for just the right item)

Although consumer user types can often be roughly defined by the combination of behavioral variables they map to, behavioral variables are also important for identifying types of business and technical users. People within a single business-role definition may have different motivations for being there and aspirations for what they plan to do in the future. Behavioral variables can capture this, though usually not until user data has been gathered.

Given the difficulty in accurately anticipating behavioral variables before user data is gathered, another helpful approach in building a persona hypothesis is making use of *demographic variables*. When planning your interviews, you can use market research to identify ages, locations, gender, and incomes of the target markets for the product. Interviewees should be distributed across these demographic ranges.

DOMAIN EXPERTISE VERSUS TECHNICAL EXPERTISE   One important type of behavioral distinction to note is the difference between technical expertise (knowledge of digital technology) and domain expertise (knowledge of a specialized subject area pertaining to a product). Different users will have varying amounts of technical expertise; similarly, some users of a product may be less expert in their knowledge of the product's domain (for example, accounting knowledge in the case of a general ledger application). Thus, depending on who the design target of the product is, domain support may be a necessary part of the product's design, as well as technical ease of use.

A relatively naive user will likely never be able to use more than a small subset of a domain-specific product's functions without domain support provided in the interface. If naive users are part of the target market for a domain-specific product, care must be taken to support domain-naive behaviors.

ENVIRONMENTAL CONSIDERATIONS   A final consideration, especially in the case of business products, is the cultural differences between organizations in which the users are employed. Small companies, for example, tend to have more interpersonal contact between workers; huge companies have layers of bureaucracy. These environmental variables also fall into ranges:

✓ Company size (small — multinational)

✓ IT presence (ad hoc — draconian)

✓ Security level (lax — tight)

Like behavioral variables, these may be difficult to identify without some domain research, because patterns do vary significantly by industry and geographic region.

PUTTING A PLAN TOGETHER

After you have created a persona hypothesis, complete with potential roles, behavioral, demographic, and environmental variables, you then need to create an interview plan that can be communicated to the person in charge of providing access to users.

Each identified role, behavioral variable, demographic variable, and environmental variable identified in the persona hypothesis should be explored in four to six interviews (sometimes more if a domain is particularly complex). However, these interviews can overlap: It is perfectly acceptable to interview a female in her twenties who loves to shop; this would count as an interview for each of three different variables: gender, age group, and desire to shop. By being clever about mapping variables to interviewee screening profiles, you can keep the number of interviews to a manageable number.

Conducting ethnographic interviews

After the persona hypothesis has been formulated and an interview plan has been derived from it, you are ready to interview — assuming you get access to interviewees! While formulating the interview plan, designers should work closely with project stakeholders who have access to users. Stakeholder involvement is generally the best way to make interviews happen, especially for business and technical products.

If stakeholders can't help you get in touch with users, you can contact a market or usability research firm that specializes in finding people for surveys and focus groups. These firms are useful for reaching consumers with diverse demographics. The difficulty with this approach is that it can sometimes be challenging to get interviewees who will permit you to interview them in their homes or places of work.

As a last alternative for consumer products, designers can recruit friends and relatives. This makes it easier to observe the interviewees in a natural environment, but also is quite limiting as far as diversity of demographic and behavioral variables are concerned.

INTERVIEW TEAMS AND TIMING

The authors favor a team of two designers per interview, one to drive the interview and take light notes, and the other to take detailed notes (these roles can switch halfway through the interview). One hour per user interviewed should be sufficient, except in the case of interviewing consumers in their homes or traveling with them as they interact with a product (for which you should budget extra time). Teams should try to limit interviews to six per day, so that there is adequate time for debriefing and strategizing between interviews, and so that the interviewers do not get fatigued.

PHASES OF ETHNOGRAPHIC INTERVIEWS

A complete set of ethnographic interviews for a project can be grouped into three distinct, chronological phases. The approach of the interviews in each successive phase is subtly different from the last, reflecting the growing knowledge of user behaviors that results from each additional interview. Focus tends to be broad at the start, aimed at gross structural and goal-oriented issues; and more narrow for interviews at the end of the cycle, zooming in on specific functions and task-oriented issues.

- ✓ Early-phase interviews are exploratory in nature, and focused on gathering domain knowledge from the point of view of the user. Broad, open-ended questions are common, with a lesser degree of drill-down into details.

- ✓ Mid-phase interviews are where designers begin to see patterns of use and ask open-ended and clarifying questions to help connect the dots. Questions in general are more focused on domain specifics, now that the designers have absorbed the basic rules, structures, and vocabularies of the domain.

- ✓ Late-phase interviews confirm previously observed patterns, further clarifying user roles and behaviors and making fine adjustments to assumptions about task and information needs. Closed-ended questions are used in greater number, tying up loose ends in the data.

After you have an idea who your actual interviewees will be, it can be helpful, if you have the opportunity, to work with stakeholders to schedule individuals most appropriate for each phase in the interview cycle. In some cases, you may also want to loop back and interview a particularly knowledgeable and articulate subject both at the beginning and the end of the interview cycle.

BASIC METHODS

The basic methods of ethnographic interviewing are simple, straightforward, and very low-tech. Although the nuances of interviewing subjects takes some time to master, any practitioner should, if they follow the suggestions below, be rewarded with a wealth of useful qualitative data:

- ✓ Interview where the interaction happens

- ✓ Avoid a fixed set of questions

- ✓ Focus on goals first, tasks second

✓ Avoid making the user a designer

✓ Avoid discussion of technology

✓ Encourage storytelling

✓ Ask for a show and tell

✓ Avoid leading questions

We describe each of these methods in more detail in the following sections.

INTERVIEW WHERE THE INTERACTION HAPPENS   Following the first principle of contextual inquiry, it is of critical importance that subjects be interviewed in the places where they actually use the products. Not only does this give the interviewers the opportunity to witness the product being used, but it also gives the interview team access to the environment in which the interaction occurs. This can give tremendous insight into product constraints and user needs and goals.

Observe the environment closely: It is likely to be crawling with clues about tasks the interviewee might not have mentioned. Notice, for example, the kind of information they need (papers on desks or adhesive notes on screen borders); inadequate systems (cheat sheets and user manuals); frequency and priority of tasks (inbox and outbox); and the kind of workflows they follow (memos, charts, calendars). Don't snoop without permission, but if you see something that looks interesting, ask your interviewee to discuss it.

AVOID A FIXED SET OF QUESTIONS   If you approach ethnographic interviews with a fixed questionnaire, you not only run the risk of alienating the interview subject, but you can also cause the interviewers to miss out on a wealth of valuable user data. The entire premise of ethnographic interviews (and contextual inquiry) is that we as interviewers don't know enough about the domain to presuppose the questions that need asking: We must learn what is important from the people we talk to. This said, it's certainly useful to have *types* of questions in mind.

Here are some **goal-oriented questions** to consider:

✓ *Opportunity*: What activities currently waste your time?

✓ *Goals*: What makes a good day? A bad day?

✓ *Priorities*: What is most important to you?

✓ *Information*: What helps you make decisions?

Another useful type of question is the **system-oriented question**:

✓ *Function*: What are the most common things you do with the product?

✓ *Frequency*: What parts of the product do you use most?

✓ *Preference*: What are your favorite aspects of the product? What drives you crazy?

✓ *Failure*: How do you work around problems?

✓ *Expertise*: What shortcuts do you employ?

For business products, **workflow-oriented questions** can be helpful:

✓ *Process*: What did you do when you first came in today? And after that?

✓ *Occurrence and recurrence*: How often do you do this? What things do you do weekly or monthly, but not every day?

✓ *Exception*: What constitutes a typical day? What would be an unusual event?

To better understand user motivations, you can employ **attitude-oriented questions**:

✓ *Aspiration*: What do you see yourself doing five years from now?

✓ *Avoidance*: What would you prefer not to do? What do you procrastinate on?

✓ *Motivation*: What do you enjoy most about your job (or lifestyle)? What do you always tackle first?

FOCUS ON GOALS FIRST, TASKS SECOND   Unlike contextual inquiry and the majority of other qualitative research methods, the first priority of ethnographic interviewing is understanding the *why* of users — what motivates the behaviors of individuals in different roles, and *how* they hope to ultimately accomplish this goal — not the *what* of the tasks they perform. Understanding the tasks is important, and the tasks must be diligently recorded. But these tasks will ultimately be restructured to better match user goals in the final design.

AVOID MAKING THE USER A DESIGNER   Guide the interviewee towards examining problems and away from expressing solutions. Most of the time, those solutions sound good to *him*, but are either not well considered, or they represent idiosyncratic solutions that the user-modeling tool of personas actively seeks to avoid. That said, if a user blurts out an interesting idea, by all means record it for later reference, thank the user for his input, and move on.

AVOID DISCUSSIONS OF TECHNOLOGY   Just as you don't want to treat the user as a designer, you also don't want to treat him as a programmer or engineer. In the case of technical or scientific products, where technology is always an issue, distinguish between domain-related technology and product-related technology, and steer away from the latter.

ENCOURAGE STORYTELLING   Far more useful than asking users for design advice is encouraging them to tell specific stories about their experiences with a product (whether an old version of the one you're redesigning, or an analogous product): how they use it, what they think of it, who else they interact with when using it, where they go with it, and so forth. Detailed stories of this kind are some of the best ways to understand how users relate to and interact with products. Try to encourage stories that deal with both typical cases and more exceptional ones.

ASK FOR A SHOW-AND-TELL   After you have a good idea of the flow and structure of a user's activities and interactions and you have exhausted other questions, it is often useful to ask the interviewee for a show-and-tell or **grand tour** of artifacts related to the design problem. These can be domain-related artifacts, software interfaces, paper systems, tours of the work environment, and ideally all the above. Be careful to not only record the artifacts themselves (digital or video cameras are very handy at this stage), but also pay attention to *how* the interviewee describes them. Be sure to ask plenty of clarifying questions as well.

AVOID LEADING QUESTIONS   One important thing to avoid in interviews is the use of *leading questions*. Just as in a courtroom, where lawyers can, by virtue of their authority, bias witnesses by suggesting answers to them, designers can inadvertently bias interview subjects by implicitly (or explicitly) suggesting solutions or opinions about behaviors. Examples of leading questions include:

- ✓ Would feature X help you?
- ✓ You like X, don't you?
- ✓ Do you think you'd use X if it were available?

AFTER THE INTERVIEWS

After each interview, teams compare notes and discuss any particularly interesting trends observed or specific points brought up in the most recent interview. If they have the time, they should also look back at old notes to see whether unanswered questions from other interviews and research have been properly answered. This information should be used to strategize about the approach to take in subsequent interviews.

After the interview process is finished, it is useful to once again make a pass through all the notes, marking or highlighting trends and patterns in the data. This is very useful for the next step, creating personas from the cumulative research. If it is helpful, the team can create a binder of the notes, review any videotapes, and print out artifact images to place in the binder or on a public surface like a wall where they are all visible simultaneously. This will be useful in later design phases.

Other Types of Research

This chapter has focused on qualitative research aimed at gathering user data that will later be used (as described in the next chapter) to construct robust user and domain models that form the key tools in the synthesis of Goal-Directed Design. Designers are likely familiar with, and will encounter, other forms of research, most of which are unsuitable as design tools, but which have their uses at other points in the development process. In this section, we will discuss several of the more prominent research methods and how they fit into the overall development effort.

Focus groups

Marketing organizations are particularly fond of gathering user data via **focus groups**, in which representative users, usually chosen to match previously identified demographics, are gathered together in a room and asked a structured set of questions and/or provided a structured set of choices. Often the meeting is recorded on audio or video media for later reference. Focus groups are a standard technique in traditional product marketing. They are useful for gauging initial reactions to the *form* of a product, its visual appearance, or industrial design. Focus groups can also gather reactions to a product that the respondents have been using for some time.

Although focus groups may appear to provide the requisite user contact, the method is in many ways not appropriate as a design tool. Focus groups excel at eliciting information about products that people own or are willing (or unwilling) to purchase, but are weak for gathering data about what people actually do with those products or how they do it. As already mentioned, people have trouble assessing exactly what they do and when: Their behaviors require observation to adequately capture them. Finally, focus groups, because they are a group activity, tend to drive to consensus: The majority or loudest opinion becomes the group opinion. This is anathema to the design process, because designers must understand all the different patterns of behavior a product must address. Focus groups tend to stifle exactly the diversity of opinion that designers need to understand.

Market demographics and market segments

The marketing profession has taken much of the guesswork out of determining what motivates people to buy. One of the most powerful tools for doing so is market segmentation, which groups people by their distinct needs to determine what types of consumers will be most receptive to a particular product or marketing message.

Marketers classify consumers according to a set of demographic and geographic variables such as age, race, education, income and location, the raw data of which is usually gathered by a combination of market surveys and focus groups. More sophisticated consumer data also include psychographics and behavioral variables including attitudes, lifestyle, values, ideology, risk aversion, and decision-making patterns. Classification systems such as SRI's VALS segmentation (SRI, 2002) and Jonathan Robbin's geodemographic PRIZM clusters (Weiss, 2000) can add greater clarity to the data by predicting consumers' purchasing power, motivation, self-orientation, and resources. These market-modeling techniques are not only able to forecast marketplace acceptance of products and services, but they can also be powerful tools for convincing executives to build a product. After all, if you know X people might buy a product or service for Y dollars, it is easy to evaluate the potential return on investment.

However, understanding why somebody wants to buy something is not the same thing as actually defining the product — what it is, how it will work, and how it will be used. Market segmentation is a great tool for defining markets, but an ineffective tool for defining *products*.

It turns out, however, that data gathered via market research, and that gathered via qualitative user research complement each other quite well. As already discussed, ethnographic interviewers should use market research to help them select interview targets. We will discuss the differences between segmentation models and user models in more detail in Chapter 5.

Usability and user testing

Usability, or user testing, focuses on measurable characteristics of a user's interaction with a product. Assessing the usability of a product focuses on standardized tests that yield quantifiable data. In usability testing, results often reveal trends pointing toward problem areas, as well as successful aspects of the product.

Usability testing requires a design artifact to test against. This places usability testing fairly late in the design cycle, after there is a coherent concept and sufficient detail to generate paper or other prototypes. User testing should also be performed as part of the test cycle on the product itself, with results provided to both the designers and developers.

Because the findings of user testing are generally measurable and quantitative, usability research is especially useful in comparing specific design variants to choose the most effective solution. Customer feedback gathered from usability testing is most useful when you need to validate or refine the interaction mechanisms or the form and expression of specific design elements.

Usability is especially effective at testing:

✓ **Naming:** Do section/button labels make sense? Do certain words resonate better than others do?

✓ **Organization:** Especially true for products that deliver information (as opposed to providing a service). Is information grouped into the right number of categories? Are items located in the places customers might look for them?

✓ **First-time use and discoverability:** Are common items easy to find for new users? Are instructions clear? Are instructions necessary?

✓ **Effectiveness:** Can customers efficiently complete specific tasks? Are they making missteps? Where? How often?

When user testing, be sure that what you are testing is actually measurable and that the results will be useful in correcting design issues. Jakob Nielsen's *Usability Engineering* (1993) is the classic volume on usability, and provides excellent guidance on the subject.

Take the time to plan your user research. Match the appropriate technique to the appropriate place in your development cycle. Your product will benefit, and you'll avoid wasting time and resources. Putting a product to the test in a lab to see whether it passes or fails may provide a lot of data, but not necessarily a lot of value. Using ethnographic interviews at the beginning of the process allows you, as a designer, to truly understand your users, their needs and their motivations. Once you have a solid design concept based on qualitative user research and the models that research feeds, your usability testing will become an even more efficient tool for judging the effectiveness of design choices you have made. Qualitative research allows you to do the heavy lifting up front in the process.

Chapter 5

Modeling Users: Personas and Goals

The most powerful tools are simple in concept, but must be applied with some sophistication. The most powerful interaction design tool used by the authors is simple on the surface: *a precise descriptive model of the user, what he wishes to accomplish, and why*. The sophistication becomes apparent in the way we construct and use that model.

These user models, which we call **personas**, are not real people, but they are based on the behaviors and motivations of real people and represent them throughout the design process. They are *composite archetypes* based on behavioral data gathered from many actual users through ethnographic interviews. We *discover* our personas during the course of the Research phase and formalize them in the Modeling phase. By understanding our personas, we achieve an understanding of our users' goals in specific contexts—a critical tool for translating user data into design frameworks.

There are many useful models that can serve as tools for the interaction designer, but the authors feel that personas are among the strongest. This chapter focuses on personas and goals and the process for creating personas; other models are briefly considered at the end of the chapter.

Why Model?

Models are used extensively in design, development, and the sciences. They are powerful tools for representing complex structures and relationships for the purpose of better understanding or visualizing them. Without models, we are left to make sense of unstructured, raw data, without the benefit of the big picture or any organizing principle. Good models emphasize the salient features of the structures or relationships they represent and de-emphasize the less significant details.

Because we are designing for users, it is important that we can understand and visualize the salient aspects of their relationships with each other, with their social and physical environments, and of course, with the products we hope to design.

Just as physicists create models of the atom based on raw, observed data and intuitive synthesis of the patterns in their data, so must designers create models of users based on raw, observed behaviors and intuitive synthesis of the patterns in the data. Only after we formalize such patterns can we hope to systematically construct patterns of interactions that smoothly match the behaviors, mental models, and goals of users. Personas provide this formalization.

Personas

To create a product that must satisfy a broad audience of users, logic tells you to make it as broad in its functionality as possible to accommodate the most people. *This logic, however, is flawed.* The best way to successfully accommodate a variety of users is to design for *specific types of individuals with specific needs*.

When you broadly and arbitrarily extend a product's functionality to include many constituencies, you increase the cognitive load and navigational overhead for all users. Facilities that may please some users will likely interfere with the satisfaction of others (see Figure 5-1).

Figure 5-1: A simplified example of how personas are useful. If you try to design an automobile that pleases every possible driver, you end up with a car with every possible feature, but which pleases nobody. Software today is too often designed to please too many users, resulting in low user satisfaction. Figure 5-2 provides an alternative approach.

The key is in choosing the right individuals to design for, ones whose needs represent the needs of a larger set of key constituents (see Figure 5-2), and knowing how to prioritize design elements to address the needs of the most important users without significantly inconveniencing secondary users. Personas provide a powerful tool for understanding user needs, differentiating between different types of users, and prioritizing which users are the most important to target in the design of function and behavior.

Since they were introduced as a tool for user modeling in *The Inmates Are Running The Asylum* (Cooper, 1999), personas have gained great popularity in the usability community, but they have also been the subject of some misunderstandings. This section attempts to clarify and explain in more depth some of the concepts and the rationale behind personas.

Strengths of personas as a design tool

The persona is a powerful, multipurpose design tool that helps overcome several problems that currently plague the development of digital products. Personas help designers:

- ✓ **Determine** what a product should do and how it should behave. Persona goals and tasks provide the basis for the design effort.

- ✓ **Communicate** with stakeholders, developers, and other designers. Personas provide a common language for discussing design decisions, and also help keep the design centered on users at every step in the process.

✓ **Build consensus and commitment** to the design. With a common language comes a common understanding. Personas reduce the need for elaborate diagrammatic models because, as the authors have found, it is easier to understand the many nuances of user behavior through the narrative structures that personas employ.

✓ **Measure** the design's effectiveness. Design choices can be tested on a persona in the same way that they can be shown to a real user during the formative process. Although this doesn't replace the need to test on real users, it provides a powerful reality check tool for designers trying to solve design problems. This allows design iteration to occur rapidly and inexpensively at the whiteboard, and it results in a far stronger design baseline when the time comes to test with real users.

✓ **Contribute** to other product-related efforts such as marketing and sales plans. The authors have seen their clients repurpose personas across their organization, informing marketing campaigns, organizational structure, and other strategic planning activities. Business units outside of product development desire sophisticated knowledge of a product's users and typically view personas with great interest.

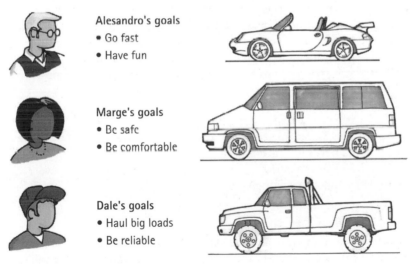

Alesandro's goals
- Go fast
- Have fun

Marge's goals
- Be safe
- Be comfortable

Dale's goals
- Haul big loads
- Be reliable

Figure 5-2: A simplified example of how personas are useful. By designing different cars for different people with different specific goals, we are able to create designs that other people with similar needs to our target drivers also find satisfying. The same holds true for the design of digital products and software.

Personas also resolve three user-centered design issues that arise during product development:

✓ The elastic user

✓ Self-referential design

✓ Design edge cases

We discuss each of these briefly in the following sections.

THE ELASTIC USER

Although satisfying the user is our goal, the term *user* causes trouble when applied to specific design problems and contexts. Its imprecision makes it unusable as a design tool — every person on a product team has his own conceptions of the user and what the user needs. When it comes time to make product decisions, this "user" becomes *elastic*, bending and stretching to fit the opinions and presuppositions of whoever has the floor.

If programmers find it convenient to simply drop a user into a confusing file system of nested, hierarchical folders to find the information she needs, they define the elastic user as an accommodating, computer-literate power user. Other times, when they find it more convenient to step the user through a difficult process with a wizard, they define the elastic user as an unsophisticated first-time user. Designing for the elastic user gives the developer license to code as he pleases while still apparently serving "the user." However, our goal is to design *software* that properly meets *real* user needs. Real users — and the personas representing them — are not elastic, but rather have specific requirements based on their goals, capabilities, and contexts.

SELF-REFERENTIAL DESIGN

Self-referential design occurs when designers or developers project their own goals, motivations, skills, and mental models onto a product's design. Most "cool" product designs fall into this category: The audience doesn't extend beyond people like the designer, which is fine for a narrow range of products and completely inappropriate for most others. Similarly, programmers apply self-referential design when they create implementation-model products. *They* understand perfectly how it works and are comfortable with such products. Few non-programmers would concur.

DESIGN EDGE CASES

Another syndrome that personas help prevent is designing for edge cases — those situations that might possibly happen, but usually won't for the target personas. Naturally, edge cases must be programmed for, but they should never be the design focus. Personas provide a reality check for the design. We can ask, "Will Julie want to perform this operation very often? Will she ever?" With this knowledge, we can prioritize functions with great clarity.

Personas are based on research

Personas must, like any model, be based on real-world observation. As discussed in the preceding chapter, the primary source of data used to synthesize personas must be from ethnographic interviews, contextual inquiry, or other similar dialogues with and observation of actual and potential users. The quality of the data gathered following the process (outlined in Chapter 4) directly impacts the efficacy of personas in clarifying and directing the synthesis of design solutions. Other data that can support and supplement the creation of personas include, in rough order of efficacy:

- ✓ Interviews with users outside of their use contexts
- ✓ Information about users supplied by stakeholders and subject matter experts (SMEs)
- ✓ Market research data such as focus groups and surveys
- ✓ Market segmentation models
- ✓ Data gathered from literature reviews and previous studies

However, none of this supplemental data can take the place of direct interaction with and observation of users in their native environments. Almost every word in a well-developed persona's description can be traced back to user quotes or observed behaviors.

Personas are represented as individuals

Personas are user models that are represented as specific, individual humans. They are not actual people, but are synthesized directly from observations of real people. One of the key elements that allow personas to be successful as user models is that they are *personifications* (Constantine and Lockwood, 2002). They are *represented* as specific individuals. This is appropriate and effective because of the unique aspects of personas as user models: They engage the *empathy* of the development team towards the human target of the design. Empathy is critical for the designers, who will be making their decisions for design frameworks and details based on both the cognitive *and* emotional dimensions of the persona, as typified by the persona's goals. (We will discuss the important connections between goals, behaviors, and personas later in this chapter.) However, the power of empathy should not be quickly discounted for other team members. The authors have observed that personas not only make the decision process for incorporating specific design elements easier from a design standpoint, but more compelling from a stakeholder-adoption standpoint. When personas have been carefully and appropriately crafted, stakeholders and programmers begin to think about them as if they are real users.

Grudin and Pruitt (2002) have noted the power of fictional characters in television programs (the authors would draw a comparison to an earlier form, the novel) to engage viewers. They note, as well, the power of method acting as a tool that actors use to understand and portray realistic characters. In fact, as we shall see in Chapter 6, the process of creating personas from user observation and later role-playing scenarios from the perspective of these personas is in many ways analogous to method acting. One designer has described the authors' Goal-Directed use of personas as the Stanislavsky Method of interaction design.

Personas represent classes of users in context

Although personas are represented as specific individuals, at the same time they represent a class or type of user of a *particular* interactive product. Specifically, a persona encapsulates a distinct set of **usage patterns**, behavior patterns regarding the use of a particular product (or analogous activities in the domain if a product does not yet exist). These patterns are identified through an analysis of ethnographic interviews, supported by supplemental data if necessary or appropriate. These patterns, along with work- or lifestyle-related roles define personas as user archetypes (Mikkelson N. and Lee, W. O., 2000). The authors refer to personas as **composite user archetypes** because personas are in a sense composites assembled by clustering related usage patterns observed across individuals in similar roles during the Research phase.

PERSONAS AND REUSE

Organizations with more than one product often want to reuse the same personas. However, to be effective, personas must be context-specific — they should be focused on the behaviors and goals related to the specific domain of a particular product. Personas, because they are constructed from specific observations of users interacting with specific products in specific contexts, cannot easily be reused across products (Grudin and Pruitt, 2002) even when those products form a closely linked suite. Even then, the focus of behaviors may be quite different in one product than in another, so researchers must take care to perform supplemental user research. The authors believe that, in most cases, personas should be researched and developed individually for different products.

ARCHETYPES VERSUS STEREOTYPES

Don't confuse persona archetypes with stereotypes. Stereotypes are, in most respects, the antithesis of well-developed personas. Stereotypes represent designer or researcher biases and assumptions, rather than factual data. Personas developed drawing on inadequate research (or synthesized with insufficient empathy and sensitivity to interview subjects) run the risk of degrading to stereotypical caricatures. Personas must be developed and treated with dignity and respect for the people whom they represent. If the designer doesn't respect his personas, nobody else will either. Personas also bring to the forefront issues of social and political consciousness (Grudin and Pruitt, 2002). Because personas provide a precise design target and also serve as a communication tool to the development team, the designer much choose particular demographic characteristics with care. Ideally, persona demographics should be a composite reflection of what researchers have observed in the interview population, modulated by broad market research. Personas should be *typical* and believable, but not stereotypical. If the data is not conclusive or the characteristic is not important to the design or its acceptance, the authors prefer to err on the side of gender, ethnic, age, and geographic diversity.

Personas explore ranges of behavior

The target market for a product describes demographics as well as lifestyles and sometimes job roles. What it does not describe are the ranges of different behaviors that members of that target market exhibit regarding the product itself and product-related contexts. Ranges are distinct from *averages*: Personas do not seek to establish an average user, but rather to identify *exemplary types* of behaviors along identified ranges.

Personas fill the need to understand how users behave within a given product domain — how they think about it and what they do with it — as well as how they behave in other contexts that may affect the scope and definition of the product. Because personas must describe *ranges* of behavior to capture the various possible ways people behave with the product, designers must identify a collection or **cast of personas** associated with any given product. Multiple personas carve up continuous ranges of behavior into discrete clusters. Different personas represent different correlated groups of behaviors. These correlations should become evident upon examination of the research and should be logically connected. The process of clustering behaviors is discussed in greater detail later in this chapter.

Personas must have motivations

All humans have motivations that drive their behaviors; some are obvious, and many are subtle. It is critical that personas capture these motivations in the form of goals. The goals we enumerate for our personas (which we will discuss at length later in this chapter) are shorthand notation for motivations that not only point at specific usage patterns, but also provide a reason why those behaviors exist. Understanding *why* a user performs certain tasks gives designers great power to improve or even eliminate those tasks, yet still accomplish the same goals.

Personas versus user roles

User roles and user profiles each share similarities with personas; that is, they both seek to describe relationships of users to products. But personas and the methods by which they are employed as a design tool differ significantly from roles and profiles in several key aspects.

User roles or role models, as defined by Larry Constantine (1999), are an *abstraction*, a defined relationship between a class of users and their problems, including needs, interests, expectations, and patterns of behavior. Holtzblatt and Beyer's (1998) use of roles in consolidated flow, cultural, physical, and sequence models is similar in that it attempts to isolate various relationships abstracted from the people possessing these relationships.

It is the authors' argument that these methods can be problematic for these reasons:

✓ It is more difficult to properly identify relationships in the abstract, isolated from people who possess them — the human power of empathy cannot easily be brought to bear on abstract classes of people.

✓ Both methods focus on *tasks* almost exclusively and neglect the use of goals as an organizing principle for design thinking and synthesis.

✓ Holzblatt and Beyer's consolidated models, although useful and encyclopedic in scope, are difficult to bring together as a coherent tool for developing, communicating, and measuring design decisions.

Personas address each of these problems. Well-developed personas incorporate the same type of relationships as user roles do, but express them in terms of goals and examples in narrative. This makes it easier for both designers and stakeholders to understand the implications of design decisions in more human terms. Personas also use goals to provide contexts to and structure for tasks, incorporating cultural and workflow information and translating it into behavioral drivers.

In general, personas provide a more holistic model of users and their contexts, where many other models seek to be more reductive. In any case, personas can certainly be used in combination with these other modeling techniques; and as we'll discuss at the end of the chapter, some models make extremely useful complements to personas.

Personas versus user profiles

Many usability practitioners use the terms **persona** and **user profile** synonymously. There is no problem with this if the profile is truly generated from ethnographic data and encapsulates the depth of information the authors have described. Unfortunately, all too often, the authors have seen user profiles that reflect Webster's definition of **profile** as a "brief biographical sketch." In other words, user profiles are often a name (and possibly a picture) attached to brief, usually demographic data, along with a short, *fictional* paragraph describing the kind of car this person drives, how many kids he has, where he lives, and what he does for a living. This kind of user profile is likely to be a user stereotype and is not useful as a design tool. Although we give our personas names, and sometimes even cars and family members, these are employed sparingly as narrative tools to help better communicate the real data and are not ends in themselves. Supporting fictional detail plays only the most minor part in persona creation and is used just enough to make the persona come to life in the minds of the designers and the product team.

Personas versus market segments

Marketing professionals may be familiar with a process similar to persona development because it shares some process similarities with market definition. The main difference between market segments and design personas is that the former are based on demographics and distribution channels, whereas the latter are based on user behaviors and goals. The two are not the same and don't serve the same purpose. The marketing personas shed light on the sales process, whereas the design personas shed light on the development process. This said, market segments play a role in persona development: They can help determine the demographic range within which to frame the persona hypothesis (see Chapter 4). Personas are segmented along ranges of behavior, not demographics or attitudes, so there is seldom a one-to-one mapping of market segments to personas. Rather, market segments can act as an initial filter to limit the scope of interviews to people within target markets (see Figure 5-3).

User personas versus non-user personas

A frequent product definition error is to target people who review, purchase, or administer the product, but who are not end users. Many products are designed for columnists who review the product in consumer publications. IT managers who purchase enterprise products are, typically, not the users of the products. Designing for the purchaser is a frequent mistake in the development of digital products.

Although you cannot ignore the IT managers' needs, they will ultimately be better served if the product serves the *real* end user well. If the end user is satisfied and productive, the IT managers are successful as well.

In certain cases, such as for enterprise systems that require maintenance and administrator interfaces, it is appropriate to create non-user personas. This requires that research be expanded to include these types of people. These personas may have their own, separate interfaces, or they may simply be useful from a rhetorical standpoint to delineate what the product should and shouldn't do. Non-user personas also often provide additional business goals that must be balanced with the user goals embodied by the user personas.

Goals

If personas provide the context for sets of observed behaviors, goals are the drivers behind those behaviors. A persona without goals can still serve as a useful communication tool, but it remains useless as a design tool. User goals serve as a lens through which designers must consider the functions of a product. The function and behavior of the product must address goals via tasks — typically, as few tasks as absolutely necessary. Remember, tasks are only a means to an end; goals are the end themselves.

Goals motivate usage patterns

People's or personas' goals motivate them to behave the way they do. Thus, goals provide not only an answer to why and how personas desire to use a product, but can also serve as a shorthand in the designer's mind for the sometimes complex behaviors in which a persona engages and, therefore, for the tasks as well.

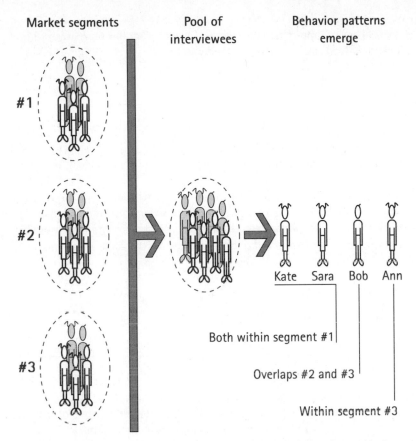

Figure 5-3: Personas versus market segments. Market segments can be used in the Research phase to limit the range of personas to target markets. However, there is seldom a one-to-one mapping between market segments and personas.

Goals must be inferred from qualitative data

You can't ask a person what his goals are directly: Either he won't be able to articulate them, or he won't be accurate or even perfectly honest. People simply aren't well prepared to answer such questions accurately. Therefore, designers and researchers need to carefully reconstruct goals from observed behaviors, answers to other questions, non-verbal cues, and clues from the environment such as book titles on shelves. One of the most critical tasks in the modeling of personas is identifying goals and expressing them succinctly: Each goal should be expressed as a simple sentence.

Types of goals

Goals come in many different varieties. The most important goals from a user-centered design standpoint are the goals of users. These are, generally, first priority in a design, especially in the design of consumer products. Non-user goals can also come into play, especially in enterprise environments. The goals of organizations, employers, customers, and partners all need to be acknowledged, if not addressed directly, by the product's design.

USER GOALS

User personas have user goals. These range from broad aspirations to highly pragmatic product expectations. User goals fall into three basic categories (Goodwin, 2001):

✓ Life goals

✓ Experience goals

✓ End goals

We describe each of these in detail in the following sections.

LIFE GOALS   Life goals represent personal aspirations of the user that typically go beyond the context of the product being designed. These goals represent deep drives and motivations that help explain *why* the user is trying to accomplish the end goals he seeks to accomplish. These can be useful in understanding the broader context of relationships the user may have with others and her expectations of the product from a brand perspective.

✓ Be the best at what I do

✓ Get onto the fast track and win that big promotion

✓ Learn all there is to know about this field

✓ Be a paragon of ethics, modesty, and trust

Life goals rarely figure directly into the design of specific elements of an interface. However, they are very much worth keeping in mind. A product that the user discovers will take him closer to his life goals, and not just his end goals, will win him over more decisively than any marketing campaign. Addressing life goals of users makes the difference (assuming other goals are also met) between a satisfied user and a fanatically loyal user.

EXPERIENCE GOALS   Experience goals are simple, universal, and personal. Paradoxically, this makes them difficult for many people to talk about, especially in the context of impersonal business. Experience goals express how someone wants to *feel* while using a product or the quality of their interaction with the product.

✓ Don't feel stupid

✓ Don't make mistakes

✓ Feel competent and confident

✓ Have fun (or at least not be too bored)

Experience goals represent the unconscious goals that people bring to any software product. They bring these goals to the context without consciously realizing it and without necessarily even being able to articulate the goals. People have an unconscious desire to be treated with decency and dignity and to be supported, not chastised. When software makes users feel stupid, their self-esteem drops and their effectiveness plummets, regardless of their other goals. Their level of discomfort and resentment also increases. Enough of this type of treatment and users will be primed to use any chance to subvert the system. Any system that violates personal goals will ultimately fail, regardless of how well it purports to achieve other goals.

END GOALS End goals represent the user's expectation of the tangible outcomes of using a specific product. When you pick up a cell phone, you likely have an outcome in mind. Similarly, when you search the Web for a particular item or piece of information, you have some clear end goals. When you open a document with a word processor, you have something in mind that you expect to accomplish. End goals must be met for users to think that a product is worth their time and money; most of the goals a product needs to concern itself with are, therefore, end goals such as the following:

- ✓ Find the best price
- ✓ Finalize the press release
- ✓ Process the customer's order
- ✓ Create a numerical model of the business

COMBINING END GOALS AND EXPERIENCE GOALS End goals have more appeal than experience or life goals, especially to sober businesspeople and programmers. True to their nature, they create software that — although it admirably fulfills the end goals — fails utterly to satisfy the experience goals of the user. Even if end goals are recognized and satisfied, users feel poorly about themselves and the product if experience goals are not also met. Sure, they get their work accomplished, but it's not a pleasant or empowering experience. On the other hand, if your software ignores the practical and serves *only* the user's experience goals, you have designed a toy, not a business application.

NON-USER GOALS

Customer goals, corporate goals, and technical goals are all non-user goals. Typically, these goals must be acknowledged and considered, but they do not form the basis for the design direction. Although these goals need to be addressed, they must not be addressed at the expense of the user.

CUSTOMER GOALS Customers, as already discussed, have different goals than users. The exact nature of these goals varies quite a bit between consumer and enterprise products. Consumer customers are often parents, relatives, or friends who often have concerns about the safety and happiness of the persons for whom they are purchasing the product. Enterprise customers are typically IT managers, and they often have concerns about security, ease of maintenance, and ease of customization. Customer personas also may have their own life, experience, and especially end goals in relation to the product if they use it in any capacity. Customer goals should never trump end goals, but need to be considered within the overall design.

CORPORATE GOALS Businesses and other organizations have their own requirements for software, and they are as high level as the personal goals of the individual. "To increase our profit" is pretty fundamental to the board of directors or the stockholders. The designer uses these goals to stay focused on the bigger issues and to avoid getting distracted by tasks or other false goals. Corporate goals include the following:

- ✓ Increase profit

- ✓ Increase market share

- ✓ Defeat the competition

- ✓ Use resources more efficiently

- ✓ Offer more products or services

Psychologists who study the workplace have a term, **hygienic factors**, which Saul Gellerman (1963) defines as "prerequisites for effective motivation but powerless to motivate by themselves." The lights in your office, for example, are hygienic. You don't go to work because the lights are nice; but if there were no lights at all, you wouldn't bother showing up.

Corporate goals are hygienic factors in this sense. From the corporation's point of view, it has important goals. But the corporation isn't doing the work; its people are, and their more personal life, experience, and end goals are equally decisive.

Corporate goals can't be slighted, however. Software that fails to achieve them will fail just as readily as software that fails to meet user goals.

TECHNICAL GOALS   Most of the software-based products we use everyday are created with technical goals in mind. Many of these goals ease the task of software creation, which is a programmer's goal. This is why they take precedence at the expense of the users' goals.

- ✓ Save memory

- ✓ Run in a browser

- ✓ Safeguard data integrity

- ✓ Increase program execution efficiency

- ✓ Use "cool" technology or features

- ✓ Maintain consistency across platforms

Technical goals in particular are very important to the development staff. It is important to stress early in the education process that these goals need to serve user and business goals. Technical goals should derive from the need to meet other more human-oriented goals. It might be a software company's *task* to use new technology, but it is never a *user's goal* to do so. As users, we don't care if we get our job done with hierarchical databases, relational databases, object-oriented databases, flat-file systems, or black magic. What we care about is getting our job done swiftly with a modicum of ease and dignity.

Successful products meet user goals first

Designing a *good* interactive product has meaning only for a person using an artifact for some purpose in some context. You cannot have purposes without people. The two are inseparable. That is why a key tool in the process of designing behavior is personas: specific people working towards specific purposes or goals.

The most important purposes or goals to consider are those of the individuals making actual use of the artifact or application, not necessarily those of its purchaser. A real person interacts with your product, not a corporation or even an IT manager, so you must regard his personal goals as more significant than those of the corporation who employs him or the IT manager who supports him. Your users will do their best to achieve their employer's business goals, while at the same time looking after their own personal goals. A user's most important goal is always to retain his human dignity: not to feel stupid.

We can reliably say that we make the user feel stupid if we let him make big mistakes, keep him from getting an adequate amount of work done, or bore him.

Don't make the user feel stupid.

This is probably the most important interaction design guideline. In the course of this book, we examine numerous ways in which existing software makes the user feel stupid, and we explore ways to avoid that trap.

The essence of good interaction design is devising interactions that achieve the goals of the manufacturer or service provider and their partners without violating the goals of users.

Constructing Personas

As previously discussed, personas are derived from patterns observed during interviews with and observations of users and potential users (and sometimes customers) of a product. Gaps in this data are filled by supplemental research and data provided by SMEs, stakeholders, and available literature. In constructing a set of personas, we are looking to segment use across a set of observed behavioral variables (also called axes or ranges). Well-developed personas incorporate information about goals, attitudes, work or activity flow, environment, skills and skill levels, and frustrations.

Creating believable and useful personas requires an equal measure of detailed analysis and creative synthesis. A standardized process aids both of these activities significantly. The process described in this section, developed by Robert Reimann, Kim Goodwin, and Lane Halley, is the result of an evolution in practice over the span of dozens of interaction design projects.

1. Revisit the persona hypothesis.

2. Map interview subjects to behavioral variables.

3. Identify significant behavior patterns.

4. Synthesize characteristics and relevant goals.

5. Check for completeness.

6. Develop narratives.

7. Designate persona types.

We will discuss each of these steps in detail in the following sections.

Revisit the persona hypothesis

After you have completed your research and performed a cursory organization of the data, you next compare patterns identified in the data to the assumptions made in the persona hypothesis. Were the possible roles that you identified truly distinct? Were the behavioral variables (see Chapter 4) you identified valid? Were there additional, unanticipated ones, or ones you anticipated that weren't supported by data?

List the complete set of behavioral variables observed. Demographic variables such as age or technical skill may also seem to affect behavior, but be wary of focusing on demographics during persona creation because behavioral variables have far more impact on the design. For enterprise applications, behavioral (and demographic) variables are often closely associated with job roles. Although the number of variables will differ from project to project, it is typical to find 15 to 30 variables per role.

If your data is at variance with your assumptions, you need to add, subtract, or modify the roles and behaviors you anticipated. If the variance is significant enough, you may consider additional interviews to cover any gaps in the new behavioral ranges that you've discovered.

Map interview subjects to behavioral variables

After you are satisfied that you have identified the entire set of behavioral variables exhibited by your interview subjects, the next step is to map each interviewee against each variable range that applies. The precision of this mapping isn't as critical as identifying the placement of interviewees in relationship to each other. In other words, it doesn't matter if an interviewee falls at precisely 45% or 50% on the scale (there's often no good way to measure this precisely; you must rely on your gut feel based on your observations of the subject). It is the way multiple subjects cluster on each variable axis that is significant (see Figure 5-4).

Identify significant behavior patterns

After you have mapped your interview subjects, you see clusters of particular subjects that occur across multiple ranges or variables. A set of subjects who cluster in six to eight different variables will likely represent a significant behavior pattern that will form the basis of a persona (Goodwin, 2002). Some specialized roles may exhibit only one significant pattern, but typically you will find two or even three such patterns.

For a pattern to be valid, there must be a logical or causative connection between the clustered behaviors (Goodwin, 2002), not just a spurious correlation. For example, there is clearly a logical connection if data shows that people who regularly purchase CDs also like to download MP3 files, but there is probably no logical connection if the data shows that interviewees who frequently purchase CDs also seem to enjoy stamp collecting.

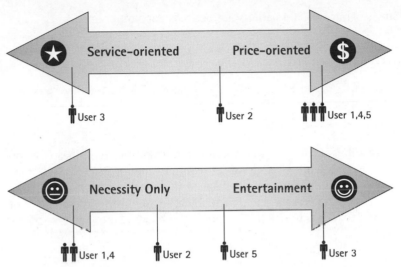

Figure 5-4: Mapping interview subjects to behavioral variables. This example is from e-commerce. Interview subjects are mapped across each behavioral axis. Precision of the absolute position of an individual subject on an axis is less important than its relative position to other subjects. Clusters of subjects across multiple axes indicate significant behavior patterns.

Synthesize characteristics and relevant goals

For each significant behavior pattern you identify, you must synthesize details from your data. Describe the potential use environment, typical workday (or other relevant time period), current solutions and frustrations, and relevant relationships with others (Goodwin, 2002a).

Brief bullet points describing characteristics of the behavior are sufficient. Stick to observed behaviors as much as possible; a description or two that sharpen the personalities of your personas can help bring them to life. Too much fictional, idiosyncratic biography, however, is a distraction and makes your personas less credible (Goodwin, 2002a). Remember that you are creating a design tool, not a character sketch for a novel. Only concrete data can support the design and business decisions your team will ultimately make.

One fictional detail at this stage *is* important: the personas' first and last names. The name should be evocative of the type of person the persona is, without tending toward caricature or stereotype. The authors use a baby name book as a reference tool in creating persona names. You can also, at this time, add in some demographic information such as age, geographic location, relative income (if appropriate), and job title. This information is primarily to help you visualize the persona better as you assemble the behavioral details. From this point on, you should refer to the persona by his or her name.

PERSONA INTERRELATIONSHIPS

It sometimes makes sense for the set of personas for a product to be part of the same family or corporation and to have interpersonal or social relationships with each other. The typical case, however, is for individual personas to be completely unrelated to each other and often from completely different geographic locations and social groups.

It makes sense for personas to have social relationships between each other only if:

1. You did not observe any behavioral variations in your interview subjects related to variations in company size, industry, or family/social dynamic.

2. Doing so is critical to illustrate workflow or social interactions between co-workers or members of a family or social group.

If you create personas that work for the same company or have social relationships with each other, you might run into difficulties if you need to express a significant goal that doesn't belong with the pre-established relationship. While a single social relationship between your set of personas is easier to define than several different, unrelated social relationships between individual personas and minor players outside the persona set, it's much better to put the initial effort into development of diverse personas than it is to risk the temptation of bending more diverse scenarios to fit a single social dynamic.

SYNTHESIZING GOALS

Goals are the most critical detail to synthesize from your interviews and observations of behaviors. Goals are best derived from an analysis of the group of behaviors comprising each persona. By identifying the logical connections between each persona's behaviors, you can begin to infer the goals that lead to those behaviors. You can infer goals both by observing actions (what interview subjects in each persona cluster are trying to accomplish and why) and by analyzing subject responses to goal-oriented interview questions (see Chapter 4).

To be effective as design tools, goals must always directly relate, in some way, to the product being designed. Typically, the majority of useful goals for a persona are *end goals*. You can expect most personas to have three to five end goals associated with them. Life goals are most useful for personas of consumer-oriented products, but they can also make sense for enterprise personas in transient job roles. Zero or one life goal is appropriate for most personas. General experience goals such as "don't feel stupid" and "don't waste time" can be taken as implicit for almost any persona. Occasionally, a specific domain may dictate the need for more specific experience goals; zero to two experience goals is appropriate for most personas.

Check for completeness and distinctiveness

At this point, your personas should be starting to come to life. You should check your mappings and personas' characteristics and goals to see if there are any important gaps that need filling. This again may point to the need to perform additional research directed at finding particular behaviors missing from your behavioral axes. You might also want to check your notes to see if there are any political personas that you need to add to satisfy stakeholder assumptions or requests.

If you find that two personas seem to vary only by demographics, you may choose to eliminate one of the redundant personas or tweak the characteristics of your personas to make them more distinct. Each persona must vary from all others in at least one significant behavior. If you've done a good job of mapping, this shouldn't be an issue.

By making sure that your persona set is both distinct and complete, you will be able to maintain a manageable set of personas.

Develop narratives

Your list of bullet point characteristics and goals point to the essence of complex behaviors, but leaves much implied. Third-person narrative is far more powerful in conveying the persona's attitudes, needs, and problems to other team members. It also deepens the designer/authors' connection to the personas and their motivations.

A typical persona narrative should be no longer than one or two pages of prose. The persona narrative does not need to contain every observed detail because, ideally, the designers also performed the research, and most people outside the design team do not require more detail than this.

The narrative must, by nature, contain some fictional events and reactions, but as previously discussed, it is not a short story. The best narrative quickly introduces the persona in terms of his job or lifestyle (enterprise versus consumer), and briefly sketches a day in his life, including peeves, concerns, and interests that have direct bearing on the product. Details should be an expansion of your list of characteristics, with additional data derived from your observations and interviews. The narrative should express what the persona is looking for in the product by way of a conclusion.

Be careful about precision of detail in your descriptions. The detail should not exceed the depth of your research. In scientific disciplines, if you record a measurement of 35.421 m, this implies that your measurements are accurate to .001 m. Likewise a detailed persona description implies a similar level of observation in your research (Goodwin, 2002a).

When you start developing your narrative, choose photographs of your personas. Photographs make them feel more real as you create the narrative and engage others on the team when you are finished. You should take great care in choosing a photograph. The best photos capture demographic information, hint at the environment (a persona for a nurse should be wearing a nurse's uniform and be in a clinical setting, perhaps with a patient), and capture the persona's general attitude (a photo for a clerk overwhelmed by paperwork might look harried). The authors keep several searchable databanks of stock photography available for finding the right persona pictures.

Designate persona types

By now your personas should feel very much like a set of real people that you feel you know. The final step in persona construction finishes the process of turning your qualitative research into a powerful set of design tools.

All design requires a design target—the audience upon whom the design is focused. The personas, which we have created, represent the possible *candidates* for that design target. A single interface can only be designed for a single persona.

Design each interface for a single, primary persona.

What we then must do is *prioritize* our personas to determine which should be the primary design target. The goal is to find a single persona from the set whose needs and goals can be completely and happily satisfied by a single interface without disenfranchising any of the other personas. We accomplish this through a process of designating **persona types**. There are six types of persona, and they are typically designated in roughly the order listed here:

- ✓ Primary
- ✓ Secondary
- ✓ Supplemental
- ✓ Customer
- ✓ Served
- ✓ Negative

We discuss each of these persona types and their significance from a design perspective in the following sections.

PRIMARY PERSONAS

Primary personas represent the primary target for the design of an interface. There can be only one primary persona per interface for a product, but it is possible for some products (especially enterprise products) to have multiple distinct interfaces, each targeted at a distinct primary persona (for example, a healthcare information system might have separate clinical and financial interfaces, each targeted at a different persona).

A **primary persona** is not satisfied by a design targeted at any other persona in the set. However, if the primary persona is the target, all other personas are at least minimally satisfied (and thus not unhappy).

Choosing the primary persona is a process of elimination: Each persona must be tested by comparing the goals of that persona against goals of the others. If no clear primary persona is evident, it could mean one of two things: Either the product needs multiple interfaces, each with a suitable primary (often the case for enterprise and technical products), or the product is trying to accomplish too much. If your consumer product has multiple primary personas, the scope of the product may be too broad.

SECONDARY PERSONAS

Sometimes a situation arises in which a persona would be entirely satisfied by a primary persona's interface if one or two specific additional needs (not required by the primary) were addressed by the interface. This indicates that the persona in question is a **secondary persona** for that interface, and the design of that interface must address those needs without getting in the way of the primary persona. Typically, an interface will have zero to two secondary personas. More than that again indicates scope problems with the product.

SUPPLEMENTAL PERSONAS

User personas that are not primary or secondary are **supplemental personas**: They are completely satisfied by one of the primary interfaces. There can be any number of supplemental personas associated with an interface. Often political personas — the ones added to the cast to address stakeholder assumptions — become supplemental personas.

CUSTOMER PERSONAS

Customer personas address the needs of customers, not end users, as discussed earlier in this chapter. Typically, customer personas are treated like secondary personas. However, in some enterprise environments, some customer personas may be primary personas for their own administrative interface.

SERVED PERSONAS

Served personas are somewhat different from the persona types already discussed. They are not users of the product at all; however, they are *directly affected by the use of the product*. A patient being treated by a radiation therapy machine is not a user of the machine's interface, but she is very much *served* by a good interface. Served personas provide a way to track second-order social and physical ramifications of products. These are treated like secondary personas.

NEGATIVE PERSONAS

Like served personas, negative personas aren't users of the product. Unlike served personas, their use is purely rhetorical, to help communicate to other members of the team who should definitely *not* be the design target for the product. Good candidates for negative personas are often technology-savvy early-adopter personas for consumer products and IT specialists for end-user enterprise products.

Other Models

Personas are extremely useful tools, but they are certainly not the only tool to help model users and their environment. Holzblatt and Beyer's *Contextual Design* provides a wealth of information on the models briefly discussed here. Workflow or sequence models are useful for capturing information flow and decision-making processes inside organizations and are usually expressed as directed graphs that capture several phenomena:

- ✓ What initiates a process
- ✓ Information the user produces and consumes
- ✓ Decisions the user makes
- ✓ Actions the user takes
- ✓ Results that follow from actions

A well-developed persona should capture personal workflows, but workflow models are still necessary for capturing interpersonal and organizational workflows.

Artifact models represent, as the name suggests, different artifacts that users employ in their tasks and workflows. Often these artifacts are online or paper forms. Artifact models typically capture commonalities and significant differences between similar artifacts for the purpose of extracting and replicating best practices in the eventual design. Artifact models can be useful later in the design process, with the caveat that direct translation of paper systems to digital systems, without a careful analysis of goals and application of design principles (especially those found in Section Two of this book), usually leads to usability issues.

Physical models, like artifact models, endeavor to capture elements of the user's environment. Physical models focus on capturing the layout of physical objects that comprise the user's workspace, which can provide insight into frequency of use issues and physical barriers to productivity. Good persona descriptions will incorporate some of this information, but it may be helpful in complex physical environments (such as shop floors and assembly lines) to create discrete, detailed physical models (maps) of the user environment.

Personas and other models make sense out of otherwise overwhelming and confusing user data. Now that you are empowered with sophisticated models as design tools, the next chapter will show you how to employ these tools to translate user goals and needs into workable design solutions.

Chapter 6

Scenarios: Translating Goals into Design

In the two previous chapters, we described how to capture qualitative information about users. Through careful analysis of this information and synthesis of user models, we can get a clear picture of our users and their respective goals. We also explained how to prioritize which users are the most appropriate design targets. The missing piece to the puzzle, then, is the process of translating this knowledge into coherent design solutions that meet the needs of users while simultaneously addressing business needs and technical constraints.

This chapter describes a process for bridging the research-design gap. It employs personas as the main characters in set of techniques that rapidly arrive at design solutions in an iterative, repeatable, and testable fashion. This process has three major milestones: defining user requirements; using these requirements to in turn define the fundamental interaction framework for the product; and filling in the framework with ever-increasing amounts of design detail. The glue that holds the processes together is *narrative*: the use of personas to tell stories that point to design.

Narrative as a Design Tool

Narrative, or storytelling, is one of the oldest human activities. Much has been written about the power of narrative to *communicate* ideas. However, narrative can also, through its efficacy at engaging and stimulating creative visualization skills, serve as a powerful tool in generating and validating design ideas (Rheinfrank & Evenson, 1996). Because interaction design is first and foremost the design of behavior that occurs over time, a narrative structure, combined with the support of minimal visualization tools such as the whiteboard, is perfectly suited for envisioning and representing interaction concepts. Detailed refinement calls for more sophisticated visual and interactive tools, but the initial work of defining requirements and frameworks is best done fluidly and flexibly, with minimal reliance on technologies that will inevitably impede ideation.

Scenarios in design

Scenario is a term familiar to usability professionals, commonly used to describe a method of *design problem solving by concretization* (Carroll, 2001): making use of a specific story to both construct and illustrate design solutions. Scenarios are anchored in the concrete, but permit fluidity; any member of the design team can modify them at will. As Carroll states in his book, *Making Use*:

> Scenarios are paradoxically concrete but rough, tangible but flexible . . . they implicitly encourage 'what-if?' thinking among all parties. They permit the articulation of design possibilities without undermining innovation. . . . Scenarios compel attention to the use that will be made of the design product. They can describe situations at many levels of detail, for many different purposes, helping to coordinate various aspects of the design project.

Carroll's use of **scenario-based design** focuses on describing how *users accomplish tasks* (Carroll, 2001). It consists of an environmental *setting* and includes *agents* or *actors* that are abstracted stand-ins for users, with role-based names such as Accountant or Programmer.

Although Carroll certainly understands the power and importance of scenarios in the design process, the authors see two problems with scenarios as Carroll approaches them:

✓ Carroll's scenarios are not concrete enough in their representation of the human actor. It is impossible to design appropriate behaviors for a system without understanding in specific detail the users of the system. Abstracted, role-oriented models are not sufficiently concrete to provide understanding or empathy with users.

✓ Carroll's scenarios jump too quickly to the elaboration of tasks without considering the user's goals and motivations that drive and filter these tasks. Although Carroll does briefly discuss goals, he refers only to *goals of the scenario*. These goals are somewhat circularly defined as the completion of specific tasks. Carroll's scenarios begin at the wrong level of detail: User goals need to be considered before user tasks can be identified and prioritized. Without addressing human goals, high-level product definition becomes difficult.

The authors believe that the missing ingredient in scenario-based design methods is the use of personas. A persona provides a sufficiently tangible representation of the user to act as a believable agent in the setting of a scenario. This enhances the designer's ability to empathize with user mental models and perspectives. At the same time, it permits an exploration of how user motivations inflect and prioritize tasks. Because personas model *goals* and not simply tasks, the scope of the problem that scenarios address can also be broadened to include product definition. They help answer the questions, "What should this product *be*?" and "How should this product look and behave?" The authors address the issues surrounding task-based scenarios with the introduction of **persona-based scenarios** — scenarios incorporating the use of personas and goals.

Using personas in scenarios

Persona-based scenarios are concise narrative descriptions of one or more personas using a product to achieve specific goals. Scenarios capture the *non-verbal dialogue* (Buxton, 1990) between artifact and user over time, as well as the structure and behavior of interactive functions. Goals serve as a filter for tasks and as guides for structuring the display of information and controls during the iterative process of constructing the scenarios.

Scenario content and context are derived from information gathered during the Research phase and analyzed during the Modeling phase. Designers role-play personas as the characters in these scenarios (Verplank, et al, 1993), similar to actors performing improvisation. This process leads to real-time synthesis of structure and behavior—typically, at a whiteboard—and later informs the detailed look and feel. Finally, personas and scenarios are used to test the validity of design ideas and assumptions throughout the process. Three types of persona-based scenarios are employed at different points in the process, each time with a successively narrower focus. These scenario types—context scenarios, key path scenarios, and validation scenarios—are described in detail in this chapter.

Persona-based scenarios versus use cases

Scenarios and use cases are both methods of describing a digital system. However, they serve very different functions. Goal-directed scenarios are an iterative means of defining the *behavior* of a product from the standpoint of specific users (personas). This includes not only the functionality of the system, but the priority of functions and the way those functions are expressed in terms of what the user sees and how he interacts with the system.

Use cases, on the other hand, are a technique that has been adopted from software engineering by some usability professionals. They are usually exhaustive descriptions of functional requirements of the system, often of a transactional nature, focusing on low-level user action and system response pairs (Wirfs-Brock, 1993). The precise *behavior* of the system—precisely *how* the system responds—is not, typically, part of a conventional or *concrete* use case; many assumptions about the form and behavior of the system to be designed remain implicit (Constantine and Lockwood, 1999). Use cases permit a complete cataloguing of user tasks for different classes of users, but say little or nothing about how these tasks are presented to the user or how they should be prioritized in the interface. Use cases may be useful in identifying edge cases and for determining that a product is functionally complete, but they should be deployed only in the later stages of design validation.

Envisioning Solutions with Persona-Based Design

As discussed briefly in Chapter 1, the translation from robust models to design solutions really consists of two major phases. **Requirements Definition** answers the broad questions about what a product is and what it should do, and **Framework Definition** answers question about how a product behaves and how it is structured to meet user goals. In this section, we'll discuss both these phases in detail, and the persona-based scenario methodology developed at Cooper by Robert Reimann, Kim Goodwin, Dave Cronin, Wayne Greenwood, and Lane Halley.

Defining the requirements

The Requirements Definition phase determines the *what* of the design: what functions our personas need to use and what kind of information they must access to accomplish their goals. The following five steps comprise this process:

1. Creating problem and vision statements

2. Brainstorming

3. Identifying persona expectations

4. Constructing the context scenario

5. Identifying needs

Although these steps proceed in roughly chronological order, they represent an iterative process. Designers can expect to cycle through steps 3 through 5 several times until the requirements are stable. This is a necessary part of the process and shouldn't be short-circuited. A detailed description of each of these steps follows.

STEP 1: CREATING PROBLEM AND VISION STATEMENTS

Before beginning any process of ideation, it's important for designers to have a clear mandate for moving forward, even if it is a rather high-level mandate. Problem and vision statements provide just such a mandate and are extremely helpful in building consensus among stakeholders before the design process moves forward.

At a high level, the **problem statement** defines the objective of the design (Newman & Lamming, 1995). A design problem statement should concisely reflect a situation that needs changing, for both the personas *and* for the business providing the product to the personas. Often a cause-and-effect relationship exists between business concerns and persona concerns. For example:

> Company X's customer satisfaction ratings are low and market share has diminished by 10% over the past year *because* users don't have adequate tools to perform X, Y, and Z tasks that would help them meet their goal of G.

The connection of business issues to usability issues is critical to drive stakeholders' buy-in to design efforts and to frame the design effort in terms of both user and business goals.

The **vision statement** is an inversion of the problem statement that serves as a high-level design vision or mandate. In the vision statement, you lead with the user's needs, and you transition from those to how business goals are met by the design vision:

> The new design of Product X will help users achieve G by giving them the ability to perform X, Y, and Z with greater [accuracy, efficiency, and so on], and without problems A, B, C that they currently experience. This will dramatically improve Company X's customer satisfaction ratings and lead to increased market share.

The content of both the problem and vision statement should come directly from research and user models. User goals and needs should derive from the primary and secondary personas, and business goals should be extracted from stakeholder interviews.

Problem and vision statements are of most use when you are redesigning an existing product. However, even for new technology products, or products being designed for unexplored market niches, when you formulate user goals and frustrations into problem and vision statements you are helping to establish team consensus on the design activity to follow.

STEP 2: BRAINSTORMING

Brainstorming performed at this early stage of Requirements Definition assumes a somewhat ironic purpose. As designers, you may have been researching and modeling users and the domain for days or even weeks. It is almost impossible that you have not had design ideas percolating in your head. Thus, the reason we brainstorm at this point in the process is to get these ideas out of our heads so we can "let them go," at least for the time being. This serves a primary purpose of eliminating as much designer bias as possible before launching into scenarios, preparing the designers to take on the roles of the primary personas during the scenario process.

Brainstorming should be unconstrained and uncritical — put all the wacky ideas you've been considering (plus some you haven't) out on the table and then be prepared to record them and file them away for safekeeping until much later in the process. It's not likely any of them will be useful in the end, but there might be the germ of something wonderful that will fit into the design framework you later create. Holtzblatt & Beyer (1998) describe a facilitated method for brainstorming that can be useful for getting a brainstorming session started, especially if your team includes non-designers.

Don't spend too much time on the brainstorming step; a few hours (less than half a day) should be more than sufficient for you and your teammates to get all those crazy ideas out of your systems. If you find your ideas are beginning to get repetitious, that's a good time to stop.

STEP 3: IDENTIFYING PERSONA EXPECTATIONS

The expectations that your persona has for a product and its context of use are, collectively, that persona's **mental model** of the product. As we discussed in Chapter 2, it's important that the **represented model** of the interface — how the design behaves and presents itself — should match the user's mental model as closely as possible, rather than reflecting the implementation model of how the product is actually constructed internally.

For each primary persona, you must identify:

✓ General expectations and desires each may have about the experience of using the product

✓ Behaviors each will expect or desire from the product

✓ Attitudes, past experiences, aspirations, and other social, cultural, environmental and cognitive factors that influence these desires

Your persona descriptions may contain enough information to answer some of these questions directly; however, you should return to your research data to analyze the language and grammar of how user subjects define and describe objects and actions that are part of their usage patterns. Some things to look for include:

- ✓ What do the subjects mention first?
- ✓ Which action words (verbs) do they use?
- ✓ Which intermediate steps, tasks, or objects in a process *don't* they mention?

After you have compiled a good list of expectations and influences, do the same for secondary and customer personas and crosscheck similarities and differences.

STEP 4: CONSTRUCTING CONTEXT SCENARIOS

Scenarios are stories about people and their activities (Carroll, 2001). Context scenarios are, in fact, the most story-like of the three types of scenario we employ in that the focus is very much on the persona, her mental models, goals, and activities. Context scenarios describe the broad context in which usage patterns are exhibited and include environmental and organizational (in the case of enterprise systems) considerations (Kuutti, 1995). Context scenarios establish the primary **touch-points** that each primary and secondary persona has with the system (and possibly with other personas via the system) over the course of a day, or some other meaningful length of time that illuminates modes of frequent and regular use. Context scenarios are sometimes, for this reason, called day-in-the-life scenarios.

Context scenarios address questions such as the following (Goodwin, 2002):

- ✓ What is the setting in which the product will be used?
- ✓ Will it be used for extended amounts of time?
- ✓ Is the persona frequently interrupted?
- ✓ Are there multiple users on a single workstation/device?
- ✓ What other products is it used with?
- ✓ How much complexity is permissible, based on persona skill and frequency of use?
- ✓ What primary activities does the persona need to accomplish to meet her goals?
- ✓ What is the expected end result of using the product?

To ensure effective context scenarios, keep them broad and relatively shallow in scope. Resist the urge to dive immediately into interaction detail. It is important to map out the big picture first and systematically identify needs. Doing this and using the steps that follow prevent you from getting lost in design details that may not fit together coherently later.

Context scenarios should *not* represent system behaviors as they currently are. These scenarios represent the brave new world of goal-directed products, so, especially in the initial phases, focus on the goals. Don't yet worry about exactly *how* things will get accomplished — you can initially treat the design as a bit of a magic black box.

Sometimes more than one context scenario is necessary. This is true especially when there are multiple primary personas, but sometimes even a single primary persona may have two or more distinct contexts of use.

Context scenarios are also entirely *textual*. We are not yet discussing form, only the behaviors of the user and the system. This discussion is best accomplished as a textual narrative.

AN EXAMPLE CONTEXT SCENARIO   The following is an example of a first iteration of a context scenario for a primary persona for a PDA/phone convergence device and service: Vivien Strong, a real-estate agent in Indianapolis. Vivien's goals are to balance work and home life, cinch the deal, and make each client feel like he is her *only* client.

Vivien's context scenario might be as follows:

1. Getting ready in the morning, Vivien uses her phone to check e-mail. It has a large enough screen and quick connection time so that it's more convenient than booting up a computer as she rushes to make her daughter, Alice, a sandwich for school.

2. Vivien sees an e-mail from her newest client, Frank, who wants to see a house this afternoon. Vivien entered his contact info a few days ago, so now she can call him with a simple action right from the e-mail screen.

3. While on the phone with Frank, Vivien switches to speakerphone so she can look at the screen while talking. She looks at her appointments to see when she's free. When she creates a new appointment, the phone automatically makes it an appointment with Frank, because it knows with whom she is talking. She quickly keys the address of the property into the appointment as she finishes her conversation.

4. After sending Alice off to school, Vivien heads into the real-estate office to gather the papers she needs for the plumber working on another property. Her phone has already updated her Outlook appointments, so the rest of the office knows where she'll be in the afternoon.

5. The day goes by quickly, and she's running a bit late. As she heads towards the property she'll be showing Frank, the phone alerts her that her appointment is in 15 minutes. When she flips open the phone, it shows not only the appointment, but a list of all documents related to Frank, including e-mails, memos, phone messages, call logs to Frank's number, and even thumbnail pictures of the property that Vivien sent as e-mail attachments. Vivien presses the call button, and the phone automatically connects to Frank because it knows her appointment with him is soon. She lets him know she'll be there in 20 minutes.

6. Vivien knows the address of the property, but is a bit unsure exactly where it is. She pulls over and taps the address she put into the appointment. The phone downloads directions along with a thumbnail map showing her location relative to the destination.

7. Vivien gets to the property on time and starts showing it to Frank. She hears the phone ring from her purse. Normally while she is in an appointment, the phone will automatically transfer directly to voicemail, but Alice has a code she can press to get through. The phone knows it's Alice calling, and uses a distinctive ring tone.

8. Vivien takes the call—Alice missed the bus and needs a pickup. Vivien calls her husband to see if he can do it. She gets his voicemail; he must be out of service range. She tells him she's with a client, and asks if he can get Alice. Five minutes later the phone makes a brief tone Vivien recognizes as her husband's; she sees he's sent her an instant message: "I'll get Alice; good luck on the deal!"

Note how the scenario remains at a fairly high level, not getting too specific about interfaces or technologies. It's important to create scenarios that are within the realm of technical possibility, but at this stage the details of reality aren't yet important. It's always possible to scale back; we are ultimately trying to describe an *optimal*, yet still feasible experience. Note also how the activities in the scenario tie back to Vivien's goals and try to strip out as many tasks as possible.

PRETENDING IT'S MAGIC   A powerful tool in the early stages of developing scenarios is to *pretend the interface is magic* (Cooper, 1999). If your persona has goals and the product has magical powers to meet them, how simple could the interaction be? This kind of thinking is useful to help designers look outside the box. Magical solutions obviously won't suffice, but figuring out creative ways to technically accomplish interactions that are as close to magical solutions as possible(from the personas' perspective) is the essence of great interaction design. Products that meet goals with the minimum of hassle and intrusion seem almost magical to users. Some of the interactions in the preceding scenario may seem a bit magical, but all are possible with technology available today. It's the goal-directed behavior, not the technology alone, that provides the magic.

In early stage design, pretend the interface is magic.

STEP 5: IDENTIFYING NEEDS

After you are satisfied with an initial draft of your context scenario, you can begin to analyze it to extract the personas' needs. These **needs** consist of *objects* and *actions* (Shneiderman, 1998) as well as *contexts*. The authors prefer not to think of needs as identical to **tasks**. The implication is that tasks must be manually performed by the user, whereas the term **needs** implies simply that certain objects need to exist and that certain actions on them need to happen (whether initiated by the user or the system) in certain contexts. Thus, a need from the scenario above might be:

Call (action) a person (object) directly from an appointment (context)

If you are comfortable extracting needs in this format, it works quite well; otherwise, you can separate them as described in the following sections.

DATA NEEDS   Personas' data needs are the objects and information that must be represented in the system. Charts, graphs, status markers, document types, attributes to be sorted, filtered, or manipulated, and graphical object types to be directly manipulated (in authoring and art software) are all examples of data needs.

FUNCTIONAL NEEDS   Functional needs are the operations that need to be performed on the objects of the system and which are eventually translated into interface controls. Functional needs also define places or containers where objects or information in the interface must be displayed.

CONTEXTUAL NEEDS AND REQUIREMENTS   Contextual needs describe relationships between sets of objects or sets of controls, as well as possible relationships between objects and controls. This can include which types of objects to display together to make sense for workflow or to meet specific persona goals, as well as how certain objects must interact with other objects (for example, when choosing items for purchase, a summed list of items already selected needs to be visible). Other contextual requirements include considerations of the product's physical environment(s) (an office, on the go, indoors, outdoors.) and the skills and capabilities of the personas using the product.

OTHER REQUIREMENTS   After you've gone through the exercise of pretending it's magic, it's important to get a firm idea of the realistic requirements of the business and technology you are designing for (although we hope that designers have some influence over technology choices when it directly affects user goals).

✓ Business requirements can include development timelines, regulations, pricing structures, and business models.

✓ Technical requirements can include weight, size, form-factor, display, power constraints, and software platform choices.

✓ Customer and partner requirements can include ease of installation, maintenance, configuration, support costs, and licensing agreements.

Now your design team should have a mandate in the form of the problem and vision statements, a rough, creative overview of how the product is going to address user goals in the form of context scenarios, and a reductive list of needs and requirements extracted from your research, user models, and the scenarios. Now you are ready to delve deeper into the details of your product's behaviors, and begin to consider how the product and its functions will be represented. You are ready to define the framework of the interaction.

Defining the interaction framework

The Requirements Definition phase sets the stage for the core of the design effort: defining the interaction framework of the product. The interaction framework defines not only the skeleton of the interaction — its structure — but also the flow and behavior of the product. The following six steps describe the process of defining the interaction framework:

1. Defining form factor and input methods

2. Defining views

3. Defining functional and data elements

4. Determining functional groups and hierarchy

5. Sketching the interaction framework

6. Constructing key path scenarios

Like previous processes, this is not a linear effort, but requires iteration. The steps are described in more detail in the following sections.

STEP 1: DEFINING FORM FACTOR AND INPUT METHODS

The first step in creating a framework is defining the form factor of the product you'll be designing. Is it a Web application that will be viewed on a high-resolution computer screen? Is it a phone that must be small, light, low-resolution, and visible in the dark and as well as in bright sunlight? Is it a kiosk that must be rugged to withstand a public environment with thousands of distracted, novice users? What are the constraints that each of these imply for any design? Answering these questions sets the stage for all subsequent design efforts.

After you have defined this basic *posture* (see Chapter 8) of the product, you should then determine the valid input methods for the system: Keyboard, mouse, keypad, thumboard, touch screen, voice, game controller, remote control, and many other possibilities exist. Which combination is appropriate for your primary and secondary personas? What is the *primary* input method for the product?

STEP 2: DEFINING VIEWS

The next step, after basic form factor and input methods are defined, is to consider which primary screens or states the product can be in. Initial context scenarios give you a feel for what these might be: They may change or rearrange somewhat as the design evolves (particularly in step 4), but it is often helpful to put an initial stake in the ground to serve as a means for organizing your thoughts. If you know that a user has several end goals and needs that don't closely relate to each other in terms of data overlap, it might be reasonable to define separate views to address them. On the other hand, if you see a cluster of related needs (for example, to make an appointment, you need to see a calendar and possibly contacts), you might consider defining a view that incorporates all these together, assuming the form factor allows it.

STEP 3: DEFINING FUNCTIONAL AND DATA ELEMENTS

Functional and data elements are the visible representations of functions and data in the interface. They are the concrete manifestations of the functional and data needs identified during the Requirements Definition phase. Where those needs were purposely described in terms of real-world objects and actions, functional and data elements are described in the language of user interface representations:

✓ Panes, frames, and other containers on screen

✓ Groupings of on-screen and physical controls

✓ Individual on-screen controls

✓ Individual buttons, knobs, and other physical affordances on a device

✓ Data objects (icons, listed items, images, graphs) and associated attributes

In early framework iterations, containers are the most important to specify; later as you focus on the design of individual containers, you will get to more detailed interface elements.

Many persona needs will spawn multiple interface elements to meet those needs. For example, Vivien needs to be able to telephone her contacts. Functional elements to meet that need include:

- ✓ Voice activation (voice data associated with contact)

- ✓ Assignable quick-dial buttons

- ✓ Selecting from a list of contacts

- ✓ Selecting the name from e-mail header, appointment, or memo

- ✓ Auto-assignment of a call button in proper context (appointment coming up)

Multiple vectors are often a good idea, but sometimes not all possible vectors will be useful to the persona. Use persona goals, design principles, and patterns (see Chapter 7), as well as business and technical constraints to winnow your list of elements for meeting particular needs. You will also need to determine data elements. Some of Vivien's data elements might include appointments, memos, to-do items, and messages.

STEP 4: DETERMINING FUNCTIONAL GROUPS AND HIERARCHY
After you have a good list of top-level functional and data elements, you can begin to group them into functional units and determine their hierarchy (Shneiderman, 1998). Because these elements facilitate specific tasks, the idea is to group elements to best facilitate the persona's flow (see Chapter 9) both within a task and between related tasks. Some issues to consider include:

- ✓ Which elements need a large amount of real estate and which do not?

- ✓ Which elements are *containers* for other elements?

- ✓ How should containers be arranged to optimize flow?

- ✓ Which elements are used together and which aren't?

- ✓ In what sequence will a set of related elements be used?

- ✓ What interaction patterns and principles apply?

- ✓ How do the personas' mental models affect organization? (Goodwin, 2002)

The most important initial step is determining the top-level container elements for the interface, and how they are best arranged given the form factor and input methods that the product requires. Containers for objects that must be compared or used together should be adjacent to each other. Objects representing steps in a process should, in general, be adjacent and ordered sequentially. Use of interaction design principles and patterns is extremely helpful at this juncture; Chapter 7 and Part II of this book provide many principles that can be of assistance at this stage of organization.

STEP 5: SKETCHING THE INTERACTION FRAMEWORK

You may want to sketch different ways of fitting top-level containers together in the interface. Sketching the framework is an iterative process that is best performed with a small, collaborative group of one or two interaction designers and a visual or industrial designer. This visualization of the interface should be extremely simple at first: boxes representing each functional group and/or container with names and descriptions of the relationships between the different areas (see Figure 6-1).

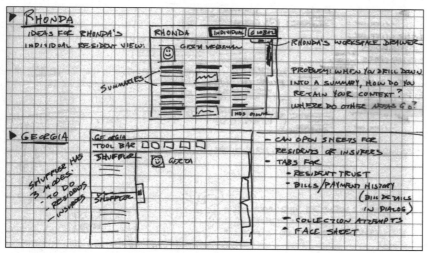

Figure 6-1: Example of an early framework sketch. Framework sketches should be simple, starting with rectangles, names, and simple descriptions of relationships between functional areas. Details can be visually hinted at to give an idea of contents, but don't fall into the trap of designing detail at this stage.

Be sure to look at the entire, top-level framework first; don't let yourself get distracted by the details of a particular area of the interface. There will be plenty of time to explore the design at the widget level and, by going there too soon, you risk a lack of coherence in the design later.

STEP 6: CONSTRUCTING KEY PATH SCENARIOS

Key path scenarios result from exploring details hinted at, but not addressed, in the context scenarios. Key path scenarios describe at the task level the primary actions and pathways through the interface that the persona takes with the greatest frequency, often on a daily basis. In an e-mail application, for example, viewing and composing mail are key path activities; configuring a new mail server is not.

Key path scenarios generally require the greatest interaction support. New users must master key path interactions and functions quickly, so they need to be supported by built-in pedagogy (see Chapters 18 and 27). However, because these functions are used frequently, users do not remain dependent on that pedagogy for long: They will rapidly demand shortcuts. In addition, as users become very experienced, they will want to customize daily use interactions so that they conform to their individual work styles and preferences.

SCENARIOS AND STORYBOARDING Unlike the goal-oriented context scenarios, key path scenarios are more task-oriented; focusing on task details broadly described and hinted at in the context scenarios (Kuutti, 1995). This doesn't mean that goals are ignored — goals and persona needs are the constant measuring stick throughout the design process, used to trim unnecessary tasks and streamline necessary ones. However, **key path scenarios** *must describe in exacting detail the precise behavior of each major interaction* and provide a walkthrough (Newman & Lamming, 1995) of each major pathway.

Typically, key path scenarios begin at a whiteboard and reach a reasonable level of detail. At some point, depending on the complexity and density of the interface, it becomes useful to graduate to computer-based tools. The authors are fond of Microsoft PowerPoint as a tool for aiding in the **storyboarding** of key path scenarios. Storyboarding is a technique borrowed from filmmaking and cartooning. Each step in an interaction, whether between the user and the system, multiple users, or some combination thereof (Holtzblatt & Beyer, 1998) can be portrayed on a slide, and clicking through them provides a reality check for the coherence of the interaction (see Figure 6-2). PowerPoint is sufficiently fast and low-resolution to allow rapid drawing and iterating without succumbing to creating excessive detail.

Figure 6-2: Examples of storyboards from Shared Healthcare Systems' Orcas product.

PRETENDING THE SYSTEM IS HUMAN Just as pretending it's magic is a powerful tool for constructing concept-level, context scenarios, pretending the system is human is a powerful tool at the interaction-level appropriate to key path scenarios. The principle is simple (and discussed at length in Chapter 14): Interactions with a digital system should be similar in tone and helpfulness to interactions with a polite, considerate human (Cooper, 1999). As you construct your interactions, you should ask yourself: Is the primary persona being treated humanely by the product? What would a thoughtful, considerate interaction look like? In what ways can the software offer helpful information without getting in the way? How can it minimize the persona's effort in reaching his goals? What would a helpful human do?

PRINCIPLES AND PATTERNS   Critical to the translation of key path scenarios to storyboards (as well as the grouping of elements in step 3) is the application of general interaction principles and specific interaction patterns. These tools leverage years of interaction design knowledge — not to take advantage of such knowledge would be tantamount to re-inventing the wheel. Key path scenarios provide an inherently top-down approach to interaction design, iterating through successively more-detailed design structures from main screens down to tiny subpanes or dialogs. Principles and patterns add a bottom-up approach to balance the process. Principles and patterns can be used to organize elements at all levels of the design. Chapter 7 discusses the uses and types of principles and patterns in detail, and the chapters of Section Three provide a wealth of useful interaction principles appropriate to this step in the process.

Refining the form and behavior

When a solid, stable framework definition is reached, designers see the remaining pieces of the design begin to smoothly fall into place: Every iteration of the key path scenarios adds detail that strengthens the overall coherence and flow of the product. At this stage, a smooth transition can be made into the Refinement phase, where the final translation of the design into a more concrete form occurs. The process of refinement includes these steps:

1. Drafting the look and feel

2. Constructing validation scenarios

3. Finalizing the design

In this phase, principles and patterns remain important in giving the design a fine formal and behavioral finish. Chapter 19 and many chapters in Section Three provide useful principles for the Refinement phase. It is also critical for the development team to be involved from the start of the Refinement phase — now that the design has a solid conceptual and interaction basis, developer input is critical to creating a finished design that can both be built and remain true to concept.

STEP 1: DRAFTING THE LOOK AND FEEL

By the time the interaction framework has reached the key path scenario stage, interaction designers should begin to work with visual interface designers to develop both the branding and functional components of the visual design (see Chapter 19 for some basic visual design principles). Similarly, industrial designers should be involved at this stage. Visual and industrial designers should walk through the key path scenarios with interaction designers. The different design perspectives are complementary, and result in a better, more desirable product as long as all parties are able to keep within the character of the persona for whom the scenario is being created.

Visual and industrial designers (or interaction designers with these skills) should begin to translate detailed wireframes and storyboards to representative, full-resolution bitmap screens (see Figure 6-3).

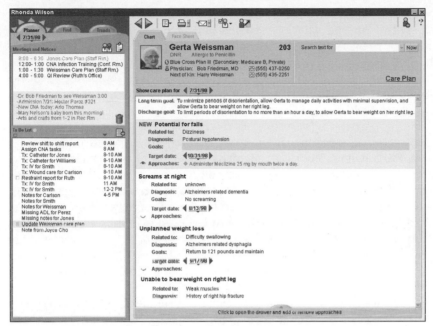

Figure 6-3: Full-resolution bitmap screens for SHS Orcas based on the storyboards from the previous figure. Note that there are minor changes to the layout that naturally result from the realities of pixels and screen resolution. Visual and interaction designers need to work closely together at this stage to ensure that visual changes to the design continue to reinforce appropriate product behaviors and meet the goals of the primary personas.

Every primary view and dialog should be addressed. Visual designers should create style guides so that developers can apply visual design elements consistently to the low-level, lower priority parts of the interface that the designers may have lacked time and resources to complete themselves.

STEP 2: CONSTRUCTING VALIDATION SCENARIOS

If a user performs a task frequently, its interaction must be well crafted. Likewise, if a task is critical but performed infrequently, its interaction, although designed with different objectives, must still be well designed. After you have walked through key path scenarios extensively and storyboarded, it is time to shift focus to less frequently used corners of the interface. You develop these scenarios in the same manner as key path scenarios and prioritize them in this general order:

KEY PATH VARIANTS   Key path variant scenarios are less-traveled interactions that split off from key pathways at some point along the persona's decision tree. These could include lesser-used functions that still belong on a main palette or toolbar, less frequently used views of documents, and major dialogs that are not critical to the basic operation of the product. Key path variants have all the same requirements as key path scenarios, with a slightly greater emphasis on pedagogy because they are used less often.

NECESSARY USE   Necessary use scenarios include all actions that *must* be performed, but that are performed infrequently. Purging databases, configuring, and making other exceptional requests might fall into this category. Necessary use interactions demand pedagogy because they are used infrequently: Users may forget how to access the function or how to perform tasks related to it. However, users won't ever require parallel interaction idioms such as keyboard equivalents because the function is rarely used. Also, because of their infrequent use, necessary functions don't need to be user-customizable.

EDGE CASE USE   Edge case use scenarios, as the name implies, are activities that are both optional and infrequent. Programmers often want to emphasize the edge cases handled by validation scenarios because of their natural tendency to view all features and functions as equally important, but edge cases should not be the focus of the design effort. Designers can't ignore edge case functions and situations, but the interaction needed for them is of lower priority and can, typically, be buried fairly deeply in the interface. Although the *code* may succeed or fail on its capability to successfully handle edge cases, the *product* will succeed or fail on its capability to successfully handle daily use and necessary cases.

FINALIZE THE DESIGN

After you have checked the design through validation scenarios, you are ready, in concert with your visual and industrial design teams, to craft the final look and feel of the design. From there, you can produce a variety of outputs, including a printed form and behavior specification. The form and behavior spec includes screen mockups and storyboards with callouts sufficiently detailed for a programmer to code from. You can, instead, produce an interactive prototype in HTML or an application like Flash or Director that serves much the same purpose. Regardless of your choice of design deliverable, your team should continue to work closely with the development team throughout implementation to ensure that the design vision is accurately translated from the design document to a final product that is faithful to it.

Chapter 7

Synthesizing Good Design: Principles and Patterns

In the last three chapters, we've discussed a process through which we can achieve superior inter-action design. But what makes a design superior? Design that meets the goals and needs of users (without sacrificing business goals or ignoring technical constraints) is one measure of design superiority. But what are the *attributes* of a design that enable it to accomplish this successfully? Are there general, context-specific attributes and features that a design can possess to make it a "good" design?

The authors strongly believe that the answer to these questions lies in the use of interaction design **principles** — guidelines for design of useful and useable form and behavior, and also in the use of interaction design **patterns** — exemplary, generalizable solutions to specific classes of design problem. This chapter defines these ideas in more detail. In addition to design-focused principles and patterns, we must also consider some larger **design imperatives** to set the stage for the design process. These are addressed at the end of this chapter.

Interaction Design Principles

Interaction design principles are generally applicable guidelines that address issues of behavior, form, and content. They represent characteristics of product behavior that help users better accomplish their goals and feel competent and confident while doing so. Principles are applied throughout the design process, helping us to translate tasks that arise out of scenario iterations into formalized structures and behaviors in the interface.

Principles minimize work

One of the primary purposes principles serve is to optimize the experience of the user when he engages with the system. In the case of productivity tools and other non–entertainment-oriented products, this optimization of experience means the *minimization of work* (Goodwin, 2002a). Kinds of work to be minimized include:

- ✓ **Logical work** — comprehension of text and organizational structures
- ✓ **Perceptual work** — decoding visual layouts and semantics of shape, size, color, and representation

✓ **Mnemonic work** — recall of passwords, command vectors, names and locations of data objects and controls, and other relationships between objects

✓ **Physical/motor work** — number of keystrokes, degree of mouse movement, use of gestures (click, drag, double-click), switching between input modes, extent of required navigation

Most of the principles in this book attempt to minimize work while providing greater levels of feedback and contextually useful information up front to the user.

Principles operate at different levels of detail

Design principles operate at three levels of organization: the conceptual level, the interaction level, and the interface level. This book addresses all three levels to some degree, although the focus is on interaction-level principles.

✓ **Conceptual**-level principles help define *what a product is* and how it fits into the broad context of use required by its primary personas. Chapters 3, 8, and 9 discuss conceptual-level design principles.

✓ **Interaction**-level principles help define *how a product should behave*, in general, and in specific situations. The chapters in Parts II, III, V, VI, and VII discuss general interaction-level principles, and Part VIII discusses interaction-level principles for the Web and device interfaces.

✓ **Interface**-level principles help define *the look and feel of interfaces*. Part IV and some of the chapters in Parts V and VI contain interface-level principles.

Most interaction design principles are cross-platform, although some platforms, such as the Web and embedded systems, have special considerations based on the extra constraints imposed by that platform.

Principles versus style guides

Style guides rather rigidly define the look and feel of an interface according to corporate branding and usability guidelines (see Chapter 19 for further discussion of look-and-feel issues). They typically focus at the detailed widget level: How many tabs are in a dialog? What should button highlight states look like? What is the pixel spacing between a control and its label? These are all questions that must be answered to create a finely tuned look and feel for a product, but they don't say much about the bigger issues of what a product should be or how it should behave.

The authors recommend that designers pay attention to style guides when they are available and when fine-tuning interaction details, but there are many bigger and more interesting issues in the design of behavior that rarely find their way into style guides. Most of the remainder of this book provides just such guidelines for the design of well-behaved interactive systems. They include principles and some patterns as well, but are not specified in terms of any particular style guide. The remainder of this chapter and both Section Two and Section Three of this book seek to address these bigger issues of what makes good behavior.

Interaction Design Patterns

Design patterns serve two important functions. The first function is to capture useful design decisions and generalize them to address similar classes of problems in the future (Borchers, 2001). In this sense, patterns represent both the capture and formalization of design knowledge, which can serve many purposes. These include reducing design time and effort on new projects, educating designers new to a project, or — if the pattern is sufficiently broad in its application — educating designers new to the field.

Although the application of patterns in design pedagogy and efficiency is certainly important, the key factor that makes patterns exciting is that they can represent optimal or near-optimal interactions for the user and the class of activity that the pattern addresses.

Interaction and architectural patterns

Interaction design patterns are far more akin to the architectural design patterns first envisioned by Christopher Alexander in his seminal volumes *A Pattern Language* (1977) and *The Timeless Way of Building* (1979) than they are to the popular engineering use of patterns. Alexander sought to capture in a set of building blocks something that he called "the quality without a name," that essence of architectural design that creates a feeling of well-being in the inhabitants of architectural structures. It is this human element that differentiates interaction design patterns (and architectural design patterns) from engineering design patterns, whose sole concern is efficient reuse of code.

One singular and important way that interaction design patterns differ from architectural design patterns is their concern, not only with structure and organization of elements, but with dynamic behaviors and changes in elements in response to user activity. It is tempting to view the distinction simply as one of change over time, but these changes are interesting because they occur in response to human activity. This differentiates them from preordained temporal transitions that can be found in artifacts of broadcast and film media (which have their own distinct set of design patterns). Jan Borchers (2001) aptly describes interaction design patterns:

> [Interaction design] Patterns refer to relationships between physical elements and the events that happen there. Interface designers, like urban architects, strive to create environments that establish certain behavioral patterns with a positive effect on those people 'inside' these environments . . . 'timeless' architecture is comparable to user interface qualities such as 'transparent' and 'natural.'

Types of interaction design patterns

Like most other design patterns, interaction design patterns can be hierarchically organized from the system level down to the level of individual interface widgets. Like principles, they can be applied at different levels of organization (Goodwin, 2002a):

✓ **Postural** patterns can be applied at the conceptual level and help determine the overall product stance in relation to the user. The concept of product posture and its most significant patterns are discussed in Chapter 8.

✓ **Structural** patterns solve problems that relate to the management of information display and access, and to the way containers of data and functions are visually manipulated to best suit user goals and contexts. They consist of views, panes, and element groupings discussed briefly in Chapter 6. We discuss some issues concerning structural patterns in more detail later in this chapter.

✓ **Behavioral** patterns solve wide-ranging problems relating to specific interactions with individual functional or data objects or groups of such objects. What most people think of as system and widget behaviors fall into this category, and many such lower-level patterns are discussed in Sections Two and Three. Figure 16-1 provides a particularly good example of a relatively new behavioral pattern pioneered at Cooper: a **natural language output query** construction for attribute-based retrieval engines.

Structural patterns are perhaps the least-documented patterns, but they are nonetheless in widespread use. One of the most commonly used high-level structural patterns is apparent in Microsoft Outlook with its navigational pane on the left, overview pane on the upper right, and detail pane on the lower right (see Figure 7-1).

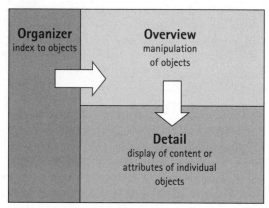

Figure 7-1: The primary structural pattern used by Microsoft Outlook is widely copied in the industry, across many diverse product domains. The left-vertical pane provides navigation and drives the content of the overview pane in the upper right. A selection in this pane populates the lower-right pane with detail or document content.

This pattern is optimal for full-screen applications that require user access to many different kinds of objects, manipulation of those objects in groups, and display of detailed content or attributes of individual objects or documents. The pattern permits all this to be done smoothly in a single screen without the need for additional windows. Many e-mail clients make use of this pattern, and variations of it appear in many authoring and information management tools where rapid access to and manipulation of many types of objects is common.

Structural patterns, pattern nesting, and pre-fab design

Structural patterns often contain other structural patterns; you might imagine that a comprehensive catalogue of structural patterns could, given a clear idea of user needs, permit designers to assemble coherent, Goal-Directed designs fairly rapidly. Although there is some truth in this assertion, which the authors have observed in practice, it is simply never the case that patterns can be mechanically assembled in cookie-cutter fashion. As Christopher Alexander is swift to point out (1979), architectural patterns are the antithesis of the pre-fab building, because context is of absolute importance in defining the actual rendered form of the pattern in the world. The environment where the pattern is deployed is critical, as are the other patterns that comprise it, contain it, and abut it. The same is true for interaction design patterns. The core of each pattern lies in the relationships between represented objects and between those objects and the goals of the user. The precise form of the pattern is certain to be somewhat different for each instance, and the objects that define it will naturally vary from domain to domain. But the relationships between objects remain essentially the same.

Interaction Design Imperatives

Beyond the need for principles of the type described previously, the authors also feel a need for some even more fundamental principles for guiding the design process as a whole. The following set of top level design imperatives (developed by Robert Reimann, Hugh Dubberly, Kim Goodwin, David Fore, and Jonathan Korman) apply to interaction design, but could almost equally well apply to any design discipline.

Interaction designers should create design solutions that are:

- ✓ Ethical [*considerate, helpful*]
  Do no harm
  Improve human situations

- ✓ Purposeful [*useful, usable*]
  Help users achieve their goals and aspirations
  Accommodate user contexts and capacities

- ✓ Pragmatic [*viable, feasible*]
  Help commissioning organizations achieve their goals
  Accommodate business and technical requirements

- ✓ Elegant [*efficient, artful, affective*]
  Represent the simplest complete solution
  Possess internal (self-revealing, understandable) coherence
  Appropriately accommodate and stimulate cognition and emotion

Ethical interaction design

Interaction designers are faced with ethical questions when they are asked to design a system that has fundamental effects on the lives of people. These may be direct effects on users of the system, or second-order effects on other people whose lives the system touches in some way. This can become a particular issue for interaction designers because the product of their design work is not simply the persuasive communication of a policy or the marketing of a product. It is, in fact, the means of executing policy or the creation of a product itself. It is relatively straightforward to design a system that does well by its users, but what effect the system has on others that the system is *used on* is sometimes more difficult to calculate.

DO NO HARM

Ideally, products shouldn't harm anyone, particularly not the users. Possible types of harm that interactive system could be a party to include:

- ✓ **Interpersonal** harm (loss of dignity, insult, humiliation)
- ✓ **Psychological** harm (confusion, discomfort, frustration, coercion, boredom)
- ✓ **Physical** harm (pain, injury, deprivation, death, compromised safety)
- ✓ **Environmental** harm (pollution, elimination of biodiversity)
- ✓ **Social and societal** harm (exploitation, creation or perpetuation of injustice)

The first three of these are somewhat easier to address than the last two and are largely the subject of Part III of this book. The first two require a deep understanding of the domain acquired by research. They also require a buy-in from stakeholders that these issues are within a scope that can be addressed by the project. (Obviously, these last two are not issues for most products; but the reader can surely imagine some examples that are relevant, such as the control system for an offshore oil rig or a voter-ballot–reading system).

IMPROVE HUMAN SITUATIONS

Not doing harm is, of course, not sufficient for a truly ethical design; it should be improving things as well. Some types of situations that interactive systems might improve broadly include:

- ✓ **Increasing understanding** (individual, social, cultural)
- ✓ **Increasing efficiency/effectiveness** of individuals and groups
- ✓ **Improving communication** between individuals and groups
- ✓ **Reducing socio-cultural tensions** between individuals and groups
- ✓ **Improving equity** (financial, social, legal)
- ✓ **Balancing cultural diversity with social cohesion**

Designers should always keep such broad issues at the back of their minds as they engage in new design projects. Opportunities to do good should always be considered, even if they are slightly outside the box.

Purposeful interaction design

The primary theme of this book is purposeful design based on an understanding of user goals and motivations. If nothing else, the Goal-Directed process described in the chapters of Part I should help you to achieve purposeful design. Part of purposefulness, however, is not only understanding user goals, but understanding their limitations as well. Personas serve well in this regard, as the behavior patterns you will observe in researching and creating them will give you a good idea of your users' strengths *and* their blind spots. Goal-Directed design helps designers to create products that support users where they are weak and empower them where they are strong.

Pragmatic interaction design

Design specifications that gather dust on a shelf are of no use to anyone: A design must get built to be of value. Once built, it needs to be deployed in the world. And once deployed, it needs to generate profitable revenue for its owners. It is critical that business goals and technical requirements be taken into account in the course of design. This doesn't imply that designers necessarily need to take everything they are told by their stakeholders and developers at face value: There needs to be an active dialog between the business, engineering, and design groups about where the boundaries are and what areas are flexible. Developers will often state that a design is *impossible* when what they mean is that it is *impossible given the current schedule*. Marketing organizations may create business plans without fully understanding whether their users will accept the ramifications of that plan. The designers, who have gathered detailed, qualitative research on users, may have insight into the business model from a unique perspective. Design works best when there is a relationship of mutual trust and respect between Design, Business, and Engineering.

Elegant interaction design

Elegance is defined in the dictionary as both "gracefulness and restrained beauty of style," and as "scientific precision, neatness, and simplicity." The authors believe that elegance in design, or at least interaction design, incorporates both of these ideals.

REPRESENT THE SIMPLEST COMPLETE SOLUTION

One of the classic elements of good design is *economy of form*: using less to accomplish more. In interaction design, this economy extends to behavior: a simple set of tools for the user that allows him to accomplish great things. Less is more in good design, and designers should endeavor to solve design problems with the fewest additions of form and behavior, in conformance with the mental models of your personas. This concept is well known to programmers, who recognize that better algorithms are clearer and shorter.

POSSESS INTERNAL COHERENCE

Good design has the feeling of a unified whole, in which all parts are in balance and harmony. Software that is poorly designed, or not designed at all, often looks and feels like it is cobbled together from disparate pieces haphazardly knit together. Often this is the result of implementation model construction, where different development teams work on different interface modules without communicating with each other. This is the antithesis of what we want to achieve. The Goal-Directed design process, in which product concepts are conceived of as a whole at the top level and then iteratively refined to detail, provides an ideal environment for creating internally coherent designs.

APPROPRIATELY ACCOMMODATE AND STIMULATE COGNITION AND EMOTION

Many traditionally trained designers speak frequently of desire and its importance in the design of communications and products. They're not wrong, but the authors feel that in placing such emphasis on a single (albeit, complex) emotion, they may sometimes be seeing only part of the picture.

Desire is a narrow emotion to appeal to when designing a product that serves a purpose, especially when that product is located in an enterprise, or its purpose is highly technical or specialized. One would hardly wish to make a technician operating a radiation therapy system feel desire for the system. We, instead, want her to feel cautious and perhaps reverent of the rather dangerous energies the system controls. Therefore, we do everything we can as designers to keep her focus on the patient and his treatment. Thus, in place of what we might call *desire*, the authors believe that elegance (in the sense of gracefulness) means that the user is stimulated and supported both cognitively and emotionally in whatever context she is in.

The remaining chapters of this book enumerate what the authors view as the most critical interaction principles in interaction design—there are, no doubt, many more you will discover, but this set will more than get you started. The chapters also contain a sprinkling of design patterns throughout.

The chapters in Part I have provided the process and concepts behind the practice of Goal-Directed interaction design. The chapters to come provide a healthy dose of design insight that will help you to transform this knowledge into excellent design, whatever your domain.

Section Two

Designing Behavior and Form

Using most of today's digital products is like driving a car that has been rolled down a cliff: You must climb in through the window, none of the lights seem to work, the engine makes a suspicious clunking noise, and spans of sheet metal fly off at inopportune moments. Why must it be that the manufactured artifacts in our lives are increasingly harder to use and understand as they incorporate more technology?

We have many noble experiments, successes, and failures to observe in interaction design today—but designers can often barely agree on the details, let alone the larger issues. The bulk of what passes for interaction design is either guesswork or imitation. The frustrating thing is that it doesn't have to be that way. The chapters in this section address these larger issues of interaction design.

Part II

Achieving Goals and Removing Barriers

Chapter 8

Software Posture

Most people have a predominant behavioral stance that fits their working role on the job: The soldier is wary and alert; the toll-collector is bored and disinterested; the actor is flamboyant and bigger than life; the service representative is upbeat and helpful. Programs, too, have a predominant manner of presenting themselves to the user.

A program may be bold or timid, colorful or drab, but it should be so for a specific, goal-directed reason. Its manner shouldn't result from the personal preference of its designer or programmer. The presentation of the program affects the way the user relates to it, and this relationship strongly influences the usability of the product. Programs whose appearance and behavior conflict with their purposes will seem jarring and inappropriate, like fur in a teacup or a clown at a wedding.

The look and behavior of your program should reflect how it is used, rather than an arbitrary standard. A program's behavioral stance — the way it presents itself to the user — is its **posture**. The look and feel of your program from the perspective of posture is *not* an aesthetic choice: It is a behavioral choice. Your program's posture is its behavioral foundation, and whatever aesthetic choices you make should be in harmony with this posture.

The posture of your interface tells you much about its behavioral stance, which, in turn, dictates many of the important guidelines for the rest of the design. As an interaction designer, one of your first design concerns should be ensuring that your interface presents the posture that is most appropriate for its behavior and that of your users. This chapter explores the different postures for applications on the desktop, the Web, and devices.

Postures for the Desktop

Desktop applications fit into four categories of posture: **sovereign**, **transient**, **daemonic**, and **auxiliary**. Because each describes a different set of behavioral attributes, each also describes a different type of user interaction. More importantly, these categories give the designer a point of departure for designing an interface. A sovereign posture program, for example, won't feel right unless it behaves in a "sovereign" way. Web and other non-desktop applications have their own variations of posture, which we will discuss at the end of this chapter.

Sovereign posture

Programs that are best used full-screen, monopolizing the user's attention for long periods of time, are **sovereign posture** application. Sovereign applications offer a large set of related functions and features, and users tend to keep them up and running continuously. Good examples of this type of application are word processors, spreadsheets, and e-mail applications. Many vertical applications are also sovereign applications because they often deploy on the screen for long periods of time, and interaction with them can be very complex and involved. Users working with sovereign programs often find themselves in a state of flow. Sovereign programs are usually used **maximized** (we'll talk more about window states in Chapter 25). For example, it is hard to imagine using Outlook in a 3x4 inch window—at that size it's not really appropriate for its main job: creating and viewing e-mail and appointments (see Figure 8-1).

Figure 8-1: Microsoft Outlook is a classic example of a sovereign posture application. It stays on screen interacting with the user for long, uninterrupted periods, and with its multiple adjacent panes for navigation and supporting information, it begs to take up the full screen.

Sovereign programs are characteristically used for long, continuous stretches of time. A sovereign program dominates a user's workflow as his primary tool. PowerPoint, for example, is open full screen while you create a presentation from start to finish. Even if other programs are used for support tasks, PowerPoint maintains its sovereign stance.

AXIOM

Users of sovereign applications are perpetual intermediates.

The implications of sovereign behavior are subtle, but quite clear after you think about them. The most important implication is that users of sovereign programs are intermediate users, as discussed in Chapter 3. Each user spends time as a novice, but only a short period of time *relative to the amount of time he will eventually spend* using the product. Certainly a new user has to get over the painful hump of an initial learning curve, but seen from the perspective of the entire relationship of the user with the application, the time he spends getting acquainted with the program is small.

From the designer's point of view, this means that the program should be designed for optimal use by perpetual intermediates and not be aimed primarily for beginners (or experts). Sacrificing speed and power in favor of a clumsier but easier-to-learn idiom is out of place here, as is providing only nerdy power tools. Of course, if you can offer easier idioms without compromising the interaction for intermediate users; that is always best.

Between first-time users and intermediate users there are many people who use sovereign applications only on occasion. These infrequent users cannot be ignored. However, the success of a sovereign application is still dependent on its intermediate, frequent users until someone else satisfies both them *and* inexperienced users. WordStar, an early word processing program, is a good example. It dominated the word processing marketplace in the late 70s and early 80s because it served its intermediate users exceedingly well, even though it was extremely difficult for infrequent and first-time users. WordStar Corporation thrived until its competition offered the same power for intermediate users while simultaneously making it much less painful for infrequent users. WordStar, unable to keep up with the competition, rapidly dwindled to insignificance.

TAKE THE PIXELS

Because the user's interaction with a sovereign program dominates his session at the computer, the program shouldn't be afraid to take as much screen real estate as possible. No other program will be competing with yours, so expect to take advantage of it all. Don't waste space, but don't be shy about taking what you need to do the job. If you need four toolbars to cover the bases, use four toolbars. In a program of a different posture, four toolbars may be overly complex, but the sovereign posture has a defensible claim on the pixels.

In most instances, sovereign programs run maximized. In the absence of explicit instructions from the user, your sovereign application should default to maximized (full-screen) presentation. The program needs to be fully resizable and must work reasonably well in other screen configurations, but it must optimize its interface for full-screen instead of the less likely cases.

DESIGN TIP

Optimize sovereign applications for full-screen use.

Because the user will stare at a sovereign application for long periods, you should take care to mute the colors and texture of the visual presentation. Keep the color palette narrow and conservative. Big colorful controls may look really cool to newcomers, but they seem garish after a couple of weeks of daily use. Tiny dots or accents of color will have more effect in the long run than big splashes, and they enable you to pack controls together more tightly than you could otherwise.

Sovereign interfaces should use conservative visual style.

Your user will stare at the same palettes, menus, and toolbars for many hours, gaining an innate sense of where things are from sheer familiarity. This gives you, the designer, freedom to do more with fewer pixels. Toolbars and their controls can be smaller than normal. Auxiliary controls like screen-splitters, rulers, and scroll bars can be smaller and more closely spaced.

RICH VISUAL FEEDBACK

Sovereign applications are great platforms for creating an environment rich in visual feedback for the user. You can productively add extra little bits of information into the interface. The status bar at the bottom of the screen, the ends of the space normally occupied by scroll bars, the title bar, and other dusty corners of the program's visible extents can be filled with visual indications of the program's status, the status of the data, the state of the system, and hints for more productive user actions. However, be careful: While enriching the visual feedback, you must be careful not to create an interface that is hopelessly cluttered.

The first-time user won't even notice such artifacts, let alone understand them, because of the subtle way they are shown on the screen. After a couple of months of steady use, however, he will begin to see them, wonder about their meaning, and experimentally explore them. At this point, the user will be willing to expend a little effort to learn more. If you provide an easy means for him to find out what the artifacts are, he will become not only a better user, but a more satisfied user, as his power over the program grows with his understanding. Adding such richness to the interface is like adding a variety of ingredients to a meat stock — it enhances the entire meal. We discuss this idea of rich **modeless** visual feedback in Chapter 34.

RICH INPUT

Sovereign programs similarly benefit from rich input. Every frequently used aspect of the program should be controllable in several ways. Direct manipulation, dialog boxes, keyboard mnemonics, and keyboard accelerators are all appropriate. You can make more aggressive demands on the user's fine motor skills with direct-manipulation idioms. Sensitive areas on the screen can be just a couple of pixels across because you can assume that the user is established comfortably in his chair, arm positioned in a stable way on his desk, rolling his mouse firmly across a resilient mouse pad.

Sovereign applications can exploit rich input.

Go ahead and use the corners and edges of the program's window for controls. In a jet cockpit, the most frequently used controls are situated directly in front of the pilot; those needed only occasionally or in an emergency are found on the armrests, overhead, and on the side panels. In Word, Microsoft has put the most frequently used functions on the two main toolbars (see Figure 8-2).

They put the frequently used but visually dislocating functions on small controls to the left of the horizontal scroll bar near the bottom of the screen. These controls change the appearance of the entire visual display—Normal view, Page Layout view and Outline view. Neophytes do not often use them and, if accidentally triggered, they can be confusing. By placing them near the bottom of the screen, they become almost invisible to the new user. Their segregated positioning subtly and silently indicates that caution should be taken in their use. More experienced users, with more confidence in their understanding and control of the program, will begin to notice these controls and wonder about their purpose. They can experimentally select them when they feel fully prepared for their consequence. This is a very accurate and useful mapping of control placement to usage.

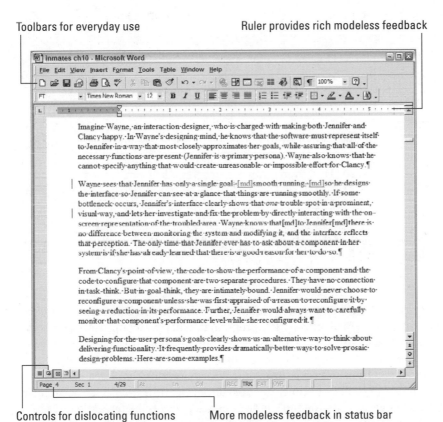

Figure 8-2: Microsoft Word has placed controls at both the top and the bottom of the application. Those at the top are more benign than those at the bottom. The latter are segregated because they can cause significant visual dislocation.

The user won't appreciate interactions that cause a delay. Like a grain of sand in your shoe, a one- or two-second delay gets painful after a few repetitions. It is perfectly acceptable for functions to take time, but they should not be frequent or repeated procedures during the normal use of the product. If, for example, it takes more than a fraction of a second to save the user's work to disk, the user quickly comes to view that delay as unreasonable. On the other hand, inverting a matrix or changing the entire formatting style of a document can take a few seconds without causing irritation because the user can plainly see what a big job it is. Besides, he won't invoke it very often.

DOCUMENT-CENTRIC APPLICATIONS

The dictum that sovereign programs should fill the screen is also true of document windows within the program itself. Child windows containing documents should always be maximized inside the program unless the user explicitly instructs otherwise.

Maximize document views within sovereign applications.

Many sovereign programs are also document-centric (their primary functions involve the creation and viewing of documents containing rich data), making it easy to confuse the two, but they are not the same. Most of the documents we work with are 8½-by-11 inches and won't fit on a standard computer screen (the authors still wonder why portrait displays never caught on). We strain to show as much of them as possible, which naturally demands a full-screen stance. If the document under construction were a 32x32 pixel icon, for example, a document-centric program wouldn't need to take the full screen. The sovereignty of a program does not come from its document-centricity nor from the size of the document — it comes from the nature of the program's use.

If a program manipulates a document but only performs some very simple, single function, like scanning in a graphic, it isn't a sovereign application and shouldn't exhibit sovereign behavior. Such single-function applications have a posture of their own, the transient posture.

Transient posture

A **transient** posture program comes and goes, presenting a single, high-relief function with a tightly restricted set of accompanying controls. The program is called when needed, appears, performs its job, and then quickly leaves, letting the user continue his more normal activity, usually with a sovereign application.

The salient characteristic of transient programs is their temporary nature. Because they don't stay on the screen for extended periods of time, the user doesn't get the chance to become very familiar with them. Consequently, the program's user interface needs to be unsubtle, presenting its controls clearly and boldly with no possibility of mistakes. The interface must spell out what it does: This is not the place for artistic-but-ambiguous images or icons — it *is* the place for big buttons with precise legends spelled out in a slightly oversized, easy-to-read typeface.

Transient applications must be simple, clear, and to the point.

Although a transient program can certainly operate alone on your desktop, it usually acts in a supporting role to a sovereign application. For example, calling up the Explorer to locate and open a file while editing another with Word is a typical transient scenario. So is setting your speaker volume (see Figure 8-3). Because the transient program borrows space at the expense of the sovereign, it must respect the sovereign by not taking more space on screen than is absolutely necessary. Where the sovereign can dig a hole and pour a concrete foundation for itself, the transient program is just on a weekend campout. It cannot deploy itself on screen either graphically or temporally. It is the taxicab of the software world.

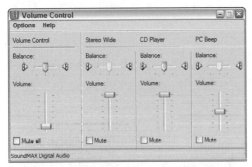

Figure 8-3: The Windows Volume Control is a typical example of a transient application, used briefly and infrequently in the service of some more sovereign activity, and then dismissed. Microsoft could have done a bit more to reinforce this panel's transient stature by conserving white space a bit more, enlarging its controls, and using a more colorful palette to differentiate it from the sovereign application that it is likely launched on top of.

BRIGHT AND CLEAR

Whereas a transient program must conserve the total amount of screen real estate it consumes, the controls on its surface can be proportionally larger than those on a sovereign application. Where such heavy-handed visual design on a sovereign program would pall within a few weeks, the transient program isn't on screen long enough for it to bother the user. On the contrary, the bolder graphics help the user to orient himself more quickly when the program pops up. The program shouldn't restrict itself to a drab palette, but should instead paint itself in brighter colors to help differentiate it from the hosting sovereign, which will be more appropriately shaded in muted hues. Transient programs should use their brighter colors and bold graphics to clearly convey their purpose—the user needs big, bright, reflective road signs to keep him from making the wrong turn at 100 kilometers per hour.

Transient programs should have instructions built into their surface. The user may only see the program once a month and will likely forget the meanings of the choices presented. Instead of a button captioned Setup, it might be better to make the button large enough to caption it Setup

User Preferences. The meaning is clearer, and the button more reassuring. Likewise, nothing should be abbreviated on a transient program—everything should be spelled out to avoid confusion. The user should be able to see without difficulty that the printer is busy, for example, or that the audio is five seconds long.

KEEP IT SIMPLE

After the user summons a transient program, all the information and facilities he needs should be right there on the surface of the program's single window. Keep the user's focus of attention on that window and never force him into supporting subwindows or dialog boxes to take care of the main function of the program. If you find yourself adding a dialog box or second view to a transient application, that's a key sign that your design needs a review.

DESIGN TIP

Keep transient applications to a single window and view.

Transient programs are not the place for tiny scroll bars and fussy point-click-and-drag interfaces. You want to keep the demands here on the user's fine motor skills down to a minimum. Simple push-buttons for simple functions are better. Anything directly manipulable must be big enough to move to easily: at least twenty pixels square. Keep controls off the borders of the window. Don't use the window bottoms, status bars, or sides in transient programs. Instead, position the controls up close and personal in the main part of the window.

You should definitely provide a keyboard interface, but it must be a simple one (see Figure 8-4). It shouldn't be more complex than Enter, Escape, and Tab. You might add the arrow keys, too, but that's about it.

Of course, there are exceptions to the monothematic nature of transient programs, although they are rare. If a transient program performs more than just a single function, the interface should communicate this visually. For example, if the program imports and exports graphics, the interface should be evenly and visually split into two halves by bold coloration or other graphics. One half could contain the controls for importing and the other half the controls for exporting. The two halves must be labeled unambiguously. Whatever you do, don't add more windows or dialogs.

Keep in mind that any given transient program may be called upon to assist in the management of some aspect of a sovereign program. This means that the transient program, as it positions itself on top of the sovereign, may obscure the very information that it is chartered to work on. This implies that the transient program must be movable, which means it must have a title bar.

It is vital to keep the amount of management overhead as low as possible with transient programs. All the user wants to do is call the program up, request a function, and then end the program. It is completely unreasonable to force the user to add non-productive window-management tasks to this interaction.

Figure 8-4: The Calculator accessory in Windows and on the Mac is another good example of a transient application, with large, obvious buttons and functions. The program can also be operated using the key-board, which is good, because the hardware-style buttons are somewhat awkward, though acceptable for infrequent use.

REMEMBERING STATE

The most appropriate way to help the user with both transient and sovereign apps is to give the program a memory. If the transient program remembers where it was the last time it was used, the chances are excellent that the same size and placement will be appropriate next time, too. It will almost always be more apt than any default setting might chance to be. Whatever shape and position the user morphed the program into is the shape and position the program should reappear in when it is next summoned. Of course, this holds true for its logical settings, too.

On the other hand, if the use of the program is really simple and single-minded, go ahead and specify its shape — omit the frame, the directly resizable window border. Save yourself the work and remove the complexity from the program (be careful, though, as this can certainly be abused). The goal here is not to save the programmer work — that's just a collateral benefit — but to keep the user aware of as few complexities as possible. If the program's functions don't demand resizing and the overall size of the program is small, the principle that simpler is better takes on more importance than usual. The calculator accessory in Windows and on the Mac, for example, isn't resizable. It is always the correct size and shape.

No doubt you have already realized that almost all dialog boxes are really transient programs. You can see that all the preceding guidelines for transient programs apply equally well to the design of dialog boxes (for more on dialog boxes, see Chapters 30 and 31).

Daemonic posture

Programs that do not normally interact with the user are **daemonic posture** programs. These programs serve quietly and invisibly in the background, performing possibly vital tasks without the need for human intervention. A printer driver is an excellent example.

As you might expect, any discussion of the user interface of daemonic programs is necessarily short. Too frequently, though, programmers give daemonic programs full-screen control panels that are better suited to sovereign programs. Designing your fax manager in the image of Excel, for example, is a fatal mistake. At the other end of the spectrum, daemonic programs are, too frequently, unreachable by the user, causing no end of frustration when adjustments need to be made.

Where a transient program controls the execution of a function, daemonic programs usually manage processes. Your heartbeat isn't a function that must be consciously controlled; rather, it is a process that proceeds autonomously in the background. Like the processes that regulate your heartbeat, daemonic programs generally remain completely invisible, competently performing their process as long as your computer is turned on. Unlike your heart, however, daemonic programs must occasionally be installed and removed and, also occasionally, they must be adjusted to deal with changing circumstances. It is at these times that the daemon talks to the user. Without exception, the interaction between the user and a daemonic program is transient in nature, and all the imperatives of transient program design hold true here also.

The principles of transient design that are concerned with keeping the user informed of the purpose of the program and of the scope and meaning of the user's available choices become even more critical with daemonic programs. In many cases, the user will not even be consciously (or unconsciously) aware of the existence of the daemonic program. If you recognize that, it becomes obvious that reports about status from that program can be quite dislocating if not presented in an appropriate context. Because many of these programs perform esoteric functions — like printer drivers or communications concentrators — the messages from them must take particular care not to confuse the user or lead to misunderstandings.

A question that is often taken for granted with programs of other postures becomes very significant with daemonic programs: If the program is normally invisible, how should the user interface be summoned on those rare occasions when it is needed? One of the most frequently used methods is to represent the daemon with an on-screen program icon found either in the status area (system tray) in Windows or in the far right of the Mac OS menu bar. Putting the icon so boldly in the user's face when it is almost never needed is a real affront, like pasting an advertisement on the windshield of somebody's car. If your daemon needs configuring no more than once a day, get it off of the main screen. Windows XP now hides daemonic icons that are not actively being used. Daemonic icons should only be employed permanently if they provide continuous, useful status information.

Microsoft makes a bit of a compromise here by setting aside an area on the far-right side of the taskbar as a status area wherein icons belonging to daemonic posture programs may reside. This area, also known as the system tray, has been abused by programmers, who often use it as a quick launch area for sovereign applications. As of Windows XP, Microsoft set the standard that only status icons are to appear in the status area (a quick launch area is supported next to the Start button on the taskbar), and unless the user chooses otherwise, only icons actively reporting status changes will be displayed. Any others will be hidden. These decisions are very appropriate handling of transient programs (see Figure 8-5).

An effective approach for configuring daemonic programs is employed by both the Mac and Windows: **control panels**, which are transient programs that run as launchable applications to configure daemons. These give the user a consistent place to go for access to such process-centric applications.

Figure 8-5: The status area of the taskbar in Windows XP. The mouse cursor is pointed at an icon representing a daemonic process that monitors the connection to Windows Messenger. The icon provides modeless visual status and also provides a launch-point for the Windows Messenger application. It is a variation on the axiom: *Allow input wherever you have output* (Chapter 10).

Auxiliary posture

Programs that blend the characteristics of sovereign and transient programs exhibit **auxiliary posture**. The auxiliary program is continuously present like a sovereign, but it performs only a supporting role. It is small and is usually superimposed on another application the way a transient is. The Windows taskbar, clock programs, performance monitors on many Unix platforms, and Stickies on the Mac are all good examples of auxiliary programs. People who continuously use instant messaging applications are also using them in an auxiliary manner. In Windows XP's version of Internet Explorer, Microsoft has recognized the auxiliary role that streaming audio can play while the user is browsing the Web. It has integrated its audio player into a side pane in the browser (see Figure 8-6).

Figure 8-6: Microsoft has recognized the potential auxiliary role of streaming audio to Web browsing, and has integrated its audio player into a collapsible side panel in Internet Explorer. The audio controls themselves can also be popped out of the browser window as a standalone window.

Auxiliary programs are typically silent reporters of ongoing processes, although some, like Stickies or stock tickers, are for displaying other data the user is interested in. In some cases, this reporting may be a function that they perform in addition to actually managing processes, but this is not necessarily true. An auxiliary application may, for example, monitor the amount of system resources either in use or available. The program constantly displays a small bar chart reflecting the current resource availability.

A process-reporting auxiliary program must be simple and often bold in reporting its information. It must be very respectful of the pre-eminence of sovereign programs and should be quick to move out of the way when necessary.

Auxiliary programs are not the locus of the user's attention; that distinction belongs to the host application. For example, take an automatic call distribution (ACD) program. An ACD is used to evenly distribute incoming calls to teams of customer-service representatives trained either to take orders, provide support, or both. Each representative uses a computer running an application specific to his or her job. This application, the primary reason for the system's purchase, is a sovereign posture application; the ACD program is an auxiliary application on top of it. For example, a sales agent fields calls from prospective buyers on an incoming toll-free number. The representative's order entry program is the sovereign, whereas the ACD program is the auxiliary application, riding on top to feed incoming calls to the agent. The ACD program must be very conservative in its use of pixels because it always obscures some of the underlying sovereign application. It can afford to have small features because it is on the screen for long periods of time. In other words, the controls on the auxiliary application can be designed to a sovereign's sensibilities.

Postures for the Web

Designers may be tempted to think that the Web is, by necessity, different from desktop applications in terms of posture. Although there are variations that exhibit combinations of these postures, the basic four stances really do cover the needs of most Web sites and Web applications (we discuss more details of designing for the Web in Chapter 37).

Information-oriented sites

Sites that are purely informational, which require no complex transactions to take place beyond navigating from page to page and limited search, must balance two forces: the need to display a reasonable density of useful information, and the need to allow first time and infrequent users to easily learn and navigate the site. This implies a tension between sovereign and transient attributes in informational sites. Which stance is more dominant depends largely on who the target personas are and what their behavior patterns are when using the site: Are they infrequent or one-time users, or are they repeat users who will return weekly or daily to view content?

The frequency at which content can be updated on a site does, in some respects, influence this behavior: Informational sites with daily-updated information will naturally attract repeat users more than a monthly-updated site. Infrequently updated sites may be used more as occasional reference (assuming the information is not too topical) rather than heavy repeat use and should then be given more of a transient stance than a sovereign one. What's more, the site can configure itself into a more sovereign posture by paying attention to how often that particular user visits.

SOVEREIGN ATTRIBUTES

Detailed information display is best accomplished by assuming a sovereign stance. By assuming full-screen use, designers can take advantage of all the possible space available to clearly present both the information itself and the navigational tools and cues to keep users oriented.

The only fly in the ointment of sovereign stance on the Web is choosing which full-screen resolution is appropriate. In fact, this is an issue for desktop applications as well. The only difference between the desktop and the Web in this regard is that Web sites have little leverage in influencing what screen resolution users will have. Users, however, who are spending money on expensive desktop productivity applications, will probably make sure that they have the right hardware to support the needs of the software. Thus, Web designers need to make a decision early on what the lowest common denominator they wish to support will be. Alternatively, they must code more complex sites that may be optimal on higher resolution screens, but which are still usable (without horizontal scrolling) on lower-resolution monitors.

TRANSIENT ATTRIBUTES

The less frequently your primary personas access the site, the more transient a stance the site needs to take. In an informational site, this manifests itself in terms of ease and clarity of navigation.

Sites used for infrequent reference might be bookmarked by users: You should make it possible for them to bookmark any page of information so that they can reliably return to it at any later time.

Users will likely visit sites with weekly to monthly updated material intermittently, and so navigation there must be particularly clear. If the site can retain information about past user actions via cookies or server-side methods and present information that is organized based on what interested them previously, this could dramatically help less frequent users find what they need with minimal navigation.

Transactional sites and Web applications

Transactional Web sites and Web applications have many of the same tensions between sovereign and transient stances that informational sites do. This is a particular challenge because the level of interaction can be significantly more complex.

Again, a good guide is the goals and needs of the primary personas: Are they consumers, who will use the site at their discretion, perhaps on a weekly or monthly basis, or are they employees who (for an enterprise or B2B Web application) must use the site as part of their job on a daily basis? Transactional sites that are used for a significant part of an employee's job should be considered full sovereign applications.

On the other hand, e-commerce, online banking, and other consumer-oriented transactional sites must, like informational sites, balance between sovereign and transient stances very similarly to informational sites. In fact, many consumer transactional sites have a heavy informational aspect because users like to research and compare products, investments, and other items to be transacted upon. For these types of sites, navigational clarity is very important, as is access to supporting information and the streamlining of transactions. Amazon.com has addressed many of these issues quite well, via one-click ordering, good search and browsing capability, online reviews of items, recommendation lists, persistent shopping cart, and tracking of recently viewed items. If Amazon has a fault, it may be that it tries to do a bit too much: Some of the navigational links near the bottom of the pages likely don't get hit very often.

Web portals

Early search engines allowed people to find and access content and functions distributed throughout the world on the Web. They served as **portals** in the original sense of the word — ways to get somewhere else. Nothing really happens in these **navigational portals**; you get in, you go somewhere, you get out. They are used exclusively to gain access quickly to unrelated information and functions.

If the user requires access via a navigational portal relatively infrequently, the appropriate posture is transient, providing clear, simple navigational controls and getting out of the way. If the user needs more frequent access, the appropriate posture is auxiliary: a small and persistent panel of links (like the Windows taskbar).

As portal sites evolved, they offered more integrated content and function and grew beyond being simple stepping-stones to another place. **Consumer-oriented** portals provide unified access to content and functionality related to a specific topic, and **enterprise** portals provide internal access to important company information and business tools. In both cases, the intent is essentially to create an environment in which users can access a particular kind of information and accomplish a particular kind of work: **environmental portals**. Actual work is done in an environmental portal. Information is gathered from disparate sources and acted upon; various tools are brought together to accomplish a unified purpose.

An environmental portal's elements need to relate to one another in a way that helps users achieve a specific purpose. When a portal creates a working environment, it also creates a sense of place; the portal is no longer a way to get somewhere else, but a destination in and of itself. The appropriate posture for an environmental portal is thus sovereign.

Within an environmental portal, the individual elements function essentially as small applications running simultaneously — as such, the elements themselves also have postures:

✓ **Auxiliary elements:** Most of the elements in an environmental portal have an auxiliary posture; they typically present aggregated sets of information to which the user wants constant access (such as dynamic status monitors), or simple functionality (small applications, link lists, and so on). Auxiliary elements are, in fact, the key building block of environmental portals. The sovereign portal is, therefore, composed of a set of auxiliary posture mini-applications.

✓ **Transient elements:** In addition to auxiliary elements, an environmental portal often provides transient portal services as well. Their complexity is minimal; they are rich in explanatory elements, and they are used for short periods on demand. Designers should give a transient posture to any embedded portal service that is briefly and temporarily accessed (such as a to-do list or package-tracking status display) so that it does not compete with the sovereign/auxiliary posture of the portal itself. Rather it becomes a natural, temporary extension of it.

When migrating traditional applications into environmental portals, one of the key design challenges is breaking the application apart into a proper set of portal services with auxiliary or transient posture. Sovereign, full-browser applications are not appropriate within portals because they are not perceived as part of the portal once launched.

Postures for Other Platforms

Handheld devices, kiosks, and software-enabled appliances each have slightly different posture issues. Like Web interfaces, these other platforms typically express a tension between several postures. (For information on other design issues regarding these platforms, see Chapter 38.)

Kiosks

The large, full-screen nature of kiosks would appear to bias them towards sovereign posture, but there are several reasons why the situation is not quite that simple. First, users of kiosks are often first-time users (with the exception, perhaps, of ATM users), and are in most cases not daily users. Second, most people do not spend any significant amount of time in front of a kiosk: They perform a simple transaction or search, get what information they need, and then move on. Third, most kiosks employ either touchscreens or bezel buttons to the side of the display, and neither of these input mechanisms support the high data density you would expect of a sovereign application. Fourth, kiosk users are rarely comfortably seated in front of an optimally placed monitor, but are standing in a public place with bright ambient light and many distractions. These user behaviors and constraints should bias most kiosks towards transient posture, with simple navigation, large controls, and rich visuals to attract attention and hint at function.

Educational and entertainment kiosks vary somewhat from the strict transient posture required of more transactional kiosks. In this case, exploration of the kiosk environment is more important than the simple completion of single transactions or searches. In this case, more data density and more complex interactions and visual transitions can sometimes be introduced to positive effect, but the limitations of the input mechanisms need to be carefully respected, lest the user lose the ability to successfully navigate the interface.

Handheld devices

Designing for handheld devices is an exercise in hardware limitations: input mechanisms, screen size and resolution, and power consumption, to name a few. One of the most important insights that many designers have now realized with regard to handheld devices is that handhelds are often not standalone systems. They are, as in the case of personal information managers like Palm and Pocket PC devices, satellites of a desktop system, used more to view information than perform heavy input on their own. Although folding keyboards can be purchased for many handhelds, this, in essence, transforms them into desktop systems (with tiny screens). In the role of satellite devices, an auxiliary posture is appropriate for the most frequently used handheld applications — typical PIM, e-mail, and Web browsing applications, for example. Less frequently or more temporarily used handheld applications (like alarms) can adopt a more transient posture.

Cellular telephones are an interesting type of handheld device. Phones are *not* satellite devices; they are primary communication devices. However, from an interface posture standpoint, phones are really transient. You place a call as quickly as possible and then abandon the interface to your conversation. The best interface for a phone is arguably non-visual. Voice activation is perfect for placing a call; opening the flip lid on a phone is probably the most effective way of answering it (or again using voice activation for hands-free use). The more transient the phone's interface is, the better.

In the last couple of years, handheld data devices and handheld phones have been converging. These convergence devices run the risk of making phone operation too complex and data manipulation too difficult, but the latest breed of devices like the Handspring Treo has delivered a successful middle ground. In some ways, they have made the phone itself more usable by allowing the satellite nature of the device to aid in the input of information to the phone: Treos make use of desktop contact information to synchronize the device's phonebook, for example, thus removing the previously painful data entry step and reinforcing the transient posture of the phone functionality. It is important, when designing for these devices, to recognize the auxiliary nature of data functions and the transient nature of phone functions, using each to reinforce the utility of the other. (The data dialup should be minimally transient, whereas the data browsing should be auxiliary.)

Appliances

Most appliances have extremely simple displays and rely heavily on hardware buttons and dials to manipulate the state of the appliance. In some cases, however, major appliances (notably washers and dryers) will sport color LCD touch screens allowing rich output and direct input.

Appliance interfaces, like the phone interfaces mentioned in the previous section, should primarily be considered transient posture interfaces. Users of these interfaces will seldom be technology-savvy and should, therefore, be presented the most simple and straightforward interfaces possible. These users are also accustomed to hardware controls. Unless an unprecedented ease of use can be achieved with a touch screen, dials and buttons (with appropriate audible feedback, and visual feedback via a view-only display or even hardware lamps) may be a better choice. Many appliance makers make the mistake of putting dozens of new — and unwanted — features into their new, digital models. Instead of making it easier, that "simple" LCD touchscreen becomes a confusing array of unworkable controls.

Another reason for a transient stance in appliance interfaces is that users of appliances are trying to get something very specific done. Like the users of transactional kiosks, they are not interested in exploring the interface or getting additional information; they simply want to put the washer on normal cycle or cook their frozen dinners.

One aspect of appliance design demands a different posture: Status information indicating what cycle the washer is on or what the VCR is set to record should be provided as a daemonic icon, providing minimal status quietly in a corner. If more than minimal status is required, an auxiliary posture for this information then becomes appropriate.

Chapter 9

Orchestration and Flow

To make software more productive, we must make its users more productive. To make users more productive, we must ensure that they remain in a harmonious frame of mind while using our applications. It is the user's mental state that ultimately dictates how effective he is at using our program. This chapter discusses how we can help ensure that our software reinforces user effectiveness and efficiency and how we can avoid disrupting the state of productive concentration that we wish our users to maintain.

Flow and Transparency

When people are able to concentrate wholeheartedly on an activity, they lose awareness of peripheral problems and distractions. The state is called flow, a concept first identified by Mihaly Csikszentmihalyi, professor of psychology at the University of Chicago, and author of *Flow: The Psychology of Optimal Experience* (HarperCollins, 1991).

In *Peopleware: Productive Projects and Teams* (Dorset House, 1987), Tom DeMarco and Timothy Lister, describe flow as a "condition of deep, nearly meditative involvement." Flow often induces a "gentle sense of euphoria" and can make you unaware of the passage of time. Most significantly, a person in a state of flow can be extremely productive, especially when engaged in process-oriented tasks such as "engineering, design, development, and writing." Today, these tasks are typically performed on computers while interacting with software. Therefore, it behooves us to create a software interaction that promotes and enhances flow, rather than one that includes potentially flow-breaking or flow-disturbing behavior. If the program consistently rattles the user out of flow, it becomes difficult for him to regain that productive state.

If the user could achieve his goals magically, without your program, he would. By the same token, if the user needed the program but could achieve his goals without going through its user interface, he would. Interacting with software is not an aesthetic experience (except perhaps in games, entertainment, and exploration-oriented interactive systems). For the most part, it is a pragmatic exercise that is best kept to a minimum.

AXIOM

No matter how cool your interface is, less of it would be better.

Directing your attention to the interaction itself puts the emphasis on the side effects of the tools rather than on the user's goals. A user interface is an artifact, not directly related to the goals of the user. Next time you find yourself crowing about what cool interaction you've designed, just remember that the ultimate user interface for most purposes is no interface at all.

To create flow, our interaction with software must become **transparent**. In other words, the interface must not call attention to itself as a visual artifact, but must instead, at every turn, be at the service of the user, providing what he needs at the right time and in the right place. There are several excellent ways to make our interfaces recede into invisibility. They are:

1. Follow mental models.

2. Direct, don't discuss.

3. Keep tools close at hand.

4. Provide modeless feedback.

We will now discuss each of these methods in detail.

Follow mental models

We introduced the concept of user mental models in Chapter 2. Different users will have different mental models of a process, but they will rarely visualize them in terms of the detailed innards of the computer process. Each user naturally forms a mental image about how the software performs its task. The mind looks for some pattern of cause and effect to gain insight into the machine's behavior.

For example, in a hospital information system, the physicians and nurses have a mental model of patient information that derives from the patient records that they are used to manipulating in the real world. It therefore makes most sense to find patient information by using names of patients as an index. Each physician has certain patients, so it makes additional sense to filter the patients in the clinical interface so that each physician can choose from a list of her own patients, organized alphabetically by name. On the other hand, in the business office of the hospital, the clerks there are worried about overdue bills. They don't initially think about these bills in terms of who or what the bill is for, but rather in terms of how late the bill is (and perhaps how big the bill is). Thus, for the business office interface, it makes sense to sort first by time overdue and perhaps by amount due, with patient names as a secondary organizational principle.

Direct, don't discuss

Many developers imagine the ideal interface to be a two-way conversation with the user. However, most users don't see it that way. Most users would rather interact with the software in the same way they interact with, say, their cars. They open the door and get in when they want to go somewhere. They step on the accelerator when they want the car to move forward and the brake when it is time to stop; they turn the wheel when they want the car to turn.

This ideal interaction is not a dialog — it's more like using a tool. When a carpenter hits nails, she doesn't discuss the nail with the hammer; she directs the hammer onto the nail. In a car, the driver—the user—gives the car direction when he wants to change the car's behavior. The driver expects direct feedback from the car and its environment in terms appropriate to the device: the view out the windshield, the readings on the various gauges on the dashboard, the sound of rushing air and tires on pavement, the feel of lateral g-forces and vibration from the road. The carpenter expects similar feedback: the feel of the nail sinking, the sound of the steel striking steel, and the heft of the hammer's weight.

The driver certainly doesn't expect the car to interrogate him with a dialog box, nor would the carpenter appreciate one (like the one in Figure 9-1) appearing on her hammer.

Figure 9-1: Just because programmers are accustomed to seeing messages like this, it doesn't mean that people from other walks of life are. Nobody wants his machine to scold him. If we guide our machines in a dunderheaded way, we *expect* to get a dunderheaded response. Sure, they can protect us from fatal errors, but scolding isn't the same thing as protecting.

One of the reasons software often aggravates users is that it doesn't act like a car or a hammer. Instead, it has the temerity to try to engage us in a dialog—to inform us of our shortcomings and to demand answers from us. From the user's point of view, the roles are reversed: It should be the user doing the demanding and the software doing the answering.

With direct manipulation, we can point to what we want. If we want to move an object from A to B, we click on it and drag it there. As a general rule, the better, more flow-inducing interfaces are those with plentiful and sophisticated direct manipulation idioms.

Keep tools close at hand

Most programs are too complex for one mode of direct manipulation to cover all their features. Consequently, most programs offer a set of different tools to the user. These tools are really different modes of behavior that the program enters. Offering tools is a compromise with complexity, but we can still do a lot to make tool manipulation easy and to prevent it from disturbing flow. Mainly, we must ensure that tool information is plentiful and easy to see and attempt to make transitions between tools quick and simple.

Tools should be close at hand, preferably on palettes or toolbars. This way, the user can see them easily and can select them with a single click. If the user must divert his attention from the application to search out a tool, his concentration will be broken. It's as if he had to get up from his desk and wander down the hall to find a pencil. He should never have to put tools away manually.

Modeless feedback

As we manipulate tools, it's usually desirable for the program to report on their status, and on the status of the data we are manipulating with the tool. This information needs to be clearly posted and easy to see without obscuring or stopping the action.

When the program has information or feedback for the user, it has several ways to present it. The most common method is to pop up a dialog box on the screen. This technique is modal: It puts the program into a mode that must be dealt with before it can return to its normal state, and before the user can continue with her task. A better way to inform the user is with **modeless feedback**.

Feedback is *modeless* whenever information for the user is built into the main interface and doesn't stop the normal flow of system activities and interaction. In Word, you can see what page you are on, what section you are in, how many pages are in the current document, what position the cursor is in, and what time it is modelessly just by looking at the status bar at the bottom of the screen.

If you want to know how many words are in your document, however, you have to call up the Word Count dialog from the Tools menu (see Figure 9-2). For people writing magazine articles, who need to be careful about word count, this information would be better delivered modelessly.

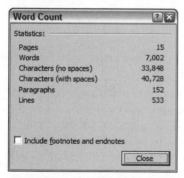

Figure 9-2: In Word, if you want to know the number of words in your document, you choose Word Count . . . from the Tools menu. This opens a dialog box. To get back to work, you must first click the Close button on the Word Count dialog. This behavior is the opposite of modeless feedback, and it hampers flow.

Jet fighters have a heads-up display, or HUD, that superimposes the readings of critical instrumentation onto the forward view of the cockpit's windscreen. The pilot doesn't even have to use peripheral vision, but can read vital gauges while keeping her eyes glued on the opposing fighter.

Our software should display information like a jet fighter's HUD. The program could use the edges of the display screen to show the user information about activity in the main work area of applications. Many drawing applications, such as Adobe Photoshop, already provide ruler guides, thumbnail maps, and other modeless feedback in the periphery of their windows. We will further discuss these types of rich modeless feedback in Chapter 34.

Orchestration

When a novelist writes well, the craft of the writer becomes invisible, and the reader sees the story and characters with clarity undisturbed by the technique of the writer. Likewise, when a program interacts well with a user, the interaction mechanics precipitate out, leaving the user face-to-face with his objectives, unaware of the intervening software. The poor writer is a visible writer, and a poor interaction designer looms with a clumsily visible presence in his software.

AXIOM

Well-orchestrated user interfaces are transparent.

To a novelist, there is no such thing as a "good" sentence. There are no rules for the way sentences should be constructed to be transparent. It all depends on what the protagonist is doing, or the effect the author wants to create. The writer knows not to insert an obscure word in a particularly quiet and sensitive passage, lest it sound like a sour note in a string quartet. The same goes for software. The interaction designer must train his ears to hear sour notes in the **orchestration** of software interaction. It is vital that all the elements in an interface work coherently together towards a single goal. When a program's communication with the user is well orchestrated, it becomes almost invisible.

Webster defines orchestration as "harmonious organization," a reasonable phrase for what we should expect from interacting with software. Harmonious organization doesn't yield to fixed rules. You can't create guidelines like, "Five buttons on a dialog box are good" and "Seven buttons on a dialog box are too many." Yet it is easy to see that a dialog box with 35 buttons is probably to be avoided. The major difficulty with such analysis is that it treats the problem *in vitro*. It doesn't take into account the problem being solved; it doesn't take into account what the user is doing at the time or what he is trying to accomplish.

Adding finesse: Less is more

For many things, more is better. In the world of interface design, the contrary is true, and we should constantly strive to reduce the number of elements in the interface without reducing the power of the system. In order to do this, we must do more with less; this is where careful orchestration becomes important. We must coordinate and control all the power of the product without letting the interface become a gaggle of windows and dialogs, covered with a scattering of unrelated and rarely used controls.

It's easy to create interfaces that are complex but not very powerful. They typically allow the user to perform a single task without providing access to related tasks. For example, most desktop software allows the user to name and save a data file, but they never let him delete, rename, or make a copy of that file at the same time. The dialog leaves that task to the operating system. It may not be trivial to add these functions, but isn't it better that the programmer perform the non-trivial activities than that the user to be forced to? Today, if the user wants to do something simple, like edit a copy of a file, he must go through a non-trivial sequence of actions: going to the desktop, selecting the file, requesting a copy from the menu, changing its name, and then opening the new file. Why not streamline this interaction?

It's not as difficult as it looks. Orchestration doesn't mean bulldozing your way through problems; it means finessing them wherever possible. Instead of adding the File Copy and Rename functions to the File Open dialog box of every application, why not just discard the File Open dialog box from every application and replace it with the shell program itself? When the user wants to open a file, the program calls the shell, which conveniently has all those collateral file manipulation functions built-in, and the user can double-click on the desired document. True, the application's File Open dialog does show the user a filtered view of files (usually limited to those formats recognized by the application), but why not add that functionality to the shell — filter by type in addition to sort by type?

Following this logic, we can also dispense with the Save As . . . dialog, which is really the logical inverse of the File Open dialog. If every time we invoked the Save As . . . function from our application, it wrote our file out to a temporary directory under some reasonable temporary name and then transferred control to the shell, we'd have all the shell tools at our disposal to move things around or rename them.

Yes, there would be a chunk of code that programmers would have to create to make it all seamless, but look at the upside. Countless dialog boxes could be completely discarded, and the user interfaces of thousands of programs would become more visually and functionally consistent, all with a single design stroke. That is finesse!

Distinguishing possibility from probability

There are many cases where interaction, usually in the form of a dialog box, slips into a user interface unnecessarily. A frequent source for such clinkers is when a program is faced with a choice. That's because programmers tend to resolve choices from the standpoint of logic, and it carries over to their software design. To a logician, if a proposition is true 999,999 times out of a million and false one time, the proposition is false — that's the way Boolean logic works. However, to the rest of us, the proposition is overwhelmingly true. The proposition has a *possibility* of being false, but the *probability* of it being false is minuscule to the point of irrelevancy. One of the most potent methods for better orchestrating your user interfaces is segregating the possible from the probable.

Programmers tend to view possibilities as being the same as probabilities. For example, a user has the choice of ending the program and saving his work, or ending the program and throwing away the document he has been working on for the last six hours. Mathematically, either of these choices is equally possible. Conversely, the probability of the user discarding his work is, at least, a thousand to one against; yet the typical program always includes a dialog box asking the user if he wants to save his changes, like the one shown in Figure 9-3.

The dialog box in Figure 9-3 is inappropriate and unnecessary. How often do you choose to abandon changes you make to a document? This dialog is tantamount to your spouse telling you not to spill soup on your shirt every time you eat. We'll discuss the implications of removing this dialog in Chapter 13.

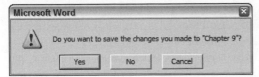

Figure 9-3: This is easily the most unnecessary dialog box in the world of GUI. Of course, we want to save our work! It is the normal course of events. *Not* saving it would be something out of the ordinary that should be handled by some dusty dialog box. This single dialog box does more to force users into knowing and understanding the useless and confusing facts about RAM and disk storage than anything else in their entire interaction with their computer. This dialog box should never be used.

Another example of confusing possibility and probability could be found in Microsoft Excel's (now obsolete) Version 4.0. When you selected one or more cells and press the Delete key to clear the field, a small dialog box popped up asking what you wanted to delete. This dialog box, shown in Figure 9-4, "conveniently" allowed the option of clearing the formats, formulas, or notes from the selected cells.

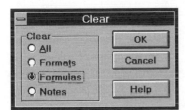

Figure 9-4: In Excel, Version 4.0, this dialog box popped up every time you pressed the delete key. This is quite reasonable if you are a computer, but if you are a human it means that you have to deal with the remote possibilities of deletion every time you try to do the high-probability clearing of the formula. Using Excel with this dialog was like listening to the symphony pause every time the conductor had to turn a page on the score. Thankfully, Microsoft fixed this in later versions.

This dialog drove users crazy with its unnecessary obtrusiveness. It is true that there are three types of deletion operations: format, formula, and notes. However, it is also true that, although people delete formulas with great frequency, they rarely delete formats or notes. Just because something is possible doesn't mean that it is probable. An advanced delete function, available from a drop-down or pop-up menu, solves the problem much more cleanly.

Programmers are judged by their ability to create software that handles the many possible, but improbable, conditions that crop up inside complex logical systems. This doesn't mean, however, that they should render that readiness to handle offbeat possibilities directly into the user interface.

The obtrusive presence of edge-case possibilities is a dead giveaway for user interfaces designed by programmers. Dialogs, controls, and options that are used a hundred times a day sit side-by-side with dialogs, controls, and options that are used once a year or never.

AXIOM

Design for the probable case; provide for the possible case.

You *might* get hit by a bus, but you probably *will* drive safely to work this morning. You don't stay home out of fear of the killer bus, so don't let what might possibly happen alter the way you treat what almost certainly will happen in your interface.

Providing comparisons

The way that a program represents information is another way that it can obtrude noisily into a user's consciousness. One area frequently abused is the representation of quantitative, or numeric, information. If an application needs to show the amount of free space on disk, it can do what the Microsoft Windows 3.x File Manager program did: give you the *exact* number of free bytes, as shown in Figure 9-5.

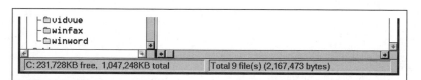

Figure 9-5: The Windows 3.x File Manager took great pains to report the exact number of bytes used by files on the disk. Does this precision help us understand whether we need to clear space on the disk? Certainly not. Furthermore, is a seven-digit number the best way to indicate the disk's status? Wouldn't a graphical representation that showed the space usage in a proportional manner (like a pie chart) be more meaningful? Luckily, Microsoft Windows now uses pie charts to indicate disk usage.

In the lower-left corner, the program tells us the number of free bytes and the total number of bytes on the disk. These numbers are hard to read and hard to interpret. With more than ten thousand million bytes of disk storage, it ceases to be important to us just how many hundreds are left, yet the display rigorously shows us down to the kilobyte. But even while the program is telling us the state of our disk with precision, it is failing to communicate. What we really need to know is whether or not the disk is getting full, or whether we can add a new 20 MB program and still have sufficient working room. These raw numbers, precise as they are, do little to help make sense of the facts.

Visual presentation expert Edward Tufte says that quantitative presentation should answer the question, "Compared to what?" Knowing that 231,728 KB are free on your hard disk is less useful than knowing that it is 22 percent of the disk's total capacity. Another Tufte dictum is, "Show the data," rather than simply telling about it textually or numerically. A pie chart showing the used and unused portions in different colors would make it much easier to comprehend the scale and proportion of hard disk use. It would show us what 231,728 KB really means. The numbers shouldn't go away, but they should be relegated to the status of labels on the display and not be the display itself. They should also be shown with more reasonable and consistent precision. The meaning of the information could be shown visually, and the numbers would merely add support.

In Windows XP, Microsoft's right hand giveth while its left hand taketh away. The File Manager (shown in Figure 9-5) is long dead, replaced by the Explorer dialog box shown in Figure 9-6. This replacement is the properties dialog associated with a hard disk. The Used Space is shown in blue and the Free Space is shown in magenta, making the pie chart an easy read. Now you can see at a glance the glad news that GranFromage is mostly empty.

Unfortunately, that pie chart isn't built into the Explorer's interface. Instead, you have to seek it out with a menu item. To see how full a disk is, you must bring up a modal dialog box that, although it gives you the information, takes you away from the place where you need to know it. The Explorer is where you can see, copy, move, and delete files; but it's not where you can easily see if things need to be deleted. That pie chart should have been built into the face of the Explorer. In Windows 2000, it *is* shown on the left-hand side when you select a disk in an Explorer window. In XP, however, Microsoft took a step backwards, and the graphic has once again been relegated to a dialog. It really should be visible at all times in the Explorer, along with the numerical data, unless the user chooses to hide it.

Using graphical input

Software frequently fails to present numerical information in a graphical way. Even rarer is the capability of software to enable graphical input. A lot of software lets users enter numbers; then, on command, it converts those numbers into a graph. Few products let the user enter a graph and, on command, convert that graph into a vector of numbers. By contrast, most modern word processors let you set tabs and indentations by dragging a marker on a ruler. The user can say, in effect, "Here is where I want the paragraph to start," and let the program calculate that it is precisely 1.347 inches in from the left margin instead of forcing the user to enter 1.347.

"Intelligent" drawing programs like Microsoft Visio are getting better at this. Each polygon that the user manipulates on screen is represented behind the scenes by a small spreadsheet, with a row for each point and a column each for the X and Y coordinates. Dragging a polygon's vertex on screen causes the values in the corresponding point in the spreadsheet, represented by the X and Y values, to change. The user can access the shape either graphically or through its spreadsheet representation.

This principle applies in a variety of situations. When items in a list need to be reordered, the user may want them ordered alphabetically, but he may also want them in order of personal preference; something no algorithm can offer. The user should be able to drag the items into the desired order directly, without an algorithm interfering with this fundamental operation.

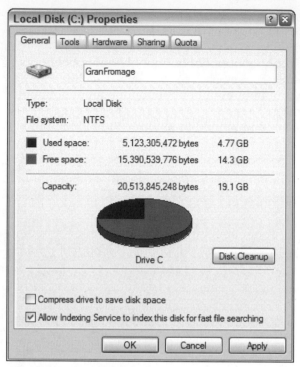

Figure 9-6: In Windows XP, Microsoft has replaced the electric chair with lethal injection. Instead of long, inscrutable numbers at the bottom of the File Manager, you can request a propertiesdialog box from the Explorer. The good news is that you can finally see how your disk is doing in a meaningful, graphic way with the pie chart. The bad news is that you have to stop what you're doing and open a dialog box to see fundamental information that should be readily available. In Windows 2000, this graph was automatically displayed on the left side of the Explorer window when a disk was selected; XP's solution represents a step backward.

Reflecting program status

When someone is asleep, he usually looks asleep. When someone is awake, he looks awake. When someone is busy, he looks busy: His eyes are focused on his work and his body language is closed and preoccupied. When someone is unoccupied, he looks unoccupied: His body is open and moving, his eyes are questing and willing to make contact. People not only expect this kind of subtle feedback from each other, they depend on it for maintaining social order.

Our programs should work the same way. When a program is asleep, it should look asleep. When a program is awake, it should look awake; and when it's busy, it should look busy. When the computer is engaged in some significant internal action like formatting a diskette, we should see some significant external action, such as the icon of the diskette slowly changing from grayed to active state. When the computer is sending a fax, we should see a small representation of the fax being scanned and sent (or at least a modeless progress bar). If the program is waiting for a response from a remote database, it should visually change to reflect its somnolent state. Program state is best communicated using forms of rich modeless feedback, briefly discussed earlier in this chapter. More detailed examples of rich modeless feedback may be found in Chapter 34.

Avoiding unnecessary reporting

For programmers, it is important to know exactly what is happening process-wise in a program. This goes along with being able to control all the details of the process. For users, it is disconcerting to know all the details of what is happening. Non-technical people may be alarmed to hear that the database has been modified, for example. It is better for the program to just do what has to be done, issue reassuring clues when all is well, and not burden the user with the trivia of *how* it was accomplished.

Many programs are quick to keep users apprised of the details of their progress even though the user has no idea what to make of this information. Programs pop up dialog boxes telling us that connections have been made, that records have been posted, that users have logged on, that transactions were recorded, that data have been transferred, and other useless factoids. To software engineers, these messages are equivalent to the humming of the machinery, the babbling of the brook, the white noise of the waves crashing on the beach: They tell us that all is well. They were, in fact, probably used while debugging the software. To the user, however, these reports can be like eerie lights beyond the horizon, like screams in the night, like unattended objects flying about the room.

As discussed before, the program should make clear that it is working hard, but the detailed feedback can be offered in a more subtle way. In particular, reporting information like this with a modal dialog box brings the interaction to a stop for no particular benefit.

It is important that we not stop the proceedings to report normalcy. When some event has transpired that was supposed to have transpired, never report this fact with a dialog box. Save dialogs for events that are outside of the normal course of events.

DESIGN TIP

Don't use dialogs to report normalcy.

By the same token, don't stop the proceedings and bother the user with problems that are not serious. If the program is having trouble getting through a busy signal, don't put up a dialog box to report it. Instead, build a status indicator into the program so the problem is clear to the interested user but is not obtrusive to the user who is busy elsewhere.

The key to orchestrating the user interaction is to take a goal-directed approach. You must ask yourself whether a particular interaction moves the user rapidly and directly to his goal. Contemporary programs are often reluctant to take any forward motion without the user directing it in advance. But users would rather see the program take some "good enough" first step and then adjust it to what is desired. This way, the program has moved the user closer to his goal.

Avoiding blank slates

It's easy to assume nothing about what your users want and rather ask a bunch of questions of the user up front to help determine what they want. How many programs have you seen that start with a big dialog asking a bunch of questions? But users — not power users, but *normal* people — are very uncomfortable with explaining to a program what they want. They would much rather see what the program *thinks* is right and then manipulate that to make it exactly right. In most cases, your program can make a fairly correct assumption based on past experience. For example, when you create a new document in Microsoft Word, the program creates a blank document with preset margins and other attributes rather than opening a dialog that asks you to specify every detail. PowerPoint does a less adequate job, asking you to choose the base style for a new presentation each time you create one. Both programs could do better by remembering frequently and recently used styles or templates, and making those the defaults for new documents.

Just because we use the word *think* in conjunction with a program doesn't mean that the software needs to be intelligent (in the human sense) and try to determine the right thing to do by reasoning. Instead, it should simply do something that has a statistically good chance of being correct, then provide the user with powerful tools for shaping that first attempt, instead of merely giving the user a blank slate and challenging him to have at it. This way the program isn't asking for permission to act, but rather asking for forgiveness after the fact.

Ask forgiveness, not permission.

For most people, a completely blank slate is a difficult starting point. It's so much easier to begin where someone has already left off. A user can easily fine-tune an approximation provided by the program into precisely what he desires with less risk of exposure and mental effort than he would have from drafting it from nothing. As we will discuss in Chapter 15, endowing your program with a good memory is the best way to accomplish this.

Command invocation versus configuration

Another problem crops up quite frequently, whenever functions with many parameters are invoked by users. The problem comes from the lack of differentiation between a function and the *configuration* of that function. If you ask a program to perform a function itself, the program should simply perform that function and not interrogate you about your precise configuration details. To express precise demands to the program, you would request the configuration dialog.

For example, when you ask many programs to print a document, they respond by launching a complex dialog box demanding that you specify how many copies to print, what the paper orientation is, what paper feeder to use, what margins to set, whether the output should be in monochrome or color, what scale to print it at, whether to use Postscript fonts or native fonts, whether to print the current page, the current selection, or the entire document, and whether to print to a file and if so, how to name that file. All those options are useful, but all we wanted was to print the document, and that is all we thought we asked for.

A much more reasonable design would be to have a command to print and another command for print setup. The print command would not issue any dialog, but would just go ahead and print, either using previous settings or standard, vanilla settings. The print setup function would offer up all those choices about paper and copies and fonts. It would also be very reasonable to be able to go directly from the configure dialog to printing.

The print control on the Word toolbar offers immediate printing without a dialog box. This is perfect for many users, but for those with multiple printers or printers on a network, it may offer too little information. The user may want to see which printer is selected before he either clicks the control or summons the dialog to change it first. This is a good candidate for some simple modeless output placed on a toolbar or status bar (it is currently provided in the ToolTip for the control, which is good, but the feedback could be better still). Word's print setup dialog is called Print . . . and is available from the File menu. Its name could be more clear, although the ellipsis does, according to GUI standards, give some inkling that it will launch a dialog.

There is a big difference between configuring and invoking a function. The former may include the latter, but the latter shouldn't include the former. In general, any user invokes a command ten times for every one time he configures it. It is better to make the user ask explicitly for configuration one time in ten than it is to make the user reject the configuration interface *nine* times in ten.

Microsoft's printing solution is a reasonable rule of thumb. Put immediate access to functions on buttons in the toolbar and put access to function-configuration dialog boxes on menu items. The configuration dialogs are better pedagogic tools, whereas the buttons provide immediate action.

Asking questions versus providing choices

Asking questions is quite different from providing choices. The difference between them is the same as that between browsing in a store and conducting a job interview. The individual asking the questions is understood to be in a position superior to the individual being asked. Those with authority ask questions; subordinates respond. Asking users questions makes them feel inferior.

AXIOM

Asking questions isn't the same as providing choices.

Dialog boxes (confirmation dialogs in particular) ask questions. Toolbars offer choices. The confirmation dialog stops the proceedings, demands an answer, and it won't leave until it gets what it wants. Toolbars, on the other hand, are always there, quietly and politely offering up their wares like a well-appointed store, offering you the luxury of selecting what you would like with just a flick of your finger.

Contrary to what many software developers think, questions and choices don't necessarily make the user feel empowered. More commonly, it makes the user feel badgered and harassed. *Would you like soup or salad?* Salad. *Would you like cabbage or spinach?* Spinach. *Would you like French, Thousand Island, or Italian?* French. *Would you like lo-cal or regular?* Stop! Just bring me the soup! *Would you like chowder or chicken noodle?*

Users don't like to be asked questions. It cues the user that the program is:

✓ Ignorant

✓ Forgetful

✓ Weak

✓ Lacking initiative

✓ Unable to fend for itself

✓ Fretful

✓ Overly demanding

These are qualities that we typically dislike in people. Why should we desire them in software? The program is not asking us our opinion out of intellectual curiosity or desire to make conversation, the way a friend might over dinner. Rather, it is behaving ignorantly or presenting itself with false authority. The program isn't interested in our opinions; it requires information — often information it didn't really need to ask us in the first place (for more discussion on how to avoid questions, see Chapters 15 and 34).

Worse than single questions are questions that are asked repeatedly and unnecessarily. Do you want to save that file? Do you want to save that file *now*? Do you *really* want to save that file? Software that asks fewer questions appears smarter to the user, and more polite, because if users fail to know the answer to a question, *they* then feel stupid.

In *The Media Equation* (Cambridge University Press, 1996), Stanford sociologists Clifford Nass and Byron Reeves make a compelling case that humans treat and respond to computers and other interactive products *as if they were people*. We should thus pay real attention to the "personality" projected by our software. Is it quietly competent and helpful, or does it whine, nag, badger, and make excuses? We'll discuss more about how to make software more polite and considerate in Chapter 14.

Choices are important, but there is a difference between being free to make choices based on presented information and being interrogated by the program in modal fashion. Users would much rather direct their software the way they direct their automobiles down the street. An automobile offers the user sophisticated choices without once issuing a dialog box. Imagine the situation in Figure 9-7.

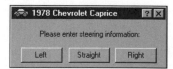

Figure 9-7: Imagine if you had to steer your car by clicking buttons on a dialog box! This will give you some idea of how normal people feel about the dialog boxes on *your* software. Humbling, isn't it?

Directly manipulating a steering wheel is not only a more appropriate idiom for communicating with your car, but it puts you in the superior position, directing your car where it should go. No user likes to be questioned like a suspect in a lineup, yet that is exactly what our software often demands of us.

Hiding ejector seat levers

In the cockpit of every jet fighter is a brightly painted lever that, when pulled, fires a small rocket engine underneath the pilot's seat, blowing the pilot, still in his seat, out of the aircraft to parachute safely to earth. Ejector seat levers can only be used once, and their consequences are significant and irreversible.

Just like a jet fighter needs an ejector seat lever, complex desktop applications need configuration facilities. The vagaries of business and the demands placed on the software force it to adapt to specific situations, and it had better be able to do so. Companies that pay millions of dollars for custom software or site licenses for thousands of copies of shrink-wrapped products will not take kindly to a program's inability to adapt to the way things are done in that particular company. The program must adapt, but such adaptation can be considered a one-time procedure, or something done only by the corporate IT staff on rare occasion. In other words, ejector seat levers may need to be used, but they won't be used very often.

AXIOM

Hide the ejector seat levers.

Programs must have ejector seat levers so that users can — occasionally — move *persistent objects* (see Chapter 11) in the interface, or dramatically (sometimes irreversibly) alter the function or behavior of the application. The one thing that must never happen is accidental deployment of the ejector seat (see Figure 9-8). The interface design must assure that the user can never inadvertently fire the ejector seat when all he wants to do is make some minor adjustment to the program.

Ejector seat levers come in two basic varieties: those that cause a significant visual dislocation (large changes in the layout of tools and work areas) in the program, and those that perform some irreversible action. Both of these functions should be hidden from inexperienced users. Of the two, the latter variety is by far the more dangerous. In the former, the user may be surprised and dismayed at what happens next, but she can at least back out of it with some work. In the latter case, she and her colleagues are likely to be stuck with the consequences.

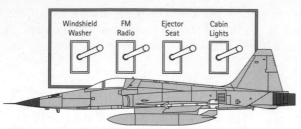

Figure 9-8: Ejector seat levers have catastrophic results. One minute, the pilot is safely ensconced in her jet, and the next she is tumbling end-over-end in the wild blue yonder while her jet goes on without her. The ejector seat is necessary for the pilot's safety, but a lot of design work has gone into ensuring that it never gets fired inadvertently. Allowing an unsuspecting user to configure a program by changing permanent objects is comparable to firing the ejection seat by accident. Hide those ejector seat levers!

By keeping in mind principles of flow and orchestration, your software can keep users engaged at maximum productivity for extended periods of time. Productive users are happy users, and customers with productive, happy users are the goal of any digital product manufacturer. In the next chapter, we further discuss ways to enhance user productivity by eliminating unnecessary barriers to use that arise as a result of implementation-model thinking.

Chapter 10

Eliminating Excise

Software too often contains interactions that are top-heavy with extra work for the user. Programmers typically focus so intently on the enabling technology that they don't carefully consider the human actions required to operate the technology from a goal-directed point-of-view. The result is software that charges its users a tax, or **excise**, of cognitive and sometimes even physical effort every time it is used.

This chapter focuses on the nature of this excise, and discusses the means by which it can be reduced and even eliminated altogether.

What Is Excise?

When we decide to drive to the office, we must open the garage door, get in, start the motor, back out, and close the garage door before we even begin the forward motion that will take us to our destination. All these actions are in support of the automobile rather than in support of getting to the destination. If we had Star Trek transporters instead, we'd dial up our destination coordinates and appear there instantaneously—no garages, no motors, no traffic lights. Our point is not to complain about the intricacies of driving, but rather to distinguish between two types of actions we take to accomplish our daily tasks.

Any large task, such as driving to the office, involves many smaller tasks. Some of these tasks work directly toward achieving the goal; these are tasks like steering down the road toward your office. **Excise tasks**, on the other hand, don't contribute directly to reaching the goal, but are necessary to accomplishing it just the same. Such tasks include opening and closing the garage door, starting the engine, and stopping at traffic lights, in addition to putting oil and gas in the car and performing periodic maintenance.

Excise is the extra work that satisfies either the needs of our tools or those of outside agents as we try to achieve our objectives. The distinction is sometimes hard to see because we get so used to the excise being part of our tasks. Most of us drive so frequently that differentiating the act of opening the garage door from the act of driving towards the destination is difficult. Manipulating the garage door is something we do for the car, not for us, and it doesn't move us towards our destination the way the accelerator pedal and steering wheel do. Stopping at red lights is something imposed on us by our society that, again, doesn't help us achieve our true goal. (In this case, it does help us achieve a related goal of arriving *safely* at our office.)

Software, too, has a pretty clear dividing line between goal-directed tasks and excise tasks. Like automobiles, some software excise tasks are trivial, and performing them is no great hardship. On the other hand, some software excise tasks are as obnoxious as fixing a flat tire. Installation leaps to mind here, as do such excise tasks as configuring networks, making backups, and connecting to online services.

The problem with excise tasks is that the effort we expend in doing them doesn't go directly towards accomplishing our goals. Where we can eliminate the need for excise tasks, we make the user more effective and productive and improve the usability of the software. As a software designer, you should become sensitive to the presence of excise and take steps to eradicate it with the same enthusiasm a doctor would apply to curing an infection.

Eliminating excise makes the user more effective.

There are many such instances of petty excise, particularly in GUIs. Virtually all window management falls into this category. Dragging, reshaping, resizing, reordering, tiling and cascading windows qualify as excise actions.

GUI Excise

One of the main criticisms leveled at graphical user interfaces by experienced computer users — notably those trained on command-line systems — is that getting to where you want to go is made slower and more difficult by the extra effort that goes into manipulating windows and icons. Users complain that, with a command line, they can just type in the desired command and the computer executes it immediately. With windowing systems, they must open various folders looking for the desired file or program before they can launch it. Then, after it appears on the screen, they must stretch and drag the window until it is in the desired location and configuration.

These complaints are well founded. Extra window manipulation tasks like these are, indeed, excise. They don't move the user towards his goal; they are overhead that the programs demand before they deign to assist the user. But everybody knows that GUIs are easier to use than command-line systems. Who is right?

The confusion arises because the real issues are hidden. The command-line interface forces an even more expensive excise budget on the user: He must first memorize the commands. Also, he cannot easily configure his screen to his own personal requirements. The excise of the command-line interface becomes smaller only after the user has invested significant time and effort in learning it.

On the other hand, for the casual or first-time user, the visual explicitness of the GUI helps him navigate and learn what tasks are appropriate and when. The step-by-step nature of the GUI is a great help to users who aren't yet familiar with the task or the system. It also benefits those users who have more than one task to perform and who must use more than one program at a time.

Excise and expert users

Any user willing to learn a command-line interface automatically qualifies as a power user. And any power user of a command-line interface will quickly become a power user of any other type of interface, GUI included. These users will easily learn each nuance of the programs they use. They will start up each program with a clear idea of exactly what it is they want to do and how they want to do it. To this user, the assistance offered to the casual or first-time user is just in the way.

We must be careful when we eliminate excise. We must not remove it just to suit power users. Similarly, however, we must not force power users to pay the full price of our providing help to new or infrequent users.

Training wheels

One of the areas where software designers can inadvertently introduce significant amounts of excise is in support for first-time or casual users. It is easy to justify adding facilities to a program that will make it easy for newer users to learn how to use the program. Unfortunately, these facilities quickly become excise as the users become familiar with the program — perpetual intermediates, as discussed in Chapter 3. Facilities added to software for the purpose of training beginners must be easily turned off. Training wheels are rarely needed for extended periods of time, and training wheels, although they are a boon to beginners, are a hindrance to advanced learning and use when they are left on permanently.

AXIOM

Don't weld on training wheels.

"Pure" excise

There are a number of actions that are excise of such purity that nobody needs them, from power users to first-timers. These include most hardware-management tasks that the computer could handle itself, like telling a program which COM port to use. Any demands for such information should be struck from user interfaces and replaced with more intelligent program behavior behind the scenes.

Visual excise

Designers sometimes paint themselves into excise corners by relying too heavily on visual metaphors. Visual metaphors like desktops with telephones, copy machines, staplers, and fax machines — or file cabinets with folders in drawers — are cases in point. These visual metaphors may make it easy to understand the relationships between program elements and behaviors; but after these fundamentals are learned, the management of the metaphor becomes pure excise (for more discussion on the limitations of visual metaphors, see Chapter 19). In addition, the screen space consumed by the images becomes increasingly egregious, particularly in sovereign posture applications. The more we stare at the program from day to day, the more we resent the number of pixels it takes to tell us what we already know. The little telephone that so charmingly told us how to dial on that first day long ago is now a barrier to quick communications.

Transient posture applications can tolerate more training and explanation excise than sovereign applications. Transient posture programs aren't used frequently, so their users need more assistance in understanding what the program does and remembering how to control it. For sovereign posture applications, however, the slightest excise becomes agonizing over time.

The second type of visual excise was not a significant issue before the advent of the Web: overemphasis of visual design elements to the extent that they interfere with user goals and comprehension. The late 90s attracted a large number of graphic and new media designers to the Web, people who viewed this medium as a predominantly visual one, the experience of which was defined by rich, often animated, visuals. Although this might have been (and perhaps still is) appropriate for **brochure-ware** Web sites that serve primarily as marketing collateral, it is highly inappropriate for transactional Web sites and Web applications. As we will discuss more in Chapter 37, these latter types of sites, into which the majority of e-commerce falls, have far more in common, from a behavioral standpoint, with sovereign desktop applications than with multimedia kiosk-ware or brochure-ware.

The result was that many visually arresting, visually innovative sites were spawned that ignored the two most critical elements: an understanding of user goals and a streamlined behavior that helped users achieve them. A pre-eminent example of this was Boo.com, one of the first major implosions of the dot.com bust. This fashion e-tailor made use of hip visuals and flash-based interactive agents, but didn't seem to spend much effort addressing user goals. The site was sluggish due to flash, visually distracting, confusingly laid out, and difficult to navigate due to multiple windows and confusing links. Boo attempted to be high-concept, but its users' goals were simply to buy products more quickly, cheaply, and easily on-line than they could elsewhere. By the time some of these problems were remedied, Boo's customers had abandoned them. One can only wonder how much difference a goal-directed design might have made to Boo and many other e-commerce failures of that time.

Unfortunately, some of these visual excesses are slowly creeping into desktop applications, as programmers and designers borrow flashy but inappropriate idioms from the Web. We will discuss appropriate design of visual interfaces more in Chapter 19.

Determining what is excise

Sometimes we find certain tasks like window management, which, although they are mainly for the program, are useful for occasional users or users with special preferences. In this case, the function itself can only be considered excise if it is forced on the user rather than made available at his discretion.

The only way to determine whether a function or behavior is excise is by comparing it to the user's goals. If the user needs to see two programs at a time on the screen in order to compare or transfer information, the ability to configure the main windows of the programs so that they share the screen space is not excise. If the user doesn't have this specific goal, a requirement that the user must configure the main window of either program is excise.

Stopping the Proceedings

There is a particular form of excise that is so prevalent that it deserves special attention. In Chapter 9, we introduced the concept of **flow**, where the user enters a highly productive mental state by working in harmony with his tools. Flow is a natural state, and people will enter it without much prodding. It takes some effort to break into flow after someone has achieved it. Interruptions like a ringing telephone will do it, as will an error message box. Some interruptions are unavoidable, but most others are easily dispensable. But interrupting a user's flow for no good reason is *stopping the proceedings with idiocy* and is one of the most disruptive forms of excise.

AXIOM

Don't stop the proceedings with idiocy.

Poorly designed software will make assertions that no self-respecting individual would ever make. It states unequivocally, for example, that a file doesn't exist merely because it is too stupid to look for it in the right place, and then it implicitly blame *you* for losing it! A program cheerfully executes an impossible query that hangs up your system until you decide to reboot. Users view such software behavior as idiocy, and with just cause.

Errors, notifiers, and confirmation messages

There are probably no more prevalent excise elements than error message and confirmation message dialogs. These are so ubiquitous that eradicating them takes a lot of work. In Part VII, we discuss these issues at length, but for now, suffice it to say that they are high in excise and should be eliminated from your applications whenever possible.

The typical error message box is unnecessary. It either tells the user something that he doesn't care about or demands that he fix some situation that the program can and should usually fix just as well. Figure 10-1 shows an error message box displayed by Adobe Illustrator 6 while the user is trying to save a document. We're not exactly sure what it's trying to tell us, but it sounds dire.

The message stops an already annoying and time-consuming procedure, making it take even longer. The user cannot reliably fetch a cup of coffee after telling the program to save his artwork, because he might return only to see the function incomplete and the program mindlessly holding up the process. We'll discuss how to eliminate these sorts of error messages in Chapter 33.

Another frustrating example, this time from Microsoft Outlook, is shown in Figure 10-2. This dialog is asking us to make an irreversible and potentially costly decision based on no information whatsoever! If the dialog occurs just after you changed some rules, doesn't it stand to reason that you want to keep them? And if you don't, wouldn't you like a bit more information, like exactly what rules are in conflict and which of them are the more recently created? We also don't have a clear idea what happens when we press Cancel . . . . Are we canceling the dialog and leaving the rules mismatched? Are we discarding recent changes that led to the mismatch? The kind of fear and uncertainty that this poorly designed interaction arouses in users is completely unnecessary. We discuss how to improve this kind of situation in Chapter 34.

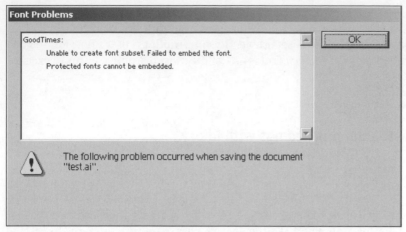

Figure 10-1: This is an ugly, useless error message box that stops the proceedings with idiocy. We can't verify or identify what it tells us, and it gives us no options for responding other than to admit our own culpability with the OK button. This message only comes up when the program is saving; that is, when we have entrusted it to do something simple and straightforward for us. The program can't even save a file without help, and it won't even tell us what help it needs.

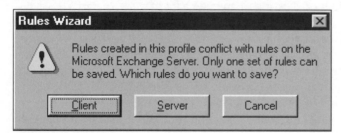

Figure 10-2: Here is a horrible confirmation box that stops the proceedings with idiocy. If the program is smart enough to detect the difference, why can't it correct the problem itself? The options the dialog gives us are scary. It is telling us that we can explode one of two boxes: one contains garbage, and the other contains the family dog — but the program won't say which is which. And if we click Cancel, what does that mean? Will it still go ahead and explode our dog?

Making the user ask permission

Back in the days of command lines and character-based menus, interfaces often offered services to the user indirectly. If you wanted to change an item, such as your address, you had to first ask the program permission to change it. The program would then display a screen where your address could be changed. Asking permission is pure excise. If you want to change a displayed value, you should be able to change it right there. You shouldn't have to ask permission or go to a different room.

Never make the user ask permission.

Many file selection dialogs do this. They show you the proposed directory, but if you don't like the choice shown, you can't just change it in place. You instead click a button that says Browse, and then get another dialog box in which to change it. This is unnecessary. The dialog could easily track those changes, verify their validity, and assure that things get installed correctly without forcing the user to ask permission.

Allow input wherever you have output.

As in the last example, many programs have one place where the values (such as filenames, numeric values, and selected options) are displayed for output and another place where input to them is accepted from the user. This follows the implementation model, which treats input and output as different processes. The user's mental model, however, doesn't recognize a difference. He thinks, "There is the number. I'll just click on it and enter a new value." If the program can't accommodate this impulse, it is needlessly inserting excise into the interface. If options are modifiable by the user, he should be able to do so right where the program displays them.

The opposite of asking permission can be useful in certain circumstances. Rather than asking the program to launch a dialog, the user tells a dialog to go away and not come back again. In this way, a user can make an unhelpful dialog box stop badgering him, even though the program mistakenly thinks it is helping. Microsoft now makes heavy use of this idiom. (If a beginner inadvertently dismisses a dialog box and can't figure out how to get it back, he may benefit from another easy-to-identify safety-net idiom in a prominent place: a Help menu item saying, "Bring back all dismissed dialogs," for example.)

Protecting us from ourselves

Another place where the proceedings are regularly stopped with idiocy is in password protection systems. Security is an important issue in a professional environment, but it doesn't mean much to Grandma and the PC she uses for Web surfing. Passwords aren't appropriate for everyone or in all contexts, and there should be ways to turn them off when they simply get in the way.

Unresponsiveness

A program can become slow or unresponsive when it talks to remote devices like servers, printers, networks, and modems, or when it performs a large amount of local processing on large data structures. Every program that executes potentially time-consuming tasks must make sure that it occasionally checks to see if the user is still out there, banging away on the keyboard or madly clicking on the mouse, whimpering "No, no, I didn't mean to reorganize the *entire* database. That will take 4.3 million years!"

Common Excise Traps

You should be vigilant in finding and rooting out each small item of excise in your interface. These myriad little extra unnecessary steps can add up to a lot of extra work for users. This list should help you spot excise transgressions:

✓ Don't force the user to go to another window to perform a function that affects this window.

✓ Don't force the user to remember where he put things in the hierarchical file system.

✓ Don't force the user to resize windows unnecessarily. When a child window pops up on the screen, the program should size it appropriately for its contents. Don't make it big and empty or so small that it requires constant scrolling.

✓ Don't force the user to move windows. If there is open space on the desktop, put the program there instead of directly over some other already-open program.

✓ Don't force the user to reenter her personal settings. If she has ever set a font, a color, an indentation, or a sound, make sure that she doesn't have to do it again unless she wants a change.

✓ Don't force the user to fill fields to satisfy some arbitrary measure of completeness. If the user wants to omit some details from the transaction entry screen, don't force him to enter them. Assume that he has a good reason for not entering them. The completeness of the database (in most instances) isn't worth badgering the user over.

✓ Don't force the user to ask permission. This is frequently a symptom of not allowing input in the same place as output.

✓ Don't ask the user to confirm his actions (this implies a robust undo facility).

✓ Don't let the user's actions result in an error.

The existence of excise in user interfaces is, along with navigational issues, the primary cause for user dissatisfaction with software-enabled products. It behooves every designer and product manager to be on the lookout for GUI excise in all its forms and to take the time and energy to see that it is *excised* from their products.

Chapter 11

Navigation and Inflection

Desktop applications, Web sites, and devices all have one particular attribute in common that, if improperly designed, becomes a critical obstacle to usability: navigation. The user must be able to **navigate** efficiently through the features and facilities of a program, Web site, or device. He must also be able to stay oriented in the program as he moves from screen to screen.

A user can navigate if he always understands what he has to do next, knows what state the program, site, or device is in, and knows how to find the tools he needs. This chapter discusses the issues surrounding navigation, and how to better help users navigate through interactive products.

Navigation Is Excise

As hinted at in Chapter 10, the most important thing to realize about navigation is that, in almost all cases, it represents pure excise, or something close to it. Except in games where the *goal* is to navigate successfully through a maze of obstacles, navigating through software does not meet user goals, needs, or desires. Unnecessary or difficult navigation thus becomes a major frustration to users. In fact, it is the authors' opinion that poorly designed navigation presents the *number-one problem* in the design of any software application or system — desktop, Web-based, or otherwise. It is also the place where the programmer's implementation model is made most apparent to the user. The authors have yet to see an application or Web site that could not benefit from additional attention paid to its navigational structures.

Types of Navigation

Navigation through software occurs at multiple levels. The following list enumerates the most common types of navigation:

- ✓ Navigation between multiple windows or screens
- ✓ Navigation between panes within a window (or frames in a page)
- ✓ Navigation between tools or menus in a pane
- ✓ Navigation within information displayed in a pane or frame (for example: scrolling, panning, zooming, following links)

Some readers may question the inclusion of some of the bullets above as types of navigation. The authors are purposely using a broad definition of navigation: any action that takes the user to a new part of the interface *or which requires him to otherwise locate objects, tools, or data*. The reason for this is simple: When we start thinking about these actions as navigation, it becomes clear that they are excise and should, therefore, be minimized or eliminated. We'll now discuss each of these types of navigation in more detail.

Navigation between multiple windows or pages

Navigation between multiple windows is perhaps the most disorienting kind of navigation for users. Navigating between windows involves a gross shifting of attention that disrupts the user's flow and forces him into a new context. The act of navigating to another window also often means that the contents of the original window are partly or completely obscured. At the very least, it means that the user needs to worry about window management, an excise task that further disrupts his flow. If users must constantly shuttle back and forth between windows to achieve their goals, their productivity will drop, and their disorientation and frustration levels will rise. If the number of windows is large enough, the user will become sufficiently disoriented that he may experience **navigational trauma**: He gets lost in the interface. Sovereign posture applications avoid this problem by placing all main interactions in a single primary window, which may contain multiple independent panes.

Navigation between panes

Windows can contain multiple panes, either adjacent to each other and separated by splitters (see Chapters 25 and 26), or stacked on top of each other and denoted by tabs. Adjacent panes can solve many navigation problems by placing useful supporting functions, links, or data directly adjacent to the primary work or display area, thus reducing navigation to almost nil. If objects can be dragged between panes, those panes should be adjacent to each other.

Problems arise when adjacent supporting panes become too numerous, or when they are not placed on the screen in a way that matches the user's workflow. Too many adjacent panes result in visual clutter and confusion: The user does not know where to go to find what he needs. Also, crowding forces the introduction of scrolling, which is another navigational hit. Navigation within the single screen thus becomes a problem. Some Web portals, trying to be everything to everyone, have such navigational problems; we'll discuss them more in Chapter 37.

In some cases, depending on user workflows, tabbed panes can be appropriate. Tabbed panes bring with them a level of navigational excise and potential for disorientation because they obscure what was on the screen before the user navigated to them. However, this idiom is appropriate for the main work area when multiple documents or independent views of a document are required (such as in Microsoft Excel; see Figure 11-1).

Some programmers interpret tabs as permission to break complex facilities into smaller chunks and place one per pane. They reason that using these facilities will somehow become easier if the functionality is simply cut into pieces. Actually, by putting parts of a single facility onto separate panes, the excise increases, whereas the user's understanding and orientation decrease. What's more, doing this violates the axiom: *A dialog box (or pop-up window) is another room; have a good reason to go there* (Chapter 25). Most users of most programs simply don't require that their software tools have dozens of controls for normal use.

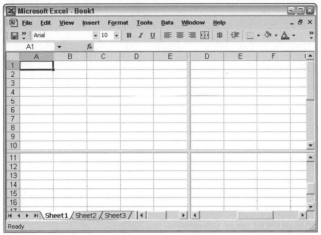

Figure 11-1: Microsoft Excel makes use of tabbed panes (visible in the lower left) to let the user navigate between related worksheets. Excel also makes use of splitters to provide adjacent panes for viewing multiple, distant parts of a single spreadsheet without constant scrolling. Both these idioms help reduce navigational excise for Excel users.

Tabbed panes can be appropriate when there are multiple supporting panes for a work area that are not used at the same time. The support panes can then be stacked, and the user can choose the pane suitable for his current tasks, which is only a single click away. Microsoft Internet Explorer for the Macintosh uses a variant of these stacked panes. If no pane is selected (users can deselect by clicking on the active tab), the program shuts the adjacent pane like a drawer, leaving only the tabs visible (see Figure 11-2). This variant is useful if space is at a premium.

Navigation between tools and menus

Another important and overlooked form of navigation results from the user's need to make use of different tools, palettes, and functions. Spatial organization of these within a pane or window is critical to minimizing extraneous mouse movements that, at best, could result in user annoyance and fatigue, and at worst, result in repetitive stress injury. Tools that are used frequently and in conjunction with each other should be grouped together spatially and also be immediately available. Menus require more navigational effort on the part of the user because their contents are not visible prior to clicking. Frequently used functions should be provided in toolbars, palettes, or the equivalent. Menu use should be reserved only for infrequently accessed commands (we'll discuss organizing controls again later in this chapter and discuss toolbars in depth in Chapter 29).

Adobe Photoshop 6.0 exhibits some annoying behaviors in the way it forces users to navigate between palette controls. For example, the Paint Bucket tool and the Gradient tool each occupy the same location on the tool palette; you must select between them by clicking and holding on the visible control, which opens a menu that lets you select between them (shown in Figure 11-3). However, both are fill tools, and both are frequently used. It would have been better to place each of them on the palette next to each other to avoid that frequent, flow-disrupting tool navigation.

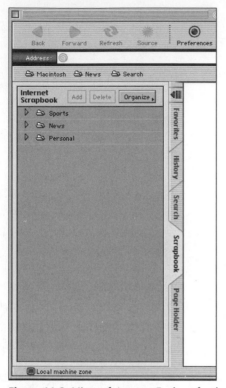

Figure 11-2: Microsoft Internet Explorer for the Mac uses tabbed panes accessible with a vertical tab bar. The PC version has a similar idiom, but uses more standard toolbar controls to select which pane is visible. The Mac version more closely ties the function to the control, but requires users to tilt their heads to read the tab labels.

Navigation of information

Navigation of information, or of the content of panes or windows, can be accomplished by several methods: scrolling (panning), linking (jumping), and zooming. The first two methods are common: scrolling is ubiquitous in most software and linking is ubiquitous on the Web (though increasingly, linking idioms are being adopted in non-Web applications). Zooming is primarily used for visualization of 3D and detailed 2D data.

Scrolling is often a necessity, but the need for it should be minimized when possible. Often there is a tradeoff between paging and scrolling information: You should understand your users' mental models and workflows to determine what is best for them.

In 2D visualization and drawing applications, vertical and horizontal scrolling is common. These kinds of interfaces benefit from a thumbnail map to ease navigation. We'll discuss this technique as well as other visual signposts later in this chapter.

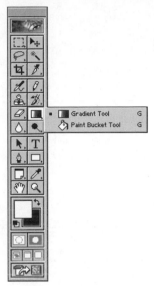

Figure 11-3: Adobe hides the Paint Bucket in a combutcon (see Chapter 26) on its tool palette. Even though users make frequent use of both the Gradient tool and the Paint Bucket, users are forced to access this menu any time they need to switch between these tools.

Linking is the critical navigational paradigm of the Web. Because it is a visually dislocating activity, extra care must be taken to provide visual and textual cues that help orient users. We will discuss Web navigation in more detail in Chapter 37.

Zooming and **panning** are navigational tools for exploring 2D and 3D information. These methods are appropriate when creating 2D or 3D drawings and models or for exploring representations of real-world 3D environments (architectural walkthroughs, for example). They typically fall short when used to examine arbitrary or abstract data presented in more than two dimensions. Some information visualization tools use zoom to mean, "display more attribute details about objects," a logical rather than spatial zoom. As the view of the object enlarges, attributes (often textual) appear superimposed over its graphical representation. This kind of interaction is almost always better served through an adjacent supporting pane that displays the properties of selected objects in a more standard, readable form. Users find spatial zoom difficult enough to understand; logical zoom is arcane to all but visualization researchers and the occasional programmer.

Panning and zooming, especially when paired together, create enormous navigation difficulties for users. Humans are not used to moving in unconstrained 3D space, and they have difficulty perceiving 3D properly when it is projected on a 2D screen (see Chapter 24 for more discussion of 3D manipulation).

Improving Navigation

There are many ways to begin improving (eliminating, reducing, or speeding) navigation in your applications, Web sites, and devices. Here are the most effective:

- ✓ Reduce the number of places to go
- ✓ Provide signposts
- ✓ Provide overviews
- ✓ Provide appropriate mapping of controls to functions
- ✓ Inflect your interface to match user needs
- ✓ Avoid hierarchies

We'll discuss these in detail below.

Reduce the number of places to go

The most effective method of improving navigation sounds quite obvious: Reduce the number of places to which one must navigate. These "places" include modes, forms, dialogs, pages, windows, and screens. If the number of modes, pages, or screens is kept to a minimum, the user's ability to stay oriented increases dramatically. In terms of the four types of navigation presented earlier, this directive means:

- ✓ Keep the number of pages and windows to a minimum: One full-screen window with two or three views (maximum) is best. Keep dialogs, especially modeless dialogs, to a minimum. Programs or Web sites with dozens of distinct types of pages, screens, or forms are not navigable under any circumstances.

- ✓ Keep the number of adjacent panes in your window or Web page limited to the minimum number needed for users to achieve their goals. In sovereign applications, three panes is a good maximum. On Web pages, anything more than two navigation areas and one content area begins to get busy.

- ✓ Keep the number of controls limited to as few as your users really need to meet their goals. Having a good grasp of your users via personas will enable you to avoid functions and controls that your users don't really want or need and that, therefore, only get in their way.

- ✓ Scrolling should be minimized when possible. This means giving supporting panes enough room to display information so that they don't require constant scrolling. Default views of 2D and 3D diagrams and scenes should be such that the user can orient himself without too much panning around. Zooming, particularly continuous zooming, is the most difficult type of navigation for most users so its use should be discretionary, not a requirement.

Many e-commerce sites present confusing navigation because the designers are trying to serve everyone with one generic site. If a user buys books but never CDs from a site, access to the CD portion of the site could be de-emphasized in the main screen for that user. This makes more room for that user to buy books, and the navigation becomes simpler. Conversely, if he visits his account page frequently, his version of the site should have his account button (or tab) presented prominently.

Provide signposts

In addition to reducing the number of navigable places, another way to enhance the user's ability to find his way around is by providing better points of reference — **signposts**. In the same way that sailors navigate by reference to shorelines or stars, users navigate by reference to **persistent objects** placed in the user interface.

Persistent objects, in a desktop world, always include the program's windows. Each program most likely has a main, top-level window. The salient features of that window are also considered persistent objects: menu bars, toolbars, and other palettes or visual features like status bars and rulers. Generally, each window of the program has a distinctive look that will soon become instantly recognizable.

On the Web, similar rules apply. The best Web applications, such as Amazon.com, make careful use of persistent objects that remain constant throughout the shopping experience, especially the tab bar along the top of the page and the Search and Browse areas on the left of the page. Not only do these areas provide clear navigational options, but their consistent presence and layout also help orient customers (see Figure 11-4).

In devices, similar rules apply to screens, but hardware controls themselves can take on the role of signposts — even more so when they are able to offer visual or tactile feedback about their state. Radio buttons that, for example, light when selected, even a needle's position on a dial, can provide navigational information if integrated appropriately with the software.

Depending on the application, the contents of the program's main window may also be easily recognizable (especially true in kiosks and small-screen devices). Some programs may offer a few different views of their data, so the overall aspect of their screens will change depending on the view chosen. A desktop application's distinctive look, however, will usually come from its unique combination of menus, palettes, and toolbars. This means that menus and toolbars must be considered aids to navigation. You don't need a lot of signposts to navigate successfully. They just need to be visible. Needless to say, signposts can't aid navigation if they are removed, so it is best if they are permanent fixtures of the interface.

Making each page on a Web site look just like every other one may appeal to marketing, but it can, if carried too far, be disorienting. Certainly, you should use common elements consistently on each page, but by making different rooms look visually distinct, — that is making the purchase page look very different from the new account page — you will help to orient your users better.

MENUS

The most prominent permanent object in a program is the main window and its title and menu bars. Part of the benefit of the menu comes from its reliability and consistency. Unexpected changes to a program's menus can deeply reduce the user's trust in them. This is true for menu items as well as for individual menus. It is okay to add items to the bottom of a menu, but the standard suite of items in the main part of it should change only for a clearly demonstrable need.

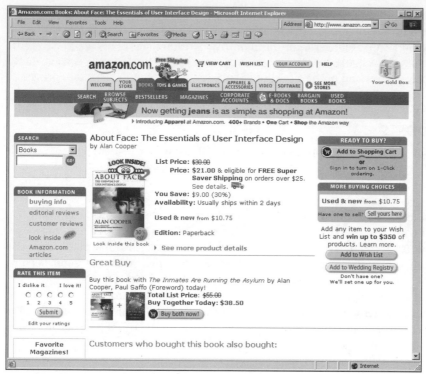

Figure 11-4: Amazon.com makes use of many persistent areas on the majority of its pages, such as the tab bar at the top and the Search and Browse areas on the sides. These not only help users figure out where they can go, but help keep them oriented as to where they are.

TOOLBARS

If the program has a toolbar, it should also be considered a recognizable signpost. Because toolbars are idioms for perpetual intermediates rather than for beginners, the strictures against changing menu items don't apply quite as strongly to individual toolbar controls. Removing the toolbar itself is certainly a dislocating change to a persistent object. Although the ability to do so should be there, it shouldn't be offered casually, and the user should be protected against accidentally triggering it. Some programs put controls on the toolbar that made the toolbar disappear! This is a completely inappropriate ejector seat lever.

OTHER INTERFACE SIGNPOSTS

Tool palettes and fixed areas of the screen where data is displayed or edited should also be considered persistent objects that add to the navigational ease of the interface. Judicious use of white space and legible fonts is important so that these signposts remain clearly evident and distinct.

Provide overviews

Overviews serve a similar purpose to signposts in an interface: They help to orient the user. The difference is that overviews help orient users within the content rather than within the application as a whole. Because of this, the overview area should itself be persistent; its content is dependent on the data being navigated.

Overviews can be graphical or textual, depending on the nature of the content. An excellent example of a graphical overview is the aptly named Navigator palette in Adobe Photoshop (see Figure 11-5).

Figure 11-5: Adobe makes use of an excellent overview idiom: the Navigator palette, which provides a thumbnail view of a large image with an outlined box that represents the portion of the image currently visible in the main display. The palette not only provides navigational context, but it can be used to pan and zoom the main display as well.

In the Web world, the most common form of overview area is textual: the ubiquitous breadcrumb display (see Figure 11-6). Again, most breadcrumbs provide not only a navigational aid, but a navigational control as well: They not only show where in the data structure the user is, but they give him tools to move to different nodes in the structure in the form of links.

Figure 11– 6: A typical breadcrumb display from Amazon.com. Users see where they've been and can click anywhere in the breadcrumb trail to navigate to that link.

A final interesting example of an overview tool is the **annotated scrollbar**. Annotated scrollbars are most useful for scrolling through text. They make clever use of the linear nature of both scrollbars and textual information to provide location information about the locations of selections, highlights, and potentially many other attributes of formatted or unformatted text. Hints about the locations of these items appear in the "track" that the thumb of the scrollbar moves in, at the appropriate location. When the thumb is over the annotation, the annotated feature of the text is visible in the display (see Figure 11-7). Microsoft Word uses a variant of the annotated scrollbar; it shows the page number and nearest header in a ToolTip that remains active during the scroll.

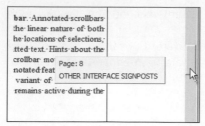

Figure 11-7: An annotated scrollbar. Marks on the scrollbar denote locations in the text, such as the highlighted passage shown here. When the thumb of the scrollbar passes over the mark, the location denoted by the mark is visible on the screen.

Provide appropriate mapping of controls to functions

Mapping describes the relationship between a control, the thing it affects, and the intended result. Poor mapping is evident when a control does not relate visually or symbolically with the object it affects. Poor mapping requires the user to stop and think about the relationship, breaking flow. Poor mapping of controls to functions increases the cognitive load for users and can result in potentially serious user errors.

An excellent example of mapping problems comes from the non-digital world of gas and electric ranges. Almost anyone who cooks has run into the annoyance of a stovetop whose burner knobs do not map appropriately to the burners they control. The typical stovetop, such as the one shown in Figure 11-8, features four burners arranged in a flat square with a burner in each corner. However, the knobs that operate those burners are laid out in a straight line on the front of the unit.

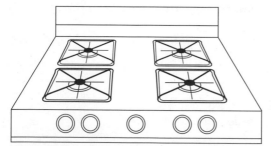

Figure 11-8: A stovetop with poor physical mapping of controls. Does the knob on the far-left control the left-front or left-rear burner? Users must figure out the mapping anew each time they use the stovetop.

In this case, we have a **physical mapping** problem. The *result* of using the control is reasonably clear: A burner will heat up when you turn a knob. However, the *target* of the control — which burner will get warm — is unclear. Does twisting the left-most knob turn on the left-front burner, or does it turn on the left-rear burner? Users must find out by trial and error or by referring to the tiny icons next to the knobs. The unnaturalness of the mapping compels users to figure this relationship out anew every time they use the stove. This cognitive work may become semi-conscious over time, but it still exists, making users prone to error if they are rushed or distracted (as people often are while preparing meals). In the best-case scenario, users feel stupid because they've twisted the wrong knob, and their food doesn't get hot until they notice the error. In the worst-case scenario, they might accidentally burn themselves or set fire to the kitchen.

The solution requires moving the physical locations of the stovetop knobs so that they better suggest which burners they control. The knobs don't have to be laid out in exactly the same pattern as the burners, but they should be positioned so that the target of each knob is clear. The stovetop in Figure 11-9 is a good example of an effective mapping of controls:

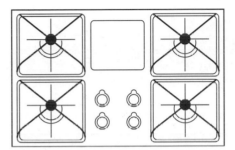

Figure 11-9: Clear spatial mapping. On this stovetop, it is clear which knob maps to which burner because the spatial arrangement of knobs clearly associates each knob with a burner.

In this layout, it's clear that the upper-left knob controls the upper-left burner. The placement of each knob visually suggests which burner it will turn on. Donald Norman (1989) calls this more intuitive layout "natural mapping."

Another example of poor mapping — of a different type — is pictured in Figure 11-10. In this case, it is the **logical mapping** of concepts to actions that is unclear.

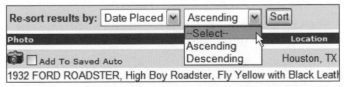

Figure 11-10: An example of a logical mapping problem. If the user wants to see the most recent items first, does he choose Ascending or Descending? These terms don't map well to how users conceive of time.

The Web site uses a pair of drop-down menus to sort a list of search results by date. The selection in the first drop-down determines the choices present in the second. When Re-sort Results by: Date Placed is selected in the first menu, the second drop-down presents the options Ascending and Descending.

Unlike the poorly mapped stovetop knobs, the *target* of this control is clear — the drop-down menu selections will affect the list below them. However, the *result* of using the control is unclear: Which sort order will the user get if he chooses Ascending?

The terms chosen to communicate the date sorting options make it unclear what users should choose if they wish to see the most recent items first in the list. Ascending and Descending do not map well to the user's mental models of time. People don't think of dates as ascending or descending; rather, they think of dates and events as being recent or ancient. A quick fix to this problem is to change the wording of the options to Most Recent First and Oldest First, as in Figure 11-11.

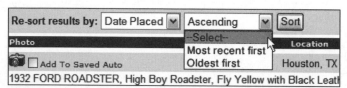

Figure 11-11: Clear logical mapping. Most Recent and Oldest are terms that users can easily map to time-based sorting.

Whether you make appliances, desktop applications, or Web sites, your product may have mapping problems. Mapping is an area where attention to detail pays off — you can measurably improve a product by seeking out and fixing mapping problems, even if you have very little time to make changes. The result? A product that is easier to understand and more pleasurable to use.

Inflect your interface to match user needs

Inflecting an interface means organizing it to minimize typical navigation. In practice, this means placing the most frequently desired functions and controls in the most immediate and convenient locations for the user to access them, while pushing the less frequently used functions deeper into the interface, where the user won't stumble over them. Rarely used facilities shouldn't be removed from the program, but they should be removed from the user's everyday workspace.

Inflect the interface for typical navigation.

The most important principle in the proper inflection of interfaces is **commensurate effort**. Although it applies to all users, it is particularly pertinent to perpetual intermediates. This principle merely states that people will willingly work harder for something that is more valuable to get. The catch, of course, is that value is in the eye of the beholder. It has nothing to do with how technically difficult a feature is to implement, but rather has entirely to do with the user's goals.

If the user really want something, he will work harder to get it. If a person wants to become a good tennis player, for example, he will get out on the court and play very hard. To someone who doesn't like tennis, any amount of the sport is tedious effort. If a user needs to format beautiful documents with multiple columns, several fonts, and fancy headings to impress his boss, he will be highly motivated to explore the recesses of the program to learn how. He will be putting *commensurate effort* into the project. If some other user just wants to print plain old documents in one column and one font, no amount of inducement will get him to learn those more-advanced formatting features.

AXIOM

Users make commensurate effort if the rewards justify it.

This means that if you add features to your program that are necessarily complex to manage, users will be willing to tolerate that complexity only if the rewards are worth it. This is why a program's user interface can't be complex to achieve simple results, but it *can* be complex to achieve *complex* results (as long as such results aren't needed very often).

It is acceptable from an interface perspective to make advanced features something that the user must expend a little extra effort to activate, whether that means searching in a menu, opening a dialog, or opening a drawer. The principle of commensurate effort allows us to **inflect** interfaces so that simple, commonly used functions are immediately at hand at all times. Advanced features, which are less frequently used but have a big payoff for the user, can be safely tucked away where they can be brought up only when needed. In general, controls and displays should be organized in an interface according to three attributes: frequency of use, degree of dislocation, and degree of exposure.

- ✓ **Frequency of use** means how often the controls, functions, objects, or displays are used in typical day-to-day patterns of use. Items and tools that are most frequently used (many times a day) should be immediately in reach, as discussed in Chapter 9. Less frequently used items, used perhaps once or twice a day, should be no more than a click or two away. Other items can be two or three clicks away.

- ✓ **Degree of dislocation** refers to the amount of sudden change in an interface or in the document/information being processed by the application caused by the invocation of a specific function or command. Generally speaking, it's a good idea to put these types of functions deeper into the interface (see "Hiding ejector seat levers," in Chapter 9, for an explanation).

- ✓ **Degree of exposure** deals with functions that are irreversible or which may have other dangerous ramifications. ICBMs require two humans turning keys simultaneously on opposite sides of the room to arm them. As with dislocating functions, you want to make these types of functions more difficult for your users to stumble across.

Of course, as users get more experienced with these features, they will search for shortcuts, and you must provide them. When software follows commensurate effort, the learning curve doesn't go away, but it disappears from the user's mind—which is just as good.

Avoid hierarchies

Hierarchies are one of the programmer's most durable tools. Much of the data inside programs, along with much of the code that manipulates it, is in hierarchical form. For this reason, many programmers present hierarchies (the implementation model) in user interfaces. Early menus, as we've seen, were hierarchical. But abstract hierarchies are very difficult for users to successfully navigate. This truth is often difficult for programmers to grasp because they themselves are so comfortable with hierarchies.

Most humans are familiar with hierarchies in their business and family relationships, but hierarchies are not natural concepts for most people when it comes to storing and retrieving arbitrary information. Most mechanical storage systems are simple, composed either of a single sequence of stored objects (like a bookshelf) or a series of sequences, one level deep (like a file cabinet). This method of organizing things into a single layer of groups is extremely common and can be found everywhere in your home and office. Because it never exceeds a single level of nesting, we call this storage paradigm **monocline grouping**.

Programmers are very comfortable with nested systems where an instance of an object is stored in another instance of the same object. Most other humans have a very difficult time with this idea. In the mechanical world, complex storage systems, by necessity, use different mechanical form factors at each level: In a file cabinet, you never see folders inside folders or file drawers inside file drawers. Even the dissimilar nesting of folder-inside-drawer-inside-cabinet rarely exceeds two levels of nesting. In the current desktop metaphor used by most window systems, you can nest folder within folder ad infinitum. It's no wonder most computer neophytes get confused when confronted with this paradigm.

Most people store their papers (and other items) in a series of stacks or piles based on some common characteristic: The Acme papers go here; the Project M papers go there; personal stuff goes in the drawer. Donald Norman (1994) calls this a *pile cabinet*. Only inside computers do people put the Project M documents inside the Active Clients folder, which, in turn, is stored inside the Clients folder, stored inside the Business folder.

Computer science gives us hierarchical structures as tools to solve the very real problems of managing massive quantities of data. But when this implementation model is reflected in the manifest model presented to users (see Chapter 2 for more on these models), they get confused because it conflicts with their mental model of storage systems. Monocline grouping is the mental model the user typically brings to the software. Monocline grouping is so dominant outside the computer that interaction designers violate this model at their peril.

Monocline grouping is an inadequate system for physically managing the large quantities of data we commonly find on computers, but that doesn't mean it isn't useful as a *manifest model*. The solution to this conundrum is to render the structure as the user imagines it — as monocline grouping — but to provide the search and access tools that only a deep hierarchical organization can offer. In other words, rather than forcing users to navigate deep, complex tree structures, give them tools to *bring appropriate information to them*. We'll discuss some design solutions that help to make this happen in Chapter 16.

Chapter 12

Understanding Undo

Undo is the remarkable facility that lets us reverse a previous action. Simple and elegant, the feature is of obvious value. Yet, when we examine undo from a goal-directed point of view, there appears to be a considerable variation in purpose and method. Undo is critically important for users, and it's not quite as simple as one might think. This chapter explores the different ways users think about undo and the different uses for such a facility.

Users and Undo

Undo is the facility traditionally thought of as the rescuer of users in distress; the knight in shining armor; the cavalry galloping over the ridge; the superhero swooping in at the last second.

As a computational facility, undo has no merit. Mistake-free as they are, computers have no need for undo. Human beings, on the other hand, make mistakes all the time, and undo is a facility that exists for their exclusive use. This singular observation should immediately tell us that of all the facilities in a program, undo should be modeled the least like its construction methods—its implementation model—and the most like the user's mental model.

Not only do humans make mistakes, they make mistakes as part of their everyday behavior. From the standpoint of a computer, a false start, a misdirected glance, a pause, a hiccup, a sneeze, a cough, a blink, a laugh, an "uh," a "you know" are all errors. But from the standpoint of the human user, they are perfectly normal. Human mistakes are so commonplace that if you think of them as "errors" or even as abnormal behavior, you will adversely affect the design of your software.

User mental models of mistakes

Users don't believe, or at least don't want to believe, that they make mistakes. This is another way of saying that the user's mental model doesn't typically include error on his part. Following the user's mental model means absolving the user of blame. The implementation model, however, is based on an error-free CPU. Following the implementation model means proposing that all culpability must rest with the user. Thus, most software assumes that it is blameless, and any problems are purely the fault of the user.

The solution is for the user interface designer to completely abandon the idea that the user can make a mistake—meaning that everything the user does is something he or she considers to be valid and reasonable. Users don't like to admit to mistakes in their own minds, so the program shouldn't contradict these actions in its interactions with users.

Undo enables exploration

If we design software from the point of view that nothing users do should constitute a mistake, we immediately begin to see things differently. We cease to imagine the user as a module of code or a peripheral that drives the computer, and we begin to imagine him as an explorer, probing the unknown. We understand that exploration involves inevitable forays into blind alleys and box canyons, down dead ends and into dry holes. It is natural for humans to experiment, to vary their actions, to probe gently against the veil of the unknown to see where their boundaries lie. How can they know what they can do with a tool unless they experiment with it? Of course the degree of willingness to experiment varies widely from person to person, but most people experiment at least a little bit.

Programmers, who are highly paid to think like computers (Cooper, 1999), view such behavior only as errors that must be handled by the code. From the implementation model — necessarily the programmer's point of view — such gentle, innocent probing represents a continuous series of "mistakes." From our more-enlightened, mental model point-of-view, these actions are natural and normal. The program has the choice of either rebuffing those perceived mistakes or assisting the user in his explorations. Undo is thus the primary tool for supporting exploration in software user interfaces. It allows the user to reverse one or more previous actions if he decides to change his mind.

A significant benefit of undo is purely psychological: It reassures users. It is much easier to enter a cave if you are confident that you can get back out of it at any time. The undo function is that comforting rope ladder to the surface, supporting the user's willingness to explore further by assuring him that he can back out of any dead-end caverns.

Curiously, users often don't think about undo until they need it, in much the same way that homeowners don't think about their insurance policies until a disaster strikes. Users frequently charge into the cave half-prepared, and only start looking for the rope ladder — for undo — after they have encountered trouble.

Designing an Undo Facility

Although users need undo, it doesn't directly support a particular goal they bring to their tasks. Rather, it supports a necessary condition — trustworthiness — on the way to a real goal. It doesn't contribute positively to attaining the user's goal, but keeps negative occurrences from spoiling the effort.

Users visualize the undo facility in many different ways depending on the situation and their expectations. If the user is very computer-naive, he might see it as an unconditional panic button for extricating himself from a hopelessly tangled misadventure. A more experienced computer user might visualize undo as a storage facility for deleted data. A really computer-sympathetic user with a logical mind might see it as a stack of procedures that can be undone one at a time in reverse order. In order to create an effective undo facility, we must satisfy as many of these mental models as we expect our users will bring to bear.

The secret to designing a successful undo system is to make sure that it supports typically used tools and avoids any hint that undo signals (whether visually, audibly, or textually) a failure by the user. It should be less a tool for reversing errors and more one for supporting exploration. Errors are generally single, incorrect actions. Exploration, by contrast, is a long series of probes and steps, some of which are keepers and others that must be abandoned.

Undo works best as a global, program-wide function that undoes the last action regardless of whether it was done by direct manipulation or through a dialog box. This can make undo problematic for embedded objects. If the user makes changes to a spreadsheet embedded in a Word document, clicks on the Word document, and then invokes undo, the most recent Word action is undone instead of the most recent spreadsheet action. Users have a difficult time with this. It fails to render the juncture between the spreadsheet and the word-processing document seamlessly: The undo function ceases to be global and becomes modal. This is not an undo problem per se, but a problem with the embedding technology.

Types and Variants of Undo

As is so common in the software industry, there is no adequate terminology to describe the types of undo that exist—they are uniformly called undo and left at that. This language gap contributes to the lack of innovation in new and better variants of undo. In this section, we define several undo variants and explain their differences.

Incremental and procedural actions

First, consider what objects undo operates on: the user's actions. A typical user action in a typical application has a procedure component—what the user did—and an optional data component—what information was affected. When the user requests an undo function, the procedure component of the action is reversed, and if the action had an optional data component—the user added or deleted data—that data will be deleted or added back, as appropriate. Cutting, pasting, drawing, typing, and deleting are all actions that have a data component, so undoing them involves removing or replacing the affected text or image parts. Those actions that include a data component are called **incremental actions**.

Many undoable actions are data-free transformations such as a paragraph reformatting operation in a word processor or a rotation in a drawing program. Both these operations act on data but neither of them add or delete data. Actions like these (with only a procedure component) are **procedural actions**. Most existing undo functions don't discriminate between procedural and incremental actions but simply reverse the most recent action.

Blind and explanatory undo

Normally, undo is invoked by a menu item or toolbar control with an unchanging label or icon. The user knows that triggering the idiom undoes the last operation, but there is no indication of what that operation is. This is called a **blind undo**. On the other hand, if the idiom includes a textual or visual description of the particular operation that will be undone it is an **explanatory undo**.

If, for example, the user's last operation was to type in the word **design**, the undo function on the menu says Undo Typing **design**. Explanatory undo is, generally, a much more pleasant feature than blind undo. It is fairly easy to put on a menu item, but more difficult to put on a toolbar control, although putting the explanation in a ToolTip (see Chapter 29) is a good compromise.

Single and multiple undo

The two most-familiar types of undo in common use today are single undo and multiple undo. Single undo is the most basic variant, reversing the effects of the most recent user action, whether procedural or incremental. Performing a single undo twice usually undoes the undo, and brings the system back to the state it was in before the first undo was activated.

This facility is very effective because it is so simple to operate. The user interface is simple and clear, easy to describe and remember. The user gets precisely one free lunch. This is by far the most frequently implemented undo, and it is certainly adequate, if not optimal, for many programs. For some users, the absence of this simple undo is sufficient grounds to abandon a product entirely.

The user generally notices most of his command mistakes right away: Something about what he did doesn't feel or look right, so he pauses to evaluate the situation. If the representation is clear, he sees his mistake and selects the undo function to set things back to the previously correct state; then he proceeds.

Multiple undo can be performed repeatedly in succession — it can revert more than one previous operation, in reverse temporal order. Any program with simple undo must remember the user's last operation and, if applicable, cache any changed data. If the program implements multiple undo, it must maintain a stack of operations, the depth of which may be settable by the user as an advanced preference. Each time undo is invoked, it performs an incremental undo; it reverses the most recent operation, replacing or removing data as necessary and discarding the restored operation from the stack.

LIMITATIONS OF SINGLE UNDO

The biggest limitation of single-level, functional undo is when the user accidentally short-circuits the capability of the undo facility to rescue him. This problem crops up when the user doesn't notice his mistake immediately. For example, assume he deletes six paragraphs of text, then deletes one word, and then decides that the six paragraphs were erroneously deleted and should be replaced. Unfortunately, performing undo now merely brings back the one word, and the six paragraphs are lost forever. The undo function has failed him by behaving literally rather than practically. Anybody can clearly see that the six paragraphs are more important than the single word, yet the program freely discarded those paragraphs in favor of the one word. The program's blindness caused it to keep a quarter and throw away a fifty-dollar bill, simply because the quarter was offered last.

In some programs any click of the mouse, however innocent of function it might be, causes the single undo function to forget the last meaningful thing the user did. Although multiple undo solves these problems, it introduces some significant problems of its own.

LIMITATIONS OF MULTIPLE UNDO

The response to the weaknesses of single-level undo has been to create a multiple-level implementation of the same, incremental undo. The program saves each action the user takes. By selecting undo repeatedly, each action can be undone in the reverse order of its original invocation. In the above scenario, the user can restore the deleted word with the first invocation of undo and restore the precious six paragraphs with a second invocation. Having to redundantly re-delete the single word is a small price to pay for being able to recover those six valuable paragraphs. The excise of the one-word re-deletion tends to not be noticed, just as we don't notice the cost of ambulance trips: Don't quibble over the little stuff when lives are at stake. But this doesn't change the fact that the undo mechanism is built on a faulty model, and in other circumstances, undoing functions in a strict LIFO (Last In, First Out) order can make the cure as painful as the disease.

Imagine again our user deleting six paragraphs of text, then calling up another document and performing a global find-and-replace function. In order to retrieve the missing six paragraphs, the user must first unnecessarily undo the rather complex global find-and-replace operation. This time, the intervening operation was not the insignificant single-word deletion of the earlier example. The intervening operation was complex and difficult and having to undo it is clearly an unpleasant, excise effort. It would sure be nice to be able to choose which operation in the queue to undo and to be able to leave intervening—but valid—operations untouched.

THE MODEL PROBLEMS OF MULTIPLE UNDO

The problems with multiple undo are not due to its behavior as much as they are due to its manifest model. Most undo facilities are constructed in an unrelentingly function-centric manner. They remember what the user does function-by-function and separate the user's actions by individual function. In the time-honored way of creating manifest models that follow implementation models, undo systems tend to model code and data structures instead of user goals. Each click of the Undo button reverses precisely one function-sized bite of behavior. Reversing on a function-by-function basis is a very appropriate mental model for solving most simple problems caused by the user making an erroneous entry. Users sense it right away and fix it right away, usually within a two- or three-function limit. The Paint program in Windows 95, for example, had a fixed, three-action undo limit. However, when the problem grows more convoluted, the incremental, multiple undo model doesn't scale up very well.

YOU BET YOUR LIFO

When the user goes down a logical dead-end (rather than merely mistyping data), he can often proceed several complex steps into the unknown before realizing that he is lost and needs to get a bearing on known territory. At this point, however, he may have performed several interlaced functions, only some of which are undesirable. He may well want to keep some actions and nullify others, not necessarily in strict reverse order. What if the user entered some text, edited it, and then decided to undo the entry of that text but not undo the editing of it? Such an operation is problematic to implement and explain. Neil Rubenking offers this pernicious example: Suppose the user did a global replace changing *tragedy* to *catastrophe* and then another changing *cat* to *dog*. To undo the first without undoing the second, can the program reliably fix all the *dogastrophes*?

In this more complex situation, the simplistic representation of the undo as a single, straight-line, LIFO stack doesn't satisfy the way it does in simpler situations. The user may be interested in studying his actions as a menu and choosing a discontiguous subset of them for reversion, while keeping some others. This demands an explanatory undo with a more robust presentation than might otherwise be necessary for a normal, blind, multiple undo. Additionally, the means for selecting from that presentation must be more sophisticated. Representing the operation in the queue to clearly show the user what he is actually undoing is a more difficult problem.

Redo

The **redo** function came into being as the result of the implementation model for undo, wherein operations must be undone in reverse sequence, and in which no operation may be undone without first undoing all of the valid intervening operations. Redo essentially undoes the undo and is easy to implement if the programmer has already gone to the effort to implement undo.

Redo avoids a diabolical situation in multiple undo. If the user wants to back out of a half-dozen or so operations, he clicks the Undo control a few times, waiting to see things return to the desired state. It is very easy in this situation to press Undo one time too many. He immediately sees that he has undone something desirable. Redo solves this problem by allowing him to undo the undo, putting back the last good action.

Many programs that implement single undo treat the last undone action as an undoable action. In effect, this makes a second invocation of the undo function a minimal redo function.

Group multiple undo

Microsoft Word has an unusual undo facility, a variation of multiple undo we will call **group multiple undo**. It is multiple-level, showing a textual description of each operation in the undo stack. You can examine the list of past operations and select some operation in the list to undo; however, you are not undoing that one operation, but rather all operations back to that point, inclusive (see Figure 12-1).

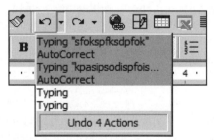

Figure 12-1: Microsoft's Undo/Redo facility is a little unusual. You can undo multiple actions, but only as a group; you can't choose to undo only the thing you did three actions ago. Redo works in the same manner.

Essentially, you cannot recover the six missing paragraphs without first reversing all the intervening operations. After you select one or more operations to undo, the list of undone operations is now available in reverse order in the Redo control. Redo works exactly the same way as undo works. You can select as many operations to redo as desired and all operations up to that specific one will be redone.

The program offers two visual cues to this fact. If the user selects the fifth item in the list, that item and all four items previous to it in the list are selected. Also, the text legend says "Undo 5 actions." The fact that the designers had to add that text legend tells me that, regardless of how the programmers constructed it, the users were applying a different mental model. The users imagined that they could go down the list and select a single action from the past to undo. The program didn't offer that option, so the signs were posted. This is like the door with a pull handle pasted with Push signs—which everybody still pulls on anyway.

Other Models for Undo-Like Behavior

The manifest model of undo in its simplest form, single undo, conforms to the user's mental model: "I just did something I now wish I hadn't done. I want to click a button and undo that last thing I did." Unfortunately, this manifest model rapidly diverges from the user's mental model as the complexity of the situation grows. In this section, we discuss models of undo-like behavior that work a bit differently from the more standard undo and redo idioms.

Comparison: What would this look like?

Besides providing robust support for the terminally indecisive, the paired undo-redo function is a convenient comparison tool. Say you'd like to compare the visual effect of ragged-right margins against justified right margins. Beginning with ragged-right, you invoke Justification. Now you click Undo to see ragged-right and now you press Redo to see justified margins again. In effect, toggling between Undo and Redo implements a **comparison** or what-if function; it just happens to be represented in the form of its implementation model. If this same function were to be added to the interface following the user's mental model, it might be manifested as a comparison control. This function would let you repeatedly take one step forward or backward to visually compare two states.

Some Sony TV remote controls include a function labeled Jump, which switches between the current channel and the previous channel — very convenient for viewing two programs concurrently. The jump function provides the same usefulness as the undo-redo function pair with a single command — a 50% reduction in excise for the same functionality.

When used as comparison functions, undo and redo are really one function and not two. One says "Apply this change," and the other says "Don't apply this change." A single Compare button might more accurately represent the action to the user. Although we have been describing this tool in the context of a text oriented word processing program, a compare function might be most useful in a graphic manipulation or drawing program, where the user is applying successive visual transformations on images. The ability to see the image *with* the transformation quickly and easily compared to the image *without* the transformation would be a great help to the digital artist.

Doubtlessly, the compare function would remain an advanced function. Just as the jump function is probably not used by a majority of TV users, the Compare button would remain one of those niceties for frequent users. This shouldn't detract from its usefulness, however, because drawing programs tend to be used very frequently by those who use them at all. For programs like this, catering to the frequent user is a reasonable design choice.

Category-specific undo

The Backspace key is really an undo function, albeit a special one. When the user mistypes, the Backspace key "undoes" the erroneous characters. If the user mistypes something, then enters an unrelated function such as paragraph reformatting, then presses the Backspace key repeatedly, the mistyped characters are erased and the reformatting operation is ignored. Depending on how you look at it, this can be a great flexible advantage giving the user the ability to undo discontiguously at any selected location. You could also see it as a trap for the user because he can move the cursor and inadvertently backspace away characters that were not the last ones keyed in.

Logic says that this latter case is a problem. Empirical observation says that it is rarely a problem for users. Such discontiguous, incremental undo — so hard to explain in words — is so natural and easy to actually use because everything is visible: The user can clearly see what will be backspaced away. Backspace is a classic example of an incremental undo, reversing only some data while ignoring other, intervening actions. Yet if you imagined an undo facility that had a pointer that could be moved and that could undo the last function that occurred where the pointer points, you'd probably think that such a feature would be patently unmanageable and would confuse the bejabbers out of a typical user. Experience tells us that Backspace does nothing of the sort. It works as well as it does because its behavior is consistent with the user's mental model of the cursor: Because it is the source of added characters, it can also reasonably be the locus of deleted characters.

Using this same knowledge, we could create different categories of incremental undo, like a format-undo function that would only undo preceding format commands and other types of **category-specific undo** actions. If the user entered some text, changed it to italic, entered some more text, increased the paragraph indentation, entered some more text, then pressed the Format-Undo key, only the indentation increase would be undone. A second press of the Format-Undo key would reverse the italicize operation. But neither invocation of the format-undo would affect the content.

What are the implications of category-specific undo in a non-text program? In a graphics drawing program, for example, there could be separate undo commands for pigment application tools, transformations, and cut-and-paste. There is really no reason why we couldn't have independent undo functions for each particular class of operation in a program.

Pigment application tools include all drawing implements — pencils, pens, fills, sprayers, brushes — and all shape tools — rectangles, lines, ellipses, arrows. Transformations include all image-manipulation tools — shear, sharpness, hue, rotate, contrast, line weight. Cut-and-paste tools include all lassos, marquees, clones, drags, and other repositioning tools. Unlike the Backspace function in the word processor, undoing a pigment application in a draw program would be temporal and would work independently of selection. That is, the pigment that is removed first would be the last pigment applied, regardless of the current selection. In text, there is an implied order from the upper-left to the lower-right. Deleting from the lower-right to the upper-left maps to a strong, intrinsic mental model; so it seems natural. In a drawing, no such conventional order exists so any deletion order other than one based on entry sequence would be disconcerting to the user.

A better alternative might be to undo within the current selection only. The user selects a graphic object, for example, and requests a transformation-undo. The last transformation to have been applied to that *selected object* would be reversed.

Most software users are familiar with the incremental undo and would find a category-specific undo novel and possibly disturbing. However, the ubiquitousness of the Backspace key shows that incremental undo is a learned behavior that users find to be helpful. If more programs had modal undo tools, users would soon adapt to them. They would even come to expect them the way they expect to find the Backspace key on word processors.

Deleted data buffers

As the user works on a document for an extended time, his desire for a repository of deleted text grows. It is not that he finds the ability to incrementally undo commands useless but rather that reversing actions can cease to be so function-specific. Take for example, our six missing paragraphs. If they are separated from us by a dozen complex formatting commands, they can be as difficult to reclaim by undo as they are to re-key. The user is thinking, "If the program would just remember the stuff I deleted and keep it in a special place, I could go get what I want directly."

What the user is imagining is a repository of the data components of his actions, rather than merely a LIFO stack of procedurals — a **deleted data buffer**. The user wants the missing text without regard to which function elided it. The usual manifest model forces him not only to be aware of every intermediate step but to reverse each of them, in turn. To create a facility more amenable to the user, we can create, in addition to the normal undo stack, an independent buffer that collects all deleted text or data. At any time, the user can open this buffer as a document and use standard cut-and-paste or click-and-drag idioms to examine and recover the desired text. If the entries in this deletion buffer are headed with simple date stamps and document names, navigation would be very simple and visual.

The user could browse the buffer of deleted data at will, randomly, rather than sequentially. Finding those six missing paragraphs would be a simple, visual procedure, regardless of the number or type of complex, intervening steps he had taken. A deleted data buffer should be offered in addition to the regular, incremental, multiple undo because it complements it. The data must be saved in a buffer, anyway. This feature would be quite useful in all programs, too, whether spreadsheet, drawing program, or invoice generator.

Milestoning and reversion

Users occasionally want to back up long distances, but when they do, the granular actions are not terrifically important. The need for an incremental undo remains, but discerning the individual components of more than the last few operations is overkill in most cases. **Milestoning**, discussed in Chapter 13, simply makes a copy of the entire document the way a camera snapshot freezes an image in time. Because milestoning involves the entire document, it is always implemented by direct use of the file system. The biggest difference between milestoning and other undo systems is that the user must explicitly request the milestone — recording a copy or snapshot of the document. After he has done this, he can proceed to safely modify the original. If he later decides that his changes were undesirable, he can return to the saved copy — a previous version of the document.

Many tools exist to support the milestoning concept in source code; but as yet, no programs the authors are aware of present it directly to the user. Instead, they rely on the file system's interface, which, as we have seen, is difficult for many users to understand. If milestoning were rendered in a non-file–system user model, implementation would be quite easy, and its management would be equally simple. A single button control could save the document in its current state. The user could save as many versions at any interval as he desires. To return to a previously milestoned version, the user would access a **reversion** facility.

The reversion facility discussed in Chapter 13 is extremely simple — too simple, perhaps. Its menu item merely says, Revert to Milestone. This is sufficient for a discussion of the file system; but when considered as part of an undo function, it should offer more information. For example, it should display a list of the available saved versions of that document along with some information about each one, such as the time and day it was recorded, the name of the person who recorded it, the size, and some optional user-entered notes. The user could choose one of these versions, and the program would load it, discarding any intervening changes.

Freezing

Freezing, the opposite of milestoning, involves locking the data in a document so that it cannot be changed. Anything that has been entered becomes unmodifiable, although new data can be added. Existing paragraphs are untouchable, but new ones can be added between older ones.

This method is much more useful for a graphic document than for a text document. It is much like an artist spraying a drawing with fixative. All marks made up to that point are now permanent, yet new marks can be made at will. Images already placed on the screen are locked down and cannot be changed, but new images can be freely superimposed on the older ones. Procreate Painter offers a similar feature with its Wet Paint and Dry Paint commands.

Undo-Proof Operations

Some operations simply cannot be undone because they involve some action that triggers a device not under the direct control of the program. After an e-mail message has been sent, for example, there is no undoing it. After a computer has been turned off without saving data, there is no undoing the loss. Many operations, however, masquerade as undo-proof, but they are really easily reversible. For example, when you save a document for the first time in most programs, you can choose a name for the file. But almost no program lets you rename that file. Sure, you can Save As under another name, but that just makes *another* file under the new name, leaving the old file untouched under the old name. Why isn't a filename undo provided? Because it doesn't fall into the traditional view of what undo is for, programmers generally don't provide a true undo function for changing a filename. Spend some time looking at your own application and see if you can find functions that seem as if they should be undoable, but currently aren't. You may be surprised by how many you find.

Chapter 13

Rethinking Files and Save

If you have ever tried to teach your mom how to use a computer, you will know that *difficult* doesn't really do the problem justice. Things start out all right: Start up the word processor and key in a letter. She's with you all the way. When you are finally done, you click the Close button, and up pops a dialog box asking "Do you want to save changes?" You and Mom hit the wall together. She looks at you and asks, "What does this mean? Is everything okay?"

The part of modern computer systems that is the most difficult for users to understand is the file system, the facility that stores programs and data files on disk. Telling the uninitiated about disks is very difficult. The difference between **main memory** and **disk storage** is not clear to most people. Unfortunately, the way we design our software forces users — even your mom — to know the difference. This chapter provides a different way of presenting interactions involving files and disks — one that is more in harmony with the mental models of our users.

What's Wrong with Saving Changes to Files?

Every program exists in two places at once: in memory and on disk. The same is true of every file. However, most users never truly grasp the difference between memory and disk storage and how it pertains to the tasks they perform on documents in a computer system. Without a doubt, the file system — along with the disk storage facility it manages — is the primary cause of disaffection with computers among non-computer–professionals.

When that Save Changes? dialog box, shown in Figure 13-1, opens, users suppress a twinge of fear and confusion and click the Yes button out of habit. A dialog box that is always answered the same way is a redundant dialog box that should be eliminated.

The Save Changes dialog box is based on a poor assumption: that saving and not saving are equally probable behaviors. The dialog gives equal weight to these two options even though the Yes button is clicked orders of magnitude more frequently than the No button. As discussed in Chapter 9, this is a case of confusing possibility and probability. The user *might* say no, but the user *will almost always* say yes. Mom is thinking, "If I didn't want those changes, why would I have closed the document with them in there?" To her, the question is absurd.

There's something else a bit odd about this dialog: Why does it only ask about saving changes when you are all done? Why didn't it ask when you actually made them? The connection between closing a document and saving changes isn't all that natural, even though power users have gotten quite familiar with it.

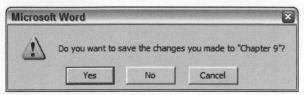

Figure 13-1: This is the question Word asks when you close a file after you have edited it. This dialog is a result of the programmer inflicting the implementation model of the disk file system on the hapless user. This dialog is so unexpected by new users that they often choose No inadvertently.

The program issues the Save Changes dialog box when the user requests Close or Quit because that is the time when it has to reconcile the differences between the copy of the document in memory and the copy on the disk. The way the technology actually implements the facility associates saving changes with Close and Quit, but the user sees no connection. When we leave a room, we don't consider discarding all the changes we made while we were there. When we put a book back on the shelf, we don't first erase any comments we wrote in the margins.

As experienced users, we have learned to use this dialog box for purposes for which it was never intended. There is no easy way to undo massive changes, so we use the Save Changes dialog by choosing No. If you discover yourself making big changes to the wrong file, you use this dialog as a kind of escape valve to return things to the status quo. This is handy, but it's also a hack: There are better ways to address these problems (such as an obvious Revert function).

So what is the real problem? The file systems on modern personal computer operating systems, like Windows XP or Mac OS X, are technically excellent. The problem Mom is having stems from the simple mistake of faithfully rendering that excellent implementation model as an interface for users.

Problems with the Implementation Model

The computer's file system is the tool it uses to manage data and programs stored on disk. This means the large hard disks where most of your information resides, but it also includes your floppy disks, ZIP disks, CD-ROMs, and DVDs if you have them. The Finder on the Mac and the Explorer in Windows graphically represent the file system in all its glory.

Disks and files don't help users achieve their goals.

Even though the file system is an internal facility that shouldn't — by all rights — affect the user, it creates a large problem because the influence of the file system on the interface of most programs is very pervasive. Some of the most difficult problems facing interaction designers concern the file system and its demands. It affects our menus, our dialogs, even the procedural framework of our programs; and this influence is likely to continue indefinitely unless we make a concerted effort to stop it.

Currently, most software treats the file system in much the same way that the operating system shell does (Explorer, Finder). This is tantamount to making you deal with your car in the same way a mechanic does. Although this approach is unfortunate from an interaction perspective, it is a de facto standard, and there is considerable resistance to improving it.

Closing and unwanted changes

We computer geeks are conditioned to think that Close is the time and place for abandoning unwanted changes if we make some error or are just noodling around. This is not correct because the proper time to reject changes is when the changes are made. We even have a well-established idiom to support this: The Undo function is the proper facility for eradicating changes.

Save As

When you answer Yes to the Save Changes dialog, many programs then present you with the Save As dialog box. A typical example is shown in Figure 13-2.

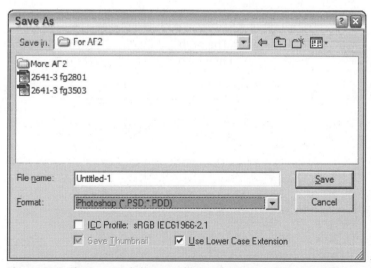

Figure 13-2: The Save As dialog provides two functions: It lets you name your file, and it lets you place it in a directory you choose. Users, however, don't have a concept of **saving**, so the title of the dialog does not match their mental models of the function. Furthermore, if a dialog allows you to name and place a document, you might expect it would allow you to *rename* and *replace* a document as well. Unfortunately, our expectations are confounded by poor design.

Most users don't understand the concept of manual saving very well, so from their point of view, the existing name of this dialog box doesn't make much sense. Functionally, this dialog offers two things: It lets users name a file, and it lets them choose which directory to place it in. Both of these functions demand intimate knowledge of the file system. The user must know how to formulate a filename and how to navigate through the file directory. Many users who have mastered the name portion have completely given up on understanding the directory tree. They put their documents in the directory that the program chooses for a default. All their files are stored in a single directory. Occasionally, some action will cause the program to forget its default directory, and these users must call in an expert to find their files for them.

The Save As dialog needs to decide what its purpose truly is. If it is to name and place files, then it does a very poor job. After the user has named and placed a file, he cannot then change its name or its directory — at least not with this dialog, which purports to offer naming and placing functions — nor can he with any other tool in the application itself. In fact, in Windows XP, you can rename *other* files using this dialog, but *not* the ones you are currently working on. Huh? The idea, one supposes, is to allow you to rename other previously saved milestones of your document because you can't rename the current one. But both operations ought to be possible and be allowed.

Beginners are out of luck, but experienced users learn the hard way that they can close the document, change to the Explorer, rename the file, return to the application, summon the Open dialog from the File menu, and reopen the document. In case you were wondering, the Open dialog doesn't allow renaming or repositioning either, except in the bizarre cases mentioned in the previous paragraph.

Forcing the user to go to the Explorer to rename the document is a minor hardship, but therein lies a hidden trap. The bait is that Windows easily supports several applications running simultaneously. Attracted by this feature, the user tries to rename the file in the Explorer without first closing the document in the application. This very reasonable action triggers the trap, and the steel jaws clamp down hard on his leg. He is rebuffed with a rude error message box shown in Figure 13-3. He didn't first close the document — how would he know? Trying to rename an open file is a sharing violation, and the operating system rejects it with a patronizing error message box.

Figure 13-3: If a user attempts to rename a file using the Explorer while Word is still editing it, the Explorer is too stupid to get around the problem. It is also too rude to be nice about it and puts up this patronizing error message. Rebuffed by both the editing program and the OS, it is easy for a new user to imagine that a document cannot be renamed at all.

The innocent user is merely trying to rename his document, and he finds himself lost in an archipelago of operating system arcana. Ironically, the one entity that has both the authority and the responsibility to change the document's name while it is still open, the application itself, refuses to even try.

Archiving

There is no explicit function for making a copy of, or archiving, a document. The user must accomplish this with the Save As dialog, and doing so is as clear as mud. Even if there were a Copy command, users visualize this function differently. If we are working, for example, on a document called Alpha, some people imagine that we would create a file called Copy of Alpha and store that away. Others imagine that we put Alpha away and continue work on Copy of Alpha.

The latter option will likely only occur to those who are already experienced with the implementation model of file systems. It is how we do it today with the Save As dialog: You have already saved the file as Alpha; and then you explicitly call up the Save As dialog and change the name. Alpha is closed and put away on disk, and Copy of Alpha is left open for editing. This action makes very little sense from a single-document viewpoint of the world, and it also offers a really nasty trap for the user.

Here is the completely reasonable scenario that leads to trouble: Let's say that you have been editing Alpha for the last twenty minutes and now wish to make an archival copy of it on disk so you can make some big but experimental changes to the original. You call up the Save As dialog box and change the file name to New Alpha. The program puts Alpha away on disk leaving you to edit New Alpha. But Alpha was never saved, so it gets written to disk without any of the changes you made in the last twenty minutes! Those changes only exist in the New Alpha copy that is currently in memory—in the program. As you begin cutting and pasting in New Alpha, trusting that your handiwork is backed up by Alpha, you are actually modifying the sole copy of this information.

Everybody knows that you can use a hammer to drive a screw or pliers to bash in a nail, but any skilled craftsperson knows that using the wrong tool for the job will eventually catch up with you. The tool will break or the work will be hopelessly ruined. The Save As dialog is the wrong tool for making and managing copies, and it is the user who will eventually have to pick up the pieces.

Implementation Model versus Mental Model

The implementation model of the file system runs contrary to the mental model almost all users bring to it. Most users picture electronic files like printed documents in the real world, and they imbue them with the behavioral characteristics of those real objects. In the simplest terms, users visualize two salient facts about all documents: First, there is only one document; and second, it belongs to them. The file system's implementation model violates both these rules: There are always two copies of the document, and they both belong to the program.

Every data file, every document, and every program, while in use by the computer, exists in two places at once: on disk and in main memory. The user, however, imagines his document as a book on a shelf. Let's say it is a journal. Occasionally, it comes down off the shelf to have something added to it. There is only one journal, and it either resides on the shelf or it resides in the user's hands. On the computer, the disk drive is the shelf, and main memory is the place where editing takes place, equivalent to the user's hands. But in the computer world, the journal doesn't come off the shelf. Instead a copy is made, and that *copy* is what resides in computer memory. As the user makes changes to the document, he is actually making changes to the copy in memory, while the original remains untouched on disk. When the user is done and closes the document, the program is faced with a decision: whether to replace the original on disk with the changed copy from memory, or to discard the altered copy. From the programmer's point of view, equally concerned with all possibilities, this choice could go either way. From the software's implementation model point of view, the choice is the same either way. However, from the user's point of view, there is no decision to be made at all. He made his changes, and now he is just putting the document away. If this were happening with a paper journal in the physical world, the user would have pulled it off the shelf, penciled in some additions, and then replaced it on the shelf. It's as if the shelf suddenly were to speak up, asking him if he really wants to keep those changes!

Dispensing with the Implementation Model of the File System

Right now, serious programmer-type readers are beginning to squirm in their seats. They are thinking that we're treading on holy ground: A pristine copy on disk is a wonderful thing, and we'd better not advocate getting rid of it. Relax! There is nothing wrong with our file systems. We simply need to hide its existence from the user. We can still offer to him all the advantages of that extra copy on disk without exploding his mental model.

If we begin to render the file system according to the user's mental model we achieve a significant advantage: We can all teach our moms how to use computers. We won't have to answer her pointed questions about the inexplicable behavior of the interface. We can show her the program and explain how it allows her to work on the document; and, upon completion, she can store the document on the disk as though it were a journal on a shelf. Our sensible explanation won't be interrupted by that Save Changes? dialog. And Mom is representative of the mass-market of computer buyers.

Another big advantage is that interaction designers won't have to incorporate clumsy file system awareness into their products. We can structure the commands in our programs according to the goals of the user instead of according to the needs of the operating system. We no longer need to call the left-most menu the File menu. This nomenclature is a bold reminder of how technology currently pokes through the facade of our programs. We'll discuss some alternatives later in this chapter.

Changing the name and contents of the File menu violates an established, though unofficial, standard. But the benefits will far outweigh any dislocation the change might cause. There will certainly be an initial cost as experienced users get used to the new presentation, but it will be far less than you might suppose. This is because these power users have already shown their ability and tolerance by learning the implementation model. For them, learning the better model will be no problem, and there will be no loss of functionality for them. The advantage for new users will be immediate and significant. We computer professionals forget how tall the mountain is after we've climbed it, but everyday newcomers approach the base of this Everest of computer literacy and are severely discouraged. Anything we can do to lower the heights they must scale will make a big difference, and this step will tame some of the most perilous peaks.

Designing a Unified File Presentation Model

Properly designed software will always treat documents as single instances, never as a copy on disk and a copy in memory: a unified file model. It's the file system's job to manage information not in main memory, and it does so by maintaining a second copy on disk. This method is correct, but it is an implementation detail that only confuses the user. Application software should conspire with the file system to hide this unsettling detail from the user.

If the file system is going to show the user a file that cannot be changed because it is in use by another program, the file system should indicate this to the user. Showing the filename in red or with a special symbol next to it would be sufficient. A new user might still get an error message as shown in Figure 13-3; but, at least, some visual clues would be present to show him that there was a *reason* why that error cropped up.

Not only are there two copies of all data files in the current model, but when they are running, there are two copies of all programs. When the user goes to the Taskbar's Start menu and launches his word processor, a button corresponding to Word appears on the Taskbar. But if he returns to the Start menu, Word is still there! From the user's point of view, he has pulled his hammer out of his toolbox only to find that there is still a hammer in his toolbox!

This should probably not be changed; after all, one of the strengths of the computer is its capability to have multiple copies of software running simultaneously. But the software should help the user to understand this very non-intuitive action. The Start menu could, for example make some reference to the already running program.

Unified Document Management

The established standard suite of file management for most applications consists of the Save As dialog, the Save Changes dialog, and the Open File dialog. Collectively, these dialogs are, as we've shown, confusing for some tasks and completely incapable of performing others. The following is a different approach that manages documents according to the user's mental model.

Besides rendering the document as a single entity, there are several goal-directed functions that the user may have need for, and each one should have its own corresponding function.

- ✓ Automatically saving the document
- ✓ Creating a copy of the document
- ✓ Creating a milestone/milestoned copy of the document
- ✓ Naming and renaming the document
- ✓ Placing and repositioning the document
- ✓ Specifying the stored format of the document
- ✓ Reversing some changes
- ✓ Abandoning all changes

Automatically saving the document

One of the most important functions every computer user must learn is how to **save** a document. Invoking this function means taking whatever changes the user has made to the copy in computer memory and writing them onto the disk copy of the document. In the unified model, we abolish all user interface recognition of the two copies, so the Save function disappears completely from the mainstream interface. That *doesn't* mean that it disappears from the program; it is still a very necessary operation.

DESIGN TIP

Save documents and settings automatically.

The program should *automatically* save the document. At the very least, when the user is done with the document and requests the Close function, the program will merely go ahead and write the changes out to disk without stopping to ask for confirmation with the Save Changes dialog box.

In a perfect world, that would be enough, but computers and software can crash, power can fail, and other unpredictable, catastrophic events can conspire to erase your work. If the power fails before you have clicked Close, all your changes are lost as the memory containing them scrambles. The original copy on disk will be all right, but hours of work can still be lost. To keep this from happening, the program must also save the document at intervals during the user's session. Ideally, the program will save every single little change as soon as the user makes it, in other words, after each keystroke. For most programs, this is quite feasible. Most documents can be saved to hard disk in just a fraction of a second. Only for certain programs—word processors leap to mind—would this level of saving be difficult (but not impossible).

Word will automatically save according to a countdown clock, and you can set the delay to any number of minutes. If you ask for a save every two minutes, for example, after precisely two minutes the program will stop to write your changes out to disk regardless of what you are doing at the time. If you are typing when the save begins, it just clamps shut in a very realistic and disconcerting imitation of a broken program. It is a very unpleasant experience. If the algorithm would pay attention to the user instead of the clock, the problem would disappear. Nobody types continuously. Everybody stops to gather his thoughts, or flip a page, or take a sip of coffee. All the program needs to do is wait until the user stops typing for a couple of seconds and *then* save.

This automatic saving every few minutes and at close time will be adequate for almost everybody. Some people though, like the authors, are so paranoid about crashing and losing data that they habitually press Ctrl+S after *every* paragraph, and sometimes after every sentence (Ctrl+S is the keyboard accelerator for the manual save function). All programs should have manual save controls, but users should not be *required* to invoke manual saves.

Right now, the save function is prominently placed on the primary program menu. The save dialog is forced on all users whose documents contain unsaved changes when users ask to close the document or to quit or exit the program. These artifacts must go away, but the manual save functionality can and should remain in place exactly as it is now.

Creating a copy of the document

This should be an explicit function called Snapshot Copy. The word **snapshot** makes it clear that the copy is identical to the original, while also making it clear that the copy is not tied to the original in any way. That is, subsequent changes to the original will have no effect on the copy. The new copy should automatically be given a name with a standard form like Copy of Alpha, where Alpha is the name of the original document. If there is already a document with that name, the new copy should be named Second Copy of Alpha. The copy should be placed in the same directory as the original.

It is very tempting to envision the dialog box that accompanies this command, but there should be no such interruption. The program should take its action quietly, efficiently, and sensibly, without badgering the user with silly questions like Make a Copy? In the user's mind it is a simple command. If there are any anomalies, the program should make a constructive decision on its own authority.

Naming and renaming the document

The name of the document should be shown on the application's title bar. If the user decides to rename the document, he can just click on it and edit it in place. What could be simpler and more direct than that?

Placing and moving the document

Most desktop productivity documents that are edited already exist. They are opened rather than created from scratch. This means that their position in the file system is already established. Although we think of establishing the home directory for a document at either the moment of creation or the moment of first saving, neither of these events is particularly meaningful outside of the implementation model. The new file should be put somewhere reasonable where the user can find it again.

DESIGN TIP   Put files where users can find them.

If the user wants to explicitly place the document somewhere in the file system hierarchy, he can request this function from the menu. A relative of the Save As dialog appears with the current document highlighted. The user can then move the file to any desired location. The program thus places all files automatically, and this dialog is used only to *move* them elsewhere.

Specifying the stored format of the document

There is an additional function implemented on the Save As dialog in Figure 13-2. The combobox at the bottom of the dialog allows the user to specify the physical format of the file. This function should not be located here. By tying the physical format to the act of saving, the user is confronted with additional, unnecessary complexity added to saving. In Word, if the user innocently changes the format, both the save function and any subsequent close action is accompanied by a frightening and unexpected confirmation box. Overriding the physical format of a file is a relatively rare occurrence. Saving a file is a very common occurrence. These two functions should not be combined.

From the user's point-of-view, the physical format of the document—whether it is rich text, ASCII, or Word format, for example—is a characteristic of the document rather than of the disk file. Specifying the format shouldn't be associated with the act of saving the file to disk. It belongs more properly in a Document Properties dialog.

The physical format of the document should be specified by way of a small dialog box callable from the main menu. This dialog box should have significant cautions built into its interface to make it clear to the user that the function could involve significant data loss.

In the case of some drawing programs, where saving image files to multiple formats is desirable, an Export dialog (which some drawing programs already support) is appropriate for this function.

Reversing changes

If the user inadvertently makes changes to the document that must be reversed, the tool already exists for correcting these actions: undo. The file system should not be called in as a surrogate for undo. The file system may be the mechanism for supporting the function, but that doesn't mean it should be rendered to the user in those terms. The concept of going directly to the file system to undo changes merely undermines the undo function.

The milestoning function described later in this chapter shows how a file-centric vision of undo can be implemented so that it works well with the unified file model.

Abandoning all changes

It is not uncommon for the user to decide that she wants to discard all the changes she has made after opening or creating a document, so this action should be explicitly supported. Rather than forcing the user to understand the file system to achieve her goal, a simple Abandon Changes function on the main menu would suffice. Because this function involves significant data loss, the user should be protected with clear warning signs. Making this function undoable would also be relatively easy to implement and highly desirable.

Creating a milestone copy of the document

Milestoning is very similar to the Copy command. The difference is that this copy is managed by the application after it is made. The user can call up a Milestone dialog box that lists each milestone along with various statistics about it, like the time it was recorded and its length. With a click, the user can select a milestone and, by doing so, he also immediately selects it as the active document. The document that was current at the time of the new milestone selection will be milestoned itself, for example, under the name Milestone of Alpha 12/17/03, 1:53 PM. Milestoning is, in essence, a lightweight form of **versioning**.

A new File menu

Our new File menu now looks like the one shown in Figure 13-4.

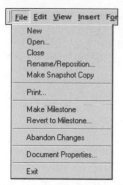

Figure 13-4: The revised file menu now better reflects the user's mental model, rather than the programmer's implementation model. There is only one file, and the user owns it. If she wants, she can make tracked or one-off copies of it, rename it, discard any changes she's made, or change the file format. She no longer needs to understand or worry about the copy in RAM versus the copy on disk.

New and Open function as before, but Close closes the document without a dialog box or any other fuss, after an automatic save of changes. Rename/Move brings up a dialog that lets the user rename the current file or move it to another directory. Make Snapshot Copy creates a new file that is a copy of the current document. Print collects all printer-related controls in a single dialog. Make Milestone is similar to Copy, except that the program manages these copies by way of a dialog box summoned by the Revert to Milestone menu item. Abandon Changes discards all changes made to the document since it was opened or created. Document Properties opens a dialog box that lets the user change the physical format of the document. Exit behaves as it does now, closing the document and application.

A new name for the File menu

Now that we are presenting a unified model of storage instead of the bifurcated implementation model of disk and RAM, we no longer need to call the left-most application menu the *File* menu — a reflection on the implementation model, not the user's model. There are two reasonable alternatives.

We could label the menu after the type of documents the application processes. For example, a spreadsheet application might label its left-most menu Sheet. An invoicing program might label it Invoice.

Alternatively, we can give the left-most menu a more generic label such as Document. This is a reasonable choice for applications like word processors, spreadsheets, and drawing programs, but may be less appropriate for more specialized niche applications.

Conversely, those few programs that do represent the contents of disks as files — generally operating system shells and utilities — *should* have a File menu because they are addressing files *as files*.

Are Disks and Files Systems a Feature?

From the user's point of view, there is no reason for disks to exist. From the hardware engineer's point of view, there are three:

✓ Disks are cheaper than solid-state memory.

✓ Once written to, disks don't forget when the power is off.

✓ Disks provide a physical means of moving information from one computer to another.

Reasons two and three are certainly useful, but they are also not the exclusive domains of disks. Other technologies work as well or better. There are varieties of RAM that don't forget their data when the power is turned off. Some types of solid-state memory can retain data with little or no power. Networks and phone lines can be used to physically transport data to other sites, often more easily than with removable disks.

Reason number one — cost — is the *real* reason why disks exist. Non-volatile solid-state memory is a lot more expensive than disk drives. Reliable, high-bandwidth networks haven't been around as long as removable disks, and they are more expensive.

Disk drives have many drawbacks compared to RAM. Disk drives are much slower than solid-state memory. They are much less reliable, too, because they depend on moving parts. They generally consume more power and take up more space, too. But the biggest problem with disks is that the computer, the actual CPU, can't directly read or write to them! Its helpers must first bring data into solid-state memory before the CPU can work with it. When the CPU is done, its helpers must once again move the data back out to the disk. This means that processing that involves disks is necessarily orders of magnitude slower and more complex than working in plain RAM.

Disks are a hack, not a design feature.

The time and complexity penalty for using disks is so severe that nothing short of enormous cost-differential could compel us to rely on them. Disks do not make computers better, more powerful, faster, or easier to use. Instead, they make computers weaker, slower, and more complex. They are a compromise, a dilution of the solid-state architecture of digital computers. If computer designers could have economically used RAM instead of disks they would have done so without hesitation — and in fact they do, in the newest breeds of handheld communicators and PDAs that make use of Compact Flash and similar solid-state memory technologies.

Wherever disk technology has left its mark on the design of our software, it has done so for implementation purposes only, and not in the service of users or any goal-directed design rationale.

Time for Change

There are only two arguments that can be mounted in favor of application software implemented in the file system model: Our software is already designed and built that way, and users are used to it.

Neither of these arguments is valid. The first one is irrelevant because new programs written with a unified file model can freely coexist with the older implementation model applications. The underlying file system doesn't change at all. In much the same way that toolbars quickly invaded the interfaces of most applications in the last few years, the unified file model could also be implemented with similar success and user acclaim.

The second argument is more insidious, because its proponents place the user community in front of them like a shield. What's more, if you ask users themselves, they will reject the new solution because they abhor change, particularly when that change affects something they have already worked hard to master — like the file system. However, users are not always the best predictors of design successes, especially when the designs are different from anything they've already experienced.

In the eighties, Chrysler showed consumers early sketches of a dramatic new automobile design: the minivan. The public gave a uniform thumbs-down to the new design. Chrysler went ahead and produced the Caravan anyway, convinced that the design was superior. They were right, and the same people who initially rejected the design have not only made the Caravan the one of the best-selling minivans, but also made the minivan the most popular new automotive archetype since the convertible.

Users aren't interaction designers, and they cannot be expected to visualize the larger effects of interaction paradigm shifts. But the market has shown that people will gladly give up painful, poorly designed software for easier, better software even if they don't understand the explanations behind the design rationale.

Part III

Providing Power and Pleasure

Chapter 14

Making Software Considerate

As we briefly discussed in Chapter 9, two Stanford sociologists, Clifford Nass and Byron Reeves, discovered that humans seem to have instincts that tell them how to behave around other sentient beings. As soon as any artifact exhibits sufficient levels of interactivity—such as that found in your average software application—these instincts are activated. Our reaction to software as sentient is both unconscious and unavoidable.

The implication of this research is profound: If we want users to like our software, we should design it to behave in the same manner as a likeable person. If we want users to be productive with our software, we should design it to behave like a supportive human colleague.

Designing Considerate Software

Nass and Reeves suggest that software should be *polite*, but the authors prefer the term *considerate*. Although politeness could be construed as a matter of protocol—saying *please* and *thank you*, but doing little else helpful—being truly *considerate* means putting the needs of others first. Considerate software has the goals and needs of its users as its primary concern beyond its basic functions.

If software is stingy with information, obscures its process, forces the user to hunt around for common functions, and is quick to blame the user for its own failings, the user will dislike the software and have an unpleasant experience. This will happen regardless of how cute, how representational, how visually metaphoric, how content-filled, or how anthropomorphic the software is.

On the other hand, if the interaction is respectful, generous, and helpful, the user will like the software and will have a pleasant experience. Again, this will happen regardless of the composition of the interface; a green-screen command-line interface will be well liked if it can deliver on these other points.

AXIOM

Software should behave like a considerate human.

What Makes Software Considerate?

Humans have many wonderful characteristics that make them considerate but whose definitions are fuzzy and imprecise. The following list enumerates some of the characteristics of considerate interactions that software-based products (and humans) should possess:

- ✓ Considerate software takes an interest.
- ✓ Considerate software is deferential.
- ✓ Considerate software is forthcoming.
- ✓ Considerate software uses common sense.
- ✓ Considerate software anticipates needs.
- ✓ Considerate software is conscientious.
- ✓ Considerate software doesn't burden you with its personal problems.
- ✓ Considerate software keeps you informed.
- ✓ Considerate software is perceptive.
- ✓ Considerate software is self-confident.
- ✓ Considerate software doesn't ask a lot of questions.
- ✓ Considerate software takes responsibility.
- ✓ Considerate software knows when to bend the rules.

We'll now discuss the characteristics in detail.

Considerate software takes an interest

A considerate friend wants to know more about you. He remembers likes and dislikes so he can please you in the future. Everyone appreciates being treated according to his or her own personal tastes.

Most software, on the other hand, doesn't know or care who is using it. Little, if any, of the *personal* software on our *personal* computers seems to remember anything about us, in spite of the fact that we use it constantly, repetitively, and exclusively.

Software should work hard to remember our work habits and, particularly, everything that we say to it. To the programmer writing the program, it's a just-in-time information world, so when the program needs some tidbit of information, it simply demands that the user provide it. The program then discards that tidbit, assuming that it can merely ask for it again if necessary. Not only is the program better suited to remembering than the human, the program is also *inconsiderate* when, acting as a supposedly helpful tool, it forgets. We'll discuss this topic of software memory in detail in Chapter 15.

Considerate software is deferential

A good service provider defers to her client. She understands the person she is serving is the boss. When a restaurant host shows us to a table in a restaurant, we consider his choice of table to be a suggestion, not an order. If we politely request another table in an otherwise empty restaurant, we expect to be accommodated. If the host refuses, we are likely to choose a different restaurant where *our* desires take precedence over the host's.

Inconsiderate software supervises and passes judgment on human actions. Software is within its rights to express its *opinion* that we are making a mistake, but it is being presumptuous when it judges our actions. Software can *suggest* that we not Submit our entry until we've typed in our telephone number. It should also explain the consequences, but if we wish to Submit without the number, we expect the software to do as it is told. (The very word *Submit* and the concept it stands for are a reversal of the deferential role. The software should submit to the user, and any program that proffers a Submit button is being rude. Take notice, almost every transactional site on the World Wide Web!)

Considerate software is forthcoming

If we ask a store employee where to locate an item, we expect him to not only answer the question, but to volunteer the extremely useful collateral information that a more expensive, higher quality item like it is currently on sale for a similar price.

Most software doesn't attempt to provide related information. Instead, it only narrowly answers the precise questions we ask it, and it is typically not forthcoming about other information even if it is clearly related to our goals. When we tell our word processor to print a document, it doesn't tell us when the paper supply is low, or when forty other documents are queued up before us, or when another nearby printer is free. A helpful human would.

Considerate software uses common sense

Offering inappropriate functions in inappropriate places is a hallmark of software-based products. Most software-based products put controls for constantly used functions adjacent to never-used controls. You can easily find menus offering simple, harmless functions adjacent to irreversible ejector-seat–lever expert functions. It's like seating you at a dining table right next to an open grill.

Horror stories also abound of customers offended by computer systems that repeatedly sent them checks for $0.00 or bills for $957,142,039.58. One would think that the system might alert a human in the accounts receivable or payable departments when an event like this happens, especially more than once, but common sense remains a rarity in most information systems.

Considerate software anticipates needs

A human assistant knows that you will require a hotel room when you travel to another city, even when you don't ask explicitly. She knows the kind of room you like and reserves one without any request on your part. She anticipates needs.

A Web browser spends most of its time idling while we peruse Web pages. It could easily anticipate needs and prepare for them while we are reading. It could use that idle time to preload all the links that are visible. Chances are good that we will soon ask the browser to examine one or more of those links. It is easy to abort an unwanted request, but it is always time-consuming to wait for a request to be filled. We'll discuss more ways for software to use idle time to our advantage in the remaining chapters of Part III.

Considerate software is conscientious

A conscientious person has a larger perspective on what it means to perform a task. Instead of just washing the dishes, for example, a conscientious person also wipes down the counters and empties the trash because those tasks are also related to the larger *goal*: cleaning up the kitchen. A conscientious person, when drafting a report, also puts a handsome cover page on it and makes enough photocopies for the entire department.

Here's an example: If we hand our imaginary assistant, Rodney, a manila folder and tell him to file it away, he checks the writing on the folder's tab — let's say it reads MicroBlitz Contract — and proceeds to find the correct place in the filing cabinet for it. Under M, he finds, to his surprise, that there is a manila folder already there with the identical MicroBlitz Contract legend. Rodney notices the discrepancy and investigates. He finds that the already-filed folder contains a contract for 17 widgets that were delivered to MicroBlitz four months ago. The new folder, on the other hand, is for 32 sprockets slated for production and delivery in the next quarter. Conscientious Rodney changes the name on the old folder to read MicroBlitz Widget Contract, 7/03 and then changes the name of the new folder to read MicroBlitz Sprocket Contract, 11/03. This type of initiative is why we think Rodney is conscientious.

Our former imaginary assistant, Elliot, was a complete idiot. He was not conscientious at all, and if he were placed in the same situation he would have dumped the new MicroBlitz Contract folder next to the old MicroBlitz Contract folder without a second thought. Sure, he got it filed safely away, but he could have done a better job. That's why Elliot isn't our imaginary assistant anymore.

If, on the other hand, we rely on a word processor to draft the new sprocket contract and then try to save it in the MicroBlitz directory, the program offers the choice of either overwriting and destroying the old widget contract or not saving it at all. The program not only isn't as capable as Rodney, it isn't even as capable as Elliot. It is stupider than a complete idiot. The software is dumb enough to make an assumption that because they have the same name, I meant to throw the old one away.

The program should, at the very least, mark the two files with different dates and save them. Even if the program refuses to take this "drastic" action unilaterally, it could at least show us the old file (letting us rename *that* one) before saving the new one. There are numerous actions that the program can take that would be more conscientious.

Considerate software doesn't burden you with its personal problems

At a service desk, the agent is expected to keep mum about her problems and to show a reasonable interest in yours. It might not be fair to be so one-sided, but that's the nature of the service business. Software, too, should keep quiet about its problems and show interest in ours. Because computers don't have egos or tender sensibilities, they should be perfect in this role; but they typically behave the opposite way.

Software whines at us with error messages, interrupts us with confirmation dialog boxes, and brags to us with unnecessary notifiers (Document Successfully Saved! How nice for you, Mr. Software: Do you ever *unsuccessfully* save?). We aren't interested in the program's crisis of confidence about whether or not to purge its Recycle bin. We don't want to hear its whining about not being sure where to put a file on disk. We don't need to see information about the computer's data transfer rates and its loading sequence, any more than we need information about the customer service agent's unhappy love affair. Not only should software keep quiet about its problems, but it should also have the intelligence, confidence, and authority to fix its problems on its own. We discuss this subject in more detail in Chapters 33 and 34.

Considerate software keeps us informed

Although we don't want our software pestering us incessantly with its little fears and triumphs, we do want to be kept informed about the things that matter to *us*. We don't want our local bartender to grouse to us about his recent divorce, but we appreciate it when he posts his prices in plain sight and when he writes what time the pregame party begins on his chalkboard, along with who's playing and the current Vegas spread. Nobody is interrupting us to tell us this information: It's there in plain view whenever we need it. Software, similarly, can provide us with this kind of rich modeless feedback about what is going on. We discuss how in Chapter 34.

Considerate software is perceptive

Most of our existing software is not very perceptive. It has a very narrow understanding of the scope of most problems. It may willingly perform difficult work, but only when given the precise command at precisely the correct time. If, for example, you ask the inventory query system to tell you how many widgets are in stock, it will dutifully ask the database and report the number as of the time you ask. But what if, twenty minutes later, someone in the Dallas office cleans out the entire stock of widgets. You are now operating under a potentially embarrassing misconception, while your computer sits there, idling away billions of wasted instructions. It is not being perceptive. If you want to know about widgets once, isn't that a good clue that you probably will want to know about widgets again? You may not want to hear widget status reports every day for the rest of your life, but maybe you'll want to get them for the rest of the week. Perceptive software observes what the user is doing and uses those patterns to offer relevant information.

Software should also watch our preferences and remember them without being asked explicitly to do so. If we always maximize an application to use the entire available screen, the application should get the idea after a few sessions and always launch in that configuration. The same goes for placement of palettes, default tools, frequently used templates, and other useful settings.

Considerate software is self-confident

Software should stand by its convictions. If we tell the computer to discard a file, it shouldn't ask, "Are you sure?" Of course we're sure, otherwise we wouldn't have asked. It shouldn't second-guess us or itself.

On the other hand, if the computer has any suspicion that we might be wrong (which is always), it should anticipate our changing our minds by being prepared to undelete the file upon our request.

How often have you clicked the Print button and then gone to get a cup of coffee, only to return to find a fearful dialog box quivering in the middle of the screen asking, "Are you sure you want to print?" This insecurity is infuriating and the antithesis of considerate human behavior.

Considerate software doesn't ask a lot of questions

As discussed in Chapter 9, inconsiderate software asks lots of annoying questions. Excessive choices quickly stop being a benefit and become an ordeal.

Choices can be offered in different ways. They can be offered in the way that we window shop. We peer in the window at our leisure, considering, choosing, or ignoring the goods offered to us — no questions asked. Alternatively, choices can be forced on us like an interrogation by a customs officer at a border crossing: *Do you have anything to declare?* We don't know the consequences of the question. Will we be searched or not? Software should never put users through this kind of intimidation.

Considerate software fails gracefully

When a friend of yours makes a serious faux pas, he tries to make amends later and undo what damage can be undone. When a program discovers a fatal problem, it has the choice of taking the time and effort to prepare for its failure without hurting the user, or it can simply crash and burn. In other words, it can either go out like a psychotic postal employee, taking the work of a dozen coworkers and supervisors with it, or it can tidy up its affairs, ensuring that as much data as possible is preserved in a recoverable format.

Most programs are filled with data and settings. When they crash, that information is normally just discarded. The user is left holding the bag. For example, say a program is computing merrily along, downloading your e-mail from a server when it runs out of memory at some procedure buried deep in the internals of the program. The program, like most desktop software, issues a message that says, in effect, "You are completely hosed," and terminates immediately after you click OK. You restart the program, or sometimes the whole computer, only to find that the program lost your e-mail and, when you interrogate the server, you find that it has also erased your mail because the mail was already handed over to your program. This is not what we should expect of good software.

In our e-mail example, the program accepted e-mail from the server — which then erased its copy — but didn't ensure that the e-mail was properly recorded locally. If the e-mail program had made sure that those messages were promptly written to the local disk, even before it informed the server that the messages were successfully downloaded, the problem would never have arisen.

Even when programs don't crash, inconsiderate behavior is rife, particularly on the Web. Users often need to enter detailed information into a set of forms on a page. After filling in ten or eleven fields, a user might press the Submit button, and, due to some mistake or omission on his part, the site rejects his input and tells him to correct it. The user then clicks the back arrow to return to the page, and lo, the ten valid entries were inconsiderately discarded along with the single invalid one. Remember Mr. Jones, that incredibly mean geography teacher in junior high school who ripped up your entire report on South America and threw it away because you wrote using a pencil instead of an ink pen? Don't you hate geography to this day? Mr. Jones could easily have been a programmer.

Considerate software knows when to bend the rules

When manual information processing systems are translated into computerized systems, something is lost in the process. Although an automated order entry system can handle millions more orders than a human clerk can, the human clerk has the ability to *work the system* in a way most automated systems ignore. There is almost never a way to jigger the functioning to give or take slight advantages in an automated system.

In a manual system, when the clerk's friend from the sales force calls on the phone and explains that getting the order processed speedily means additional business, the clerk can expedite that one order. When another order comes in with some critical information missing, the clerk can go ahead and process it, remembering to acquire and record the information later. This flexibility is usually absent from automated systems.

In most computerized systems, there are only two states: non-existence or full-compliance. No intermediate states are recognized or accepted. In any manual system, there is an important but paradoxical state — unspoken, undocumented, but widely relied upon — of suspense, wherein a transaction can be accepted although still not being fully processed. The human operator creates that state in his head or on his desk or in his back pocket.

For example, a digital system needs both customer and order information before it can post an invoice. Whereas the human clerk can go ahead and post an order in advance of detailed customer information, the computerized system will reject the transaction, unwilling to allow the invoice to be entered without it.

The characteristic of manual systems that let humans perform actions out of sequence or before prerequisites are satisfied is called fudgeability. It is one of the first casualties when systems are computerized, and its absence is a key contributor to the inhumanity of digital systems. It is a natural result of the implementation model. The programmers don't see any reason to create intermediate states because the computer has no need for them. Yet there are strong human needs to be able to bend the system slightly.

One of the benefits of fudgeable systems is the reduction of mistakes. By allowing many small temporary mistakes into the system and entrusting humans to correct them before they cause problems downstream, we can avoid much bigger, more permanent mistakes. Paradoxically, most of the hard-edged rules enforced by computer systems are imposed to prevent just such mistakes. These inflexible rules cast the human and the software as adversaries, and because the human is prevented from fudging to prevent big mistakes, he soon stops caring about protecting the software from really colossal problems. When inflexible rules are imposed on flexible humans, both sides lose. It is invariably bad for business to prevent humans from doing what they want, and the computer system usually ends up having to digest invalid data anyway.

In the real world, both missing information and extra information that doesn't fit into a standard field are important tools for success. Information processing systems rarely handle this real-world data. They only model the rigid, repeatable data portion of transactions, a sort of skeleton of the actual transaction, which may involve dozens of meetings, travel and entertainment, names of spouses and kids, golf games and favorite sports figures. Maybe a transaction can only be completed if the termination date is extended two weeks beyond the official limit. Most companies would rather fudge on the termination date than see a million-dollar deal go up in smoke. In the real world, limits are fudged all the time. Considerate software needs to realize and embrace this fact.

Considerate software takes responsibility

Too much software takes the attitude: "It isn't my responsibility." When it passes a job along to some hardware device, it washes its hands of the action, leaving the stupid hardware to finish up. Any user can see that the software isn't being considerate or conscientious, that the software isn't shouldering its part of the burden for helping the user become more effective.

In a typical print operation, for example, a program begins sending the 20 pages of a report to the printer and simultaneously puts up a print process dialog box with a Cancel button. If the user quickly realizes that he forgot to make an important change, he clicks the Cancel button just as the first page emerges from the printer. The program immediately cancels the print operation. But unbeknownst to the user, while the printer was beginning to work on page 1, the computer has already sent 15 pages into the printer's buffer. The program cancels the last five pages, but the printer doesn't know anything about the cancellation; it just knows that it was sent 15 pages, so it goes ahead and prints them. Meanwhile, the program smugly tells the user that the function was canceled. The program lies, as the user can plainly see.

The user isn't very sympathetic to the communication problems between the application and the printer. He doesn't care that the communications are one-way. All he knows is that he decided not to print the document before the first page appeared in the printer's output basket, he clicked the Cancel button, and then the stupid program continued printing for 15 pages even though he acted in plenty of time to stop it. It even acknowledged his Cancel command. As he throws the 15 wasted sheets of paper in the trash, he growls at the stupid program.

Imagine what his experience would be if the application could communicate with the print driver and the print driver could communicate with the printer. If the software were smart enough, the print job could easily have been abandoned before the second sheet of paper was wasted. The printer certainly has a Cancel function—it's just that the software is too indolent to use it, because its programmers were too indolent to make the connection.

Considerate Software Is Possible

Our software-based products irritate us because they aren't considerate, not because they lack features. As this list of characteristics shows, considerate software is usually no harder to build than rude or inconsiderate software. It simply means that someone has to envision interaction that emulates the qualities of a sensitive and caring friend. None of these characteristics is at odds with the other, more obviously pragmatic goals of business computing. Behaving more humanely can be the most pragmatic goal of all.

Chapter 15

Making Software Smart

Because every instruction in every program must pass single-file through the CPU, we tend to optimize our code for this needle's eye. Programmers work hard to keep the number of instructions to a minimum, assuring snappy performance for the user. What we often forget, however, is that as soon as the CPU has hurriedly finished all its work, it waits idle, doing nothing, until the user issues another command. We invest enormous efforts in reducing the computer's reaction time, but we invest little or no effort in putting it to work proactively when it is not busy reacting to the user. Our software commands the CPU as though it were in the army, alternately telling it to hurry up and wait. The hurry up part is great, but the waiting needs to stop.

The computer does the work, and the user does the thinking.

The division of labor in the computer age is very clear: The computer does the work, and the user does the thinking. Computer scientists tantalize us with visions of artificial intelligence: computers that think for themselves. However, users don't really need much help in the thinking department. They *do* need a lot of help with the work of information management — activities like finding and organizing information — but the actual decisions made from that information are best made by the wetware — us.

There is some confusion about **smart** software. Some naive observers think that smart software is actually capable of behaving intelligently, but what the term really means is that these programs are capable of working hard even when conditions are difficult and even when the user isn't busy. Regardless of our dreams of thinking computers, there is a much greater and more immediate opportunity in simply getting our computers to work harder. This chapter discusses some of the most important ways that software can work a bit harder to serve humans better.

Putting the Idle Cycles to Work

In our current computing systems, users need to remember too many things, such as the names they give to files and the precise location of those files in the file system. If a user wants to find that spreadsheet with the quarterly projections on it again, he must either remember its name or go browsing. Meanwhile, the processor just sits there, wasting billions of cycles.

Most current software also takes no notice of context. When a user is struggling with a particularly difficult spreadsheet on a tight deadline, for example, the program offers precisely as much help as it offers when he is noodling with numbers in his spare time. Software can no longer, in good conscience, waste so much idle time while the user works. It is time for our computers to begin to shoulder more of the burden of work in our day-to-day activities.

Wasted cycles

Most users in normal situations can't do anything in less than a few seconds. That is enough time for a typical desktop computer to execute at least a *billion* instructions. Almost without fail, those interim cycles are dedicated to idling. The processor does *nothing* except wait. The argument against putting those cycles to work has always been: "We can't make assumptions; those assumptions might be wrong." Our computers today are so powerful that, although the argument is still true, it is frequently irrelevant. Simply put, it doesn't matter if the program's assumptions are wrong; it has enough spare power to make several assumptions and discard the results of the bad ones when the user finally makes his choice.

With Windows and Mac OS X's pre-emptive, threaded multitasking, you can perform extra work in the background without affecting the performance the user sees. The program can launch a search for a file, and if the user begins typing, merely abandon it until the next hiatus. Eventually, the user stops to think, and the program will have time to scan the whole disk. The user won't even notice.

Every time the program puts up a modal dialog box, it goes into an idle waiting state, doing no work while the user struggles with the dialog. This should never happen. It would not be hard for the dialog box to hunt around and find ways to help. What did the user do last time? The program could, for example, offer the previous choice as a suggestion for this time.

We need a new, more proactive way of thinking about how software can help people with their goals and tasks.

Putting the cycles to better use

If your program, Web site, or device could predict what the user is going to do next, couldn't it provide a better interaction? If your program could know which selections the user will make in a particular dialog box or form, couldn't that part of the interface be skipped? Wouldn't you consider advance knowledge of what actions your users take to be an awesome secret weapon of interface design?

Well, you *can* predict what your users will do. You *can* build a sixth sense into your program that will tell it with uncanny accuracy exactly what the user will do next! All those billions of wasted processor cycles can be put to great use: All you need to do is give your interface a memory.

Giving Software a Memory

When we use the term **memory** in this context, we don't mean RAM, but rather a program facility for tracking and responding to user actions over multiple sessions. If your program simply remembers what the user did the last time (and how), it can use that remembered behavior as a guide to how it should behave the next time. As we'll see later in this chapter, your program should remember more than one previous action, but this simple principle is one of the most effective tools available for designing software behavior.

You might think that bothering with a memory isn't necessary; it's easier to just ask the user each time. Programmers are quick to pop up a dialog box to request any information that isn't lying conveniently around. But as we discussed in Chapter 9, *people don't like to be asked questions*. Continually interrogating users is not only a form of excise, but from a psychological perspective, it is a subtle way of expressing doubt about their authority.

Most software is forgetful, remembering little or nothing from execution to execution. If our programs *are* smart enough to retain any information during and between uses, it is usually information that makes the job easier for the *programmer* and not for the user. The program willingly discards information about the way it was used, how it was changed, where it was used, what data it processed, who used it, and whether and how frequently the various facilities of the program were used. Meanwhile, the program fills initialization files with driver-names, port assignments, and other details that ease the programmer's burden. It is possible to use the exact same facilities to dramatically increase the smarts of your software from the perspective of the user.

Task Coherence

Does this kind of memory really work? Predicting what a user will do by remembering what he did last is based on the principle of **task coherence**: the idea that our goals and the way we achieve them (via tasks) is generally the same from day to day. This is not only true for tasks like brushing our teeth and eating our breakfasts, but it also describes how we use our word processors, e-mail programs, cell phones, and e-commerce sites.

When a consumer uses your product, there is a high percentage chance that the functions he uses and the way he uses them will be very similar to what he did last time he used your program. He may even be working on the same documents, or at least the same types of documents, located in similar places. Sure, he won't be doing the exact same thing each time, but it will likely be variants of a small number of repeated patterns. With significant reliability, you can predict the behavior of your users by the simple expedient of remembering what they did the last several times they used the program. This allows you to greatly reduce the number of questions your program must ask the user.

Sally, for example, though she may use Excel in dramatically different ways than Kazu, will herself tend to use Excel the same way each time. Although Kazu likes 9-point Times Roman and Sally prefers 12-point Helvetica, Sally will use 12-point Helvetica with dependable regularity. It isn't really necessary for the program to ask Sally which font to use. A very reliable starting point would be 12-point Helvetica, every time.

Remembering choices and defaults

The way to determine what information the program should remember is with a simple rule: If it's worth the user entering, it's worth the program remembering.

If it's worth the user entering, it's worth the program remembering.

Any time your program finds itself with a choice, and especially when that choice is being offered to the user, the program should remember the information from run to run. Instead of choosing a hard-wired default, the program can use the previous setting as the default, and it will have a much better chance of giving the user what he wanted. Instead of asking the user to make a determination, the program should go ahead and make the same determination the user made last time, and let the user change it if it was wrong. Whatever options the user set should be remembered, so that the options remain in effect until manually changed. If the user ignored facilities of the program or turned them off, they should not be offered to the user again. The user will seek them out when and if he is ready for them.

One of the most annoying characteristics of programs without memories is that they are so parsimonious with their assistance regarding files and disks. If there is one place where the user needs help, it's with files and disks. A program like Word remembers the last place the user looked for a file. Unfortunately, if the user always puts his files in a directory called Letters, then edits a document template stored in the Template directory just one time, all his subsequent letters will be stored in the Template directory rather than in the Letters directory. So the program must remember more than just the last place the files were accessed. It must remember the last place files *of each type* were accessed.

The position of windows should also be remembered, so if you maximized the document last time it should be maximized next time. If the user positioned it next to another window, it is positioned the same way the next time without any instruction from the user. Microsoft Office applications now do a good job of this.

Remembering patterns

The user can benefit in several ways from a program with a good memory. Memory reduces excise, the useless effort that must be devoted to managing the tool and not doing the work. A significant portion of the total excise of an interface is in having to explain things to the program that it should already know. For example, in your word processor, you might often reverse-out text, making it white on black. To do this, you select some text and change the font color to white. Without altering the selection, you then set the background color to black. If the program paid enough attention, it would notice the fact that you requested two formatting steps without an intervening selection option. As far as you're concerned, this is effectively a single operation. Wouldn't it be nice if the program, upon seeing this unique pattern repeated several times, automatically created a new format style of this type — or better yet, created a new Reverse-Out toolbar control?

Most mainstream programs allow their users to set defaults, but this doesn't fit the bill as a memory would. Configuration of this kind is an onerous process for all but power users, and many users will never understand how to customize defaults to their liking.

Actions to Remember

Everything that users do should be remembered. There is plenty of storage on our hard drives, and a memory for your program is a good investment of storage space. We tend to think that programs are wasteful of disk space because a big horizontal application might consume 30 or 40 MB of space. That is typical usage for a program, but not for user data. If your word processor saved 1 KB of execution notes every time you ran it, it still wouldn't amount to much. Let's say that you use your word processor ten times every business day. There are approximately 200 workdays per year, so you run the program 2,000 times a year. The net consumption is still only 2 MB, and that gives an exhaustive recounting of the entire year! This is probably not much more than the background image you put on your desktop.

File locations

All file-open facilities should remember where the user gets his files. Most users only access files from a few directories for each given program. The program should remember these source directories and offer them on a combobox on the File-Open dialog. The user should never have to step through the tree to a given directory more than once.

Deduced information

Software should not simply remember these kinds of explicit facts, but should also remember useful information that can be deduced from these facts. For example, if the program remembers the number of bytes changed in the file each time it is opened, it can help the user with some reasonableness checks. Imagine that the changed-byte-count for a file was 126, 94, 43, 74, 81, 70, 110, and 92. If the user calls up the file and changes 100 bytes, nothing would be out of the ordinary. But if the number of changed bytes suddenly shoots up to 5000, the program might suspect that something is amiss. Although there is a chance that the user has inadvertently done something about which he will be sorry, the probability of that is low, so it isn't right to bother him with a confirmation dialog. It is, however, very reasonable for the program to make sure to keep a milestone copy of the file before the 5000 bytes were changed, just in case. The program probably won't need to keep it beyond the next time the user accesses that file, because the user will likely spot any mistake that glaring immediately, and he would then demand an undo.

Multi-session undo

Most programs discard their stack of undo actions when the user closes the document or the program. This is very shortsighted on the program's part. Instead, the program could write the undo stack to a file. When the user reopens the file, the program could reload its undo stack with the actions the user performed the last time the program was run — even if that was a week ago!

Past data entries

A program with a better memory can reduce the number of errors the user makes. This is simply because the user has to enter less information. More of it will be entered automatically from the program's memory. In an invoicing program, for example, if the software enters the date, department number, and other standard fields from memory, the user has fewer opportunities to make typing errors in these fields.

If the program remembers what the user enters and uses that information for future reasonableness checks, the program can work to keep erroneous data from being entered. Imagine a data entry program where zip codes and city names are remembered from run to run. When the user enters a familiar city name along with an unfamiliar zip code, the field can turn yellow, indicating uncertainty about the match. And when the user enters a familiar city name with a zip code already associated with another city, the field can turn pink, indicating a more serious ambiguity. He wouldn't necessarily have to take any action because of these colors, but the warning is there if he wants it.

Some Windows 2000 and XP applications, notably Internet Explorer, have a facility of similar nature: Named data entry fields remember what has been entered into them before, and allow the user to pick those values from a combobox. For security-minded individuals, this feature can be turned off, but for the rest of us, it saves time and prevents errors.

Foreign application activities on program files

Applications might also leave a small thread running between invocations. This little program can keep an eye on the files it worked on. It can track where they go and who reads and writes to them. This information might be helpful to the user when he next runs the application. When he tries to open a particular file, the program can help him find it, even if it has been moved. The program can keep the user informed about what other functions were performed on his file, such as whether or not it was printed or faxed to someone. Sure, this information might not be needed, but the computer can easily spare the time, and it's only bits that have to be thrown away, after all.

Applying Memory to Your Applications

A remarkable thing happens to the software design process when developers accept the power of task coherence. Designers find that their thinking takes on a whole new quality. The normally unquestioned recourse of popping up a dialog box gets replaced with a more studied process, where the designer asks questions of much greater subtlety. Questions like: How *much* should the program remember? Which aspects should be remembered? Should the program remember more than just the last setting? What constitutes a change in pattern? Designers start to imagine situations like this: The user accepts the same date format 50 times in a row, and then manually enters a different format once. The next time the user enters a date, which format should the program use? The format used 50 times or the more recent one-time format? How many times must the new format be specified before it becomes the default? Just because there is ambiguity here, the program still shouldn't ask the user. It must use its initiative to make a reasonable decision. The user is free to override the program's decision if it is the wrong one.

The following sections explain some characteristic patterns in the ways people make choices that can help us resolve these more complex questions about task coherence.

Decision-set reduction

People tend to reduce an infinite set of choices down to a small, finite set of choices. Even when you don't do the exact same thing each time, you will tend to choose your actions from a small, repetitive set of options. People unconsciously perform this **decision-set reduction**, but software can take notice and act upon it.

For example, just because you went shopping at Safeway yesterday doesn't necessarily mean that you will be shopping at Safeway exclusively. However, the next time you need groceries, you will probably shop at Safeway again. Similarly, even though your favorite Chinese restaurant has 250 items on the menu, chances are that you will usually choose from your own personal subset of five or six favorites. When people drive to and from work, they usually choose from a small number of favorite routes, depending on traffic conditions. Computers, of course, can remember four or five things without breaking a sweat.

Although simply remembering the last action is better than not remembering anything, it can lead to a peculiar pathology if the decision-set consists of precisely two elements. If, for example, you alternately read files from one directory and store them in another, each time the program offers you the last directory, it will be guaranteed to be wrong. The solution is to remember more than just one previous choice.

Decision-set reduction guides us to the idea that pieces of information the program must remember about the user's choices tend to come in groups. Instead of there being one right way, there will be several options that are all correct. The program should look for more subtle clues to differentiate which one of the small set is correct. For example, if you use a check-writing program to pay your bills, the program may very quickly learn that only two or three accounts are used regularly. But how can it determine from a given check which of the three accounts is the most likely to be appropriate? If the program remembers the payees and amounts on an account-by-account basis, that decision would be easy. Every time you pay the rent, it is the exact same amount! It's the same with a car payment. The amount paid to the electric company might vary from check to check, but it probably stays within 10 or 20 percent of the last check written to them. All this information can be used to help the program recognize what is going on, and use that information to help the user.

Preference thresholds

The decisions people make tend to fall into two primary categories: important and unimportant. Any given activity may involve potentially hundreds of decisions, but only a very few of them are important. All the rest are insignificant. Software interfaces can use this idea of preference thresholds to simplify tasks for users.

After you decide to buy that car, you don't really care who finances it as long as the terms are competitive. After you decide to buy groceries, the particular checkout aisle you select is not important. After you decide to ride the Matterhorn, you don't really care which toboggan they seat you in.

Preference thresholds guide us in our user interface design by demonstrating that asking the user for successively detailed decisions about a procedure is unnecessary. After the user asks to print, we don't have to ask him how many copies he wants or whether the image is landscape or portrait. We can make an assumption about these things the first time out, and then remember them for all subsequent invocations. If the user wants to change them, he can always request the Printer Options dialog box.

Using preference thresholds, we can easily track which facilities of the program the user likes to adjust and which are set once and ignored. With this knowledge, the program can offer choices where it has an expectation that the user will want to take control, not bothering the user with decisions he won't care about.

Mostly right, most of the time

Task coherence predicts what the user will do in the future with reasonable, but not absolute, certainty. If our program relies on this principle, it's natural to wonder about the uncertainty of our predictions. If we can reliably predict what the user will do 80% of the time, it means that 20% of the time we will be wrong. It might seem that the proper step to take here is to offer the user a choice, but this means that the user will be bothered by an unnecessary dialog 80% of the time. Rather than offering a choice, the program should go ahead and do what it thinks is most appropriate and allow the user to override or undo it. If the undo facility is sufficiently easy to use and understand, the user won't be bothered by it. After all, he will have to use undo only two times out of ten instead of having to deal with a redundant dialog box eight times out of ten. This is a much better deal for humans.

Memory Makes a Difference

One of the main reasons our software is often so difficult to use is because its designers have made rational, logical assumptions that, unfortunately, are very wrong. They assume that the behavior of users is random and unpredictable, and that users must be interrogated to determine the proper course of action. Although human behavior certainly isn't deterministic like that of a digital computer, it is rarely random, and asking silly questions is predictably frustrating for users.

However, when we apply memory via task coherence to our software, we can realize great advantages in user efficiency and satisfaction. We would all like to have an assistant who is intelligent and self-motivated, one who shows initiative and drive, and who demonstrates good judgment and a keen memory. A program that makes effective use of its memory would be more like that self-motivated assistant, remembering helpful information and personal preferences from execution to execution without needing to ask. Simple things can make a big difference: the difference between a product your users tolerate, and one that they *love*. The next time you find your program asking your users a question, make it ask itself one instead.

Chapter 16

Improving Data Retrieval

In the physical world, storing and retrieving are inextricably linked; putting an item on a shelf (storing it) also gives us the means to find it later (retrieving it). In the digital world, the only thing linking these two concepts is our faulty thinking. Computers will enable remarkably sophisticated retrieval techniques if only we are able to break our thinking out of its traditional box. This chapter discusses methods of data retrieval from an interaction standpoint and presents some more human-centered approaches to the problem of finding useful information.

Storage and Retrieval Systems

A **storage system** is a method for safekeeping goods in a repository. It is a physical system composed of a container and the tools necessary to put objects in and take them back out again. A **retrieval system** is a method for finding goods in a repository. It is a logical system that allows the goods to be located according to some abstract value, like name, position or some aspect of the contents.

As we discussed in Chapter 13, disks and files are usually rendered in implementation terms rather than in accord with the user's mental model of how information is stored. This is also true in the methods we use for *finding* information after it has been stored. This is extremely unfortunate because the computer is the one tool capable of providing us with significantly better methods of finding information than those physically possible using mechanical systems. But before we talk about how to improve retrieval, let's briefly discuss how it works.

Storage and Retrieval in the Physical World

We can own a book or a hammer without giving it a name or a permanent place of residence in our houses. A book can be identified by characteristics other than a name — a color or a shape, for example. However, after we accumulate a large number of items that we need to find and use, it helps to be a bit more organized.

Everything in its place: Storage and retrieval by location

It is important that there be a proper place for our books and hammers, because that is how we find them when we need them. We can't just whistle and expect them to find us; we must know where they are and then go there and fetch them. In the physical world, the actual location of a thing is the means to finding it. Remembering where we put something — its address — is vital both to finding it, and putting it away so it can be found again. When we want to find a spoon, for example, we go to the place where we keep our spoons. We don't find the spoon by referring to any inherent characteristic of the spoon itself. Similarly, when we look for a book, we either go to where we left the book, or we guess that it is stored with other books. We don't find the book by association. That is, we don't find the book by referring to its contents.

In this model, which works just fine in your home, the storage system is the same as the retrieval system: Both are based on remembering locations. They are coupled storage and retrieval systems.

Indexed retrieval

This system of everything in its proper place sounds pretty good, but it has a flaw: It is limited in scale by human memory. Although it works for the books, hammers, and spoons in your house, it doesn't work at all for the volumes stored, for example, in the Library of Congress.

In the world of books and paper on library shelves, we make use of another tool to help us find things: the Dewey Decimal system (named after its inventor, American philosopher and educator John Dewey). The idea was brilliant: Give every book title a unique number based on its subject matter and title and shelve the books in this numerical order. If you know the number, you can easily find the book, and other books related to it by subject would be near by—perfect for research. The only remaining issue was how to discover the number for a given book. Certainly nobody could be expected to remember every number.

The solution was an **index**, a collection of records that allows you to find the *location* of an item by looking up an **attribute** of the item, such as its name. Traditional library card catalogs provided lookup by three attributes: author, subject, and title. When the book is entered into the library system and assigned a number, three index cards are created for the book, including all particulars and the Dewey Decimal number. Each card is headed by the author's name, the subject, or the title. These cards are then placed in their respective indices in alphabetical order. When you want to find a book, you look it up in one of the indices and find its number. You then find the row of shelves that contains books with numbers in the same range as your target by examining signs. You search those particular shelves, narrowing your view by the lexical order of the numbers until you find the one you want.

You *physically* retrieve the book by participating in the system of storage, but you *logically* find the book you want by participating in a system of retrieval. The shelves and numbers are the storage system. The card indices are the retrieval system. You identify the desired book with one and fetch it with the other. In a typical university or professional library, customers are not allowed into the stacks. As a customer, you identify the book you want by using only the retrieval system. The librarian then fetches the book for you by participating only in the storage system. The unique serial number is the bridge between these two interdependent systems. In the physical world, both the retrieval system and the storage system may be very labor intensive. Particularly in older, non-computerized libraries, they are both inflexible. Adding a fourth index based on acquisition date, for example, would be prohibitively difficult for the library.

Storage and Retrieval in the Digital World

Unlike in the physical world of books, stacks, and cards, it's not very hard to add an index in the computer. Ironically, in a system where easily implementing dynamic, associative retrieval mechanisms is at last possible, we often don't implement *any* retrieval system. Astonishingly, we don't use indices at all on the desktop.

In most of today's computer systems, there is no retrieval system other than the storage system. If you want to find a file on disk you need to know its name and its place. It's as if we went into the library, burned the card catalog, and told the patrons that they could easily find what they want by just remembering the little numbers painted on the spines of the books. We have put 100 percent of the burden of file retrieval on the user's memory while the CPU just sits there idling, executing billions of NOP instructions.

Although our desktop computers can handle hundreds of different indices, we ignore this capability and have no indices at all pointing into the files stored on our disks. Instead, we have to remember where we put our files and what we called them in order to find them again. This omission is one of the most destructive, backward steps in modern software design. This failure can be attributed to the interdependence of files and the organizational systems in which they exist, an interdependence that doesn't exist in the mechanical world.

Retrieval methods

There are three fundamental ways to find a document on a computer. You can find it by remembering where you left it in the file structure, by **positional retrieval**. You can find it by remembering its identifying name, by **identity retrieval**. The third method, **associative** or **attributed-based retrieval**, is based on the ability to search for a document based on some inherent quality of the document itself. For example, if you want to find a book with a red cover, or one that discusses light rail transit systems, or one that contains photographs of steam locomotives, or one that mentions Theodore Judah, the method you must use is associative.

Both positional and identity retrieval are methods that also function as storage systems, and on computers, which can sort reasonably well by name, they are practically one and the same. Associative retrieval is the one method that is not also a storage system. If our retrieval system is based solely on storage methods, we deny ourselves any attribute-based searching and we must depend on memory. Our user must know what information he wants and where it is stored in order to find it. To find the spreadsheet in which he calculated the amortization of his home loan he has to know that he stored it in the directory called Home and that it was called amort1. If he doesn't remember either of these facts, finding the document can become quite difficult.

An attribute-based retrieval system

For early GUI systems like the original Macintosh, a positional retrieval system almost made sense: The desktop metaphor dictated it (you don't use an index to look up papers on your desk), and there were precious few documents that could be stored on a 144K floppy disk. However, our current desktop systems can now easily hold 250,000 times as many documents! Yet we still use the same metaphors and retrieval model to manage our data. We continue to render our software's retrieval systems in strict adherence to the implementation model of the storage system, ignoring the power and ease-of-use of a system for *finding* files that is distinct from the system for *keeping* files.

An attribute-based retrieval system would enable us to find our documents by their contents. For example, we could find all documents that contain the text string "superelevation". For such a search system to really be effective, it should know where all documents can be found, so the user doesn't have to say "Go look in such-and-such a directory and find all documents that mention "superelevation." This system would, of course, know a little bit about the domain of its search so it wouldn't try to search the entire Internet, for example, for "superelevation" unless we insist.

A well-crafted, attribute-based retrieval system would also enable the user to browse by synonym or related topics or by assigning attributes to individual documents. The user can then dynamically define sets of documents having these overlapping attributes. For example, imagine a consulting business where each potential client is sent a proposal letter. Each of these letters is different and is naturally grouped with the files pertinent to that client. However, there is a definite relationship between each of these letters because they all serve the same function: proposing a business relationship. It would be very convenient if a user could find and gather up all such proposal letters while allowing each one to retain its uniqueness and association with its particular client. A file system based on place — on its single storage location — must of necessity store each document by a single attribute rather than multiple characteristics.

The system can learn a lot about each document just by keeping its eyes and ears open. If the attribute-based retrieval system remembers some of this information, much of the setup burden on the user is made unnecessary. The program could, for example, easily remember such things as:

✓ The program that created the document

✓ The type of document: words, numbers, tables, graphics

✓ The program that last opened the document

✓ If the document is exceptionally large or small

✓ If the document has been untouched for a long time

✓ The length of time the document was last open

✓ The amount of information that was added or deleted during the last edit

✓ Whether or not the document has been edited by more than one type of program

✓ Whether the document contains embedded objects from other programs

✓ If the document was created from scratch or cloned from another

✓ If the document is frequently edited

✓ If the document is frequently viewed but rarely edited

✓ Whether the document has been printed and where

✓ How often the document has been printed, and whether changes were made to it each time immediately before printing

✓ Whether the document has been faxed and to whom

✓ Whether the document has been e-mailed and to whom

The retrieval system could find documents for the user based on these facts without the user ever having to explicitly record anything in advance. Can you think of other useful attributes the system might remember?

One product on the market provides much of this functionality for Windows. Enfish Corporation sells a suite of personal and enterprise products that dynamically and invisibly create an index of information on your computer system, across a LAN if you desire it (the Professional version), and even across the Web. It tracks documents, bookmarks, contacts, and e-mails — extracting all the reasonable attributes. It also provides powerful sorting and filtering capability. It is truly a remarkable set of products. We should all learn from the Enfish example.

There is nothing wrong with the disk file storage systems that we have created for ourselves. The only problem is that we have failed to create adequate disk file *retrieval* systems. Instead, we hand the user the storage system and call it a retrieval system. This is like handing him a bag of groceries and calling it a gourmet dinner. There is no reason to change our file storage systems. The Unix model is fine. Our programs can easily remember the names and locations of the files they have worked on, so they aren't the ones who need a retrieval system: It's for us human users.

Relational Databases versus Digital Soup

Software that uses database technology makes two simple demands of its users: First, the user must define the form of the data in advance; second, the user must then conform to that definition. There are also two facts about human users of software: First, they never know what they are going to want in advance; and second, even if they did, more often than not they change their minds.

Organizing the unorganizable

Now that we live in the Internet age, we find ourselves more and more frequently confronting information systems that fail the relational database litmus: We can neither define information in advance, nor can we reliably stick to any definition we might conjure up. In particular, two phenomena, both experiencing exponential growth, exemplify this dilemma.

The first phenomenon is electronic mail. Whereas a record in a database has a specific identity, and thus belongs in a table of objects of the same type, an e-mail message doesn't fit this paradigm very well. We can divide our e-mail into incoming and outgoing, but that doesn't help us much. For example, if you receive a piece of e-mail from Jerry about Sally, regarding the Ajax Project, and how it relates to Jones Consulting and your joint presentation at the board meeting. You can file this away in the "Jerry" folder, or the "Sally" folder, or the "Ajax" folder, but what you really want to do is to file it in all of them. In six months, you might try to find this message for any number of unpredictable reasons, and you'll want to be able to find it, regardless of your reason.

The second phenomenon is the Web. Like an infinite, chaotic, redundant, unsupervised hard disk, the Web defies being structured. Enormous quantities of information are available on the Internet, but its sheer quantity and heterogeneity guarantee that no regular system could ever be imposed on it (we'll see where the Semantic Web initiatives engaged in by the W3C take us; perhaps there is hope). Even if the Web could be organized, the method would likely have to exist on the outside, because its contents are owned by millions of individuals, none of whom are subject to any authority. Unlike records in a database, we cannot expect to find a predictable identifying mark in a record on the Internet.

Problems with databases

There's a further problem with databases: All database records are of a single, predefined type, and all instances of a record type are grouped together. A record may represent an invoice or a customer, but it never represents an invoice *and* a customer. Similarly, a field within a record may be a name or a social security number, but it is never a name *and* a social security number. This is the fundamental concept underlying all databases—it serves the vital purpose of allowing us to impose order on our storage system. Unfortunately, it fails miserably to address the realities of retrieval for our e-mail problem: It is not enough that the e-mail from Jerry is a record of type "e-mail". Somehow, we must also identify it as a record of type "Jerry", type "Sally", type "Ajax", type "Jones Consulting", and type "Board Meeting". We must also be able to add and change its identity at will, even after the record has been stored away. What's more, a record of type "Ajax" may refer to documents other than e-mail messages—a project plan for example. Because the record format is unpredictable, the value that identifies the record as pertaining to Ajax cannot be stored reliably within the record itself. This is in direct contradiction to the way databases work.

Databases do provide us with retrieval tools with a bit more flexibility than matching simple record types. They allow us to find and fetch a record by examining its contents and matching them against search criteria. For example, we search for invoice number "77329" or for the customer with the identifying string "Goodyear Tire and Rubber". Yet, this *still* fails for our e-mail problem. If we allow the user to enter the keywords "Jerry", "Sally", "Ajax", "Jones Consulting", and "Board Meeting" into the message record, we must define such fields in advance. But as we've said, defining things in advance doesn't guarantee that the user will follow that definition later. He may now be looking for messages about the company picnic, for example. Besides, adding a series of keyword fields leads you into one of the must fundamental and universal conundrums of data processing: If you give users ten fields, someone is bound to want eleven.

The attribute-based alternative

So, if relational database technology isn't right, what is? If users find it hard to define their information in advance as databases require, is there an alternative storage and retrieval system that might work well for them?

Once again, the key is separating the storage and retrieval system. If an *index* were used as the retrieval system, the storage technique could still remain a database. We can imagine the storage facility as a sort of **digital soup** where we could put our records. This soup would accept any record we dumped into it, regardless of its size, length, type, or contents. Whenever a record was entered, the program would return a token that could be used to retrieve the record. All we have to do is give it back that token, and the soup instantly returns our record. This is just our storage system, however; we still need a retrieval system that manages all those tokens for us.

Attribute-based retrieval thus comes to our rescue: We can create an index that stores a key value along with a copy of the token. The real magic, though, is that we can create an infinite number of indices, each one representing its own key and containing a copy of the token. For example, if our digital soup contained all our e-mail messages, we could establish an index for each of our old friends, "Jerry", "Sally", "Ajax", "Jones Consulting", and "Board Meeting". Now, when we need to find e-mail pertinent to the board meeting, we don't have to paw manually and tediously through dozens of folders. Instead, a single query brings us everything we are looking for.

Of course, someone or something must fill those indices, but that is a more mundane exercise in interaction design. There are two components to consider. First, the system needs to be able to read e-mail messages and automatically extract and index information like proper names, Internet addresses, street addresses, phone numbers, and other significant data. Second, the system must make it very easy for a user to add ad hoc pointers to messages. He should be able to explicitly specify that a given e-mail message pertains to a specific value, whether or not that value is quoted verbatim in the message. Typing is okay, but selecting from pick-lists, clicking-and-dragging, and other more advanced user interface idioms can make the task almost painless.

Significant advantages arise from a world where the storage system is reduced in importance and the retrieval system is separated from it and significantly enhanced. Some form of digital soup will help us to get control of the unpredictable information that is beginning to make up more and more of our everyday information universe. We can offer users powerful information management tools without demanding that they configure their information in advance or that they conform to that configuration in the future. After all, they can't do it. So why insist?

Natural Language Output: An Ideal Interface for Attribute-Based Retrieval

In the previous sections of this chapter, we've discussed the merits of attribute-based retrieval. This kind of a system, to be truly successful, requires a front end that allows users to very easily make sense of what could be quite complex and interrelated sets of attributes.

One alternative is to use natural language processing, where the user can key in his request in English. The problem with this method is that it is not possible for today's run-of-the-mill computers to effectively understand natural language queries in most commercial situations. It might work reasonably in the laboratory under tightly controlled conditions, but not in the real world where it is subject to whim, dialect, colloquialism, and misunderstanding. In any case, the programming of a natural language recognition engine is beyond the capabilities and budget of your average programming team.

A better approach, which the authors have used successfully, is a technique for which we've coined the name **natural language output**. Using this technique, the program proffers to the user an array of bounded controls to choose from. The controls line up so that they can be read like an English sentence. The user chooses from a grammar of valid alternatives, so the design is in essence a self-documenting, bounded query facility. Figure 16-1 shows how it works.

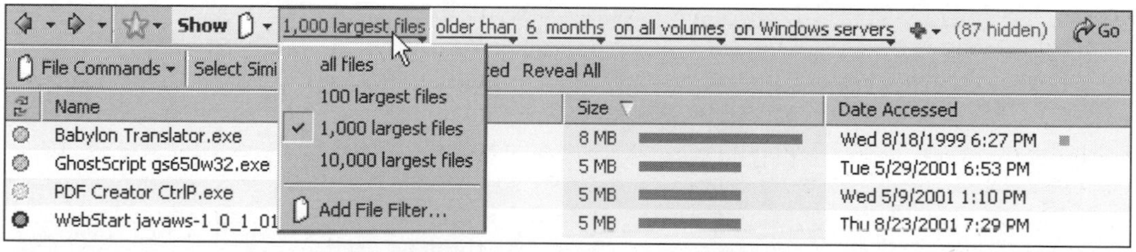

Figure 16-1: An example of a natural language output interface to an attribute-based retrieval engine, part of a Cooper design created for Softek's Storage Manager. These controls produce natural language as output, rather than attempting to accept natural language as input, for database queries. Each underlined phrase, when clicked, provides a drop-down menu with a list of selectable options. The user constructs a sentence from a dynamic series of choices that always guarantees a valid result.

A natural language output interface is also a natural for expressing everything from queries to plain old relational databases. Querying a database in the usual fashion is very hard for most people because it calls for Boolean notation and arcane database syntax, ala SQL. We discussed the problems with Boolean notation in Chapter 2. We determined that just because the program needs to understand Boolean queries, users shouldn't be forced to as well.

English isn't Boolean, so the English clauses aren't joined with AND and OR, but rather with English phrases like "all of the following apply" or "not all of the following apply." The user finds that choosing among these phrases is easy because they are very clear and bounded, and when he is done, he can read it like a sentence to check its validity.

The trickiest part of natural language output from a programming perspective is that choosing from controls on the left may, in many circumstances, change the content of the choices in controls to the right of them, in a cascading fashion. This means that in order to effectively implement natural language output, the grammars of the choices need to be well mapped out in advance, and also that the controls need to be dynamically changeable or hidable, depending on what is selected in other controls. It also means the controls themselves must be able to display or, at least, load data dynamically.

The other concern is localization. If you are designing for multiple languages, those with very different word orders (for example, German and English) may require different grammar mappings.

Both attribute-based retrieval engines and natural language output interfaces require a significant design and programming effort, but users will reap tremendous benefits in terms of the power and flexibility in managing their data. Because the amount of data we all must manage is growing at an exponential rate, it makes sense to invest now in these more powerful, goal-directed tools wherever data must be managed.

Chapter 17

Improving Data Entry

In Chapter 14, we discussed the need for considerate software that knows when to bend the rules. One of the ways in which software is least capable is in regard to how it handles data entry. This is an artifact of the history of software development—in particular, the development of database software. In this chapter, we'll discuss the problems with existing ways of dealing with data entry and some possible ways to make this process more focused on human needs and less focused on the needs of the database.

Data Integrity versus Data Immunity

The development imperative regarding data entry and data processing is simple: Never let tainted, unclean data get into the software. The programmer erects barriers in the user interface so that bad data can never enter the system. This pure internal state is commonly called **data integrity**.

The imperative of data integrity posits that there is a world of chaotic information out there, and before any of it gets inside the computer it must be filtered and cleaned up. The software must maintain a vigilant watch for bad data, like customs officials at a border crossing (see Figure 17-1). All data is made valid at its point of entry. Anything on the outside is assumed to be suspect, and after it has run the gauntlet and been allowed inside, it is assumed to be pristine. The advantage is that once inside the database, the code doesn't have to bother with successive, repetitive checks on the validity or appropriateness of the data.

The disadvantage of this method is simple: It places the needs of the database before that of the user, subjecting him to the equivalent of a shakedown every time he enters a scrap of data into the computer. Note that this isn't a problem with most personal software: PowerPoint doesn't know or care if you've formatted your presentation correctly. But as soon as you deal with a large corporation, whether you are a clerk performing data entry for an enterprise management system, or a Web surfer buying DVDs online, you come face to face with the border patrol.

Humans, especially those filling out lots of forms every day as part of their job, know that data isn't provided to them in the pristine form that their software demands. They know that their information is incomplete, and sometimes wrong. They know that sometimes they need to expedite processing to make their customers happy. But when confronted with a system that is entirely inflexible in such matters, data processors must either grind to a halt or find some way to subvert the system to get things done. If, however, the software recognized these facts of human existence and allowed for them in its interface, everyone would benefit.

Make no mistake: When our software shakes down data at the point of entry, when it strip-searches the user to assure that he isn't carrying any contraband into the high-security depths of the computer, it makes a very clear statement. It tells us that the user is insignificant and that the program is omnipotent—that the user works for the good of the program and not vice versa.

This is not the impression that we want to give. We want the user to feel in charge; to feel that the program works for him; that the program is doing the work while the user makes the decisions.

Happily, there's more than one way to protect software from bad data. Instead of keeping it out of the system, the programmer needs to make the system *immune* to inconsistencies and gaps in the information. This method involves writing much smarter, more sophisticated code that can robustly handle all permutations of data, giving the program a kind of **data immunity**.

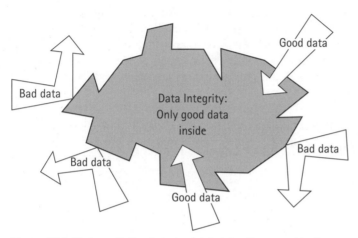

Figure 17-1: Underneath the rhetoric of data integrity — an objective imperative of protecting the user and computer with sanctified data — there is a disturbing subtext: that humans are ill-intentioned screw-ups and that users will, given the chance, enter the most bizarre garbage possible in a deliberate attempt to bring the system to its knees. This is not true. Users will *inadvertently* enter erroneous data, but that is different from implying that they do it intentionally. Users are very sensitive to subtext; they will quickly perceive that the program doesn't trust them. Data integrity not only hampers the system from serving the user for the dubious benefit of easing the programmer's burden, but it also offends the user with its high-handed attitude. It's another case of requiring users to adapt to the needs of the computer, rather than the computer meeting the needs of users.

Data immunity

To implement data immunity, our programs must be trained to look before they leap, and they must be trained to ask for help. Most software blindly performs arithmetic on numbers without actually examining them first. The program assumes that a number field must contain a number — data integrity tells it so. If the user entered the word "nine" instead of the number "9", the program would croak, but a human reading the form wouldn't even blink. If the program simply looked at the data before it acted, it would see that a simple math function wouldn't do the trick.

We must train our programs to believe that the user will enter what he means to enter, and if the user wants to correct things, he will do so without our paranoid insistence. But the program can look elsewhere in the computer for assistance. Is there a module that knows how to make numeric sense of alphabetic text? Is there a history of corrections that might shed some light on the user's intent?

If all else fails, the program must add annotations to the data so that when — and if — the user comes to examine the problem, he finds accurate and complete notes that describe what happened and what steps the program took.

Yes, if users enter "asdf" instead of "9.38" the program won't be able to arrive at satisfactory results. But stopping the program to resolve this *right now* is not a satisfactory process either; the entry process is just as important as the end report. If the user interface is designed correctly, the program provides visual feedback when the user enters "asdf", so the likelihood of the user entering hundreds of bad records is very low. Generally, users only act stupidly when programs treat them stupidly.

Most often, the incorrect data that the user enters is still reasonable for the situation. If the program expects a two-letter state code, the user may enter "TZ" by accident. However, if that same user enters "Dallas" for the city name, it doesn't take a lot of intelligence to figure out the problem. Fixing missing postal codes won't tax our modern, powerful computers. In the rare cases where a postal code locator program might fail, most humans would likely fail, too.

What about lost data?

It is clearly counter to everyone's wishes if information is lost. The data entry clerk who fails to key in the invoice amount and then discards the invoice creates a real problem. But is it really the righteous duty of the program to stop the user and point out this failure? No, it isn't. You have to consider the situation. If the application is a desktop productivity program, the user is interacting with it, and the results of his error will likely become apparent. In any case, the user will be driving the program like a car, and he won't take kindly to having the steering wheel lock up because the Chevy discovered it was low on windshield-washer fluid.

On the other hand, let's say the user is a full-time data-entry clerk keying forms into a corporate data-entry program. Our clerk does this one job for a living, and he has spent hundreds — maybe thousands — of hours using the program. He has a sixth sense for what is happening on the screen and knows at a glance whether he has entered bad data, particularly if the program is using subtle, modeless visual and audible cues to keep him informed of the status of the data.

The program is also helping out: Data items, like part numbers that *must* be valid, aren't going to be typed in, but are entered through List views or other bounded controls. Addresses and phone numbers are entered more naturally into smart fields that can help parse the data. The program gives the user frequent positive feedback, so the program begins to act as a partner, helping him stay aware of the status of his work. So, how serious is the loss of data?

In a data-entry situation, a missing field can be serious, but the field is usually entered incorrectly rather than just omitted. The program can easily help the clerk detect the problem and change it to a valid entry without stopping the proceedings. If the clerk is determined to omit necessary fields, the problem is the clerk and not the program. The percentage of clerks who fail either because of lack of ability or sociopathic tendencies is likely quite low. It isn't the job of the data-entry program to treat all data entry clerks as though they can't be trusted to do a simple job just because one out of a hundred can't.

Most of our information processing systems *are* tolerant of missing information. A missing name, code, number, or price can almost always be reconstructed from other data in the record. If not, the data can always be reconstructed by asking the various parties involved in the transaction. The cost is high, but not as high as the cost of technical help centers, for example. Our information processing systems can work just fine with missing data. The programmers who write these systems just don't like all the extra work involved in dealing with missing data, so they invoke data integrity as an unbreakable, deified law. Thousands of clerks must, therefore, interact with rigid fascist-ware to keep databases from crashing — not to prevent their business from failing.

It is obviously counter-productive to treat all your workers like idiots to protect against those few who are. It lowers everyone's productivity, encourages rapid, expensive, and error-causing turnover, and it decreases morale, which increases the unintentional error rate of the clerks who want to do well. It is a self-fulfilling prophecy to assume that your information workers are untrustworthy.

The stereotypical role of the data-entry clerk mindlessly keypunching from stacks of paper forms while sitting in a boiler room among hundreds of identical clerks doing identical jobs is rapidly evaporating. The task of data entry is becoming less a mass-production job and more of a productivity job: a job performed by intelligent, capable professionals and, with the advent of e-commerce, directly by customers. In other words, the population interacting with data-entry software is increasingly less tolerant of being treated like unambitious, uneducated, unintelligent peons. Users won't tolerate stupid software that insults them, not when they can push a button and surf for another few seconds until they find another vendor who presents an interface that treats them with respect.

Data entry and fudgeability

When entry systems work to keep bad data out of the system, they almost never allow the user to *fudge*. There is no way to make marginal comments or to add an annotation next to a field. For example, a vitally necessary item of data may be missing, an interest rate, say. If the system won't allow the transaction to be entered without a valid interest rate, it stops the company from doing business. What if the interest rate field on the loan application had a penciled note next to it, initialed by the bank president, that said: "Prime plus three the day the cash is delivered"? The system, working hard to maintain perfection, fails the reality test.

If an automated data processing system is too rigid, it won't model the real world. A system that rejects reality is not helpful, even if all its fields are valid. In this case, you must ask yourself the question: "Which is more important, the database or the business it is trying to support?" The people who manage the database and create the data-entry programs that feed it are serving only the CPU. It is a significant conflict of interest that only interaction design, knowledgeable in but detached from development, can resolve.

Fudgeability can be difficult to build into a computer system because it demands a considerably more capable interface. The clerk cannot move a document to the top of the queue unless the queue, the document, and its position in the queue can be easily seen. The tools for pulling a document out of the electronic stack and placing it on the top must also be present and obvious in their functions. Fudgeability also requires facilities to hold records in suspense, but an undo facility has similar requirements. A more significant problem is that fudging admits the potential for abuse.

The saving grace to avoid abuse is that the computer also has the power to easily track all the user's actions, recording them in detail for any outside observer. The principle is a simple one: Let the user do whatever he wants, but keep very detailed records of those actions so that full accountability is easy.

Auditing versus Editing

Many programmers believe that it is their duty to inform the user when he has made an error in entering data. It is certainly the program's duty to inform *other programs* when they make an error, but this rule shouldn't extend to users. The customer is always right, so the program must accept whatever the user tells it, regardless of what the program does or doesn't know. This is similar to the concept of data immunity because whatever the user enters should be acceptable, regardless of how incorrect the program believes it to be.

This doesn't mean that the program can wipe its hands and say, "All right, he doesn't want a life preserver, so I'll just let him drown." Just because the program must act as though the user is always right, this doesn't mean that the user actually *is* always right. Humans are always making mistakes, and your users are no exception. Users' errors may not be your program's fault, but they are its responsibility. How are you going to fix it?

An error may not be your fault, but it's your responsibility.

The program can provide warnings — as long as they don't stop the proceedings with idiocy — but if the user chooses to do something suspect, the program can do nothing but accept the fact and work to protect the user from harm. Like a faithful guide, it must follow its master into the jungle, making sure to bring along an elephant gun and plenty of ammunition.

Warnings should use modeless techniques on the surface of the active window to inform the user of what he has done, much like the way the speedometer silently reports our speed violations. It is not reasonable, however, for the program to stop the proceedings with modal idiocy, just like it is not right for the speedometer to cut the gas when we edge above 65 miles per hour. Instead of an error message box, for example, edit fields can highlight any user input it evaluates as suspect.

When the user does something that the program is sure is wrong, there is only one way to protect him. If we edit his work without telling him, he will be proceeding into the jungle on false pretenses, so we cannot do that. If we edit his work and ensure that he knows about it, we will have to use an error message or a confirmation dialog box. This is also not acceptable. The only choice we have is to run along behind our brave user, making sure that he doesn't come to harm. We keep track of his path into the jungle; we remember each of his actions; we ensure that each action can be cleanly reversed; we ensure that no collateral information is lost and that the user can figure out where we think the problems might be. Essentially, we maintain a clear audit trail of his actions. Thus, the axiom: Audit, don't edit.

AXIOM

Audit, don't edit.

If you can't manage entered data by using bounded controls, you must accept whatever the user gives you. Then keep track of what you did and didn't get, and if anybody demands that things get straightened out, you will have full records that will enable you to do so. You could, for example, make an internal note that the data wasn't quite right yet and make that information available to the user. The user can then judge whether the absence of the data will cause the planets to halt in their orbits. This means that the software should keep track of who, what, where, how, and when the user is doing things, so the situation can be modified, rectified, or just plain understood at some later date. This is much more human than merely forcing the data into some arbitrary format whose correctness is judged mostly on its compliance to a file schema rather than to a human need.

Microsoft Word has an excellent example of auditing, as well as a nasty counter-example. The excellent example is the way it handles spell checking: Little wavy underlines appear in the text as you type, identifying words that its spelling and grammar dictionaries don't recognize (see Figure 17-2). Right-clicking on these words pops up a menu of alternatives you can choose from — but you don't have to change anything, and you are not interrupted by dialogs or other modal idiocy.

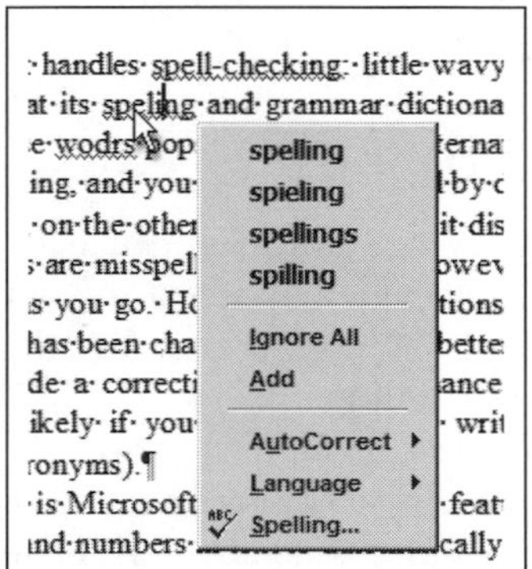

Figure 17–2: Microsoft Word's automatic spelling checker audits misspelled words with a wavy red underline, providing modeless feedback to users. Right-clicking on an underlined word pops open a menu of possible alternatives to choose from.

Word's AutoCorrect feature, on the other hand, is a little bit disturbing at first. As you type, it silently changes words it thinks are misspelled. It turns out, however, that this feature is incredibly useful for fixing minor typos as you go. However, the corrections leave no audit trail, so the user has no idea that what he typed has been changed. It would be better if Word could provide some kind of mark that indicates it has made a correction on the off chance that it has miscorrected something (which becomes much more likely if you are, for instance, writing a technical paper heavy in specialized terminology and acronyms).

More frightening, however, is Microsoft's AutoFormat feature, which tries to interpret user behaviors like use of asterisks and numbers in text to automatically format numbered lists and other paragraph formats. When this works, it seems magical; but frequently the program does the wrong thing, and once it does so, the action is difficult to undo. The problem with AutoFormat is that the software is trying to be just a bit too smart; it should leave the thinking to the human. Luckily, this feature can be turned off.

In the real world, humans accept partially and incorrectly filled-in documents all the time. We make a mental (or otherwise) note to fix it later, and we usually do. If we forget, we fix it when we eventually discover the omission. Even if we never fix it, we somehow muddle through. Who said that these behaviors should be different for computer software than it is for humans? Programmers, that's who. They say they reject incomplete or inaccurate data for our own good, but actually they do so for *their* own good — so they don't have to write the more difficult code that deals with the unexpected. Humans don't die if they try to divide by zero, but computer programs do.

Chapter 18

Designing for Different Needs

As we discussed in Part I, personas and scenarios provide designers with strong guidance for establishing and designing for the basic goals, behavior patterns, and needs of users. However, even though we optimize our design for personas, individual needs shift over time, and there are variations in behavior among individuals and subgroups of users that ought to be addressed by a truly robust interface. This chapter explores various concepts and design ideas for coping with the different needs of different users within the larger context of a design framework.

Command Vectors and Working Sets

Two concepts are particularly useful in sorting out the needs of users with different levels of experience: command vectors and working sets. **Command vectors** are distinct techniques for allowing users to issue instructions to the program. Direct manipulation handles, drop-down and pop-up menus, toolbar controls, and keyboard accelerators are all examples of command vectors.

Good user interfaces provide **multiple command vectors**, where key functions in the program are provided in the form of menu commands, toolbar commands, keyboard accelerators, and direct manipulation controls, each with the parallel capability to invoke a particular command. This redundancy enables users of different skill sets and preferences to command the program according to their desires and abilities.

Immediate and pedagogic vectors

Direct manipulation controls, like push-buttons and toolbar controls, are **immediate vectors**. There is no delay between clicking a button and seeing the results of the function. Direct manipulation also has an immediate effect on the information without any intermediary. Neither menus nor dialog boxes have this immediate property. Each one requires an intermediate step, sometimes more than one.

Some command vectors offer more support to new users. Typically, menus and dialog boxes offer the most, which is why we have named them **pedagogic vectors**. Beginners avail themselves of the pedagogy of menus as they get oriented in a new program, but perpetual intermediates often want to leave them behind to find slimmer, more immediate vectors.

Working sets and personas

Because each user unconsciously memorizes commands that are used frequently, perpetual intermediates memorize a moderate subset of commands and features, a **working set**. The commands that comprise any user's working set are unique to that individual, although it will likely overlap significantly with other users who exhibit similar use patterns when working with the application. In Excel, for example, almost every user will enter formulas and labels, specify fonts, and print; but Sally's working set might include goal-seeking, whereas Elliot's working set includes linked spreadsheets.

Although, strictly speaking, there is no such thing as a standard working set that will cover the needs of all users, research and modeling of users and their use patterns can yield a smaller subset of functions which designers can be reasonably confident are accessed frequently by most users. This **minimal working set** can be determined via goal-directed design methods: by using scenarios to discover the functional needs of your personas. These needs translate directly to the contents of the minimal working set.

The commands in any person's working set are those used frequently. The user wants those commands to be especially quick and easy to invoke. This means that the designer must, at least, provide immediate command vectors for the minimal working set of the most likely users of the application.

Although a program's minimal working set is almost certainly part of each user's full working set, his individual preferences and job requirements will dictate which additional features are included. Even custom software written for corporate operations can offer a range of features from which each user can pick and choose. This means that the designer must, while providing immediate access to the minimal working set, also provide means for promoting other commands to immediate vectors. Similarly, immediate commands also require more pedagogic vectors to enable beginners to learn the interface. This implies that most functions in the interface should have multiple command vectors.

There is an exception to the rule of multiple vectors: Dangerous commands (like Erase All, Clear Undo, Abandon Changes, and so on) should not have easy, parallel command vectors. Instead, they need to be protected within menus and dialog boxes (in keeping with the axiom: *Hide the ejector seat levers* (Chapter 9).

Graduating Users from Beginners to Intermediates

Donald Norman (1989) provides another useful perspective on command vectors. Norman uses the phrases, **information in the world** and **information in the head** to refer to different ways that users access information. When he talks about information in the world, Norman refers to situations in which there is sufficient information available by looking in an environment or interface to accomplish something. A kiosk showing a printed map of downtown, for example, is information in the world. We don't have to bother remembering exactly where the Transamerica Building is, because we can find it by reading a map. Opposing this is information in your head, which refers to knowledge that you have learned or memorized, like the back-alley shortcut that isn't printed on any map. Information in your head is much faster and easier to use than information in the world, but you are responsible for ensuring that you learn it, that you don't forget it, and that it stays up to date. Information in the world is slower and more cumbersome, but very dependable.

World vectors and head vectors

A pedagogic vector is necessarily filled with information in the world, which is why it is a **world vector**. Conversely, keyboard accelerators constitute a **head vector** because using them requires the user to have filled his head with information about the functions and their keyboard equivalents. World vectors are required by beginners and by more experienced users accessing advanced or seldom-used functions. Head vectors are used extensively by intermediates and even more so by experts.

For example, when you first moved into your neighborhood, you probably had to use a map — a world vector. After living there a couple of days, you abandoned the map because you had learned how to get home — a head vector. On the other hand, even though you know your house intimately, when you have to adjust the temperature setting on the water heater, you need to read the instructions — a world vector — because you didn't bother to memorize them when you moved in.

Our relationship to our software works the same way. We find ourselves easily memorizing facilities and commands that we use frequently and ignoring the details of commands that we use only rarely. This means that any vector that is used frequently will automatically become a candidate for a head vector. After daily use, for example, we no longer really read the menus, but find what we need by recognizing patterns: Pull down the second menu and select the bottom-most item in the next-to-last section. Pattern recognition is much faster for the human mind than reading is. We read only to verify our choices.

Memorization vectors

New users are happy with world vectors, but as they progress to become perpetual intermediates they begin to develop their working set, and the (pedagogic) world vectors will start to seem tedious. Users like to find more immediate head vectors for the contents of their working sets. This is a natural and appropriate user desire and, if our software is to be judged easy-to-use, we must satisfy it. The solution consists of two components. First, we must provide a head vector in parallel to the world vector, and second, we must provide a path by which the user can learn the head vector corresponding to each world vector. This path is a vector itself: a **memorization vector**.

There are several ways to provide memorization vectors for users. The least effective method is to mention the vector only in the user documentation. The slightly better, but still ineffective method is to mention it in the program's main online help system. These methods put the onus of finding the memorization vector on the user, and also leave it up to the user to realize that she needs to find it in the first place.

Superior memorization vectors are built right into the interface, or are at least offered in the program's interface by way of its own world vector. The latter can be minimally implemented just by adding a menu item to the standard Help menu called Shortcuts. This item takes the user directly to a section of Help that describes available shortcuts. This method has the benefit of being explicit and, therefore, pedagogic. New users can see that multiple command vectors exist and that there is an easy-to-find resource for learning them. All programs should have this Shortcut item.

DESIGN TIP   Offer shortcuts from the Help menu.

Integrating memorization vectors directly into the main interface is less problematic than it sounds. There are already two on the menus of most programs. As defined by Microsoft, a typical Windows application has two keyboard head vectors: mnemonics and accelerators. In Microsoft Word, for example, the mnemonic for Save is Alt+F+S. The memorization vector for this mnemonic is achieved visually by underlining the F and S in the menu title and the menu item, respectively. The accelerator for Save is Ctrl+S. Ctrl+S is noted explicitly on the right side of the menu on the same line as the Save item, which acts as a memorization vector.

Neither of these vectors intrudes on the new user. He may not even notice their existence until he has the opportunity to use the program at some length — that is, until he becomes an intermediate user. Eventually, he will notice these visual hints and will wonder about their meaning. Most reasonably intelligent people — most users — will get the accelerator connection without any help. The mnemonic is slightly tougher, but once the user is clued into the use of the Alt meta-key, either by direction or accident, the idiom is extremely easy to remember and use wherever it occurs.

If you look ahead at Figure 30-4 in Chapter 30, you can see an excellent technique whereby small icons are used to provide memorization vectors for transitioning from menus to toolbar — **butcons** (iconic buttons). The icon identifying each function or facility should be shown on every artifact of the user interface that deals with it: each menu, each butcon, each dialog box, every mention in the help text, and every mention in the printed documentation. A memorization vector formed of visual symbols in the interface is the most effective technique, yet it remains underexploited in the industry at large.

Personalization and Configuration

User interface designers often face the conundrum of whether to make their products user-customizable. It is easy to be torn between the user's need to have things done his way, and the clear problem this creates when the program's navigation suffers due to familiar elements being moved or hidden. The solution is to cast the problem in a different light.

People like to change things around to suit themselves. Even beginners, not to mention perpetual intermediates, like to put their own personal stamps on a program, changing it so that it looks or acts the way they prefer, uniquely suiting their tastes. People will do this for the same reason they fill their identical cubicles with pictures of their spouses and kids, plants, favorite paintings, quotes, and Dilbert cartoons.

Decorating the persistent objects — the walls — gives them individuality without removing them. It also allows you to recognize a hallway as being different from dozens of identical hallways because it is the one with the M. C. Escher poster hanging in it. The term **personalization** describes the decoration of persistent objects.

Personalization makes the places in which we work more likable and familiar. It makes them more human and pleasant to be in. The same is true of software, and giving the user the ability to decorate his personal program is both fun and useful as a navigational aide.

On the other hand, moving persistent objects *themselves* can hamper navigation. If the facilities people come into your office over the weekend and rearrange all the cubicles, Dilbert cartoons notwithstanding, finding your office again on Monday morning will be tough (persistent objects and their importance to navigation is discussed in Chapter 11).

Is this an apparent contradiction? Not really. Adding decoration to persistent objects helps navigation, whereas moving the persistent objects hinders navigation. The term **configuration** describes moving, adding, or deleting persistent objects.

Configuration is desirable for more experienced users. Perpetual intermediates, after they have established a working set of functions, will want to configure the interface to make those functions easier to find and use. They will also want to tune the program itself for speed and ease, but in all cases, the level of custom configuration will be light to moderate.

Configuration is a necessity for expert users. They are already beyond the need for more traditional navigation aids because they are so familiar with the product. Experts may use the program for several hours every day; in fact, it may be the main application for accomplishing the bulk of their jobs.

Moving controls around on the toolbar is a form of personalization. However, the three leftmost toolbar controls on many programs, which correspond to File New, File Open, and File Save, are now so common that they can be considered persistent objects. A user who moves these around is *configuring* his program as much as he is personalizing it. Thus, there is a gray boundary between configuration and personalization.

Changing the color of objects on the screen is clearly a personalization task. Windows has always been very accommodating in this respect, allowing users to independently change the color of each component of the windows interface, including the color and pattern of the desktop itself. Windows gives users a *practical* ability to change the system font, too. Personalization is **idiosyncratically modal** (see the next section); people either love it or they don't. You must accommodate both categories of users.

Tools for personalizing must be simple and easy to use, giving the user a visual preview of her selections. Above all, they must be easy to undo. A dialog box that lets users change colors should offer a function that returns everything to the factory settings.

Most end users won't squawk if they can't configure your program as long as it does its job well. Some really expert users may feel slighted, but they will still use and appreciate your program if it works the way they expect.

Corporate IT managers value configuration. It allows them to subtly coerce corporate users into practicing common methods. They appreciate the ability to add macros and commands to menus and toolbars that make the off-the-shelf software work more intimately with established company processes, tools, and standards. Many IT managers base their buying decisions on the configurability of programs. If they are buying ten or twenty thousand copies of a program, they rightly feel that they should be able to adapt it to their particular style of work. It is, thus, not on a whim that Microsoft Office applications are among the most configurable shrink-wrapped software titles available.

Idiosyncratically Modal Behavior

Many times user testing indicates that a user population divides relatively equally on the effectiveness of an idiom. Half of the users clearly prefer one idiom, whereas the other half prefers another. This sort of clear division of a population's preferences into two or more large groups indicates that their preferences are **idiosyncratically modal**.

Development organizations can become similarly emotionally split on issues like this. One group becomes the menu-item camp while the rest of the developers are the butcon camp. They wrangle and argue over the relative merits of the two methods although the real answer is staring them in the face: Use both!

When the user population splits on preferred idioms, the software designers *must* offer both idioms. Both groups must be satisfied. It is no good to satisfy one half of the population while angering the other half, regardless of which particular group you or your developers align yourselves with.

Windows offers an excellent example of how to cater to idiosyncratically modal desires in its menu implementation. Some people like menus that work the way they did on the original Macintosh. You click the mouse button on a menu bar item to make the menu appear; then — while still holding down the button — you drag down the menu and release the mouse button on your choice. Other people find this procedure difficult and prefer a way to accomplish it without having to awkwardly hold the mouse button down while they drag. Windows neatly satisfies this by letting the user click and release on the menu bar item to make the menu appear. Then the user can move the mouse — button released — to the menu item of her choice. Another click and release selects the item and closes the menu. The user can also still click and drag to select a menu item. The brilliance of these idioms is that they coexist quite peacefully with each other. Any user can freely intermix the two idioms, or stick consistently with one or the other. The program requires no change. There are no preferences or options to be set; it just works.

Starting in Windows 95, Microsoft added a third idiosyncratically modal idiom to the menu behavior: The user clicks and releases as before, but now he can drag the mouse along the menu bar and the other menus are triggered in turn. Amazingly, now all three idioms are accommodated seamlessly. The Mac now, too, supports all three of these idioms.

Localization and Globalization

Designing applications for use in different languages and cultures present some special challenges to designers. Here again, however, consideration of command vectors can provide guidance.

Immediate vectors such as direct manipulation and toolbar butcons are idiomatic (see Chapter 20) and visual rather than textual. They are, therefore, capable of being globalized with considerable ease. It is, of course, important for designers to do their homework to ensure that colors or symbols chosen for these idioms do not have particular meanings in different cultures that the designer would not intend. (In Japan, for example, an X in a check box would likely be interpreted as *de*selection rather than selection.) However, non-metaphorical idioms should, in general, be fairly safe for globalized interfaces.

The pedagogic vectors such as menu items, field labels, ToolTips, and instructional hints are language dependent, and thus must be the subject of localization via translation to appropriate languages. Some issues to bear in mind when creating interfaces that must be localized include:

✓ In some languages, words and phrases tend to be longer than in others (German text labels, for example, are significantly longer than those in English on average).

✓ Words in some languages, Asian languages in particular, can be difficult to sort alphabetically.

✓ Ordering of day-month-year and the use of 12- or 24-hour notation for time vary from country to country.

✓ Decimal points in numbers and currency are represented differently (some countries use periods and commas the opposite of the way they are used in the US).

✓ Some countries make use of week numbers (for example, week 50 is in mid-December), and some countries make use of calendars other than the Gregorian calendar.

Menu items and dialogs, when they are translated, need to be considered holistically. It is important to make sure that translated interfaces remain coherent as a whole. Items and labels that translate straightforwardly in a vacuum may become confusing when grouped with other independently translated items. Semantics of the interface need to be preserved at the higher level as well as at the detail level.

Galleries and Templates

Not all users of applications that create documents are capable of building them completely from scratch. Most programs, however, offer atomic tools to users, the equivalent of hammers, saws, and chisels. That is fine for some users, but others require more: the equivalent of an unfinished table or chair that they can then sand and paint.

For example, consider a program that lets you configure your own personalized newspaper from information on the Internet. Some users will really appreciate being able to put sports at the top of page one. Most users, however, will probably want a more traditional view, with world news at the top and sports at the back. Even these more-traditional users will appreciate the fact that they can add their local news and news concerning topics of particular personal interest. They should be able to pick a premade newspaper and then make the few small changes to it needed to get their custom version. Constructing a whole newspaper from a blank slate would be an unpleasant task for all but the closet journalists among us.

In other words, users should be allowed to choose a starting design or document structure in any application from a gallery of possible designs, if they don't have the need or desire to create one from scratch.

DESIGN TIP

Offer the user a gallery of good-solution templates.

Some programs already offer galleries of predesigned templates, but more should do the same. Blank slates intimidate most people, and users shouldn't have to deal with one if they don't want to. A gallery of basic designs is a fine solution.

Part IV

Applying Visual Design Principles

Chapter 19

Designing Look and Feel

The commonly accepted wisdom of the post-Macintosh era is that graphical user interfaces, or GUIs, are better than character-based user interfaces. However, although there are certainly GUI programs that dazzle us with their ease of use and their look and feel, most GUI programs still irritate and annoy us in spite of their graphical nature. It's easy enough, so it seems, to create a program with a graphical user interface that has a difficulty-of-use on par with a command-line Unix application. Why is this the case?

To find an answer to this question, we need to better understand the role of visual design in the creation of user interfaces.

Visual Art versus Visual Design

Practitioners of visual art and practitioners of visual design share a visual medium. Each must be skilled and knowledgeable about that medium, but there the similarity ends. The goal of the artist is to produce an observable artifact that provokes an aesthetic response. Art is thus a means of self-expression on topics of emotional or intellectual concern to the artist, and sometimes, to society at large. Few constraints are imposed on the artist; and the more singular and unique the product of the artist's exertions, the more highly it is valued.

Designers, on the other hand, create artifacts that meet the goals of *people other than themselves*. Whereas the concern of contemporary artists is primarily *expression* of ideas or emotions, visual designers, as Kevin Mullet and Darrell Sano note in their excellent book *Designing Visual Interfaces* (1995), "are concerned with finding the *representation* best suited to the communication of some specific information." Visual interface designers, moreover, are concerned with finding the representation best suited to communicating the *behavior* of the software that they are designing.

Graphic Design and Visual Interface Design

Design of user interfaces does not entirely exclude aesthetic concerns, but rather it places such concerns within the constraints of a functional framework. Visual design in an interface context thus requires several related skills, depending on the scope of the interface in question. Any designer working on interfaces needs to understand the basics: color, typography, form, and composition. However, designers working on interfaces also need some understanding of interaction, the behavior of the software, as well. It is rare to find visual designers with an even balance of these skills, although both types of visual perspectives are required for a truly successful interactive design.

Graphic design and user interfaces

Graphic design is a discipline that has, until the last twenty years or so, been dominated by the medium of print, as applied to packaging, advertising, and document design. Old-school graphic designers are uncomfortable designing in a digital medium and are unused to dealing with graphics at the pixel level, a requirement for most interface-design issues. However, a new breed of graphic designers has been trained in digital media and quite successfully applies the concepts of graphic design to the new, pixilated medium.

Graphic designers typically have a strong understanding of visual principles and a weaker understanding of concepts surrounding software behavior and interaction over time. Talented, digitally-fluent graphic designers excel at providing the sort of rich, clean, visually consistent, aesthetically pleasing, and exciting interfaces we see in Windows XP, Mac OS X, and some of the more visually sophisticated computer-game interfaces and consumer-oriented applications. These designers excel at creating beautiful and appropriate *surfaces* of the interface and are also responsible for the interweaving of corporate branding into software look and feel. For them, design is first about legibility and readability of information, then about tone, style, and framework that communicate a brand, and finally about communicating behavior through affordances (see Chapter 20).

Visual interface design and visual information design

Visual interface designers share some of the skills of graphic designers, but they focus more on the organizational aspects of the design and the way in which affordances communicate behavior to users. Although graphic designers are more adept at defining the *syntax* of the visual design — what it looks like — visual interface designers are more knowledgeable about principles of interaction. Typically, they focus on how to match the visual structure of the interface to the logical structure of both the user's and the program's behavior. Visual interface designers are also concerned with communication of program states to the user and with cognitive issues surrounding user perception of functions (layout, grids, figure-ground issues, and so on).

Visual *information* designers fulfill a similar role regarding content and navigation rather than more interactive functions. Their role is particularly important in Web design, where content often outweighs function. Their primary focus tends to be on controlling information hierarchy through the use of visual language. Visual information designers work closely with information architects, just as visual interface designers work closely with interaction designers.

Industrial design

Although it is beyond the scope of this book to discuss industrial design issues in any depth, as interactive appliances and handheld devices become widespread, industrial design is playing an ever-growing role in the creation of new interactive products. Much like the difference in skills between graphic designers and visual interface and information designers, there is a similar split among the ranks of industrial designers. Some are more adept at the creation of arresting and appropriate shapes and skins of objects, whereas others' talents lie more in the logical and ergonomic mapping of physical controls in a manner that matches user behaviors and communicates device behaviors. As more physical artifacts become software-enabled and sport sophisticated visual displays, it will become more important that interaction designers, industrial designers, and visual designers of all flavors work closely together to produce usable products.

Principles of Visual Interface Design

The human brain is a superb pattern-processing computer, making sense of the dense quantities of visual information that bombard us everywhere we look. Our brains manage this chaotic input by discerning visual patterns and establishing a system of priorities for the things we see, which in turn allows us to make conscious sense of the visual world. The ability of the brain's visual system to assemble portions of our visual field into patterns based on visual cues is what allows us to process visual information so quickly and efficiently. Visual interface design must take advantage of our innate visual processing capabilities to help programs communicate their behavior and function to users.

One small section of a chapter is far too small to do justice to the topic of visual interface design. However, there are some important principles that can help make your visual interface as easy and pleasurable to use as possible. Kevin Mullet and Darrell Sano (1995) provide a superb detailed analysis of these principles; we will summarize some of the most important visual interface design concepts here.

Visual interfaces should:

✓ Avoid visual noise and clutter

✓ Use contrast, similarity, and layering to distinguish and organize elements

✓ Provide visual structure and flow at each level of organization

✓ Use cohesive, consistent, and contextually appropriate imagery

✓ Integrate style and function comprehensively and purposefully

We discuss each of these principles in more detail in the following sections.

Avoid visual noise and clutter

Visual noise in interfaces is the result of superfluous visual elements that distract from those visual elements that directly communicate software function and behavior. Imagine trying to hold a conversation in an exceptionally crowded and loud restaurant. It can become impossible to communicate if the atmosphere is too noisy. The same is true for user interfaces. Visual noise can take the form of over-embellished and unnecessarily dimensional elements, overuse of rules and other visual elements to separate controls, insufficient use of white space between controls, and inappropriate or overuse of color, texture, and typography.

Cluttered interfaces attempt to provide an excess of functionality in a constrained space, resulting in controls that visually interfere with each other. Visually baroque, jumbled, or overcrowded screens raise the cognitive load for the user and hamper the speed and accuracy of user attempts at navigation.

In general, interfaces—non-entertainment interfaces, in particular—should use simple geometric forms, minimal contours, and less-saturated colors. Typography should not vary widely in an interface: Typically one or two typefaces in a few sizes are sufficient. When multiple, similar design elements (controls, panes, windows) are required for similar or related logical purpose, they should be quite similar in visual attributes such as shape, size, texture, color, weight, orientation, spacing, and alignment. Elements intended to stand out should be visually contrasted with any regularized elements.

Good visual interfaces, like any good visual design, are visually *efficient*. They make the best use out of the minimal set of visual and functional elements. A popular technique used by graphic designers is to experiment with the removal of individual elements in order to test their contribution to the clarity of the intended message.

Pilot and poet Antoine de Saint Exupery once expressed, "Perfection is attained not when there is no longer anything to add, but when there is no longer anything to take away." As you create your interfaces, you should constantly be looking to simplify visually. The more useful work a visual element can accomplish, while retaining clarity, the better. As Albert Einstein suggested, things should be as simple as possible, but no simpler.

Another related concept is that of **leverage**, using elements in an interface for multiple, related purposes. A good example is a visual symbol that communicates the type of an object in a list, which when clicked on also opens a properties dialog for that object type. The interface could include a separate control for launching the properties display, but the economical and logical solution is to combine it with the type marker. In general, interaction designers, not visual designers, are best suited to tackle the assignment of multiple functions to visual elements. Such mapping of elements requires significant insight into the behavior of users in context, the behavior of the software, and programming issues.

Use contrast and layering to distinguish and organize elements

There are two needs addressed by providing contrast in the elements of an interface. The first is to provide visual contrast between active, manipulable elements of the interface, and passive, non-manipulable visual elements. The second is to provide contrast between different logical sets of active elements to better communicate their distinct functions. Unintentional or ambiguous use of contrast should be avoided, as user confusion almost certainly results. Proper use of contrast will result in visual patterns that users register and remember, allowing them to orient themselves much more rapidly. Contrast also provides a gross means of indicating the most or least important elements in an interface's visual hierarchy. In other words, contrast is a tool for the communication of function and behavior.

A visual interface is based on visual patterns.

DIMENSIONAL, TONAL, AND SPATIAL CONTRAST

The manipulable controls of an interface should visually stand out from non-manipulable regions. Use of pseudo-3D to give the feel of a manual affordance (see Chapter 20 for a further discussion of affordance) is perhaps the most effective form of contrast for controls. Typically, buttons and other items to be clicked or dragged are given a raised look, whereas data entry areas like text fields are given indented looks. These techniques provide **dimensional contrast**.

In addition to the dimensionality of affordance, *hue*, *saturation*, or *value* (brightness) can be varied to distinguish controls from the background or to group controls logically. When using such **tonal contrast**, you should in most cases vary along a single "axis"—hue or saturation or value, but not all at once. Also, be aware that contrasting by hue runs the risk of disenfranchising individuals with color perception problems; saturation or brightness is probably a safer alternative. In grayscale displays, **tonal contrast** by value is the only choice the designer has. Depending on the context, tonal contrast of either the controls, of the background area the controls rest on, or of both may be appropriate.

Spatial contrast is another way of making logical distinctions between controls and data entry areas. By positioning related elements together spatially, you help make clear to the user what tasks relate to each other. Good grouping by *position* takes into account the order of tasks and subtasks and how the eye scans the screen (left to right in most Western countries, and generally from top to bottom), which we discuss more in a following section. Shape is also an important form of contrast: Check boxes, for example, are square, whereas radio buttons are round—a design decision not made by accident. Another type of spatial contrast is *orientation*: up, down, left, right, and the angles in between. Icons on the Mac and in Windows provide subtle orientation cues: Document icons are more vertical, folders more horizontal, and application icons, at least on the original Mac, had a diagonal component. Contrast of *size* is also useful, particularly in the display of quantitative information, as it easily invites comparison. We talk more about information design later in this chapter. Contrast in size is also useful when considering the relative sizes of titles and labels, as well as the relative sizes of modular regions of an interface grid. Size, in these cases, can relate to broadness of scope, to importance, and to frequency of use. Again, as with tonal contrast, sticking to a single "axis" of variation is best with spatial contrast.

LAYERING

Interfaces can be organized by **layering** visual cues in individual elements or in the background on which the active elements rest. Several visual attributes control the perception of layers. Color affects perception of layering: Dark, cool, desaturated colors recede, whereas light, warm, saturated colors advance. Size also affects layering: Large elements advance whereas small elements tend to recede. Positionally overlapping elements are perhaps the most straightforward examples of visual layering.

To layer elements effectively, you must use a minimum amount of contrast to maintain close similarity between the items you wish to associate in a layer on the screen. After you have decided what the groups are and how to best communicate about them visually, you can begin to adjust the contrast of the groups to make them more or less prominent in the display, according to their importance in context. Maximize differences between layers, but minimize differences between items within a layer.

FIGURE AND GROUND

One side effect of the way humans visually perceive patterns is the tension between the **figure**, the visual elements that should be the focus of the user's attention, and the **ground**, the background context upon which the figure appears. People tend to perceive light objects as the figure and dark objects as the ground. Figure and ground need to be integrated in a successful design: Poorly positioned and scaled figure elements may end up emphasizing the ground. Well-integrated designs feature figure and ground that are about equal in their scale and visual weight and in which the figure is centered on the ground.

THE SQUINT TEST

A good way to help ensure that a visual interface design employs contrast effectively is to use what graphic designers refer to as the **squint test**. Close one eye and squint at the screen with the other eye in order to see which elements pop out and which are fuzzy, which items seem to group together, and whether figure or ground seem dominant. Other tests include viewing the design through a mirror (the mirror test) and looking at the design upside down to uncover imbalances in the design. Changing your perspective can often uncover previously undetected issues in layout and composition.

Provide visual structure and flow at each level of organization

Your interfaces are most likely going to be composed of visual and behavioral elements used in groups, which are then grouped together into panes, which then may, in turn, be grouped into screens or pages. This grouping, as discussed elsewhere, can be by position (or proximity), by alignment, by color (value, hue, temperature, saturation), by texture, by size, or by shape. There may be several such levels of structure in a sovereign application, and so it is critical that you maintain a clear visual structure so that the user can easily navigate from one part of your inter-face to another, as his workflow requires. The rest of this section describes several important attributes that help define a crisp visual structure.

ALIGNMENT, GRIDS, AND THE USER'S LOGICAL PATH

Alignment of visual elements is one of the key ways that designers can help users experience a product in an organized, systematic way. Grouped elements should be aligned both horizontally and vertically (see Figure 19-1). In particular, designers should take care to

- ✓ **Align labels.** Labels for controls stacked vertically should be aligned with each other; left-justification is easier for users to scan than right justification, although the latter may look visually cleaner — if the input forms are the same size. (Otherwise, you get a Christmas tree, ragged-edge effect on the left and right.)

- ✓ **Align within a set of controls.** A related group of check boxes, radio buttons, or text fields should be aligned according to a regular grid.

- ✓ **Align across controls.** Aligned controls (as described previously) that are grouped together with other aligned controls should all follow the same grid.

- ✓ **Follow a regular grid structure** for larger-scale element groups, panes, and screens, as well as for smaller grouping of controls.

A **grid structure** is particularly important for defining an interface with several levels of visual or functional complexity. After interaction designers have defined the overall framework for the application and its elements (as discussed in Chapter 6), visual interface designers should help regularize the layout into a grid structure that properly emphasizes top-level elements and struc-tures but still provides room for lower-level or less important controls. The most important thing to remember about grids is that simple is better. If the atomic grid unit is too small, the grid will become unrecognizable in its complexity. Ambiguity and complexity are the enemies of good design. Clear, simple grids help combat ambiguity.

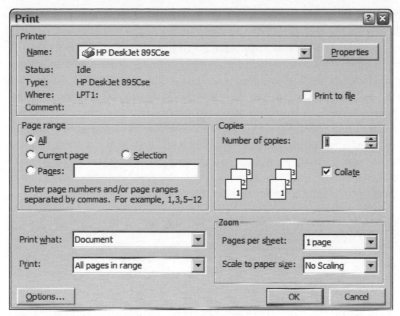

Figure 19-1: Microsoft Word's Print dialog is a good example of elements meticulously aligned both vertically and horizontally in conformity with a grid. Note the group boxes around related functional elements. It is easy to get carried away with the use of these boxes, which can visually clutter the interface. The Print dialog treads a fine line. With a proper balance of white space around grouped elements, an explicit box is often not required to indicate grouping.

The layout, although conforming to the grid, must also properly mirror the user's **logical path** through the application, taking into account the fact that (in Western countries) the eye will move from top to bottom and left to right (see Figure 19-2).

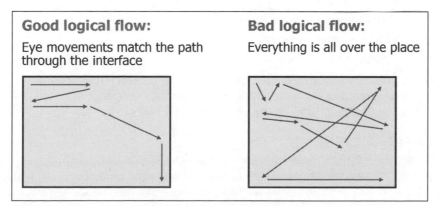

Figure 19-2: Eye movement across an interface should mirror the logical path through the interface that the user takes to accomplish goals and tasks.

SYMMETRY AND BALANCE

Symmetry is a useful tool in organizing interfaces from the standpoint of providing visual balance. Interfaces that don't employ symmetry tend to look unbalanced, as if they are going to topple over to one side. Experienced visual designers are adept at achieving asymmetrical balance by controlling the visual weight of individual elements much as you might balance children of different weights on a seesaw. Asymmetrical design is difficult to achieve in the context of user interfaces because of the high premium placed on white space by screen real-estate constraints. The squint test, the mirror test, and the upside down test are again useful for seeing whether a display looks lopsided.

Two types of symmetry are most often employed in interfaces: vertical axial symmetry (symmetry along a vertical line, usually drawn down the middle of a group of elements) or diagonal axial symmetry (symmetry along a diagonal line). Most typical dialog boxes exhibit one or the other of these symmetries — most frequently diagonal symmetry (see Figure 19-3).

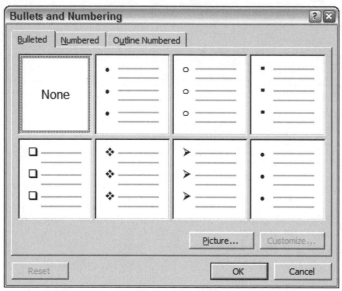

Figure 19-3: Diagonal symmetry in Microsoft Word's Bullets and Numbering dialog. The axis of symmetry runs from lower left to upper right.

Sovereign applications typically won't exhibit such symmetry at the top level (they achieve balance through a well-designed grid), but elements within a well-designed sovereign interface will almost certainly exhibit use of symmetry to some degree (see Figure 19-4).

SPATIAL HARMONY AND WHITE SPACE

Spatial harmony considers the interface (or at least each screen) as a whole. Designers have discovered that certain proportions seem to be more pleasing than others to the human eye. The best known of these is the Golden Section ratio, discovered in antiquity — likely by the Greeks — and probably coined by Leonardo Da Vinci. Unfortunately, for the time being, most computer monitors have a ratio of 1.33:1, which puts visual designers at a bit of a disadvantage when laying out full-screen, sovereign applications (see Chapter 8). Nonetheless, the understanding of such ratios makes a big difference in developing comfortable layouts for user interfaces.

Figure 19-4: Vertical symmetry in the Macromedia Fireworks 4 tool palette.

Proper dimensioning of interface functional regions adds to spatial harmony, as does a proper amount of white space between elements and surrounding element groups. Just as well-designed books enforce proper margins and spacing between paragraphs, figures, and captions, the same kind of visual attention is critical to designing an interface that does not seem cramped or uncomfortable. Especially in the case of sovereign applications, which users will be inhabiting for many hours at a time, it is critical to get proportions right. The last thing you want is for your user to feel uncomfortable and irritated every time she uses your product or service. The key is to be decisive in your layout. Almost a square is no good. Almost a double square is also no good. Make your proportions bold, crisp, and exact.

Use cohesive, consistent, and contextually appropriate imagery

Use of icons and other illustrative elements can help users understand an interface, or if poorly executed, can irritate, confuse, or insult. It is important that designers understand both what the program needs to communicate to users and how users think about what must be communicated. A good understanding of personas and their mental models should provide a solid foundation for both textual and visual language used in an interface. Cultural issues are also important. Designers should be aware of different meanings for colors in different cultures (red is not a warning color in China), for gestures (thumbs up is a terrible insult in Turkey), and for symbols (an octagonal shape means a stop in the US, but not in many other countries). Also, be aware of domain-specific color coding. Yellow means radiation in a hospital. Red usually means something life-threatening. Make sure you understand the visual language of your users' domains and environments before forging ahead.

Visual elements should also be part of a cohesive and globally applied visual language. This means that similar elements should share visual attributes, such as how they are positioned, their size, line weight, and overall style, contrasting only what is important to differentiate their meaning. The idea is to create a system of elements that integrate together to form a cohesive whole. A design that achieves this seems to fit together perfectly; nothing looks stuck on at the last minute.

FUNCTION-ORIENTED ICONS

Designing icons to represent functions or operations performed on objects leads to interesting challenges. The most significant challenge is to represent an abstract concept in iconic, visual language. In these cases, it is best to rely on idioms rather than force a concrete representation where none makes sense and to consider the addition of ToolTips (see Chapter 29) or text labels.

For more obviously concrete functions, some guidelines apply:

- ✓ Represent both the **action** and an **object** acted upon to improve comprehension. Nouns and verbs are easier to comprehend together than verbs alone (for example, for a Cut command, representing a document with an X through it may be more readily understood than a more metaphorical image of a pair of scissors).

- ✓ Beware of metaphors and representations that may not have the intended meanings for your target audience.

- ✓ Group related functions visually to provide context, either spatially or, if this is not appropriate, using color or other common visual themes.

- ✓ Keep icons simple; avoid excessive visual detail.

- ✓ Reuse elements when possible, so users need to learn them only once.

ASSOCIATING VISUAL SYMBOLS TO OBJECTS

Creating unique symbols for types of objects in the interface supports user recognition. These symbols can't always be representational or metaphoric — they are thus often idiomatic (see Chapter 20 for more information on the strengths of idioms). Such visual markers help the user navigate to appropriate objects faster than text labels alone would allow. To establish the connection between symbol and object, use the symbol wherever the object is represented on the screen.

AXIOM

Visually distinguish elements that behave differently.

Designers must also take care to visually differentiate symbols representing different object types. Discerning a particular icon within a screen full of similar icons is as difficult as discerning a particular word within a screen full of words. It's also particularly important to visually differentiate (contrast) objects that exhibit different behaviors, including variants of controls such as buttons, sliders, and check boxes.

RENDERING ICONS AND VISUAL SYMBOLS

Especially as the graphics capabilities of color screens increase, it is tempting to render icons and visuals with ever-increasing detail, producing an almost photographic quality. However, this trend does not ultimately serve user goals, especially in productivity applications. Icons should remain simple and schematic, minimizing the number of colors and shades and retaining a modest size. Both Windows XP and Mac OS X have recently taken the step towards more fully rendered icons (OS X more so, with its 128x128 pixel, nearly photographic icons). Although such icons may look great, they draw undue attention to themselves and render poorly at small sizes, meaning that they must necessarily take up extra real estate to be legible. They also encourage a lack of visual cohesion in the interface because only a small number of functions (mostly those related to hardware) can be adequately represented with such concrete photo-realistic images. Photographic icons are like all-capitalized text; the differences between icons aren't sharp and easy to distinguish, so we get lost in the complexity. The Mac OS X Aqua interface is filled with photo-realistic touches that ultimately distract (see Figure 19-5). None of this serves the user particularly well.

Figure 19-5: Photo-realistic icons in Mac OS X. This level of detail in icons serves only to distract from data and function controls. In addition, although it might, in some instances, make sense to render in detail objects people are familiar with, what is the sense of similarly rendering unfamiliar objects and abstract concepts (for example, a network)? How many users have seen what a naked hard disk drive looks like (far right)? Ultimately, users must rely on accompanying text to make sense of these icons, unless they are quite frequently used.

VISUALIZING BEHAVIORS

Instead of using words alone to describe the results of interface functions (or worse, not giving any description at all), use visual elements to *show* the user what the results will be. Don't confuse this with use of icons on control affordances. Rather, in addition to using text to communicate a setting or state, render an illustrative picture or diagram that communicates the *behavior*. Although visualization often consumes more space, its capability to clearly communicate is well worth the pixels. In recent years, Microsoft has discovered this fact, and the dialog boxes in Windows Word, for example, have begun to bristle with visualizations of their meaning in addition to the textual controls. Photoshop and other image-manipulation applications have long shown thumbnail previews of the results of visual processing operations.

AXIOM

Visually communicate function and behavior.

The Word Page Setup dialog box offers an image labeled Preview. This is an output-only control, showing a miniature view of what the page will look like with the current margin settings on the dialog. Most users have trouble visualizing what a 1.2 inch left margin looks like. The Preview control shows them. Microsoft could go one better by allowing input on the Preview control in addition to output. Drag the left margin of the picture and watch the numeric value in the corresponding spinner ratchet up and down.

The associated text field is still important—you can't just replace it with the visual one. The text shows the precise values of the settings, whereas the visual control accurately portrays the look of the resulting page.

Integrate style and function comprehensively and purposefully

When designers choose to apply stylistic elements to an interface, it must be from a global perspective. Every aspect of the interface must be considered from a stylistic point of view, not simply individual controls or other visual elements. You do not want your interface to seem as though someone applied a quick coat of paint. Rather you need to make sure that the functional aspects of your program's visual interface design are in complete harmony with the visual brand of your product. Your program's behavior is part of its brand, and your user's experience with your product should reflect the proper balance of form, content, and behavior.

FORM VERSUS FUNCTION

Although visual style is a tempting diversion for many visual designers, use of stylized visual elements needs to be carefully controlled within an interface—particularly when designing for sovereign applications. Designers must be careful not to affect the basic shape, visual behavior, and visual affordance (see Chapter 20) of controls in the effort to adapt them to a visual style. The point is to be aware of the value each element provides. There's nothing wrong with an element that adds style, as long as it accomplishes what you intend and doesn't interfere with the meaning of the interface or the user's ability to interact with it.

That said, educational and entertainment applications, especially those designed for children, leave room for a bit more stylistic experimentation. The visual experience of the interface and content are part of the enjoyment of these applications, and a greater argument can also be made for thematic relationships between controls and content. Even in these cases, however, basic affordances should be preserved so that users can, in fact, reach the content easily.

BRANDING AND THE USER INTERFACE

Most successful companies make a significant investment in building brand equity. A company that cultivates substantial brand equity can command a price premium for its products, while encouraging greater customer loyalty. Brands indicate the positive characteristics of the product and suggest discrimination and taste in the user.

In its most basic sense, brand value is the sum of all the interactions people have with a given company. Because an increasing number of these interactions are occurring through technology-based channels, it should be no surprise that the emphasis placed on branding user interfaces is greater than ever. If the goal is consistently positive customer interactions, the verbal, visual, and behavioral brand messages must be consistent.

Although companies have been considering the implications of branding as it relates to traditional marketing and communication channels for some time now, many companies are just beginning to address branding in terms of the user interface. In order to understand branding in the context of the user interface, it can be helpful to think about it from two perspectives: the first impression and the long-term relationship.

Just as with interpersonal relationships, first impressions of a user interface can be exceedingly important. The first five-minute experience is the foundation that long-term relationships are built upon. To ensure a successful first five minute experience, a user interface must clearly and immediately communicate the brand. Visual design, typically, plays one of the most significant roles in managing first impressions largely through color and image. By selecting a color palette and image style for your user interface that supports the brand, you go a long way toward leveraging the equity of that brand in the form of a positive first impression.

After people have developed a first impression, they begin to assess whether the behavior of the interface is consistent with its appearance. You build brand equity and long-term customer relationships by delivering on the promises made during the first impression. Interaction design and the control of behavior are often the best ways to keep the promises that visual branding makes to users.

Principles of Visual Information Design

Like visual interface design, visual information design also has many principles that the prospective designer can use to his advantage. Information design guru Edward Tufte asserts that good visual design is "clear thinking made visible," and that good visual design is achieved through an understanding of the viewer's "cognitive task" (goal) and a set of design principles.

Tufte claims that there are two important problems in information design:

1. It is difficult to display multidimensional information (information with more than two variables) on a two-dimensional surface.

2. The resolution of the display surface is often not high enough to display dense information. Computers present a particular challenge — although they can add motion and interactivity, computer displays have a low information density compared to that of paper.

Interaction and visual interface designers may not be able to escape the limitations of 2D screens or overcome the problems of low-resolution displays. However, some universal design principles — indifferent to language, culture, or time — help maximize the effectiveness of any information display, whether on paper or digital media.

In his beautifully executed volume, *The Visual Display of Quantitative Information* (1983), Tufte introduces seven Grand Principles, which we briefly discuss in the following sections as they relate specifically to digital interfaces and content.

Visually displayed information should, according to Tufte

1. Enforce visual comparisons

2. Show causality

3. Show multiple variables

4. Integrate text, graphics, and data in one display

5. Ensure the quality, relevance, and integrity of the content

6. Show things adjacently in space, not stacked in time

7. Not de-quantify quantifiable data

We will briefly discuss each of these principles as they apply to the information design of software-enabled media.

Enforce visual comparisons

You should provide a means for users to compare related variables and trends or to compare before and after scenarios. Comparison provides a context that makes the information more valuable and more comprehensible to users. Adobe Photoshop, along with many other graphics tools, makes frequent use of previews, which allow users to easily achieve before and after comparisons interactively (see Figure 19-6, as well as Figures 19-7 and 19-8).

Show causality

Within information graphics, clarify cause and effect. In his books, Tufte provides the classic example of the space shuttle Challenger disaster, which could have been averted if charts prepared by NASA scientists had been organized to more clearly present the relationship between air temperature at launch and severity of O-ring failure. In interactive interfaces, modeless visual feedback (see Chapter 34) should be employed to inform users of the potential consequences of their actions or to provide hints on how to perform actions.

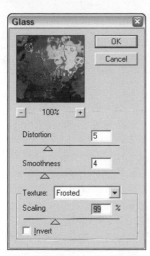

Figure 19-6: Visual comparison. Photoshop filters provide interactive previews that allow users to compare results of an operation with the original before the operation has been executed. Some Photoshop filters permit the preview (which can be flipped on and off instantaneously by the user) to occur over the entire image, or a selection thereof, in addition to the thumbnail shown in the preceding dialog.

Show multiple variables

Data displays that provide information on multiple, related variables should be able to display them all simultaneously without sacrificing clarity. In an interactive display, the user should be able to selectively turn off and on the variables to make comparisons easier and correlations (causality) clearer. Figure 19-7 shows an example of an interactive display that permits manipulation of multiple variables.

Integrate text, graphics, and data in one display

Diagrams that require separate keys or legends to decode are less effective and require more cognitive processing on the part of users. Reading and deciphering diagram legends is yet another form of navigation-related excise. Users must move their focus back and forth between diagram and legend and then reconcile the two in their minds. Figure 19-8 shows an interactive example that integrates text, graphics, and data, as well as input and output: a highly efficient combination for users.

Ensure the quality, relevance, and integrity of the content

Don't show information simply because it's technically possible to do so. Make sure that any information you display will help your users achieve particular goals that are relevant to their context. Unreliable or otherwise poor-quality information will damage the trust you must build with users through your product's content, behavior, and visual brand.

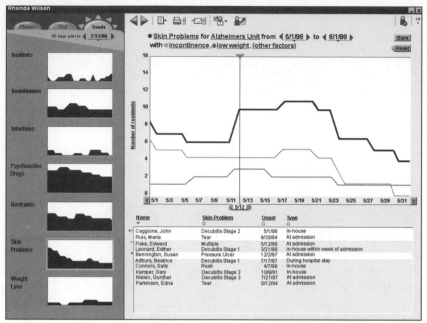

Figure 19-7: Showing multiple variables. This design created for Shared Healthcare Systems' Orcas long-term healthcare system allows nurses to compare and correlate trends in a single full-screen display. Nurses at long-term care facilities need to be proactive about quality of care issues. Cooper designers created a trend-analysis tool that allows nurses to choose which care issues to track and to interactively correlate them against other potentially related concerns. Graphs on the left show major trends as live thumbnails; these and other attributes can be added to the chart on the right. The sliding vertical vernier determines the day being looked at in the area below the chart, which breaks out all incidents according to affected residents. Clicking on a resident's name takes the nurse to that resident's chart.

Show things adjacently in space, not stacked in time

If you are showing changes over time, it's much easier for users to understand the changes if they are shown adjacently in space, rather than superimposed on one another. Cartoon strips are a good example of showing flow and change over time arranged adjacently in space.

Of course, this advice applies to static information displays; in software, **animation** can be used even more effectively to show change over time, as long as technical issues (such as memory constraints or connection speed over the Internet) don't come into play.

Don't de-quantify quantifiable data

Although you may want to use graphs and charts to make perception of trends and other quantitative information easier to grasp, you should not abandon the display of the numbers themselves. For example, in the Windows Disk Properties dialog, a pie chart is displayed to give users a rough idea of their free disk space, but the numbers of kilobytes free and used are also displayed in numerical form.

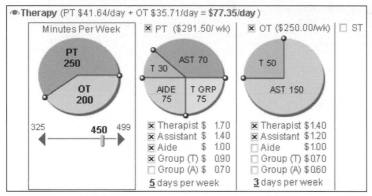

Figure 19-8: Combining text, graphics, and data in a single display. This interface, also designed for Shared Healthcare Systems, permits case managers at long-term healthcare facilities to appropriately balance the quality of care and cost of care for new residents interactively. The ability to see what if scenarios visually, as well as the details in text, allows the users to better and more quickly plan what's best for each new resident and her family.

Use of Text and Color in Visual Interfaces

Text and color are both becoming indispensable elements of the visual language of user interfaces (text always has been). This section discusses some useful visual principles concerning the use of these two important visual tools.

Use of text

Humans process visual information more easily than they do textual information, which means that navigation by visual elements is faster than navigation by textual elements. For navigation purposes, text words are best considered as visual elements. They should, therefore, be short, easily recognized, and easily remembered.

Text forms a recognizable shape that our brains categorize as a visual object. Each word has a recognizable shape, which is why WORDS TYPED IN ALL CAPITAL LETTERS ARE HARDER TO READ than upper/lowercase — the familiar pattern-matching hints are absent in capitalized words, so we must pay much closer attention to decipher what is written. Avoid using all caps in your interfaces.

Recognizing words is also different from *reading*, where we consciously scan the individual words and interpret their meaning in context. Interfaces should try to minimize the amount of text that must be read in order to navigate the interface successfully: After the user has navigated to something interesting, he should be able to read in detail if appropriate. Using visual objects to provide context facilitates navigation with minimal reading.

Our brains can rapidly differentiate objects in an interface if we represent *what* objects are by using visual symbols and idioms. After we have visually identified the type of object we are interested in, we can read the text to distinguish *which* particular object we are looking at. In this scheme, we don't need to read about types of objects we are not interested in, thus speeding navigation and eliminating excise. The accompanying text only comes into play after we have decided that it is important.

AXIOM

Visually show what; textually show which.

When text must be read in interfaces, some guidelines apply:

✓ Make sure that the text is in high contrast with the background and do not use conflicting colors that may affect readability.

✓ Choose an appropriate typeface and point size. Point sizes less than 10 are difficult to read. For brief text, such as on a label or brief instruction, a crisp sans-serif font, like Arial, is appropriate; for paragraphs of text, a serif font, like Times, is more appropriate.

✓ Phrase your text to make it understandable by using the least number of words necessary to clearly convey meaning. Phrase clearly, and avoid abbreviation. If you must abbreviate, use standard abbreviations.

Use of color

Color is an important part of most visual interfaces whose technology can support it. In these days of ubiquitous color LCDs, users have begun to expect color screens even in devices like PDAs and phones. However, color is much more than a marketing checklist item; it is a powerful information design and visual interface design tool that can be used to great effect, or just as easily abused.

Color communicates as part of the visual language of an interface, and users will impart meaning to its use. For non-entertainment, sovereign applications in particular, color should integrate well into the other elements of the visual language: symbols and icons, text, and the spatial relationships they maintain in the interface. Color, when used appropriately, serves the following purposes in visual interface design:

✓ **Color draws attention.** Color is an important element in rich visual feedback, and consistent use of it to highlight important information provides an important channel of communication.

✓ **Color improves navigation and scanning speed.** Consistent use of color in signposts can help users quickly navigate and home in on information they are looking for.

✓ **Color shows relationships.** Color can provide a means of grouping or relating objects together.

Misuse of color

There are a few ways that color can be misused in an interface if one is not careful. The most common of these misuses are as follows:

✓ **Too many colors.** A study by Human Factors International indicated that one color significantly reduced search time. Adding additional colors provides less value, and at seven or more, search performance degraded significantly. It isn't unreasonable to suspect a similar pattern in any kind of interface navigation.

✓ **Use of complementary colors.** Complementary colors are the inverse of each other in color computation. These colors, when put adjacent to each other or when used together as figure and ground, create perceptual artifacts that are difficult to perceive correctly or focus on. A similar effect is the result of **chromostereopsis**, in which colors on the extreme ends of the spectrum "vibrate" when placed adjacently. Red text on a blue background (or vice versa) is extremely difficult to read.

✓ **Excessive saturation.** Highly saturated colors tend look garish and draw too much attention. When multiple saturated colors are used together, chromostereopsis and other perceptual artifacts often occur.

✓ **Inadequate contrast.** When figure colors differ from background colors only in hue, but not in saturation or value (brightness), they become difficult to perceive. Figure and ground should vary in brightness or saturation, in addition to hue, and color text on color backgrounds should also be avoided when possible.

✓ **Inadequate attention to color impairment.** Roughly ten percent of the male population has some degree of color-blindness. Thus care should be taken when using red and green hues (in particular) to communicate important information. Any colors used to communicate should also vary by saturation or brightness to distinguish them from each other. If a grayscale conversion of your color palette is easily distinguishable, color-blind users should be able to distinguish the color version.

Consistency and Standards

Many in-house usability organizations view themselves, among other things, as the gatekeepers of consistency in digital product design. **Consistency** implies a similar look, feel, and behavior across the various modules of a software product, and this is sometimes extended to apply across all the products a vendor sells. For at-large software vendors, such as Macromedia and Adobe, who regularly acquire new software titles from smaller vendors, the branding concerns of consistency take on a particular urgency. It is obviously in their best interests to make acquired software look as though it belongs, as a first-class offering, alongside products developed in-house. Beyond this, both Apple and Microsoft have an interest in encouraging their own and third-party developers to create applications that have the look and feel of the OS platform on which the program is being run, so that the user perceives their respective platforms as providing a seamless and comfortable user experience.

Benefits of interface standards

User interface standards provide benefits that address these issues, although they come at a price. Standards provide benefits to users when executed appropriately. According to Jakob Nielsen (1993), relying on a single interface standard improves users' ability to quickly learn interfaces and enhances their productivity by raising throughput and reducing errors. These benefits accrue because users are more readily able to predict program behavior based on past experience with other parts of the interface, or with other applications following similar standards.

At the same time, interface standards also benefit software vendors. Customer training and technical support costs are reduced because the consistency that standards bring improves ease of use and learning. Development time and effort are also reduced because formal interface standards provide ready-made decisions on the rendering of the interface that development teams would otherwise be forced to debate during project meetings. Finally, good standards can lead to reduced maintenance costs and improved reuse of design and code.

Risks of interface standards

The primary risk of any standard is that the product that follows it is only as good as the standard itself. Great care must be made in developing the standard in the first place to make sure, as Nielsen says, that the standard specifies a truly usable interface, and that it is usable by the *developers* who must build the interface according to its specifications.

It is also risky to see interface standards as a panacea for good interfaces. Most interface standards emphasize the *syntax* of the interface, its visual look and feel, but say little about deeper behaviors of the interface or about its higher-level logical and organizational structure. There is a good reason for this: A general interface standard has no knowledge of context incorporated into its formalizations. It takes into account no specific user behaviors and usage patterns within a context, but rather focuses on general issues of human perception and cognition and, sometimes, visual branding as well. These concerns are important, but they are presentation details, not the interaction framework upon which such rules hang.

Standards, guidelines, and rules of thumb

Although standards are unarguably useful, they need to evolve as technology and our understanding of users and their goals evolve. Some practitioners and programmers invoke Apple's or Microsoft's user interface standards as if they were delivered from Mt. Sinai on a tablet. Both companies publish user interface standards, but both companies also freely and frequently violate them and update the guidelines post facto. When Microsoft proposes an interface standard, it has no qualms about changing it for something better in the next version. This is only natural — interface design is still in its infancy, and it is wrongheaded to think that there is benefit in standards that stifle true innovation. In some respects, Apple's dramatic visual shift from OS 9 to OS X has helped to dispel the notion among the Mac faithful that interface standards are etched in granite.

The original Macintosh was a spectacular achievement precisely because it transcended all Apple's previous platforms and standards. Conversely, much of the strength of the Mac came from the fact that vendors followed Apple's lead and made their interfaces look, work, and act alike. Similarly, many successful Windows programs are unabashedly modeled after Word, Excel, and Outlook.

Interface standards are thus most appropriately treated as detailed *guidelines* or *rules of thumb*. Following interface guidelines too rigidly or without careful consideration of the needs of users in context can result in force-fitting an application's interface into an inappropriate interaction model.

When to violate guidelines

So, what should we make of interface guidelines? Instead of asking if we should *follow* standards, it is more useful to ask: When should we *violate* standards? The answer is when, and only when, we have a very good reason.

Obey standards unless there is a truly superior alternative.

But what constitutes a very good reason? Is it when a new idiom is measurably better? Usually, this sort of measurement can be quite elusive because it rarely reduces to a quantifiable factor alone. The best answer is: When an idiom is clearly seen to be significantly better by most people in the target user audience (your personas) who try it, there's a good reason to keep it in the interface. This is how the toolbar came into existence, along with outline views, tabs, and many other idioms. Researchers may have been examining these artifacts in the lab, but it was their useful presence in real-world software that confirmed the success.

Your reasons for diverging from guidelines may ultimately not prove to be good enough and your product may suffer. But you and other designers will learn from the mistake. This is what Christopher Alexander (1964) calls the "unselfconscious process," an indigenous and unexamined process of slow and tiny forward increments as individuals attempt to improve solutions. New idioms (as well as new uses for old idioms) pose a risk, which is why careful, goal-directed design and appropriate testing with real users in real working conditions are so important.

Consistency and standards across applications

Using standards or guidelines has special challenges when a company that sells multiple software titles decides that all its various products must be completely consistent from a user-interface perspective.

From the perspective of visual branding, as discussed earlier, this makes a great deal of sense, although there are some intricacies. If an analysis of personas and markets indicates that there is little overlap between the users of two distinct products and that their goals and needs are also quite distinct, you might question whether it makes more sense to develop two visual brands that speak specifically to these different customers, rather than using a single, less-targeted look. When it comes to the behavior of the software, these issues become even more urgent. A single standard *might* be important if customers will be using the products together as a suite. But even in this case, should a graphics-oriented presentation application, like PowerPoint, share an interface structure with a text processor like Word? Microsoft's intentions were good, but it went a little too far enforcing global style guides. PowerPoint doesn't gain much from having a similar menu structure to Excel and Word, and it loses quite a bit in ease-of-use by conforming to an alien structure that diverges from the user's mental models. On the other hand, the designers did draw the line somewhere, and PowerPoint does have a slide-sorter display, an interface unique to that application.

AXIOM

Consistency doesn't imply rigidity.

Designers, then, should bear in mind that consistency doesn't imply rigidity, especially where it isn't appropriate. Interface and interaction style guidelines need to grow and evolve like the software they help describe. Sometimes you must bend the rules to best serve your users and their goals (and sometimes even your company's goals). When this has to happen, try to make changes and additions that are compatible with standards. The spirit of the law, not the letter of the law, should be your guide.

Chapter 20

Metaphors, Idioms, and Affordances

Interface designers, especially those of a visual bent, often speak of finding the right metaphor upon which to base their interface designs. They imagine that filling their interface with images of familiar objects from the real world will give their users a pipeline to easy learning. So they create an interface masquerading as an office filled with desks, file cabinets, telephones, and address books, or as a pad of paper or a street of buildings. If you, too, search for that magic metaphor, you will be in august company. Some of the best and brightest designers in the interface world consider metaphor selection as one of their first and most important tasks.

The authors believe that this approach is in error. Strict adherence to metaphors tie interfaces unnecessarily to the workings of the physical world. They have a host of other problems as well: There aren't enough good metaphors to go around; they don't scale well; and the ability of users to recognize them is often questionable, especially across cultural boundaries. Metaphors, especially physical and spatial metaphors, have an extremely limited place in the design of most information-age, software-enabled products. In this chapter, we discuss the reasons for this, as well as the alternatives to design based on metaphors.

Interface Paradigms

There are three dominant paradigms in the conceptual and visual design of user interfaces: **implementation-centric**, **metaphoric**, and **idiomatic**. The implementation-centric interfaces are based on *understanding* how things work—a difficult proposition. Metaphoric interfaces are based on *intuiting* how things work—a risky method. Idiomatic interfaces, however, are based on *learning* how to accomplish things—a natural, human process.

The field of user-interface design progressed from a heavy focus on technology (implementation) to an equally heavy focus on metaphor. There is ample evidence of all three paradigms in contemporary software design, even though the metaphoric paradigm is the only one that has been named and described. Although metaphors are great tools for humans to communicate with each other (this book is filled with them), they are a weak tool for the design of software, and all too often they hamper the creation of truly superior interfaces.

Implementation-centric interfaces

Implementation-centric user interfaces are widespread in the computer industry. These interfaces are expressed in terms of their construction, of how they are built. In order to successfully use them, the user must understand how the software works internally. Following the implementation-centric paradigm means user-interface design based exclusively on the implementation model.

The overwhelming majority of software programs today are implementation-centric in that they show us, without any hint of shame, precisely how they are built. There is one button per function, one dialog per module of code, and the commands and processes precisely echo the internal data structures and algorithms.

We can see how an implementation model interface ticks by learning how to run its program. The problem is that the reverse is also true: We *must* learn how the program works in order to successfully use the interface.

AXIOM

Users would rather be successful than knowledgeable.

Engineers want to know how things work, so the implementation-centric paradigm is very satisfying to them (which is the reason, in addition to ease of construction, why so much of our software follows it). Engineers prefer to see the gears and levers and valves because it helps them understand what is going on inside the machine. That those artifacts needlessly complicate the interface seems a small price to pay. Engineers may want to understand the inner workings, but most users don't have either the time or desire. They'd much rather be successful than be knowledgeable, a preference that is often hard for engineers to understand.

Metaphoric interfaces

Metaphoric interfaces rely on intuitive connections that the user makes between the visual cues in an interface and its function. There is no need to understand the mechanics of the software, so it is a step forward from implementation-centric interfaces, but its power and usefulness has been inflated to unrealistic proportions.

When we talk about metaphors in the context of user interface and interaction design, we really mean visual metaphors: a picture used to represent the purpose or attributes of a thing. Users recognize the imagery of the metaphor and, by extension, can understand the purpose of the thing. Metaphors can range from the tiny images on toolbar buttons to the entire screen on some programs — from a tiny scissors on a button indicating Cut to a full-size checkbook in Quicken. We understand metaphors intuitively, but what does that really mean? Webster's Dictionary defines intuition like this:

> in·tu·i·tion \in-'tu-wi-shen\ n 1 : quick and ready insight 2 a : immediate apprehension or cognition b : knowledge or conviction gained by intuition c : the power or faculty of attaining to direct knowledge or cognition without evident rational thought and inference

This definition highlights the magical quality of intuition, but it doesn't say *how* we intuit something. Intuition works by inference, where we see connections between disparate subjects and learn from these similarities, while not being distracted by their differences. We grasp the meaning of the metaphoric controls in an interface because we mentally connect them with other things we have already learned. This is an efficient way to take advantage of the awesome power of the human mind to make inferences. However, this method also depends on the idiosyncratic human minds of users, which may not have the requisite language, knowledge, or inferential power necessary to make those connections.

LIMITATIONS OF METAPHORS

The idea that metaphors are a firm foundation for user-interface design is misleading. It's like worshipping floppy disks because so much good software once came on them. Metaphors have many limitations when applied to modern, information-age systems.

For one thing, metaphors don't scale very well. A metaphor that works well for a simple process in a simple program will often fail to work well as that process grows in size or complexity. File icons were a good idea when computers had floppies or 10MB hard disks with only a couple of hundred files, but in these days of 60 gigabyte hard disks and tens of thousands of files, file icons become too clumsy to use effectively.

Metaphors also rely on associations perceived in similar ways by both the designer and the user. If the user doesn't have the same cultural background as the designer, it is easy for metaphors to fail. Even in the same or similar cultures, there can be significant misunderstandings. Does a picture of an airplane mean "check flight arrival information" or "make airline reservations?"

Finally, although a metaphor offers a small boost in learnability to first-time users, it exacts a tremendous cost after they become intermediates. By reflecting the physical world of mechanisms, most metaphors firmly nail our conceptual feet to the ground, forever limiting the power of our software. We'll discuss this issue with metaphors later in this chapter.

Our definition of intuition indicates that rational thought is not required in the process of intuiting. In the computer industry, and particularly in the user-interface design community, the word *intuitive* is often used to mean easy-to-use or easy-to-understand. Ease-of-use is obviously important, but it doesn't promote our craft to attribute its success to metaphysics. Nor does it help us to devalue the precise meaning of the word. There are very real reasons why people understand certain interfaces and not others.

INTUITION, INSTINCT, AND LEARNING

There are certain sounds, smells, and images that make us respond without any previous conscious learning. When a small child encounters an angry dog, she *instinctively* knows that bared fangs signal great danger even without any previous learning. The encoding for such recognition goes deep. Instinct is a hard-wired response that involves no conscious thought. Intuition is one step above instinct because, although it also requires no conscious thought, it is based on a web of knowledge learned consciously.

Examples of instinct in human-computer interaction include the way we are startled and made apprehensive by gross changes in the image on the screen, find our eyes drawn inexorably to the flashing advertisement on a Web page, or the way we react to sudden noises from the computer or the smell of smoke rising from the CPU.

Intuition is a middle ground between having consciously learned something and knowing something instinctively. If we have learned that things glowing red can burn us, we tend to classify all red-glowing things as potentially dangerous until proven otherwise. We don't necessarily know that the particular red-glowing thing is a danger, but it gives us a safe place to begin our exploration.

What we commonly refer to as intuition is actually a mental comparison between a new experience and the things we have already learned. You instantly intuit how to work a wastebasket icon, for example, because you once learned how a real wastebasket works, thereby preparing your mind to make the connection years later. But you didn't *intuit* how to use the original wastebasket. It was just an extremely easy thing to learn. This brings us to the third type of interface, based on the fact that the human mind is an incredibly powerful learning machine that constantly and effortlessly learns new things.

Idiomatic interfaces

Idiomatic design, what Ted Nelson has called "the design of principles," (1990) is based on the way we learn and use idioms — figures of speech like "beat around the bush" or "cool." Idiomatic user interfaces solve the problems of the previous two interface types by focusing not on technical knowledge or intuition of function, but rather on the learning of simple, non-metaphorical visual and behavioral idioms to accomplish goals and tasks.

Idiomatic expressions don't provoke associative connections the way metaphors do. There is no bush and nobody is beating anything. Idiomatically speaking, something can be both cool and hot and be equally desirable. We understand the idiom simply because we have learned it and because it is distinctive, not because we understand it or because it makes subliminal connections in our minds. Yet, we are all capable of rapidly memorizing and using such idioms: We do so almost without realizing it.

If you cannot intuit an idiom, neither can you reason it out. Our language is filled with idioms that, if you haven't been taught them, make no sense. If we say, "Uncle Joe kicked the bucket," you know what we mean even though there is no bucket or kicking involved. You can't know this by thinking through the various permutations of smacking pails with your feet. You can only learn this from context in something you read or by being consciously taught it. You remember this obscure connection between buckets, kicking, and dying only because humans are good at remembering things like this.

The human mind has a truly amazing capacity to learn and remember large numbers of idioms quickly and easily without relying on comparisons to known situations or an understanding of how or why they work. This is a necessity, because most idioms don't have metaphoric meaning at all, and the stories behind most others were lost ages ago.

GRAPHICAL INTERFACES ARE LARGELY IDIOMATIC

It turns out that most of the elements of intuitive graphical interfaces are actually visual idioms. Windows, title bars, close boxes, screen-splitters, hyperlinks, and drop-downs are things we learn idiomatically rather than intuit metaphorically. The Macintosh's use of the trashcan to eject a floppy or ZIP disk is purely idiomatic (and many designers consider it a poor idiom), despite the visual metaphor of the trash can itself.

The ubiquitous mouse input device is not metaphoric of anything, but rather is learned idiomatically. There is a scene in the movie *Star Trek IV* where Scotty returns to twentieth-century Earth and tries to speak into a mouse. There is nothing about the physical appearance of the mouse that indicates its purpose or use, nor is it comparable to anything else in our experience, so learning it is not intuitive. However, learning to point at things with a mouse is incredibly easy. Someone probably spent all of three seconds showing it to you the first time, and you mastered it from that instant on. We don't know or care how mice work, and yet even small children can operate them just fine. That is idiomatic learning.

Ironically, many of the familiar GUI elements that are often thought of as metaphoric are actually idiomatic. Artifacts like resizable windows and endlessly nested file folders are not really metaphoric — they have no parallel in the real world. They derive their strength only from their easy idiomatic learnability.

GOOD IDIOMS MUST BE LEARNED ONLY ONCE

We are inclined to think that learning interfaces is hard because of our conditioning based on experience with implementation-centric software. These interfaces are very hard to learn because you need to understand how the software works internally to use them effectively. Most of what we know we learn *without* understanding: things like faces, social interactions, attitudes, melodies, brand names, the arrangement of rooms, and furniture in our houses and offices. We don't *understand* why someone's face is composed the way it is, but we *know* that face. We recognize it because we have looked at it and automatically (and easily) memorized it.

All idioms must be learned; good idioms need to be learned only once.

The key observation about idioms is that although they must be learned, they are very easy to learn, and good ones only need to be learned once. It is quite easy to learn idioms like "neat" or "politically correct" or "the lights are on but nobody's home" or "in a pickle" or "take the red-eye" or "grunge." The human mind is capable of picking up idioms like these from a single hearing. It is similarly easy to learn idioms like radio buttons, close boxes, drop-down menus, and comboboxes.

BRANDING AND IDIOMS

Marketing and advertising professionals understand well the idea of taking a simple action or symbol and imbuing it with meaning. After all, synthesizing idioms is the essence of product branding, in which a company takes a product or company name and imbues it with a desired meaning. The golden arches of McDonalds, the three diamonds of Mitsubishi, the five interlocking rings of the Olympics, even Microsoft's flying window are non-metaphoric idioms that are instantly recognizable and imbued with common meaning. The example of idiomatic branding shown in Figure 20-1 illustrates its power.

Figure 20-1: Here is an idiomatic symbol that has been imbued with meaning from its use, rather than by any connection to other objects. For anyone who grew up in the 1950s and 1960s, this otherwise meaningless symbol has the power to evoke a shiver of fear because it represents nuclear radiation. Visual idioms, such as the American flag, can be just as powerful as metaphors, if not more so. The power comes from how we use them and associate them, rather than from any innate connection to real-world objects.

Further Limitations of Metaphors

If we depend on metaphors to create user interfaces, we encounter not only the minor problems already mentioned, but also two more major problems: Metaphors are hard to find and they constrict our thinking.

Finding good metaphors

It may be easy to discover visual metaphors for physical objects like printers and documents. It can be difficult or impossible to find metaphors for processes, relationships, services, and transformations—the most frequent uses of software. It can be extremely daunting to find a useful visual metaphor for buying a ticket, changing channels, purchasing an item, finding a reference, setting a format, rotating a tool, or changing resolution; yet these operations are precisely the type of processes we use software to perform most frequently.

The problems with global metaphors

The most significant problem with metaphors, however, is that they tie our interfaces to mechanical age artifacts. An extreme example of this was Magic Cap, a handheld communicator interface introduced with some fanfare by General Magic in the mid-1990s. It relies on metaphor for almost every aspect of its interface. You access your messages from an inbox or a notebook on a desk. You walk down a hallway that is lined with doors representing secondary functions. You go outside to access third-party services, which as you can see in Figure 20-2, are represented by buildings on a street. You enter a building to configure a service, and so on. The heavy reliance on this metaphor means that you can intuit the basic functioning of the software; but the downside is that, after you understand its function, the metaphor adds significantly to the overhead of navigation. You *must* go back out onto the street to configure another service. You *must* go down the hallway and into the game room to play Solitaire. This may be normal in the physical world, but there is no reason for it in the world of software. Why not abandon this slavish devotion to metaphor and give the user *easy* access to functions? It turns out that a General Magic programmer later created a bookmarking shortcut facility as a kludgy add-on, but alas, too little too late.

Figure 20-2: The Magic Cap interface from General Magic was used in products from Sony and Motorola in the mid-1990s. It is a tour de force of metaphoric design. All the navigation in the interface, and most other interactions as well, were subordinated to the maintenance of spatial and physical metaphors. It was surely fun to design, but not particularly easy to use after you became an intermediate. This was a shame, because some of the lower-level, non-metaphoric data-entry interactions were quite sophisticated and well designed for the time.

General Magic's interface relies on what is called a **global metaphor**. This is a single, overarching metaphor that provides a framework for all the other metaphors in the system. The desktop of the original Macintosh is also considered a global metaphor.

A hidden problem of global metaphors is the mistaken belief that other lower-level metaphors consistent with them enjoy cognitive benefits by association. The temptation is irresistible to stretch the metaphor beyond simple function recognition: That software telephone also lets you dial with buttons just like those on our desktop telephones. We see software that has address books of phone numbers just like those in our pockets and purses. Wouldn't it be better to go beyond these confining, industrial-age technologies and deliver some of the real power of the computer? Why shouldn't our communications software allow multiple connections or make connections by organization or affiliation, or just hide the use of phone numbers altogether?

It may seem clever to represent your dial-up service with a picture of a telephone sitting on a desk, but it actually imprisons you in a limited design. The original makers of the telephone would have been ecstatic if they could have created a phone that let you call your friends just by pointing to pictures of them. They couldn't because they were restricted by the dreary realities of electrical circuits and Bakelite moldings. On the other hand, today we have the luxury of rendering our communications interfaces in any way we please—showing pictures of our friends is completely reasonable—yet we insist on holding these concepts back with representations of obsolete technology.

There are two snares involved in extending metaphors, one for the user and one for the designer. After the user depends on the metaphor for recognition, he expects consistency of behavior with the real-world object to which the metaphor refers. This causes the snare for the designer, who now, to meet user expectations, is tempted to render the software in terms of the metaphor's mechanical age referent. As we saw in Part I, transliterating mechanical processes onto the computer usually makes them worse than they were before.

Brenda Laurel has said (1991), "Interface metaphors rumble along like Rube Goldberg machines, patched and wired together every time they break, until they are so encrusted with the artifacts of repair that we can no longer interpret them or recognize their referents." It amazes me that software designers, who can finally create that dream-phone interface, give us the same old telephone simply because they were taught that a strong, global metaphor is a prerequisite to good user-interface design. Of all the misconceptions to emerge from Xerox PARC, the global metaphor myth is the most debilitating and unfortunate.

Idiomatic design is the future of interaction design. Using this paradigm, we depend on the natural ability of humans to learn easily and quickly as long as we don't force them to understand how and why. There is an infinity of idioms waiting to be invented, but only a limited set of metaphors waiting to be discovered. Metaphors give first-timers a penny's worth of value but cost them many dollars' worth of problems as they continue to use the software. It is always better to design idiomatically, using metaphors only when a truly appropriate and powerful one falls in our lap.

Use metaphors if you can find them, but don't bend your interface to fit some arbitrary metaphoric standard.

Never bend your interface to fit a metaphor.

Macs and metaphors: A revisionist view

In the mid-1970s, the modern graphical user interface (GUI) was invented at Xerox Palo Alto Research Center (PARC). The GUI — as defined by PARC — consisted of many things: windows, buttons, mice, icons, visual metaphors, and drop-down menus. Together they have achieved an unassailable stature in the industry by association with the empirical superiority of the ensemble.

The first commercially successful implementation of the PARC GUI was the Apple Macintosh, with its desktop metaphor: the wastebasket, overlapping sheets of paper (windows), and file folders. The Mac didn't succeed because of these metaphors, however. It succeeded for several other reasons, including an overall attention to design and detail. The interaction design advances that contributed were:

- ✓ It defined a tightly restricted but flexible vocabulary for users to communicate with applications, based on a very simple set of mouse actions.

- ✓ It offered sophisticated direct manipulation of rich visual objects on the screen.

- ✓ It used square pixels at high resolution, which enabled the screen to match printed output very closely, especially the output of Apple's other new product: the laser printer.

Metaphors helped structure these critical design features and made for good marketing copy, but were never the main appeal. In fact, the early years were rather rocky for the Mac as people took time to grow accustomed to the new, GUI way of doing things. Software vendors were also initially gun-shy about developing for such a radically different environment (Microsoft being the exception).

However, people were eventually won over by the *capability* of the system to do what other systems couldn't: WYSIWYG (what you see is what you get) desktop publishing. The combination of WYSIWYG interfaces and high-quality print output (via the LaserWriter printer) created an entirely new market that Apple and the Mac owned for years. Metaphors were but a bit-player (no pun intended) in the Mac's success.

Building Idioms

When graphical user interfaces were first invented they were so clearly superior that many observers credited the success to the interfaces' graphical nature. This was a natural, but incorrect, assumption. The first GUIs, such as the original Mac, were better primarily because the graphical nature of their interfaces required a restriction of the range of vocabulary by which the user interacted with the system. In particular, the input they could accept from the user went from an unrestricted command line to a tightly restricted set of mouse-based actions. In a command line interface, the user can enter any combination of characters in the language—a virtually infinite number. In order for the user's entry to be correct, he needs to know exactly what the program expects. He must remember the letters and symbols with exacting precision. The sequence can be important, and sometimes even capitalization matters.

In modern GUIs, the user can point to images or words on the screen with the mouse cursor. Most of these choices migrated from the user's head to the screen, eliminating any need to memorize them. Using the buttons on the mouse, the user can click, double-click, or click-and-drag. The keyboard is used for data entry, but not typically for command entry or navigation. The number of atomic elements in the user's input vocabulary has dropped from dozens (if not hundreds) to just three, even though the range of tasks that can be performed by GUI programs isn't any more restricted than that of command-line systems.

The more atomic elements there are in an interaction vocabulary, the more time-consuming and difficult the learning process is. A vocabulary like that of the English language takes at least ten years to learn thoroughly, and its complexity requires constant use to maintain fluency, but it can be extraordinarily expressive for a skilled user. Restricting the number of elements in our interaction vocabulary reduces its expressiveness at the atomic level. However, more complex interactions can be easily built from the atomic ones, much the way that letters combine to form words, and words to form sentences.

A properly formed interaction vocabulary can be represented by an inverted pyramid. All easy-to-learn communications systems obey the pattern shown in Figure 20-3. The bottom layer contains **primitives**, the atomic elements of which everything in the language is comprised. In modern GUIs, these primitives consist of pointing, clicking, and dragging.

The middle layer contains **compounds**. These are more complex constructs created by combining one or more of the primitives. These include simple visual objects that are acted upon and which reveal state, actions such as double-clicking, click-and-dragging, and manipulable objects like pushbuttons, check boxes, hyperlinks, and direct manipulation handles.

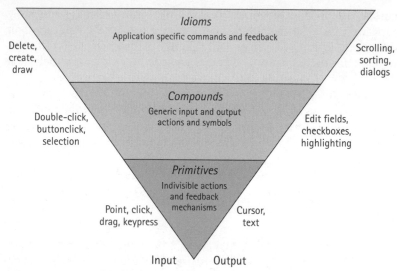

Figure 20-3: One of the primary reasons that GUIs are easy to use is that they enforce a restricted interaction vocabulary that builds complex idioms from a very small set of primitives: pointing, clicking, and dragging. These primitives can build a larger set of simple compounds, which in turn can be assembled into a wide variety of complex, domain-specific idioms, all of which are based on the same small set of easily learned actions.

The uppermost layer contains **idioms**. Idioms combine and structure compounds using **domain knowledge** of the problem under consideration: information related to the user's work patterns and goals, and not specifically to the computerized solution. The set of idioms opens the vocabulary to information about the particular problem the program is trying to address. In a GUI, it includes things like labeled buttons and fields, navigation bars, list boxes, icons, and even groups of fields and controls, or entire panes and dialogs.

Any language that does not follow this form will be very hard to learn. Many effective communications systems outside of the computer world follow similar vocabularies. Street signs in the United States follow a simple pattern of shapes and colors: Yellow triangles are cautionary, red octagons are imperatives, and green rectangles are informative.

Manual Affordances

Donald Norman (1989) has given us the term **affordance**, which he defines as "the perceived and actual properties of the thing, primarily those fundamental properties that determine just how the thing could possibly be used."

This definition is fine as far as it goes, but it omits the key connection: *How* do we know what those properties offer to us? If you look at something and understand how to use it — you comprehend its affordances — you must be using some method for making the mental connection.

We will thus alter Norman's definition by omitting the phrase "and actual." By doing this, affordance becomes a purely cognitive term, referring to what we *think* the object can do rather than what it can actually do. If a push-button is placed on the wall next to the front door of a residence, its affordances are 100% doorbell. If, when we push it, it causes a trapdoor to open beneath us and we fall into it, it turns out that it wasn't a doorbell; but that doesn't change its affordance as one.

So how do we know it's a doorbell? Simply because we have learned about doorbells and door etiquette and push-buttons from our complex and lengthy socialization and maturation process. We have learned about this class of pushable things by exposure to electrical and electronic devices in our environs and because — years ago — we stood on doorsteps with our parents, learning how to approach another person's home.

But there is another force at work here, too. If we see a push-button in an unlikely place such as the hood of a car, we cannot imagine what its purpose is, but we do recognize it as a finger-pushable object. How do we know this? Undoubtedly, we recognize it because of our tool-manipulating nature. We, as a species, see things that are finger-sized, placed within reach, and we automatically push them. We see things that are long and rounded, and we wrap our fingers around them and grasp them like handles. This is what Norman was getting at with his term **affordance**. For clarity, however, we'll call this instinctive understanding of how objects are manipulated with our hands **manual affordance**. When artifacts are clearly shaped to fit our hands or feet, we recognize that they can be directly manipulated and require no written instructions. In fact, this act of understanding how to use a tool based on the relationship of its shape to our hands is a clear example of intuiting an interface.

Norman discusses at length how [manual] affordances are much more compelling than written instructions. A typical example he uses is a door that must be pushed open using a metal bar for a handle. The bar is just the right shape, height and position to be grasped by the human hand. The manual affordances of the door scream, "Pull me." No matter how often someone uses this diabolical door, he will always attempt to pull it open, because the affordances are strong enough to drown out any number of signs affixed to the door saying Push.

There are only a few manual affordances. We pull handle-shaped things with our hands or, if they are small, we pull them with our fingers. We push flat plates with our hands or fingers. If they are on the floor we push them with our feet. We rotate round things, using our fingers for small ones — like dials — and both hands on larger ones, like steering wheels. Such manual affordances are the basis for much of our visual user-interface design.

The popular faux-3D design of systems like Windows, Mac OS, and Motif rely on shading and highlighting to make screen images appear more dimensional. These images offer virtual manual affordances in the form of button-like images that say "Push me" to our tool-manipulating brains.

Semantics of manual affordances

What's missing from an unadorned, virtual manual affordance is any idea of what function it performs. We can see that it looks like a button, but how do we know what it will accomplish when we press it? Unlike mechanical objects, you can't figure out a virtual lever's function just by tracing its connections to other mechanisms — software can't be casually inspected in this manner. Instead, we must rely either on supplementary text and images, or, most often, on our previous learning and experience. The affordance of the scrollbar clearly shows that it can be manipulated, but the only things about it that tell us what it does are the arrows, which hint at its directionality. In order to know that a scrollbar controls our position in a document, we have to either be taught or learn through experimentation.

Controls must have text or iconic labels on them to make sense. If the answer isn't written directly on the control, we can only learn what it does by one of two methods: experimentation or training. Either we read about it somewhere, ask someone, or try it and see what happens. We get no help from our instinct or intuition. We can only rely on the empirical.

Fulfilling user expectations of affordances

In the real world, an object does what it can do as a result of its physical form and its connections with other physical objects. A saw can cut wood because it is sharp and flat and has a handle. A knob can open a door because it is connected to a latch. However, in the digital world, an object does what it can do because a programmer imbued it with the power to do something. We can discover a great deal about how a saw or a knob works by physical inspection, and we can't easily be fooled by what we see. On a computer screen, though, we can see a raised, three-dimensional rectangle that clearly wants to be pushed like a button, but this doesn't necessarily mean that it *should* be pushed. It could, literally, do almost anything. We can be fooled because there is no natural connection — as there is in the real world — between what we see on the screen and what lies behind it. In other words, we may not know how to work a saw, and we may even be frustrated by our inability to manipulate it effectively, but we will never be fooled by it. It makes no representations that it doesn't manifestly live up to. On computer screens, canards and false impressions are very easy to create.

When we render a button on the screen, we are making a contract with the user that that button will visually change when she pushes it: It will appear to depress when the mouse button is clicked over it. Further, the contract states that the button will perform some reasonable work that is accurately described by its legend. This may sound obvious, but it is frankly astonishing how many programs offer bait-and-switch manual affordances. (This is relatively rare for pushbuttons, but all too common for other controls.) Make sure that your program delivers on the expectations it sets via the use of manual affordances.

Section Three

Interaction Details

The scientists who invented computers gave us the complex symbology of language as the tool for communicating with software. It has the advantage of precision, but it is far too labor-intensive and error-prone. Pundits outside of the industry — and some inside it who should know better — advocate instead an interface based on speaking to our computers. Words, however — especially spoken words — are prone to misinterpretation and quotation out of context. Communication by *demonstration* is far less ambiguous. The idea of pointing with a mouse or stylus or finger follows this concept. Because these actions are more direct, we *show* the computer (or other digital product) what to do, instead of trying to *tell* it what to do. The details of this paradigm have been refined over the last 25 years, and apply broadly to desktop software, as well as (with some necessary constraints) to the Web and to embedded systems. The intricate details of these interactions deserve a closer look, which this section provides.

Part V

Mice and Manipulation

Chapter 21

Direct Manipulation and Pointing Devices

Modern graphical user interfaces are founded on the concept of direct manipulation of graphical objects on the screen: buttons, sliders, and other function controls, as well as icons and other representations of data objects. The ability to choose, group, and move objects on the screen is fundamental to the interfaces we design today. But to perform these manipulations, we also require input mechanisms that give us the flexibility to do so. This chapter discusses both the basics of direct manipulation and the various devices that have been employed to make such manipulation possible.

Direct Manipulation

Ben Shneiderman, professor of Computer Science at University of Maryland, coined the term direct manipulation in 1974. Its three elements (paraphrased by the authors) consist of:

✓ Visual representation of the manipulated objects

✓ Physical actions instead of text entry

✓ Immediately visible impact of the operation

A less-rigorous definition would say that direct manipulation is clicking and dragging things; and although this is true, it can easily miss the point that Shneiderman subtly makes. Notice that of his three points, two of them concern the visual feedback the program offers the user and only the second point concerns the user's actions. It might be more accurate to call it "visual manipulation" because of the importance of what we see during the process. Unfortunately, I've seen many instances of direct-manipulation idioms implemented without adequate visual feedback, and these idioms fail to satisfy the definition of effective direct manipulation.

AXIOM

Rich visual interaction is the key to successful direct manipulation.

Yet another observation about direct manipulation—one that is hidden by its obviousness—is that we can only directly manipulate information that is already displayed by the program; it must be visible for us to manipulate it, which again emphasizes the visual nature of direct manipulation. If you want to create effective direct-manipulation idioms in your software, you must take care to render data, objects, controls, and cursors with fine graphic detail and richness.

Direct manipulation is simple, straightforward, easy-to-use, and easy-to-remember. However, most users, when first exposed to a given direct-manipulation idiom, cannot intuit or discover it independently. Direct manipulation idioms must be taught, but the teaching of them is trivial—usually consisting of merely pointing them out—and, once taught, they are seldom forgotten. It is a classic example of idiomatic design. Adding metaphoric images may help, but you cannot depend on finding an appropriate one; and if you do, you cannot depend on it communicating clearly to all users. Resign yourself to the burden of teaching direct manipulation idioms. Console yourself with the ease of that teaching.

With regard to direct manipulation, Apple's Human Interface Style Guide says, "Users want to feel that they are in charge of the computer's activities." These published guidelines and the Macintosh user interface itself make clear that Apple believes in direct manipulation as a fundamental tenet of good user-interface design. However, user-centered design guru Don Norman (1989) says "Direct manipulation, first-person systems have their drawbacks. Although they are often easy to use, fun, and entertaining, it is often difficult to do a really good job with them. They require the user to do the task directly, and the user may not be very good at it." Whom should we believe?

The answer, of course, is both of them. As Apple says, direct manipulation is an extremely powerful tool; and as Norman says, the tool must be put into the hands of someone qualified to use it.

This contradiction should illustrate the differences between two distinct types of direct manipulation. Pushing a button is direct manipulation and so is drawing with the pen tool in a paint program. Although almost any user can push a button, few are capable of drawing well with the pen tool (or for that matter with a real pen). These examples illustrate the two variants of direct manipulation: **program manipulation** and **content manipulation**.

Program manipulation versus content manipulation

Program manipulation includes actions like button pushing and scrolling and is equally accessible to all (non-handicapped) users. Program manipulation should require no special skills or training and is typically focused on the *management* of the program and its interface.

Content manipulation, on the other hand, is involved primarily with the *direct, manual creation, modification, and movement* of data with the pointing device; and although it can be performed by anyone, its results will always be commensurate with the skill and talent of the manipulator.

Applications like Corel Draw!, Adobe Photoshop, and Macromedia Fireworks are focused on drawing operations, and these fit into the definition of content manipulation. The same holds for 3D modeling applications like SketchUp or Alias|Wavefront Maya. Programs like Visio or even PowerPoint strain the definition, but even their more-structured interfaces are still content-centered and require some graphic talent from the user. We'll discuss drawing idioms in more detail in Chapter 24.

In the program manipulation category, we find five varieties of direct manipulation:

✓ Selection

✓ Drag and drop

✓ Control manipulation

✓ Resizing, reshaping, and repositioning

✓ Connecting objects

We will discuss each of these in the remaining chapters of Part V.

Three phases of the direct manipulation process

We can divide the direct manipulation process into three distinct phases:

1. **Free Phase:** Before the user takes any action

2. **Captive Phase:** After the user has begun the drag

3. **Termination Phase:** After the user releases the mouse button

In the **free phase**, nothing has happened yet. The job of the interface is to indicate direct-manipulation pliancy at the appropriate time.

In the **captive phase**, the interface has two tasks. It must positively indicate that the direct-manipulation process has begun, and it must visually identify the potential participants in the action.

In the **termination phase**, the interface must plainly indicate to the user that the action has terminated and show exactly what the result is.

Visual feedback for direct manipulation idioms

As we've discussed, the key to successful direct manipulation is rich visual feedback. Let's take a more detailed look at some visual feedback methods.

Depending on which phase you are in, there are two variants of cursor hinting. During the free phase, any visual change the cursor makes as it passes over something on the screen is called **free cursor hinting**. After the captive phase has begun, changes to the cursor represent **captive cursor hinting**. Many programs use a hand-shaped cursor to indicate that the document itself, rather than the information in it, can be dragged.

If you are holding down a meta-key during the drag to drag away a copy of the object instead of the object itself, the cursor may change from an arrow to an arrow with a little plus sign over it to indicate that the operation is a copy rather than a move. This is a clear example of captive cursor hinting.

When an object is dragged, the cursor must drag either the full representation of the object or some simulacrum of that representation. In a drawing program, for example, when you drag a complex visual element from one position to another, it may be too difficult for the program to actually drag the image (due to the computer's performance limitations), so it often simply drags an outline of the object.

Direct manipulation is critical to effective interaction

The advent of the Web and HTML in the early 1990s in some ways represented a giant step back for the industry in terms of interface and interaction design. The industry suddenly got hold of the notion that an interaction limited to scrolling a page and single-clicking a link was not only acceptable, but that it was superior. Well, why not? What could be simpler than a single click to do something? This view was, and is, shortsighted. Although single clicks are (barely) adequate for moving from one document to another (you still need to scroll, after all), they are supremely inadequate for most other tasks, such as moving, grouping or organizing things, drawing and sculpting things, positioning and sizing things, and other human tasks. There is no reason to limit either the Web or the desktop to the single click, and we can hopefully look forward to Web applications that are as rich in their interaction as desktop applications, as technology improves. Luckily, the hardware we have is more than up to the task of rich use of direct manipulation; we need only make sure our software continues to keep pace. In the next section of this chapter, we discuss common pointing devices and the capabilities they provide.

Pointing Devices

Direct manipulation of objects on a 2D screen is made possible through the use of a **pointing device**. Clearly, the best way to point to something is with your fingers. They're always handy; you probably have several of these convenient pointing devices nearby right now. The only real drawback they have is that their ends are too blunt for precisely pointing at high-resolution screens, and high-resolution screens also can't, on their own, recognize being pointed at. Because of this limitation, other pointing devices have taken the place of fingers, and each substitute has its own strengths and weaknesses. The mouse is the most omnipresent today, but it's not clear that the mouse will reign supreme forever.

Light Pens and CRTs

The first computer pointing device, the light pen, was a very logical extension of the finger. You held the light pen in your hand and pointed it at the screen like a pen. It was the perfect tool for direct manipulation, except for the tragic fact that it was completely unusable with computers.

When we use a stylus or any other writing device, we exercise fine motor control of our hand muscles to manipulate the tip of the stylus with our fingers. To do this reliably we have to have something to rest the heel of our hand on; otherwise, our movements are cast adrift. No matter how precise our finger motions are, they drift unless we provide our hand with a firm foundation.

Computers use big, clunky cathode ray tubes or flimsy, delicate liquid crystal display panels as their display screens. These typically face us vertically rather than lying flat on our desks like books and papers. As easy as it is to use a stylus on a sheet of paper on a firm horizontal surface, it is terribly difficult to make precise movements with that same stylus on a vertical surface with your arm and hand in the air, unsupported. Using a pen on vertical display squanders the fine motor control of our fingers and forces us to rely on the gross motor control of the muscles in our arms. These muscles are well suited for moving much greater distances, but they cannot give us the precision we expect for accurate pointing.

It is also extremely difficult to draw on a vertical surface while resting the ball of your hand on it—try it on your wall. Your wrist just won't bend backwards far enough. Sign painters, who must paint on the vertical surfaces of walls, doors, and windows, frequently use a tool called a *mahlstick*—a half-meter–long wooden dowel with a padded end. The artist rests the padded end on the wall and holds the other end in her free hand. Then she rests the heel of her drawing hand on the center of the stick. The mahlstick enables her to change the relative incidence of the painting surface from pure vertical to one that is better suited to keeping her drawing hand under control.

Unfortunately, a mahlstick is impractical for computer users, so we invented other tools, like the mouse.

Mice and indirect manipulation

As you roll the mouse around on your desktop, you see a visual symbol, the cursor, move around on the video screen in the same way. Move the mouse left and the cursor moves left; move the mouse up and the cursor moves up. As you first use the mouse, you immediately get the sensation that the mouse and cursor are connected, a sensation that is extremely easy to learn and equally hard to forget. This is good, because perceiving how the mouse works by inspection is nearly impossible. There is a scene in the movie *Star Trek IV: The Voyage Home*, where a character from the 24th century comes to 20th century Earth and tries to work a computer. He picks up the mouse, holds it to his mouth, and speaks into it. This scene is funny because of its underlying truth: The mouse has no visual affordance that it is a pointing device until someone shows us how the movements of the cursor are related to its movements. At that point, understanding is instantaneous. All idioms must be learned. Good idioms need only be learned once, and the mouse is certainly a good idiom in that regard.

The motion of the mouse to the cursor is not usually one-to-one, however. Instead, the motion is proportional. On most PCs, the cursor crosses an entire 30-centimeter screen in about 4 centimeters of mouse movement. With the heel of your hand resting firmly on the tabletop, your fingers can move the mouse with great accuracy. The fine motor control of the muscles in your hand enables you to precisely place the cursor, even with a 1:8 movement ratio. Those users who have a difficult time mastering the mouse usually don't place the heel of their palm firmly on their desk.

Although we use the term **direct manipulation** when we talk about pointing and moving things with the mouse, we are actually manipulating these things *indirectly*. A light pen points directly to the screen and can more properly be called a direct-manipulation tool because we actually point to the object. With the mouse, however, we are only manipulating a mouse on the desk, not the object on the screen.

With a thin-bodied stylus, we can get very precise control of the point, but with the palm-sized mouse, the muscles in our fingertips don't come into play the way they can with a pen. This is why we cannot enter handwriting practically with a mouse. Although we utilize fine motor control with a mouse, it is nothing like the extremely detailed control we exercise with the tip of a pen. With our hand wrapped around the much larger mouse, we can easily move the cursor to a particular place, but we cannot effectively define shapes or make the continuous self-relative movements that are required either for cursive or block printing. Thus the mouse is great for pointing at things on the screen, but miserable for entering graphical data. The stylus is fine for both tasks, assuming a horizontal surface for data entry.

Other pointing devices

The mouse is a clever tool that allows us to point to things on a vertical screen without entangling ourselves with the drawbacks of pointing or drawing on a vertical surface. In all other cases, it is worse than a pen. The fact that you can enter cursive handwriting with a pen and that you cannot do so with a mouse should be clue enough that the pen can be more precisely manipulated than the mouse. It is only when the writing surface goes vertical that the mouse emerges as the better tool.

There are many other pointing devices that have competed with the mouse for years but have not been universally accepted. These include trackballs, digitizing tablets, and touchpads.

TRACKBALLS

Trackballs have been around almost as long as microcomputers, but besides their use in games and early laptops, they have never really caught on. There's a good reason for this — trackballs are simply more awkward to use than mice. The biggest issue is placement of buttons. It is arguable that trackballs provide a degree of precision equal to or greater than that of mice, as far as moving the cursor goes. A trackball doesn't need to slide and is, therefore, more compact in terms of footprint on a desk. However, the buttons on the trackball, by necessity, need to be off to the side where they are awkward to click. Perhaps, if the button (for a Mac anyway) could be placed under the ball so that pressing gently on the ball itself activates a click (similar in concept to the no-button Apple mouse), the trackball might gain greater acceptance.

DIGITIZING TABLETS

Digitizing tablets have also been around for years, and although they have a dedicated following among artists and graphic designers, most people find them almost impossible to use to navigate a computer desktop. Part of the problem might be that people have been too well trained in using the mouse. The mouse is a relative pointing device — picking it up and putting it down elsewhere doesn't alter the position of the cursor on the screen; only motion of the mouse on a surface affects cursor location. Tablets are generally absolute pointing devices — each location on the tablet maps directly to an analogous location on the screen. So if you pick up the pen from the top-left corner and put it down in the bottom-right, the cursor will immediately jump from the top-left to the bottom-right of the screen. The really big problem with the digitizer tablet is that the display and digitizing area are separate. For some reason, this really causes ease of use problems for most people. Add to that the high price of these tablets, and you can see why they've never gone mainstream.

TOUCHPADS

Touchpads (Apple calls them trackpads, with some good reason) are, to date, the most successful pointing device after the mouse, largely because of their ubiquitous placement on laptop computers, which are quickly becoming more popular than desktop systems. Touchpads are fascinating because they combine behaviors of mouse, trackball, and digitizing pad. They use a tiny digitizing surface like a tablet, but like a trackball or mouse, you use your fingers, not a specialized pen. Like a mouse, they are relative pointing devices — movement of the cursor depends only on you moving your finger on the pad surface, not on your finger's position on the surface. Like a trackball, their buttons are placed, by necessity, in an awkward position where it is hard to access them except with the thumb. More recent touchpad drivers let you tap or double-tap the pad to click and double-click. This works well as long as you don't accidentally slide your finger while tapping, which moves the cursor. Of course, if you need to right-click (in Windows), you're stuck with the awkward hardware button. Although they are not perfect, touchpads have one great advantage to which they owe their success: You don't need to bring along a mouse when you travel with your laptop.

THE TRACKPOINT

IBM and Toshiba laptops, as well as a few other brands, make use of a somewhat bizarre pointing device called a TrackPoint, which consists of a pencil-eraser–sized nub stuck in the middle of its keyboard, nestled between the G, H, and B keys. Nudging this eraser-head with your finger moves the cursor in the direction of the nudge. Although some people swear by these devices, many users find them difficult to control, and they suffer from the same button placement problem as touchpads.

The return of the pen?

About 10 years ago, the first affordable products that made use of a technology that merged LCD displays and digitizing tablets — touchscreens — appeared. One of the earliest and best known of these was, undoubtedly, the Apple Newton. This device allowed users to use either a stylus or their fingers to directly manipulate objects on the screen, to write on the screen directly, and even to translate handwriting to computer-readable text (though the original Newton became notorious for its handwriting recognition problems). The design was such that you could hold the Newton in your hand like a notepad, thus providing the much-needed horizontal orientation of the display. This, in turn, allowed users to execute the precision movements that a pen is capable of. The device was large enough to support the hand properly, and this was perhaps part of its downfall — many people found it too large to stick in a pocket, thus critically weakening its purported function as an electronic notepad.

Palm Computing quickly followed Apple's lead. They created a similar, smaller device that did *not* recognize handwriting, but instead recognized a simplified alphabet called Graffiti. Oddly, you could not enter graffiti characters on the screen itself without third-party software; instead you needed to enter them in a digitizing area below the screen — perhaps the weakest part of the Palm interaction, and one that Palm licensees like Sony have since fixed. You *could*, however, use a stylus or your finger to directly manipulate objects on its small, square, digitized display. The most important success factor for Palm was that its device was small and simple. It was and still is a runaway success, and the Palm OS has now even found its way into some cellular phones.

By the time you read this book, Microsoft will have introduced its Tablet PC platform. Microsoft had released a version of Windows for pen-based computers years ago, but the hardware technology was still too slow, big, and heavy for it to catch on. This time around, the Tablet PCs will be light and fast, with high-resolution displays and powerful handwriting recognition. But most important, they will be in a form-factor that is comfortable for the pen-wielding human hand. Will the pen finally be in a position to challenge the mouse? Only time will tell.

For the time being, however, we must still contend with the mouse. Let's explore its interaction model further.

Using the Mouse

When you mouse around on the screen, there is a distinct dividing line between near motions and far motions: Your destination is either near enough that you can keep the heel of your hand stationary on your desktop, or you must pick up your hand. When the heel of your hand is down and you move the cursor from place to place, you use the fine-motor skills of the muscles in your fingers. When you lift the heel of your hand from the desktop to make a larger move, you use the gross motor skills of the muscles in your arm. Gross motor skills are no faster or slower than fine motor skills, but transitioning between the two is difficult. It takes both time and concentration, because the user must integrate the two groups of muscles. Touch-typists dislike anything that forces them to move their hands from the home position on the keyboard because it requires a transition between their muscle groups. For the same reason, moving the mouse cursor across the screen to manipulate a control forces a change from fine to gross and back to fine motor skills.

Clicking the button on the mouse also requires fine motor control — you use your finger to push it — and if your hand is not firmly planted on the desktop, you cannot click it without inadvertently moving the mouse and the cursor. Some compromise is possible between fine and gross motor control for the movement aspect of working a mouse. However, when it comes time to actually click the button — to pull the trigger — the user must first plant the heel of his hand, forcibly going into fine-motor control mode. To manipulate a control with a mouse, the user must use fine motor control to precisely position the cursor over the check box or push-button. However, if the cursor is far away from the desired control, the user must first use gross motor control to move the cursor near the control, then shift to fine motor control to finish the job. Some controls compound the problem with their interactions (see Figure 21-1).

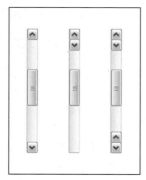

Figure 21-1: The familiar scrollbar, shown on the left, is one of the more difficult-to-use GUI controls. To shift from scrolling up to scrolling down, you must transition from the fine motor control required by clicking the button to the gross motor control you need to move your hand to the opposite end of the bar. You then change back to fine motor control to accurately position the mouse and click the button again. If the scrollbar were modified only slightly, as in the center, so that the two buttons were adjacent, the problem would go away. (Macintosh scrollbars can be similarly configured to place both arrow buttons at the bottom.) The scrollbar on the right is a bit visually cluttered, but has the most flexible interaction. For more on scrollbars, see Chapter 26.

It should be obvious at this point that any program that places its clickable areas more than a few pixels apart is inviting trouble. If a control demands a click nearby followed by a click far away, the control is poorly designed. Yet the ubiquitous scrollbar is just such a creature. If you are trying to scroll through a document, you click the down arrow several times, using fine motor control, until you find what you are looking for; but you are likely to click it one too many times and overrun your destination. At this point you must click the up arrow to get back to where you want to go. Of course, to move the cursor to the up arrow, you must pick up the heel of your hand and make a gross-motor movement. You then place the heel of your hand back down and make a fine-motor movement to precisely locate the arrow and keep the mouse firmly positioned while you click the button.

Why are the arrows on scroll-bars separated by the entire length of the bar itself? Yes, it looks visually more symmetrical this way, but it is much more difficult to use. If the two arrows were instead placed adjacent to each other at one end of the scrollbar, as shown in Figure 21-1, a single fine-motor movement could change the direction of the scroll, instead of the difficult dance of fine-gross-fine. Microsoft and mouse manufacturers have made an effort to address this problem in hardware by adding a **scroll wheel** to the mouse, located between the left and right button. Scrolling this wheel forward or back scrolls up or down, respectively, in the active window (if the application supports the scroll wheel).

Not only do the less manually dexterous find the mouse problematic, but also many experienced computer users, particularly touch-typists, find the mouse difficult at times. For many data-intensive tasks, the keyboard is superior to the mouse. It is frustrating to have to pull your hands away from the keyboard to reposition a cursor with the mouse, only to have to return to the keyboard again. In the early days of personal computing, it was the keyboard or nothing, and today, it is often the mouse or nothing. Programs should fully support both the mouse and the keyboard for all motion and selection tasks.

DESIGN TIP

Support both mouse and keyboard use for motion and selection tasks.

A significant percentage of computer users have trouble with the mouse, so if we want to be successful, we must design our software in sympathy with them as well as with expert mouse users. This means that for each mouse-idiom there should be at least one non-mouse alternative. Of course, this may not always be possible. It would be ridiculous to try to support some very graphic-oriented actions in a drawing program, for example, without a mouse, but these examples are in a clear minority. Most business or personal software lends itself pretty well to keyboard commands. Most users will actually use a combination of mouse and keyboard commands, sometimes starting commands with the mouse and ending them with the keyboard and vice versa.

How many mouse buttons?

The inventors of the mouse tried to figure out how many buttons to put on it, and they couldn't agree. Some said one button was correct, whereas others swore by two buttons. Still others advocated a mouse with several buttons that could be clicked separately or together so that five buttons could yield up to 32 distinct combinations. Ultimately, though, Apple settled on one button for its Macintosh, Microsoft went with two, and the Unix community (Sun Microsystems in particular) went with three.

One of the major drawbacks of the Macintosh is its single-button mouse. Apple's extensive user testing determined that the optimum number of buttons for beginners (who wasn't, back in 1984?) was one, thereby enshrining the single-button mouse in the pantheon of Apple history. This is unfortunate, as the right mouse button usually comes into play soon after a person graduates from beginner status and becomes a perpetual intermediate. A single button sacrifices power for the majority of computer users in exchange for simplicity for beginners.

There are fewer differences between the one- and two-button camps than you might think. The established purpose of the left mouse button is tacitly defined as "the same as the single button on the Macintosh mouse." In other words, the right mouse button is widely regarded as an extra button, and the left button is the only one the user really needs. This statement is no longer true today, however, with the evolution of the right-button context menu.

Even though many of the Unix workstation providers chose to provide a three-button mouse with their systems, the middle button is seldom used and is often claimed to be "reserved for application use." Needless to say, there are few applications that ever use it.

The left mouse button

In general, the left mouse button is used for all the major direct-manipulation functions of triggering controls, making selections, drawing, and so on. By deduction, this means that the functions the left button doesn't support must be secondary functions. Secondary functions are either accessed with the right mouse button or are not available by direct manipulation, residing only on menus or the keyboard.

The most common meaning of the left mouse button is activation or selection. For controls such as a push-button or check box, clicking the left mouse button means pushing the button or checking the box. If you are clicking in data, the left mouse button generally means selecting. We'll discuss this in greater detail in the next chapter.

The right mouse button

The right mouse button was long treated as nonexistent by Microsoft and many others. Only a few brave programmers connected actions to the right mouse button, and these actions were considered to be extra, optional, or advanced functions. When Borland International used the right mouse button as a tool for accessing a dialog box that showed an object's properties, the industry seemed ambivalent towards this action although it was, as they say, critically acclaimed. Of course, most usability critics have Macs, which have only one button, and Microsoft disdains Borland, so the concept didn't initially achieve the popularity it deserved. This changed with Windows 95, when Microsoft finally followed Borland's lead. Today the right mouse button serves an important and extremely useful role: enabling direct access to properties and other context-specific actions on objects and functions.

The middle mouse button

Although application vendors can confidently expect a right mouse button (except on the Mac), they can't depend on the presence of a middle mouse button. Because of this, no vendor can use the button as anything other than a shortcut. In fact, in its style guide, Microsoft states that the middle button "should be assigned to operations or functions already in the interface," a definition it once reserved for the right mouse button.

The authors have some friends who do use the middle button. Actually, they swear by it. They use it as a shortcut for double-clicking with the left mouse button — a feature they create by configuring the mouse driver software, trickery of which the application remains blissfully ignorant.

Pointing and clicking with a mouse

At its most basic, there are two atomic operations you can do with a mouse: You can move it to point at different things, and you can click the buttons. Any further mouse actions beyond pointing and clicking will be made up of a combination of one or more of those actions. The vocabulary of mouse actions is canonically formed and this is a significant reason why mice make such good computer peripherals.

Mouse actions can also be altered by using the meta-keys: Ctrl, Shift, and Alt. We will discuss these keys later in this chapter. The complete set of mouse actions that can be accomplished without using meta-keys is summarized in the following list. For the sake of discussion, we have assigned a short name to each of the actions (shown in parenthesis).

✓ Point (Point)

✓ Point, click, release (Click)

✓ Point, click, drag, release (Click and drag)

✓ Point, click, release, click, release (Double-click)

✓ Point, click, click other button, release, release (Chord-click)

✓ Point, click, release, click, drag, release (Double-drag)

Each of these actions (except chord-clicking) can also be performed on either button of a two-button mouse. An expert mouse user may perform all six actions, but only the first five items on the list are within the scope of normal users. Of these, only the first three can be considered reasonable actions for mouse-phobic users. Windows and the Mac OS are designed to be usable with only the first three actions. To avoid double-clicking in either OS, the user may have to take circuitous routes to perform his desired tasks, but at least the access is possible.

POINTING

This simple operation is a cornerstone of the graphical user interface and is the basis for all mouse operations. The user moves the mouse until the on-screen cursor is pointing to, or placed over, the desired object. Objects in the interface can take notice of when they are being pointed at, even when they are not clicked. Objects that can be directly manipulated often change their appearance subtly to indicate this attribute when the mouse cursor moves over them. This behavior is called pliancy and is discussed in detail later in this chapter.

CLICKING

While the user holds the mouse in a steady position, he clicks the button down and releases it. In general, this action is defined as triggering a state change in a control or selecting an object. In a matrix of text or cells, the click means, "Bring the selection point over here." For a push-button control, a state change means that while the mouse button is down and directly over the control, the button will enter and remain in the pushed state. When the mouse button is released, the button is triggered, and its associated action occurs.

Single-click selects data or changes the control state.

If, however, the user, while still holding the mouse button down, moves the cursor off of the control, the push-button control returns to its unpushed state (though input focus is still on the control until the mouse button is released). When the user releases the mouse button, input focus is severed, and nothing happens. This provides a convenient escape route if the user changes his mind. The mechanics of mouse-down and mouse-up events in clicking are discussed in more detail later in this chapter.

CLICKING AND DRAGGING

This versatile operation has many common uses including selecting, reshaping, repositioning, drawing and dragging and dropping. We'll discuss all of these in the remaining chapters of Part V.

The scrollbar treads an interesting gray area, because it embodies a drag function, but is a control, not an object (like a desktop icon). Windows scrollbars retain full input while the mouse button is clicked, allowing users to scroll successfully without having the mouse directly over the scrollbar. However, if the user drags too far astray from the scrollbar, it resets itself to the position it was in before being clicked on. This behavior makes sense, since scrolling over long distances requires gross motor movements that make it harder to keep within the bounds of the narrow scrollbar control. If the drag is too far off base, the scrollbar makes the reasonable assumption that the user didn't mean to scroll in the first place. Some programs set this limit too close, resulting in frustratingly temperamental scroll behavior.

DOUBLE-CLICKING

If double-clicking is composed of single-clicking twice, it seems logical that the first thing double-clicking should do is the same thing that a single-click does. This is indeed its meaning when the mouse is pointing into data. Single-clicking selects something; double-clicking selects something and then takes action on it.

Double-click means single-click plus action.

This fundamental interpretation comes from the Xerox Alto/Star by way of the Macintosh, and it remains a standard in contemporary GUI applications. The fact that double-clicking is difficult for less dexterous users — painful for some and impossible for a few — was largely ignored. The industry needs to confront this awful truth: Although a significant number of users have problems, the majority of users have no trouble double-clicking and working comfortably with the mouse. We should not penalize the majority for the limitations of the relative few. The answer is to go ahead and include double-click idioms, while ensuring that their functions have equivalent single-click idioms.

While double-clicking on data is well defined, double-clicking on most controls has no meaning (if you class icons as data, not controls), and the extra click is discarded. Or, more often, it will be interpreted as a second, independent click. Depending on the control, this can be benign or problematic. If the control is a toggle-button, you may find that you've just returned it to the state it started in (rapidly turning it on, then off). If the control is one that goes away after the first click, like the OK button in a dialog box, for example, the results can be quite unpredictable — whatever was directly below the push-button gets the second button-down message.

CHORD-CLICKING

Chord-clicking means clicking two buttons simultaneously, although they don't really have to be either clicked or released at precisely the same time. To qualify as a chord-click, the second mouse button must be clicked before the first mouse button is released.

There are two variants to chord-clicking. The first is the simplest, whereby the user merely points to something and clicks both buttons at the same time. This idiom is very clumsy and has not found much currency in existing software, although some creatively desperate programmers have implemented it as a substitute for a Shift key on selection.

The second variant is using chord-clicking to cancel a drag. The drag begins as a simple, one-button drag; then the user adds the second button. Although this technique sounds more obscure than the first variant, it actually has found wider acceptance in the industry. It is perfectly suited for canceling drag operations, and we'll discuss it in more detail in the next chapter.

DOUBLE-DRAGGING

This is another expert-only idiom. Faultlessly executing a double-click and drag can be like patting your head and rubbing your stomach at the same time. Like triple-clicking, it is useful only in mainstream, horizontal, sovereign applications. Use it as a variant of selection extension. In Word, for example, you can double-click in text to select an entire word; so, expanding that function, you can extend the selection word-by-word by double-dragging.

In a big sovereign application that has many permutations of selection, idioms like this one are appropriate. But unless you are creating such a monster, stick with more basic mouse actions.

Up and down events

Each time the user clicks a mouse button, the program must deal with two discrete events: the mouse-down event and the mouse-up event. With the lack of consistency exhibited elsewhere in the world of mouse management, the definitions of the actions to be taken on mouse-down and mouse-up can vary with the context and from program to program. These actions should be made rigidly consistent.

When selecting an object, the selection should always take place on the button-down. This is so because the button-down may be the first step in a dragging sequence. By definition, you cannot drag something without first selecting it, so the selection *must* take place on the mouse-down. If not, the user would have to perform the demanding double-drag.

DESIGN TIP

Mouse-down over data means select.

On the other hand, if the cursor is positioned over a control rather than selectable data, the action on the button-down event is to *tentatively* activate the control's state transition. When the control finally sees the button-up event, it then commits to the state transition.

DESIGN TIP

Mouse-down over controls means propose action; mouse-up means commit to action.

This is the mechanism that allows the user to gracefully bow out of an inadvertent click. In a push-button, for example, the user can just move the mouse outside of the button and the selection is deactivated even though the mouse button is still down. For a check box, the meaning is similar: On mouse-down the check box visually shows that it has been activated, but the check doesn't actually appear until the mouse-up transition.

The cursor

The cursor is the visible representation of the mouse's position on the screen. By convention, it is normally a small arrow pointing diagonally up and left, but under program control it can change to any shape as long as it stays relatively small: 32x32 pixels. Because the cursor frequently must resolve to a single pixel — pointing to things that may occupy only a single pixel — there must be some way for the cursor to indicate precisely which pixel is the one pointed to. This is accomplished by always designating one single pixel of any cursor as the actual locus of pointing, called the **hotspot**. For the standard arrow, the hotspot is, logically, the tip of the arrow. Regardless of the shape the cursor assumes, it always has a single hotspot pixel.

Pliancy and hinting

As you move the mouse across the screen, some things that the mouse points to are inert: Clicking the mouse button while the cursor's hotspot is over them provokes no reaction. **Pliant** objects or areas, on the other hand, react to mouse actions. A push-button control is pliant because it can be "pushed" by the mouse cursor. Any object that can be picked up and dragged is pliant; thus any directory or file icon in the File Manager or Explorer is pliant. In fact, every cell in a spreadsheet and every character in a text document is pliant.

When objects on the screen are pliant, this fact must be communicated to the user. If this fact isn't made clear, the idiom ceases to be useful to any user other than experts (conceivably, this could be useful, but in general, the more information we can communicate to every user the better).

AXIOM

Visually hint at pliancy.

There are three basic ways to communicate the pliancy of an object to the user: by static visual affordances of the object itself, by dynamically changing visual affordances, or by changing the visual affordances of the cursor as it passes over the object.

STATIC AND DYNAMIC VISUAL HINTING

Static visual hinting — when the pliancy of an object is communicated by the static visual affordance of the object itself — is provided by the way the object is drawn on the screen. For example, the three-dimensional sculpting of a push-button is static visual hinting because of its manual affordance for pushing.

Some visual objects that are pliant are not obviously so, either because they are too small or because they are hidden. If the pliant object is not in the central area of the program's main window and is unique-looking, the user simply may not understand that the object can be manipulated. This case calls for more aggressive visual hinting: dynamic visual hinting.

It works like this: When the cursor passes over the pliant object, it changes its appearance with an animated motion. Remember, this action occurs before any mouse buttons are clicked and is triggered by cursor fly-over only. A good example of this is behavior of butcons (icon-like buttons) on toolbars since Windows 98: Although the button-like affordance of the butcon has been removed to reduce visual clutter on toolbars, passing the cursor over any single butcon causes the affordance to reappear. The result is a powerful hint that the control has the behavior of a button, which, of course, it does. This idiom has also become quite common on the Web.

Active visual hinting at this level is powerful enough to act as a training device, in addition to merely reminding the user of where the pliant spots are.

CURSOR HINTING

Cursor hinting communicates pliancy by changing the appearance of the cursor as it passes over an object.

Most popular software intermixes visual hinting and cursor hinting freely, and we think nothing of it. For example, push-buttons are rendered three-dimensionally, and the shading clearly indicates that the object is raised and affords to be pushed; when the cursor passes over the raised button, however, it doesn't change. On the other hand, when the cursor passes over a window's frame, the cursor changes to a double-ended arrow showing the axis in which the window edge can be stretched. This is the only definite visual affordance that the frame can be stretched. Although cursor hinting usually involves changing the cursor to some shape that indicates what type of direct-manipulation action is acceptable, its most important role is in making it clear to the user that the object is pliant. It is difficult to make data visually hint at its pliancy without disturbing its normal representation, so cursor hinting is the most effective method. Some controls are small and difficult for users to spot as readily as a button, and cursor hinting is vital for the success of such controls. The column dividers and screen splitters in Microsoft's Excel are good examples, as you can see in Figure 21-2.

In a broad generalization, controls usually offer static or dynamic visual hinting, whereas *pliant* (manipulable) data more frequently offers cursor hinting. We talk more about hinting in Chapter 23.

DESIGN TIP   Indicating pliancy is the most important role of cursor hinting.

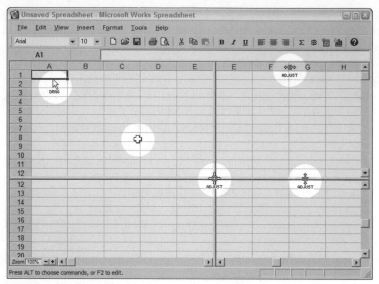

Figure 21-2: Microsoft Works Spreadsheet uses cursor hinting to highlight several controls that, by visual inspection, are not obviously pliant. The width of the individual columns and height of rows can be set by dragging on the short vertical lines between each pair of columns, so the cursor changes to a two-headed horizontal arrow hinting at both the pliancy and indicating the permissible drag direction. The same is true for the screen-splitter controls. When the mouse is over an unselected editable cell, it shows the plus cursor; and when it is over a selected cell, it shows the drag cursor. The addition of text to these cursors makes them almost like ToolTips.

WAIT CURSOR HINTING

There is a variant of cursor hinting, called wait cursor hinting. Whenever the program is doing something that takes significant amounts of time in human terms—like accessing the disk or rebuilding directories—the program changes the cursor into a visual indication that the program has become unresponsive. In Windows, this image is the familiar hourglass. Other operating systems have used wristwatches, spinning balls, and steaming cups of coffee. Informing the user when the program becomes stupid is a good idea, but the cursor isn't the right tool for the job. After all, the cursor belongs to everybody and not to any particular program.

The user interface problem arises because the cursor belongs to the system and is just "borrowed" by a program when it invades that program's airspace. In the pre-emptive multitasking world of Windows or Mac OS X, when one program gets stupid, it won't necessarily make other running programs get stupid. If the user points to one of these programs, it will need to use the cursor. Therefore, the cursor must not be used to indicate a busy state for any single program.

If the program must turn a blind eye and deaf ear to the user while it scratches some digital itch, it should make this known through an indicator on its own screen real estate, and it should leave the cursor alone. It can graphically indicate the corresponding function and show its progress either on its main window or in a dialog box that appears for the duration of the procedure, and offer the user a means to cancel the operation. The dialog box is a weaker idiom than drawing the same graphics right in the main window of the program.

Windows only displays the hourglass cursor within its own windows, which is logically correct. However, this means the program that is busy now offers no visual feedback of its state of stupidity. If the user inadvertently moves the cursor off of a busy program's main window and onto that of another running program, the cursor will revert to a normal arrow. The visual hinting is thus circumvented.

Ultimately, each program must indicate its busy state by some visual change to its own display. Using the cursor to indicate a busy state doesn't work if that busy state depends on where the cursor is pointing.

Input focus

Input focus is an obscure technical state that is so complex it has confounded more than one GUI programming expert.

Windows and most other desktop OS platforms are multitasking, which means that more than one program can be performing useful work at any given time. But no matter how many programs are running concurrently, only one program can be in direct contact with the user at one time. That is why the concept of input focus was derived. Input focus indicates which program will receive the next input from the user. For the purposes of our discussion here, we can think of input focus as being the same as *activation*: There is only one program active at a time. This is purely from the user's point of view. Programmers will generally have to do more homework. The active program is the one with the most prominent title bar.

In its simplest case, the program with input focus will receive the next keystroke. Because a normal keystroke has no location component, input focus cannot change because of it, but a mouse button click does have a location component and can cause input focus to change as a side effect of its normal command, a **new-focus click**. However, if you click the mouse somewhere in a window that already has input focus, an **in-focus click**, there is no change to input focus.

An in-focus click is the normal case, and the program will deal with it as just another mouse click, selecting some data, moving the insertion point, or invoking a command. The conundrum arises for the new-focus click: What should the program do with it? Should the program discard it (from a functional standpoint) after it has performed its job of transferring input focus, or should it do double-duty, first transferring input focus and then performing its normal task within the application?

For example, let's assume that two file system folder windows are visible on the screen simultaneously. Only one of them can be active. By definition, if folder Foo's window is active, it has input focus and visibly indicates this with a highlighted caption bar. Pressing keys sends messages only to folder Foo's window. Mouse clicks inside the already-active folder Foo window are in-focus and go only to folder Foo's window.

Now, if you move the mouse cursor over to the window for folder Bar and click the mouse, you are telling Windows that you want folder Bar's window to become the active window and take over input focus. This new-focus click causes both caption bars to change color, indicating that folder Bar's window is active and folder Foo's window is now inactive.

The question then arises: Should folder Bar's window interpret that new-focus click within its own context? Let's say that new-focus click was on a visible file icon. Should that icon also become selected or should the click be discarded after transferring input focus? If folder Bar's window was already active and you in-focus clicked on that same icon, the file would be selected. As a matter of fact, in real life, the file *does* get selected. The window interprets the new-focus click as a valid in-focus click.

Microsoft Windows interprets new-focus clicks as in-focus clicks with some uniformity. For instance, if you change focus to Word by clicking and dragging on its title bar, Word not only gets input focus, but is repositioned, too. Ah, but here is where it gets sticky! If you change input focus to Word by clicking on a document inside Word, Word gets input focus, but the click is discarded — it is *not* also interpreted as an in-focus click within the document.

Experts hold contradictory positions on the issue of interpreting new focus clicks, so neither policy is necessarily "right." Generally, ignoring the new-focus click is a safer and more conservative course of action. On the other hand, demanding extra clicks from the user contributes to excise. If you do choose to ignore the click, like Word and Excel do, it is difficult to explain the contradiction that a new-focus click in the window frame will be also used as an in-focus click, even though the interaction somehow *feels* right.

Meta-keys

Using meta-keys in conjunction with the mouse can extend direct manipulation idioms. Meta-keys include the Control key, the Alt key, and either of the two Shift keys.

In the Windows world, no single voice articulated user interface standards with the iron will that Apple did for the Macintosh, and the result was chaos in some important areas. This is evident when we look at meta-key usage. Although Microsoft has finally articulated meta-key standards, its efforts now are about as futile as trying to eliminate kudzu from Alabama roadsides.

Even Microsoft freely violates its own standards for meta-keys. Each program tends "to roll its own," but some meanings predominate, usually those that were first firmly defined by Apple. Unfortunately, the mapping isn't exactly the same. Apples have a Clover key and an Apple key that roughly correspond to the Ctrl and Alt keys, respectively. Keep in mind that the choice of which meta-key to use, or which program to model your choices after, is less important than remaining consistent within your own interface.

Using cursor hinting to dynamically show the meanings of meta-keys is a good idea, and more programs should do it. While the meta-key is pressed, the cursor should change to reflect the new intention of the idiom.

 DESIGN TIP   Use cursor hinting to show the meanings of meta-keys.

We will discuss the specific meanings and usage of the Control and Shift meta-keys and how they affect selection and drag and drop in Chapters 22 and 23.

Chapter 22

Selection

There are really only two things you can do with a mouse: Choose an object, and choose something to do with that object. These choosing actions are referred to as **selection**, and they have many nuances. This chapter discusses the various types of selection, when they should be applied, and how they should be visually indicated.

Object-Verb Ordering and Selection

A fundamental issue in user interfaces is the sequence in which commands are issued. Almost every command has an operation and one or more operands. The **operation** describes what action will occur, and the **operands** are the things acted upon by the operation. Operation and operand are programmers' terms; interface designers prefer to borrow linguistic terminology, referring to the operation as the **verb**, and to the operand as the **object**.

You can specify the verb first, followed by the object, or you can specify the object first, followed by the verb. These are commonly called verb-object and object-verb orders, respectively. Modern user interfaces use both orders.

When graphical user interfaces first emerged, it became clear that verb-object ordering created a problem. In an interactive interface, if the user chooses a verb, the system must then enter a state — a mode — that differs from the norm: waiting for an object. Normally, the user will then choose an object, and all will be well. However, if the user wants to act on more than one object, how does the system know this? It can only know if the user tells it in advance how many operands he will enter. Requiring the user to do this, however, violates the axiom: *Never make the user ask permission* (see Chapter 10). Otherwise, the program must accept all operands until the user enters some special object-list–termination command, also a very clumsy idiom. See the problem? What works just fine in a highly structured linguistic environment falls apart completely in the looser universe of interactivity.

If we change the command order to object-verb, we don't need to worry about termination. The user selects which objects will be operated upon, and then he indicates which verb to execute on them. The software then executes the indicated function on the selected data. A benefit of this is that the user can easily execute a series of verbs on the same complex selection. Notice, however, that a new concept has crept into the equation that didn't exist — and wasn't needed — in a verb-object world. That new concept is called **selection**.

Rather than the program remembering the verb while the user specifies one or more objects, we are asking the program to remember one or more objects while the user chooses the verb. This means, however, that we need a mechanism for identifying, marking, and remembering the chosen operands. Selection is the mechanism by which the user informs the program which objects to remember.

The object-verb model can be difficult to understand intellectually, but selection is an idiom that is very easy to grasp and, once shown, it is rarely forgotten (CTRL-clicking multiple e-mails in Outlook and deleting them, for example, quickly becomes second nature). Explained through the linguistic context of the English language, it is nonsensical that we must choose an object first (although it's probably not an issue for German speakers). On the other hand, we use this model frequently in our non-linguistic actions. We purchase groceries by first selecting the objects—by placing them in our shopping cart—then specifying the operation to execute on them by bringing the cart up to the checkout counter and expressing our desire to purchase. But we never say, "Corn flakes, buy" in English conversation.

In a non-interactive interface, like a modal dialog box, the concept of selection isn't always needed. Dialog boxes naturally come with one of those object-list–termination commands: the OK button. The user can choose a function first and an object second or vice versa because the whole operation won't actually occur until the confirming OK button is clicked. This is not to say that object-verb ordering isn't used in most dialog boxes. It merely shows that no particular command ordering has a divine right, but rather that the two orderings have strengths and weaknesses that complement each other in the complex world of user interfaces. Both are powerful tools for the software designer and should be used where they are best suited.

In its simplest variant, selection is trivial: The user points to a data object with the mouse cursor and clicks: The object is selected. However, this operation is deceptively simple and, in practice, many interesting variants are exposed.

Discrete and Contiguous Selection

Users generally select data objects, not verbs, which are operations on objects. When you invoke a verb (in other words, a command), you may do it with the same type of click action you used to select the data; however, commands are rarely presented as objects that possess a selection state. Selectable objects are typically those that can be operated upon, and that means data. The basic variants of selection, then, depend on the basic variants of selectable data, and there are two broad categories of data.

Some programs represent data as distinct visual objects that can be manipulated independently of other objects. The icons on the desktop and graphic objects in draw programs are examples. These objects are also selected independently of each other. They are **discrete data**, and selection of them is **discrete selection**.

Discrete data is not necessarily homogeneous, and discrete selection is not necessarily contiguous.

Conversely, some programs represent their data as a matrix of many little contiguous pieces of data. The text in a word processor or the cells in a spreadsheet are made up of hundreds or thousands of similar little objects that together form a coherent whole. These objects are often selected in contiguous groups, and so we call them **contiguous data** and selection within them **contiguous selection**.

Both contiguous selection and discrete selection support single-click selection and click-and-drag selection. Single-clicking selects the smallest possible discrete amount and clicking and dragging selects some larger quantity, but there are other significant differences.

There is a natural order to the text in a word processor's document — it consists of contiguous data. Scrambling the order of the letters destroys the sense of the document. The characters flow from the beginning to the end in a meaningful continuum and selecting a word or paragraph makes sense in the context of the data, whereas random, disconnected selections are generally meaningless. Although it is theoretically possible to allow a discontiguous selection — several disconnected paragraphs, for example — the user's task of visualizing the selections and avoiding inadvertent, unwanted operations on them is more trouble than it is worth. Generally, if contiguous data can be scrolled off-screen, it shouldn't be discontiguously selectable.

Discrete data, on the other hand, has no inherent order, like peas on your plate; the order in which you select and eat them is immaterial. In a drawing program, where various graphic objects reside on the screen, the objects are independent. No relationship is integral to their meaning, and even the z-order, the order in which they overlay each other on the screen, is only significant if they directly overlay each other. Scrambling the order of the objects might have no effect whatsoever on the collective image (again, except where objects overlay each other). Because there is no inherent order in these objects, contiguous selection has no meaning in this context, and each object is selected discretely.

Most drawing programs offer a grouping facility that allows two or more discrete objects to be logically grouped together to form a single, new discrete object. That group object now behaves as though it were a single discrete object regardless of the number of component pieces it contains.

Of course, you can always select more than one discrete object, but it remains a series of independent selections rather than a subset of ordered data.

Mutual Exclusion

Typically, when a selection is made, any previous selection is unmade. This behavior is called **mutual exclusion**, as the selection of one excludes the selection of the other. Typically, the user clicks on an object and it becomes selected. That object remains selected until the user selects something else. Mutual exclusion is the rule in both discrete and contiguous selection.

Some discrete systems allow a selected object to be deselected by clicking on it a second, canceling time. This can lead to a curious condition in which nothing at all is selected, and there is no insertion point. You must decide whether this condition is appropriate for your application.

Additive Selection

Mutual exclusion is necessary in contiguous selection because the user cannot see or know what effect his actions will have if his selections can readily be scrolled off the screen. Imagine being able to select several independent paragraphs of text in a long document. It might be useful, but it isn't easily controllable. Scrolling, not the contiguous selection, creates the problem, but most programs that manage contiguous data *are* scrollable.

However, if mutual exclusion is turned off in *discrete* selection, the user can select many independent objects by clicking on them sequentially, in what is called **additive selection**. A list box, for example, can allow the user to make as many selections as desired. An entry is then deselected by clicking it a second time. After the user has selected the desired objects, the terminating verb acts on them collectively.

Most discrete-selection systems implement mutual exclusion by default and allow additive selection only by using a meta-key. The Shift meta-key is used most frequently for this; the Ctrl key is also frequently used. In a draw program, for example, after you've clicked to select one graphical object, you typically can add another one to your selection by Shift-clicking.

Contiguous selection systems generally should not allow additive selection because of the control issues discussed previously (one could, however, imagine an interface with an overview display that might make additive selections manageable). However, contiguous-selection systems do need to enable their single allowable selection to be *extended*, and again, meta-keys are used. Unfortunately, there is little consensus regarding whether it should be the Ctrl or the Shift key that performs this role. In Word, the Shift key causes everything between the initial selection and the Shift-click to be selected. It is easy to find programs with similar additive selection functions that have made different choices of meta-key variations. There is little practical difference between choices, so this is an area where following the market leader is best because it offers the user the small-but-real advantage of consistency.

Some list boxes, as well as the file views in Windows (both examples of discrete data), do something a bit strange with additive selection. They use the Ctrl key to implement "normal" discrete additive selection; but then they use the Shift key to *extend* the selection, as if it were contiguous, not discrete data. In most cases this mapping simply adds to confusion, because it conflicts with the common idiom for discrete additive selection. There are also few times that someone would want to select, say, three adjacent items in a list box *simply because they are adjacent*, which is really the purpose of the contiguous selection extension idiom that is being misapplied here. There's a bit more argument for this idiom in file views, but group selection (see the next section) handles this almost equally well. The Macintosh uses the more typical (and more appropriate) mapping of Shift-click to discontiguously add to the selection in file views, which adds to the cognitive overhead of switching between the Mac and Windows, if like the authors, you work on both systems.

Insertion and Replacement

As we've established, selection indicates on which data the next function will operate. If that next function is a write command, the incoming data (keystrokes or a PASTE command) writes onto the selected object. In discrete selection, one or more discrete objects are selected, and the incoming data is handed to the selected discrete objects, which process the data in their own ways. This may cause a **replacement** action, where the incoming data replaces the selected object. Alternatively, the selected object may treat the incoming data as fodder for some standard function. In PowerPoint, for example, when a shape is selected, incoming keystrokes result in a text annotation of the selected shape.

In contiguous selection, however, the incoming data always replaces the currently selected data. When you type in a word processor or text entry box, you replace what is selected with what you are typing. Contiguous selection exhibits a unique quirk: The selection can simply indicate a location *between* two elements of contiguous data, rather than any particular element of the data. This in-between place is called the **insertion point**.

In a word processor, the **caret** (usually a dark, blinking, vertical line indicating where the next character will go) indicates a position between two characters in the text, without actually selecting either one of them. By pointing and clicking anywhere else, you can easily move the caret, but if you drag to extend the selection, the caret disappears and is replaced by the contiguous selection of text.

Another way to think of the insertion point is as a null selection. By definition, typing into a selection replaces that selection with the new characters, but if the selection is null, the new characters replace nothing; they are merely inserted. In other words, insertion is the trivial case of replacement.

Spreadsheets also use contiguous selection but implement it somewhat differently than word processors. The selection is contiguous because the cells form a contiguous matrix of data, but there is no concept of selecting the space between two cells. In the spreadsheet, a single-click will select exactly one whole cell. There is currently no concept of an insertion point in a spreadsheet, although the design possibilities are intriguing (that is, select the line between the top and bottom of two vertically adjacent cells and start typing to insert a row and fill a new cell in a single action).

A blend of these two idioms is possible as well. In PowerPoint's slide-sorter view, insertion-point selection is allowed, but single slides can be selected, too. If you click on a slide, that slide is selected, but if you click in between two slides, a blinking insertion-point caret is placed there.

If a program allows an insertion point, objects must be selected by clicking and dragging. To select even a single character in a word processor, the mouse must be dragged across it. This means that the user will be doing quite a bit of clicking and dragging in the normal course of using the program, with the side effect that any drag-and-drop idiom will be more difficult to express. You can see this in Word, where dragging and dropping text involves first a click-and-drag operation to make the selection, then another mouse move back into the selection to click and drag again for the actual move. To do the same thing, Excel makes you find a special pliant zone (only a pixel or two wide) on the border of the selected cell. To move a discrete selection, the user must click and drag on the object in a single motion.

To relieve the click-and-drag burden of selection in word processors, other direct manipulation shortcuts are also implemented, like double-clicking to select a word.

Group Selection

The click-and-drag operation is also the basis for group selection. For contiguous data, it means "extend the selection" from the mouse-down point to the mouse-up point. This can also be modified with meta-keys. In Word, for example, Ctrl-click selects a complete sentence, so a Ctrl-drag extends the selection sentence-by-sentence. Sovereign applications should rightly enrich their interaction with these sorts of variants as appropriate. Experienced users will eventually come to memorize and use them, as long as the variants are manually simple.

In a collection of discrete objects, the click-and-drag operation generally begins a drag-and-drop move. If the mouse button is clicked in an area between objects, rather than on any specific object, it has a special meaning. It creates a **drag rectangle**, shown in Figure 22-1.

A drag rectangle is a dynamically sizable rectangle whose upper-left corner is the mouse-down point and whose lower-right corner is the mouse-up point. When the mouse button is released, any and all objects enclosed within the drag rectangle are selected as a group.

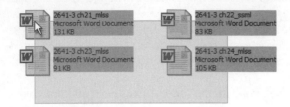

Figure 22-1: When the cursor is not on any particular object at mouse-down time, the click-and-drag operation normally creates a drag rectangle that selects any object wholly enclosed by it when the mouse button is released. This is a familiar idiom to users of drawing programs and many word processors. This example is taken from Windows XP, selecting files displayed within a file folder. The rectangle has been dragged from lower right to upper left.

Visual Indication of Selection

Selected objects must be clearly, boldly indicated as such to the user. The selected state must be easy to spot on a crowded screen, unambiguous, and must not obscure normally visible details of the object.

Make selection visually bold and unambiguous.

You must ensure that, in particular, users can easily tell which items are selected and which are not. It's not good enough just to be able to see that the items are different. Keep in mind that a significant portion of the population is colorblind, so color alone is insufficient to distinguish between selections.

Inversion

Selection is often accomplished by **inversion** — by inverting the pixels of the selected object. On a monochrome screen, this means turning all the white pixels black and all the black pixels white, but how many of you are still using black-and-white monitors? When the original Macintosh was released in 1984, it was a monochrome computer in spirit as well as in hardware. Because of this, Apple felt justified in using the inversion technique for indicating selections. Inversion was accomplished by the expedient of exclusive-ORing (or XORing) the pixels of the selected object with all 1 bits (or all 0 bits, depending on the processor). The XOR happens to be one of the fastest operations a CPU can execute, and, with the limited computing power available in 1984, this was an easily justifiable choice. XORs are naturally fast and, by a curious quirk of Boolean logic, the action of a XOR can be undone by repeating the identical XOR. Fast! Microsoft continued the XOR technique in the first releases of Windows even though it was never a monochrome system in thought or in deed.

The hidden gotcha is that the result of the XOR operation is only defined when its operands are binary: on or off, one or zero, white pixels or black pixels. XOR is inappropriate for color video. Sure, it works, but the colors are defined differently for different video drivers. What is the inverse of blue? In art class, it's yellow; but in Boolean algebra, who knows? Beyond this, color brings meaning with it; and it's a bad idea to let your users' video hardware be the arbiter of meaning. Finally, some inverted colors may lead to illegibility of the selection, which should be avoided at all costs.

Microsoft's PowerPoint is color-intensive and the slide view is rarely monochrome. When characters within text objects are selected for editing, the background turns black and the actual characters are inverted. The consistent black background can be reassuring, whereas the inverted pixels are okay — sometimes. However, when the text is white (as it commonly is), its background turns black and the characters are inverted from white to black, and this makes for very difficult editing. The program should make sure text is easily legible under all circumstances when selected.

In controls, inverting colors for selection causes more aesthetic and legibility problems. For example, in early releases of Windows, if you used the Control Panel program to configure your screen colors, and you set your menus to yellow instead of gray, they inverted to blue. This was certainly noticeable, but not necessarily desirable due to the legibility issues it introduced.

Microsoft acknowledged this problem in Windows 3.0 by defining two new system color settings: COLOR_HIGHLIGHT and COLOR_HIGHLIGHTTEXT. Of course, these manifest constants merely represent changeable colors rather than some fixed color. Each user can change these variable definitions, which then remain constant for all applications (until the user changes them again). Along with these new colors came a corresponding standard for use: When an object is selected, its color changes to whatever color is represented by COLOR_HIGHLIGHT. Any text or other contrasting pixels within the selected object change to whatever color is represented by COLOR_HIGHLIGHTTEXT. If the selection is contiguous, as in a word processor, the background becomes COLOR_HIGHLIGHT, and the foreground text becomes COLOR_HIGHLIGHTTEXT. This new standard normalizes the visual behavior of selection on a color platform. The Mac OS and most Unix window systems have similar user-configurable settings.

Use system highlight colors to show selection.

Selecting multicolor objects

In drawing, painting, animation, and presentation programs, where we deal with multicolor objects, it's easy for selections to get visually lost. The most reasonable solution is to *add* selection indicators to the object, rather than indicating selection by changing any of the selected object's visual properties. Most graphic arts programs take this approach, adding a form of visual scaffolding to the selected object without obscuring the object itself. This is often done with **handles** (discussed in Chapter 24): little boxes that surround the selected object, providing points of control. Handles can still get lost in the clutter, particularly with complex image-manipulation programs. There is, however, one way to assure that the selection will always be visible, regardless of the colors used: Indicate the selection by movement.

One of the first programs on the Macintosh, MacPaint, had a wonderful idiom where a selected object was outlined with a simple dashed line, except that the dashes all moved in synchrony around the object. The dashes looked like ants in a column; thus this effect earned the colorful sobriquet **marching ants** (it was also called the **marquee**, after the flashing lights on old cinema signs that exhibited a similar behavior).

Adobe Photoshop uses this idiom to show selected regions of photographs, and it works extremely well (expert users can toggle it off and on with a keystroke so that they can see their work without visual distraction). The animation is not hard to do, although it takes some care to get it right, and it works regardless of the color mix and intensity of the background.

Now that you understand the basics of selection, you can move on to how selected objects can be further controlled using direct manipulation. The remaining chapters of this section discuss dragging, dropping, and other ways to visually manipulate selected objects.

Chapter 23

Drag and Drop

Of all the direct-manipulation idioms characteristic of the GUI, nothing defines it more than the drag-and-drop operation, clicking and holding the button while moving some object across the screen. Surprisingly, drag-and-drop isn't used as widely as we imagine, and it certainly hasn't lived up to its full potential. In particular, the popularity of the Web and the myth that Web-like behavior is synonymous with superior ease of use have set back the development of drag-and-drop on the desktop, as developers mistakenly emulated the crippled interactions of Web browsers in other, far less appropriate contexts.

Defining Drag-and-Drop

Any mouse action is very efficient because it combines two command components in a single user action: a geographical location and a specific function. Drag-and-drop is doubly efficient because, in a single, smooth action, it adds a second geographical location. Although drag-and-drop was accepted immediately as a cornerstone of the modern GUI, it is remarkable that drag-and-drop is found so rarely outside of programs that specialize in drawing and painting. Thankfully, this seems to be changing, as more programs make use of this idiom.

We might define **drag-and-drop** as "clicking on an object and moving it to a new location," although that definition is somewhat narrow in scope for such a broad idiom. A more accurate description of drag-and-drop is "clicking on some object and moving it to imply a transformation."

The Macintosh was the first successful system to offer drag-and-drop. It raised a lot of expectations with the idiom that were never fully realized for two simple reasons. First, drag-and-drop wasn't a system-wide facility, but rather an artifact of the Finder, a single program. Second, as the Mac was at the time a single-tasking computer, the concept of drag-and-drop between applications didn't surface as an issue for many years.

To Apple's credit, they described drag-and-drop in its first user interface standards guide. On the other side of the fence, Microsoft not only failed to put drag-and-drop aids in its early releases of Windows, but didn't even describe the procedure in its programmer documentation. However, Microsoft eventually caught up and even pioneered some novel uses of the idiom, such as movable toolbars and dockable palettes.

Interior and Exterior Drag-and-Drop

Fundamentally, you can drag-and-drop something from one place to another inside your program, or you can drag-and-drop something from inside your program into some other program. These variants are called **interior drag-and-drop** and **exterior drag-and-drop**, respectively.

Interior drag-and-drop is fairly simple, both from a conceptual and from a coding point-of-view. Exterior drag-and-drop demands significantly more sophisticated support because both the programs involved must subscribe to the same concepts, and they must be implemented in compatible ways.

Critical to both variants of the drag-and-drop idiom is an understanding of the **source-and-target** paradigm.

The Source-and-Target Paradigm

When the user clicks on a discrete object and drags it to another discrete object in order to perform a function, what goes on behind the scenes embodies the **source-and-target paradigm**.

The object within which the dragging originates controls the entire process: It is the **source object**, which will be a window. If you are dragging an icon, that icon is its own window. If you are dragging a paragraph of text, the enclosing editor is the window. When the user ultimately releases the mouse button, whatever was dragged is dropped on some **target object**.

The main purpose of the term **source-and-target** is to differentiate this operation from the kind of drag-and-drop operations we find in drawing and painting programs, where tools and graphical objects are dragged around on an open canvas. Source-and-target is an idiom in which manipulating logical objects represents some behind-the-scenes processing. The most familiar form of source-and-target drag-and-drop is moving icons from folder to folder in the Program Manager or in the Macintosh Finder.

Dragging data objects to target functions

Instead of dragging a file or folder to another folder, you can drag it to a control that represents a function. This idiom is arguably the most famous expression of direct manipulation because of the Macintosh's familiar trashcan. Windows copies this familiar idiom with its Recycle Bin. As we build software with better object-orientation, we'll be able to drag-and-drop objects onto icons or controls representing functions other than just Delete. Apple has already extended this idea to printers, and the authors have also seen file decompression programs implemented in this manner. There is a lot of room for innovation in exploring this idiom!

Notice that all the idioms in the previous paragraph involve *exterior* drag-and-drop, because the target objects are separate programs. Within a single program, the code knows what objects can be dragged — usually one type — and any control that it gets dropped on will easily handle it. In exterior drag-and-drop, the source object can come from any program, and the target control may not have any direct knowledge of the originating program or the dropped object. The target must be able to handle the unknown object in some reasonable way without necessarily understanding what it is or what is in it. A file folder, for example, can do this because it knows that it will be handed only files. What would it do if it were handed a paragraph of dragged text from a word processor, for example? If it can't handle the text, it isn't truly exterior capable. To Microsoft's credit, the Recycle Bin in Windows can actually accept paragraphs of text dragged from Word or cells dragged from Excel.

To be truly **exterior capable**, an object must be able to accept a drop of anything from any other object, regardless of the originating program. At first, this sounds like a dauntingly complex implementation problem, but it doesn't have to be. Mostly, it's a matter of defining interface standards. When data is dragged to an object, all the target object has to say is, "Yes, I can accept the drop" to the source object. The two objects then must negotiate over formats, because it is unreasonable to expect every object to accept data in every other program's proprietary formats. If the source object is Excel, say, it may initially offer the data in its internal format. Another Microsoft program may know how to decipher this format, but a Brand X product might not. So the Brand X target object politely demurs — not to the drop, but to the *format* of the drop's contents. Excel, the source, must then re-offer the data in successively more generic formats: SYLK, CSV, ASCII. The target object can turn up its nose at SYLK or CSV, but by convention, it must accept ASCII; ASCII is the lowest common denominator format on all platforms. Every exterior capable object must minimally accept ASCII, simple bitmaps, pointers to files, and as we'll see, functions. Objects that hope to become successful in the open market will accept many more formats than these, but these four guarantee compatibility with everything. Even an audio file, for example, can ultimately be passed as a simple pointer to a disk file. Exterior drag-and-drop protocols that support this type of haggling over formats are **negotiated drag-and-drop protocols**. Protocols that don't negotiate formats can only accept known formats and are thus called **known-format drag-and-drop protocols**.

Dragging function objects to target data

A proper, negotiated, exterior drag-and-drop capability includes dragging and dropping functions onto data as well as dragging and dropping data onto functions. Defining the scope of such actions could be problematic when working in contiguous data, and there again arises the issue of verb-object ordering and termination, but in the authors' opinion, it is an idiom worthy of more research.

For now, there is no standard exterior drag-and-drop protocol, although OLE and ActiveX purport to offer one. Certainly, there is no negotiated drag-and-drop protocol.

Source-and-Target Interactions

A well-designed object will visually hint at its pliancy, either statically, in the way it is drawn or actively, by animating as the cursor passes over it.

The idea that an object can be dragged is easily learned idiomatically. It is difficult for a user to forget that an icon, selected text, or other distinct object can be directly manipulated after he has been shown that it can. He may forget the details of the action (so other feedback forms are very important *after* the user clicks on the object), but the fact of direct-manipulation pliancy itself is easy to remember. The first-timer or very infrequent user will probably require some additional help. This help will come either through additional training or by advice built right into the interface. In general, a program with a forgiving interaction encourages users to try direct manipulation on various objects in the program.

As soon as the user clicks the mouse button over an object, that object becomes the source object for the duration of the drag-and-drop. On the other hand, there is no corresponding target object because the mouse-up point hasn't yet been determined: It could be on another object or in the open space between objects. However, as the user moves the mouse around with the button held down, the cursor may pass over a variety of objects inside or outside the source object's program. If these objects are drag-and-drop compliant, they are possible targets, called **drop candidates**.

There can only be one source and one target in a drag, but there may be many drop candidates. Depending on the drag-and-drop protocol, the drop candidate may not know how to accept the particular dropped value; it just has to know how to accept the offered drop protocol. Other protocols may require that the drop candidate recognize immediately whether it can do anything useful with the offered source object. The latter method is slower but offers much better feedback to the user. If the protocol requires extensive conversing between the source object and each drop candidate, however, the interaction can become very sluggish, at which point it may not be worth the trouble.

Visual feedback while dragging

The only task of each drop candidate is to visually indicate that the hotspot of the captive cursor is over it, meaning that it will accept the drop — or at least comprehend it — if the user releases the mouse button. Such an indication is, by its nature, active visual hinting.

DESIGN TIP   Drop candidates must visually indicate their receptivity.

The weakest way to offer the visual indication of receptivity to being dropped upon is by changing the cursor. It is the job of the cursor to represent what is being dragged. It is best to leave all indications of drop candidacy to the drop candidate itself.

DESIGN TIP   The drag cursor must visually indicate the source object.

It is important that these two visual functions not be confused. Unfortunately, Microsoft seems to have done so in Windows. This decision was likely made more for the ease of coding than for any design considerations. It is much easier to change the cursor than it is to have drop candidates highlight to show their drop receptivity. The role of the cursor is to represent the master, the dragged object. It should not be used to represent the drop candidate.

As if that weren't bad enough, Microsoft performs cursor hinting using the detestable circle with a bar sinister, the universal icon for Not Permitted.

This symbol is an unpleasant idiom because it tells users what they can't do. It is negative feedback. A user can easily construe its meaning to be, "Don't let go of the mouse now, or you'll do some irreversible damage," instead of "Go ahead and let go now and nothing will happen." Adding the Not Permitted symbol to cursor hinting is an unfortunate combination of two weak idioms and should be avoided, regardless of what the Microsoft style guide says.

After the user finally releases the mouse button, the current drop candidate becomes the **target**. If the user releases the mouse button in the interstice between valid drop candidates, or over an invalid drop candidate, there is no target and the drag-and-drop operation ends with no action.

Silence, or visual inactivity, is a good way to indicate this termination. It isn't a cancellation, exactly, so there is no need to show a cancel stamp.

INDICATING DRAG PLIANCY

Active cursor hinting to indicate drag pliancy is a problematic solution. In an increasingly object-oriented world, more things can be dragged than not. A cursor flicking and changing rapidly can be more visual distraction than help. One solution is to just assume that things can be dragged and let the user experiment. This method is reasonably successful in the Windows Explorer and Macintosh Finder windows. Without cursor hinting, drag pliancy can be a hard-to-discover idiom, so you might consider building some other indication into the interface, maybe a textual hint or a ToolTip-style pop-up.

After the source object is picked up and the drag operation begins, there must be some visual indication of this. The most visually rich method is to fully animate the drag operation, showing the entire source object moving in real-time. This method is hard to implement, can be annoyingly slow, and very probably isn't the proper solution. The problem is that a master-and-target operation requires a pretty precise pointer. For example, the source object may be six-centimeters square, but it must be dropped on a target that is one-centimeter square. The source object must not obscure the target and, because the source object is big enough to span multiple drop candidates, we need to use a cursor hotspot to precisely indicate which candidate it will be dropped on. What this means is that, in master-and-target, dragging a transparent outline of the object may be much better than actually dragging a fully animated, exact image of the source object. It also means that the dragged object can't obscure the normal arrow cursor. The tip of the arrow is needed to indicate the exact hotspot.

Dragging an outline also is appropriate for most repositioning, as the outline can be moved relative to the source object, still visible in its original position.

INDICATING DROP CANDIDACY

As the cursor traverses the screen, carrying with it an outline of the source object, it passes over one drop candidate after another. These drop candidates must visually indicate that they are aware of being considered as potential drop targets. By visually changing, the drop candidate alerts the user that it can do something constructive with the dropped object.

A point, so obvious that it is difficult to see, is that the only objects that can be drop candidates are ones that are currently visible. A running application doesn't have to worry about visually indicating its readiness to be a target if it isn't visible. Usually, the number of objects occupying screen real estate is very small — a couple of dozen at most. This means that the implementation burden should not be overwhelming.

Internally, the source object should be communicating with each drop candidate as it passes over it. A brief conversation should occur, where the source asks the target whether it can accept a drop. If it can, the target indicates it with visual hinting. The target also needs to know when the cursor leaves its airspace, so it can turn off the hinting.

Microsoft not only doesn't insist on drop candidate visual hinting, it suggests that changing the cursor is sufficient. This decision is unfortunate for users. It is difficult to understand what is being dragged, what the target is, and whether the target can make sense of the drop. At least on the desktop, Windows icons now correctly indicate their drop candidacy by visually highlighting. Is this a shallow imitation of the Macintosh Finder specific only to the Windows desktop, or a system-wide standard for how source-and-target drag-and-drop should work? We hope it is the latter.

Completing the drag-and-drop operation

When the source object is finally dropped on a drop candidate, the candidate becomes a bona-fide target. At this point, the source and target must engage in a more detailed conversation than the brief one that occurred between the source and all the other drop candidates. After all, the user has committed, and we now know the target. The target may know how to accept the drop, but that does not necessarily mean that it can swallow the particular source object dropped in this specific operation.

The implication of this more-detailed conversation is that the transfer may fail. That is okay. It is better to show drop receptivity and fail on the actual drop than it is not to indicate receptivity if there is any likelihood of it succeeding. (If minimum common format standards are adhered to, there will never be a physical failure.) If the drag-and-drop is negotiated, the format of the transfer remains to be resolved. If information is transferred, the source and target may wish to negotiate whether the transfer will be in some proprietary format known to both or whether the data will have to reduced in resolution to some weaker but more common format, like ASCII text.

Insertion targets

As the user drags a source object around the screen, each drop candidate visually changes as it is pointed to, which indicates its capability to accept the drop. In some programs, the source object can instead be dropped in the spaces between other objects. Dragging text in Word is such an operation, as are most reordering operations in lists or arrays.

The vital visual feedback of drag-and-drop is showing where the source object will fall if the user releases the mouse button. In source-and-target, the drop candidate becomes visually highlighted to indicate the potential drop, but in this kind of **reordering drag-and-drop**, the potential drop will be in some space where there is no object at all. The visual hinting is drawn on the background of the program or in its contiguous data: an **insertion target**.

Rearranging slides in PowerPoint's slide-sorter view is a good example of this type of (interior) drag-and-drop. The user can pick up a slide and drag it into a different presentation order. As you drag, the insertion target (a vertical black bar that looks like a big text edit caret) appears between slides. Word, too, shows an insertion target when you drag text. Not only is the loaded cursor apparent, but you also see a vertical gray bar showing the precise location, in between characters, where the dropped text will land.

Whenever something can be dragged-and-dropped on the space between other objects, the program must show an insertion target. Like a drop candidate in source-and-target drag-and-drop, the program must visually indicate where the dragged object can be dropped.

Visual feedback at completion

If the target and the source can agree, the appropriate operation then takes place. A vital step at this point is visual feedback that the operation has occurred. If the operation is a transfer, the source object must disappear from its source and reappear in the target. If the target represents a function rather than a container (such as a print icon), the icon must visually hint that it received the drop and is now printing. It can do this with animation or by otherwise changing its visual state.

A richly visual source-and-target drag-and-drop operation is one of the most powerful operations in the GUI designer's bag of tricks. If tool vendors better support this idiom, it will grow in popularity with application developers. Users will be the beneficiaries.

Other Drag-and-Drop Interaction Issues

When we are first exposed to the drag-and-drop idiom, it seems simple; but for frequent users and in some special conditions, it can exhibit problems and difficulties that are not so simple. As usual, the iterative refinement process of software design has exposed these shortcomings, and in the spirit of invention, clever designers have devised equally clever solutions.

Auto-scrolling

What interpretation should the program make when the selected object is dragged beyond the border of the enclosing application? The correct interpretation is, of course, that the object is being dragged to a new position. But is that new position inside or outside of the enclosing application?

Take Microsoft Word, for example. When a piece of selected text is dragged outside the visible text window, is the user saying "I want to put this piece of text into another program" or is he saying "I want to put this piece of text somewhere else in this same document, but that place is currently scrolled off the screen"? If the former, we proceed as already discussed. But if the user desires the latter, the application must automatically scroll (auto-scroll) in the direction of the drag to reposition the selection at a distant, not currently visible location in the same document.

Auto-scroll is a very important adjunct to drag-and-drop. Where you implement one, you will likely have to implement the other. Wherever the drop target can possibly be scrolled off-screen, the program needs to auto scroll.

DESIGN TIP

Any scrollable drag-and-drop target must auto-scroll.

In early implementations, auto-scrolling worked if you dragged outside of the application's window. This had two fatal flaws. First, if the application filled the screen, how could you get the cursor outside of the app? Second, if you want to drag the object to another program, how can the app tell the difference between that and the desire to auto-scroll?

Microsoft developed an intelligent solution to this problem. Basically, it begins auto-scrolling just *inside* the application's border instead of just *outside* the border. As the drag cursor approaches the borders of the scrollable window—but is still inside it—a scroll in the direction of the drag is initiated. If the drag cursor comes within three or four millimeters of the bottom of the text area, Word begins to scroll the window's contents upward. If the drag cursor comes equally close to the top edge of the text area, Word scrolls down. Unfortunately, Word's implementation doesn't take into account the power of the microprocessor, and the action occurs too fast to be useful on the authors' computers (to be fair, some Microsoft products do implement auto-scrolling right). Besides compensating for processor speed, a better way to implement this same idiom would be to use a variable auto-scroll rate as shown in Figure 23-1, where the automatic scrolling increases in speed as the cursor gets closer to the window edge. For example, when the cursor is five millimeters from the upper edge, the text scrolls down at one line per second. At four millimeters, the text scrolls at two lines per second, and so on. This gives the user sufficient control over the auto-scroll to make it useful. The auto-scroll should always be constrained; computers are only getting faster.

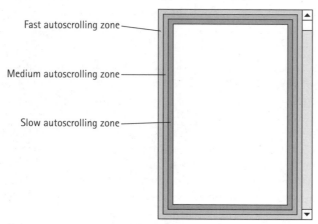

Fast autoscrolling zone

Medium autoscrolling zone

Slow autoscrolling zone

Figure 23-1: Microsoft, unfortunately, auto-scrolls at whatever speed the computer is capable of, or at least far too fast for users to control. Not only should there be a maximum speed limit on auto-scroll, the movement should also be graduated and user-controllable. The auto-scroll should go faster the closer the user gets to the edge of the window. To its credit, Microsoft's idea of auto-scrolling as the cursor approaches the *inside* edges of the enclosing scrollbox, rather than the outside, is very clever indeed.

Another important detail required by auto-scrolling is a time delay. If auto-scrolling begins as soon as the cursor enters the sensitive zone around the edges, it is too easy for a slow-moving user to inadvertently auto-scroll. To cure this, auto-scrolling should only begin after the drag-cursor has been in the auto-scroll zone for some reasonable time cushion—about a half-second.

If the user drags the cursor completely outside of the Word's scrollable text window, no auto-scrolling occurs. Instead, the repositioning operation will terminate in a program other than Word. For example, if the drag cursor goes outside of Word and is positioned over PowerPoint, when the user releases the mouse button, the selection will be pasted into the PowerPoint slide at the position indicated by the mouse. Furthermore, if the drag cursor moves within three or four millimeters of any of the borders of the PowerPoint Edit window, PowerPoint begins auto-scrolling in the appropriate direction. This is a very convenient feature, as the confines of contemporary screens mean that we often find ourselves with a loaded drag cursor and no place to drop its contents.

Avoiding drag-and-drop twitchiness

When an object can be either selected or dragged, it is vital that the mouse be biased towards the selection operation. Because it is so difficult to click on something without inadvertently moving the cursor a pixel or two, the frequent act of selecting something must not accidentally cause the program to misinterpret the action as the beginning of a drag-and-drop operation. Users rarely want to drag an object only one or two pixels across the screen. The time it takes to perform a drag is usually much greater than the time it takes to perform a selection. Dragging is often accompanied by a redraw operation, causing objects on the screen to flicker (although this will cease as computers get faster). This unexpected visual paroxysm can be disturbing to users expecting a simple selection. In addition, the object is now displaced by a couple of pixels. The user probably had the object just where he wanted it, so having it displaced by even one pixel will not please him.

In the hardware world, controls like pushbuttons that have mechanical contacts can exhibit what engineers call **bounce**, which means that the tiny metal contacts of the switch literally bounce when someone presses them. For electrical circuits like doorbells, the milliseconds the bounce takes aren't meaningful, but in modern electronics, those extra clicks can be significant. The circuitry backing up such switches has special logic to ignore extra transitions if they occur within a few milliseconds of the first one. This keeps your stereo from turning back off a thousandth of a second after you've turned it on. This situation is analogous to the oversensitive mouse problem, and the solution is to copy switch makers and debounce the mouse.

To avoid this situation, programs should establish a **drag threshold**, in which all mouse-movement messages that arrive after the mouse-down event are ignored unless the movement exceeds a small threshold amount, such as three pixels. This provides some protection against initiating an inadvertent drag operation. If the user can keep the mouse button within three pixels of the mouse-down point, the entire click action is interpreted as a selection command, and all tiny, spurious moves are ignored. The object has been debounced. As soon as the mouse moves beyond the three-pixel threshold, the program can confidently change the operation to a drag. This is shown in Figure 23-2. Any time you have a situation where an object can be selected and dragged, the drag operation should be debounced.

The Program Manager in Windows 3.x had a one-pixel drag threshold, which was too small. It was far too easy to accidentally move an icon out of position when all you wanted to do was select it. Icons on the Windows XP desktop appear to have a three-pixel debounce threshold.

DESIGN TIP   Debounce all drags.

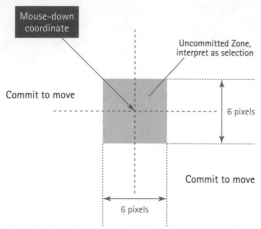

Figure 23-2: Any object that can be both selected and dragged must be debounced. When the user clicks on the object, the action must be interpreted as a selection rather than a drag, even if the user accidentally moves the mouse a pixel or two between the click and the release. The program must ignore any mouse movement as long as it stays within the uncommitted zone, which extends three pixels in each direction. After the cursor moves more than three pixels away from the mouse-down coordinate, the action changes to a drag, and the object is considered "in play." This is called a *drag threshold*, and it is used to debounce the mouse.

Some applications may require more-complex drag thresholds. 3D applications often require drag thresholds that enable movement in three projected axes on the screen. Another such example arose in the design of a report generator for one of our clients. The user could reposition columns on the report by dragging them horizontally; for example, he could put the Firstname column to the left of the Lastname column by dragging it into position from anywhere in the column. This was, by far, the most frequently used drag-and-drop idiom. There was, however, another, infrequently used drag operation. This one allowed the values in one column to be interspersed *vertically* with the values of another column—for example, an address field and a state field (see Figure 23-3).

We wanted to follow the user's mental model and enable him to drag the values of one column on top of the values of another to perform this stacking operation, but this conflicted with the simple horizontal reordering of columns. We solved the problem by differentiating between horizontal drags and vertical drags. If the user dragged the column left or right, it meant that he was repositioning the column as a unit. If the user dragged the column up or down, it meant that he was interspersing the values of one column with the values of another.

Before

1	NAME	ADDRESS	CITY
2	Ginger Beef	342 Easton Lane	Waltham
3	C. U. Lator	339 Disk Drive	Borham
4	Justin Case	68 Elm	Albion
5	Creighton Barrel	9348 N. Blenheim	Five Islands
6	Dewey Decimal	1003 Water St.	Freeport

After

1	NAME	ADDRESS/CITY	
2	Ginger Beef	342 Easton Lane Waltham	
3	C. U. Lator	339 Disk Drive Borham	
4	Justin Case	68 Elm Albion	
5	Creighton Barrel	9348 N. Blenheim Five Islands	
6	Dewey Decimal	1003 Water St. Freeport	

Figure 23-3: This report-generator program offered an interesting feature that enabled the contents of one column to be interspersed with the contents of another by dragging and dropping it. This direct-manipulation action conflicted with the more-frequent drag-and-drop action of reordering the columns (like moving City to the left of Address). We used a special, two-axis drag threshold to accomplish this.

Because the horizontal drag was the predominant user action and vertical drags were rare, we biased the drag threshold towards the horizontal axis. Instead of a square uncommitted zone, we created the spool-shaped zone shown in Figure 23-4. By setting the horizontal-motion threshold at four pixels, it didn't take a big movement to commit the user to the normal horizontal move, while still insulating the user from an inadvertent vertical move. To commit to the far less-frequent vertical move, the user had to move the cursor eight pixels on the vertical axis without deviating more than four pixels left or right. The motion is quite natural and easily learned.

This axially non-symmetric threshold can be used in other ways, too. Visio implements a similar idiom to differentiate between drawing a straight and a curved line.

Mouse vernier

The weakness of the mouse as a precision pointing tool is readily apparent, particularly when dragging objects around in drawing programs. It is darned hard to drag something to the exact desired spot, especially when the screen resolution is 100 or more pixels-per-inch and the mouse is running at a six-to-one ratio to the screen. To move the cursor one pixel, you must move the mouse precisely one six-hundredth of an inch. Not easy to do.

This is solved by adding a **mouse vernier** function, where the user can quickly shift into a mode that allows much finer-resolution for mouse-based manipulation of objects.

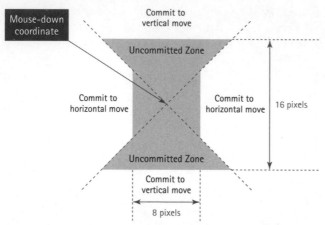

Figure 23-4: This spool-shaped drag threshold allowed a bias toward horizontal dragging in a client's program. Horizontal dragging was, by far, the most frequently used type of drag in this application. This drag threshold made it difficult for the user to inadvertently begin a vertical drag. However, if the user really wanted to drag vertically, a bold move either up or down would cause the program to commit to the vertical mode with a minimum of excise. Before this method was instituted, a vertical move involved a semipermanent mode change by using a toolbar butcon.

During a drag, if the user decides that he needs more precise maneuvering, he can change the ratio of the mouse's movement to the object's movement on the screen. Any program that might demand precise alignment must offer a vernier facility. This includes, at a minimum, all drawing and painting programs, presentation programs, and image-manipulation programs.

DESIGN TIP

Any program that demands precise alignment must offer a vernier.

There are several acceptable variants of this idiom. A key can be pressed during the drag operation, like the Enter key, and the mouse shifts into vernier mode. In vernier mode, each ten pixels of mouse movement will be interpreted as a single pixel of object movement.

Another effective method is to make the arrow keys active during a drag operation. While holding down the mouse button, the user can manipulate the arrow keys to move the selection up, down, left, or right — one pixel at a time. The drag operation is still terminated by releasing the mouse button.

The problem with such a vernier is that the simple act of releasing the mouse button can often cause the user's hand to shift a pixel or two, causing the perfectly placed object to slip out of alignment just at the moment of acceptance. The solution to this is, upon receipt of the first vernier keystroke, to **desensitize** the mouse. This is accomplished by making the mouse ignore all subsequent movements under some reasonable threshold, say five pixels. This means that the user can make the initial gross movements with the mouse, then make a final, precise placement with the arrow keys, and release the mouse button without disturbing the placement. If the user wants to make additional gross movements after beginning the vernier, he simply moves the mouse beyond the threshold, and the system shifts back out of vernier mode.

If the arrow keys are not otherwise spoken for in the interface, as in a drawing program, they can be used to control vernier movement of the selected object. This means the user does not have to hold the mouse button down. Adobe Illustrator and Photoshop do this, as does PowerPoint. In PowerPoint, the arrow keys move the selected object one step on the grid — about two millimeters using the default grid settings. If you hold the Alt key down while using the arrow keys, the movement is one pixel per arrow keystroke. This is nicely done.

Chapter 24

Manipulating Controls, Objects, and Connections

In the previous two chapters, we discussed two important kinds of direct manipulation: selection and drag-and-drop. In this chapter, we'll discuss the remaining kinds: control manipulation, object manipulation, and object connection.

Control Manipulation

We can categorize the types of direct manipulation on controls by examining which mouse actions they require: clicking or clicking and dragging.

Beyond simple one-click controls, most direct-manipulation idioms demand a click-and-drag operation. This is a fundamental building block of visual interaction using a mouse, and we will explore it in some detail.

Click-and-drag

A drag begins when the user clicks the mouse button and then moves it without releasing the button. The set of cursor screen coordinates when the user first clicks the mouse button is called the **mouse-down point** and that when the user releases the button is called the **mouse-up point**. The mouse-down point is a known quantity throughout any direct manipulation operation. The mouse-up point only becomes known at the end of the process.

After a drag begins, the entire interaction between the user and the computer enters a special state. In programmer lingo, we say that all interaction between the system and the user is **captured**, meaning that no other program can interact with the user until the drag is completed.

Any actions the user might take with the mouse or keyboard or any other input device go directly to the program — technically, the window — in which the mouse button was first clicked (the one that received the mouse-down event). This window that owns the mouse-down point is the **source object**. If this source object is contiguous data or a control, the drag will indicate a selection extension or a control state change. However, if the source object is a discrete object, it more likely indicates the beginning of a direct-manipulation operation like drag-and-drop, and capture will play an important part.

Technically, a state of capture exists the instant the user clicks the mouse button, and it doesn't end until that mouse button is released, regardless of the distance the mouse moves between the two button actions. To the human, a simple click-and-release without motion seems instantaneous, but to the program, hundreds of thousands of instructions can be executed in the time it takes to click and release the button. If the user inadvertently moves the mouse before releasing the button, capture protects him from wildly triggering adjacent controls. The source object will simply reject such spurious commands.

Escaping from capture

One of the most important — yet most frequently ignored — parts of a drag operation is a mechanism for getting out of it. The user not only needs a way to abort the drag; if he does, he needs to have solid assurance that he did so successfully.

If the communication to the user that the drag action was canceled is clear, bold, and unambiguous, he will be reassured and confident in using the cancel idiom, whatever it may be. Most applications, though, have no means of drag cancellation whatsoever. This is a grave lapse in user interface terms because any good interface provides consistent and reliable ways out of a user's ill-starred action.

AXIOM

Provide an escape from dragging and inform the user about it.

At a minimum, the Escape key on the keyboard should always be recognized as a general-purpose cancel mechanism for any mouse operation, either clicking or dragging. If the user presses the Escape key while holding down the mouse button, the system should abandon the state of capture and return the system to the state it was in before the mouse button was clicked. When the user subsequently releases the mouse button, the program must remember to discard that mouse-up input before it has any side effect.

Because the meta-keys are often the only keys that have any meaning during drags, we could actually use any non-meta–keystroke to cancel a mouse stroke, rather than offering up only the Escape. However, some programs allow the use of the arrow keys in conjunction with the mouse (we'll discuss this in the next chapter), so there are some exceptions to work around.

One less-known idiom is the chord-click, where the user clicks left and right mouse buttons together. In Windows, a chord-click cancels a drag operation in many instances. Typically, the user begins a drag with the left mouse button, and then discovers that he doesn't really want to finish what he has begun. He clicks the right mouse button, then safely releases both. The idiom is insensitive to the timing or sequence of the release and works equally well if the drag was begun with the right mouse button.

DESIGN TIP

Cancel a drag on chord-click.

Microsoft used chord-clicking for drag cancel in its Word for DOS software, but unfortunately discarded the idiom when it went to Windows. Admittedly, the idiom is for experts, but why hobble an interface for mouse experts simply to pander to mouse novices? At least the current version of Word recognizes the Escape key as a drag cancel.

Windows Explorer (and even the desktop) in XP supports Escape and chord-clicking as drag cancel idioms, but if you actually try to use the chord-click, a problem arises. The Windows designers have chosen to launch the context (right-click) pop-up menu on a *mouse-up* event, rather than on mouse-down. This means when you lift your finger off the right mouse button, you are confronted with an unwanted menu that you have to actively navigate away from and dismiss (with another mouse click). Yuck! There's a reason why menus should launch on mouse-down events!

Because Microsoft was so tentative in committing to the presence of a second mouse button, it is only fitting that it has been tentative about committing the chord-click to a cancel idiom. But now that Microsoft seems to have admitted that all its users will have at least two mouse buttons, adopting the chord-click as a universal cancel idiom would only make good sense (assuming it was done right!). Write your congressperson today.

If your program is well designed and enables the user to cancel out of a drag operation with an Escape key or a chord-click, the problem still remains of assuring the user that he is now safe. The cursor may have been changed to indicate that a drag was in progress, or an outline of the dragged object may have been moving with the cursor. The cancellation makes these visual hints go away, but the user may still wonder if he is truly safe. A user may have pressed the Escape key, but is still holding the mouse button down, unsure whether it is entirely safe to let go of it (or perhaps he has just chord-clicked, and is holding down two mouse buttons). The user should now be informed that the operation has been effectively canceled and that releasing the mouse button (or buttons) is okay. It can't hurt — and can only help — to make sure that he gets a reassuring message.

Of course, the user will get visual feedback that whatever object he was dragging is no longer being dragged because it will vanish from underneath the cursor or snap back to where it came from. This snap-back could be enhanced with a brief animation indicating the snap-back, rather like the original Macintosh animation that accompanied windows opening and closing. (This was such wonderful visual hinting; Windows should learn a lesson in general from this.)

Alternately, or perhaps in addition to this, you could imagine a brief message, rather like a ToolTip, appearing for a second or two in the vicinity of the cursor. One could also imagine that a little "snip" sound to indicate premature termination of the drag operation would help reinforce the idiom.

Pliant response

Let's return to the drag operation itself: Once the drag begins, the meaning of the user's actions varies depending on the type of drag action. The drag action depends on the program, the context, and the master object.

In the simplest case, involving contiguous data, dragging means, "extend the selection." The text or other data is selected contiguously from the mouse-down point to the mouse-up point.

If the mouse is clicked while the cursor is inside a control, the control must visually show that it is poised to undergo a state change. This action is important and is often neglected by those who create their own controls. It is a form of active visual hinting: **pliant response**.

A push-button needs to change from a visually raised state to a visually indented state; a check box should highlight its box but not show a check just yet. Pliant response is an important feedback mechanism for any control that either invokes an action or changes its state, letting the user know that some action is forthcoming if she releases the mouse button. The pliant response is also an important part of the cancel mechanism. When the user clicks down on a button, that button responds by indenting. If the user moves the mouse away from that button while still holding the button down, the button should return to its quiescent, raised state. If the user then releases the mouse, the button will not be activated (consistent with the lack of pliant response).

Click-and-drag controls

Many controls, particularly menus, require the moderately difficult motion of a click-and-drag rather than a mere click. This direct-manipulation operation is more demanding of the user because of its juxtaposition of fine motions with gross motions to click, drag, and then release the mouse button. Although menus are not used as frequently as toolbar controls, they are still used very often, particularly by new or infrequent users. Thus, we find one of the more intractable conundrums of GUI design: The menu is the primary control for beginners, yet it is one of the more difficult controls to physically operate.

There is no solution to this problem other than to provide additional idioms to accomplish the same task. If a function is available from the menu, and it is one that will be used more than just rarely, make sure to provide other idioms for invoking the function — idioms that don't require a click-and-drag operation.

One of the nice features of Windows, which recent versions of the Mac OS have also adopted, is the capability to work its menus with a series of single clicks rather than clicking and dragging. You click on the menu, and it drops down. You point to the desired item, click once to select it and close the menu. Microsoft further extended this idea by putting programs into a sort-of **menu mode** (as soon as you click once on any menu). When in menu mode, all the top-level menus in the program and all the items on those menus are active, just as though you were clicking and dragging. As you move the mouse around, each menu, in turn, drops down without your having to use the mouse button at all. This can be disconcerting if you are unfamiliar with it; but after the initial shock has worn off, the action is generally more pleasant, mostly because it is easier on the wrist.

Palette tool behaviors

In drawing and painting programs, after a tool or shape is selected from a palette, the user manipulates it by dragging. Palette tools have their own unique behaviors, which are worthy of separate mention here. There are two basic variants of palette tool behavior: modal tools and charged cursor tools.

MODAL TOOLS

With **modal tools**, the user selects a tool from a list or specialized toolbar, usually called a toolbox or palette. The display area of the program is now completely in the mode of that tool: It will only do that one tool's job. The cursor usually changes to indicate the active tool.

When the user clicks and drags with the tool on the drawing area, the tool does its thing. If the active tool is a spray can, for example, the program enters Spray Can mode and it can only spray. The tool can be used over and over, spraying as much ink as desired until the user clicks on a different tool. If the user wants to use some other tool on the graphic, like an eraser, he must return to the toolbox and select the eraser tool. The program then enters Eraser mode and can only erase things until another tool is chosen. There is usually a selection-cursor tool on the palette to let the user return the cursor to a selection-oriented pointer, as in Adobe Photoshop, for example.

Modal tools work both for tools that perform **actions** on drawings — like an eraser — or for **shapes** that can be drawn — like ellipses. The cursor can become an eraser tool and erase anything previously entered, or it can become an ellipse tool and draw any number of new ellipses. The mouse-down event anchors a corner or center of the shape (or its bounding-box), the user drags to stretch out the shape to the desired size and aspect, and the mouse-up event confirms the draw.

Modal tools are not bothersome in a program like Paint, where the number of drawing tools is very small. In a more advanced drawing program such as Adobe Photoshop, however, the modality is very disruptive because, as the user gets more facile with the cursor and the tools, the percentage of time and motion devoted to selecting and deselecting tools — the excise — increases dramatically. Modal tools are excellent idioms for introducing users to the range of features of such a program, but they don't usually scale well for experienced users of more sophisticated programs. Luckily, Photoshop makes extensive use of keyboard commands for power users.

The difficulty of managing a modal tool application isn't caused by the modality as much as it is by the sheer quantity of tools. More precisely, the efficiencies break down when the quantity of tools in the user's working set gets too large. A working set of more than about five modal tools tends to get hard to manage. If the number of necessary tools in Adobe Illustrator could be reduced from 24 to eight, for example, its user interface problems might diminish below the threshold of user pain.

To compensate for the profusion of modal tools, products like Adobe Illustrator use meta-keys to modify the various modes. The shift key is commonly used for constrained drags, but Illustrator adds many non-standard meta-keys and uses them in non-standard ways. For example, holding down the Alt key while dragging an object drags away a *copy* of that object, but the Alt key is also used to promote the selector tool from single vertex selection to object selection. The distinction between these uses is subtle: If you click something, then press the Alt key, you drag away a copy of it. Alternately, if you press the Alt key and *then* click on something, you select all of it, rather than a single vertex of it. But then, to further confuse matters, you must *release* the Alt key or you will drag away a copy of the entire object. To do something as simple as selecting an entire object and dragging it to a new position, you must press the Alt key, point to the object, click and hold the mouse button without moving the mouse, release the Alt key, and then drag the object to the desired position! What were these people thinking?

Admittedly, the possible combinations are powerful, but they are very hard to learn, hard to remember, and hard to use. If you are a graphic arts professional working with Illustrator for eight hours a day, you can turn these shortcomings into benefits in the same way that a race car driver can turn the cantankerous behavior of a finely tuned automobile into an asset on the track. The casual user of Illustrator, however, is like the average driver behind the wheel of an Indy car: way out of his depth with a temperamental and unsuitable tool.

Adobe Illustrator is firmly rooted in the Macintosh world. One of the errors that Adobe made in its Windows interface design was refusing to take advantage of the benefits of the two-button mouse, something that comes cheap or free with Windows. Illustrator doesn't use the right mouse button at all. Undoubtedly, someone in the company felt that interoperability with the Mac was more important. Adobe could have put all selection tools on the left button and all drawing tools on the right button, for example. Users could then go back and forth between drawing things and manipulating them just by deciding which mouse button to use, and even better, each button would then have available to it three meta-keys: Alt, Ctrl, and Shift.

CHARGED CURSOR TOOLS

With **charged cursor** tools, the user again selects a tool or shape from a palette, but this time, rather than the cursor switching permanently (until the user switches again) to the selected tool, the cursor becomes loaded — or **charged** — with a single instance of the selected object.

When the user clicks once in the drawing area, an instance of the object is created on the screen at the mouse-up point. The charged cursor doesn't work too well for functions (though Microsoft uses it ubiquitously for its Format Painter function), but it is nicely suited for graphic objects. PowerPoint, for example, uses it extensively. The user selects a rectangle from the graphics palette, and the cursor then becomes a modal rectangle tool charged with exactly one rectangle.

Many common drawing programs work this way, but it is also very popular for graphic direct-manipulation idioms in programs that aren't normally thought of as drawing programs. A good example is Visual Basic. When the user clicks on one of the controls on the tool palette, the cursor becomes charged with that control. The user then clicks again to create a single instance of the control on a form. Borland's Delphi uses charged cursor too, but if you Shift-click on a control in the palette, you, instead, get a modal tool for creating multiple instances of a control. Nice touch.

In many charged cursor programs like PowerPoint, the user cannot always deposit the object with a simple click, but must drag a bounding rectangle to determine the size of the deposited object. Some programs, like Visual Basic, allow either method. A single click of a charged cursor creates a single instance of the object in a default size. The new object is created in a state of selection, surrounded by **handles** (which we'll discuss in the next section), and ready for immediate precision reshaping and resizing. This dual-mode, allowing either a single-click for a default-sized object or dragging a rectangle for a custom-sized object is certainly the most flexible and discoverable method that will satisfy most users.

Sometimes charged cursor programs forget to change the appearance of the cursor. For example, although Visual Basic changes the cursor to crosshairs when it's charged, Delphi doesn't change it at all. If the cursor has assumed a modal behavior — if clicking it somewhere will create something — it is important that it visually indicate this state. Charged cursor also demands good cancel idioms. Otherwise, how do you harmlessly discharge the cursor?

Object Manipulation

Like controls, data objects on the screen, particularly graphical objects in drawing and modeling programs, can be manipulated by clicking and dragging. Objects (other than icons, which were discussed in the previous chapter) depend on click-and-drag motions for three main operations: repositioning, resizing, and reshaping.

Repositioning

Repositioning is the simple act of clicking on an object and dragging it to a new location. The most significant design issue regarding repositioning is that it usurps the place of other direct-manipulation idioms. The repositioning function demands the click-and-drag action, making it unavailable for other purposes. If the object is repositionable, the meaning of click-and-drag is taken and cannot be devoted to some other action, like scrolling or pressing a button, within the object itself.

The most common solution to this conflict is to dedicate a specific physical area of the object to the repositioning function. For example, you can reposition a window in Windows or on the Macintosh by clicking and dragging its title bar. The rest of the window is not pliant for repositioning, so the click-and-drag idiom is available for functions within the window, as you would expect. The only hint of the window's capability to be dragged is the color of the title bar, a subtle visual hint that is purely idiomatic: There is no way to intuit the presence of the idiom. But the idiom is very effective, and it merely proves the efficacy of idiomatic interface design. In general, however, you need to provide more explicit visual hinting of an area's pliancy. (Title bars could, for instance, use a slight shift in brightness as a pliancy hint, or you could use cursor hinting). The cost of this solution is the number of pixels devoted to the title bar. Mitigating this is the fact that the title bar does multiple-duty as a program identifier, active status indicator, and repository for certain other system-standard controls such as minimize, maximize, and close functions.

To move an object, it must first be selected. This is why selection must take place on the mouse-down transition: The user can drag without having to first click and release on an object to select it, then click and drag it to reposition it. It feels so much more natural to simply click it and then drag it to where you want it in one easy motion.

This creates a problem for moving contiguous data. In Word, for example, Microsoft uses this clumsy click-wait-click operation to drag chunks of text. You must click and drag to select a section of text and then wait a second or so and click and drag again to move it. This is unfortunate, but there is no good alternative for contiguous selection. If Microsoft were willing to dispense with its meta-key idioms for extending the selection, those same meta-keys could be used to select a sentence and drag it in a single movement, but this still wouldn't solve the problem of selecting and moving arbitrary chunks of text.

Resizing and reshaping

When referring to the desktop of Windows and other similar GUIs, there isn't really any functional difference between resizing and reshaping. The user adjusts a rectangular window's size and aspect ratio at the same time and with the same control by clicking and dragging on a dedicated control. On the Macintosh, there is a special resizing control on each window in the lower-right corner. Dragging this control allows the user to change both the height and width of the rectangle. Windows 3.x eschewed this idiom in favor of using the frame surrounding each window to allow resizing from any frame edge. It offered both generous visual hinting and cursor hinting, so it was easily discovered. Windows 95 added to this a reshaping-resizing control remarkably similar to the Macintosh's lower-right-corner reshaper/resizer, although it narrowed its window frame (resizing from the frame still works, though). Today Windows retains the frame and its cursor hinting, but virtually no visual hinting of the frame remains. For users who notice the cursor hinting, it provides the best of both worlds.

Such idioms are appropriate for resizing windows, but when the object to be resized is a graphical element in a drawing or modeling program, it is not acceptable to permanently superimpose such controls on objects. A resizing idiom for graphical objects must be visually bold to differentiate itself from parts of the drawing, especially the object it controls, and it must be respectful of the user's view of the object and the area around it. The resizer must also not obscure the resizing action.

A popular idiom accomplishes these goals; it consists of eight little black squares positioned one at each corner of a rectangular object and one centered on each side. These little black squares, shown in Figure 24-1, are called **resize handles** (or, simply, **handles**).

Handles are a boon to designers because they can also indicate selection. This is a naturally symbiotic relationship because an object must usually be selected to be resizable.

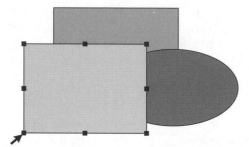

Figure 24-1: The selected object has eight handles, one at each corner and one centered on each side. The handles indicate selection and are a convenient idiom for resizing and reshaping the object. Handles are sometimes implemented with pixel inversion, but in a multicolor universe they can get lost in the clutter.

The handle centered on each side moves only that side, while the other sides remain motionless. The handles on the corners simultaneously move both the sides they touch, an interaction which is quite visually intuitive.

Handles tend to obscure the object they represent, so they don't make very good permanent controls. This is why we don't see them on top-level resizable windows (although windows in some versions of Sun's Open Look GUI come close). For that situation, frame or corner resizers are better idioms. If the selected object is larger than the screen, the handles may not be visible. If they are hidden off-screen, not only are they unavailable for direct manipulation, but they are useless as indicators of selection.

Notice that the assumption in this discussion of handles is that the object under scrutiny is rectangular or can be easily bounded by a rectangle. Certainly in the Windows world, things that are rectangular are easy for programs to handle, and non-rectangular things are best handled by enclosing them in a bounding rectangle. If the user is creating an organization chart this may be fine, but what about reshaping more complex objects? There is a very powerful and useful variant of the resize handle: a **vertex handle**.

Many programs draw objects on the screen with **polylines**. A **polyline** is a graphics programmer's term for a multisegment line defined by an array of vertices. If the last vertex is identical to the first vertex, it is a closed form and the polyline forms a polygon. When the object is selected, the program, rather than placing eight handles as it does on a rectangle, places one handle on top of every vertex of the polyline. The user can then drag any vertex of the polyline independently and actually change one small aspect of the object's internal shape rather than affecting it as a whole. This is shown in Figure 24-2.

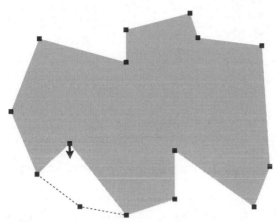

Figure 24-2: These are vertex handles, so named because there is one handle for each vertex of the polygon. The user can click and drag any handle to reshape the polygon, one segment at a time. This idiom is useful for drawing programs, but it may have application in desktop productivity programs, too.

Freeform objects in PowerPoint are rendered with polylines. If you click on a freeform, it is given a bounding rectangle with the standard eight handles. If you right-click on the freeform and choose Edit Points from the context menu, the bounding rectangle disappears and vertex handles appear instead. It is important that both these idioms are available, as the former is necessary to scale the image in proportion, whereas the latter is necessary to fine-tune the shape.

Resizing and reshaping meta-key variants

In the context of dragging, a meta-key is often used to constrain the drag to an orthogonal direction. This type of drag is called a **constrained drag**, and is shown in Figure 24-3.

A constrained drag is a drag whose path is limited to a straight line up, down, left, right, or at 45-degree angles regardless of what path the user might take the mouse. Usually, the Shift meta-key is used, but this convention varies from program to program. Constrained drags are extremely helpful in drawing programs, particularly when drawing neatly organized diagrams. The predominant motion of the first few millimeters of the drag determines the angle of the drag. If the user begins dragging on a predominantly horizontal axis, for example, the drag will henceforth be constrained to the horizontal axis. Some programs interpret constraints differently, letting the user shift angles in mid-drag by dragging the mouse across a threshold.

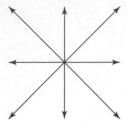

Figure 24-3: When a drag is constrained, usually by holding down the Shift key, the object is only dragged along one of the four axes shown here. The program selects which one by the direction of the initial movement of the mouse, an implementation of the drag threshold discussed later in the chapter.

The Paint program that comes with Windows doesn't constrain drags when moving an object around, but it does constrain the drawing of a few shapes, like lines and circles. Most drawing programs (like PowerPoint) that treat their graphics as objects instead of bits (as Paint does) allow constrained drags, and more sophisticated paint applications like Adobe Photoshop support the constrained drag idiom.

The use of meta-keys gives rise to a curious question: Where in the drag does the meta-key become meaningful? In other words, must the meta-key be held down when the drag begins — when the mouse button descends — or is it merely necessary for the meta-key to be pressed at some point during the drag? Or must the meta-key remain pressed at the time the user releases the mouse button? The best answer is this: The user should be able to switch to and receive visual feedback of constrained drag by pressing the meta-key at any time after he starts to drag. If he lets go of the meta-key during the drag, it reverts to unconstrained drag. Finally, if the computer detects that the meta-key is held down at the instant when the mouse button is released, the constrained drag is confirmed. This is true in PowerPoint and Paint, for example.

In an interesting bit-drawing variant, Paint also allows drag constraints in its pencil tool; any time the meta-key is held down during dragging, the constraint affects what is drawn during the drag. Mouse-up stops the flow of digital ink.

3D object manipulation

Working with precision on three-dimensional objects presents considerable interaction challenges for users equipped with 2D input devices and displays. Some of the most interesting research in UI design involves trying to develop better paradigms for 3D input and control. So far, however, there seem to be no real revolutions, but merely evolutions of 2D idioms extended into the world of 3D.

Most 3D applications are concerned either with precision drafting (for example, architectural CAD) or with 3D animation. When models are being created, animation presents problems similar to those of drafting. An additional layer of complexity is added, however, in making these models move and change over time. Often, animators create models in specialized applications and then load these models into different animation tools.

There is such a depth of information about 3D-manipulation idioms that an entire chapter or even an entire book could be written about them. We will thus briefly address some of the broader issues of 3D object manipulation.

DISPLAY ISSUES AND IDIOMS

Perhaps the most significant issue in 3D interaction on a 2D screen is that surrounding lack of parallax, the binocular ability to perceive depth. Without resorting to expensive, esoteric goggle peripherals, designers are left with a small bag of tricks with which to conquer this problem. Another important issue is one of occlusion: near objects obscuring far objects. These navigational issues, along with some of the input issues discussed in the next section, are probably a large part of the reason virtual reality hasn't yet become the GUI of the future.

MULTIPLE VIEWPOINTS   Use of **multiple viewpoints** is perhaps the oldest method of dealing with both of these issues, but it is, in many ways, the least effective from an interaction standpoint. Nonetheless, most 3D modeling applications present multiple views on the screen, each displaying the same object or scene from a different angle. Typically, there is a top view, a front view, and a side view, each aligned on an absolute axis, which can be zoomed in or out. There is also usually a fourth view, an orthographic or perspective projection of the scene, the precise parameters of which can be adjusted by the user. When these views are provided in completely separate windows, each with its own frame and controls, this idiom becomes quite cumbersome: Windows invariably overlap each other, getting in each other's way, and valuable screen real estate is squandered with repetitive controls and window frames. A better approach is to use a multipane window that permits 1-, 2-, 3-, and 4-pane configurations (the 3-pane configuration has one big pane and 2 smaller panes). Configuration of these views should be as close to single-click actions as possible, using a toolbar or keyboard shortcut.

The shortcoming of multiple viewpoint displays is that they require the user to look in several places at the same time to figure out the position of an object. Forcing the user to locate something in a complex scene by looking at it from the top, side, and front, and then expecting him to triangulate in his head in real-time is a bit much to expect, even from modeling whizzes. Nonetheless, multiple viewpoints *are* helpful for precisely aligning objects along a particular axis.

BASELINE GRIDS, DEPTHCUEING, SHADOWS, AND POLES   Baseline grids, depthcueing, shadows, and poles are idioms that help to get around some of the problems created by multiple viewpoints. The idea behind these idioms is to allow users to successfully perceive the location and movement of objects in a 3D scene projected in an orthographic or perspective view.

Baseline grids provide virtual floors and walls to a scene, one for each axis, which serve to orient users. This is especially useful when (as is usually the case) the camera viewpoint can be freely rotated.

Depthcueing is a means by which objects deeper in the field of view appear dimmer. This effect is typically continuous, so even a single object's surface will exhibit depthcueing, giving useful clues about its size, shape, and extent. Depthcueing, when used on grids, helps disambiguate the orientation of the grid in the view.

One method used by some 3D applications for positioning objects is the idea of **shadows** — outlines of selected objects projected onto the grids as if a light is shining perpendicularly to each grid. As the user moves the object in 3D space, she can track, by virtue of these shadows or silhouettes, how she is moving (or sizing) the object in each dimension.

Shadows work pretty well, but all those grids and shadows can get in the way visually. An alternative is the use of a single **floor grid** and a **pole**. Poles work in conjunction with a horizontally oriented grid. When the user selects an object, a vertical line extends from the center of the object to the grid. As she moves the object, the pole moves with it, but the pole remains vertical. The user can see where in 3D space she is moving the object by watching where the base of the pole moves on the surface of the grid (x and y axes), and also by watching the length and orientation of the pole in relation to the grid (z axis).

GUIDELINES AND OTHER RICH VISUAL HINTS   The idioms described in the previous section are all examples of rich visual modeless feedback, which we will discuss in detail in Chapter 34. However, for some applications lots of grids and poles may be overkill. For example, @Last Software's SketchUp is an architectural sketching program where users can lay down their own drafting lines using tape measure and protractor tools and, as they draw out their sketches, get color-coded hinting that keep them oriented to the right axes. Users can also turn on a blue-gradient sky and a ground color to help keep them oriented. Because the application is focused on architectural sketching, not general purpose 3D modeling or animation, the designers were able to pull off a spare, powerful, and simple interface that is both easy to learn and use (see Figure 24-4).

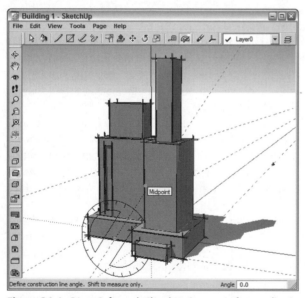

Figure 24-4: @Last Software's SketchUp is a gem of an application that combines powerful 3D architectural sketching capability with smooth interaction, rich feedback, and a manageable set of design tools. Users can set sky color and real-world shadows according to location, orientation, and time of day and year. These not only help in presentation, but help orient the user while building. Users also can lay down 3D grid and measurement guides just as in a 2D sketching application; the protractor tool is visible above. Camera rotate and zoom functions are cleverly mapped to the mouse scroll wheel, allowing fluid access while using other tools. ToolTips provide textual hints that assist in drawing lines and aligning objects.

WIRE FRAMES AND BOUNDING BOXES   Wire frames and **bounding boxes** solve problems of object visibility. In the days of slower processors, all objects needed to be represented as wire frames because computers weren't fast enough to render solid surfaces in real time. It is fairly common these days for modeling applications to render a rough surface for selected objects, while leaving unselected objects as wire frames. Transparency would also work, but is still very computing-intensive. In highly complex scenes, it is sometimes necessary or desirable, but not ideal, to render only the bounding boxes of non-selected objects.

INPUT ISSUES AND IDIOMS

3D applications make use of many idioms such as drag handles and vertex handles that have been adapted from 2D to 3D. However, there are some special issues surrounding 3D input.

DRAG THRESHOLDS   One of the fundamental problems with direct manipulation in a 2D projection of a 3D scene is the problem of translating 2D motions of the cursor in the plane of the screen into a more meaningful movement in the virtual 3D space.

In a 3D projection, a different kind of drag threshold is required to differentiate between movement in three, not just two, axes. Typically, up and down mouse movements translate into movement along one axis, whereas 45-degree–angle drags are used for each of the other two axes. SketchUp provides color-coded hinting in the form of dotted lines when the user drags parallel to a particular axis, and it also hints with ToolTips. In a 3D environment, rich feedback in the form of cursor and other types of hinting becomes a necessity.

THE PICKING PROBLEM   The other significant problem in 3D manipulation is known as **the picking problem**. Because objects need to be in wireframe or otherwise transparent when assembling scenes, it becomes difficult to know which of many overlapping items the user wants to select when she mouses over it. Locate highlighting can help, but is insufficient because the object may be completely occluded by others. Group selection is even trickier.

Many 3D applications resort to less direct techniques, such as an object list or object hierarchy that users can select from outside of the 3D view. Although this kind of interaction has its uses, there are more direct approaches.

For example, hovering over a part of a scene could open a ToolTip-like menu that lets users select one or more overlapping objects (this menu wouldn't be necessary in the simple case of one unambiguous object). If individual facets, vertices, or edges can be selected, each should hint at its pliancy as the mouse rolls over it.

Although it doesn't address the issue directly, a smooth and simple way to navigate around a scene can also ameliorate the picking problem. SketchUp has mapped both zoom and **orbit** functions to the mouse scroll wheel. Spin the wheel to zoom in towards or away from the central zero point in 3D space; press and hold the wheel to switch from whatever tool you are using to orbit mode, which allows the camera to circle around the central axes in any direction. This fluid navigation makes manipulation of an architectural model almost as easy as rotating it in your hand.

OBJECT ROTATION, CAMERA MOVEMENT, ROTATION, AND ZOOM   One more issue specific to 3D applications is the number of spatial manipulation functions that can be performed. Objects can be repositioned, resized, and reshaped in three axes. They can also be rotated in three axes.

Beyond this, the camera viewpoint can be rotated in place or revolved around a focal point, also in three axes. Finally, the camera's field of view can be zoomed in and out.

Not only does this mean that assignment of meta-keys and keyboard shortcuts is critical in 3D applications. (Obviously, some of these controls can be put in toolbars, but dedicated users will almost exclusively use the keyboard to control these modes.) There is another problem: It can be difficult to tell the difference between camera transformations and object transformations by looking at a camera viewpoint, even though the actual difference between the two can be quite significant. One way around this problem is to include a thumbnail, absolute view of the scene in a corner of the screen. It could be enlarged or reduced as needed, and could provide a reality check and global navigation method in case the user gets lost in space (note that this kind of thumbnail view is useful for navigating large 2D diagrams as well).

Object Connection

A direct-manipulation idiom that can be very powerful in some applications is **connection**, in which the user clicks and drags from one object to another, but instead of dragging the first object onto the second, a connecting line or arrow is drawn from the first object to the second one.

If you use project management or organization chart programs, you are undoubtedly familiar with this idiom. For example, to connect one task box in a project manager's network diagram (often called a PERT chart) with another, you click and drag an arrow between them. In this case the direction of the connection is significant: The task where the mouse button went down is the *from* task and the task where the mouse button is released is the *to* task.

As a connection is dragged between objects, it provides visual feedback in the form of **rubber-banding**: The arrow forms a line that extends from the exact mouse-down point to the current cursor position. The line is animated, following the movement of the cursor with one end, while remaining anchored at the mouse-down point with its other end.

After the user releases the mouse button, the mouse-up point is known and the program can decide whether it was within a valid target location. If so, the program draws a more permanent line or arrow between the two objects. In some applications, it also links the objects logically.

As the user drags the end of the arrow around the screen, input is captured and the rules of dragging for discrete data apply.

The left button can't normally trigger the connection function because it would collide with selection and repositioning. In some programs, the right button triggers it, but Windows makes that problematic with its usurpation of the right click for the context menu. A better solution might be to provide either a dedicated connection area or handle from which to drag the connection, or to use a modal or cursor-charged tool from a palette, or a meta-key mapping (is Alt still unused?).

Connections can also be full-fledged objects themselves, with reshape handles and editable properties. This sort of implementation would mean connections could be independently selected, moved, and deleted as well. For programs where connections between objects need to contain information (such as in a project-planning application), it makes sense for connections to be first-class citizens.

Connection doesn't require as much cursor hinting as other idioms because the rubber-banding effect is so clearly visible. However, it would be a big help in programs where objects are connected logically, to show which currently pointed-to objects are valid targets for the arrow. In other words, if the user drags an arrow until it points to some icon or widget on the screen, how can he tell if that icon or widget can legally be connected to? The answer is to have the potential target object engage in some active visual hinting. This hinting for potential targets can be quite subtle, or even eschewed completely when all objects in the program are equally valid targets for any connection. Target objects should always highlight, however, when a connection is actually dragged over them, to indicate willingness to accept the connection.

Also indisputably vital is a convenient means of canceling the action. Chord-clicking and Escape still work for this idiom.

Part VI

Controls and Their Behaviors

Chapter 25

Window Behaviors

Any book on user interface design must discuss windows (with a lowercase w). We will first place these omnipresent rectangles in some historical perspective to keep the reader from imbuing them with too much intrinsic value. The remainder of the chapter discusses important behavioral attributes of windows and multiwindowed applications, and when their use is (and isn't) appropriate.

PARC and the Alto

Modern GUIs all derive their appearance from the Xerox Alto, an experimental desktop computer system developed in the mid-1970s at Xerox's Palo Alto Research Center (PARC), now PARC, Inc. PARC's Alto was the first computer with a graphical interface and was designed to explore the potential of computers as desktop business systems. The Alto was designed as a networked office system where documents could be composed, edited, and viewed in WYSIWYG (What You See Is What You Get) form, stored, retrieved, transferred electronically between workstations, and printed. The Alto system contributed many significant innovations to the vernacular of desktop computing that we now regard as commonplace: the mouse, the rectangular window, the scrollbar, the push-button, the "desktop metaphor," object-oriented programming, drop-down menus, the Ethernet, and laser printing.

PARC's effect on the industry and contemporary computing was profound. Both Steve Jobs and Bill Gates, chairmen of Apple Computer and Microsoft, respectively, saw the Alto at PARC and were indelibly impressed.

Xerox tried to commercialize the Alto itself, and later a derivative computer system called the Star, but both were expensive, complex, agonizingly slow, and commercial failures. It was widely felt that executive management at Xerox, then primarily a copy machine company, didn't have the vision or the gumption to put a concerted effort behind marketing and selling the "paperless office." The brain trust at PARC, realizing that Xerox had blown an opportunity of legendary proportions, began an exodus that greatly enriched other software companies, particularly Apple and Microsoft.

Steve Jobs and his PARC refugees immediately tried to duplicate the Alto/Star with the Lisa. In many ways they succeeded, including copying the Star's failure to deal with reality. The Lisa was remarkable, accessible, exciting, too expensive ($9995 in 1983), and frustratingly slow. Even though it was a decisive commercial failure, it ignited the imagination of many people in the small but booming microcomputer industry.

Meanwhile, Bill Gates was less impressed by the sexy "graphicalness" of the Alto/Star than he was by the advantages of an object-oriented presentation and communication model. Software produced by Microsoft in the early 1980s, notably the spreadsheet Multiplan (the forerunner of Excel), reflected this thinking.

Steve Jobs wasn't deterred by the failure of the Lisa. He was convinced that PARC's vision of a truly graphical personal computer was an idea whose time had come. He added to his cadre of PARC refugees by raiding Apple's various departments for skilled and energetic individuals, then set up a skunk works to develop a commercially viable incarnation of the Alto. The result was the legendary Macintosh, a machine that has had enormous influence on our technology, design, and culture. The Mac single-handedly brought an awareness of design and aesthetics to the industry. It not only raised the standards for user-friendliness, but it also enfranchised a whole population of skilled individuals from disparate fields who were previously locked out of computing because of the industry's self-absorption in techno-trivia.

The almost-religious aura surrounding the Macintosh was also associated with many aspects of the Mac's user interface. The drop-down menus, metaphors, dialog boxes, rectangular overlapping windows and other elements all became part of the mystique. Unfortunately, because its design has acquired these heroic proportions, its failings have often gone unexamined.

PARC's Principles

The researchers at PARC, in addition to developing a revolutionary set of hardware and software technologies to create the Alto, also pioneered many of the concepts held as gospel today in the world of GUI design and development.

Visual metaphors

One of the ideas that emerged from PARC was the visual metaphor. At PARC, the global visual metaphor was considered critical to the user's ability to understand the system, and thus critical to the success of the product and its concept. In Part IV, we discuss some of the problems of relying completely on such metaphoric design.

Avoiding modes

Another principle associated with the modern GUI is the notion that modes should be avoided. A mode is a state the program can enter where the effects of a user's action changes from the norm — essentially a behavioral detour.

For example, older programs demanded that you shift into a special state to enter records, and then shift into another state to print them out. These behavioral states are modes, and they can be extremely confusing and frustrating. Larry Tesler, former PARC researcher and former Chief Scientist at Apple, was an early advocate of eliminating modes from software and was pictured in an influential magazine wearing a T-shirt with the bold legend "Don't mode me in." His license plate read, "NOMODES." In a command-line environment, modes are indeed poisonous. However, in the object-verb world of a GUI, they aren't inherently evil, although *poorly designed* modes can be terribly frustrating. Unfortunately, the don't-mode-me-in principle has become an unquestioned part of our design vernacular.

Arguably, the most influential program on the Macintosh was MacPaint, a program with a thoroughly modal interface. This program enables the user to draw pixel-by-pixel on the computer screen. The user selects one tool from a palette of a dozen or so and then draws on the screen with it. Selecting a tool is entering a mode because, when a tool is selected, the behavior of the program conforms to the attributes of that tool. The program can only behave in one way.

The PARC researchers weren't wrong, just misunderstood. The user interface benefits of MacPaint, when compared with contemporary programs, were great; but they didn't accrue from its imagined modelessness. Rather, they resulted from the ease with which the user could see which mode the program was in and the effortlessness of changing that mode.

Modes based on implementation models are confusing modes. Edit mode versus Preview mode is convenient only for the program, not the user. Modes based on the user's mental model are often harmless, such the Spray Can or the Paintbrush modes in MacPaint, for example.

Overlapping windows

Another Mac fundamental that emerged from PARC (and which has metastasized in Microsoft Windows) is the idea of overlapping rectangular windows. The rectangular theme of modern GUIs is so dominating and omnipresent that it is often seen as vital to the success of visual interaction.

There are good reasons for displaying data in rectangular panes. Probably the least important of these is that it is a good match for our display technology: CRTs and LCDs have an easier time with rectangles than with other shapes. More important is the fact that most data output used by humans is in a rectangular format: We have viewed text on rectangular sheets since Gutenberg; and most other forms, such as photographs, film, and video also conform to a rectangular grid. Rectangular graphs and diagrams are also the easiest for us to make sense of. There's something about rectangles that just seems to work cognitively for humans. Rectangles are also quite space-efficient.

Overlapping windows demonstrated clearly that there are better ways to transfer control between concurrently running programs other than typing in obscure commands.

Overlapping rectangular windows were initially intended to represent overlapping sheets of paper on the user's desktop. Okay, but why? The answer again goes back to the global metaphor of the desktop. Your desk, if it is like the authors', is covered with papers; when you want to read or edit one, you pull it out of the pile, lay it on top, and get to work. The problem is that this works only as well as it does on a real desktop and that isn't particularly well, especially if your desk is covered with papers and is only 17 inches across diagonally.

The overlapping window *concept* is good, but its execution is impractical in the real world. The overlapping-sheets-of-paper metaphor starts to suffer when you get three or more applications and documents on the screen — it just doesn't scale up well. The idiom has other problems, too. A user who clicks the mouse just one pixel away from where he thought he was can find his program disappearing, to be replaced by another one. User testing at Microsoft has shown that a typical user might launch the same word processor several times in the mistaken belief that he has somehow "lost" the program and must start over. It is problems like these that prompted Microsoft to introduce the taskbar; Apple still hasn't completely sorted out the problem.

Another part of the confusion regarding overlapping windows comes from several other idioms that are also implemented using an overlapping window. The familiar dialog box is one, as are menus and floating tool palettes. Such overlapping within a single application is completely natural and a well-formed idiom. It even has a faint metaphoric trace: that of someone handing you an important note.

Microsoft and Tiled Windows

In the grand tradition of focusing on the most visible aspect of the new PARC GUI, Bill Gates named his hastily cobbled together response to the Macintosh's success "Windows."

The first version of Microsoft Windows diverged somewhat from the pattern established by Xerox and Apple. Instead of using overlapping rectangular windows to represent the overlapping sheets of paper on one's desktop, Windows 1.0 relied on what was called **tiling** to allow the user to have more than one application on screen at a time. Tiling meant that applications would divide up the available pixels in a uniform, rectilinear tessellation, evenly parsing out the available space to running programs. Tiling was invented as an idealistic means to solve the orientation and navigation problems caused by overlapping windows. Navigation between tiled windows is much easier than between overlapped windows, but the cost in pixels is horrendous. And besides, as soon as the user moves neatly tiled windows, he is thrust right back into overlapping window **excise** (see Chapter 10). Tiling died as a mainstream idiom, although it can still be found in the most interesting places: Try right-clicking on the current Windows taskbar.

Full-Screen Applications

Overlapping windows fail to make it easy to navigate between multiple, running programs; so other vendors continue to search for new ways to achieve this. The **virtual desktop** of session managers on some Unix-based platforms extends the desktop to six times the size of the visible window. In a corner of the screen are small superimposed, thumbnail images of all six desktop-spaces, all of which can be running different things simultaneously and each of which can have many open windows. You switch between these virtual desktops by clicking on the one you want to make active. In some versions, you can even drag tiny window thumbnails from one desktop to another.

Microsoft braved a double-barreled breach-of-contract and patent infringement lawsuit from Apple in order to add overlapping to Windows 2.0. In all this controversy, the basic problem seemed to have been forgotten: How can the user easily navigate from one program to another? Multiple windows sharing a small screen — whether overlapping or tiled — is not a good general solution (although it certainly may have its occasional uses). We are moving rapidly to a world of full-screen programs. Each application occupies the entire screen when it is "at bat." A tool like the taskbar borrows the minimum quantity of pixels from the running application to provide a visual method of changing the line-up. (Amusingly, this concept is similar to the early days of the Mac with its Switcher, which would toggle the Mac display between one full-screen application and another). This solution is much more pixel-friendly, less confusing to users, and highly appropriate when an application is being used for an extended period of time. In Windows, users have the choice of making their applications full-screen or overlapping at will. Apple is sticking to the overlapping window model alone, at its peril.

Much contemporary software design begins with the assumption that the user interface will consist of a series of overlapping windows, without modes, informed by a global metaphor. The PARC legacy is a strong one. Most of what we know about modern graphical user interface design came from these origins, whether right or wrong. But the well-tempered designer will push the myths aside and approach software design from a fresh viewpoint, using history as a guide, not as a mandate.

Multipaned Applications

It turns out that there is an idiom that takes the best elements of tiled windows and provides them within a sovereign, full-screen application, the idiom of **multipaned windows**. Multipaned windows consist of independent views or **panes** that share a single window. **Adjacent panes** are separated by fixed or movable dividers or **splitters**. (We'll discuss splitters more in Chapter 26.) The classic example of a multipaned application is Microsoft Outlook, where separate panes are used to display the list of mailboxes, contents of the selected mailbox, and a selected message, all on one screen. In calendar view, a monthly view, weekly view, and to-do list are similarly displayed.

The advantage of multipaned windows is that independent but related information can be easily displayed in a single, sovereign screen in a manner that reduces navigation and window management excise to almost nil. For a sovereign application of any complexity, adjacent pane designs are practically a requirement. Specifically, designs that provide navigation and/or building blocks in one pane and allow viewing or construction of data in an adjacent pane seem to represent an efficient pattern that bears repeating.

The concept of adjacent panes was also adopted on the Web in the form of **frames**, but thanks to a poorly designed implementation out of the gate and a standards war between then preeminent Netscape and Microsoft, frames have been tainted as awkward and complex. Hopefully, as Web technologies progress and highly interactive Web applications become more prevalent, the concept behind frames will re-emerge inside the browser (the browsers themselves *already* make use of multiple panes).

Another form of multiple panes are **stacked panes** or **tabs**. Although these are seen most frequently in dialogs (see Chapter 31), they are also sometimes useful in sovereign windows. A good example of this is Microsoft Excel, which allows related spreadsheets to be accessible via inverted tabs at the bottom of the screen. Excel makes use of both multiple adjacent panes and stacked panes (see Figure 25-1).

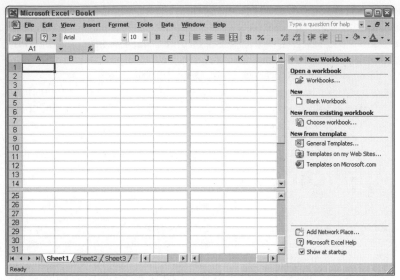

Figure 25-1: Microsoft Excel provides an excellent example of both tabbed and adjacent panes. Inverted tabs are an unusual visual twist on the tab idiom (see Chapter 31), but seem to work well in context. Excel allows you to split your view of a single spreadsheet into multiple adjacent panes. Other applications like Outlook have completely different (but usually related) information in adjacent panes. The pane on the far right in this figure is an example of this type of adjacent pane being used for navigation and construction support.

Choosing Your Windows

Our programs are constructed of two kinds of windows: main windows and subordinate windows (like documents and dialog boxes). Determining which windows to use for a program is a primary step in determining its look and feel. If we expect to create an effective user interface, we cannot simply guess at which windows to use. We must choose them carefully and understand *why* we make our choices.

Unnecessary rooms

If we imagine our program as a house, we can picture each window as a separate room. The house itself is represented by the program's main window, and each room is a document window or dialog box. In real life, we don't add a room to our house unless it has a purpose that cannot be served by other rooms. Similarly, we shouldn't add windows to our program unless they have a special purposes that can't or shouldn't be served by existing windows.

Purpose is a goal-directed term. It implies that using a room is associated with a goal, but not necessarily with a particular task or function. For example, you might shake someone's hand at your front door, but it will probably have quite different connotations from shaking someone's hand in the kitchen or bedroom.

If someone you just met held out his hand to shake yours, you would think it odd if he suddenly jerked it away and said, "Wait! Let's go into the kitchen." Moving to another room just to shake hands is simply weird. The task can be performed just as well right where you are. It would be especially ridiculous if, after shaking hands in the kitchen, you both then trudged back to the foyer to continue what you were doing.

AXIOM

A dialog box is another room; have a good reason to go there.

In most drawing programs, for example, the depth of a drop-shadow is usually set by selecting a menu item that triggers a dialog box. A text field or similar control on the dialog then sets the shadow depth. After the setting is made, the program returns to the main screen that contains the drawing. This sequence is so commonplace that it is completely unremarkable, and yet it is undeniably poor design. In a drawing program, changing the image is the primary task. The image is in the main window, so that's where the tools that affect it should be also. Setting the depth of a drop-shadow isn't a tangential task but one quite integral to the drawing process. If the drawing were being done with pencil on paper, the artist might bring a new tool to bear — an eraser — but he would not shift to a different table or sheet of paper just to change the depth of the drop-shadow. The drop-shadow depth could be set with a control right on the toolbar, for example, or — better yet — by letting the user click on the shadow with the mouse and simply drag the shadow to a new position.

Putting functions in a dialog box emphasizes their separateness from the main task. Putting the drop-shadow adjustment in a dialog box works just fine, but it creates an interaction that is awkward. Going into an adjacent room to shake hands works fine as far as the handshake goes, but it is a distracting waste of effort in the context of the larger interaction.

From the programmer's point of view, changing the drop-shadow is a separate function, so it seems natural to treat it like one. From the user's point of view, however, it is an integral function and should be integrated into the main window.

DESIGN TIP

Build functions into the window where they are used.

This is one of the most frequently violated tips in user interface design. Because the construction of programs is so function-centric, the user interface is often constructed in close parallel. Combine this with the incredible ease with which we can build dialog boxes, and the result is one dialog box per function. Our modern GUI-building tools tend to make dialogs easy to create, but adding controls to the surface of a document window or creating direct-manipulation idioms is generally not supported by these handy tools. The developer who wants to create a better user interface often must build his own without much help from the tool vendors.

Necessary rooms

When you want to go swimming, it would be odd if you were offered a living room full of guests as a place to change your clothes. Decorum and modesty are excellent reasons for you to want a separate room in which to change. It is entirely appropriate to provide a separate room when one is needed.

When users perform a function that is outside of the normal sequence of events for them, that program should provide a special place in which to perform it. For example, purging a database is not a normal activity. It involves setting up and using features and facilities that are not part of the normal operation of the database program. The more prosaic parts of the program will support daily tasks like entering and examining records, but erasing records en masse is not an everyday occurrence. The purge facility correctly belongs in a separate dialog box. It is entirely appropriate for the program to lead the user into a separate room — a window or dialog — to handle that function.

Using goal-directed thinking, we can examine each function to good effect. If someone is using a graphics program to develop a drawing, his goal is to create an appealing and effective image. All the drawing tools are directly related to this goal, but the pencils and paintbrushes and erasers are the most tightly connected functions. These tools should be intimately integrated into the workspace itself in the same way that the conventional artist will arrange his pencils, pens, knives, tweezers, erasers, and other drawing equipment right on his drawing board, close at hand. The tools are ready for immediate use without his having to reach far, let alone having to get up and walk into the next room. In the program, drawing tools should be arrayed on the edges of the drawing space, available with a single click of the mouse. The user shouldn't have to go to the menu or to dialog boxes to accomplish these tasks. Procreate's Painter 7 arranges artists' tools in trays, and lets you move the things that you use frequently to the front of the tray. Although you can hide the various trays and palettes if you want, they appear as the default and are part of the main drawing window. They can be positioned anywhere on the window, as well. And if you create a brush that is, for example, thin charcoal in a particular shade of red that you're going to need again, you simply "tear it off" the palette and place it wherever you want on your workspace — just like laying that charcoal in the tray on your easel. This tool selection design closely mimics the way we manipulate tools while drawing.

If, on the other hand, the user decides to import a piece of clip art, although the function is related to the goal of producing a good drawing, the tools used are not related to drawing. The clip art directory is clearly not congruent with the user's goal of drawing — it is only a means to an end. The conventional artist probably does not keep a book of clip art right on his drawing board, but you can expect that it is close by, probably on a bookshelf immediately adjacent to the drawing board and available without even getting up. In the program, the clip art facility should be very easy to access but, because it involves a whole suite of tools that aren't normally needed, it should be placed in a separate facility: a dialog box.

When the user is done creating the artwork, he has achieved his initial goal of creating an effective image. At this point, his goals change. His new goal is to preserve the picture, protect it, and communicate through it. The need for pens and pencils is over. The need for clip art is over. Leaving these tools behind now is no hardship. The conventional artist would now unpin the drawing from his board, take it into the hall and spray it with fixative, then roll it up and put it in a mailing tube. He purposely leaves behind his drawing tools — he doesn't want them affected by fixative overspray and doesn't want accidents with paint or charcoal to mar the finished work.

Mailing tubes are used infrequently and are sufficiently unrelated to the drawing process that he stores them in a closet. In the software equivalent of this process, the user ends the drawing program, puts away his drawing tools, finds an appropriate place on the hard disk to store the image, and sends it to someone else via electronic mail. These functions are clearly separated from the drawing process by the goals of the user.

By examining the user's goals, we are naturally guided to an appropriate form for the program. Instead of merely putting every function in a dialog box, we can see that some functions shouldn't be enclosed in a dialog at all. Others should be put into a dialog that is integral to the main body of the interface, and still other functions should be completely removed from the program.

Windows pollution

Some designers take the approach that each dialog box should embody a single function. What they end up with is windows pollution.

Achieving many user goals involves executing a series of functions. If there is a single dialog box for each function things can quickly get visually crowded and navigationally confusing. The CompuServe Navigator (Version 1.0.1), shown in Figure 25-2, is the case in point.

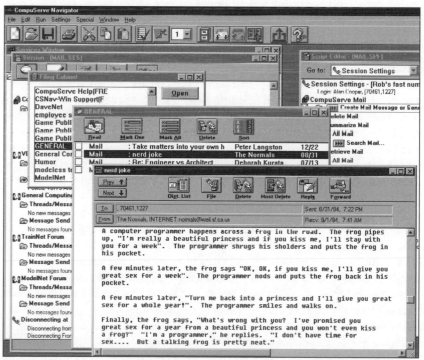

Figure 25-2: Version 1.0 of CompuServe's Navigator suffered from tragic windows pollution. Normal downloading of e-mail required three windows to be opened. To examine a filed message required three more windows. Examining mail is one integral activity and should occupy a single, integrated window. But the worst is yet to come: The user had to put every window away individually, in the reverse order of opening them.

Adding a squirt of oil to a bicycle makes it pedal more easily, but that doesn't mean that dumping a gallon of oil on it will make it pedal itself. The designer of Navigator was on a mission to put more windows in our lives, perhaps in the mistaken belief that windows are inherently good.

The utility of any interaction idiom is context-dependent.

Another possibility is that Navigator was the result of a large team of programmers working without an integrated framework for the design. Thus each module of functionality is expressed in a window or dialog, simply because it's easier than trying to fit them cleanly together post facto: classic implementation model. This example was presented in the first edition of *About Face* in 1995, and we wish we could say things have improved. But one need only look at America Online's interface today to see how little things have changed. AOL, despite the disservice it does to its huge user base in terms of excise and confusion, continues to be one of the worst windows polluters on the planet.

Let's look at one example from Navigator: e-mail. From the user's point of view, examining a saved piece of e-mail is not three functions (choosing a mailbox, sorting mail in a mailbox, and reading a message), but rather, a single activity. One window would not only be perfectly sufficient to accomplish this task, it would also more closely correspond to the user's goal and mental model of viewing an e-mail. The programmer has instead faithfully rendered the actual processing to the user, somewhat like forcing the driver to turn two steering wheels, one for each front wheel, instead of combining the two functions into a single, conceptual whole.

A much better solution to the Navigator problem would have been to create a single mailbox with tools strategically positioned along the top row—a toolbar would be perfect—for managing searches. Intermediate results of the search could be shown in the window along with the final message itself. One goal—finding and reading a message—should be implemented as one dialog box. Microsoft Outlook has made strides in this area: Multiple mailboxes, the list of mail in each box, and the e-mail messages themselves can be accessed within a single, multipane, sovereign window that is designed to remain maximized. Replying to a message opens a single additional window.

There is no way to show the connections between lots of windows, so don't create lots of windows. This is a particularly annoying problem with Visual Basic (VB) where it is easy to create forms. Forms are independent, top-level windows. In terms of behavior, they are the same as modeless dialog boxes. Creating applications as collections of several modeless dialog boxes is a questionable strategy that was never very common until VB made it easy to do. Just because it's easy to do doesn't mean it is good design. Modal dialogs always get you immediately back to the point of departure so they don't count against you, but each added window contributes more to the user's burden of window management excise. This overhead can grow to obnoxious proportions if the program is used daily.

A VB programmer once explained that his program was especially difficult to design because it had 57 forms. No program can be used effectively with 57 forms. Each form may be excellent in its own right, but collectively, it's simply too many. It's like saying you're going to taste 57 vintage Chardonnays at a sitting or test drive 57 sedans on Saturday.

Window States

A programmer would call an application's primary window its **top-level window**. The intrinsic behavior of a top-level window includes the capability to overlap other top-level windows, but this is not how they are normally used. Each top-level window has the native capability to be in one of three states (in Windows and some Unix GUI platforms), depending on how they are programmed. Oddly, only two of these three states have been given names by Microsoft: **minimized** and **maximized**.

In Unix GUIs like Motif, and on pre-95 versions of Windows, **minimized** windows were shrunk to boxy icons (usually larger than normal desktop icons) that stacked on the desktop. As of Windows 95, minimizing a window collapses the window into the button that represents it on the taskbar. **Maximized** windows fill the entire screen, covering up whatever is beneath them.

Microsoft somehow manages to avoid directly referring to the third state, and the only hint of a name is on the system menu (click the upper left corner of the title bar to see it) where the verb **Restore** describes how to get to it. This function restores a maximized or minimized top-level window to that *other* state. In the interests of sanity, we will call this third state **pluralized**, although it has also been called **restored**.

The pluralized state is that in-between condition where the window is neither an icon nor maximized to cover the entire screen. When a window is pluralized, it shares the screen with icons and other pluralized windows. In Mac OS X, all windows are pluralized if they aren't iconized (Mac OS 9 only permits windows to be collapsed to their title bars, not fully iconized). Pluralized windows can be either tiled or overlapping.

Back in the days of Windows 1.0, the states of minimization and maximization were called **iconized** and **zoomed**, terms that were more descriptive and certainly more engaging. IBM, then enjoying a cozy relationship with Microsoft, demanded the change to corporate-speak in the mistaken impression that America's executives would feel more comfortable. The weaker appellations have stuck.

The normal state for a sovereign application is the maximized state. There is little reason for such a program to be pluralized, other than to support switching between programs or dragging and dropping data between programs or documents (the latter could be cleverly accomplished using a toolbar control instead). Some transient applications, like the File Manager or the Explorer are appropriately run pluralized, but these transient programs are used primarily as springboards for sovereign applications.

Why minimize?

Any application in Windows can be minimized, but why go to the trouble? On systems without a Taskbar or similar idiom, it is often necessary to minimize to switch from one application to another, an ungainly procedure. You minimize the active program (which was likely maximized), then maximize (or pluralize) the icon of the desired program—if it isn't already pluralized or maximized, but lurking behind the previous application. To switch back, you reverse the sequence. You must move the mouse all over the screen; and the process is slow, complicated, and tiresome.

The Windows 3.*x* Alt+Tab key sequence was a much more useful method of switching between applications (and still supported even in XP). However, it's obscure, not visual, demands a high level of user expertise, is relatively unknown outside of the power-user community, and operates unlike any other idiom in Windows. Pressing Alt+Tab moves you quickly and directly to the next running program. Holding down the Alt key and repeatedly pressing the Tab key cycles you through each running program. It does this by showing a small window in the center of the screen with the name and icon of the candidate program. The trick is that the actual selection of a program occurs when the user *releases* the Alt key! Nowhere else in Windows does an action occur on the release of a shifting key. This idiom is weird enough that most people don't know about it, and learning it can be difficult. After the idiom is learned, however, it is a remarkably fast way to navigate between applications. Besides the speed of the technique for switching from program to program, the great advantage is that the various programs can each remain in their natural state, either maximized or pluralized, but usually maximized.

The Alt+Tab idiom is a classic example of how a programming team can ingeniously solve a significant problem that baffled the experts. Many sharp software designers tried to create convenient program-switching idioms, but none are the equal of this one. The solution is brilliant, but virtually undiscoverable — it's not documented and it doesn't appear on any menu, so someone must tell you about it. The solution is fabulously economical in overhead but requires a deep familiarity and dexterity with the computer, coupled with a clear sense of dominance over it — a good description of your average code-slinger. What we really needed was a more benign version of Alt+Tab that wasn't just for power-users and hackers. In Windows 95, we got this solution with the Taskbar.

The Windows Taskbar finally acknowledges that most people want to work on one maximized sovereign application at a time, and that they want a more accessible idiom for accomplishing this. A significant slice of the screen's real estate is devoted to this ever-present gray bar, but it is worth it for everyone but the most hard-core programmer (who can always hide it). The Taskbar contains a button for every running program/open document, regardless of its current state (except daemonic posture programs, and even some of these make it into the status area). The button for the active program is shown in its pushed-in state.

The Taskbar is a simple and visual implementation of the Alt+Tab idiom: You click the button of the application you want and it moves to the front of the screen and becomes active. If it was last in a maximized state, it will still be maximized. If it was last in a pluralized state, it will still be pluralized and in the same position it was in before, just moved to the top of the window pile. If it was minimized, it will open to its prior maximized or pluralized state. You can imagine the running programs as channels on your TV — pressing buttons that allow you to jump from channel to channel.

The other reason to minimize a program is to reduce clutter on your screen. If you run several pluralized sovereign applications, it can simplify your screen to minimize some of them. However, this is treating the symptom rather than the cause of the problem. If each application is maximized in turn, there will be no apparent clutter, and minimizing won't be necessary, as long as you have the Taskbar or the Alt+Tab to navigate between them. The only remaining rationale for minimization is to clear space to get at icons on the desktop. The Taskbar in windows includes a button in its quick start area that instantly minimizes all windows. On the other hand, Windows 2000 and XP Taskbars include a desktop access toolbar that eliminates even this need (although this feature is off by default).

Current versions of Windows remove the few rationales for minimizing a program. Managing your programs as a set of channels is superior given adequate tools. The Alt+Tab has long allowed power users to work this way, and the Taskbar finally brings the capability to the rest of us.

Minimized applications before the advent of the Taskbar, as well as those on Unix GUI platforms, were sometimes used in innovative ways to display dynamic or animated status information. This is still the case on Unix, and it may end up being the case for Mac OS X, now that it has true minimized apps but no fully maximized ones. But on Windows, using items on the desktop to display useful information has all but died as an idiom, as programmers have come to realize that maximized program windows almost always obscure these items.

Why pluralize?

Is there any reason for a program to be pluralized? Well, maybe. Sometimes obscure situations require two or more programs to be juxtaposed. If all the user wants to do is run one sovereign program after another, with a sprinkling of smaller transient programs temporarily overlaid on them, pluralization is unnecessary. If the user wants to cut and paste information between sovereign programs, the clipboard will work just fine. However, if the user wishes to take advantage of the program-to-program drag-and-drop facility, the two programs doing the dragging and dropping must both be visible, sharing the screen. In other words, both programs must be pluralized. At least this was true until the advent of the Taskbar in Windows, which allows you to drag and hold an object over a minimized application to open it. Although this idiom requires some excise dragging, it eliminates excise window manipulation: Take your pick.

Modern XGA computer screens range from 640x480 pixels to 1600x1200 pixels. 1024x768 is probably the most common resolution at the beginning of the 21st century. In such limited physical environments, modern sovereign programs such as word processors or graphics programs are difficult and unpleasant to use when they own less than half of the screen. When giving demonstrations to the press or captains of industry, Microsoft proudly demonstrates the drag-and-drop of a spreadsheet into a word processor. The windows of the two applications are carefully posed in advance to illustrate this single function in isolation. What they don't show you is that the management overhead of pluralizing two windows and then adjusting them manually so that each one gets sufficient exposure is considerably greater than the management overhead of using the clipboard and Taskbar and merely swapping between the two sovereign programs.

Program-to-program drag-and-drop is a powerful idiom, and one that we may see with increasing frequency in the future. However, we won't see it used too often between sovereign applications until our computer screens get a lot bigger, which doesn't promise to happen for several more years. However, program-to-program drag-and-drop can be a boon for moving information between a sovereign application and a transient application. For example, look at the process of adding a piece of clip art to a word processing document.

The word processor is the sovereign application, and it is running maximized. The clip art librarian is a transient application and would normally run as a fixed-size window approximately one-quarter of the full size of the screen (one half of the width and one half of the height). The clip art librarian could be easily positioned in the least obtrusive quadrant of the screen and, after the desired image is located, the image could be dragged directly into the appropriate place in the word processor. Another click and the clip art librarian is stored away on the Taskbar, and the user can proceed. Window management overhead is a mere two clicks, one to open and one to close the librarian, with a possible click-and-drag operation to move the librarian out of the way so the critical area of the word processor's display can be seen more easily. Neither application needs to be pluralized.

Windows software can be effectively built without supplying the capability to either minimize or pluralize. Programs occupying the in-between state of pluralization are dying out, and Windows is helping to kill them. The programs never have to pass through the pluralized or minimized state. Of course, that doesn't mean that you can actually dispense with these options. You must be able to minimize for backwards compatibility, and every program that can maximize must be able to be pluralized for those cases when a user needs to tile the screen with the application. Experienced users will probably be upset if the application can't acquit itself of this basic expectation, even though it is more an exercise in adaptability than in practical software design.

For practical purposes, we are left with only two program configurations: maximized sovereign programs and pluralized transient programs. The sovereign programs endure while the transient programs appear briefly on top of them. When you design your application, you must make this fundamental design decision: dominant or temporary. This will dictate the type of main window you will use.

MDI versus SDI

About 15 years ago, Microsoft began proselytizing a new method for organizing the functions in a Windows application. The company called this the **multiple document interface**, or **MDI**. It satisfied a need apparent in certain categories of applications, namely those that handled multiple instances of a single type of document simultaneously. Notable examples were Excel and Word.

Microsoft backed up its new standard with code built into the operating system, so the emergence of MDI as a standard was inevitable. For a time in the late 80s and early 90s, MDI was regarded by some at Microsoft as a kind of cure-all patent medicine for user interface ills. It was prescribed liberally for all manner of ailments.

These days, Microsoft has turned its back on MDI and embraced **single document interface**, or **SDI**. It seems that MDI didn't fix all the problems after all.

If you want to copy a cell from one spreadsheet and paste it to another, opening and closing both spreadsheets, in turn, is very tedious. It would be much better to have two spreadsheets open simultaneously. Well, there are two ways to accomplish this: You can have one spreadsheet program that can contain two or more spreadsheet instances inside of it. Or you can have multiple instances of the entire spreadsheet program, each one containing a single instance of a spreadsheet. The second option is technically superior but it demands high-performance equipment.

In the early days of Windows, Microsoft chose the first option for the simple, practical reason of resource frugality. One program with multiple spreadsheets (documents) was more conservative of bytes and CPU cycles than multiple programs, and performance was an issue then.

Unfortunately, the one-program–multiple-documents model violated a fundamental design rule established early on in Windows: Only one window can be active at a time. What was needed was a way to have one program active at a time along with one document window active at a time within it. MDI was the hack that implemented this solution.

Two conditions have emerged in the years since MDI was made a standard. First, well-meaning but misguided programmers tragically abused the facility. Second, our computers have gotten much more powerful—to the point where multiple instances of programs, each with a single document, are very feasible. Thus Microsoft has made it clear that MDI is no longer politically correct, if not actually doomed.

The winds of change at Microsoft notwithstanding, MDI is actually reasonable enough, as long as it is not abused. The main way to abuse it is to have more than one type of document window in a single program. Figure 25-2 shows this clearly. The CompuServe Navigator program offers a dozen or more different types of document windows, making it very difficult to understand what is going on (and AOL does this today). This is one of the main reasons why many designers would like to see the facility abandoned. But there is nothing wrong with MDI in a sovereign application, such as a word processor or spreadsheet, as long as there is only one type of document and the minimize/pluralize functions are suppressed in favor of choosing fully maximized documents from the Window menu or perhaps from a set of tabs. Otherwise, confusion sets in as functions lose their sharp edges, and navigation becomes oppressive. The reason for enforcing these limitations is twofold. First, as document windows of different types are selected, the menus must change to keep up. The user depends on the permanency of menus to help keep him oriented on the screen. Changing them bleeds away this reliability. Second, everything described in our earlier discussion about minimizing, maximizing, and pluralizing windows goes double for document windows inside an MDI application. The user is forced to manage little windows inside a big window, a truly heinous example of excise. It is much better to go cleanly from one window to the next. Going from one fully maximized spreadsheet to another fully maximized spreadsheet is powerful and effective.

Today there is little effective difference between MDI and SDI, as Microsoft implements them. In most Microsoft applications, you can go either to the Window menu or the Taskbar to change from spreadsheet to spreadsheet, and you can go to the Taskbar to change from Excel to Word.

Chapter 26

Using Controls

Controls are manipulable, self-contained screen objects that allow communication between users and software. Controls, widgets, gadgets, or gizmos — whatever you choose to call them — are primary building blocks for creating graphical user interfaces. They are closely identified with GUI development, being as fundamental to GUI construction as windows, menus, and dialog boxes.

When examined in light of users' goals, controls come in four basic flavors: **imperative controls**, used to initiate a function; **selection controls**, used to select options or data; **entry controls**, used to enter data; and **display controls**, used to directly manipulate the program visually. Some controls combine one or more of these flavors.

Most of the controls that we are familiar with are those that come standard with Windows, the Mac OS, and other common windowing interfaces. This set of canned controls has always been very limited in scope and power.

Avoiding Control-Laden Dialog Boxes

The easiest thing to build in most window systems is a dialog box. The dialog box facility offers automatic tools for specifying how and where controls will be placed. The de facto definition of a dialog box is a modal window covered with controls. The ease with which developers can create user interfaces based on one control-laden dialog box after another is significant. Equally significant is the difficulty involved in creating windowing interfaces using any other visual, directly manipulated idioms. Thus most host GUI systems divide the universe of interaction into two worlds: the extremely easy to implement world of canned controls (radio buttons, check boxes, drop-down menus, and so on), and the extremely difficult-to-implement world of direct visual interaction. Consistent with this, most existing literature covers the canned-control world reasonably well, while ignoring other approaches. However, control-laden dialog boxes are *not* the key to successful user interface design. We'll discuss more about appropriate use of dialog boxes in Chapters 30 and 31.

A multitude of control-laden dialog boxes doth not a good user interface make.

The authors are not suggesting the elimination of standard controls. However, although the use of these controls may guarantee ease-of-implementation, it won't guarantee ease-of-use. Controls must be used judiciously and in the proper context, like all elements of a good interface.

We'll now look at each of the four types of controls—imperative, selection, entry, and display—in more detail.

Imperative Controls

In the interaction between humans and computers, there is a language of nouns (sometimes called objects), verbs, adjectives, and adverbs. When we issue a command, we are specifying the verb—the action of the statement. When we describe what the action will affect, we are specifying the noun of the sentence. Sometimes we choose a noun from an existing list, and sometimes we enter a new one. We can modify both the noun and the verb with adjectives and adverbs, respectively.

The control type that corresponds to a verb is called the **imperative control** because it commands immediate action. Imperative controls take action, and they take it immediately. Menu items, which we will discuss in Chapters 27 and 28, are also imperative idioms. In the world of controls, the quintessential imperative idiom is the push-button; in fact, it is the only one, although it comes in numerous guises. Click the button and the associated action—the verb—executes immediately.

Push-buttons

Push-buttons are most often identified by their simulated-3D raised aspect. If the control is rectangular (or sometimes oval) and appears raised (due to its shadow on the right and bottom and highlight on the top and left), it has the visual affordance of an imperative. It will execute as soon as the user clicks and releases it with the mouse cursor. In dialogs, a **default button** is often highlighted to indicate the most reasonable typical action for a user to take.

The push-button is arguably the most visually compelling control in the designer's toolkit. It isn't surprising that it has evolved with such diversity across the user interface. The manipulation affordances of contemporary faux three-dimensional push-buttons have prompted their widespread use. It's a good thing—so why *not* use it a lot? Designers of hyperlinks on the Web have even borrowed the look of the push-button, though often at the cost of pliant feedback.

Part of the affordance of a push-button is its visual pliancy, which indicates its "pressability." When the user points to it and clicks the mouse button, the push-button on screen visually changes from raised to indented, indicating that it is activated. This is an example of dynamic visual hinting, as discussed in Part V. Poorly-designed programs and many Web sites contain buttons that are painted on the screen but don't actually move when clicked. This is cheap and easy for the developer to do (especially on the Web), but it is very disconcerting for the user, because it generates a mental question: "Did that actually do something?" The user expects to see the button move—the pliant response—and you must satisfy his expectations.

This is important in Web pages and multimedia applications, many of which, for reasons both artistic and technological, eschew the desktop rules of pliancy but still set aside portions of their display that are sensitive to clicking.

Cursor hinting isn't enough in these cases, although it's a desirable supplement. Even if the entire screen is consumed by a collage of, say, baseball collectibles, when the user clicks on a Louisville Slugger to perform some function, that bat should move to visually confirm to the user that it is an imperative push-button — or, in this case, a push-bat!

Butcons

Concurrent with the release of Windows 3.0 came the introduction of the **toolbar** (which we discuss at length in Chapter 29), an idiom that has grown into a de facto standard as familiar as the menu bar. To populate the toolbar, the push-button was adapted from its traditional home on the dialog box. On its way, it expanded significantly in function, role, and visual aspect.

On dialog boxes, the push-button is rectangular (with rounded edges on the Mac) and exclusively labeled with text. When it moved to the toolbar, it became square, lost its text, and acquired a pictograph, an iconic legend. Thus was born the **butcon**: half button, half icon. In Windows 98, the butcon, or toolbar button, continued to develop, losing its raised affordance except when used — a move to reduce visual clutter in response to the overcrowding of toolbars. Unfortunately, this makes it more difficult for newcomers to understand the idiom; the toolbar butcon in Windows 2000 now reveals its button affordance only when pointed at. Windows XP has continued the evolution of the butcon away from its "button-ness." Office XP application butcons have a rather confusing visual hint in which the icon lifts from the surface of the toolbar on a little square platform. The authors wonder why Microsoft couldn't leave well enough alone and continue to visually associate butcons strongly with their function as buttons.

Butcons are, in theory, easy to use: They are always visible and don't demand as much time or dexterity as a drop-down menu does. Because they are constantly visible, they are easy to memorize, particularly in sovereign applications. The advantages of the butcon are hard to separate from the advantages of the toolbar — the two are inextricably linked. The consistently annoying problem with the butcon derives not from its button part, but from its icon part. We instantly decipher the visual affordance — it screams, "click me!" (or did, in any case, before Windows 98). The problem is that the image on the face of the butcon is seldom that clear.

Icons, in general, are hard to decipher with certainty, and icons of verbs are much harder to decipher than icons of nouns. Because butcons are imperative controls, their icons represent verbs, and thus remain problematic. It isn't really a matter of coming up with better visual metaphors or finding a better graphic artist. The problem is that actions and relationships are difficult, if not impossible, to portray in the limited visual resolution of an icon. If you can find an appropriate icon, it may have good mnemonic qualities, but will usually be inadequate to teach newcomers its purpose.

The dilemma arises because images do have such good mnemonic qualities. These qualities are good enough that the visual image is more than enough to remind the daily user of the command represented by the butcon. The visual butcon is very space-efficient compared to the older, text-legend button. As long as there is a way to learn it initially, and it is part of the user's working set of commands, he will remember the image as an idiom and have no problem with the lack of innate learnability. Thus, to be successful, the butcon's image must be visually distinct from other butcons and memorable as an idiom.

Without any mechanism for explaining their purpose, however, butcons and toolbars would be significantly less useful than they are. The rapid spread of butcons on toolbars initially caused widespread grumbling about incomprehensible icons for just this reason. In response, some companies enlarged their butcons until they were big enough to hold text legends in addition to icons. Yet others required users to choose which commands would be displayed as butcons, adding another annoying layer of excise to the interface. But Microsoft's ToolTips neatly solved the inscrutable butcon problem once and for all. ToolTips provide initial learning without getting in the way of the frequent user. The grumbling over inscrutable butcons has since subsided to inaudibility due to ToolTips, a testament to the efficacy of the idiom.

We'll speak more about butcons, toolbars, and ToolTips in Chapter 29.

Selection Controls

Because the imperative control is a verb, it needs a noun upon which to operate. Selection and entry controls are the two controls used to select nouns. A **selection control** allows the user to choose an operand from a group of valid choices.

No action is associated with selection controls. Selection controls can either present a single choice (to which the user can only say Yes or No), or it can present a group of choices (from which the user can select one or more choices, depending on how the control is configured). The list box and the check box are good examples of selection controls.

Check boxes

The **check box** was one of the earliest visual control idioms invented, and it is the favorite for presenting a single, binary choice. The check box has a strong visual affordance for clicking; it appears as a pliant area because of a mouseover highlight or a 3D "recessed" visual treatment. After the user clicks on it and sees the checkmark appear, he has learned all he needs to know to make it work at will: Click to check; click again to uncheck. The check box is simple, visual, and elegant.

The check box is, however, primarily a text-based control. The checkable box acts as a visually recognizable icon next to its discriminating text. This works in just the way that icons to the left of text items in a list box help the user visually discriminate their types. Like those list box entries, however, the graphic supports the text, rather than the other way around. The check box is a familiar, effective idiom; but it has the same strengths and weaknesses as menus. The exacting text makes check boxes unambiguous. The exacting text forces the user to slow down to read it, and takes a considerable amount of real estate.

Traditionally, check boxes are square. Users recognize visual objects by their shape, and the square check box is an important standard. There is nothing inherently good or bad about squareness; it just happens to have been the shape originally chosen and many users have already learned to recognize this shape. There is no good reason to deviate from this pattern. Don't make them diamond-shaped or round, regardless of what the marketing or graphic arts people say.

Perhaps we could do to the check box what the butcon did to the menu. Perhaps we could develop a check-box control that dispenses with text and uses an icon instead. Well, sort of. We won't get far trying to iconize the check box, but we can replace the check-box function with another evolving idiom: the butcon.

The push-button evolved into the butcon by replacing its text with an icon, then migrating onto the toolbar. Once there, the metamorphosis of the button continued by the simple expedient of allowing it to stay in the recessed—or pushed-in—state when it is clicked, then returning to the raised aspect when it is clicked again, a **latching butcon** (see Figure 26-1). The state of the latching butcon is no longer momentary, but rather locks in place until it is clicked again. The character of the control has changed sufficiently to move it into an entirely different category, from imperative to selection control!

Figure 26-1: Butcons in their flat, mouseover (raised), and clicked states on Windows 2000 (left) and XP (right). The button affordance on the left is clearer. The controls pictured are also examples of latching butcons, invented by applying the simple expedient of not letting the button pop back out after it has been clicked. What is remarkable about this idiom is that it moves the butcon idiom from the imperative category—a verb—into the selection category—a noun. It has all the idiomatic and space-saving advantages of the butcon, except that it sets state rather than invoking an immediate command.

The default toolbar configuration on Microsoft's Office suite of programs seems tacitly to separate the momentary, imperative butcons from the latching, selection butcons. Generally Microsoft only put imperative butcons on the top bar and put mostly selection butcons on the others.

The latching butcon is widely superseding the check box as a single-selection idiom and is especially appropriate in modeless interactions that do not require interruption of a user's flow to make a decision. Latching butcons are more space-efficient than check boxes: They are smaller because they can rely on visual recognition instead of text labels to indicate their purpose. Of course, this means that they exhibit the same problem as imperative butcons: the inscrutability of the icon. We are saved once again by ToolTips. Those tiny, pop-up windows give us just enough text to disambiguate the butcon without permanently consuming too many pixels.

Flip-flop buttons: A selection idiom to avoid

Flip-flop buttons are an all-too-common control variant used to save interface real estate, but at the cost of considerable user confusion. The verb on the flip-flop button is always one of multiple states that the control can be in. For example, if a flip-flop button were designed to control print resolution, it might say Draft Output until you click it, and then it might say Quality Output.

The control affords that you can click it, so when it says Quality Output it intends to mean that by clicking it you will get into quality output mode. The button then changes to say, Draft Output to indicate that clicking it again will put the application in draft output mode. The problem with this technique is that the control could be interpreted to serve as an indicator of which state you are in. Unfortunately, because it shows Draft Output when you are in quality output mode and vice versa, it is, in fact, doing exactly the opposite of what might be expected. The control can either serve as a state indicator or as a state-switching imperative control, but not both (see Figure 26-2).

The solution to this one is to either spell it out on the button as a verb phrase—Switch to Quality Output—or to use some other technique entirely. Replacing it with two radio buttons is a popular choice. The downside is that this consumes more screen real estate.

Another approach is pictorial. Draw a picture of the page in portrait. When the user clicks on it, it rolls over onto its side to show that you are in landscape orientation. This is very memorable and engaging, but it is not necessarily very discoverable. That depends on how well the rest of your program has influenced the user to expect that a small picture is pliant and will have some effect. Cursor hinting will help. However, it's important not to put the image on top of a button. If you do, you will have just created a pictographic flip-flop butcon with the same conflicting messages as those with a text label.

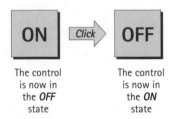

The control is now in the *OFF* state

The control is now in the *ON* state

Figure 26-2: Flip-flop button controls are very efficient. They save space by controlling two mutually exclusive options with a single control. The problem with flip-flop controls is that they fail to fulfill the second duty of every control — to inform the user of their current state. If the button says ON when the state is off, it is unclear what the setting is. If it says OFF when the state is off, however, where is the ON button? Don't use them. Not on buttons and not on menus!

Radio buttons

A variant of the check box is the **radio button**. The name says it all. When radios were first put in automobiles, we all discovered that manually tuning an analog radio with a rotating knob while driving was dangerous to your health. So automotive radios were offered with a newfangled panel consisting of a half-dozen chrome-plated push-buttons, each of which would twist the tuner to a preset station. Now you could tune to your favorite station, without taking your eyes off of the road, just by pushing a button. The idiom is a powerful one, and it still has many practical uses in interaction design.

The behavior of radio buttons is **mutually exclusive**, which means that when one option is selected, the previously selected option automatically deselects. Only one button can be selected at a time. (Techno-geeks frequently use the word **mux** as a convenient contraction of the phrase **mutually exclusive**, and we often use it in reference to these controls.)

In consequence of mutual exclusion, radio buttons always come in groups of two or more, and one radio button in each group is always selected. (Technically speaking, there is no enforcement of this mutual exclusion, nor is there enforcement of the always-one-selected rule. The individual developer is quite free to break the rules.) A single radio button is undefined—it must act like a check box instead. (You should use a check box or similar non-mux selection control in this instance.)

Radio buttons are even more wasteful of screen real estate than check boxes. They waste the same amount of space as check boxes, and for the same reasons, but radio buttons are only meaningful in groups, so their waste is always multiplied. In some cases, the waste is justified, particularly where it is important to show the user the full set of available choices at all times. This should sound vaguely pedagogic, and it is. Radio buttons are well suited to a teaching role, which means they can be justified in infrequently used dialog boxes, but they should not be visible on the surface of a sovereign application which must cater to daily users.

For the same reason that check boxes are traditionally square — that's how we've always done it — radio buttons are round. There are no reasons to change this shape other than aesthetic or marketing ones, and these reasons take back seat to the established tradition. (X Windows/Motif's radio buttons are diamonds, so you might consider sticking to those if you're designing for the Unix world.)

Radio buttons are one of the oldest GUI idioms, and consequently many designers see them as somehow better than other, newer idioms, but this isn't so. In some cases, radio buttons are being supplanted by more modern idioms.

As you might imagine, the butcon has also done to the radio button what it did to the check box: replaced it on the surface of an application. If two or more latching butcons are grouped together and mux-linked — so that only one of them at a time can be latched — they behave in exactly the same way as radio buttons. They form a **radio butcon**.

They work just like radio buttons: One is always selected — latched down — and whenever another one is pressed, the first one returns to its normal — raised — position. The alignment controls on Word's toolbar are an excellent example of a radio butcon, as shown in Figure 26-3.

Figure 26-3: Word's alignment controls are a radio butcon group, acting like radio buttons. One is always selected, and when another is clicked, the first one returns to its normal, raised position. This variant is a very space-conservative idiom that is well suited for frequently used options.

Just as in all butcon idioms, these are very efficient consumers of space, letting experienced users rely on pattern recognition to identify them and letting infrequent users rely on ToolTips to remind users of their purpose. First-time users will either be clever enough to learn from the ToolTips or will learn more slowly, but just as reliably, from other, parallel, pedagogic command vectors.

Combutcons

A variant of the radio butcon is a drop-down version. Because of its similarity to the combobox control, we call this a **combutcon**. It is shown in Figure 26-4. Normally, it looks like a single, latched butcon with a small down-arrow to its right (in Windows), but if you click and hold the arrow, it drops down a menu of several (sometimes many, arranged in a 2D array) latching but-cons. You slide the cursor much the same way you do on a pull-down menu to select one of the items in the combutcon's drop-down list/array. When you release the mouse button, the selection is made and the selected butcon now appears on the toolbar next to the arrow (clicking on the butcon itself toggles the butcon state). Like menus, the menu of butcons should also deploy if the user clicks once on the arrow and releases. A second click makes the selection.

Figure 26-4: A *combutcon* is a group of latching butcons that behave like a combobox. Clicking the mouse button while over the combutcon's down-arrow drops down a menu of butcons. Slide the cursor down to the desired one and release. The newly selected butcon shows on the toolbar as the selected option. Think of this idiom as a way to cram many related latching butcons into the space of a single one. It creates more user excise than putting up separate butcons, but is useful when space is at a premium or when the functions are not used very frequently.

Variations on combutcons include drawing a small, downward- or right-pointing triangle in the lower-right corner of the combutcon icon in place of the separate down-arrow that is seen in Microsoft toolbars. Adobe products make use of this variant in their palette controls; this variant also requires a click and hold on the button itself to bring up the menu (which, in Adobe palette controls, unfolds to the right rather than down, as shown in Figure 26-5). You can vary this idiom quite a bit, and creative software designers are doing just that in the never-ending bid to cram more functions onto screens that are always too small.

You can see a Microsoft variant in Word, where the butcon for specifying the colors of high-lights and text show combutcon menus that look more like little palettes than stacks of butcons. As you can see from Figure 26-5, these menus can pack a lot of power and information into a very compact control. This facility is definitely for frequent users, particularly mouse-heavy users, and not at all for first-timers. However, for the user who has at least a basic familiarity with the avail-able tools, the idiom is instantly clear after it is discovered or demonstrated. This is an excellent control idiom for sovereign-posture programs with which users interact for long hours. It demands sufficient manual dexterity to work a menu with relatively small targets, but is much faster than going to the menu bar, pulling down a menu, selecting an item, waiting for the dialog box to deploy, selecting a color on the dialog box, and then clicking the OK button.

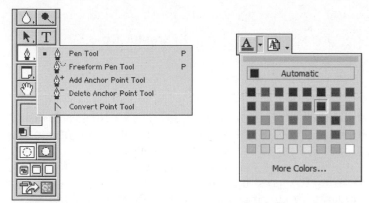

Figure 26-5: These combutcons are taken from Adobe Photoshop (left) and Microsoft Word (right). In Photoshop, the combutcon opens to the right, and includes a text description of each butcon. In the Word combutcon, clicking the butcon causes a tear-off menu to appear, which can become a floating palette. Colors are selected from the swatches at the top or from the text item, which brings up a color selection dialog. This dense packing of information, both input and output, is indicative of the direction in which superior user interfaces have moved in the last 15 years.

List controls

List controls allow users to select from a finite set of text strings, each representing a command, object, or attribute. These controls are sometimes called **picklists** because they offer lists of items from which the user can pick a selection, they are also known as **list boxes** or **listviews**, depending on which platform and which control variant you are talking about. The list control is a powerful tool for simplifying interaction because it eliminates the possibility of making an incorrect selection.

List controls are small text areas with a vertical scrollbar on the right-hand edge. The application displays objects as discrete lines of text in the box, and the scrollbar moves them up or down. The user can select a single line of text at a time by clicking on it. A list control variant allows multiple selection, where the user can select multiple items at one time, usually by pressing the Shift or Ctrl key while clicking with the mouse.

Early list controls handled text only, and that decision affects their behavior to this day. A list control filled with line after line of text unrelieved by visual symbols is a dry desert indeed. Some adventurous programmers have adapted older list controls for graphics, but most programmers probably aren't that masochistic.

However, Microsoft seems to have done a good job, as of Windows 95, with its **listview control**. Among other features, it allows each line of text to be preceded with an icon without need of custom coding. This is excellent news, because there are many instances in which users would benefit from items shown in lists with an identifying or information-providing visual icon next to important text entries. Figure 26-6 in the next section shows a modified listview control with icons.

Distinguish important text items in lists with graphic icons.

Listviews are, true to their name, good for displaying lists of items and allowing the user to select one or more of them. They are also good idioms for providing a source of draggable items. If the items are draggable within the listview itself, it makes a fine tool for enabling the user to put items in a specific order (see the "Ordering Lists" section later in this chapter).

Many lists displayed in desktop interfaces are not static and support modification by users who add, delete, and change the text of entries. To support this requires the ability to key, directly into the listview, a new text item or a modification to an existing one. Luckily, in addition to icons, listviews support drag-and-drop and edit-in-place capabilities.

The weight of history and habit still puts older list controls onto a lot of dialog boxes. Thankfully, most of those dialogs appear quickly, allow the user to select a single item, and then go away. To provide better interaction, programmers should use the newer listview control — or its equivalents on other platforms — exclusively.

EARMARKING

Generally speaking, users select items in a list control as input to some function, like selecting the name of a desired font from a list of several available fonts. Selection in a list control is conventional, with keyboard equivalents, focus rectangles, and selected items shown in highlight colors.

Occasionally, however, list controls are used to select multiple items, and this can introduce complications. The selection idiom in list controls is very well suited for single selection, but much weaker for multiple selection. In general, multiple selection of discrete objects works adequately if the entire playing field is visible at once, like the icons on a desktop. If two or more icons are selected at the same time, you can clearly see this because all the icons are visible.

But if the pool of available discrete items is too large to fit in a single view and some of it must be scrolled off screen, the selection idiom immediately becomes unwieldy. This is the normal state of affairs for list controls. Their standard mode of selection is mutual exclusion, so when you select one thing, the previous selected thing deselects. It is thus far too easy, in the case of multiple selection, for users to select an item, scroll it into invisibility, and then select a second item, forgetting that they have now *deselected* the first item because they can no longer see it.

The alternative is equally unpalatable: The list control is programmed to disable the mutual-exclusion behavior of a standard list control in its selection algorithm, allowing users to click on as many items as they like with them all remaining selected. Things now work absolutely perfectly (sort of): The user selects one item after another, and each one stays selected. The fly in the ointment is that there is no visual indication that selection is behaving differently from the norm. It is just as likely that a user will select an item, scroll it into invisibility, then spot a more desirable second item and select it *expecting the first — unseen — item to automatically deselect* by way of the mux standard. You get to choose between offending the first half of your users or the second half. Bad idea.

When objects can scroll off the screen, multiple selection requires a better, more distinct idiom. The correct action is to use a different idiom from simple selection, one that is visually distinct. But what is it?

It just so happens we already have another well-established idiom to indicate that something is selected — the check box. Check boxes communicate their purposes and their settings quite clearly and, like all good idioms, are extremely easy to learn. Check boxes are also very clearly dis-associated from any hint of mutual exclusion. If we were to add a check box to every item in our problematic list control, the user would not only clearly see which items were selected and which were not, he would also clearly see that the items were not mux-linked, solving both of our problems in one stroke. This check box alternative to multiple selection is called **earmarking**, an example of which is shown in Figure 26-6.

Figure 26-6: Selection is normally a mutually exclusive (mux) operation. When the need arises to discard mux in order to provide multiple selection, things can become confusing if some of the items can be scrolled out of sight. Earmarking is a solution to this. Put check boxes next to each text item and use them instead of selection to indicate the user's choices. Check boxes are a clearly non-mux idiom and a very familiar GUI idiom. Users grasp the workings of this idiom right away.

Earmarking also solves another niggling problem with multiple selections. Multiple selection list controls, when they are created, have no selected items. However, in some variants, once the user selects an item, there is no way to return to a state where nothing is selected. In other words, there is no idiom for selecting nothing. If the list control is used in the sense of an operand selector for a function dialog box, the Cancel button provides the escape route if the user changes his mind. However, if the list control isn't on a dialog box, he may be stuck (ideally, clicking again on a selected item should unselect it even in this case). Earmarking doesn't operate under the same rules as selection, and each item in the list is independent. One click checks the box; a second click unchecks the box.

Sometimes, as in some drawing programs like Powerpoint, it makes sense to have a None or No Color item at the top of the list. In this particular case, None is truly a valid selection, because you can have an object with no outline or no fill color. Don't, however, use this idiom as a means for general purpose deselecting of items in a list, especially if an item needs to be selected for the user to proceed! Use earmarking instead.

DRAGGING-AND-DROPPING FROM LISTS

List controls can be treated as palettes of goodies to use in a direct-manipulation idiom. If the list was part of a report-writing program, for example, you could click on an entry and drag it to the surface of the report to add a column representing that field. It's not selection in the usual sense, because it is a completely captive operation. Without a doubt, many programs would benefit if they made use of list controls that supported dragging and dropping.

Such draggable items can help users gather items in a desired set. Two adjacent list controls, one showing available items and the other showing chosen items, is a common GUI idiom. One or sometimes a bidirectional pair of push-buttons placed between them allows items to be selected and transferred from one box to the other, as shown in Figure 26-7. It is so much more pleasant when the idiom is buttressed with the capability to just click and drag the desired item from one box to another without having to go through the intermediate steps of selection and function invocation.

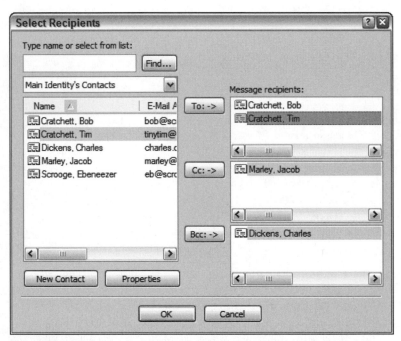

Figure 26–7: This dialog from Microsoft Outlook Express would benefit from the capability to drag a contact from the list at left into the To, Cc, and Bcc lists at right. Also notice the unfortunate use of horizontal scrollbars in all list fields. In the left-hand field, in particular, ToolTips could show the full row of information in the left-hand box.

ORDERING LISTS

Sometimes the need arises to drag an item from a list control to another position in the same list control. Actually, this need arises far more often than most interaction designers seem to think. Many programs offer automatic sort facilities for important lists. Windows Explorer, for example, allows sorting files by name, by type, by modification date, and by size. That's nice, but wouldn't be even better to be able to order them by importance to the user? Algorithmically, the program could order them by frequency of user access, but that won't always get the right results. Adding in a factor of how recently files were accessed, as well, would get closer, but still wouldn't be exactly what right. (Microsoft does this with its font picker in some applications, and it works pretty well for this purpose.) Why not let the user be able to move what's important to him to a region at the top, and sort those things separately (in alphabetical or whatever order), in addition to sorting the full directory below? For example, you might want to rearrange a list of the people in your department in descending order by how competent you think they are. There is no automatic function that will do this; you just have to drag them until it's right. Now, this is the kind of customizing that an experienced user wants to do after long hours of familiarization with an application. It takes a lot of effort to fine-tune a directory like this, and the program *must* remember the exact settings from session to session—otherwise, the capability to reorder things is worthless.

Being able to drag items from one place to another in a list control is powerful, but it demands that autoscrolling be implemented (see Chapter 23). If you pick up an item in the list but the place you need to drop it is currently scrolled out of view, you must be able to scroll the listview without putting down the dragged object.

HORIZONTAL SCROLLING

List controls normally have a vertical scrollbar for moving up and down through the list. List controls can also be made to scroll horizontally. This feature allows the programmer to put extra-long text into the list controls with a minimum of effort. However, it offers nothing to users but a major pain.

Scrolling text horizontally is a terrible thing, and it should *never, ever* be done. When a text list is scrolled horizontally, it hides from view one or more of the first letters of every single line of text showing. This makes *none* of the lines readable and the continuity of the text is utterly destroyed. To see this, take your bookmark and cover up just the first two characters of each line in this paragraph. See how hard it becomes to read? Yes, it is decipherable, but you have to strain at it. The purpose of computers is to eliminate strain from the lives of humans.

AXIOM

Never scroll text horizontally.

If you find a situation that seems to call for horizontal scrolling of text, search for alternative solutions. Begin by asking yourself why the text in your list is so long. Can you shorten the entries? Can you wrap the text to the next line to avoid that horizontal length? Can you allow the user to enter aliases for the longer entries? Can you use graphical entries instead? Can you use a smaller typeface? You should alternatively be asking yourself if there is some way to widen the control. Can you rearrange things on the window or dialog to expand horizontally?

The best answer will usually be to wrap the text onto the next line, indenting it so it is visually different from other entries. This means that you now have a list control with items of variable height, but this is still better than horizontal scrolling.

Remember, we're just talking about *text*. For graphics, there is nothing wrong with horizontal scrollbars or horizontally scrollable windows in general. But providing a text-based list with a required horizontal scrollbar is like providing a computer with a required pedal-powered electrical generator—bad news.

ENTERING DATA INTO A LIST

Little work has been done historically to enable users to make direct text entry into an item in a list control. Older list box controls punted on this, and it takes some pretty nifty coding to implement it yourself. Of course, the need to enter text where text is output is widespread, and much of the kludginess of dialog box design can be directly attributed to programmers trying to dodge the bullet of having to write edit-in-place code.

However, modern list and tree controls in Windows and other platforms offer an edit-in-place facility. Windows Explorer uses both of these controls, and you can see how they work by renaming a file or directory. To rename a file in the Mac OS or Windows 95, you click twice — but not too quickly (lest it be interpreted as a double-click and open the object in question) — on the desired name. You then enter whatever changes are desired. (This has changed a bit in Windows XP, so that in some views you need to select Rename from a right-click menu to get into Rename mode — is this progress?). Items that are editable in other circumstances should, when displayed in list controls, be editable there as well.

The edge case that makes edit-in-place a real problem is adding a new entry to the list. Most designers use other idioms to add list items: Click a button or select a menu item and a new, blank entry is added to the list and the user can then edit-in-place its name. It would be more sensible if you could, say, double-click in the space between existing entries to create a new, blank entry right there or at least have a perpetual open space at the beginning or end of the list with a Click to Add Entry label on it to make it discoverable. Ah, wishful thinking . . . . The real-world solution to this problem is the combobox, which we'll talk about next.

Comboboxes

Windows 3.0 introduced a new control called the **combobox**. It is — as its name suggests — a combination of a list box and an edit field. It provides an unambiguous method of data entry into a list control. The other attribute of the combobox that makes it a winner is its pop-up variant that is extremely conservative of screen real estate.

With the combobox control, there is a clear separation between the text-entry part and the list-selection part, minimizing user confusion. For single selection, the combobox is a superb control. The edit field can be used to enter new items, and it also shows the current selection in the list. When the current selection is showing in the edit field, the user can edit it there — sort of a poor man's edit-in-place.

Because the edit field of the combobox shows the current selection, the combobox is by nature a single-selection control. There is no such thing as a multiple-selection combobox. Single selection implies mutual exclusion, which is one of the reasons why the combobox is fast replacing groups of radio buttons for mux-linked options. (The Mac OS had pop-up menus before Windows had the combobox, and these served to replace large banks of radio buttons on that platform. The Mac versions didn't have the combobox's edit feature, however.) The other reasons include its space efficiency and its capability to add items dynamically, something that radio buttons cannot do.

When the drop-down variants of the combobox are used, the control shows the current selection without consuming space to show the list of choices. Essentially, it becomes a list-on-demand, much like a menu provides a list of immediate commands on demand. A combobox is a pop-up list control.

The screen efficiency of the combobox allows it to do something remarkable for a control of such complexity: It can reasonably reside permanently on a program's main screen. It can even fit comfortably on a toolbar. It is a very effective control for deployment on a sovereign-posture application. There are four comboboxes visible on the authors' word processors' toolbars, for example. This effectively crams a huge amount of information and usefulness into a very small space. Using comboboxes on the toolbar is more effective than putting the equivalent functions on menus, because the comboboxes display their current selection without requiring any action on the user's part, such as pulling down a menu to see the current status. Once again, the control that delivers the most information with the smallest permanent screen footprint wins the Darwinian battle for pixels.

If drag and drop is implemented in list controls, it should also be implemented in comboboxes. For example, being able to open a combobox, scroll to a choice, and then to be able to drag the choice onto a document under construction is a very powerful idiom. Because comboboxes fit so well on toolbars, the idiom has real appeal for adding direct manipulation to sovereign applications. Drag-and-drop functionality should be a standard part of comboboxes.

The utility of the combobox collapses if the situation calls for multiple selection; the idiom just can't handle it, and you must return to a plain list box. Regular list controls consume significant space on-screen, however — enough so that it shouldn't be considered practical for permanent deployment unless there is a truly great need. In general, list controls are best relegated to transient dialogs.

Tree controls

Mac OS 7 and Windows 95 both brought us general-purpose tree controls, which had already been in use in the Unix world for some time. Tree controls are listviews that can present hierarchical data. They display a sideways tree, with icons for each entry. The entries can be expanded or collapsed the way that many outline processors work. Programmers tend to like this presentation. It is often used as a file system navigator, and some find the format of the display to be effective — certainly more effective than scattering icons around in multiple windows on the desktop. Unfortunately, it is problematic for users because of the difficulty many nonprogrammer users have with understanding hierarchical data structures. In general, it makes sense to use a treeview, no matter how tempting it may be, only in the case where what is being represented is "naturally" thought of as a hierarchy (such as a family tree). Using a treeview to represent arbitrary objects organized in an arbitrary fashion at the whim of a programmer is asking for big trouble when it comes to usability.

Entry Controls

Entry controls enable the user to enter new information into the program, rather than merely selecting information from an existing list.

The most basic entry control is a text edit field. Like selection controls, entry controls represent nouns to the program. Because a combobox contains an edit field, some combobox variants qualify as entry controls, too. Also, any control that lets the user enter a numeric value is an entry control. Controls such as spinners, gauges, sliders, and knobs fit in this category.

Bounded and unbounded entry controls

Any control that restricts the available set of values that the user can enter is a **bounded entry control**. A slider that moves from 1 to 100, for example, is bounded. Regardless of the user's actions, no number outside those specified by the program can be entered with a bounded control. It is thus impossible for users to enter an invalid value with bounded entry controls.

Conversely, a simple text field can accept any alphanumeric data the user keys into it. This open-ended entry idiom is an example of an **unbounded entry control**. With an unbounded entry control, it is easy for users to enter invalid values. The program may subsequently reject it, of course, but the user can still enter it.

Simply put, bounded controls should be used wherever bounded values are needed. If the program needs a number between 7 and 35, presenting the user with a control that will accept any numeric value from −1,000,000 to +1,000,000 is not doing the user any favors. She would much rather be presented with a control that embodies 7 as its bottom limit and 35 as its upper limit. Users are smart, and they will immediately comprehend and respect the limits of their sandbox.

It is important to understand that we mean a quality of the entry control and not of the data. To be a bounded control, it needs to clearly communicate, preferably visually, the acceptable data boundaries to the user. A text field that rejects the user's input *after* he has entered it is *not* a bounded control. It is simply a *rude* control.

Most quantitative values needed by software are bounded, yet many programs allow unbounded entry with numeric fields. When the user inadvertently enters a value that the program cannot accept, the program issues an error message box. This is cruelly teasing the user with possibilities that aren't. "What would you like for dessert? We've got everything," we say. "Ice cream," you respond. "Sorry, we don't have any," we say. "How about pie?" you innocently ask. "Nope," we say. "Cookies?" "Nope." "Candy?" "Nope." "Chocolate?" "Nope." "What, then?" you scream in anger and frustration. "Don't get mad," we say indignantly. "We have plenty of fruit compote." This is how the user feels when we put up a dialog box with an unbounded edit field when the valid values are bounded. She types **17**, and we reward this innocent entry with an error message box that says "You can only enter values between 4 and 8." This is poor user-interface design; a much better scheme is to use a bounded control that automatically limits the input to 4, 5, 6, 7, or 8. If the bounded set of choices is composed of text rather than numbers, you can still use a slider of some type, or a combobox, or list box. Figure 26-8 shows a bounded slider used by Microsoft in the Windows Display Settings dialog. It works like a slider or scrollbar, but has four discrete positions that represent distinct resolution settings. Microsoft could easily have used a non-editable combobox in its place, too. In many cases, a slider is a nice choice because it telegraphs the range of valid entries. A combobox isn't much smaller but it keeps its cards hidden until clicked—a less friendly stance.

If the program requires a numeric value that must remain within specific boundaries, give the user a control that intrinsically communicates those limits and prevents him from entering a value outside of the boundaries. The scrollbar control class does this. Although scrollbars have significant drawbacks, they are exemplary in one area: They allow the user to enter quantitative information by analogy. Scrollbars allow the user to specify numeric values in relative terms, rather than by directly keying in a number. That is, the user moves the sliding thumb to indicate, by its relative position, a proportional value for use inside the program. They are less useful for entering precise numbers, though many programs use them for that purpose. Controls like spinners are better for entering exact numbers.

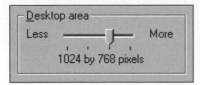

Figure 26-8: A bounded control lets you enter only valid values. It does *not* let you enter invalid values, only to reject them when you try to move on. This figure shows a bounded slider control from the Display Settings dialog in Windows 95. The little slider has four discrete positions. As you drag the slider from left to right, the legend underneath it changes from "640 by 480 pixels" to "800 by 600 pixels" to "1024 by 768 pixels" to "1280 by 1024 pixels." Why didn't they use a combobox? Which would you prefer?

Spinners

Spinner controls are a common form of numeric entry control that permit data entry using either the mouse or keyboard. Spinners contain a small edit field with two half-height buttons attached, as shown in Figure 26-9. Spinners blur the difference between bounded and unbounded controls.

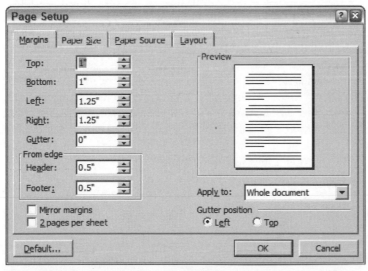

Figure 26-9: The Page Setup Dialog from MS Word makes heavy use of the spinner control. On the left side of the dialog, you see a stack of seven of these new controls, whose popularity is growing fast. By clicking on either of the small, arrowed buttons, the specific numeric value is made to increase or decrease in small, discrete steps. If the user wants to make a large change in one action or to enter a precise setting, he can use the edit field portion for direct text entry. The arrow button portion of the control embodies bounding, whereas the edit field portion does not. Does that make this a bounded control?

Spinners blur the difference between bounded and unbounded controls. Using either of the two small arrow buttons enables the user to change the value in the edit window in small, discrete steps. These steps are bounded — the value won't go above the upper limit set by the program or below the lower limit. If the user wants to make a large change in one action or to enter a specific number, he can do so by clicking in the edit window portion and directly entering keystrokes into it, just like entering text into any other edit field. Unfortunately, the edit window portion of this control is unbounded, leaving the user free to enter values that are out of bounds or even unintelligible garbage. In the page setup dialog box in the figure, if the user enters an invalid value, the program behaves like most other rude programs, issuing an error message box explaining the upper and lower boundaries (sometimes) and requiring the user to click the OK button to continue.

Overall, the spinner is an excellent idiom and can be used in place of plain edit fields for most bounded entry. In Part VII, we will discuss ways to improve control error handling.

Unbounded entry: Text edit controls

The primary unbounded entry control is the **text edit control**. This simple control allows the user to key in any alphanumeric text value. Edit fields are most often small areas where a word or two of data can be entered by the user, but they can also be fairly sophisticated text editors in their own right. The user can edit text within them using the standard tools of contiguous selection (as discussed in Chapter 22) with either the mouse or the keyboard.

Text edit controls are often used either as data entry fields in database applications (and now quite often on Web sites connected to databases), as option entry fields in dialog boxes, or as the entry field in a combobox. In all these roles, they are frequently called upon to do the work of a bounded entry control. However, if the desired values are finite, the text edit control should not be used. If the acceptable values are numeric, use a bounded numeric entry control, such as a slider or knob, instead. If the list of acceptable values is composed of text strings, a list control should be used so the user is not forced to type.

Sometimes the set of acceptable values is finite but too big to be practical for a list control. For example, a program may require a string of any 30 alphabetic characters excluding spaces, tabs, and punctuation marks. In this case, a text edit control is probably unavoidable even though its use is bounded. If these are the only restrictions, however, the text edit control can be designed to reject non-alphabetic characters and similarly disallow more than 30 characters to be entered into the field. This, however, brings up interaction issues surrounding validation.

VALIDATION

From an unbounded control's point-of-view, there is really no such thing as invalid data. Data can only be adjudged invalid in the context of the program. For example, 1995 is valid in a text entry control that gathers the year, but not in one that gathers the month. Physically, an unbounded entry control cannot recognize invalid data — only the program can make the actual determination of validity. From the program's point of view, a *bounded* entry control will only hand it valid input. Thus, by definition, an *unbounded* control *can* return invalid input to the program.

An unbounded control that is used to gather bounded data must serve two bosses: The control must blithely accept whatever data the user keys in, and then, if the program judges that input to be invalid, the control is forced to be the bearer of someone else's bad news. Putting unbounded controls in the role of accepting bounded input is one of the most significant contributors to user dissatisfaction with computers.

Use bounded controls for bounded input.

If the data is bounded—but not too heavily bounded—the program must let the user enter the data, only to reject it afterwards. Although there are some mitigating steps, there really is no good way to solve this problem. Unless . . . .

There *is* one way to solve this problem: The program could just go ahead and accept whatever the user enters. In other words, eliminate the handling of semibounded data. Either coerce the correct data with a bounded control, or accept whatever the user gives the program in an unbounded control. Most programmers reject this solution. They do not feel that their programs can accept, for example, **asdf;lkj** as input to a social security number field. However, there are some cases where this may make sense. In Chapter 33, we discuss this idea in detail.

The way programmers have dealt with this dilemma is by creating a **validation control**, or an unbounded text entry control with built-in editing. Many data entry types are commonplace, including formats such as dates, phone numbers, zip codes, and social security numbers. Specialized text edit controls are commercially available; you can purchase variants of the text entry control that will only allow numbers or letters or phone numbers, or reject spaces and tabs, for example.

Although the validation control is a very widespread idiom, it is a poor one because users must rely on the greater application context to determine what valid values might be for a given control. Tactically, though, these controls are often necessary; so we'll ignore the bigger issues for now and look at practical ways to make them better. The key to successfully designing a validation control is to give the user generous feedback. An entry control that merely refuses to accept input is just plain rude and will guarantee an angry and resentful user.

A fundamental improvement, based on the axiom: *Visually distinguish elements that behave differently* (Chapter 19), is to make validation controls visually distinct from non-validated controls, whether it is the typeface used in the text edit field, a different border color, or even a different background color for the field itself.

However, the primary way to improve validation controls is to provide rich status feedback to the user. Unfortunately, the text edit control, as we know it today, provides virtually no built-in support for feedback of any kind. The designer must specify such feedback mechanisms in detail, and the programmer will likely need to implement them himself as a custom control.

ACTIVE AND PASSIVE VALIDATION

Some controls reject the user's keystrokes as he enters them. When a control actively rejects keystrokes during the entry process, this is an example of **active validation**. A text-only entry control, for example, may accept only alphabetic characters and refuse to allow numbers to be entered. Some controls reject any keystrokes other than the numeric digits 0 through 9. Other controls reject spaces, tabs, dashes, and other punctuation in real-time. Some variants can get pretty intelligent and reject some numbers based on live calculations, for example, unless they pass a checksum algorithm.

When an active validation control rejects a keystroke, it must make it clear to the user that it has done so. It should also alert the user as to why it made the rejection. If an explanation is proffered, the user will be less inclined to assume the rejection is arbitrary. He will also be in a better position to give the program what it wants.

The user is expecting to be able to enter keystrokes at will; this is the nature of the keyboard. If the control is going to reject some keystrokes based on their value, it must clearly communicate this to the user.

Sometimes the range of possible data is such that the program cannot validate it until the user has completed his entry, rather than at each individual keystroke. The editing step then takes place only when the control loses focus, that is, when the user is done with the field and moves on to the next one. The editing step must also take place if the user closes the dialog — or invokes another function if the control is not on a dialog box (for example, selects Submit on a Web page). If the control waits until the user finishes entering data before it edits the value, this is **passive validation**.

The control may wait until a name is fully entered, for instance, before it interrogates a database to see if it is an existing entry. Each character is valid by itself, yet the whole may not pass muster. The program could attempt to verify the name as each character is entered, but that would probably bring the network and server to their knees with the extra workload. Besides, although the program would know at any given instant whether the name was valid, the user could still move on while the name was in an invalid state.

A way to address this is by maintaining a countdown timer in parallel with the input and reset it on each keystroke. If the countdown timer ever hits zero, do your validation processing. The timer should be set to around 400 milliseconds, although you may wish to user test this for a more precise number. The effect of this is that as long as the user is entering a keystroke faster than once every 400 ms, the system is extremely responsive. If the user pauses for more than 400 ms, the program reasonably assumes that the user has paused to think (something that takes months in CPU terms) and goes ahead and performs its analysis of the input so far.

To provide rich visual feedback, the entry field could change colors to reflect its estimate of the validity of the entered data. The field could show in shades of pink until the program judged the data valid, when it would change to white or green.

CLUE BOXES

Another good solution to the validation control problem is the **clue box**. This little pop-up window looks and behaves just like a ToolTip (but could be made distinguishable from a ToolTip by background color). Its function is to explain the range of acceptable data for a validation control, either active or passive. Whereas a ToolTip appears when the cursor sits for a moment on a control, a clue box would appear as soon as the control detects an invalid character (it might also display unilaterally just like a ToolTip if the cursor sits unmoving on the field for a second or so). If the user enters, for example, a non-numeric character in a numeric-only field, the program would put up a clue box near the point of the offending entry, yet without obscuring it. It would say, for example, 0–9. Short, terse, but very effective. Yes, the user is rejected, but he is not also ignored. The clue box also works for passive validation, as shown in Figure 26-10.

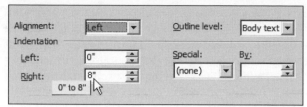

Figure 26-10: The ToolTip idiom is so effective that it could easily be extended to other uses. Instead of yellow ToolTips offering flyover labels for buttons, we could have pink ones offering flyover hints for unbounded edit fields. These clue boxes could also help eliminate error message boxes. In this example, if the user enters a value lower than allowable, the program could replace the entered value with the lowest allowable and display the cluebox that modelessly explains the reason for the substitution. The user can enter a new value or accept the minimum without being stopped by an error dialog.

HANDLING OUT OF BOUNDS DATA

Typically, an edit field is used to enter a numeric value needed by the program, like the point size of a font. The user can enter anything he wants, from 5 to 500, and the field will accept it and return the value to the owning program. If the user enters garbage, the control must make some kind of decision. In Microsoft Word, for example, if you enter asdf as a font point size, the program issues an error message box informing you: This is not a valid number. It then reverts the size to its previous value. The error dialog is rather silly, but the summary rejection of my meaningless input is perfectly appropriate. But what if you had keyed in the value nine? The program rejects it with the same curt error message box. If instead the control were programmed to think of itself as a numeric entry control, it could perhaps behave better. It doesn't bother me if the program converts the nine into a 9, but it certainly is incorrect when it says that nine is not a valid number. Without a doubt, it is valid, and the program has put its foot in its mouth.

Barring other tools, a simple rejection of input data is better than a rejection coupled with an error message box. For example, if a passive validation control can only accept a number between 5 and 25, and the user enters 50 the control should change to 25 and proceed. If the user enters 2, the control should change it to 5 and proceed. If the user enters asdf, the control should revert to the previously valid value and proceed.

UNITS AND MEASUREMENTS

It's nice when a text edit control is smart enough to recognize appropriate units. For example, if a program is requesting a measurement, and the user enters 5i or 5in or 5 inches, the control should not only report the result as five, but it should report inches as well. If the user enters 5mm the control should report it as five millimeters. SketchUp, an elegant architectural sketching application on Windows and the Mac, supports this type of feedback.

Say that the field is requesting a column width. The user can enter either a number or a number and an indicator of the measurement system as described above. The user could also be allowed to enter the word **default** and the program would set the column width to the default value for the program. The user could alternately enter **best fit** and the program would measure all the entries in the column and choose the most appropriate width for the circumstances. There is a problem with this scenario, however, because the words *default* and *best fit* must be in the user's head rather than in the program somewhere. This is easy to solve, though. All we need to do is provide the same functionality through a combobox. The user can drop down the box and find a few standard widths and the words *default* and *best fit*. Microsoft uses this idea in Word, as shown in Figure 26-11.

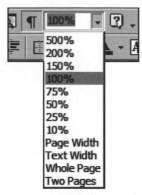

Figure 26–11: The drop-down combobox makes an excellent tool for bounded entry fields because it can accommodate entry values other than numbers. The user doesn't have to remember or type words like Page Width or Whole Page because they are there to be chosen from the drop-down list. The program interprets the words as the appropriate number, and everyone is satisfied.

The user can pull down the combobox, see items like Page Width or Whole Page and choose the appropriate one. With this idiom, the information has migrated from the user's head into the program where it is visible and choosable.

RICH TEXT CONTROLS

With the advent of **rich text controls** it is possible for simple text edit controls to take on the excise overhead of full-blown word processors. It is important for designers to be clear about the scope of options that should be exposed to the user when edit fields are implemented with rich text controls. Activating entire paragraph-formatting subsystems is not appropriate for simple entry fields that are expecting a single word or number as input.

The rich text control isn't very useful as a tool for entering structured data for fitting into rigidly structured databases. It is, however, handy for such tasks as composing e-mail messages or taking notes—in other words, unbounded text entry that will be used verbatim.

INSERT AND OVERTYPE ENTRY MODES

In most text editors there is a user-settable option toggling between insert mode, where text following the insertion point is preserved by sliding it out of the way as new text is added, and overtype mode, where text following the insertion point is lost as the user types over it. These two modes are omnipresent in the world of word processors and, like FORTRAN, never seem to die. Insert and overtype are modes that cause a significant change in the behavior of an interface, with no visible indication until after the user has interacted, and there is no clear way into or out of these modes (at least in Windows) except by means of a rather obscure keystroke.

Today, with modern GUI word processors, it's hard to imagine anyone using overtype mode, but undoubtedly such people are out there. But for edit fields of a single line, adding controls beyond simple insert-mode entry and editing is foolish — the potential for trouble is far greater than the advantages. Of course, if you are designing a word processor, the story is different.

USING TEXT EDIT CONTROLS FOR OUTPUT: A BAD IDEA

The text edit control, with its familiar system font and visually articulated white box, strongly affords data entry. Yet software developers frequently use the text edit control for read-only output fields. The edit control certainly works as an output field, but to use this control for output only is to bait-and-switch your user, and he will not be amused. If you have text data to output, use a text display control and not a text *edit* control. If you want to show the amount of free space on disk, for example, don't use a text edit field, because the user is likely to think that he can get more free space by entering a bigger number. At least, that is what the control is telling him with its equivalent of body language.

If you are going to output editable information, go ahead and output it in a fully editable text control and wire it up internally so that it works exactly as it will appear. If not, stick to display controls, described in the next section.

DESIGN TIP   Use non-editable (display) controls for output-only text.

Display Controls

Display controls are used to display and manage the *visual presentation of information* on the screen. Typical examples include scrollbars and screen splitters. Controls that manage the way objects are displayed visually on the screen fall into this category, as do those that display static, read-only information. These include paginators, rulers, guidelines, grids, group boxes, and those 3D lines called dips and bumps. Rather than discuss all of these at length, we focus on a few of the more problematic controls.

Text controls

Probably the simplest display control is the text control, which displays a written message at some location on the screen. The management job that it performs is pretty prosaic, serving only to label other controls and to output data that cannot or should not be changed by the user.

The only significant problem with text controls is that they are often used where edit controls should be (and vice versa). Most information stored in a computer can be changed by the user. Why not allow the user to change it at the same point the software displays it? Why should the mechanism to input a value be different from the mechanism to output that value? In many cases, it makes no sense for the program to separate these related functions. In almost all cases where the program displays a value that could be changed, it should do so in an editable field so the user can click on it and change it directly. Special edit modes are almost always examples of excise.

For years, Adobe Photoshop insisted on opening a dialog box in order to create formatted text in an image. Thus, the user could not see exactly how the text was going to look in the image, forcing her to repeat the procedure again and again to get things right. Finally Adobe fixed the problem, letting users edit formatted text directly into an image layer, in full WYSIWYG fashion — as it should be.

Those darned scrollbars

Scrollbars are a frustrating control, fraught with difficulties, hard to manipulate and wasteful of pixels. The scrollbar is, without a doubt, both overused and under-examined. In its role as a window content and document navigator — a display control — its application is appropriate. In many cases, though, it is used inappropriately only because designers and programmers don't seem to have any better ideas. That's a poor rationale for any aspect of software design.

The singular advantage of the scrollbar — aside from its near-universal availability — is its proportional rendering of value. The scrollbar's **thumb** is the small, draggable box that indicates the current position, and, often, the scale of the "territory" that can be scrolled.

A scrollbar can be used to grossly represent ratio. For example, the user can see that a scrollbar whose thumb is about equidistant between its endpoints represents a quantity of roughly 50 percent. The fact that the scrollbar conveys no information about its terminal values detracts considerably from its usefulness as a sliding value selector; but nonetheless, the scrollbar's proportional rendering, flawed in implementation though it may be, is an excellent type of visual feedback.

Another shortcoming of the scrollbar is its parsimonious doling out of information to the user. It should instead generously inform us about the information it is managing. The best scrollbars today use thumbs that are proportionally sized to show the percentage of the document that is currently visible. But scrollbars could also tell us:

- ✓ How many pages there are in total

- ✓ The page number (record number, graphic) as we scroll with the thumb

- ✓ The first sentence (or item) of each page as we scroll with the thumb

Additionally, the scrollbar is stingy with functions. It manages the bulk of our navigation within documents; it should give us powerful tools for going where we want to go quickly and easily. It could:

- ✓ Offer us buttons for skipping ahead by pages/chapters/sections/keywords

- ✓ Offer us buttons for jumping to the beginning and end of the document

- ✓ Give us tools for setting bookmarks that we can quickly return to

Recent versions of Microsoft Word make use of scrollbars that exhibit many of these features. The scrollbar also demands a high degree of precision with the mouse. Scrolling down or up in a document is generally much easier than scrolling down *and* up in document. You must position the mouse cursor with great care, taking your attention away from the data you are scrolling. Some scrollbars replicate both their up and down nudge arrows at each end of the scrollbar; for document viewers that will likely stretch across most of the screen, this can be helpful; for smaller windows, such replication of controls is probably overkill and simply adds to screen clutter.

One final annoyance about scrollbars: In maximized windows, the scrollbar is on the far right of the screen, so you'd expect that if you slammed the mouse to the right, clicked, and dragged, something would happen. But the right-most two pixels of the screen are not part of the scrollbar, even though they *look* like they are. This means that you must again exert fine motor control to ensure you haven't overshot to the edge of the screen before you start scrolling. If there's a reason why the active area of the scrollbar can't extend to the edge of the screen, the authors haven't been able to identify it.

Sliders and dials

Although sliders and dials are primarily used as bounded entry controls, they are sometimes used and misused as controls for changing the display of data. The most important thing to remember about sliders is that they are bounded, *non-proportional* controls. For most purposes, scrollbars do a better job of moving data in a display because the scrollbars can easily indicate the magnitude of the scrolling data, which sliders can't do.

Dials are an idiom borrowed directly from mechanical age metaphors of rotating knobs. They are very space efficient, but are extremely difficult to manipulate with a mouse because of the circular motion they imply. They are inadequate as bounded controls, and worse as unbounded controls. Even the best implementations of dials on screen are a chore for users, and this idiom should be avoided when possible.

Thumbwheels

The thumbwheel is a variant of the dial, but one that is much easier to use. On screen thumbwheels look rather like the scroll wheel on a mouse, and behave in much the same way. They are popular with some 3D applications because they are a compact, unbounded control, which is perfect for certain kinds of panning and zooming. Unlike a scrollbar, they need not provide any proportional feedback because the range of the control is infinite. It makes sense to map a control like this to unbounded movement in some direction (like zoom), or movement within data that loops back on itself.

Splitters

Splitters are useful tools for dividing a sovereign application into multiple, related panes in which information can be viewed, manipulated, or transferred. Movable splitters should always advertise their pliancy with cursor hinting. Though it is easy and tempting to make all splitters movable, you should exercise care in choosing which ones to make movable. In general, a splitter shouldn't be able to be moved in such a way that makes the contents of a pane completely unusable. In cases where panes need to collapse, a drawer may be a better idiom.

Drawers and levers

Drawers are panes in a sovereign application that can be opened and closed with a single action. They can be used in conjunction with splitters if the amount that the drawer opens is user configurable. A drawer is usually opened by clicking on a control in the vicinity of the drawer. This control needs to be visible at all times and should either be a latching button/butcon or a lever, which behaves similarly, but typically swivels to indicate an open or closed state. Microsoft Internet Explorer makes use of latching butcons to control its History and other drawers, whereas IE on the Mac uses vertically oriented tabs that extend from the edge of the drawer to accomplish the same thing. The tabs are a bit awkward and end up covering browser real estate, but they do a better job of associating themselves with the drawer than do the butcons in their sister application on Windows.

Drawers are a great place to put controls and functions that are less frequently used, but when they are used, it is in conjunction with the main work area of the application. Drawers have the benefit of not covering up the main work area the way a dialog does. Property details, searchable lists of objects or components, and histories are perfect candidates for putting in drawers.

Although the big-picture principles discussed in Section Two can provide enormous leverage in creating products that will please and satisfy users, it's always important to remember that the devil is in the details. Frustrating controls can lead to a constant low-level annoyance, even if an overall product concept is excellent. Be sure to dot your i's and cross your t's, and ensure that your controls are well-behaved.

Chapter 27

Menus: The Pedagogic Vector

The modern GUI with its drop-down menus and dialog boxes hasn't been around that long — only since 1984 and the Macintosh — as a mainstream design idiom. Still, it is now so ubiquitous that it is easy to take for granted. It is worthwhile to peer backwards and see the path we've taken in the development of the modern dialog and menu interface to best understand menus' strengths and potential pitfalls.

The Command-Line interface

If you wanted to talk to an IBM mainframe computer in the 1970s, you had to manually keypunch a deck of computer cards, use an obscure language called JCL (job control language) to tell the computer how to read your program, and submit this deck of cards to the system through a noisy, mechanical card reader. Each line of JCL or program had to be punched on a separate card. Even the first microcomputers, small, slow, and stupid, running a primitive operating system called CP/M, had a much better conversational style than those hulking dinosaurs in their refrigerated glass houses. You could communicate directly with microcomputers running CP/M merely by typing commands into a standard keyboard. What a miracle! The program issued a prompt on the computer screen that looked like this:

```
A>
```

You could then type in the names of programs, which were stored as files, as commands and CP/M would run them. We called it the **command-line** interface, and it was widely considered a great leap forward in man-machine communications.

The only catch is that you had to know what to type. For frequent users, who at that time were mostly programmers, the command-line prompt was very powerful and effective because it offered the quickest and most efficient route to getting the desired task done. With his hands on the keyboard in the best tradition of touch typists, the user could rip out `"copy a:*.* b:"` and the disk was copied. And today, if you possess the knowledge, the command line is still faster than using a mouse for many operations.

The command-line interface really separated the men (and women) from the nerds. As software got more powerful and complex, however, the memorization demands that the command-line interface made on users were just too great, and it had to give way to something better.

363

Sequential Hierarchical Menus

Finally, sometime in the late-70s, some very clever programmer came up with the idea of offering the user a list of choices. You could read the list and select an item from it the way that you choose a dish at a restaurant by reading the menu. The appellation stuck, and the age of the **sequential hierarchical menu** began.

The sequential hierarchical menu enabled the user to forget many of the commands and option details required by the command-line interface. Instead of keeping the details in his head, he could read them off the screen. Another miracle! Circa 1979, your program was judged heavily on whether or not it was menu-based. Those vendors stuck in the command-line world fell by the wayside in favor of the more modern paradigm.

Although the paradigm was called *menu-based* at the time, we refer to these menus as *sequential* and *hierarchical* to differentiate them from the menus in widespread use today. The old pre-GUI menus were deeply hierarchical: After you made a selection from one menu, it would be replaced by another, then another, drilling down into a tall tree of commands.

Because only one menu at a time could be placed on the screen and because software at that time was still heavily influenced by the batch style of mainframe computing, the hierarchical menu paradigm was sequential in behavior. The user was presented with a high-level menu for choosing between major functions as, for example:

1. Enter transactions

2. Close books for month

3. Print income statement

4. Print balance sheet

5. Exit

After the user chose a function, say 1. Enter transactions, he would then be prompted with another menu, subordinate to his choice from the first one, such as:

1. Enter invoices

2. Enter payments

3. Enter invoice corrections

4. Enter payment corrections

5. Exit

The user would choose from this list and, most likely, be confronted with a couple more such menus before the actual work would begin. Then, the Exit option would take him up only one level in the hierarchy. This meant that navigating through the menu tree was a real chore.

Once the user made his selection, it was set in concrete—there was no going back. People, of course, made mistakes all the time, and the more progressive developers of the day added confirmation menus. The program would accept the user's choice as before, then issue another menu to enquire: Press the Escape Key to Change Your Selection, Otherwise Press Enter to Proceed. This was an incredible pain, because regardless of whether you had made a mistake or not, you needed to answer this awkward and confusing meta-question, which could lead you to make exactly the kind of mistake you were hoping to avoid.

Such menu-based interfaces would be judged terrible by today's standards. Their chief failing was the necessary depth of the hierarchy. This was coupled with a striking lack of flexibility and clarity in dealing with their users. Still, they were better than command lines, where you had to remember each operand. Sequential hierarchical menus lightened the users' memorization burden, but forced them to laboriously navigate an archipelago of confusing choices and options (just like most Web sites do today). They, too, had to give way to something better.

The Lotus 1-2-3 Interface

The next great advance in user-interface technology came in 1979 from Lotus Corporation with the original 1-2-3 spreadsheet program. 1-2-3 was still controlled by a deeply hierarchical menu interface, but Lotus added its own twist to help make it the most successful piece of software ever sold up to that point, the visible hierarchical menu.

In 1979, a computer screen offered exactly 2000 characters per screen (see Figure 27-1), arranged in 25 horizontal rows of 80 characters each. 1-2-3 presented its menu horizontally along the top of the screen, where it consumed only two rows out of the 25 available. This meant that the menu could coexist on the screen with the actual spreadsheet program. Unlike the hierarchical menu programs that came before it, the user didn't have to leave a productive screen to see a menu. He could enter a menu command right where he was working in the program. This idea has been reinvented on the Web in the form of breadcrumbs, a row of links that both show the path a user has taken in the hierarchy of Web pages on a site and allows a user to navigate immediately to any level back up the chain.

Figure 27-1: The original Lotus 1-2-3, which first shipped in 1979, exhibited a remarkable new menu structure that actually coexisted with the working screen of the program. All other menu-based programs at that time forced you to leave the working screen to make menu selections. Like all great ideas, this one was invisible in foresight and obvious in hindsight.

Lotus used its new menu idiom with great abandon, creating a hierarchical menu structure of remarkable proportions. There were dozens of nodes in the menu tree, and several hundred individual choices available. Each one could be found by looking at the top line of the screen and tabbing over and down to the desired selection. The program differentiated between data for the spreadsheet and a command for the menu by detecting the presence of a backslash character (\). If the user typed a slash, the keystrokes that followed were interpreted as menu commands rather than data. To select an item on the menu, all you had to do was read it and type in its first letter preceded by a slash. Submenus then replaced the main menu on the top line.

Frequent users quickly realized that the patterns were memorable, and they didn't necessarily have to read the menu. They could just type / - s to save their work to disk. They could just type / - c - g - x to add up a column of numbers. They could, in essence, bypass the use of the menu entirely. They became power-users, memorizing the letter commands and gloating over their knowledge of obscure functions.

It seems silly now, but it illustrates a very powerful point: A good user interface enables its users to move in an ad hoc, piecemeal fashion from beginner to expert. A given power-user of 1-2-3 might be on intimate terms with a couple of dozen functions, while simultaneously being completely ignorant of several dozen others. If he has memorized a particular slash-key sequence, he can go ahead and access it immediately. Otherwise, he can read the menu to find those less-frequently used ones that he hasn't committed to memory. The importance of menus as a means of discovering and learning the functions of an interface is discussed at length later in this chapter.

But 1-2-3's hierarchical menu was hideously complex. There were simply too many commands, and every one of them had to fit into the single hierarchical menu structure. The program's designers bent over backwards to make logical connections between functions in an attempt to justify the way they had apportioned the commands in the hierarchy. In the delirium of revolutionary success and market dominance, such details were easily ignored.

As you might imagine, because of 1-2-3's success, the mid-80s were a time of widespread 1-2-3 cloning. The always-visible, hierarchical menu found its way into numerous programs, but the idiom was really the last gasp of the character-based user interface in the same way that the great, articulated steam locomotives of the late 1940s were the final, finest expression of a doomed technology. As surely as diesel locomotives completely eliminated all steam power within the span of a decade, the GUI eliminated the 1-2-3-style hierarchical menu within a few short years.

Drop-Down and Pop-Up Menus

Many concepts and technologies had to come together to make the GUI possible: the mouse, memory-mapped video, powerful processors, and pop-up windows. A pop-up window is a rectangle on the screen that appears, overlapping and obscuring the main part of the screen, until it has completed its work, whereupon it disappears, leaving the original screen behind, untouched. The pop-up window is the mechanism used to implement **drop-down menus** (also called pull-down menus) and dialog boxes.

In modern GUIs, menus are visible across the top row of a screen or window in a **menu bar**. The user points and clicks on a menu title on a menu bar and its immediately subordinate list of options appears in a small window just below it. A variant of the drop-down menu is a menu that "pops up" when you click (or more frequently, right-click) on an object, even though it has no menu title: a **pop-up** menu.

After the menu is open, the user makes a single choice by clicking once or by dragging and releasing. There's nothing remarkable about that, except that the menus generally go no deeper than this. The selection the user makes on the menu either takes immediate effect or calls up a dialog box. The hierarchy of menus has been flattened down until it is only one level deep. In other words, it has finally become a **monocline grouping** (discussed in Chapter 11).

Arguably the most significant advance of the GUI menu was this retreat from the hierarchical form into monocline grouping. The dialog box, another use of the pop-up window, was the tool that simplified the menu. The dialog box enabled the software designer to encapsulate all the sub-choices of any menu item within a single, interactive container. With dialogs, menu hierarchies could flatten out considerably, gathering all the niggling details further down the menu tree into a single dialog window. The deeply hierarchical menu was a thing of the past.

With the higher resolution of GUI displays, enough choices could be displayed on the menu bar to organize all the program's functions into about a half-dozen meaningful groups, each group represented by a one-word menu title. The menu for each group was also roomy enough to include all its related functions. The need to go to additional levels of menus was made almost superfluous.

(Of course, Philistines and reprobates are always with us, and they have created methods for turning pull-down menus back into hierarchical menus. They are called **cascading menus**, and although they are occasionally useful, more often they merely tempt the weaker souls in the development community to gum up their menus for little gain. We discuss this in more detail in Chapter 28.)

Menus Today: The Pedagogic Vector

As the modern GUI evolved, two idioms developed that fundamentally changed the role of the menu in the user interface. These two idioms are direct manipulation and toolbars. The development of direct-manipulation idioms has been a slow and steady progression from the first days of graphical user interfaces. Conversely, the toolbar was an innovation that swept the industry around 1989. Within a couple of years, virtually every Windows program sold had a toolbar filled with butcons. Only a few years before, nobody had seen a toolbar.

In the same way that a stranger to town may take a roundabout route to her destination while a native will always proceed on the most economical path, experienced users of a program will commonly invoke a function with the most immediate command rather than one that requires intermediate steps. Naturally, the most frequently used commands in a program are those that migrate onto butcons on the toolbar. These functions are still supported by items on the menu, where their use becomes increasingly the purview of beginners, while experienced users gravitate toward the immediate vectors of butcons and direct manipulation.

This bifurcation of usage along lines of experience is an important characteristic of software usage, and it affects how menus and dialog boxes are used. They are needed less and less for daily use, and instead become a teaching tool for first time and infrequent users.

The butcons and other controls on the toolbar are usually redundant with respect to commands on the menu. Butcons are immediate, whereas menu commands remain relatively slow and clunky. Menu commands have a great advantage, however, in their English descriptions of the functions, and the detailed controls and data that appear on corresponding dialog boxes. This detailed data makes menus and dialogs the most useful interaction techniques for the purpose of teaching users about the capabilities of the product: **pedagogic vectors** (for more about other types of command vectors, see Chapter 18).

One required element of effective pedagogy is the ability to examine and experiment without fear of commitment. The Cancel button on each dialog box supports this function well. Contrary to the user interface paradigms of 10 years ago, menus and dialog boxes have ceased to be the main method by which normal users perform everyday functions. Many programmers and designers haven't yet realized this fact, and they continue to confuse the purpose of the menu command vector. Its role is to teach new users, to remind those who have forgotten, and to provide a way to discover (and rediscover) infrequently-used functions.

AXIOM

Provide a pedagogic vector with menus and dialogs.

When a user looks at a program for the first time, it is often difficult to size up what that program can do. An excellent way to get an impression of the power and purpose of an application is to glance at the set of available functions by way of its menus and dialogs. We do this in the same way we look at a restaurant's menu posted at its entrance to get an idea of the type of food, the presentation, the setting, and the price.

Understanding the scope of what a program can and can't do is one of the fundamental aspects of creating an atmosphere conducive to learning. Many otherwise easy-to-use programs put the user off because there is no simple, unthreatening way for him to find out just what the program is capable of doing.

The toolbar and direct-manipulation idioms can be too inscrutable for the first time user to understand, but the textual nature of the menus serves to explain the functions. Reading Format Gallery (see Figure 27-2) is more enlightening to the new user than trying to interpret a butcon that looks like this (although ToolTips obviously help):

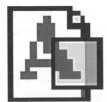

Figure 27-2: A menu item reading Format Gallery is likely to be more enlightening to new users than a butcon like this one. But after they become intermediates, it's a different story altogether.

For infrequent users who are somewhat familiar with the program, the drop-down menu/dialog vector's main task is as an index to tools: a place to look when he knows there is a function but can't remember where it is or what it's called. This works the same way as its namesake, the restaurant menu, which permits him to rediscover that delightful fish curry thing he ordered a year ago, without having to remember its precise name. The drop-down menu lets him rediscover functions whose names he's forgotten. He doesn't have to keep such trivia in his head, but can depend on the menu to keep it for him, available when he needs it.

If the main purpose of menus were to execute commands, terseness would be a virtue. But because the main justification of their existence is to teach us about what is available, how to get it, and what shortcuts are available, terseness is really the exact opposite of what we need. Our menus have to explain what a given function does, not just where to invoke it. Because of this it behooves us to be more verbose in our menu item text. We shouldn't say "Open. . .," but rather "Open the Report. . . ." We shouldn't say "Auto-arrange" but rather "Auto-arrange icons." We should stay far away from jargon, as our menu's users won't yet be acquainted with it.

Many programs also use the status bar that goes across the bottom of their main window to display an even longer line of explanatory text associated with the currently selected menu item. This idiom can enhance the teaching value of the command vector — if the user knows to look for it. The location ensures that such information will often go unnoticed.

The pedagogic vector also means that menus must be complete, offering a full selection of the actions and facilities available in the program. Every dialog box in the program should be accessible from a menu item. A scan of the menus should make clear the scope of the program and the depth and breadth of its various facilities.

Another teaching purpose is served by providing hints pointing to other command vectors in the menu itself. Putting hints in that describe keyboard equivalents teaches users about quicker command methods that are available (Figure 28-1 in the next chapter demonstrates good use of hints for keyboard equivalents). By putting this information right in the menu, the user registers it subconsciously. It won't intrude upon his conscious thoughts until he is ready to learn it, and then he will find it readily available and already familiar.

Chapter 28

Using Menus

Menus are perhaps the oldest idioms in the GUI universe — revered and surrounded by superstition and lore. We accept without question that traditional menu design is correct because so many existing programs attest to its excellence. But this belief is like snapping your fingers to keep the tigers away. There aren't any tigers here, you say? See, it works! That said, menus as currently structured aren't going away any time soon. This chapter discusses both problems with menus and how to use them appropriately.

Standard Menus

Most every GUI these days has at least a File and an Edit menu in its two leftmost positions and a Help menu to the right. The Windows, Macintosh, and even the Motif style guides state that these File, Edit and Help menus are standard. You might also think that this de facto cross-platform standard is a strong indication of the proven correctness of the idiom. Wrong! It is a strong indication of the development community's willingness to blithely accept mediocre design, changing it only when the competition forces us to do better. The File menu's name is the result of implementation model thinking about how our operating systems work. The Edit menu is based on a very weak clipboard. And the Help menu is frequently the least helpful source of insight and information for the befuddled user.

These menu conventions can trap us into designing weak user interfaces. The menus on most of our programs may be familiar, but are they good ways to organize functions? Selections like View, Insert, Format, Tools, and Options sound like tools and functions, not goals. Why not organize the facilities in a more goal-directed way?

Can't you hear the programmers shouting, "How can you change something that has become a standard? People *expect* the File menu!" The reply is a simple one: People may get used to pain and suffering, but that is no reason to perpetuate them. Users will adapt without significant problems if we change the File menu so that it delivers a *better, more meaningful* model. Arbitrarily changing the menu items without considering user goals would indeed be the big mistake these programmers worry about.

The key to figuring out a reasonable menu structure goes back to understanding your users' mental models. How do they think about what they are doing? What terms make the most sense to them? If your users are computer-savvy, and you're designing a productivity application, it might make sense to stick to recognizable standards, at least at the top level. If, however, you're designing an application for children or for a specialized niche, the structure might very well need to be different.

All that said, there is obviously still a place for the standard menu structures. The rest of this chapter provides some practical advice for those instances where you need to design "inside the box" of standard menus.

The File menu

In Chapter 13 we described a better File menu. Although we removed the save command from the menu, we shouldn't dispense with the function entirely. The program should save automatically, but allow users to save on demand as well. The Save function doesn't necessarily have to overwrite the original copy on disk the way it usually does now. It just needs to save the data in an easily recoverable way that is independent of and invisible from within the application.

If we change from a file-centric view to this document-centric view, we should also change the name of the menu from File to Document.

The Most Recently Used (MRU) list on Microsoft applications is an excellent shortcut idea. You can see it in Figure 28-1.

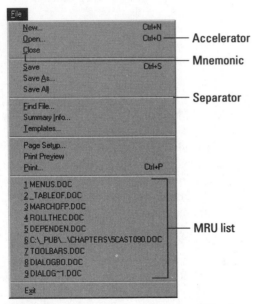

Figure 28-1: The File menu from Microsoft Word shows off the excellent Most Recently Used (MRU) list. In Chapter 13, you saw how to reconstruct the first six items so that they better reflect the user's mental model, rather than following the technically faithful implementation model as shown here.

The Edit menu

The Edit menu contains facilities for cutting and pasting and importing and exporting. Don't use it as a catch-all for functions that don't seem to fit anywhere else. Instead, gather them up into an Options or Preferences dialog that is accessible from the Tools menu.

The Windows menu

The Windows menu is for arranging, viewing, and switching between multiple windows opened by the program. It can also offer tools for laying out multiple documents on-screen simultaneously. Nothing else should go on this menu.

The Help menu

Today's Help menus are poorly designed reflections of poor help systems. We'll talk about help in general in Chapter 35, but it should be mentioned here that the Help menu sorely needs an item labeled Shortcuts that would explain how to go beyond relying on the menus. It could offer pointers on more powerful idioms such as accelerators, toolbar buttons, and direct manipulation idioms.

Optional Menus

The following menus are commonly used, but considered optional in most style guides. An application of moderate complexity is likely to make use of at least some of these menus.

The View menu

The View menu should contain all options that influence the way the user looks at the program's data. Additionally, any optional visual items like rulers, templates, or palettes should be controlled here.

The Insert menu

The Insert menu is really an extension of the Edit menu. If you only have one or two Insert items, consider putting them on the Edit menu instead and omitting the Insert menu entirely.

The Settings menu

If you have a Settings menu in your application, you are making a commitment to the user that anytime he wants to alter a setting in the program he will find the way to do it here. Don't offer up a settings menu and then scatter other setting items or dialogs on other menus. This includes printer settings, which are often erroneously found on the File menu.

The Format menu

The Format menu is one of the weakest of the optional menus because it deals almost exclusively with properties of visual objects and not functions. In a more object-oriented world, properties of visual objects are controlled by more visual direct-manipulation idioms, not by functions. The menu serves its pedagogic purpose, but you might consider omitting it entirely if you've implemented a more object-oriented format property scheme.

The page setup commands that typically reside on the File menu should be placed here. (Notice that page setup is very different from printer setup.)

The Tools menu

The Tools menu, sometimes less-clearly called the Options menu, is where big, powerful functions go. Functions like spell-checkers and goal-finders are considered tools. Also, the Tool menu is where the hard-hat items should go.

Hard-hat items are the functions that should only be used by real power users. These include various advanced settings. For example, a client/server database program has easy-to-use, direct-manipulation idioms for building a query, while behind the scenes the program is composing the appropriate SQL statement to create the report. Giving power users a way to edit the SQL statement directly is most definitely a hard-hat function! Functions like these can be dangerous or dislocating, so they must be visually set off from the more benign tools available. In the past, the authors have segregated them from the other menu items and highlighted them with icons to indicate that they are for experts only. Another possible approach is to place them in an Expert menu, to the right of the more benign Tools menu.

Problematic Menu Idioms

Over the years, programmers have seen fit to embellish simple menus with new behavioral idioms. Some of these have their (limited) uses, and others simply get in the way. This section discusses these menu idioms and their appropriate uses.

Cascading Menus

A variant of drop-down menus permits a secondary menu to appear alongside another active drop-down menu. This technique, called cascading menus, presents some serious issues for ease of use. At the same time, the temptation to make menus cascade is nearly unavoidable for most programmers, who seemingly have a fond attachment to them.

Where drop-down menus provide clear, easy-to-navigate monocline grouping, cascading menus move us into the nasty territory of nesting and hierarchies. Multiple levels of cascading menus not only make it much more difficult for users to remember where items are located, but they also require precision mouse movements to navigate them smoothly.

In the previous chapter, we talked about how the modern GUI allowed us to leave hierarchical menus behind. It seems tragic that programmers would want to revive an idiom that lies happily in its grave. Cascading menus do serve a purpose: They allow more functions to be crammed onto a single, top-level menu than would otherwise be legible on the screen. There are occasionally enough items on a menu to justify putting some of the more obscure ones onto a second level, but this should be an idiom of last resort (Figure 28-2 shows a properly-formed cascading menu with a single level). Cascading menus should never be employed for frequently used functions.

In Windows, it is difficult to say categorically that an idiom should not be used because the range of possible application software is so huge. Cascading menus, however, are a weak idiom, one that can be used as needed, but that should not be chosen before first considering other ways to solve the problem.

Windows makes extensive use of cascading menus in the Taskbar. The Start button is so overloaded with hierarchical menus that it can be jerky and unresponsive, even for adept mousers. It seems that Microsoft went to an incredible extreme just to make double-clicks unnecessary.

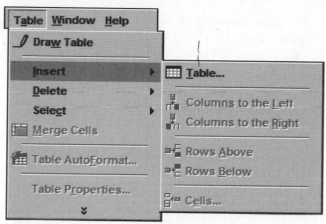

Figure 28-2: This is a cascading menu in Microsoft Word. Hierarchies make logical sense to the programmers, but rarely to users. Cascades also demand considerable skill with a mouse, which will frustrate infrequent users. Microsoft and most major software vendors keep to the standard of no more than one level of cascading menu. One other mitigating factor in this example: The cascaded items are also available from buttons, so there is an immediate alternative provided to cascading-menu access. This figure also shows examples of menu items in their disabled state.

Expanding Menus

A new menu idiom arrived with Windows 2000 and is still in use in Windows XP: the expanding menu. This menu idiom is used ubiquitously throughout Microsoft's latest Office software, and although it's well-intended, it severely cripples the underlying pedagogic role of drop-down menus. With expanding menus, Microsoft designers tried to anticipate what the frequently used items on each menu would be and to initially display only those items to users. To see the rest of the menu items, users are forced to click (or hover the mouse) on an icon at the bottom of the menu. The previously hidden items may be interspersed with the items originally shown. Because the ordering of the menu changes significantly, in Windows 2000, Microsoft differentiates between normally displayed items and normally hidden items by visually indenting the normally hidden items. This is a terribly confusing visual idiom! It conflicts with the pliant response of buttons and adds confusing visual noise to menus; fortunately, this has been changed in Windows XP (see Figure 28-3). Nonetheless, the idiom is a massive train wreck—like cascading menus, only worse—its only slight saving grace is that if you actually choose one of the hidden items, it will then be available on the list of normally displayed items the next time you look.

Microsoft was clearly trying to make its menu items more usable, but in doing so it has struck a terrible blow to the fundamental reason menus exist, to teach users what functions are available. Microsoft should realize that toolbars, not menus, are the place to send users for frequently used items. Luckily, the user can turn off this feature, but unfortunately it is on by default.

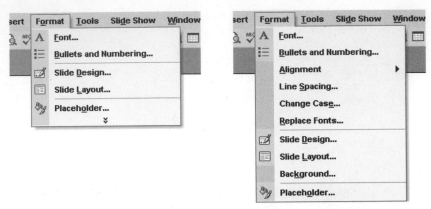

Figure 28-3: An expanding menu from PowerPoint in Windows XP, before and after expansion. Expanding menus get just about everything wrong, interaction-wise; they are even more annoying than cascading menus. They hide information in menus, subverting the pedagogic vector; they change the ordering of menu items, disrupting motor memory of menu item location. In the expanded menu, the slightly darker shade of gray on the left indicates, rather subtly, those items that are not on the contracted version of the menu. Luckily, expanding menus can be turned off completely.

Bang Menus

In the early days of the Mac and Windows, some programs were shipped with a menu variant that has, for good reason, fallen out of favor: the **immediate** menu or **bang menu**. In programmer's jargon, an exclamation mark is a **bang**, and, by convention, top-level immediate menu items were always followed with a bang. Just as its name implies, it is a menu title — directly on the menu bar next to other menu titles — that instead, behaves like a menu *item* in a drop-down. Rather than displaying a drop-down menu for a subsequent selection, the bang menu causes a function to execute right away! For example, a bang menu title for compiling source code would be called Compile!

Its behavior is so unexpected that it generates instant anger. The bang menu title has virtually no instructional value. It is dislocating and disconcerting. The same immediacy on a toolbar butcon bothers nobody, though. The difference is that butcons on a toolbar advertise their immediacy because they are *buttons*, and toolbars are where immediate commands should stay.

Menu Item Conventions and Variants

This section describes some of the conventions used in displaying and structuring items within menus and when they are best used.

Disabling menu items

A common menu standard is to disable (make non-functional) menu items when they are not relevant to the selected data object or item. (The disabled status is indicated by graying out the item on the menu). Menus have facilities that make it easy to disable them when their corresponding function is not valid, and you should take every advantage of this. The user is well served by the knowledge that the enabling and disabling of menu items reflects their appropriate use. This function helps the menu become an even better teaching tool.

DESIGN TIP

Disable menu items when they are inapplicable.

It is important that each menu item clearly show when it is or isn't applicable to fulfill its role as a teacher. Don't omit this detail.

Checkmark menu items

Checkmarks next to menu items, an idiom quickly grasped by users, is probably best used in programs with fairly simple menu structures. They are usually used for indicating and toggling attributes of the program's interface (such as turning toolbars on and off) or attributes related to the display of data objects (such as wire frame versus fully rendered images). The latter attributes could very easily be summed up on a dialog box that would allow a grouping of more powerful tools, while simultaneously freeing up valuable space on the menu itself. If the program is a complex application, the menu space will be sorely needed. If the attributes are frequently toggled, they should also be accessible from a toolbar.

Flip-flop menu items

You might consider the following trick for saving menu space. You have a function with two states. One is called, for example, Display Status Bar and the other is called Hide Status Bar. You could create a single flip-flop menu item that alternates between the two states, always showing the one currently *not* chosen.

This technique *does* save space, because otherwise it might require two menu items with mutually exclusive checkmarks. But, since instructional clarity is the goal for menus, anything that obscures understanding is undesirable. Flip-flop menus are very confusing for one simple reason: You can't tell if it is offering a choice or describing a state. If it says Display Toolbar, does that mean tools are now being displayed or does it mean that by selecting the option you can begin displaying them? By making use of a single checkmark menu item instead (Status Bar is either checked or unchecked), you can make the meaning unambiguous.

Icons on menus

Visual symbols next to text items help the user to differentiate between them without having to read, so their function is understood faster. Because of this, adding small graphics to menu items can really speed users up. They also provide a helpful visual connection to other controls that do the same task. In particular, a menu item should show the same icon as the corresponding toolbar butcon.

Use parallel visual symbols on parallel command vectors.

Windows provides powerful tools for putting graphics in menus. Too few programs take full advantage of this opportunity for providing an easy, visual learning trick. For example, the applications in Microsoft's Office suite all use an icon depicting a blank sheet of paper to indicate the New Document function on its toolbar. Microsoft puts that same icon in the File menu to the left of the New → Blank Document cascade menu item. The user soon makes the connection, probably without even thinking about it.

Microsoft Office applications have done an excellent job incorporating teaching graphics into their menus, as shown in Figure 28-4.

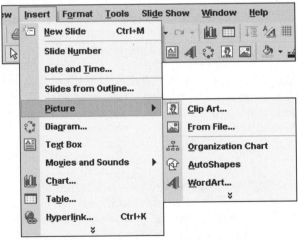

Figure 28-4: Microsoft PowerPoint offers us a regular smorgasbord of menu idioms. The Insert menu shows us separators, cascading menus, mnemonics, accelerators, and menu icons. As you can see, the icons are the same as those on butcons that perform the identical tasks. What a wonderful way to build learning into the interface without seeming pedantic or intrusive!

Accelerators

Accelerators provide an additional, optional way to invoke a function from the keyboard. Accelerators are the keystrokes, which usually are a function key (like F9) or activated with a Ctrl, Alt or Shift prefix, that are shown to the right of drop-down menu items. They are a defined standard on Windows and other platforms, but their implementation is up to the individual designer, and they are often forgotten.

There are three tips for successfully creating good accelerators:

1. Follow standards.

2. Provide for their daily use.

3. Show how to access them.

Where standard accelerators exist, use them. In particular, this refers to the standard editing set as shown on the Edit menu. Users quickly learn how much easier it is to type Ctrl+C and Ctrl+V than it is to remove their mouse hands from the home row to pull down the Edit menu, select Copy, then pull it down again and select Paste. Don't disappoint them when they use your program. Don't forget standards like Ctrl+P for print and Ctrl+S for save.

Identifying the set of commands that will comprise those needed for daily use is the tricky part. You must select the functions likely to be used frequently and assure that those menu items are given accelerators. The good news is that this set won't be large. The bad news is that it can vary significantly from user to user.

The best approach is to perform a triage operation on the available functions. Divide them into three groups: Those that are definitely part of everyone's daily use; those that are definitely not part of anyone's daily use; and everything else. The first group must have accelerators and the second group must not. The final group will be the toughest to configure, and it will inevitably be the largest. You can perform a subsequent triage on this group and assign the best accelerators, like F2, F3, F4 and so on to the winners in this group. More obscure accelerators, like Alt+7 should go to those least likely to be part of someone's everyday commands.

Don't forget to show the accelerator in the menu. An accelerator isn't going to do anyone any good if they have to go to the manual or online help to find it. Put it to the right of the corresponding menu item, where it belongs. Users won't notice it at first, but eventually they will find it, and they will be happy to make the discovery as perpetual intermediates (see Chapter 3). It will give them a sense of accomplishment and a feeling of being an insider. These are both feelings well worth encouraging in your customers.

Some programs offer user-configurable accelerators, and there are many instances where this is a good idea, and even a necessity, especially for expert users. Allowing users to customize accelerators on the sovereign applications that they use most of the time really lets them adapt the software to their own style of working. Be sure to include a Return to Defaults control along with any customization tools.

Mnemonics

Mnemonics are another Windows standard (also seen in some Unix GUIs) for adding keystroke commands in parallel to the direct manipulation of menus and dialogs.

The Microsoft style guide covers both mnemonics (which Microsoft now calls access keys) and accelerators in detail, so we will simply stress that they should not be overlooked. Mnemonics are accessed using the ALT key, arrow keys, and the underlined letter in a menu item or title. Pressing the ALT key places the application into mnemonic mode, and the arrow keys can be used to navigate to the appropriate menu. After it opens, pressing the appropriate letter key executes the function. The main purpose of mnemonics is to provide a keyboard equivalent of each menu command. For this reason, mnemonics should be complete, particularly for text-oriented programs. Don't think of them as a convenience so much as a pipeline to the keyboard. Keep in mind that your most experienced users will rely heavily on their keyboards; so to keep them loyal, assure that the mnemonics are consistent and thoroughly thought-out. Mnemonics are not optional.

For those designers among you who don't use mnemonics themselves (the authors do not), it is easy to put in bad mnemonics; to have non-unique characters within a menu, or to use inappropriate and difficult-to-remember characters (thus creating, by definition, non-mnemonic mnemonics). Make sure that someone on the development or design team tests and refines the mnemonics.

The Windows System Menu

The **system menu** is a Windows standard menu available in the upper-left corner of all independent windows, which replicates window frame controls. In Windows 3.*x*, there was a little box with a horizontal bar in it that launched this menu. In Windows 95 and later, this was replaced by the program's icon. Some Unix GUI platforms, like Motif, have a similar menu, in a similar location.

This menu is a relic. It serves no useful purpose. Originally, it was to be the home of system-level window management commands, but they have migrated to immediate controls on the title bar and window frame, and no new ones have been added.

The very existence of the window menu contributes to the level of ambient confusion; it's just another lever on the mechanism with no evident purpose except to generate worry in the user's mind. The sole remaining purpose for the system menu is as a programming support for equivalent keyboard commands for moving, resizing, maximizing, and minimizing the window. It would be no loss to the interface if the system menu were eliminated, as long as the keyboard commands were retained. Somehow it has been retained, even in Windows XP.

Chapter 29

Using Toolbars and ToolTips

Toolbars are one of the more recent GUI developments, relatively speaking. Although not an exclusive feature of Windows, they were first popularized there, unlike so many other GUI idioms popularized on the Mac. The toolbar has great strengths and weaknesses, but these are complementary to those of its partner, the menu. Whereas menus are complete toolsets with the main purpose of teaching, toolbars are for frequently used commands and offer little help to the new user.

Toolbars: Visible, Immediate Functionality

The typical toolbar is a collection of buttons, usually without text labels, in a horizontal slab positioned directly below the menu bar or in a vertical slab attached to the side of the main window. Essentially, a toolbar is a single row (or column) of immediate, graphical, always-visible menu items.

Great ideas in user interface design often seem to spring from many sources simultaneously. The toolbar is no exception. It appeared on many programs at about the same time, and nobody can say who invented it first. What is clear is that its advantages were immediately apparent to all. In a stroke, the invention of the toolbar solved the problems of the pull-down menu. Toolbar functions are always plainly visible, and the user can trigger them with a single mouse click.

Toolbars are not menus

Toolbars are often thought of as just a speedy version of the menu. The similarities are hard to avoid: They offer access to the program's functions, and they usually form a horizontal row across the top of the screen. Designers imagine that toolbars, beyond being a command vector in parallel to menus, are an *identical* command vector to menus. They think that the functions available on toolbars are supposed to be the same as those available on menus.

But the purpose of toolbars is actually quite different from the purpose of menus, and their composition shouldn't necessarily be the same. The purpose of toolbars and their controls is to provide fast access to functions used frequently by those who have already mastered the program's basics. Toolbars offer nothing to beginners and are not designed with that purpose in mind. The menu is where the beginner must turn for help.

DESIGN TIP

Toolbars provide experienced users fast access to frequently used functions.

The great strength of menus is their completeness and verbosity. Everything the user needs can be found somewhere on the program's menus. Of course, this very richness means that they get big and cumbersome. To keep these big menus from consuming too many pixels, they have to be folded away most of the time and only popped-up on request. The act of popping up excludes menus from the ranks of visible and immediate commands. The tradeoff with menus is thoroughness and power in exchange for a small but uniform dose of clunkiness applied at every step. The butcons on toolbars, on the other hand, are incomplete and inscrutable; but they are undeniably visible, immediate, and very space-efficient compared to menus.

Toolbars freed menus to teach

As we discussed in the previous chapters, it was the toolbar's invention that finally permitted menus to focus on their pedagogical purpose. After frequently used functions were put into toolbar butcons, drop-down menus ceased to be the primary function-launching idiom. For users with even slight experience, it was much faster and easier to click on a butcon than to drop down a menu and select an item—a task requiring significantly more dexterity and time. After toolbars became widespread, the menu fell into the background as a supporting character. The only programs where menus are still employed for daily-use functions are programs with poorly designed or non-existent toolbars.

Toolbars and Toolbar Controls

The toolbar gave birth to the butcon, a happy marriage between a button and an icon. As a visual mnemonic of a function, butcons are excellent. They can be hard for newcomers to interpret, but then, they're not *for* newcomers.

Icons versus text on toolbars

If the butcons on a toolbar act the same as the items on a drop-down menu, why are the menu items almost always shown with text and the toolbar buttons almost always shown with little images? There are good reasons for the difference, although we almost certainly stumbled on them accidentally.

Text labels, like those on menus, can be very precise and clear—they aren't always, but precision and clarity is their basic purpose. To achieve this, they demand that the user take the time to focus on them and read them. As we discussed in Chapter 19, reading is slower and more difficult than recognizing images. In their pedagogic role, menus must offer precision and clarity—a teacher who isn't precise and clear is a bad teacher. Taking the extra time and effort is a reasonable tradeoff in order to teach.

On the other hand, pictorial symbols are easy for humans to recognize, but they often lack the precision and clarity of text. Pictographs can be ambiguous until you actually learn their meaning. However, after you've learned their meaning, you don't easily forget it; and your recognition remains lightning fast, whereas you still have to read the text every time. In their role of providing quick access to frequently used tools, icons must elicit quick recognition from experienced users. This is their highest priority. The pictorial imagery of symbols suits that role better than text does.

Butcons have the immediacy and visibility of buttons, along with the fast-recognition capability of images. They pack a lot of power into a very small space. As usual, their great strength is also their great weakness: the icon.

Relying on pictographs to communicate is reasonable as long as the parties have agreed in advance what the icon means. They must do this because the meaning of an icon of any kind is by nature ambiguous until it is learned. Many designers think that they must invent visual metaphors for butcons that adequately convey meaning to first-time users. This is a quixotic quest that not only reflects a misunderstanding of the purpose of toolbars, but also reflects the futile hope for magical powers in metaphors, which we discussed in Chapter 20.

The image on the button *doesn't* need to teach the user its purpose; it merely needs to have a bold and unique visual identity. The user will have already learned its purpose through other means. This is not to say that the designer shouldn't strive to achieve both ends, but don't fool yourself: It can't be done very often. It's a lot easier to find images that represent *things* than it is to find images that represent actions or relationships. A picture of a trash can, printer, or chart is pretty easy to interpret, but what icon do you draw to represent Apply Style or Cancel or Connect or Merge or Convert or Measurement or Adjust? Then again, perhaps the user will find himself wondering what a picture of a printer means. It could mean find a printer, change the printer's settings, or report on the status of the printer. Of course, after he learns that the little printer means "Print one copy of the current document on the active printer now," he won't have trouble with it again.

The problem with labeling butcons

It might seem like a good idea to label butcons with both text and images. There is not only logic to this argument, but precedent, too. The original icons on the Macintosh desktop had text subtitles. Even today, some Web browsers do this by default. Icons are useful for allowing quick classification, but beyond that, we need text to tell us *exactly* what the object is for.

The problem is that using both text and images is very expensive in terms of pixels. Besides, toolbar functions can be dangerous or dislocating, and offering too-easy access to them can be like leaving a loaded pistol on the coffee table. The toolbar is for users who know what they are doing. The menu is for the rest.

Some user interface designers have gone ahead and added labels to butcons, either across them or just below them, and left the images in place. Except in rare circumstances, screen space is far too valuable to waste this way. These designers are trying to satisfy two groups of users with two different goals: One wants to learn in a gentle, forgiving environment. The other knows where the sharp edges are but sometimes needs a brief reminder. Certainly, there must be a way to bridge the gap between these two classes of users. Next, we'll discuss some methods that don't dedicate lots of precious screen real estate to solving the problem.

Explaining Toolbar Controls

The biggest problem with toolbars is that although their controls are fast and quickly memorable, they are not initially decipherable. How is the new user supposed to learn what butcons and other toolbar controls do?

Balloon help: A first attempt

Apple was the first to attempt a solution by inventing a facility for the Macintosh called **balloon help**. Balloon help is one of those frustrating ideas that everyone can clearly see is good, yet nobody actually wants to use. Balloon help is a **flyover** facility (sometimes called **rollover** or **mouseover**). This means that it appears as the mouse cursor passes over something without the user pressing a mouse button, similar to active visual hinting.

When balloon help is active, little speech bubbles like those in comic strips appear next to the object that the mouse points to. Inside the speech bubble is a brief sentence or two explaining that object's function.

Balloon help doesn't work for a good reason. It is founded on the misconception that it is acceptable to discomfit daily users for the benefit of first-timers. The balloons were too big, too obtrusive, and too condescending. They were very much in the way. Most users find them so annoyingly in-your-face that they keep them turned off. Then, when they have forgotten what some object is, they have to go up to the menu, pull it down, turn balloon help on, point to the unknown object, read the balloon, go back to the menu, and turn balloon help off. Whew, what a pain!

ToolTips

Microsoft is never one to make things easy for the beginner at the expense of the more frequent user. It has invented a true variant of balloon help called ToolTips that is one of the cleverest and most-effective user interface idioms we've ever seen.

At first, ToolTips seem the same as balloon help, but on closer inspection you can see the minor physical and behavioral differences that have a huge effect from the user's point-of-view. Unlike balloon help, ToolTips only explain the purpose of controls on the toolbar (and identify items in the Taskbar and application status bars). They don't try to explain other stuff on the screen like scroll bars, menus, and desktop icons. Microsoft obviously understands that the user doesn't need to have the very basics explained. It also shows an understanding that, although we are all beginners once, we all evolve into more-experienced daily users.

ToolTips contain a single word or a very short phrase. They don't attempt to explain in prose how the object is used; they assume that you will get the rest from context. This is probably the single most-important advance that ToolTips have over balloon help, illustrating the difference in design intent of Microsoft versus Apple. Apple wanted its bubbles to *teach* things to first-time users. Microsoft figured that first-timers would just have to learn how things work the hard way, and ToolTips would merely act as a memory jogger for frequent users.

By making the controls on the toolbar so much more accessible for normal users, Microsoft has allowed the toolbar to evolve beyond simply supporting menus. ToolTips have freed the tool-bar to take the lead as the main idiom for issuing commands to sovereign applications. This also allows the menu to quietly recede into the background as a command vector for beginners and for invoking occasionally used functions. The natural order of butcons as the primary idiom, with menus as a backup, makes sovereign applications much easier to use. For transient programs, though, most users qualify as first-time or infrequent users, so the need for butcons—short cuts—is much reduced.

ToolTip windows are very small, and they have the presence of mind to not obscure important parts of the screen. As you can see in Figure 29-1, they appear underneath the butcons they are explaining and labeling them without consuming the space needed for dedicated labels. There is a critical time delay, about a half a second, between placing the cursor on a butcon and having the ToolTip appear. This is just enough time to point to and select the function without getting the ToolTip. This design decision ensures that you aren't barraged by little pop-ups as you move the mouse across the toolbar trying to do actual work—a problem that early versions of balloon help suffered from. It also means that if you forget what a rarely used butcon is for, you only need to invest a half-second to find out.

Figure 29-1: Microsoft's ToolTips were the solution to the toolbar problem. Although toolbars are for experienced users, sometimes these users forget the purpose of a less-frequently used command. The little text box that pops up as the cursor rests for a second is all that is needed to remind the user of the butcon's function. The ToolTip succeeds because it respects the user by not being pedantic and by having a very strongly developed respect for the value of pixels. ToolTips were the gate that allowed the toolbar to develop as the primary control mechanism in sovereign applications, while letting the menu fall quietly into the background as a purely pedagogic and occasional-use command vector.

A little picture of a printer may be ambiguous until you see the word Print next to it. There is now no confusion in your mind. If the butcon were used to configure the printer it would say Configure Printer or even just Printer, referring to the peripheral rather than to its function. The context tells you the rest. The economy of pixels is superb.

The authors are both experienced users and leave ToolTips on all the time. Balloon help on our Macs is never on. Microsoft's solution is a quantum leap beyond balloon help, and yet it is almost exactly the same. It just goes to prove that the devil is in the details.

Use ToolTips with all toolbar and iconic controls.

Toolbars without ToolTips force users to sift though menus, learn their function by experimentation, or worst of all, read the documentation. Because toolbars contain immediate versions of commands that should be used by moderately experienced users, they inevitably contain some that are dislocating or dangerous. Explaining the purpose of butcons with a line of text on the status line at the bottom of the screen just isn't as good as ToolTips that appear right there where you're looking.

Do not create toolbars without ToolTips. In fact, ToolTips should be used on all iconic butcons, even those on dialog boxes.

Disabling toolbar controls

Toolbar controls should become disabled if they are not applicable to the current selection. They must not offer a pliant response: The butcon must not depress, for example, and controls should also gray themselves out to make matters absolutely clear.

Some programs make disabled toolbar controls disappear altogether, and the effect of this is ghastly. Users remember toolbar layouts by position, and with this behavior, the trusted toolbar becomes a skittish, tentative idiom that scares the daylights out of new users and disorients even those more experienced (such as the authors!). The path to modeless operation does not lie in becoming more ephemeral but rather in becoming more solid, permanent, and dependable.

Evolution of the Toolbar

After people started to regard the toolbar as something more than just an accelerator for the menu, its growth potential became more apparent. Designers began to see that there was no reason other than habit to restrict the controls on toolbars to butcons. Soon designers began to invent new idioms expressly for the toolbar. With the advent of these new constructions, the toolbar truly came into its own as a primary control device, separate from — and in many cases superior to — drop-down menus.

After the butcon, the next control to find a home on the toolbar was the combobox, as in Word's Style, Font, and Font Size controls. It is perfectly natural that these selectors be on the toolbar. They offer the same functionality as those on the drop-down menu, but they also show the current style, font and font size as a property of the current selection. The idiom delivers more information in return for less effort by the user.

After comboboxes were admitted onto the toolbar, the precedent was set, and all kinds of idioms appeared, as we have already discussed in Chapter 26. Some of these toolbar idioms are shown in Figure 29-2.

Figure 29-2: The development of the toolbar soon led to an extension of its purpose. It evolved from a mere repository of imperative command buttons to a place where controls could indicate the state of the currently selected item. This is a more object-oriented concept, and it makes our software more powerful. The toolbar has become the place for control innovation, far beyond what we have come to expect from dialog boxes. This image shows part of a toolbar from Microsoft PowerPoint XP. You can see the toolbar drag control, comboboxes, and latching butcons, retaining a state after the user releases the mouse button (see Chapter 26).

State-indicating toolbar controls

This variety of controls contributed to a broadening use of the toolbar. When it first appeared, it was merely a place for fast access to frequently used *functions*. As it developed, controls on it began to reflect the *state* of the program's data. Instead of a butcon that simply changed a word from plain to italic text, the butcon now began to indicate — by its state — whether the currently selected text was already italicized. The butcon not only controlled the application of the style, but it represented the status of the selection with respect to the style. This is a significant move towards a more object-oriented presentation of data, where the system tunes itself to the object that you have selected.

Menus on toolbars

As the variety of controls on the toolbar grows, we find ourselves in the ironic position of adding drop-down menus to it. The Word toolbar shown in Figure 29-3 shows the Undo drop-down. It is ironic that such a very menu-like idiom should migrate onto the toolbar. Immediate Undo certainly belongs on the menu, but does the associated pull-down that shows the history of past actions belong there, too? There isn't a clear answer. It is good that the historical list is positioned next to the Undo button because it makes it easy to find, but the toolbar is the place for frequently used functions. How frequently would one need to access the list? Ultimately, it comes down to pixels. As Microsoft implemented it, the pixel consumption is small enough to justify the idiom. What should be evident, though, is that the modern toolbar is pushing the old-fashioned menu bar further into the background as a secondary command vector.

Figure 29-3: Toolbars now contain drop-down lists. This example is from the Undo control in Word 2000. Irony of ironies, the drop-down menu has migrated onto the toolbar, which began as a refutation of the old-fashioned drop-down menu bar!

Movable toolbars

Microsoft has done more to develop the toolbar as a user interface idiom than any other software publisher. This is reflected in the quality of its products. In its Office suite, all the toolbars are very customizable. Each program has a standard battery of toolbars that the user can choose to be visible or invisible. If they are visible, they can be dynamically positioned in one of five locations. They can be attached — referred to as **docked** — to any of the four sides of the program's main window. You click the mouse anywhere in the interstices between butcons on the toolbar and drag it to any point near an edge and release. The toolbar attaches itself permanently to that side, top or bottom. If you drag the toolbar away from the edge, it configures itself as a floating toolbar, complete with mini-title bar, as shown in Figure 29-4.

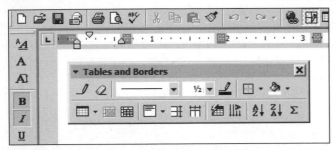

Figure 29-4: Toolbars can be docked horizontally (top), vertically (left), and dragged off the toolbar to form a free-floating palette. It's almost always preferable to use dockable palettes like these, rather than forcing users to perform windows management on undockable palettes. Complex palettes may not be able to organize themselves into toolbar-like strips, but should still be dockable against the sides of the sovereign window.

Allowing users to move toolbars around also provided the possibility for users to obscure parts of toolbars with other toolbars. Microsoft handily addresses this problem with an expansion combutton or drop-down menu that appears only when a toolbar is partly obscured, and provides access to hidden items via a drop-down menu, as shown in Figure 29-5.

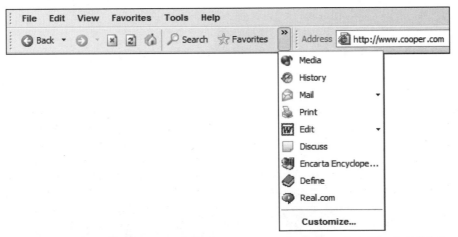

Figure 29-5: Microsoft's clever way of allowing users to overlap toolbars, but still get at all their functions. This provides a very lightweight kind of customization; power users would more likely perform full toolbar customization to address similar needs via the Customize . . . item at the bottom of the drop-down menu.

Customizable toolbars

Microsoft has clearly seen the dilemma that arises because toolbars represent the frequently used functions for all users, but those functions are different for each user. Microsoft apparently arrived at this solution: Ship the program with the best guess at what typical users' daily-use controls are, and let the others customize. This solution has been diluted somewhat, however, by the addition of non-daily use functions. For example, the Word toolbar's default button suite contains functions that certainly are not frequently used. Controls like Insert Autotext or Insert Excel Spreadsheet seem more like feature checklist items than practical, daily options for the majority of users. Although they may be useful at times, most users do not *frequently* use them.

Word gives more advanced users the ability to customize and configure the toolbars to their hearts' content. There is a certain danger in providing this level of customizability to the toolbars, as it is possible for a reckless user to create a really unrecognizable and unusable toolbar. However, it takes some effort to totally wreck things. People generally won't invest much effort into creating something that is ugly and hard to use. More likely, they will make just a few custom changes and enter them one at a time over the course of months or years. Microsoft has extended the idiom so that you can create your own completely new, completely custom toolbars. The feature is certainly overkill for normal users, but IT managers might use it to create a "corporate" look.

Microsoft's custom toolbar facility does exhibit an astounding attention to detail. You have the ability to drag buttons sideways a fraction of an inch to create a small gap between them. This allows you to create "groups" of buttons with nice visual separations. Some buttons are mutually exclusive, so grouping them is very appropriate. You can also select whether the buttons are large or small in size. This is a nice compensation for the disparity between common screen resolutions, ranging from 640x480 to 1600x1200 or more. Fixed-size buttons can be either unreadably small or obnoxiously large if their size is not adjustable. You have the option to force buttons to be rendered in grayscale instead of color. Finally, you can turn ToolTips off, although the authors can't imagine why anyone would do this.

The Windows Taskbar: Special Purpose Toolbars

With the release of Windows 95, Microsoft introduced the Taskbar, a clever and efficient means of managing running applications and displaying system status. Perhaps originally introduced to compete with the Macintosh OS 7 and its ubiquitous menubar, the Taskbar is actually much more useful and more suitable to a multitasking OS (which Mac OS was not at the time). The Taskbar also provided a somewhat cumbersome, but easily identifiable entry point to programs and the file system through the Start menu. In subsequent releases, the Taskbar evolved, adding a user-configurable quick start area for launching common applications and documents. The Taskbar can be dragged larger to hold more controls, and in past releases, it could be docked on either the top or bottom of the screen.

With each new Windows release, Microsoft seems to want to add something new to the Taskbar — a trend which could have diminishing returns fairly soon. But for now, the sum of this functionality makes the Taskbar a critical tool for users to manage their desktop.

In Mac OS X, we finally see a poor cousin to the Taskbar, the Dock, emerge as a standard on the Macintosh platform. Unfortunately, their implementation is heavy on flash and light on substance. Its gravest error is in poorly distinguishing between icons representing *launchable applications* and icons representing *running processes*, something the Taskbar has no problems presenting clearly.

The Start menu

As discussed elsewhere, the Start menu is primarily an entry point into a cascading menu structure of programs, settings, and documents. Its one major virtue is that it is behind a large friendly button that is almost always on the screen and is labeled Start in big letters. The problem is that once you click on it, especially as a new user, you're a bit at a loss as to where to go or what to do next. The Start menu has become more elaborate in Windows XP, and although the designers' apparent desire to segregate items into more readily understandable categories is evident, the whole effect becomes one of confusion and clutter.

One nice aspect of the Start menu has always been the capability to drag items onto it; but with the addition of the Quick Start area (described next), this functionality becomes a bit superfluous. Why put an item on an already crowded menu when you can put it on a toolbar?

Quick Start toolbar

To the right of the Start menu is a customizable area for dragging icons from the desktop. Items dragged there become butcons that launch the application or document in question. This is a great feature and well executed. If you want to remove an item, just drag it off. When you drop it, it becomes a desktop shortcut to the item, which you can leave or delete.

Some programmers may be tempted to install a link to their application directly in the Quick Start area without asking permission. This is an arrogant gesture that your users will not appreciate. You can make it easy for them to *choose* to do this, but don't assume they will want it there.

Window buttons

The window buttons are the primary fixture of the Taskbar; they represent every running window on the desktop. Clicking on one will open the window if it is closed and make that window the one receiving input focus. Clicking on one representing an open window will close that window. If you click on open windows, the state of the window buttons in the Taskbar mirror these selections, so that the Taskbar can always be used to tell what the current window is.

Taskbar buttons contain the application's icon and the title of the application and/or the current document it is displaying. (Microsoft currently seems to be following the standard of document title first, then application title, separated by a dash.) This works okay as long as you don't have too many windows open or too many other controls on the Taskbar because the window buttons get narrower the less space there is. ToolTips come to the rescue here.

Unfortunately, in Windows XP, Microsoft has done something which disrupts this quite workable ToolTip scheme: As space gets limited, rather than squeezing all the buttons, the Taskbar starts grouping them by application into single buttons. The ToolTip only shows the name of the application (and the fact that there is more than one window represented, which the button itself shows as well). To get a particular document from one of these group buttons, users are forced to make a menu selection after clicking on the button. This new scheme has two serious problems.

First, it is now impossible to tell, in some circumstances, which documents are open without clicking on a window button. Second, the mapping between the active window button and the active window has been thrown out of kilter by the many-to-one mapping of the grouped window buttons. Thank goodness this pathological behavior can be turned off in the Taskbar properties!

The status area

Since it was introduced in Windows 95, the status area (also known as the system tray) has become the dumping ground for little controls that probably shouldn't be there. The status area was designed to provide status information about various hardware and background processes, as well as providing a switch to turn these types of things on and off. It also displays the time (and date, in a ToolTip), which is handy and which replicated a long-standing feature found on the Mac menu bar. In Windows XP, icons that have been inactive for a while are hidden in a drawer (that the user can open), and emerge when they need attention. Status area icons typically launch a small configuration dialog when clicked and a pop-up menu when right-clicked. These should both be very simple and minimal. If you find yourself designing a status bar control that launches a full application or a complex cascading menu, it is probably inappropriate to put it in the status area in the first place.

One other behavior that some status bar icons exhibit (as of Windows 2000) is an interesting, non-flyover variant of Apple's balloon help concept, but used for a totally different purpose. In Windows 2000 and XP, status area icons occasionally launch little speech balloons that act like bulletins or process dialogs (see Chapters 30 and 31 for discussion on these and other dialogs), complete with embedded termination controls (similar to, but far less annoying than Clippy's help dialogs). They behave the way system modal dialogs really should, by not getting in the way of what the user is doing.

More toolbars on the Taskbar?

In Windows 2000 and XP, the Taskbar includes other toolbars that you can reach by right-clicking on the Taskbar — one that lets users type a URL and launch a browser, one that lets you add URLs as links, and one that replicates all the users desktop icons and folders. You can even create your own toolbars based on any folder or URL. This last seems particularly egregious. Although these might be interesting to some users, Microsoft should be aware that toolbars are not the answer to all problems. This attempt to cram everything but the kitchen sink onto the Taskbar is probably what resulted in the window button mess described earlier. Was it really worth it?

Chapter 30

Using Dialogs

Dialog boxes, or dialogs, are not part of the main program. If the program is the kitchen, the dialog box is its pantry. The pantry plays a secondary role, as does the dialog box. They are supporting actors rather than lead players, and although they may ratchet the action forward, they are not the engines of motion.

Dialogs Suspend Normal Interaction

Dialogs are superimposed over the main window of the parent program. The dialog engages the user in a conversation by offering information and requesting some input. When the user has finished viewing or changing the information presented, he has the option of accepting or rejecting his changes. The dialog then disappears and returns the user to the main program.

Many users and programmers think of dialog boxes as the primary user-interface idiom of the GUI. Many applications use dialogs to provide the main method of interaction with the program (we're not speaking of simple applications that are composed of just a single dialog box; in those cases, the dialog assumes the role of a main window). In most applications, the user is forced to bounce back and forth between the program's main window and its dialog boxes, inevitably leading to his fatigue and frustration.

AXIOM

Put primary interactions in the primary window.

When the application presents a dialog box, it temporarily moves the action out of the mainstream, abandoning the user's main focus of attention to develop a secondary issue. This understanding that dialogs are suspensions of normal processing is key to their proper design. The main interaction of the program should be contained in the main window of the program, whereas dialog boxes should be used only for secondary, and usually brief, interactions.

If you asked your dinner party guests to temporarily abandon their soup and step into the pantry, the smooth flow of conversation and warm friendship would be broken. In the same way, a dialog box breaks the smooth flow of rapport between a user and the program. Dialogs, for good or ill, interrupt the interaction and make the user react to the program instead of driving it.

Dialogs break flow.

Dialogs are appropriate for functions or features that are out of the mainstream of interaction. Anything that is confusing, dangerous, or rarely used can profitably be placed on a dialog box. **Dislocating actions** make immediate and gross changes to the screen image. Such changes can be visually disturbing to the user and should be cordoned off from users unfamiliar with them. For this reason, dialogs are tools well suited to managing dislocating actions.

Dialog boxes are good for presenting infrequently used functions and settings. The dialog box serves to isolate these operations from more frequently used functions and settings. The dialog box is generally a roomier setting to present controls than other primary control venues; you have more space for explanatory labels than you do in a toolbar, for example.

Dialog boxes are also well suited for concentrating information related to a single subject, such as the properties of an object in an application — an invoice or a customer, for example. They can also gather together all information relevant to a function performed by a program — printing reports, for example. The dialog box, when used in this way, becomes an encapsulation tool, enabling you to box up and remove functions and settings that might have a dislocating or dangerous effect on the program's normal flow of events. For example, a dialog box that allows wholesale reformatting of a document should be considered a dislocating action. The dialog helps prevent this feature from being invoked accidentally by assuring that a big, friendly Cancel button is always present, and also by providing the space to show more protective and explanatory information along with the risky controls. The dialog can graphically show the user the potential effects of the function with a thumbnail picture of what the changes will look like.

Most dialogs are invoked from a menu, so there is a natural kinship between menus and dialogs. As discussed in Chapter 27, menus provide the pedagogic command vector — their primary purpose is to teach users about the program. By extension, dialog boxes also frequently play a part in the pedagogic vector.

Dialog boxes serve two masters: the frequent user who is familiar with the program and uses them to control its more advanced or dangerous facilities; and the infrequent user who is unfamiliar with the scope and use of the program and who is using dialogs to learn the basics. This dual nature means that dialog boxes must be compact and powerful, speedy and smooth, and yet be clear and self-explanatory in use. These two goals may seem to contradict each other, but they can actually be useful complements. A dialog's speedy and powerful nature can contribute directly to its power of self-explanation.

Dialog Box Basics

Most dialogs have buttons, comboboxes, and other controls on their surface; and although there are some rudimentary conventions, generally the designer places them as she sees fit and not according to any conventional plan. The dialog's window may or may not have a title/caption bar or frame.

All dialog boxes have an owner. Normally this owner is an application program—usually the one that created it—but it can also be the window system itself. Dialog boxes are always placed visually in a layer on top of their parent program, although the windows of other programs may obscure them.

Every dialog box has at least one **terminating command**, a control that, when activated, causes the dialog box to shut down and go away. Most dialogs will offer at least two push-buttons as terminating commands, OK and Cancel, although the Close box in the upper-right corner (upper-left corner in Windows 3.x and Mac OS 9) is also a terminating command idiom.

It is technically possible for dialogs not to have terminating commands. Some dialogs are unilaterally erected and removed by the program—for reporting on the progress of a time-consuming function, for example—so their designers may have omitted terminating commands. This is poor design for a variety of reasons, as we will see.

Modal dialog boxes

There are two types of dialog boxes: modal and modeless. **Modal dialogs boxes** are, by far, the most common variety. After a modal dialog opens, the owning program cannot continue until the dialog box is closed. It stops all proceedings in their tracks. Clicking on any other window belonging to the program will only get the user a rude "beep" for his trouble. All the controls and objects on the surface of the owning application are deactivated for the duration of the modal dialog box. Of course, the user can activate *other* programs while a modal dialog box is up, but the dialog box will stay there indefinitely. When the user goes back to the program, the modal dialog box will still be there waiting.

In general, modal dialogs are the easiest for users (and designers) to understand. The operation of a modal dialog is quite clear, saying to the user, "Stop what you are doing and deal with me now. When you are done, you can return to what you were doing." The rigidly defined behavior of the modal dialog means that, although it may be abused, it will rarely be misunderstood. There may be too many modal dialog boxes and they may be weak or stupid, but their purpose and scope will usually be clear to the user. Like death and taxes, you may not like modal dialog boxes, but you grasp their meaning.

If a modal dialog box is function-oriented, it usually operates on the entire program or on the entire active document. If the modal dialog box is process- or property-oriented, it usually operates on the current selection. In any case, you can't change the selection after you've summoned the dialog. This is the most important difference between modal and modeless dialogs.

Actually, because modal dialog boxes only stop their owning application, they are more precisely named **application modal**. It is also possible to create a dialog box, called **system modal**, that brings every program in the system to a halt. No application program should ever create one of these. Their only purpose is to report truly catastrophic occurrences (such as the hard disk melting) that affect the entire system.

DESIGN TIP

Never create a system modal dialog.

Modeless dialog boxes

The other variety of dialog box is called **modeless**. They are less common than their modal siblings (although they are becoming more common with the widespread use of floating palettes in applications from Adobe and Macromedia). They are also less understood.

After the modeless dialog opens, the parent program continues without interruption. It does not stop the proceedings, and the application does not freeze. The various facilities and controls, menus, and toolbars of the main program remain active and functional. Modeless dialogs have terminating commands, too, although the conventions for them are far weaker and more confusing than for modal dialogs.

A modeless dialog box is a much more difficult beast to use and understand, mostly because the scope of its operation is unclear. It appears when you summon it, but you can go back to operating the main program while it stays around. This means that you can change the selection while the modeless dialog box is still visible. If the dialog acts on the current selection, you can select, change, select, change, select, and change all you want. For example, Microsoft Word's Find and Replace dialog allows you to find a word in text (which is automatically selected), make edits to that word, and then pop back to the dialog, which has remained open during the edit.

In some cases, you can also drag objects between the main window and a modeless dialog box. This characteristic makes them really effective as tool or object palettes in drawing-type programs.

Modeless dialog issues

Most modeless dialogs are implemented awkwardly. Their behavior is inconsistent and confusing. They are visually very close to modal dialog boxes, but they are functionally very different. There are few established behavioral conventions for them, particularly with respect to terminating commands. Microsoft is setting a disturbing precedent with terminating buttons that change legends contextually, a poor construct.

Most of the confusion arises because we are more familiar with the modal form and because of inconsistencies that arise in the way we use dialogs. When we see a dialog box, we assume that it is modal and has modal behavior. If it is modeless, users must tentatively poke and prod at it to determine how it behaves. There is just no clear archetype for it.

More confusion creeps into the situation because users are so familiar with the behavior of modal dialogs. A modal dialog can adjust itself for the current selection at the instant it was summoned. It can do this with assurance that the selection won't change during its lifetime. Conversely, the selection is quite likely to change during the lifetime of a modeless dialog box. Then what should the dialog do? For example, if the modeless dialog box modifies text, what should it do if we now select some non-text object on the main window? Should gizmos on the dialog box gray out? Freeze up? Disappear? Should the dialog box just stay there with all its controls "active" but having no effect if they are manipulated? All these options have been tried, and although each one has advantages, it is not clear which help and which hinder us. We'll take a closer look in the next few pages.

Modeless dialog boxes also lead us into complex situations. For example, in Word, request the modeless Find dialog box from the Edit menu. Now, from the Format menu request the modal Font dialog. The Find dialog vanishes. This is a good thing, sort of — it would be bizarre to have a modal dialog stuck on top of an unrelated modeless dialog — but where did the Find dialog go? If you close the Font dialog, the modeless Find dialog reappears—it was hiding behind your document window the whole time! This shuffling of windows makes logical sense: Keep the modal dialog and the window it is operating on as close together as possible visually. However, the disappearance of the modeless dialog could be a bit disturbing to inexperienced users. The simple answer would be to eliminate modeless dialog boxes entirely, but that would be cutting off our nose to spite our face.

Two solutions for better modeless dialogs

A solution must be found for the modeless dialog box problem. We offer two. The first one is easy to swallow, an evolutionary step forward from our present predicament. The second one is more radical; a revolutionary leap. As you might suspect, the first solution is less thorough and effective than the second one. You might also guess—correctly—that we're fonder of the revolutionary leap.

THE EVOLUTIONARY SOLUTION

In the evolutionary solution, we leave modeless dialog boxes pretty much the way they are, but we adopt two guiding principles and apply them consistently to all modeless dialog boxes. The first principle says that we must visually differentiate modeless dialog boxes from modal ones.

DESIGN TIP

Visually differentiate modeless dialogs from modal dialogs.

If a programmer uses the standard modeless dialog box facility in the Windows API, the resultant dialog is visually indistinguishable from a modal one. We must break this habit. The designer must assure that all modeless dialog boxes are rendered with a clearly noticeable visual difference. One possible method might be to use a distinctive hue for the dialog's background, or perhaps provide a colored border around the window, or insert a colored stripe across its corner, or make the controls visually distinct, using a different color or labeling them in, say, italics. You can also try setting apart the title/caption bar visually, by making it thinner, for example, or adding a distinctive icon to it.

Whatever method you choose, you must stick with it consistently. It would be nice if vendors agreed on a standard common to all, but that is wishful thinking. It will still be a significant improvement if each vendor adheres to his own company-wide standards for modeless dialog boxes.

The second principle says that we must adopt consistent and correct conventions for the terminating commands. It seems that each vendor, sometimes each programmer, uses a different technique on each individual dialog box. There isn't any reason for this cacophony of methods. Some dialogs say Close, some say Apply, some use Done, while some Dismiss, Accept, Yes, and some even use OK. The variety is endless. Still others dispense with terminating buttons altogether and rely only upon the Close box in the title bar. Terminating a modeless dialog box should be a simple, easy, consistent idiom, very similar—if not exactly the same—from program to program.

Give modeless dialog boxes consistent terminating commands.

One particularly obnoxious construction is the use of terminating buttons that change their legends from Cancel to Apply, or from Cancel to Close depending on whether the user has taken an action within the modeless dialog box. This dynamic change is, at best, disconcerting and hard to interpret and, at worst, frightening and inscrutable. These legends should *never* change. If the user hasn't selected a valid option but clicks OK anyway, the dialog box should assume the user means, "Dismiss the box without taking any action," for the simple reason that that is what the user actually did. Modal dialog boxes offer us the ability to cancel our actions directly, with the Cancel button. Modeless dialogs don't usually allow this direct idiom — we must resort to Undo — so changing the legends to warn the user just confuses things.

Never dynamically change the labels of terminating buttons.

The cognitive strength of *modal* dialog boxes is in their rigidly consistent OK and Cancel buttons. In modal dialogs, the OK button means, "Accept my input and close the dialog." The problem is that there is no equivalent for modeless dialog boxes. Because the controls on a modeless dialog box are always live, the equivalent concept is clouded in confusion. The user doesn't conditionally configure changes in anticipation of a terminal Execute command as he does for a modal dialog box. In modal dialogs, the Cancel button means, "Abandon my input and close the dialog." But because the changes made from a modeless dialog box are immediate — occurring as soon as an activating button is clicked — there is no concept of "Cancel all of my actions." There may have been dozens of separate actions on a number of selections. The proper idiom for this is the Undo function, which resides on the toolbar or Edit menu and is active application-wide for all modeless dialog boxes. This all fits together logically, because the Undo function is unavailable if a modal dialog box is up, but is still usable with modeless ones.

The only consistent terminating action for modeless dialog boxes is Close. Every modeless dialog box should have a Close button placed in a consistent location like the lower-right corner. It would have to be consistent from dialog to dialog: in the exact same place and with the exact same caption. Not to put too fine a point on this, but the word *Close* is the one to use, and the dialog should never deactivate or change this label.

If the Close button activates a function in addition to shutting the dialog, you have created a modal dialog box that should follow the conventions for the modal idiom instead.

Don't forget that modeless dialog boxes will frequently have several buttons that immediately invoke various functions. The dialog box should not close when one of these function buttons is clicked. It is modeless because it stays around for repetitive use and should only close when the single, consistently-placed Close button is clicked.

Modeless dialog boxes must also be incredibly conservative of pixels. They will be staying around on the screen, occupying the front and center location, so they must be extra careful not to waste pixels on anything unnecessary. For this reason, especially in the context of floating palettes, the Close box in the title bar may be the best solution for a sole terminating control.

A MORE RADICAL SOLUTION

The previous is but an interim solution. There is a more radical solution that delivers us from modeless-dialog maladies.

We currently have two modeless tool idioms in common use. The modeless dialog box is the older of the two. The other modeless idiom is a relative newcomer on the user interface scene but has achieved unprecedented success: toolbars and butcons. The toolbar idiom has by now achieved a widespread success because of its demonstrable quality and convenience. *It is also nothing more than a modeless dialog box permanently attached to the top (or side) of the program's main window.*

The modelessness of toolbar butcons is perfectly acceptable because they are not delivered to us in the visual form of a dialog. Instead, they are presented as omnipresent tools surrounding the workspace. Without the usual trappings of dialog boxes, it's a sure bet that they won't be confused with dialog boxes. We have no trouble understanding their use, even though identical controls often confound us when placed on a modeless dialog box.

Toolbar butcons can, and should (as discussed in Chapter 29) gray out when they have no effect in the context of the current selection. This behavior is easily understood by users and solves yet another modeless dialog issue.

In summary, toolbars are modeless, but they don't introduce the conundrums that modeless dialogs do. They also offer two characteristics that modeless dialog boxes don't: They are visually different from dialog boxes, and there is no need to worry about dismissing them because they are omnipresent—thus there is no need for terminating controls. They solve other problems, too. Toolbars are incredibly efficient in screen space, particularly compared to dialog boxes, *and they don't cover up what they are operating on*!

Modeless dialogs are free-floating windows, allowing users to position them on the screen wherever they like. The downside is the windows-management excise this entails. **Docking toolbars** (discussed in the previous chapter; see Figure 29-4) are the perfect solution. You can click-and-drag on a docking toolbar, pull it away from the edge of the program, and it will instantly convert into a **floating palette** (also called a palette window)—in other words, a modeless dialog. You can leave it this way or drag it to any edge of the program's main window, where it will convert back to a toolbar and become **docked** against the edge.

Elimination of windows-management excise becomes quite important, especially when we are talking about a large suite of floating palettes such as those in Adobe Photoshop and other drawing programs. Back in the days of 640x480 screen resolutions, there was a good reason to leave these floating—the user could slide them out of the way and still get access to the tools. But as screen resolutions creep higher and the numbers of these floating controls multiply, there is a point of diminishing returns where floating palettes simply get in the way. Adobe has partially acknowledged the issue by allowing palettes to snap to the edges of the main window, but they have not gone the final step of allowing them to dock in the main window so that nothing is hidden beneath them. Macromedia, on the other hand, has embraced the idea of dockable palettes in Fireworks MX and other recent application versions. Docking palettes and toolbars eliminate excise, but still give users the flexibility to float individual tools when they are needed.

Look at Figure 30-1, a toolbar from Microsoft Word that has been undocked. It is normally docked in a horizontal row at the top of the main window, just below the menu bar.

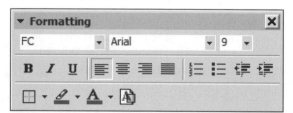

Figure 30-1: Here's a floating toolbar from Microsoft Word. It is also a modeless dialog box! The smaller title bar gives it a visual appearance distinct from modal dialog boxes, and the apparent conundrum of contextually inactive butcons is bothersome to nobody. If all modeless dialog boxes were rendered this way, much of the confusion surrounding them would disappear. What's more, if you drag this floating toolbar to an edge of the application, it docks on that edge as a familiar, fixed toolbar. Imagine if you could do that with *any* modeless dialog box — the Find dialog, for example?

Now let's imagine Word's Find dialog, shown in Figure 30-2, rendered as a floating toolbar. It would have a smaller-title bar instead of its normal one. It would lack a terminating button, relying instead on the Close box in the minicaption bar. What would happen if we were to drag this new Find dialog to the upper edge of the main window? If its behavior were consistent, it would dock: The controls on the surface of the Find dialog would distribute themselves in a horizontal toolbar the way the Format toolbar does. If it works for all those Format butcons and comboboxes, why can't it work for the Find dialog? Why can't we have a toolbar with a butcon for Find Next and with check boxes for the various options (if not for every bit of functionality, then at least for the most often-used functions)? A great example of this is the Google Toolbar, a downloadable toolbar control for Internet Explorer that implements Google's search functions along with a surprising amount of additional functionality.

Microsoft has made the floating/docking toolbar idiom a standard in its Office suite. The programs all include a facility for customizing the toolbars to the user's taste. This is a fine step in developing the user interface and should be used whenever possible as a new idiom for replacing modeless dialog boxes.

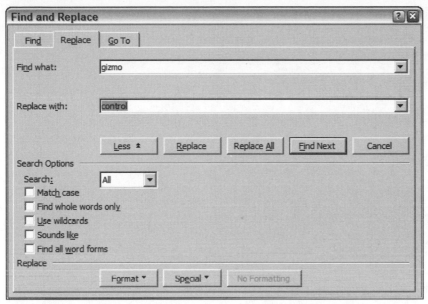

Figure 30-2: Here's a typical, modeless dialog box, from Microsoft Word. What a mess! It's big, it obscures the text it needs to search within (Word disconcertingly nudges it out of the way if a found word is underneath it), and its button labels are unclear. The Cancel button, for example: What does it cancel? Why can't functions like Find be built into the main window interface? The answer is, they can.

Goal-Directed Dialog Boxes

The concepts of modal and modeless dialogs are derived from programmers' terms. They affect our design, but we must also examine dialogs from a goal-directed point-of-view. In that light, there are four fundamental varieties of dialog box: property, function, process, and bulletin.

Property dialog boxes

A property dialog box presents the user with the settings or attributes of a selected object and enables the user to make changes to them. Sometimes the attributes may relate to the entire application or document, rather than just one object.

The Font dialog box in Word, shown in Figure 30-3, is a good example. The user selects some text in the main window and then requests the dialog box from the Format menu. The dialog enables the user to change font-related attributes of the selected characters. You can think of property dialogs as a control panel with exposed configuration controls for the selected object. Property dialog boxes can be either modal or modeless.

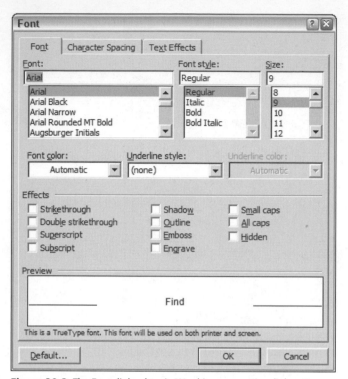

Figure 30-3: The Font dialog box in Word is a properties dialog. It reflects all the typographic characteristics of the current selection. When the user manipulates controls in this dialog, the typographic qualities of the selection change in the preview area, but not in the document until the OK button is clicked. The operation is essentially one of configuration. The preview box is great, but why can't the font field in the upper-left corner use the actual fonts, too?

A properties dialog box generally controls the current selection. This follows the object-verb form: The user selects the object, then, via the property dialog, selects new settings for the selection.

Function dialog boxes

Function dialog boxes are usually summoned from a menu. They are most frequently modal dialog boxes, and they control a single function such as printing, inserting objects, or spell checking.

Function dialog boxes not only allow the user to start an action, but they often also enable the user to configure the details of the action's behavior. In many programs, for example, when the user requests printing, she uses the Print dialog to specify which pages to print, the number of copies to print, which printer to output to and other settings directly relating to the print function. The terminating OK button on the dialog not only confirms the settings and closes the dialog, but also initiates the print operation.

This technique, though common, combines two functions into one: configuring the function and invoking it. Just because a function *can* be configured, however, doesn't necessarily mean that a user will *want* to configure it before every invocation. It's often better to make these two functions separately accessible.

Many functions available from modern software are quite complicated and have many configurable options. Their controlling dialog boxes are thus correspondingly complicated.

In the example shown in Figure 30-4, the user first configures the operation by choosing a file and then executes the configured command by clicking the terminating command button. It is very tempting to make that terminating button say Insert instead of OK, as the designers have done in this case. You should fight this urge. It may seem more logical, but the loss of a consistently labeled terminating command button is too great a price to pay. If the dialog's title bar text is appropriate, it will read like an English phrase, telling the user exactly what will happen: Insert the Picture . . . .

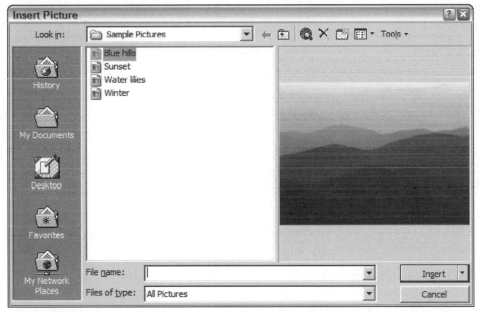

Figure 30-4: The Insert Picture dialog box from Word is a function dialog box. It is quintessentially modal, allowing the user to first configure the function by choosing a file. Nothing happens, however, until the OK button is clicked. The dialog does not have an effect on an object, but rather performs an operation.

Note also that the Insert button in this picture has a drop-down menu associated with it. Although the intent was to hide complexity (and probably to save space), the last thing you want in a terminating control on a dialog is for it to be non-standard and confusing. The designers should have taken a different approach.

Process dialog boxes

Process dialog boxes are launched at the program's discretion rather than at the user's request. They indicate to the user that the program is busy with some internal function and that performance in other areas is likely to degrade.

The process dialog box alerts the user to the program's inability to respond normally. It also warns the user not to be overcome with impatience and to resist banging on the keyboard to get the program's attention.

When a program begins a process that will take perceptible quantities of time, as measured by a human user, it must make clear that it is busy, but that everything is otherwise normal. If the program does not indicate this, the user will interpret it as rudeness at best; at worst, he will assume the program has crashed and that drastic action must be taken.

 DESIGN TIP

Programs must inform the user when they are about to become unresponsive.

As we discussed in Chapter 21, many programs currently rely on active wait cursor hinting, turning the cursor into an hourglass. A better, more informative solution is a process dialog box (we'll discuss an even better solution later in this chapter).

Each process dialog box has four tasks:

1. Make clear to the user that a time-consuming process is happening.

2. Make clear to the user that things are completely normal.

3. Make clear to the user how much more time the process will take.

4. Provide a way for the user to cancel the operation and regain control of the program.

The mere presence of the process dialog box satisfies the first requirement, alerting the user to the fact that some process is occurring. Satisfying the third requirement can be accomplished with a **progress meter** of some sort, showing the relative percentage of work performed and how much is yet to go. Satisfying the second requirement is the tough one. The program can crash and leave the dialog box up, lying mutely to the user about the status of the operation. The process dialog box must continually show, via time-related movement, that things are progressing normally. The meter should show the progress relative to the total *time* the process will consume rather than the total size of the process. Fifty percent of one process may be radically different in time than 50 percent of the next process.

The user's mental model of the computer executing a time-consuming process will quite reasonably be that of a machine cranking along. A static dialog box that merely announces that the computer is Reading Disk may *tell* the user that a time-consuming process is happening, but it doesn't *show* that this is true. The best way to show the process is by using animation on the dialog box. In Windows, when files are moved, copied, or deleted, a process dialog box shows a small animated cartoon of papers flying from one folder to another folder or the wastebasket (see Figure 30-5). The effect is remarkable: The user gets the sense that the computer is really *doing* something.

The sensation that things are working normally is visceral rather than cerebral, and users—even expert users—are reassured.

Microsoft's progress meter satisfies—barely—the third requirement by hinting at the amount of time remaining in the process. There is one dialog box per operation, but the operation can affect many files. The dialog should also show an animated countdown of the number of files in the operation (for example, "12 out of 37 files remaining"). Right now, the meter shows only the progress of the single file currently being transferred (interestingly, the standard Windows install process *does* use a meter that indicates how many documents there are to go.

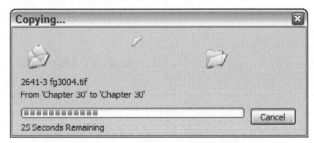

Figure 30-5: Microsoft got this one mostly right. For any move, copy, or delete operation in this Explorer, they show this reasonably well-designed process dialog box. It provides a hint of the time remaining in the operation, and the dialog uses animation to show paper documents flying out of the folder on the left into the folder (or wastebasket) on the right. The user's mental model is one of things moving inside the computer, and this little gem actually shows things moving. It is refreshing to see the outside of the computer reflect the inside of the computer in users' terms. The one thing missing is a countdown of the number of files left to move, which would provide even better feedback about the process at hand.

Notice that the copy dialog in Figure 30-5 also has a Cancel button. Ostensibly, this satisfies requirement number four, that there be a way to cancel the operation. The user may have second thoughts about the amount of time the operation will take and decide to postpone it, so the Cancel button enables him to do so. However, if the user realizes that he issued the wrong command and wishes to cancel the operation, he will not only want the operation to stop but will want all trace of the operation to be obliterated.

If the user drags 25 files from directory Alpha to directory Bravo, and halfway through the move realizes that he really wanted them placed in directory Charlie, he will try pushing the Cancel button. Unfortunately, all that does is *stop* the move at its current state and abandons the remainder of the moves. In other words, if the user clicks the Cancel button after 10 files have been copied, the remaining 15 files are still in directory Alpha, but the first 10 are now in directory Bravo. This is *not* what the user wants. If the button says Cancel, it should mean *cancel*, and that means, "I don't want any of this to happen." If the button were to accurately represent its action, it would say Halt Move or Halt Copy. Instead, it says Cancel, so cancel is what it should do. This may mean some significant buffering is needed, and the cancel operation could easily take more time than the original move, copy, or delete. But isn't this rare event one when the extra time required is easily justified? In Windows Explorer, the program can completely undo a copy, move, or delete, so there is no reason why the Cancel button can't also undo the portion that has already been performed.

A good alternative would be to have two buttons on the dialog, one labeled Cancel and other labeled Stop. The user could then choose the one he really wants.

Eliminating process dialogs

The need for process dialog boxes is unclear. They are as common as weeds in contemporary software, and about as useful, too. But what can we do to replace them?

The answer to that question is found by asking who is doing the processing. Because a dialog is a separate room, we must ask whether the process reported by the dialog is a function separate from that on the main window. If the function is an integral part of what is shown on the main window, the status of that function should be shown on the main window. For example, the Windows flying pages dialog that was shown in Figure 30-5 is attractive and appropriate, but isn't copying a file fundamental to what the Explorer does? The animation, in this case, could have been built right into the main Explorer window. The little pages could fly across the status bar, or they could fly directly across the main window from directory to directory.

Process dialogs are, of course, much easier to program than building animation right into the main window of a program. They also provide a convenient place for the Cancel button, so it is a very reasonable compromise to fling up a process dialog for the duration of a time-consuming task. But don't lose sight of the fact that, by doing this, we are still going to another room for a this-room function. It is an easy solution, but not the correct solution.

Bulletin dialog boxes

The **bulletin dialog box** is a simple, devilish little artifact that is arguably the most abused element of any graphical user interface. Like the process dialog, it is launched, unrequested, by the program.

The ubiquitous error message box best characterizes the bulletin dialog. Normally, the issuing program's name is shown in the caption bar, and a very brief text description of the problem is displayed in the body. A graphic icon that indicates the class or severity of the problem, along with an OK button, usually completes the ensemble. Sometimes a button to summon online help is added. An example from Word is shown in Figure 30-6.

The familiar message box is normally an application modal dialog that stops all further progress of the program until the user issues a terminating command — like clicking the OK button. This is called a **blocking bulletin** because the program cannot continue until the user responds.

It is also possible for a program to put up a bulletin dialog and then unilaterally take it down again. This type is a **transitory bulletin** because the dialog disappears and the program continues without user intervention.

Transitory bulletins are sometimes used for error reporting. A program that launches an error message to report a problem may correct the problem itself or may detect that the problem has disappeared via some other agency. Some programmers will issue an error or notifier bulletin merely as a warning — Your disk is getting full — and take it down again after it has been up for, say, 10 seconds. This type of behavior is fraught with usability problems.

Figure 30-6: Here's a typical bulletin dialog box. It is never requested by the user, but is always issued unilaterally by the program when the program fails to do its job or when it just wants to brag about having survived the procedure. The program decides that it is easier to blame the user than it is to go ahead and solve the problem. Users interpret this as saying, "The measurement must be between –22 inches and 22 inches, and you are an incredible buffoon for not knowing that basic, fundamental fact. You are so stupid, in fact, that I'm not even going to change it for you!"

An error or confirmation message *must* stop the program. If it doesn't, the user may not be able to read it fully; or if he is looking away, he either won't see it or worse yet, see only a fleeting glimpse out of the corner of his eye. He will be justifiably suspicious that he has missed something important, something that will come back to haunt him later. He will now begin to worry: What did I miss? Was that an important bit of intelligence that I will regret not knowing? Is the system unstable? Is it about to crash? This is true even if the problem has gone away by itself.

If a thing is worth saying with a dialog box, it's worth ensuring that the user definitely gets the message. A transitory bulletin can't make that guarantee. It should never be used in the role of error reporting or confirmation gathering.

DESIGN TIP

Never use transitory dialogs as error messages or confirmations.

Property and function dialog boxes are intentionally requested by the user — they serve the user. The program, however, issues bulletin dialogs — they serve the program, at the user's expense. Error, notification (alert), and confirmation messages are blocking bulletin dialogs. As we shall see, even these can and should be avoided in most circumstances. We will discuss this in detail in Chapters 33 and 34.

Chapter 31

Dialog Etiquette

In the last chapter, we discussed the larger design issues concerning dialog boxes. In this chapter, we zoom in closer to examine the way well-behaved dialogs should act. Even an appropriate dialog box can exhibit behavior that is unexpected or irritating. By attending to the details, we can change them from rude interrupters to polite and helpful attendants.

Politeness as a Dialog Virtue

As you recall, we divided dialog boxes into four types: property, function, bulletin, and process. One of the most important differences among these types is the way they are summoned. The first two are shown only at the user's explicit request, whereas the latter two are unilaterally issued by the program. This suggests a difference in tone and presentation. If you summon a servant, you expect him to step smartly into the room and plainly and immediately offer his services. On the other hand, when he wants to ask *you* for a raise, you want him to wait obsequiously until you are in a pleasant mood before interrupting your reverie to impose his own needs. In this spirit, bulletin and process dialogs should show much more deference than property or function dialogs. Unfortunately, the opposite is usually true.

A user-requested dialog may be large and place itself front-and-center on the screen. No unrequested dialog should take such liberties — unless there is a clear and present danger to the user. An unrequested dialog should be smaller, more compact in its use of space, and should appear off to one side of the screen so as not to obstruct the user's view of things.

The Title Bar

If a dialog box doesn't have a title bar, it cannot be moved. All dialog boxes should be movable so they don't obscure the contents of the windows they overlap. Therefore, all dialog boxes should have title bars. Is that clear? Even the Windows style guide almost agrees on this point, saying, "In general, an application should use only movable dialog boxes."

DESIGN TIP

All dialog boxes should have title bars.

There seems to be some belief that system modal messages (which, of course, you will *never* create) don't need to have title bars because they are often used to report fatal errors. The programmer's reasoning is: "Well, the system is crashed, so why bother to let the users move the dialog around?" Of course, a system crash is precisely the time you might need to get a good look at what was on your screen before you reboot. After all, you will probably lose whatever was there.

There also seems to be widespread confusion about what text string to put in the title bar of a dialog box. Some people think it should be the name of the function, whereas others think it should be the name of the program. The belt-and-suspenders crew tends to use both. The correct answer is very simple: neither of these.

If the dialog box is a function dialog, the title bar should have the function's *action* — the verb, if you will. For example, if you request Break from the Insert menu, the title bar of the dialog should say Insert Break. What are we doing? We are *inserting a break*! We are not breaking, so the title bar should not say Break. A word like that could easily scare or confuse someone.

Use verbs in function dialog title bars.

When the function will operate on some selection, the title bar should, when practical, indicate what is selected to the best of its capability. For example, if you select the sentence, "Smilin' Ed is dead," and invoke the Font item from the Format menu, the dialog's title bar should say Format Font for "Smilin' Ed is dead." If you've selected text that's too big to fit on the title bar, it should show the first and last couple of words of the selection separated by ellipses. If nothing is selected, the caption should say Format Font for Future Text.

Use object names in property dialog title bars.

If the dialog box is a property dialog, the title bar should have the name or description of the object whose properties we are setting. The properties dialogs in Windows work this way. When you request the Properties dialog for a directory named Backup, the title bar says Backup Properties.

Transient Posture

If dialog boxes were independent programs, they would be transient-posture programs. As you might expect, dialog boxes should then look and behave like transient programs, with bold, visual idioms, bright colors, and large buttons. On the other hand, dialogs borrow their pixels from sovereign applications, so they must never be wasteful of pixels. The imperative to be large is constantly at war with the imperative to be small. One solution is to make each of the individual controls slightly larger, but to make sure that the dialog itself wastes no additional space.

DESIGN TIP

Dialogs should be as small as possible, but no smaller.

Borland popularized a standard by creating extra-large buttons with bitmapped symbols on their faces: a large red X for Cancel, a large green checkmark for OK, and a big blue question mark for Help. They were cleverly designed and very attractive — at first. Most people, with good reason, now find them wasteful of space. The icons on the buttons worked well to visually identify themselves, well enough that the extra size wasn't necessary. Borland now uses the same bitmaps on buttons of a more conventional size, which is a much better solution. The visual images accomplish the job just fine without the need to waste precious pixels.

Obscuring the parent window with dialogs should be minimized. Dialog boxes should never take more room than they need. Pixels remain the most limited resource in modern desktop computers, and dialog boxes shouldn't sprawl across the screen. Compare the space efficiency of the CompuServe Navigator dialog in Figure 31-1 to the one from Word in Figure 31-2.

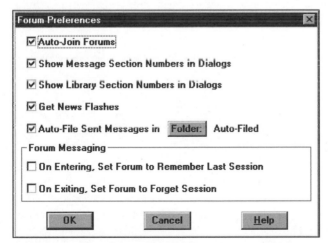

Figure 31-1: Here is a properties dialog box from CompuServe Navigator for Windows (v1.0). The sprawling check boxes consume a lot of space. At least it has a title bar, so you can move it out of the way. Also note the poor placement of the OK button at the far left rather than at the right.

Check boxes are a relatively space-inefficient control: the accompanying text requires a lot of dedicated space. Compared to the text of check boxes, buttons can be crammed together like sardines. But even check boxes don't need the kind of room they were given in the Navigator dialog.

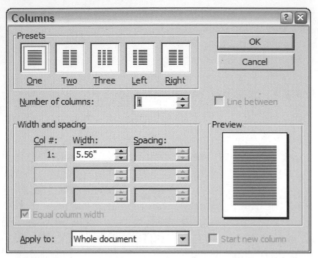

Figure 31-2: A typical function dialog box from Microsoft Word shows an excellent use of space. The controls are compact and very conservative of space. Compare this with the previous figure (Figure 31-1). Notice, also, Microsoft's willingness to use graphic objects instead of just canned, text-based controls like edit fields, check boxes, and push-buttons. Note the odd placement of the termination controls in the upper-right. In this case, the designer might have taken space efficiency a tiny bit *too* far.

Reduce Excise

Dialog boxes can be a burden on the user if they require a lot of excise—unnecessary overhead, which we discussed in Chapter 10. Users quickly tire of repositioning and reconfiguring a dialog box every time it appears. The duty of the dialog box designer is to assure that the excise is kept to a bare minimum, particularly because dialog boxes are only supporting actors in the interactive drama.

Know where you are needed

The usual ways dialog boxes fail to reduce excise are in their geographical placement and their state. Dialogs should always remember where they were placed the last time they were opened, and they should return to that place automatically. Most dialogs also start out fresh each time they are invoked, remembering nothing from their last instantiation. This is an artifact of the way dialogs are implemented: as subroutines with dynamic storage. We should not let these implementation details affect the way our programs behave. Dialogs should always remember what state they were in last time they were invoked and return to that same state. If the dialog was expanded or a certain tab was selected, the dialog should return the exact same way on subsequent visits. In Chapter 15, we discuss in more detail about how to apply memory to this type of problem.

The same idea can be applied to the contents of input fields. If a check box was checked last time, the dialog box should remember and come up with the box checked next time. Chances are good that the settings used the last time will be used the next time, too.

Know if you are needed

The most effective way that a dialog box (bulletin and process dialogs in particular) can reduce excise is to simply not appear if it is not needed. If there is some way for the dialog box to be smart enough to know whether it is really necessary, the program should — by all means — determine this and prevent the user from having to dismiss the unneeded box: an action that is pure excise.

For example, in Word, if you Save, Print, and Close a document in that order (something the authors do all the time), the repagination involved in printing marks the document as changed. This means that the program asks if you want to save it when you issue the Close command, even though you just did! The program should pay attention! Of course you want to save the document before closing. Not only should it not ask this question at all, it should be able to see that *you* didn't change it, the *program* did. The entire invocation of this dialog box is excise.

The same thing is true of bulletin dialogs that tell me that the program has completed some function normally. If it was so normal, the program shouldn't need to resort to the excise of a dialog box that stops the proceedings with idiocy.

If a program uses a dialog box to offer a selection of options every time you ask for a certain function, and you always use the same options, the program shouldn't bother to put up the dialog box. It should be able to recognize the pattern and remove the unnecessary step. Of course, it would have to inform you first (modelessly, please), so you're not surprised, and it should give you the option to override its decision.

Terminating Commands for Modal Dialogs

Every modal dialog box has one or more terminating commands. Most modal dialog boxes have three: the OK and Cancel buttons and the Close box on the title bar. The OK button means, "Accept any changes I have made and then close the dialog." The Cancel button means, "Reject any changes I have made and then close the dialog." This is such a simple and obvious formula, such a well-established standard, that it is inconceivable that anyone would vary from its familiar, trustworthy, well-trod path. Yet, for inexplicable reasons, many user interface designers do diverge from this simple formula, always to the detriment of their product and the despair of their users.

The modal dialog box makes a contract with the user that it will offer services on approval — the OK button — and a simple way to get out without hurting anything — the Cancel button. These two buttons cannot be omitted without violating the contract, and doing so deflates any trust the user might have had in the program. It is extremely expensive in terms of stretching the user's tolerance. Never omit these two buttons or change their legends.

DESIGN TIP   Offer OK and Cancel buttons on all modal dialog boxes.

A colleague countered this tip by suggesting that a dialog box asking if the user wants to *Cancel Reservation?* would cause problems when it appears with an OK and Cancel button. What does it mean to say "Cancel" to Cancel? Good question, and the solution to the problem is never to ask questions like that. If you ever need to ask a question like that — and you shouldn't — don't express it using the same words that are standard to termination controls. With a Cancel Reservation? query, users must respond with the word Cancel to avoid canceling. Confusing? You bet! Instead, the question should be stated like this: Remove the Reservation? Better yet, we'll talk about how to eliminate confirmation dialogs entirely in Part VII.

DESIGN TIP   Never use terminating command words in dialog text.

The design tip "Offer OK and Cancel buttons on all modal dialog boxes" applies to function and property dialogs. Bulletin dialogs reporting errors — those hateful things — can get away with just an OK button (as if the user wants to collude in the program's failure!). Process dialogs only need a Cancel button so the user can end a time-consuming process.

The OK and Cancel buttons are the most important controls on any dialog box. These two buttons must be immediately identifiable visually, standing out from the other controls on the dialog box, and particularly from other action buttons. This means that lining up several identical-looking buttons, including OK and Cancel, is *not* the right thing to do, regardless of how frequently it is done. Even from companies who should know better, the OK and Cancel buttons are buried in groups of other, unrelated buttons, and their familiar legends change with depressing frequency.

The Cancel button, in particular, is crucial to the dialog box's capability to serve its pedagogic purpose. As the new user browses the program, he will want to examine the dialogs to learn their scope and purposes and then cancel them so as not to get into any trouble. For the more experienced user, the OK button begins to assume greater import than the Cancel button. The user calls the dialog box, makes his changes, and exits with a confirming push of the OK button.

For a while, Microsoft adopted a new standard for terminating buttons. It demanded that the OK button be in the upper-right corner of the dialog and that the Cancel button be positioned immediately below it, with the Help button below that. Thank goodness recent releases of Windows have abolished this misstep. The majority of users read from upper-left to lower-right, so the terminating buttons make more sense in the lower-right of the dialog box. Microsoft has also gone for the executive gray look, and the terminating buttons are not visually identified by any unique color, shape, or even a unique typeface or type size. They blend right in with the other buttons on the dialog — too bad.

The OK button should be placed in the lower-right corner of the dialog box, and the Cancel button should be placed immediately to its left. The user can then dependably know that an affirmative ending of the dialog can be had by going to the extreme lower-right corner. To their credit, the folks at Apple have gotten this right from the beginning. Why do so many other companies continue to have such trouble with it?

The Close box

Because dialog boxes are windows with title bars, they have another terminating idiom. Clicking the Close box in the upper-right corner (or the upper-left corner on the Mac) terminates the dialog box. The problem with this idiom is that the disposition of the user's changes is unclear: Were the changes accepted or rejected? Was it the equivalent of an OK or a Cancel? Because of the potential for confusion, there is only one possible way for programs to interpret the idiom: as Cancel. Unfortunately, this conflicts with its meaning on a modeless dialog, where it is the same as a Close command. The Close box is needed on a modeless dialog but not on a modal dialog box. So, to avoid confusion, the close box should *not* be included in modal dialogs.

 Don't put close boxes on modal dialogs.

If the user expects an OK and gets a Cancel, he will be surprised and will have to do the work over — and he will learn. On the other hand, if the user expects a Cancel and gets an OK, he will still have to do the work over, but this time he will be angry. Don't let this situation arise.

The Help button

The Help button is often presented as a button on par with OK and Cancel. It requests context-sensitive help but doesn't terminate the dialog, so it isn't a terminating button. It is so often grouped with the terminating buttons that it has assumed the same importance by association. Online help, however, is not as important as the terminating commands. Putting Help adjacent to them is weak, but not harmful, and it has the power of a familiar standard. Help would be better placed as a control on dialog title bars. In many of their recent application versions, Microsoft is showing that it understands this issue. As you can see in Figure 31-3, Microsoft has moved Help away from the OK and Cancel terminating buttons, and put it on the title bar. Up there, it is on an area common to all dialogs, but clearly separated from the very special terminating commands (except, of course, the Close box).

Keyboard Shortcuts

Many dialogs offer services that are frequently used or used repetitively, like those for Replace or Find. As users gain experience with the program, they appreciate the presence of keyboard shortcuts for these frequently used dialogs. There are usually enough keys to go around, and there is no reason why a given function should have just a single keyboard shortcut. A function like Find should be callable with a Ctrl+F keystroke, as well as with a special function key, like F2. Replace could be Ctrl+R and F3.

Figure 31-3: This Properties modal dialog box from Windows XP shows how Microsoft has finally realized that Help is not a terminating command. It removed it from the suite of terminating buttons and put it on the title bar near the Close box. This is certainly an improvement, but then Microsoft went ahead and added another control to the terminating-button row: Apply. There is no use for an Apply function on *this* tab pane, but it is applicable on the Sharing pane. Why not put the Apply button on the pane where it means something and keep it out of the way of the terminating buttons?

Users learn these shortcuts either from the Help system or from the menus. Usually, these shortcuts go unnoticed until they are desired. New users go directly to the menus, and it is only after they find themselves actively searching for faster ways to operate that they discover them. And they will then be grateful that you had the foresight to put those shortcuts in for them. It can really please the power-user crowd, and this crowd has a big influence over new users.

One feature particularly desirable to power users is a facility for customizing and configuring these shortcuts. Although this isn't something that all (or even most) users will take advantage of, power users will likely make heavy use of it because it allows them to tweak controls to best match their work styles, something power users are always interested in.

Tabbed Dialogs

Another user interface idiom that took the world of commercial software by storm is the **tabbed dialog**. In less than two years, tabbed dialogs, as shown in Figure 31-4, went from a virtually unknown idiom to a well-established standard, which has now found its way, in a somewhat degraded form, to almost every commercial Web site in existence. When an idiom has merit, it is widely copied, and the tab control has been such a blessing to dialog box designers that it has become a standard part of all GUIs.

Tabbed dialogs allow all or part of a dialog to be set aside in a series of fully overlapping **panes**, each one with a protruding, identifying **tab**. Clicking on a tab brings its associated pane to the foreground, hiding the others. The tabs can run horizontally across the top or the bottom of the panes or vertically down either side. Arguably, the most usable of these variations is the top-oriented tabs, because side-oriented tabs either require users to rotate their heads to read the labels or take up too much space with standard labels, and bottom-oriented tabs are too easy to overlook.

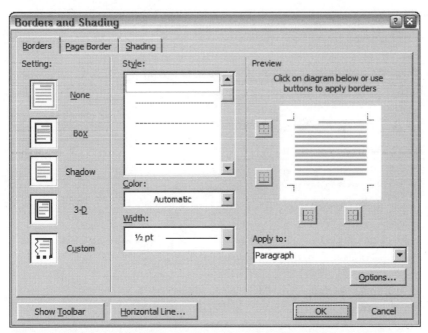

Figure 31-4: This is a tabbed dialog box from Microsoft Word. Combining borders and shading on one dialog box makes sense, if you have a convenient way to do it. Tabbing provides the way. Note that the designer correctly put the terminating controls outside the tabbed pane, in the lower-right. It would be best if the OK button were the right-most button (Apple has advocated this from the start, but Microsoft just has to be different).

Many objects with numerous properties can now have correspondingly rich property dialog boxes without making those boxes excessively large and crowded with controls. Many function dialogs that were previously jam-packed with controls now make better use of their space. Before tabbed dialogs, the problem was clumsily solved with expanding and cascading dialogs, which we'll discuss shortly.

Every tabbed dialog box is divided into two parts, the stack of panes, the **tabbed area**, and the remainder of the dialog outside of the panes, the **untabbed area**. The terminating command buttons must be placed on the untabbed area. If the terminating buttons are placed directly on the tabbed area, even if they don't change position from pane to pane, their meaning is ambiguous. The user may well ask, "If I press the Cancel button, am I canceling just the changes made on *this* pane or all the changes made on *all* the panes?" By removing the buttons from the panes and placing them on the untabbed area, their scope becomes visually clear.

DESIGN TIP

Put terminating buttons on the untabbed area of a tabbed dialog.

Breadth versus depth

A tabbed dialog allows you to cram more controls onto a single dialog box, but more controls won't necessarily mean that the user will find your interface easier to use or more powerful. The contents of the various panes on the dialog must have a meaningful rationale for being together, otherwise this capability just degrades to what is good for the programmer, rather than what is good for the user.

The panes on a dialog can be organized to manage either increased depth or increased breadth on a topic. To organize for more breadth, each pane covers additional aspects of the main topic, the way borders and shading, shown in Figure 31-4, both address ways that text is enhanced. In the case of organizing for more depth, each pane probes the same aspect of one topic in greater depth.

Stacked tabs: Dialog abuse

Tabs had such success because the idiom follows the user's mental model of how things are normally stored: in a monocline grouping. The various controls are grouped in several parallel panes, one-level deep. But even this idiom can be (and often is) abused.

Because you can cram so many controls into a tabbed dialog, the temptation is great to add more and more panes to a dialog. The Options dialog in Microsoft Word, shown in Figure 31-5, is a clear example of this problem. The ten tabs are far too numerous to show in a single line, so they are stacked two deep. The problem with this idiom, called **stacked tabs**, is that, if you click on a tab in the back row, the entire row of tabs moves forward, shunting the other two rows to the back. Very few users seem to be happy with this because it is disconcerting to click on a tab and then have it move out from under the mouse. It works, true, but at what cost?

AXIOM

All idioms have practical limits.

Stacked tabs illustrate the following axiom of user interface design: All idioms, regardless of their merits, have practical limits. A group of five radio buttons may be excellent, but a group of fifty of them is ridiculous. Five or six tabs in a row are fine, but adding enough tabs to require stacking destroys the usefulness of the idiom.

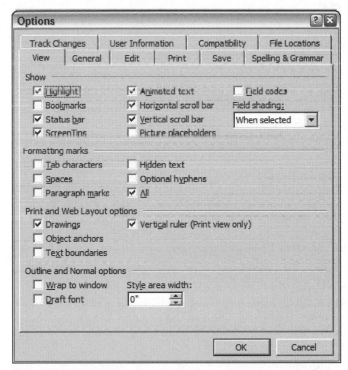

Figure 31-5: The Options dialog in Word is an extreme example of what can be done with tabs. There is certainly a lot crammed into this one dialog, which is good. The problem is that the tabs move around! The active tab must be on the bottom row, so if you click on Spelling and Grammar, for example, that row rolls down to the bottom and the other row rises to the top. Everybody hates it when the tabs move underneath the cursor. It's better just to break this up into smaller dialogs.

A better alternative would be to use several separate dialogs with fewer tabs on each. In this example, Options is just too broad a category, and lumping all this functionality in one place isn't doing the user any favors. There is little connection between the twelve panes, so there is little need to move between them. This solution may lack a certain programming elegance, but it is much better for the user.

DESIGN TIP   Don't stack tabs.

Expanding Dialogs

Expanding dialog boxes were big around 1990 but have declined in popularity since then, largely due to the omnipresence of toolbars and tabbed dialogs. You can still find them in many mainstream applications, such as the Find dialog in Word.

Expanding dialogs unfold to expose more controls. The dialog shows a button marked More or Expand, and when the user clicks it, the dialog box grows to occupy more screen space. The newly added portion of the dialog box contains added functionality, usually for advanced users or more complex, but related, operations. The Find dialog in Word is a familiar example of this idiom and is shown in the previous chapter, in Figure 30-2.

Expanding dialog boxes allow infrequent or first-time users the luxury of not having to confront the complex facilities that more frequent users don't find upsetting. You can think of the dialog as being in either beginner or advanced mode. However, these types of dialogs must be designed with care. When a program has one dialog for beginners and another for experts, it all too often simultaneously insults the beginners and hassles the experts.

Most expanding dialogs are implemented so that they always open in beginner mode. This forces the advanced user to have to promote the dialog each time. Why can't the dialog come up in the *appropriate* mode instead? It is easy enough to know which mode is appropriate: It's usually the mode it was left in. If a user expands the dialog and then closes it, it should come up expanded next time it is summoned. If it was put away in its shrunken state last time, it should come up in its shrunken state next time. This simple trait could make the expanding dialog automatically choose the mode of the user, rather than forcing the user to select the mode of the dialog box. The Find dialog from Word does exactly this. Bravo, Microsoft!

For this to happen, of course, there has to be a Shrink button as well as an Expand button (or a Less as well as More, as in the Find dialog). The most common way this is done is to have only one button, but to make its legend change between More and Less as it is clicked. Normally, changing the legend on a button is weak because it gives no clue as to the current state, only indicating the opposite state. In the case of expanding dialogs, though, the visual nature of the expanded dialog itself is clear enough evidence of the state the dialog is in.

Cascading Dialogs

Cascading dialogs are a diabolical idiom whereby controls, usually push-buttons, on one dialog box summon up another dialog box in a hierarchical nesting. The second dialog box usually covers up the first one. Sometimes the second dialog can summon up yet a third one. What a mess! Thankfully, cascading dialogs have been falling from grace, but examples can still be found. Figure 31-6 shows an example taken from Windows XP.

It is simply hard to understand what is going on with cascading dialogs. Part of the problem is that the second dialog covers up at least part of the first. That isn't the big issue — after all, comboboxes and pop-up menus do that, and some dialogs can be moved. The real confusion comes from the presence of a second set of terminating buttons. What is the scope of each Cancel? What are we OKing?

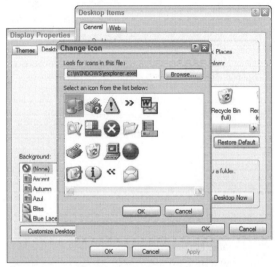

Figure 31-6: You can still find cascading dialogs in Windows. Each dialog box offers a set of terminating buttons. The resulting excise and ambiguity are not helpful.

The strength of tabbed dialogs is handling breadth of complexity, while cascading dialogs are better suited for depth. The problem is that excessive depth is a prime symptom of a too-complex interface. If you find your program requiring cascading dialogs for anything other than really obscure stuff that your users won't generally need, you should take another look at the overall complexity of your interface.

Examples of cascading are common. Most print dialogs allow print-setup dialogs to be called, and most print-setup dialogs allow print-driver-configuration dialogs to be called. Each layer of dialog box is another layer deeper into the process, and as the user terminates the uppermost dialog, the system returns control to the next lower dialog, and so on.

Cascading dialogs exist because they seem natural to programmers and because they mirror the physical processes underneath them. Sometimes they reflect the fact that two different programming teams worked on different parts of the interface, and linking dialogs was the most expedient way to stitch it all together. But this kind of baling-wire and band-aid rationalization is about as backward a motivation as one can have — it ignores the user's goals and the user's mental model of the process. Perhaps cascading dialog boxes can't be entirely avoided, but they represent a very weak idiom and should be scrutinized carefully before they are deployed. Sometimes the situation demands them, as in the print dialog example described above. Even in that case, however, the authors would combine them into a single dialog with three tabs, or at the least combine the first two dialogs and maintain only the printer driver dialog separately from the main print dialog. Three cascading dialogs are excessive for almost any purpose.

Dynamic Dialogs

Most dialogs are static, presenting a fixed array of controls. A variant, the **dynamic dialog**, changes and adapts its suite of controls based on user input, even more so than the expanding dialog.

An example of a dynamic dialog can be found in the Customize dialog of Word 95 as shown in Figure 31-7. The controls on the face of the dialog change dynamically to adapt to the user's input to other controls on the same dialog. Depending on the selection the user makes in the Categories control, the contents of the Commands control changes. It's possible to swap out the entire Container control with something different; earlier versions of this dialog displayed butcons in a group-box, but fonts and macros in a list box filled with text items.

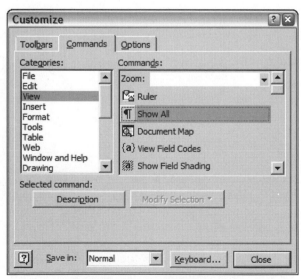

Figure 31-7: Word's Customize dialog box is an example of a dynamic dialog box. Depending on what you select in the Categories list box control, the Command list box to its right will contain controls (as shown), macros, font names, or other items.

This idiom has the potential to be confusing to users, as they wonder where certain controls went. But it is particularly effective when the user is entering settings in a clearly sequenced manner. For example, in a database access application where the user must first select a server, then a database on that server, then a table within that database, a dynamic dialog would be very appropriate. The structure of the problem calls for the server to be chosen first, so the user selects one from a list. As soon as the selection is made, the dialog configures itself to include a field for a password if the server requires it. As soon as the user selects the database, one or more fields then appear to allow the user to select the table, its owner, and other required information, in sequence.

Dialogs can become useful assistants that help your users accomplish their goals, instead of dreaded roadblocks that confound them at every step. By keeping your dialogs manageable, and invoking them only when their functions are truly those that belong in another room, you will go far towards maintaining your users' flow and ensuring their success and gratitude.

Chapter 32

Creating Better Controls

Controls are valuable tools for interacting with users because they encapsulate complex behavior in a ready-to-use package. The ready availability of controls leads us to rely on them for designing user interfaces. We use them because they are available. Unfortunately, the set of controls that come with most window system APIs is rudimentary at best. Controls remain a significant arena for invention and entrepreneurship. This chapter explores some needed areas of control innovation.

Direct Manipulation Controls

The most striking area for invention is in bounded-entry controls. So many programs offer dialog boxes with edit fields or spinners to gather data that could more easily be entered through direct manipulation. Using click-and-drag idioms in place of entry controls not only makes input clearer and easier, but it can also, by its very nature, put natural bounds on what could otherwise (using standard controls) end up as an unbounded data entry problem.

Example 1: Draggable drop shadows

For example, many drawing programs, such as PowerPoint, permit users to add drop shadows to filled objects. The "obvious" way to accomplish this is to employ a dialog box with two spinner controls, one for horizontal offset and one for vertical offset, right? Possibly you might include a preview image, so the user can see what happens when she enters a new value, so she doesn't need to hit Undo if it doesn't look right. When the user is ready, she clicks OK and the drop shadow is added to the object she selected. There's nothing really terrible about this interface, but there's nothing really useful or compelling about it either.

But what if in place of the spinners and passive preview area, the dialog had a dynamic preview area where the user could just grab the drop shadow by clicking and dragging, and move it wherever she wanted in real time? And what if, instead of a dialog box, this happened right in the main window of the program, so that the user could see exactly how the drop shadow would look in the full context of the document? She could perhaps press the Enter key to confirm or the Esc key to cancel the operation, or choose similarly from small controls that appear when the cursor is within the bounding box of the drop shadow. If the actual numeric values of the offset are important, those could be displayed as an overlay nearby the drop shadow, in the status area of the application, or even in editable fields in a toolbar or dockable palette.

Dragging a drop shadow much more closely approaches the ideal of direct manipulation. Like the carpenter swinging his hammer, the user can place the shadow just so, and clearly and immediately receive direct feedback regarding his input. He doesn't have to wonder whether three pixels are too few or four pixels are too many. He can *see* when it's just right. The more you can make use of direct manipulation, the more useful and compelling your applications and their interactions are likely to be.

In this last part of the example, you'll notice that there's a bit of modality to the interaction, but it hardly seems modal. This is part of the power of direct manipulation over the use of standard dialogs — even when there are some decisions to make, they don't *feel* the same as a dialog that stops you in your tracks because they are better integrated into the main flow of the application. Of course, the drop shadow could also be implemented as a completely independent effect layer, in which case there's no modality at all. If you don't want it there, just delete the layer.

Example 2: Specifying grids

A grid might, as in the "before" case of the drop shadow example, be controlled through a small dialog box with two edit controls for specifying the horizontal and vertical interval of the grid. Why not replace these controls with a dynamic preview swatch of grid that the user can adjust by direct manipulation? When the user moves the cursor over the swatch, the cursor changes to indicate that the sample grid is pliant. The user can then just click and drag anywhere in the swatch to adjust the spacing. Dragging down opens the vertical interval. Dragging up closes it. Dragging right or left works the same way for the horizontal axis. In order to adjust one axis without inadvertently affecting the other, you can use a drag threshold like the one described in Chapter 23, or let the user hold down a Shift key, which has become a fairly standard idiom for axis locking in drawing programs. You could also imagine a direct-manipulation grid control built directly into the rulers on the main screen — grab a handle, and pull to stretch it or compress it — this would make the interaction even more direct.

Both the drop shadow control and the grid control replace ugly, inappropriate text controls with the direct manipulation of graphical objects that were visually appropriate to the desired result. The user could stay in context, even though the tools are used rarely enough to justify their residing on dialog boxes. Both controls finesse away the need for text entry and provided visual, bounded, direct manipulation of the settings.

Extraction Controls

One of the most noticeable attributes of text edit controls is how stupid they are. If an application calls for typing an address, for example, there are no Address controls, yet that is exactly what we need. Validation controls exist, true, but their capability to adapt to variable input, like a whole address, approaches nil. A *real* address control would be an example of an **extraction control**.

Extraction controls are a better approach to the problem of formatted data entry. Extraction controls parse the contents of a free-form text entry control according to some rules about the general class of input. For example, instead of having one field for street address, one for apartment/suite/mail stop, one for city, one for state, and one for zip code, you would instead create a *single* text entry control, several lines tall. The user keys in the entire desired address in the single field, just as he would on an envelope or in a rolodex, and the control makes sense of the various parts of that address. Sounds good, huh. But how do we do it?

A normal text edit control has a method (or entry point, or value, depending on your language/coding model) to examine its **contents**. The contents of a normal zip code entry field are whatever the user enters. An extraction control has several other content examination methods in addition to the traditional one. They would include:

- ✓ Street address line
- ✓ Street
- ✓ Number
- ✓ Geographical designation
- ✓ Second address line
- ✓ Suite number
- ✓ Building
- ✓ Apartment
- ✓ Mail stop
- ✓ Floor
- ✓ City line
- ✓ City
- ✓ State
- ✓ Province
- ✓ District
- ✓ Zip code
- ✓ Postal code
- ✓ Country

Not all these values would be filled, only those that are relevant, depending on what the user enters. The control would do its best to determine which parts of the entered text belong in each category. There are basically three levels of discrimination in this process. The control would return the text verbatim as the user entered it. Each line of the address would be separated: Street address line, Second address line, City line. Then, each separate element of the address would be parsed into its appropriate category.

A control like this enables users to enter addresses the same way they manually prepare an envelope: by typing the address as a block. The computer does the work of separating the fields out for efficient categorizing in a database program. A program would then be able to, for example, sort the addresses by street name or by zip code, even though the address is entered in human-readable form.

Useful types of extraction controls include those for proper names, e-mail addresses, physical descriptions, and telephone numbers. An extraction control could easily pull a person's first name, last name, middle name, honorific, rank, and title from a single field so the user isn't forced to manually separate them at entry time.

Yes, there will be an error rate, but it won't be high and it won't be significant. An address-parsing algorithm can easily pull apart the vast majority of addresses. If someone tried to deliberately enter garbage, the extraction control would probably fail to discriminate accurately, but then again, how many users deliberately enter garbage? An end user with a shrink-wrapped application who deliberately enters garbage into his own system certainly won't blame *you* for the problem.

When coded into a dialog box, a telephone-number extraction control, for example, would recognize phone numbers by applying a series of simple lexical and semantic rules. The outputs of the field would consist of the raw text as entered by the user, along with an array of possible phone, fax, cellular, and pager numbers. If the control is unable to discern these numbers from the contents, well, it can't; but in most cases where these numbers are discernible by humans they are also discernible by software. Let's take an example: Say that we key this text into a phone number extraction control:

```
415-366-2300w, Home:367-9824 (415) 367-9976 fax 508 2031 pager
```

There's some pretty torturous stuff here: inconsistent and missing symbols and varying labels. But can you figure out what we've typed? Sure you can. A program could, too! The first number is a well-formed number with area code, prefix, and body. It has a **w** appended to it that can reasonably be interpreted as being a work phone. The comma is just a separator. The next number is prefixed by the word **Home:** so its nature is clear. The absence of an area code is not much of a crisis. The program could easily assume it is a 415 number — the same as all the others. If it were different, it is likely that we would have entered it. The third number is trickier. Certainly, it a well-formed number, but what is it? The word **fax** is ambiguous. It could be referring to the third number or the fourth number. The last word in the entry, **pager**, disambiguates the two because it must be referring to the fourth number, so **fax** must refer to the third. The lack of a hyphen in the fourth number should be no problem because the number is still a recognizable, well-formed phone number.

If we wanted to really tax the control we could enter something more problematic, like this:

```
4558, 1-800-555-1212 25433 555-FLIX
```

Well, this would certainly put a strain on things, but it is not impossible. The first number, 4558, is not a recognizable phone number, but it is a recognizable fragment of a phone number. When you want to call someone within your company through a private PBX, you often just enter a four-digit number. If the PBX's prefix were 488 — which the program is likely to already know — the number from the outside would be 488-4558. The second number is a well-formed number; it's just more complete than many others. It includes the long distance prefix 1 and adds a five-digit extension. We guess that it is an extension because it is not delimited from the 800 number. If it contained only four digits, we might have trouble discriminating between it being an extension or another in-house number. The last number is, well, recognizable even though it doesn't use all-numeric digits because its form is recognizable. Software might otherwise have difficulty determining that **555-FLIX** is a phone number, except that we are talking about a field that is designed to process phone numbers — that's a big hint.

Many of you are probably having trouble swallowing the idea of extraction controls. They seem to fly in the face of our tradition of guaranteed data integrity. This isn't really the case, however, as we discussed at length in Chapter 17. Besides, there's nothing preventing you from allowing your users to see (and correct if necessary) the results of the extraction parsing before committing it to the database, which is the solution Microsoft has chosen.

After the first edition of About Face was published, Microsoft has bravely implemented a few extraction controls just as described here. See for yourself in Figure 32-1.

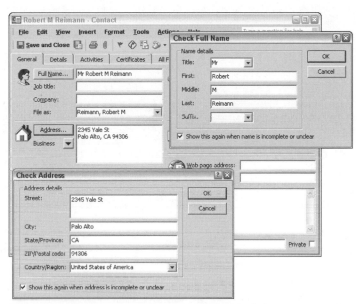

Figure 32-1: The New Contacts dialog in Outlook includes some extraction controls; look at the Full Name and Address fields in the main dialog. If you want to check the results, you can click the Full Name or Address buttons (which double as field labels), to get the dialogs that are shown. Outlook has correctly parsed one of the author's name and address — but couldn't it all have been entered into a single field?

Visual Controls

Most traditional GUI controls are encapsulations of text. Check boxes, radio buttons, menus, text edits, list views, and comboboxes are primarily text with a thin veneer of graphics added. They don't exploit the full potential of the GUI medium.

When most programs offer options to the user, they describe them in a text-based selection control like a combobox. This is fine for abstract functions or functions concerning text. However, if options can be more clearly and compellingly offered visually, we should discard the combobox and let the user point-and-click on a picture of what he wants instead of a text description alone.

Figure 32-2 is an excellent example of an almost purely visual interface, appropriate to an almost purely visual application, Photoshop. One is hard-pressed to find text in the Layers Palette, except for the names of layers and operations applied to them. But most of the controls are visual, most spectacularly, the thumbnail images of each layer in the stack.

Figure 32–2: The Layers Palette in Photoshop is an exemplary use of visual controls, especially the use of actual thumbnail images of the layers themselves, which update in real time as changes are made to them. The palette is not only able to pack a huge amount of usable functionality into a small space, but the visual nature of the controls is also appropriate for the user base of the application: artists, photographers, and other visual thinkers.

Figure 31-4 in the previous chapter shows a dialog box from Word using visual controls. The controls let the user request complex bordering options by clicking on small visual representations of borders, instead of asking for them by name. In this situation, these controls rescued Microsoft from a difficult dilemma because the number of bordering options is large. Rules can be independently specified for the top, bottom, left, right, and in-betweens of a paragraph, and each border can have its own weight and style. Offering a combobox filled with hundreds of options like "thin left, really thin right, thick top, dashed thin bottom" would have been pathological. Alternatively, a dialog box with an array of individual comboboxes for each of the five possible borders would still result in a morass of confusing interactions for the user. Microsoft's solution is an elegant way of addressing these problems.

We don't have to save visual controls for the tough stuff, though. On the left of the same figure (Figure 31-4) is another visual control that offers a simple choice from one of five options: an outline, a drop-shadow, 3D borders, a custom border, or no border at all. These could easily have been radio buttons, but clicking on the little pictures is much better. The user can click on the image of what he wants instead of having to click on the words that describe what he wants. It is less ambiguous, more easily localizable, faster, and more direct.

Most software publishers use radio buttons instead of visual controls like these because radio buttons come free with the OS and the visual controls don't. If publishers want a visual control, they must pay designers and programmers to create them. This is not an expensive thing to do relative to other custom coding, but compared to a free text-based control, it is still costly. In the long run, though, such expenditure is worth it because of usability problems it solves that would otherwise result in localization costs, customer support calls, and all the hidden costs associated with poor user satisfaction.

Figure 32-3 shows a beautifully crafted visual control in the control panel of Windows 95. Instead of picking a time zone from a text list (although such a list exists on the dialog), you choose your time zone by clicking on a blue and green map of the world. When you select a zone, the map sensuously slides so that your selection is centered in the window. *There was no need for Microsoft to do this,* just as there is no reason for an exclusive law firm to have marble floors instead of linoleum. But as you run your hand along the teak and cherry wood trim of the lobby furnishings and slide gently into a soft, supple leather wing chair, you know true comfort and luxury. For some reason, this interaction was eliminated in Windows 98 and later versions (the dialog is still there, but the zone doesn't highlight, and you're forced to use the combobox). Its removal is a mystery, and the authors of this book miss it.

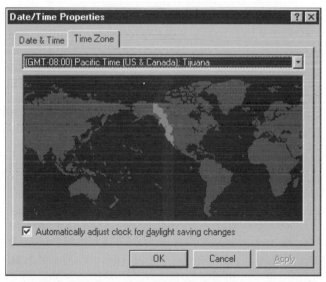

Figure 32-3: The time zone dialog box in Windows 95 is an excellent visual control. It shows the selections available to the user attractively and graphically. If you live on the East Coast of the US, for example, all you need to do is click somewhere along the eastern seaboard and the map smoothly scrolls until the Eastern US is centered and highlighted. The animation speeds up and slows down so nicely that the effect is almost sensual. It's like walking into the lobby of someone's office and finding marble, walnut, and leather instead of stucco and plywood. If you want to add a sense of aesthetics to your program, make them tactile aesthetics. Why Microsoft removed this interaction in the next OS release remains a mystery.

Paradoxically, controls are distinct objects on the surface of an application, but the path to improving them is to integrate them more intimately into the visual fabric of the program. The examples discussed in this chapter are undoubtedly hand-coded one-offs. This is an area of significant opportunity for a vendor: creating a generic visual-control development kit that allows average programmers on average budgets to create visual, animated, direct manipulation controls for their products. One place where there *has* been lots of innovation in visual controls has been on the Web, within the tight constraints of HTML. New technological developments like Macromedia's Flash MX might, if widely adopted, provide a platform for such visual controls in the future.

Part VII

Communicating with Users

Chapter 33

Eliminating Errors

In Chapter 30, we discussed the bulletin dialog, issued unilaterally by a program when it is has a problem or confronts a decision that it doesn't feel capable of answering on its own. In other words, bulletin dialog boxes are used for error messages, notifiers, and confirmations, three of the most abused components of modern GUI design. With proper design, these dialogs can all but be eliminated. In this chapter, we'll explore how and why.

Errors Are Abused

There is probably no more abused idiom in the GUI world than the error dialog. The proposal that a program doesn't have the right — even the duty — to reject the user's input is so heretical that many practitioners dismiss it summarily. Yet, if we examine this assertion rationally and from the user's — rather than the programmer's — point of view, it is not only possible, but quite reasonable.

Users never *want* error messages. Users want to avoid the *consequences* of making errors, which is very different from saying that they want error messages. It's like saying that people want to abstain from skiing when what they really want to do is avoid breaking their legs. Usability guru Donald Norman (1989) points out that users frequently blame themselves for errors in product design. Just because you aren't getting complaints from your users doesn't mean that they are happy getting error messages.

Why We Have So Many Error Messages

The first computers were undersized, underpowered, and expensive, and didn't lend themselves easily to software sensitivity. The operators of these machines were white-lab-coated scientists who were sympathetic to the needs of the CPU and weren't offended when handed an error message. They knew how hard the computer was working. They didn't mind getting a core dump, a bomb, an "Abort, Retry, Fail?" or the infamous "FU" message (File Unavailable). This is how the tradition of software treating people like CPUs began. Ever since the early days of computing, programmers have accepted that the proper way for software to interact with humans was to demand input and to complain when the human failed to achieve the same perfection level as the CPU.

Examples of this approach exist wherever software demands that the user do things its way instead of the software adapting to the needs of the human. Nowhere is it more prevalent, though, than in the omnipresence of error messages.

What's Wrong with Error Messages

Error messages, as blocking modal bulletins (see Chapter 30), must stop the proceedings with a modal dialog box. Most user interface designers — being programmers — imagine that their error message boxes are alerting the user to serious problems. This is a widespread misconception. Most error message boxes are informing the user of the inability of the program to work flexibly. You can see an example of this in Figure 30-6. Most error message boxes seem to the user like an admission of real stupidity on the program's part. In other words, to most users, error message boxes are seen not just as the program stopping the proceedings but, in clear violation of the axiom presented in Chapter 10: *Don't stop the proceedings with idiocy*. We can significantly improve the quality of our interfaces by eliminating error message boxes.

DESIGN TIP   Error message boxes stop the proceedings with idiocy.

People hate error messages

Humans have emotions and feelings: Computers don't. When one chunk of code rejects the input of another, the sending code doesn't care; it doesn't scowl, get hurt, or seek counseling. Humans, on the other hand, get angry when they are flatly told they are idiots.

When users see an error message box, it is as if another person has told them that they are stupid. Users hate this (see Figure 33-1). Despite the inevitable user reaction, most programmers just shrug their shoulders and put error message boxes in anyway. They don't know how else to create reliable software.

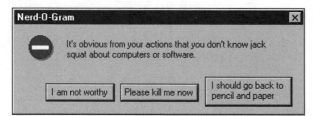

Figure 33-1: No matter how nicely your error messages are phrased, this is how they will be interpreted.

Many programmers and user interface designers labor under the misconception that people either like or need to be told when they are wrong. This assumption is false in several ways. The assumption that people like to know when they are wrong ignores human nature. Many people become very upset when they are informed of their mistakes and would rather not know that they did something wrong. Many people don't like to hear that they are wrong from anybody but themselves. Others are only willing to hear it from a spouse or close friend. Very few wish to hear about it from a machine. You may call it denial, but it is true, and users will blame the messenger before they blame themselves.

The assumption that users *need* to know when they are wrong is similarly false. How important is it for you to know that you requested an invalid type size? Most programs can make a reasonable substitution.

We consider it very impolite to tell people when they have committed some social *faux pas*. Telling someone they have a bit of lettuce sticking to their teeth or that their fly is open is equally embarrassing for both parties. Sensitive people look for ways to bring the problem to the attention of the victim without letting others notice. Yet programmers assume that a big, bold box in the middle of the screen that stops all the action and emits a bold "beep" is the appropriate way to behave.

Whose mistake is it, anyway?

Conventional wisdom says that error messages tell the user when he has made some mistake. Actually, most error bulletins report to the user when the *program* gets confused. Users make far fewer substantive mistakes than imagined. Typical "errors" consist of the user inadvertently entering an out-of-bounds number, or entering a space where the computer doesn't allow it. When the user enters something unintelligible by the computer's standards, whose fault is it? Is it the user's fault for not knowing how to use the program properly, or is it the fault of the program for not making the choices and effects clearer?

Information that is entered in an unfamiliar sequence is usually considered an error by software, but people don't have this difficulty with unfamiliar sequences. Humans know how to wait, to bide their time until the story is complete. Software usually jumps to the erroneous conclusion that out-of-sequence input means wrong input and issues the evil error message box.

When, for example, the user creates an invoice for an invalid customer number, most programs reject the entry. They stop the proceedings with the idiocy that the user must make the customer number valid *right now*. Alternatively, the program could accept the transaction with the expectation that a valid customer number will eventually be entered. It could, for example, make a special notation to itself indicating what it lacks. The program then watches to make sure the user enters the necessary information to make that customer number valid before the end of the session, or even the end of the month book closing. This is the way most humans work. They don't usually enter "bad" codes. Rather, they enter codes in a sequence that the software isn't prepared to accept.

If the human forgets to fully explain things to the computer, it can, after some reasonable delay, provide more insistent signals to the user. At day's or week's end, the program can move irreconcilable transactions into a suspense account. The program doesn't have to bring the proceedings to a halt with an error message. After all, the program will remember the transactions so they can be tracked down and fixed. This is the way it worked in manual systems, so why can't computerized systems do at least this much? Why stop the entire process just because something is missing? As long as the user remains well informed throughout that some accounts still need tidying, there shouldn't be a problem. The trick is to inform without stopping the proceedings. We'll discuss this idea more in Chapter 34.

If the program were a human assistant and it staged a sit-down strike in the middle of the accounting department because we handed it an incomplete form, we'd be pretty upset. If we were the bosses, we'd consider finding a replacement for this anal-retentive, petty, sanctimonious clerk. Just take the form, we'd say, and figure out the missing information. The authors have used Rolodex programs that demand you enter an area code with a phone number even though the person's address has already been entered. It doesn't take a lot of intelligence to make a reasonable guess at the area code. If you enter a new name with an address in Menlo Park, the program can reliably assume that their area code is 650 by looking at the other 25 people in your database who also live in Menlo Park and have 650 as their area code. Sure, if you enter a new address for, say, Boise, Idaho, the program might be stumped. But how tough is it to access a directory on the Web, or even keep a list of the 1,000 biggest cities in America along with their area codes?

Programmers may now protest: "The program might be wrong. It can't be sure. Some cities have more than one area code. It can't make that assumption without approval of the user!" Not so.

If we asked a human assistant to enter a client's phone contact information into our Rolodex, and neglected to mention the area code, he would accept it anyway, expecting that the area code would arrive before its absence was critical. Alternatively, he could look the address up in a directory. Let's say that the client is in Los Angeles so the directory is ambiguous: The area code could be either 213 or 310. If our human assistant rushed into the office in a panic shouting "Stop what you're doing! This client's area code is ambiguous!" we'd be sorely tempted to fire him and hire somebody with a greater-than-room-temperature IQ. Why should software be any different? A human might write 213/310? into the area code field in this case. The next time we call that client, we'll have to determine which area code is correct, but in the meantime, life can go on.

Again, squeals of protest: "But the area code field is only big enough for three digits! I can't fit 213/310? into it!" Gee, that's too bad. You mean that rendering the user interface of your program in terms of the underlying implementation model — a rigidly fixed field width — forces you to reject natural human behavior in favor of obnoxious, computer-like inflexibility supplemented with demeaning error messages? Not to put too fine a point on this, but error message boxes come from a failure of the program to behave reasonably, not from any failure of the user.

User interface is not only skin deep.

This example illustrates another important observation about user interface design. It is *not* only skin deep. Problems that aren't solved in the design are pushed through the system until they fall into the lap of the user. There are a variety of ways to handle the exceptional situations that arise in interaction with software—and a creative designer or programmer can probably think of a half-dozen or so off the top of her head—but most programmers just don't try. They are compromised by their schedule and their preferences, so they tend to envision the world in the terms of perfect CPU behavior rather than in the terms of imperfect human behavior.

Error messages don't work

There is a final irony to error messages: *They don't prevent the user from making errors.* We imagine that the user is staying out of trouble because our trusty error messages keep them straight, but this is a delusion. What error messages really do is prevent the *program* from getting into trouble. In most software, the error messages stand like sentries where the program is most sensitive, not where the user is most vulnerable, setting into concrete the idea that the program is more important than the user. Users get into plenty of trouble with our software, regardless of the quantity or quality of the error messages in it. All an error message can do is keep me from entering letters in a numeric field—it does nothing to protect me from entering the wrong numbers—which is a much more difficult design task.

Eliminating Error Messages

We can't eliminate error messages by simply discarding the code that shows the actual error message dialog box and letting the program crash if a problem arises. Instead, we need to rewrite the programs so they are no longer susceptible to the problem. We must replace the error-message with a kinder, gentler, more robust software that prevents error conditions from arising, rather than having the program merely complain when things aren't going precisely the way it wants. Like vaccinating it against a disease, we make the program immune to the problem, and then we can toss the message that reports it. To eliminate the error message, we must first eliminate the possibility of the user making the error. Instead of assuming error messages are normal, we need to think of them as abnormal solutions to rare problems—as surgery instead of aspirin. We need to treat them as an idiom of last resort.

Every good programmer knows that if module A hands invalid data to module B, module B should clearly and immediately reject the input with a suitable error indicator. Not doing this would be a great failure in the design of the interface between the modules. But human users are not modules of code. Not only should software not reject the input with an error message, but the software designer must also reevaluate the entire concept of what "invalid data" is. When it comes from a human, the software must assume that the input is correct, simply because the human is more important than the code. Instead of software rejecting input, it must work harder to understand and reconcile confusing input. The program may understand the state of things inside the computer, but only the user understands the state of things in the real world. Ultimately, the real world is more relevant and important than what the computer thinks.

Making errors impossible

Making it impossible for the user to make errors is the best way to eliminate error messages. By using bounded gizmos for all data entry, users are prevented from ever being able to enter bad numbers. Instead of forcing a user to key in his selection, present him with a list of possible selections from which to choose. Instead of making the user type in a state code, for example, let him choose from a list of valid state codes or even from a picture of a map. In other words, make it impossible for the user to enter a bad state.

Make errors as impossible as possible.

Another excellent way to eliminate error messages is to make the program smart enough that it no longer needs to make unnecessary demands. Many error messages say things like "Invalid input. User must type xxxx." Why can't the program, if it knows what the user must type, just enter xxxx by itself and save the user the tongue-lashing? Instead of demanding that the user find a file on a disk, introducing the chance that the user will select the wrong file, have the program remember which files it has accessed in the past and allow a selection from that list. Another example is designing a system that gets the date from the internal clock instead of asking for input from the user.

Undoubtedly, all these solutions will cause more work for programmers. However, it is the programmer's job to satisfy the user and not vice versa. If the programmer thinks of the user as just another input device, it is easy to forget the proper pecking order in the world of software design.

Users of computers aren't sympathetic to the difficulties faced by programmers. They don't see the technical rationale behind an error message box. All they see is the unwillingness of the program to deal with things in a human way. They see all error messages as some variant of the one shown in Figure 33-2.

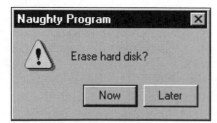

Figure 33-2: This is how most users perceive error message dialog boxes. They see them as Kafkaesque interrogations with each successive choice leading to a yet blacker pit of retribution and regret.

One of the problems with error messages is that they are usually *post facto* reports of failure. They say, "Bad things just happened, and all *you* can do is acknowledge the catastrophe." Such reports are not helpful. And these dialog boxes always come with an OK button, requiring the user to be an accessory to the crime. These error message boxes are reminiscent of the scene in old war movies where an ill-fated soldier steps on a landmine while advancing across the rice paddy. He and his buddies clearly hear the click of the mine's triggering mechanism and the realization comes over the soldier that although he's safe now, as soon as he removes his foot from the mine, it will explode, taking some large and useful part of his body with it. Users get this feeling when they see most error message boxes, and they wish they were thousands of miles away, back in the real world.

Positive feedback

One of the reasons why software is so hard to learn is that it so rarely gives positive feedback. People learn better from positive feedback than they do from negative feedback. People want to use their software correctly and effectively, and they are motivated to learn how to make the software work for them. They don't need to be slapped on the wrist when they fail. They do need to be rewarded, or at least acknowledged, when they succeed. They will feel better about themselves if they get approval, and that good feeling will be reflected back to the product.

Advocates of negative feedback can cite numerous examples of its effectiveness in guiding people's behavior. This evidence is true, but almost universally, the context of effective punitive feedback is getting people to refrain from doing things they want to do but shouldn't: Things like not driving over 55 mph, not cheating on their spouses, and not fudging their income taxes. But when it comes to *helping* people do what they want to do, positive feedback is best. Imagine a hired ski instructor who yells at you, or a restaurant host who loudly announces to other patrons that your credit card was rejected.

AXIOM

Users get humiliated when software tells them they failed.

Keep in mind that we are talking about the drawbacks of negative feedback from a computer. Negative feedback by another person, although unpleasant, can be justified in certain circumstances. One can say that the drill sergeant is at least training you in how to save your life in combat, and the imperious professor is at least preparing you for the vicissitudes of the real world. But to be given negative feedback by software — any software — is an insult. The drill sergeant and professor are at least human and have *bona fide* experience and merit. But to be told by software that you have failed is humiliating and degrading. Users, quite justifiably, hate to be humiliated and degraded. There is nothing that takes place inside a computer that is so important that it can justify humiliating or degrading a human user. We only resort to negative feedback out of habit.

AXIOM

No crisis inside a computer is worth humiliating a human.

Aren't There Exceptions?

As our technological powers grow, the portability and flexibility of our computer hardware grows, too. Modern computers can be connected to and disconnected from networks and peripherals without having to first power down. This means that it is now normal for hardware to appear and disappear ad hoc. Printers, modems, and file servers can come and go like the tides. With the development of wireless networks such as WiFi and Bluetooth, our computers can connect and disconnect from networks frequently, easily, and soon, transparently. Is it an error if you print a document, only to find that no printers are connected? Is it an error if the file you are editing normally resides on a drive that is no longer reachable? Is it an error if your communications modem is no longer plugged into the computer?

The deeper we wade into the Internet ocean, the more this conundrum of here-today-gone-tomorrow becomes commonplace. The Internet can easily be thought of as an infinite hard disk — one that is out of the control of any one person, company, or system administrator. A valid pointer today can be meaningless tomorrow. Is this an error?

None of these occurrences should be considered as errors. If you try to print something and there is no printer available, your program should just spool the print image to disk. The print manager program should quietly indicate when it reconnects to a printer while it has unprinted documents in its queue. This should be an aspect of normal, everyday computing. It is not an error. The same is true for files. If you open a file on the server and begin editing it, then wander out to a restaurant for lunch, taking your notebook with you, the program should see that the normal home of the file is no longer available and do something intelligent. It could use the built-in WiFi card to log onto the server remotely, or it could just save any changes you make locally, synchronizing with the version on the server when you return to the office from lunch. In any case, it is normal behavior, not an error.

Almost all error message boxes can be eliminated. If you examine the situation from the point of view that the error message box must be eliminated and that everything else is subject to change in search of this objective, you will see the truth of this assertion. You will also be surprised by how little else needs to be changed in order to achieve it. In those rare cases where the rest of the program must be altered too much, that is the time to compromise with the real world and go ahead and use an error message box. But the community of programmers needs to start thinking of this compromise as an admission of failure on the its part: that it has resorted to a low blow, a cheap shot, like a GOTO statement in its code.

Still, we *would* like to see an error message on our screen if the printer catches on fire. Error messages should be reserved for just such real emergencies.

Improving Error Messages: The Last Resort

Now we will discuss some methods of improving the quality of error message boxes, if indeed we are stuck using them. Use these recommendations only as a last resort, when you run out of other options.

A well-formed error message box should conform to these requirements:

✓ Be polite

✓ Be illuminating

✓ Be helpful

Never forget that an error message box is the program reporting on *its* failure to do its job, and it is interrupting the user to do this. The error message box must be unfailingly polite. It must never even hint that the user caused this problem, because that is simply not true from the user's perspective. The customer is always right.

The user may indeed have entered some goofy data, but the program is in no position to argue and blame. It should do its best to deliver to the user what he asked for, no matter how silly. Above all, the program must not, when the user finally discovers his silliness, say, in effect, "Well, you did something really stupid, and now you can't recover. Too bad." It is the program's responsibility to protect the user even when he takes inappropriate action. This may seem draconian, but it certainly isn't the user's responsibility to protect the computer from taking inappropriate action.

The error message box must illuminate the problem for the user. This means that it must give him the kind of information he needs to make an appropriate determination to solve the program's problem. It needs to make clear the scope of the problem, what the alternatives are, what the program will do as a default, and what information was lost, if any. The program should treat this as a confession, telling the user everything.

It is wrong, however, for the program to just dump the problem on the user's lap and wipe its hands of the matter. It should directly offer to implement at least one suggested solution right there on the error message box. It should offer buttons that will take care of the problem in various ways. If a printer is missing, the message box should offer options for deferring the printout or selecting another printer. If the database is hopelessly trashed and useless, it should offer to rebuild it to a working state, including telling the user how long that process will take and what side effects it will cause.

Figure 33-3 shows an example of a reasonable error message. Notice that it is polite, illuminating, and helpful. It doesn't even hint that the user's behavior is anything but impeccable.

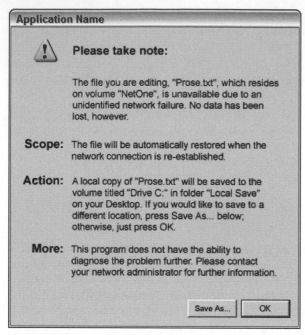

Application Name

⚠ **Please take note:**

The file you are editing, "Prose.txt", which resides on volume "NetOne", is unavailable due to an unidentified network failure. No data has been lost, however.

Scope: The file will be automatically restored when the network connection is re-established.

Action: A local copy of "Prose.txt" will be saved to the volume titled "Drive C:" in folder "Local Save" on your Desktop. If you would like to save to a different location, press Save As... below; otherwise, just press OK.

More: This program does not have the ability to diagnose the problem further. Please contact your network administrator for further information.

[Save As...] [OK]

Figure 33-3: Just as there is rarely a good reason to ever use a GOTO statement in your code, there is rarely a good reason to ever issue an error message box. However, just as programmers occasionally compromise with one or two convenient GOTOs, they might occasionally issue an error message. In that case, your error message should look something like this one. It politely illuminates the problem for the user, offering him help in extricating the program from its dilemma. This error bulletin has four sections (labeled "Please take note, Scope, Action, and More) that clearly help the user understand the options available and why he might choose each. The program is intelligent enough not to lose the file just because the volume became unavailable. The dialog offers an alternative action to the user by way of the Save As . . . button.

The End of Errors

Error message boxes validate the idea that the computer is the final arbiter of correctness, and the user is there just to serve its digital majesty. This attitude influences both programmers and users. It tempts programmers to make bad judgments in design and to take shortcuts in implementation. These compromises necessitate the use of yet more error messages. Also, users are anesthetized by error messages so they cannot visualize the possibility of error-free computing.

Chapter 34

Notifying and Confirming

We dealt with error dialogs in the previous chapter. In this chapter, we discuss alert dialogs (also known as notifiers) and confirmation dialogs, as well as the structure of these interactions, the underlying assumptions about them, and how they, too, can be eliminated in most cases.

Alerts and Confirmations

Like error dialogs, alerts and confirmations stop the proceedings with idiocy, but they do not report malfunctions. An alert notifies the user of the program's action, whereas a confirmation also gives the user the authority to override that action. These dialogs pop up like weeds in most programs and should, much like error dialogs, be eliminated in favor of more useful idioms.

Alerts: Announcing the obvious

When a program exercises authority that it feels uncomfortable with, it takes steps to inform the user of its actions. This is called an alert. Alerts violate the axiom: *A dialog box is another room; you should have a good reason to go there* (see Chapter 25). Even if an alert is justified (it seldom is), why go into another room to do it? If the program took some indefensible action, it should confess to it in the same place where the action occurred and not in a separate dialog box.

Conceptually, a program should either have the courage of its convictions or it should not take action without the user's direct guidance. If the program, for example, saves the user's file to disk automatically, it should have the confidence to know that it is doing the right thing. It should provide a means for the user to find out what the program did, but it doesn't have to stop the proceedings with idiocy to do so. If the program really isn't sure that it should save the file, it shouldn't save the file, but should leave that operation up to the user.

Conversely, if the user directs the program to do something — dragging a file to the trash can, for example — it doesn't need to stop the proceedings with idiocy to announce that the user just dragged a file to the trashcan. The program should ensure that there is adequate visual feedback regarding the action; and if the user has actually made the gesture in error, the program should silently offer him a robust Undo facility so he can backtrack.

The rationale for alerts is that they inform the user. This is a desirable objective, but not at the expense of smooth interaction flow.

The alert shown in Figure 34-1 is an example of how alerts are more trouble than help. The Find dialog (the one underneath) already forces the user to click Cancel when the search is completed, but the superimposed alert box makes it a brace of flow-breaking buttons: First the OK to the alert, then the Cancel to the Find. If the information aspect of the alert were built into the main Find dialog, the user's burden would be reduced to half. That is good economy for user interface designers.

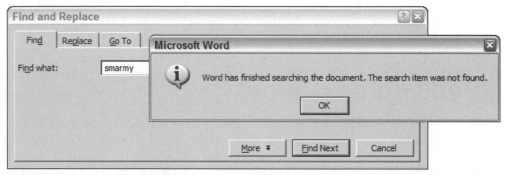

Figure 34-1: Here is a typical alert dialog box. It is unnecessary, inappropriate, and stops the proceedings with idiocy. The Find dialog in Word has finished searching the document. Is reporting that fact a different facility of Word? If not, why does it use a different dialog? It's like having to go into the dining room to use a fork and the kitchen to use a spoon. The "information" icon is a sure tip-off to clumsy interface design. Yes, software must constantly and effusively report its status to the user. But proceedings-stopping alert dialogs are an inappropriate mechanism.

Alerts are so numerous because they are so easy to create. Most languages offer some form of message box facility in a single line of code. Conversely, building an animated status display into the face of a program might require a thousand or more lines of code. Programmers cannot be expected to make the right choice in this situation. They have a conflict of interest, so designers must be sure to specify precisely where information is reported on the surface of an application. The designers must then follow up to be sure that the design wasn't compromised for the sake of rapid coding. Imagine if the contractor on a building site decided unilaterally not to add a bathroom because it was just too much trouble to deal with the plumbing. There would be consequences.

Software needs to keep the user informed of its actions. It should have visual indicators built into its main screen to make such status information available to the user, should he desire it. Launching an alert to announce an unrequested action is bad enough. Putting up an alert to announce a *requested* action is pathological.

Software needs to be flexible and forgiving, but it doesn't need to be fawning and obsequious. The dialog box shown in Figure 34-2 is a classic example of an alert that should be put out of our misery. It announces that it added the entry to our phone book. This occurs immediately after we told it to add the entry to our phone book, which happened milliseconds after we physically added the entry to what appears to be our phone book. It stops the proceedings to announce the obvious.

It's as though the program wants approval for how hard it worked: "See, dear, I've cleaned your room for you. Don't you love me?" If a person interacted with us like this, we'd suggest that they seek counseling.

Figure 34-2: This dialog, from Delrina WinFax Lite, is unnecessarily obsequious. We add an entry to our phone book, and are promptly stopped in our tracks by this important message. Do we really need the program to waste our time elaborating the obvious?

Confirmations

When a program does not feel confident about its actions, it often asks the user for approval with a dialog box. This is called a **confirmation**, like the one shown in Figure 34-3. Sometimes the confirmation is offered because the program second-guesses one of the user's actions. Sometimes the program feels that is not competent to make a decision it faces and uses a confirmation to give the user the choice instead. Confirmations always come from the program and never from the user. This means that they are a reflection of the implementation model and are not representative of the user's goals.

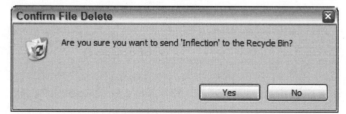

Figure 34-3: Every time we delete a file in Windows, we get this confirmation dialog box asking if we're sure. Yes, we're sure. We're always sure. And if we're wrong, we expect Windows to be able to recover the file for us. Windows lives up to that expectation with its Recycle Bin. So why does it still issue the confirmation message? When a confirmation box is issued routinely, users get used to approving it routinely. So when it eventually reports an impending disaster to the user, he goes ahead and approves it anyway, because it is routine. Do your users a favor and never create another confirmation dialog box.

As discussed in Chapter 2, revealing the implementation model to users is a sure-fire way to create an inferior user interface. This means that confirmation messages are inappropriate. Confirmations get written into software when the programmer arrives at an impasse in her coding. Typically, she realizes that she is about to direct the program to take some bold action and feels unsure about taking responsibility for it. Sometimes the bold action is based on some condition the program detects, but more often it is based on a command the user issues. Typically, the confirmation will be launched after the user issues a command that is either irrecoverable or whose results might cause undue alarm.

Confirmations pass the buck to the user. The user trusts the program to do its job, and the program should both do it and ensure that it does it right. The proper solution is to make the action easily reversible and provide enough modeless feedback so that the user is not taken off-guard.

As a program's code grows during development, programmers detect numerous situations where they don't feel that they can resolve issues adequately. Programmers will unilaterally insert buck-passing code in these places, almost without noticing it. This tendency needs to be closely watched, because programmers have been known to insert dialog boxes into the code even after the user interface specification has been agreed upon. Programmers often don't consider confirmation dialogs to be part of the user interface, but they are.

THE DIALOG THAT CRIED, "WOLF!"

Confirmations illustrate an interesting quirk of human behavior: They only work when they are unexpected. That doesn't sound remarkable until you examine it in context. If confirmations are offered in routine places, the user quickly becomes inured to them and routinely dismisses them without a glance. The dismissing of confirmations thus becomes as routine as the issuing of them. If, at some point, a truly unexpected and dangerous situation arises — one that *should* be brought to the user's attention — he will, by rote, dismiss the confirmation, exactly because it has become routine. Like the fable of the boy who cried, "Wolf," when there is finally real danger, the confirmation box won't work because it cried too many times when there was no danger.

For confirmation dialog boxes to work, they must only appear when the user will almost definitely click the No or Cancel button, and they should *never* appear when the user is likely to click the Yes or OK button. Seen from this perspective, they look rather pointless, don't they?

The confirmation dialog box shown in Figure 34-4 is a classic. The irony of the confirmation dialog box in the figure is that it is hard to determine which styles to delete and which to keep. If the confirmation box appeared whenever we attempted to delete a style that was currently *in use*, it would at least then be helpful because the confirmation would be less routine. But why not instead put an icon next to the names of styles that are in use and dispense with the confirmation? The interface then provides more pertinent status information, so one can make a more informed decision about what to delete.

ELIMINATING CONFIRMATIONS

Three axioms tell us how to eliminate confirmation dialog boxes. The best way is to obey the simple dictum: Do, don't ask. When you design your software, go ahead and give it the force of its convictions (backed up by user research, as discussed in Chapter 4). Users will respect its brevity and its confidence.

AXIOM

Do, don't ask.

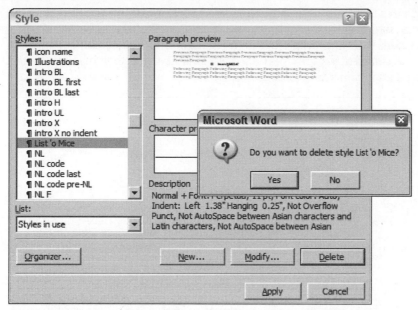

Figure 34-4: If you click the Delete button in the Style dialog box in Word, you get this confirmation box. Most people will click Yes, by rote, regardless of whether that's what they really mean to do. In the Style dialog, you might occasionally inadvertently delete a style you really want to keep. This confirmation, however, doesn't do much to prevent that, nor does it allow recovery. If its appearance were based on some criteria other than simply asking for a deletion, there is some faint chance that it would be useful. Promise that you won't ever create one of these, please?

Of course, if the program confidently does something that the user doesn't like, it must have the capability to reverse the operation. Every aspect of the program's action must be undoable. Instead of asking in advance with a confirmation dialog box, on those rare occasions when the program's actions were out of turn, let the user issue the Stop-and-Undo command.

Most situations that we currently consider unprotectable by Undo can actually be protected fairly well. Deleting or overwriting a file is a good example. The file can be moved to a suspense directory where it is kept for a month or so before it is physically deleted. The Recycle Bin in Windows uses this strategy, except for the part about automatically erasing files after a month: Users still have to manually take out the garbage.

AXIOM

Make all actions reversible.

Even better than acting in haste and forcing the user to rescue the program with Undo, you can make sure that the program offers the user adequate information so that the he never purposely issues a command that leads to an inappropriate action (or never omits a necessary command). The program should use sufficiently rich visual feedback so that the user is constantly kept informed, the same way the instruments on dashboards keep us informed of the state of our cars.

Provide modeless feedback to help users avoid mistakes.

Occasionally, a situation arises that really can't be protected by Undo. Is this a legitimate case for a confirmation dialog box? Not necessarily. A better approach is to provide users with protection the way we give them protection on the freeway: with consistent and clear markings. You can often build excellent, modeless warnings right into the interface. For instance, look at the dialog from Adobe Photoshop in Figure 34-5, telling us that our document is larger than the available print area. Why has the program waited until now to inform us of this fact? What if guides were visible on the page at all times (unless the user hid them) showing the actual printable region? What if those parts of the picture outside the printable area were highlighted when the user moused over the Print butcon in the toolbar? Clear, modeless feedback (see the next section) is the best way to address these problems.

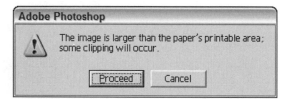

Figure 34-5: This dialog provides too little help too late. What if the program could display the printable region right in the main interface as dotted guides? There's no reason for users to be subjected to dialogs like these.

Much more common than honestly irreversible actions are those actions that are easily reversible but still uselessly protected by routine confirmation boxes. The confirmation in Figure 34-3 is an excellent specimen of this species. There is no reason whatsoever to ask for confirmation of a move to the Recycle Bin. The sole reason that the Recycle Bin exists is to implement an undo facility for deleted files.

Replacing Dialogs: Rich Modeless Feedback

Most computers now in use in the both the home and the office come with high-resolution displays and high-quality audio systems. Yet, very few programs (outside of games) even scratch the surface of using these facilities to provide useful information to the user about the status of the program, the users' tasks, and the system and its peripherals in general. It is as if an entire toolbox is available to express information to users, but programmers have stuck to using the same blunt instrument — the dialog — to communicate information. Needless to say, this means that subtle status information is simply *never* communicated to users at all, because even the most clueless designers know that you don't want dialogs to pop up *constantly*. But constant feedback is exactly what users need. It's simply the channel of communication that needs to be different.

In this section, we'll discuss **rich modeless feedback**, information that can be provided to the user in the main displays of your application, which don't stop the flow of the program or the user, and which can all but eliminate pesky dialogs.

Rich visual modeless feedback

Perhaps the most important type of modeless feedback is **rich visual modeless feedback** (RVMF). This type of feedback is *rich* in terms of giving in-depth information about the status or attributes of a process or object in the current application. It is *visual* in that it makes idiomatic use of pixels on the screen (often dynamically), and it is *modeless* in that this information is always readily displayed, requiring no special action or mode shift on the part of the user to view and make sense of the feedback.

For example, in Windows 2000 or XP, clicking on an object in a file manager window automatically causes details about that object to be displayed on the left-hand side of the file manager window. (In XP, Microsoft ruined this slightly by putting the information at the bottom of a variety of other commands and links. Also, by default, they made the Details area a drawer that you must open, although the program, at least, remembers its state.) Information includes title, type of document, its size, author, date of modification, and even a thumbnail or miniplayer if it is an image or media object. If the object is a disk, it shows a pie chart and legend depicting how much space is used on the disk. Very handy indeed! This interaction is perhaps slightly modal because it requires selection of the object, but the user needs to select objects anyway. This functionality handily eliminates the need for a properties dialog to display this information. Although most of this information is text, it still fits within the idiom. See Figure 34-6 for an example from a Cooper design project.

Here's another example, this time from the Mac: When you download a file from the Internet, the downloading file appears on the desktop as an icon with a small dynamically updating progress bar, indicating visually what percentage has downloaded.

A final example of RVMF is from the computer gaming world: Sid Meier's Civilization. This game provides dozens of examples of RVMF in its main interface, which is a map of the historical world that you, as a leader of an evolving civilization, are trying to build and conquer. Civilization uses RVMF to indicate a half-dozen things about a city, all represented visually. If a city is more advanced, its architecture is more modern. If it is larger, the icon is larger and more embellished. If there is civil unrest, smoke rises from the city. Individual troop and civilian units also show status visually, by way of tiny meters showing unit health and strength. Even the landscape has RVMF: Dotted lines marking spheres of influence shift as units move and cities grow. Terrain changes as roads are laid, forests are cleared, and mountains are mined. Although dialogs exist in the game, much of the information needed to understand what is going on is communicated clearly with no words or dialogs whatsoever.

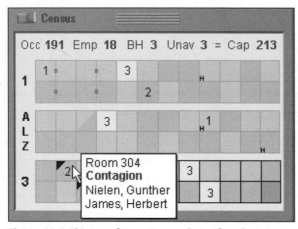

Figure 34-6: This pane from a Cooper design for a long-term healthcare information system is a good example of RVMF. The diagram is a representation of all the rooms in the facility. Color-coding indicates male, female, empty, or mixed-gender rooms; numbers indicate empty beds; tiny boxes between rooms indicate shared bathrooms. Black triangles indicate health issues, and a tiny "H" means a held bed. This RVMF is supplanted with ToolTips, which show room number, names of the occupants of the room, and highlight any important notices about the room or the residents. A numeric summary of rooms, beds, and employees is at the top. This display has a short learning curve. Once mastered, it allows nurses and facility managers to understand their facility's status at a glance.

Imagine if all the objects that had pertinent status information on your desktop or in your application were able to display their status in this manner. Printer icons could show how near they were to completing your print job. Disks and removable media icons could show how full they were. When an object was selected for drag and drop, all the places that could receive it would visually highlight to announce their receptiveness.

Think about the objects in your application, what attributes they have — especially dynamically changing ones — and what kind of status information is critical for your users. Figure out how to create a representation of this. After a user notices and learns this representation, it tells him what is going on at a glance. (There should also be a way to get fully detailed information if the user requests it.) Put this information into your main displays in the form of RVMF and see how many dialogs you can eliminate from routine use!

One important point does need to be made about rich modeless visual feedback. It isn't for beginners. Even if you add ToolTips to textually describe the details of any visual cues you add (which you should), it requires users to discover it in the first place and then realize it's meaningful. RVMF is something that users will discover over time. When they do, they'll think it's amazing; but, in the meantime, they will need the support of menus and dialogs to find what they're looking for. This means that RVMF used to replace alerts and warnings of serious trouble must be extraordinarily clear to users. Make sure that this kind of status is visually emphasized over less critical, more informational RVMF.

Audible feedback

In data-entry environments, clerks sit for hours in front of computer screens entering data. These users may well be examining source documents and typing by touch instead of looking at the screen. If a clerk enters something erroneous, he needs to be informed of it via both auditory and visual feedback. The clerk can then use his sense of hearing to monitor the success of his inputs while he keeps his eyes on the document.

The kind of auditory feedback we're proposing is *not* the same as the beep that accompanies an error message box. In fact, it isn't beep at all. The auditory indicator we propose as feedback for a problem is *silence*. The problem with much current audible feedback is the still-prevalent idea that, rather than positive audible feedback, negative feedback is desirable.

NEGATIVE AUDIBLE FEEDBACK: ANNOUNCING USER FAILURE

People frequently counter the idea of audible feedback with arguments that users don't like it. Users are offended by the sounds that computers make, and they don't like to have their computer beeping at them. This is likely true based on how computer sounds are widely used today — people have been conditioned by these unfortunate facts:

- ✓ Computers have always accompanied error messages with alarming noises.
- ✓ Computer noises have always been loud, monotonous and unpleasant.

Emitting noise when something bad happens is called **negative audible feedback**. On most systems, error message boxes are normally accompanied by loud, shrill, tinny "beeps," and audible feedback has thus become strongly associated them. That beep is a public announcement of the user's failure. It explains to all within earshot that you have done something execrably stupid. It is such a hateful idiom that most software developers now have an unquestioned belief that audible feedback is bad and should never again be considered as a part of interface design. Nothing could be further from the truth. It is the negative aspect of the feedback that presents problems, not the audible aspect.

Negative audible feedback has several things working against it. Because the negative feedback is issued at a time when a problem is discovered, it naturally takes on the characteristics of an alarm. Alarms are designed to be purposefully loud, discordant, and disturbing. They are supposed to wake sound sleepers from their slumbers when their house is on fire and their lives are at stake. They are like insurance because we all hope that they will never be heard. Unfortunately, users are constantly doing things that programs can't handle, so these actions have become part of the normal course of interaction. Alarms have no place in this normal relationship, the same way we don't expect our car alarms to go off whenever we accidentally change lanes without using our turn indicators. Perhaps the most damning aspect of negative audible feedback is the implication that success must be greeted with silence. Humans like to know when they are doing well. They *need* to know when they are doing poorly, but that doesn't mean that they like to hear about it. Negative feedback systems are simply appreciated less than positive feedback systems.

Given the choice of no noise versus noise for negative feedback, people will choose the former. Given the choice of no noise versus unpleasant noises for positive feedback, people will choose based on their personal situation and taste. Given the choice of no noise versus soft and pleasant noises for positive feedback, however, people will choose the feedback. We have never given our users a chance by putting high-quality, positive audible feedback in our programs, so it's no wonder that people associate sound with bad interfaces.

POSITIVE AUDIBLE FEEDBACK

Almost every object and system outside the world of software offers sound to indicate success rather than failure. When we close the door, we know that it is latched when we hear the click, but silence tells us that it is not yet secure. When we converse with someone and they say, "Yes" or "Uh-huh," we know that they have, at least minimally, registered what was said. When they are silent, however, we have reason to believe that something is amiss. When we turn the key in the ignition and get silence, we know we've got a problem. When we flip the switch on the copier and it stays coldly silent instead of humming, we know that we've got trouble. Even most equipment that we consider silent makes some noise: Turning on the stovetop returns a hiss of gas and a gratifying "whoomp" as the pilot ignites the burner. Electric ranges are inherently less friendly and harder to use because they lack that sound — they require indicator lights to tell us of their status.

When success with our tools yields a sound, it is called **positive audible feedback**. Our software tools are mostly silent; all we hear is the quiet click of the keyboard. Hey! That's positive audible feedback. Every time you press a key, you hear a faint but positive sound. Keyboard manufacturers could make perfectly silent keyboards, but they don't because we depend on audible feedback to tell us how we are doing. The feedback doesn't have to be sophisticated — those clicks don't tell us much — but they must be consistent. If we ever detect silence, we know that we have failed to press the key. The true value of positive audible feedback is that its absence is an extremely effective problem indicator.

The effectiveness of positive audible feedback originates in human sensitivity. Nobody likes to be told that they have failed. Error message boxes are negative feedback, telling the user that he has done something wrong. Silence can ensure that the user knows this without actually being told of the failure. It is remarkably effective, because the software doesn't have to insult the user to accomplish its ends.

Our software should give us constant, small, audible cues just like our keyboards. Our programs would be much friendlier and easier to use if they issued barely audible but easily identifiable sounds when user actions are correct. The program could issue an upbeat tone every time the user enters valid input to a field. If the program doesn't understand the input, it would remain silent and the user would be immediately informed of the problem and be able to correct his input without embarrassment or ego-bruising. Whenever the user starts to drag an icon, the computer could issue a low-volume sound reminiscent of sliding as the object is dragged. When it is dragged over pliant areas, an additional percussive tap could indicate this collision. When the user finally releases the mouse button, he is rewarded with a soft, cheerful "plonk" from the speakers for a success or with silence if the drop was not meaningful.

As with visual feedback, computer games tend to excel at positive audio feedback. Mac OS 9 also does a good job with subtle positive audio feedback for activities like documents saves and drag and drop. Of course, the audible feedback must be at the right volume for the situation. Windows and the Mac offer a standard volume control, so one obstacle to beneficial audible feedback has been overcome.

Rich modeless feedback is one of the greatest tools at the disposal of interaction designers. Replacing annoying, useless dialogs with subtle and powerful modeless communication can make the difference between a program users will despise and one they will love. Think of all the ways you might improve your own applications with RVMF and other mechanisms of modeless feedback!

Chapter 35

Other Communication with Users

This Part of the book is about communicating with your users, and we would be remiss if we did not discuss ways of communicating to the user that are not only helpful to them, but which are also helpful to you, as creator or publisher of software, in asserting your brand and identity. In the best circumstances, these communications are not at odds, and this chapter presents recommendations that will enable you to make the most out of both aspects of user communication.

Your Identity on the Desktop

The modern desktop screen is getting quite crowded. A typical user has a half-dozen programs running concurrently, and each program must assert its identity. The user needs to recognize your application when he has relevant work to be done, and you should get the credit you deserve for the program you have created. There are several conventions for asserting identity in software.

Your program's name

By convention, your program's name is spelled out in the title bar of the program's main window. This text value is the program's **title string**, a single text value within the program that is usually owned by the program's main window. Microsoft Windows introduces some complications. Since Windows 95, the title string has played a greater role in the Windows interface. Particularly, the title string is displayed on the program's **launch button** on the taskbar.

The launch buttons on the taskbar automatically reduce their size as more buttons are added, which happens as the number of open programs increases. As the buttons get shorter, their title strings are truncated to fit.

Originally, the title string contained only the name of the application and the company brand name. Here's the rub: If you add your company's name to your program's name, like, say "Microsoft Word," you will find that it only takes seven or eight running programs or open folders to truncate your program's launch-button string to "Microsoft." If you are also running "Microsoft Excel," you will find two adjacent buttons with identical, useless title strings. The differentiating portions of their names — "Word" and "Excel" — are hidden.

The title string has, over the years, acquired another purpose. Many programs use it to display the name of the currently active document. Microsoft's Office Suite programs do this. In Windows 95, Microsoft appended the name of the active document to the right end of the title string, using a hyphen to separate it from the program name. In subsequent releases, Microsoft has reversed that order: The name of the document comes first, which is certainly a more goal-directed choice as far as the user is concerned. The technique isn't a standard; but because Microsoft does it, it is often copied. It makes the title string extremely long, far too long to fit onto a launch button — but ToolTips come to the rescue!

What Microsoft could have done instead was add a new title string to the program's internal data structure. This string would be used only on the launch button (on the Taskbar), leaving the original title string for the window's title bar. This enables the designer and programmer to tailor the launch-button string for its restricted space, while letting the title string languish full-length on the always-roomier title bar.

Your program's icon

The second biggest component of your program's identity is its icon. There are two icons to worry about in Windows: the standard one at 32 pixels square and a miniature one that is 16 pixels square. Mac OS 9 and earlier had a similar arrangement; icons in OS X can theoretically be huge — up to 128x128 pixels. Windows XP also seems to make use of a 64x64 pixel, which makes sense given that screen resolutions today can exceed 1600x1200 pixels.

The 32x32 pixel size is used on the desktop, and the 16x16 pixel icon is used on the title bar, the taskbar, the Explorer, and at other locations in the Windows interface. Because of the increased importance of visual aesthetics in contemporary GUIs, you must pay greater attention to the quality of your program icon. In particular, you want your program's icon to be readily identifiable from a distance — especially the miniature version. The user doesn't necessarily have to be able to recognize it outright — although that would be nice — but he should be able to readily see that it is different from other icons.

Icon design is a craft unto itself, and is more difficult to do well than it may appear. Arguably, Susan Kare's design of the original Macintosh icons set the standard in the industry. Today, many visual interface designers specialize in the design of icons, and any applications will benefit from talent and experience applied to the effort of icon design.

Ancillary Application Windows

Ancillary application windows are windows that are not really part of the application's functionality, but are provided as a matter of convention. These windows are either available only on request or are offered up by the program only once, such as the program's credit screen. Those that are offered unilaterally by the program are erected when the program is used for the *very* first time or each time the program is initiated. All these windows, however, form channels of communication that can both help the user and better communicate your brand.

About boxes

The About box is a single dialog box that — by convention — identifies the program to the user. The About box is also used as the program's credit screen, identifying the people who created it. Ironically, the About box rarely tells the user much about the program. On the Macintosh, the About box can be summoned from the top of the Apple pop-up menu. In Windows, it is almost always found at the bottom of the Help menu.

Microsoft has been consistent with About boxes in its programs, and it has taken a simple approach to its design, as you can see in Figure 35-1. Microsoft uses the About box almost exclusively as a place for identification, a sort of driver's license for software. This is unfortunate, as it is a good place to give the curious user an overview of the program in a way that doesn't intrude on those users who don't need it. It is often, but not always, a good thing to follow in Microsoft's design footsteps. This is one place where diverging from Microsoft can offer a big advantage.

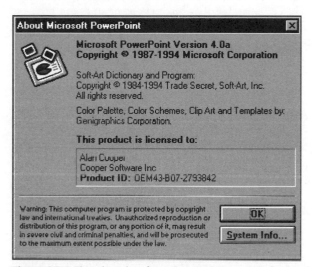

Figure 35-1: This About box from PowerPoint is a typical example of Microsoft's approach. It tells you the exact name and version of the program, states relevant copyrights, issues legal warnings (ugh!), and displays the user's name and company. The program's icon is traditionally shown in the upper-left corner. The problem is, if a friend asked you to tell her about PowerPoint, you probably wouldn't recite the relevant copyrights, but would instead describe to her what the program is *about*. What's wrong with this picture?

The main problem with Microsoft's approach is that the About box doesn't tell the user about the program. In reality, it is an *identification* box. It identifies the program by name and version number. It identifies various copyrights in the program. It identifies the user and the user's company. These are certainly useful functions, but are more useful for Microsoft customer support than for the user.

The desire to make About boxes more useful is clearly strong—otherwise, we wouldn't see memory usage and system-information buttons on them. This is admirable, but, by taking a more goal-directed approach, we can add information to the About box that really *can* help the user. The single most important thing that the About box can convey to the user is the scope of the program. It should tell, in the broadest terms, what the program can and can't do. It should also state succinctly what the program does. Most program authors forget that many users don't have any idea what the InfoMeister 3000 Version 4.0 program actually does. This is the place to gently clue them in.

The About box is also a great place to give the one lesson that might start a new user successfully. For example, if there is one new idiom — like a direct-manipulation method — that is critical to the user interaction, this is a good place to briefly tell him about it. Additionally, the About box can direct the new user to other sources of information that will help him get his bearings in the program.

Because the current design of this facility just presents the program's fine print instead of telling the user *about* the program, it should be called an **Identity box** instead of an About box, and that's how we'll refer to it from this point on. The Identity box identifies the program to the user, and the dialog in Figure 35-1 fulfills this definition admirably. It tells us all the stuff the lawyers require and the tech support people need to know. Clearly, Microsoft has made the decision that an Identity box is important, whereas a true About box is expendable.

As we've seen, the Identity box must offer the basics of identification, including the publisher's name, the program's icons, the program's version number, and the names of its authors. Another item that could profitably be placed here is the publisher's technical support telephone number.

Many software publishers don't identify their programs with sufficient discrimination to tie them to a specific software build. Some vendors even go so far as to issue the same version number to significantly different programs for marketing reasons. But the version number in the Identity — or About — box is mainly used by customer support. A misleading version number will cost the publisher a significant amount of phone-support time just figuring out precisely which version of the program the user has. It doesn't matter what scheme you use, as long as this number is very specific.

An important part of reporting the version number is telling the user which previous version it replaces. Knowing that this is version 3.2 isn't tremendously meaningful. Knowing that version 3.2 fixes bugs in version 3.1 and supersedes all versions 2.*x*, however, *is* useful. Vendors work hard to improve their software, and each version is usually intended to replace some previous version. Smaller, incremental revisions are released to fix bugs but may not entirely replace a predecessor. Similarly, a special version may be shipped that allows compatibility with certain new hardware or software. This should be stated, as well.

If you are going to display an informative version number, it wouldn't hurt to explain the details of the numbering scheme in this box. Most users will ignore it, but it will be appreciated by thousands of corporate IT managers.

Many programs are uniquely identified by their serial numbers. This, of course, is the place to display that number. The user may need to use that number in correspondence with the publisher, or for his own company records, so the program should let the user view it and select it for copying.

The About box (not the Identity box) is absolutely the right place to state the product team's names. The authors firmly believe that credit should be given where credit is due in the design, development, and testing of software. Programmers, designers, managers, and testers all deserve to see their names in lights. Documentation writers sometimes get to put their names in the manual, but the others only have the program itself. The About box is one of the few dialogs that has no functional overlap with the main program, so there is no reason why it can't be oversized. Take the space to mention everyone who contributed. Although some programmers are indifferent to seeing their names on the screen, many programmers are powerfully motivated by it and really appreciate managers who make it happen. What possible reason could there be for *not* naming the smart, hard-working people who built the program?

This last question is directed at Bill Gates (as it was in the first edition in 1995), who has a corporate-wide policy that individual programmers *never* get to put their names in the About boxes of programs. He feels that it would be difficult to know where to draw the line with individuals. But the credits for modern movies are indicative that the entertainment industry, for one, has no such worries. In fact, it is in game software that development credits are most often featured. Perhaps now that Microsoft is heavy into the game business things will change — but don't count on it.

Microsoft's policy is disturbing because its conventions are so widely copied. As a result, its no-programmer–names policy is also widely copied by companies who have no real reason for it other than blindly following Microsoft.

Splash screens

A **splash screen** is a dialog box displayed when a program first loads into memory. Sometimes it may just be the About box or Identity box, displayed automatically, but more often publishers create a separate splash screen that is more engaging and visually exciting.

The splash screen should be placed on the screen as soon as user launches the program, so that he can view it while the bulk of the program loads and prepares itself for running. After a few seconds have passed, it should disappear and the program should go about its business. If, during the splash screen's tenure, the user presses any key or clicks any mouse button, the splash screen should disappear immediately. The program must show the utmost respect for the user's time, even if it is measured in milliseconds.

The splash screen is an excellent opportunity to create a good impression. It can be used to reinforce the idea that your users made a good choice by purchasing your product. It also helps to establish a visual brand by displaying the company logo, the product logo, the product icon, and other appropriate visual symbols.

Splash screens are also excellent tools for directing first-time users to training resources that are not regularly used. If the program has built-in tutorials or configuration options, the splash screen can provide buttons that take the user directly to these facilities (in this case, the splash screen should remain open until manually dismissed).

Because splash screens are going to be seen by first-timers, if you have something to say to them, this is a good place to do it. On the other hand, the message you offer to those first-timers will be annoying to experienced users, so subsequent instances of the splash screen should be more generic. Whatever you say, be clear and terse, not long-winded or cute. An irritating message on the splash screen is like a pebble in your shoe, rapidly creating a sore spot if it isn't removed promptly.

Shareware splash screens

If your program is shareware, the splash screen can be your most important dialog (though not your users'). It is the mechanism whereby you inform users of the terms of use and the appropriate way to pay for your product. Some people refer to shareware splash screens as the **guilt screen**. Of course, this information should also be embedded in the program where the user can request it, but by presenting to users each time the program loads, you can reinforce the concept that the program *should* be paid for. On the other hand, there's a fine line you need to tread lest your sales pitch alienate users. The best approach is to create an excellent product, not to guilt-trip potential customers.

Online help

Online help is just like printed documentation, a reference tool for perpetual intermediates. Ultimately, online help is not important, the way that the user manual of your car is not important. If you find yourself needing the manual, it means that your car is badly designed. The design is what is important.

A complex program with many features and functions should come with a reference document: a place where users who wish to expand their horizons with a product can find definitive answers. This document can be a printed manual or it can be online help. The printed manual is comfortable, browsable, friendly, and can be carried around. The online help is searchable, semi-comfortable, very lightweight, and cheap.

The index

Because you don't read a manual like a novel, the key to a successful and effective reference document is the quality of the tools for finding what you want in it. Essentially, this means the index. A printed manual has an index in the back that you use manually. Online help has an automatic index search facility.

The authors suspect that few online help facilities they've seen were indexed by a professional indexer. However many entries are in your program's index, you could probably double the number. What's more, the index needs to be generated by examining the program and all its features, not by examining the help text. This is not easy, because it demands that a highly skilled indexer be intimately familiar with all the features of the program. It may be easier to rework the interface to improve it than to create a really good index.

The list of index entries is arguably more important than the text of the entries themselves. The user will forgive a poorly written entry with more alacrity than he will forgive a missing entry. The index must have as many synonyms as possible for topics. Prepare for it to be huge. The user who needs to solve a problem will be thinking "How do I turn this cell black?" not "How can I set the *shading* of this cell to 100%?" If the entry is listed under shading, the index fails the user. The more goal-directed your thinking is, the better the index will map to what might possibly pop into the user's head when he is looking for something. One index model that works is the one in *The Joy of Cooking*, Irma S. Rombaur & Marion Rombaur Becker (Bobbs-Merrill, 1962). That index is one of the most complete and robust of any the authors have used.

Shortcuts and overview

One of the features missing from almost every help system is a **shortcuts** option. It is an item in the Help menu which when selected, shows in digest form all the tools and keyboard commands for the program's various features. It is a very necessary component on any online help system because it provides what perpetual intermediates need the most: access to features. They need the tools and commands more than they need detailed instructions.

The other missing ingredient from online help systems is **overview**. Users want to know how the Enter Macro command works, and the help system explains uselessly that it is the facility that lets you enter macros into the system. What we need to know is scope, effect, power, upside, downside, and why we might want to use this facility both in absolute terms and in comparison to similar products from other vendors. @Last Software provides online streaming video tutorials for its architectural sketching application, SketchUp. This is a fantastic approach to overviews, particularly if they are also available on CD-ROM.

Not for beginners

Many help systems assume that their role is to provide assistance to beginners. This is not true. Beginners stay away from the help system because it is generally just as complex as the program. Besides, any program whose basic functioning is too hard to figure out just by experimentation is unacceptable, and no amount of help text will resurrect it. Online help should ignore first-time users and concentrate on those people who are already successfully using the product, but who want to expand their horizons: the perpetual intermediates.

Modeless and interactive help

ToolTips are modeless online help, and they are incredibly effective. Standard help systems, on the other hand, are implemented in a separate program that covers up most of the program for which it is offering help. If you were to ask a human how to perform a task, he would use his finger to point to objects on the screen to augment his explanation. A separate help program that obscures the main program cannot do this. Apple has used an innovative help system that directs the user through a task step by step by highlighting menus and buttons that the user needs to activate in sequence. Though this is not totally modeless, it is interactive and closely integrated with the task the user wants to perform, and not a separate room, like reference help systems.

Wizards

Wizards are an idiom unleashed on the world by Microsoft, and they have rapidly gained popularity among programmers and user interface designers. A wizard attempts to guarantee success in using a feature by stepping the user through a series of dialog boxes. These dialogs parallel a complex procedure that is "normally" used to manage a feature of the program. For example, a wizard helps the user create a presentation in PowerPoint.

Programmers like wizards because they get to treat the user like a peripheral device. Each of the wizard's dialogs asks the user a question or two, and in the end the program performs whatever task was requested. They are a fine example of interrogation tactics on the program's part, and violate the axiom: *Asking questions isn't the same as providing choices* (see Chapter 9).

Wizards are written as step-by-step procedures, rather than as informed conversations between user and program. The user is like the conductor of a robot orchestra, swinging the baton to set the tempo, but otherwise having no influence on the proceedings. In this way, wizards rapidly devolve into exercises in confirmation messaging. The user learns that he merely clicks the Next button on each screen without critically analyzing why.

There is a place for wizards in actions that are very rarely used, such as installation and initial configuration. In the weakly interactive world of HTML, they have also become the standard idiom for almost all transactions on the Web — something that better browser technology will eventually change.

A better way to create a wizard is to make a simple, automatic function that asks no questions of the user but that just goes off and does the job. If it creates a presentation, for example, it should create it, and then let the user have the option, later, using standard tools, to change the presentation. The interrogation tactics of the typical wizard are not friendly, reassuring, or particularly helpful. The wizard often doesn't explain to the user what is going on.

Wizards were purportedly designed to improve user interfaces, but they are, in many cases, having the opposite effect. They are giving programmers license to put raw implementation model interfaces on complex features with the bland assurance that: "We'll make it easy with a wizard." This is all too reminiscent of the standard abdication of responsibility to users: "We'll be sure to document it in the manual."

"Intelligent" agents

Perhaps not much needs to be said about Clippy and his cousins, since even Microsoft has turned against their creation in its marketing of Windows XP (not that it has actually *removed* Clippy from XP, mind you). Clippy is a remnant of research Microsoft did in the creation of BOB, an "intuitive" real-world, metaphor-laden interface remarkably similar to General Magic's Magic Cap interface, discussed briefly in Chapter 20. BOB was populated with anthropomorphic, animated characters that conversed with users to help them accomplish things. It was one of Microsoft's most spectacular interface failures. Clippy is a descendant of these help agents and is every bit as annoying as they were.

A significant issue with "intelligent" animated agents is that by employing animated anthropomorphism, the software is upping the ante on user expectations of the agent's intelligence. If it can't deliver on these expectations, users will quickly become furious, just as they would with a sales clerk in a department store who claims to be an expert on his products, but who, after a few simple questions, proves himself to be clueless.

These constructs soon become cloying and distracting. Users of Microsoft Office are trying to accomplish something, not be entertained by the antics and pratfalls of the help system. Most applications demand more direct, less distracting, and trustworthier means of getting assistance.

Chapter 36

The Installation Process

One more form of software communication deserves comment because it is the first communication your application will have with your customers: the installation process.

Most software development managers are fooled by the unproductive nature of installation programs, so they fail to see them as an opportunity (or a danger). If your installation process is a showcase of effective user interface design, the user will be in a good frame of mind as he begins to use your program in earnest. Conversely, if your installation process is cobbled together as an afterthought, your user will be disinclined to tolerate anything less than perfection in the balance of your product.

The Best Installation Is No Installation

Sometimes the best communication is none at all. Any IT manager worth his salary knows this is true for installation. Installation means maintenance updates. It means people deluging call centers with questions and problems. It means having to undo damage that users inadvertently do while trying to navigate through cumbersome, brain-dead installer interfaces.

Hatred of installation is one of the primary reasons why browser-based enterprise applications written in HTML have become omnipresent in corporate offices. No IT manager in his right mind wants to spend his time dealing with the hassle of endless installs and upgrades. To the IT manager, installation-free software is a godsend. Never mind the fact that browser-based Web applications are slow, interaction-poor, and cause no end of annoyance to users — the fact that they work across platforms and update themselves is a powerful persuasion to IT professionals, most of whom don't have to use the software they purchase.

The irony of the situation is that IT managers and even developers have conflated *browser-based* with *installation-free*. It's entirely possible to create non-browser–based, *Internet-enabled* applications that have all the interaction benefits of full desktop applications, yet have the same zero-install properties as any application you can access via a browser. Microsoft Office applications already support a shade of this in Windows XP through the Automatic Updates feature. It's a small step from there to permitting full automatic installation over the Internet or corporate intranet. Network-savvy applications have never been limited to browser technology, but the ease of cobbling together HTML-based software has done much to help developers overlook this fact. Client-server model applications can be created to provide all the benefits of browser-based software, but also to permit (depending on how much client-side processing the programmers are able to manage) the same richness of interaction that we *used* to expect of applications before HTML lowered all our expectations.

One Damned Thing after Another

Back in the world of manual installs, whether you install software off of a CD-ROM, a file server, or the Internet, the process you go through is basically the same, consisting of two steps. First, the software must be copied or loaded onto your local hard disk. Second, the software generally requires some initial configuration so that both you and it can work smoothly.

Edward Tufte, author of *The Visual Display of Quantitative Information* (Graphics Press, 1983), detests the manual software installation process, calling it "one damned thing after another." It doesn't help the user to achieve his goals; it doesn't help the program to perform its functions.

Most applications now use standard installation shells, like InstallShield on Windows or the Mac Installer. These programs are a significant improvement over the days when vendors created their own from scratch, and users now are now somewhat familiar with these standard formats. But even within these frameworks, little consideration is given to the interaction from a goal-directed point of view. Installation programs thus continue to blindly interrogate the user, force him to make uninformed decisions, and make arrogant assumptions about the way the computer is used.

The most common problems exhibited by installation programs are a microcosm of some of the nastiest software interface design problems in general. Most installation programs exhibit at least several of these design errors:

✓ Demanding responses without informing you of the consequences

✓ Not informing you of the scope of your actions

✓ Asking you questions to which you are unlikely to know the answer

✓ Asking you for answers it can determine for itself

✓ Not doing its homework

✓ Not providing for uninstallation

✓ Ignoring evidence of its previous activity

✓ Abusing system-wide files

✓ Putting files where they don't belong

✓ Overwriting shared files

✓ Not offering you any information about the program

✓ Confusing installation with configuration

✓ Demanding your active participation

We'll now discuss each of these transgressions in detail.

Demanding responses without informing you of the consequences

Without a doubt, this is the most common of all the transgressions of installation programs. The installation program puts up a dialog box that looks something like the one in Figure 36-1.

Figure 36-1: This is a typical installation program's first dialog box. As when you play a video game, you have only your wits to guide you. Is a full installation too much for me to handle? Am I smart enough to customize this program? Does it make me a wimp if I choose a minimum installation?

The program starts right off by asking you a question that will clearly have global consequences, is probably not reversible, and the effects of which you don't understand. Some more advanced installation programs, notably those from Microsoft and Apple, make a reasonable disclosure of the effects of your choice on how much disk space will be consumed. However, you are still guessing about the meaning of the choice. What the user needs to know is *exactly* what functionality he will be sacrificing if he chooses a minimal installation. It isn't enough to merely know the disk space implications, he must know the usefulness implications of his choice, too.

Some versions of this question deal with system-level resources such as communications ports, video drivers, and the like. These are particularly vexing because the wrong choice can instantly lock up the computer system, crash other programs, lose data, and sometimes even require rebooting the computer from a boot diskette and manually fixing the damage done by the installation program. Although the consequences for making a wrong choice are severe, the user is rarely made aware that this is not the time for a guess — not even an educated guess.

To counter user interactions with this kind of problem, software should practice **informed consent**. The user should only be asked questions whose consequences he understands. In particular, he must understand the consequences to *him*, not just to his computer. If the program offers configuration choices, the user must be well informed about how the various configurations affect the program's capability to help him achieve his goals.

For example, an appropriate way to create an atmosphere of informed consent is to offer an itemized list of the features, expressed in terms of what they do for the user, and which are either included or excluded from the various choices. Additionally, a prose description of the big picture from the user's point of view is necessary. Something like the following would be nice:

> A minimal installation is designed for laptop and notebook computers with available disk space of less than 100 megabytes. The MicroBlitz PIM-Meister will consume about 40% less space than a full installation on your hard disk without sacrificing any critical functions. What you will sacrifice includes: most, but not all, online help text; the tutorial program for beginners; four out of seven Wizards; and, most of the more obscure import and export utilities. If you want the minimal installation but feel that you must have one or more of the excluded facilities, you can easily request the minimal installation with *special options* and add the desired facilities back in. Also, you can always easily change your existing configuration by running the installation program a second time.

First, this statement describes the main reason why the user might want to choose the minimum installation option. Second, it describes, in some detail, exactly what is sacrificed to get it. Third, it informs the user how and why he can override the setting if he wants to. Fourth, it reassures the user by informing him how he can change things at a later time, should his needs change. This is informed consent, and the user will be able to make intelligent choices and feel good about them. Apple's installers are not quite this verbose in all instances but, in general, do a similar job of seeking informed consent.

It's a taboo in programming circles to create verbose programs, but this applies mainly to programming tools for programmers and to frequent program communications. Installation is neither exclusively for programmers nor is it frequent, so don't be afraid to explain installation issues to users at length. Your users will thank you for it.

Not informing you of the scope of your actions

A typical installation program wastes no time on what a programmer considers idle chitchat with the user, but that chitchat is important to dispel the user's uneasiness. Imagine if an appliance repairperson arrived at your house and, without a word to you, started wrenching apart your plumbing and dismantling your refrigerator. You would feel much better if the repairperson gave you the big picture first:

> The compressor on your refrigerator is completely dead because the motor has seized. I will have to replace it completely. I have the replacement motor in my truck and it will take about an hour-and-a-half to make the repair, including recharging the system with coolant in an environmentally friendly way. Your warranty will cover the cost of the parts but not my labor. I charge $45 per hour. The plumbing will need some minor work because the icemaker is directly connected to your pipes. Anytime existing iron-pipe plumbing is disturbed, there is a slight risk of starting leaks elsewhere in the system. I will make every effort to keep the pipes from moving to reduce that chance.

You are now informed of how much time the operation will take, how much money it will cost, and what the risks of failure are. You are aware of the scope of the operation. Wouldn't it be nice, then, if our install program told us something like this:

I am going to install MicroBlitz PIM-Meister on your system. This means copying the program from the distribution CD onto your hard disk, decompressing the files, and then configuring the program for your specific needs. Judging from the speed of your processor, I estimate the entire process will take about 7 minutes for a full install and as little as 2 minutes for a minimal installation. The program will occupy between 45 and 124 megabytes on your hard disk, depending on which configuration you choose. In other words, it will take between 2.7 and 4.7 percent of your total capacity. Your disk is currently less than half full, so the available space will be reduced by 4.6 to 8 percent.

I will place all parts of the program and all associated information in a special directory that I will create new. You will be given the choice of where that directory is located and what it will be called, but you can also just keep the default of PIM-Meister. By necessity, I must make at least one entry the Windows Registry. This entry will be restricted to a single parameter line that will have absolutely no effect on the operating system or any other program, even if you later decide to uninstall PIM-Meister. If you select the check box, I will also create an icon for launching PIM-Meister in the Programs folder of the Start menu.

This installation program maintains an internal status log so that, in the unlikely event it crashes, it will know how to pick up the pieces intelligently if you merely rerun it.

You can uninstall this entire program at any time simply by pushing the Uninstall button. The program will be removed from your system, leaving as few traces as possible, but leaving any data files you created with PIM-Meister untouched. If desired, you may request the space-saver uninstall, which means the program is removed but all your personal settings are saved. A subsequent execution of the install program can put PIM-Meister back exactly the way it was.

This monologue is prolix, and experienced users won't want to read it. But new users will find it very reassuring to hear what the implications of the installation process are. They will be happy to understand the scope of the process they are about to undergo.

Asking you questions to which you are unlikely to know the answer

An installation program may ask the user to specify the desired serial port. Most users don't know what a serial port is or how many they have, let alone which one is best for this program. Game and sound card installation programs frequently ask users about available interrupt vectors, a question that can't be adequately answered by most computer engineers, let alone a typical home user. Business software installations can be expected to ask about network support and the type of mouse in use. Most users have no idea what to answers to such questions.

It's a bad idea to ask users questions that they can't answer. First, it doesn't get the program the answer it needs. Instead, it gets a guess. Second, it makes the user feel bad — he just proved himself inadequate in front of a machine. How embarrassing!

If the program needs to know about serial ports, it should test them and see which ones are occupied. It can search in various configuration files for clues as to how they are currently being used. It can even ask the user to move the mouse and look for activity on the various ports to eliminate that possibility.

If the program needs to know about interrupts, it can examine them or listen to them to determine whether or not they are in use or available. The installation program can make a very good guess (and probably a much more reliable guess than the user's) about what interrupts are available by deduction and by looking at system information files and the registry, if there is one. By recording its findings and then telling the user it is about to do something that might lock up the system, the user can close all other running programs and be prepared for the program's error. If one occurs, he can then rerun the program, and it will find its earlier notes. It now knows what *didn't* work, which should be enough to enable it to deduce the correct choice. Don't force this choice onto a user who cannot be expected to know the answer.

Asking you for answers it can determine for itself

This is a common problem in all software, but the authors of installation programs are deservedly notorious for it. The program asks you what type of display device your computer has when it can easily check the system for the answer to that question. The program asks you how much disk space is available when it can interrogate the file system to get the exact answer. The program asks you where another program or file is located when it can easily search the disk to find it. The program asks you which hard disk you want to install on when you only have one hard disk.

The computer's job is to remove unnecessary trivia from our lives. Questions like these only add more pointless trivia and are offensive. Most information needed by any program can and should be determined without asking the human user.

Not doing its homework

One of the most obnoxious ways an installation program can misbehave is not being aware of its own existence. The installation program blithely installs an identical copy of a program that already exists on the disk. Or, it doesn't know that it is being used just to change a configuration, so it copies files from CD to hard disk that are already there.

The designer of an installation program should write a list of all the environmental givens that the program needs, including such things as RAM, video, disks, microphones, joysticks, mice, modems, or speakers. The installation program should then check that these assumptions are indeed true before proceeding. The program should perform a common-sense examination of the system before it starts working. It should look for previous copies of itself; it should look for other, required software; it should check for fatal or dangerous conditions like lack of memory or disk storage.

Most intermediate users make some attempt to configure and personalize their sovereign applications to make them more convenient. It is very frustrating when an upgrade for that application ignores those personalized settings. Many business executives get a new computer every year or so and then find that they must painstakingly recreate their settings by hand for each major application they use. A good installation program should know how to import these settings from other computers, as well as other versions.

Not providing a means for uninstallation

Although many software vendors seem unaware of the fact, customers often want to remove software from their computers. A customer might remove software because it is needed on another computer, because it is not needed on this computer any longer, because it takes up space needed by other more important programs, or because the user has decided that the program is not good enough to keep. Every vendor should provide a tool for removing its program, just as it provides a tool for installing it. The uninstaller should be just as robust and full-featured as the installation tool. It should follow the principle of informed consent, telling the user what the scope and consequences of the program are. The Add/Remove Programs control panel and the Program Registry provide this functionality on Windows, provided that the application has properly installed itself. Program installers also can provide this functionality, as shown in Figure 36-2. Apple, for some reason, has never understood the importance of uninstallation: It is still an onerous manual process on the Mac.

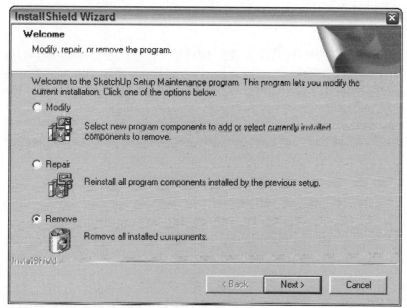

Figure 36-2: A good installer is aware of the fact that its software has already been installed and offers maintenance and removal functionality if it is launched under those circumstances. This installer could be a bit more helpful in providing useful information up front, like which files are installed and where, how much space is taken up by them, and how much is available. (This information is shown on later screens, but users need it early to make informed decisions.) Mostly, however, this installer has the right idea. InstallShield's wizard at least gives users the ability to retrace their steps or cancel if they decide they don't want to go through with an install or uninstall.

It is reasonable to assume that the user does not hate your program but is removing it because he merely wishes to regain some disk space by removing a no-longer–needed tutorial or some subsystems that have proven unnecessary. Uninstallers should give the user the ability to remove individual pieces of her program without affecting the main function of the application. The user may also wish to move the application to a different hard disk or to a different place on the same hard disk. The uninstaller should know how to make the transfer so that all references are updated and the program works smoothly despite the transition.

If a user needs to temporarily reclaim the space on disk occupied by the program (say he needs additional free space for a two-week business trip), the uninstaller should make this easy to do. It should remove all the big, space-consuming files but leave behind all the directories, configuration files, and entries in other system files. When the user returns from his business trip, the installation program can be used to put the big files back on his disk without overwriting or forgetting about his personal settings. The program would be reinstalled just as before.

Some programs such as networking, peripheral drivers, and printer-sharing software are not only installed on the hard disk, but are also activated by files at boot time, thus becoming a permanent part of the operating system. Software like this makes a special demand on its uninstaller. The uninstaller must be able to disable the program without physically removing it. If the user wants to, for example, run a game program that demands absolutely all available memory, the user should be able to disable the network drivers for the duration without physically removing them from disk.

Ignoring evidence of its previous activity

Installation programs should keep a log of their activities on the user's hard disk. This log tells the program what it has done before and what it is doing now. If the program learns anything from a previous execution, either by testing the system or by asking the user, it should be recorded here so reprocessing can be speeded up and the user doesn't have to be bothered again. The installation facility for Windows has this SmartRecovery feature. Installers should also know when their software has already been installed and offer uninstallation and update options if invoked under those circumstances (see Figure 36-2).

Abusing system-wide files

Windows applications should limit themselves to no more than two or three entries in system-wide facilities (such as the Windows Registry). If the program needs more information, it should create its own initialization file(s) and store the information there.

Putting files where they don't belong

The application should operate in its own directory. If it requires multiple directories, these should be made subordinate to the program's main directory. The program should never put files in other directories, unless required by the particular platform (for example, extensions on the Mac). Otherwise, if the user were to install a new version of the OS, the application's files might be deleted in the process. The resultant malfunctioning and confusion would be very unpleasant and completely avoidable.

Application programs often ignore the possibility that the operating system will be reinstalled or upgraded. The program is often inextricably dependent on entries in system files that, when the OS is reinstalled, will disappear. Most programs then require a complete reinstallation, including redundantly recopying the files.

Although all a program's supporting files should be placed in that one directory subtree, this is not necessarily true for the *data* files it creates. It is good practice to keep program files and data files separate, and the install program should begin with that assumption. Current practice in many Windows programs is to put all data files in the My Documents folder. The intent here is good, but when dozens of programs all put their data files in this one directory, chaos ensues. It would be much better if a program's data files were stored — by default — in a named subdirectory under My Documents instead.

Overwriting shared files

Many applications use runtime libraries of some sort. Visual Basic applications, in particular, use the VBRUN dynamic link library (DLL) and usually a few VBX or OCX DLLs for each of the installable controls used in the program. When a program installs the DLL or VBX, it may overwrite one with the same name already installed by another program. For example, if program A uses a commercially available VBX grid control named GRID.VBX and program B, from another vendor, uses a proprietary VBX grid control that is also named GRID.VBX, the installation process will cause problems. Even though the names are the same, the functionality and interfaces may be quite different. When program B is installed, it must ensure that it doesn't just overwrite the GRID.VBX file by assuming that it is an earlier version of itself. If it makes this assumption, program A will crash violently and mysteriously. The ensuing confusion will leave the user perplexed and angry.

A similar problem arises if two different programs use different versions of the same DLL. Imagine that both programs A and B use version 1.0 of a DLL called DATBASE.DLL. The user then purchases the newest release of program B that includes the newest release of DATBASE.DLL, version 2.0. The installation program for B likely assumes that it can blithely replace version 1.0 of DATBASE.DLL with version 2.0. But program A won't know how to deal with the new version of the library, and a crash is unavoidable. Crashes like this are particularly insidious because the user could install the new release of program B in January and not get around to running program A until June. He will have no clue as to what caused the problem. If anything, he will blame the completely innocent program A. Because this problem can affect any vendor, even though the vendor is not strictly at fault, it means that you must take defensive action to keep the problem from happening to you.

The problem can be avoided by following two simple guidelines. First, use names that aren't likely to collide with those from other vendors. Instead of naming a library GRID, try using XGRID, GRD or even G7QL. The user will likely never see these names, so they don't have to be mnemonic. Second, append a unique number indicating the version of the library. Name the first release XGRD1, the second release XGRD2, and so on.

Not offering you any information about the program

The installation program should keep the user informed at all times of what it is doing and what remains to be done. Contemporary installation programs put a dialog box on the screen with a small completion meter showing the amount done expressed as a percentage. Most of these meters are frustrating and confusing, however, because they don't adequately explain what they are representing. Does the meter show the progress for this file? This section? This CD? The entire installation? Is it expressed as time or as bytes copied? Users have become used to being burned by meaningless meters, and they know enough to ignore them. They know that the installation program is just being obscure.

Confusing installation with configuration

Because most programs need some rudimentary configuration before they can run well, the installation procedure usually includes a configuration step. This is reasonable, but the configuration process may need to be performed more than once, whereas the copying of files from the CD is usually a one-time operation. Installation designers frequently forget this and intertwine the two processes so that a reconfiguration cannot be done without an unnecessary copy operation. The installation program should be smart enough to recognize that it is being rerun and offer the user the option of just reconfiguring the existing instance of the program without incurring the entire overhead of recopying.

Demanding your active participation

Some installation programs make unreasonable demands on your time and attention. They require that you actively participate in the installation process, even though you would just as soon delegate the job to the software. The WordPerfect for Windows installation program, for example, interspersed questions for the user with the actual copying of the program onto the hard disk. In other words, it asked you a question, then installed a few files, then asked you another question, and then installed a few more files.

Thus you are forced to consciously baby-sit the entire process. Installers should ask all relevant questions at the beginning and then let the user get up and walk away while the installation proceeds. It should also issue an audible alert if a new CD needs to be inserted, releasing you from having to watch the screen.

Far and away, the best install process is one that demands no user involvement whatsoever.

Part VIII

Designing Beyond the Desktop

Chapter 37

Designing for the Web

The advent of the World Wide Web has been both a boon and a curse for interaction designers. On the one hand, the popularity of the Web has also popularized — even more so than Apple Computer and the Macintosh — the idea that ease of use is important. For perhaps the first time since the invention of graphical user interfaces, corporate decision makers have begun to understand and adopt the language of user-centered design. On the other hand, the limitations of Web interactivity, which are a natural result of its historical evolution, have set interaction design back at least ten years. Designers are only now beginning to take advantage of the many desktop interaction idioms (such as drag and drop) on the Web that were old news years before the first Web sites went online.

This chapter does not attempt to address the many detailed aspects of Web design that have been covered in great detail in many other volumes. Steve Krug's *Don't Make Me Think!* (2000), Louis Rosenfeld's and Peter Morville's *Information Architecture* (1998), and Jeffrey Veen's *The Art and Science of Web Design* (2000), in particular, cover the essential elements of Web design in clear, straightforward language. (Jakob Nielsen's *useit.com* Web site is also an excellent resource.) Instead, this chapter seeks to relate the process discussed in Part I to the world of Web design and to provide some perspectives on Web design from an interaction design standpoint. It focuses, in particular, on the emergence of a new breed of *Web applications* — transactional, Internet-enabled programs that exhibit complex behaviors and which must, by necessity, break the barriers of the browser.

The Good News and the Bad News

Although the popularity of the Web has obviously been good news for interaction designers and usability practitioners, whose fortunes rose (and then fell) along with the industry hype, it has also proven to be a two-edged sword as far as the evolution of design in the Web medium is concerned. In the early days of the Web boom, the industry was flooded with fresh art school graduates and traditional graphic designers, who saw the Web as an exciting and lucrative opportunity to create compelling communication through new forms of interactive visual expression. Certainly, great opportunity existed in the early days of the Web, when the biggest challenges involved working around the tight constraints of the medium (created originally to share scientific papers and their attached diagrams) to produce documents with even a rudimentary level of visual and typographic organization. Big demand and small supply led to reliance on less-skilled practitioners who designed by guesswork, making it up as they went along.

Even then, graphic designers recognized that a new design issue resulted from the support of hyperlinks in documents: the design, organization, and structuring of *content*. **Findability**, a term coined by Louis Rosenfeld (1998), is an apt way to describe the design issue in a nutshell. A new breed of designers, the information architects, built a discipline and practice to address the largely non-visual design problems of logical structure and flow of content. Information architecture, which addresses difficult design problems surrounding content, is still growing and evolving as a discipline.

In the early days of the Web, graphic-design expertise was sufficient to handle obvious Web design issues of the time. As use of the Web increased and simple Web sites transformed into large clearing-houses of information, information architecture emerged to handle the problems of navigating and organizing content on pages. But while technical restrictions have begun to relax with better browser and markup technology, the focus of most Web designers remains on visual expression and problems of content access. Only scant attention has been paid to the third distinguishing element of software that was, by historical accident, a latecomer to the Web world: the interactive *behavior* that permits people to accomplish complex transactions.

Today's Web technologies blur many of the distinctions between desktop and Web applications, but many old-school Web designers are still living in the world of the mid-1990s, when visual and information design were the most significant elements of the Web experience. With the rise of Web-delivered applications and services for markets (such as B2B e-commerce and CRM supported by technologies such as Microsoft's .NET and Macromedia's Flash MX), the design of Internet-enabled software grows less and less distinct from the design of desktop applications. Although Web browsers and browser-based content are here to stay for the foreseeable future, Web-based applications must increasingly be designed with the primary concern of appropriate behavior both within the browser and outside it. The tyranny of the browser is at an end. Sophisticated, Internet-enabled applications powered by .NET and other new technologies offer people a better, richer, and more productive user experience. Of course, good behavior doesn't come free with better technology: A lot of design work must be done. The first step is to recognize some of the many design myths that have arisen about the Web and put them in context.

Common Myths about Web Design

The hype that surrounded the Web and its concomitant New Economy led to many popular myths concerning the design of Web content and Web-based applications. We can forgive this kind of mythology, which is typical of most popular technical innovations. When commercial and industrial use of electricity became a reality at the end of the nineteenth century, it was commonly believed to have miraculous powers not only to transform business and society, but also to cure almost any conceivable ailment by "restoring the life force." Like electricity, the Web has transformed our society to some degree, even in the relatively short time span since its introduction. However, it took 50 years for our use of electricity to mature, and it will doubtless take as many years for us to realize the full benefits and socioeconomic ramifications of the Web.

Some of the most common myths about Web design follow. These myths have found their way into business and technical organizations, and are — to some degree or other — taken at face value by management, marketing, engineering, and sometimes even Web designers themselves. The sooner you can disabuse your organization of these myths, the better.

✓ **Myth #1: The Web inherently makes things easier to use.** In the early days of the Web, all that was possible in terms of interaction was single-clicking on text or images to move to a new page (or another part of the same page). This incredible dearth of interaction severely limited what was possible to implement on the Web, with the side effect of making behavior extremely simple. In this sense, the early Web was easy to use, although poor structure and layout could still easily ruin the user experience. However, with the subsequent addition of features like frames, forms, scripted actions, and embedded applets, these apparent gains in ease of use have vanished. What designers are left with now are systems that *appear* rich enough to be desktop applications. For lingering technical reasons, however, they are capable neither of supporting all the idioms we have come to expect of desktop applications nor of providing the smooth flow and rich feedback that desktop software allows. Dealing with these issues remains a substantial challenge for Web-design practitioners.

✓ **Myth #2: Designing for the Web is new and different.** For the many print-oriented graphic designers who entered the Web-design world in the mid-1990s, the Web was certainly new and different. It was more constrained, more fluid, and it introduced a new (to them) concept: hyperlinking of documents. However, little of this was news to software designers, GUI programmers, and usability professionals, who had been concerned with nearly identical problems in the design of software interfaces for many years. One area that *was* new was the emphasis on *content* over form and behavior, and thus the discipline of information architecture quickly grew to address that gap in knowledge. However, as the cutting edge of design for the Web has shifted from presentation to transaction, *behavior* is once again the dominant concern, although content must remain quite important as well. The process of design for the Web is not really different from the design of software applications, although the requirements of content and certain technical limitations affect the direction that the design solution ultimately takes.

✓ **Myth #3: Web design is about HTML, layout, and typography.** Since the beginning of the Web, there has been an unfortunate terminology problem in Web-design circles. Print and graphic designers, moving to the Web, brought with them a media-focused perspective on design. Traditional art and design schools focus considerable attention on mastery of media, and rightly so. However, this media-oriented way of thinking about design applies best to design problems that have little or no complex structure, no *architecture* to worry about. Jumping directly to the crafting of individual pages short-circuits the important *planning* phase that information architects soon recognized was required for Web sites more complex than a handful of pages. Again, this mirrors the experience of designers in the software-application world, where planning and prototyping is the primary *design* activity and where *implementation* is, subsequently, performed by programmers. Because Web implementation has historically been relatively easy at the front end, it has often been lumped together with the design process. For many graphic designers, who were recruited for Web design in the boom times, the design of a graphic image also means its implementation. However, to produce superior solutions, most commercial Web sites today require a greater division of labor between design/planning and implementation.

✓ **Myth #4: Web design is just about the front end.** As we have hoped to show in other sections of this book, design concerns the whole of the product or service — not just what it does, but what it is and what goals it serves. This is no different for the Web; the design of the user's experience, her interaction with and perception of the system, implies that the system must be considered as a whole: how form, content, and behavior are presented by the front end, and what those behaviors must imply at the back end. Web design is concerned with visual design, information design, and interaction design, in near equal parts. The latter two, in particular, can have significant ramifications for the design of the back end of a transactional system.

✓ **Myth #5: Web design is about browsers.** Although the majority of Web applications currently run inside of browsers, change is already in the air. Internet-enabled software applications have existed for a long time, and with the advent of technologies like .NET, the number of Internet-enabled programs existing outside of browsers will rapidly expand. Besides desktop applications, device-based applications that incorporate wireless connectivity are already beginning to gain popularity as products like the Handspring Treo become available. Web-enabled software of any variety promises to deliver on the same kind of rich information and media access the Web provides without the constraints of browser-based interfaces. It is up to interaction designers and the product team to decide what platform is the most appropriate for a new product or service: browser or standalone application. Browsers work reasonably well for *browsing*. Complex transactions are better handled by more sophisticated interaction models with richer idioms at their disposal.

✓ **Myth #6: Web design is about Web pages.** Before the popularity of e-commerce, Web design was very much about page design. Of course, even then, it was also about overall site structure, logical flow, and navigation. The view of Web sites as hierarchies (and other-directed graphs) of reasonably static pages persists today, and this notion is reinforced by a body of work published about the discipline of information architecture. Clearly, there is still a place today for thinking about informational Web sites from the perspective of the page. This paradigm is, at the same time, fundamentally at odds with the way most highly-transactional sites are generated — dynamically from information retrieved from databases in real time. As front-end Web technology gets more sophisticated interaction capability, it makes less and less sense to treat dynamically generated *screens* as pages. Highly transactional Web applications are best considered as what they really are: client-server applications. Breaking out of the constraints of page-oriented thinking allows designers to better address the real goals and needs of users of transactional Web applications.

✓ **Myth #7: The Web and the Internet are synonymous.** Early Web technologies (HTTP and HTML, in particular) were designed for transferring and formatting ASCII text and the occasional binary image in an asynchronous, request-driven manner. Web browsers and servers remain well suited to these kinds of operations, but not as well suited to transferring large amounts of heterogeneous data in a synchronous or streaming fashion. The Internet is a much more diverse network than the browser-accessible Web. Distributed applications that use Internet protocols (IP, TCP) can be much more flexible and powerful than browser-based Web applications.

✓ **Myth #8: Web applications are easier and faster to build than native desktop applications.** HTML allows for fast prototyping and some information-oriented Web sites have simple behavior that permits rapid construction. However, a transactional Web application with complex behavior entails the same kind of engineering challenge as the development of native code, and inevitably it needs to be approached using a similarly robust design and development methodology.

Web Sites versus Web Applications

Web browsers were originally conceived of as a means of sharing and linking documents without the need for cumbersome protocols and file transfer tools such as FTP, Gopher, and Archie. Few people anticipated the popularity of the Web — at initially, for both personal communication and community-building and, a bit later, for commercial communication and services. Thus Web protocols have grown from rather humble beginnings, and the relatively low level of interactivity supported by both browsers and these protocols is an artifact of the limited original purposes for which the Web was conceived.

Web sites

In this chapter, we refer to **Web sites** as information-centric services on the Web whose level of interaction primarily involves searching and following links. Most Web sites consist either of static pages or of complete articles or documents served up by a database. Web sites, as described, can easily be conceived of as sets of pages or documents organized sequentially, hierarchically, or in some other directed graph, with a navigation model to take users from one page to another, as well as a search facility to provide more goal-directed location of specific documents. Plenty of Web sites exist out there, in the form of personal sites, corporate marketing and support sites, and information-centric intranets. In Web sites, the dominant design concerns are the content, the organization (information hierarchy), and clarity. The behavior consists of little more than a coherent navigational schema (not to make light of this; getting navigation right is critical for Web site ease of use) and proper use of affordance and idiom to telegraph to users which elements are active.

Web applications

Web applications, on the other hand, are heavily transactional in nature. Most (if not all) screens are served up dynamically, and different information and forms appearing on the screen simultaneously may come from several different databases. Some regions of the screen may also be occupied by applets delivering data in real time, or allowing real-time manipulation of data on the client side. Web applications may live inside a browser, or they may run as standalone applications. Because the nature of Web applications is transactional, behavior rather than content becomes the primary concern. This said, the two must actually be considered hand-in-hand, because for most Web applications — e-commerce sites like Amazon.com, for example — the content drives the transaction. However, as we have seen with many e-commerce applications, even if the content (the merchandise) is presented well and there is a demand for it, if the *transaction* remains difficult, unsatisfying, or worrisome, users will abandon their efforts. The world of e-commerce is full of shopping carts abandoned by potential customers as soon as they saw the 800-pound gorilla at the checkout counter.

Web applications exist in many other domains than e-commerce. Enterprise resource planning and customer-relationship management systems like those offered by SAP, Oracle, and Siebel have moved to Web platforms in recent years. Many financial planning, online banking, and personal information management systems are available in Web version, their advantage being that they are accessible to users from any computer (or even PDA) with an Internet connection.

Enterprise and other specialized Web applications can be presented to users like desktop applications that happen to run inside a browser window, with little penalty as long as the interactions are carefully designed to reflect engineering constraints. For the time being, commerce sites located on the Internet must more closely resemble traditional Web sites because some portions of these sites may well consist of mostly static, informational pages.

TRANSIENT POSTURE WEB APPLICATIONS

Web applications, much like desktop applications, can have sovereign or transient posture. **Transient posture Web applications** typically take the form of interactive applets embedded inside of standard HTML Web pages. A good example of such a transient Web application is MSN Money Deluxe Portfolio Manager, an interactive stock-tracking tool available on Microsoft's MSN Web site. Transient Web applications are most often utilities, used occasionally to frequently, but which are not sovereign applications that users spend hours at a time in front of. Transient Web applications should follow the same guidelines as transient desktop applications (see Chapter 8), as well as these additional guidelines:

✓ **Transient Web applications should clearly telegraph their functionality.** Because users of Web sites are accustomed to limited interactivity, and transient Web applications are embedded in such a context, take extra care needs to make affordances obvious and to supply hints, if necessary, in the form of brief instructions designed integrally into the application.

✓ **Transient Web applications must be simple, direct, and to the point.** Transient, embedded Web applications are no place to allow scope creep. Make sure that your utility is doing only the minimum necessary to successfully meet user goals.

✓ **Transient Web applications should fit into the user's mental models and flow in the context of the rest of the Web site.** You should develop your transient application paying close attention to user mental models and workflow, not only in the context of their domain, but also in the context of Web site use. If your application can't be implemented in line with other content, don't make the link to your utility seem like an advertisement. Users are conditioned to ignore anything resembling a banner or inline ad, especially animations.

✓ **Carefully consider the problem of access to user data.** Because most transient Web applications can't, for technical reasons, save user data at the client side, users may need to sign in to retrieve or manipulate their data. Similarly, you must ask users to manually save data they have entered. These operations should be presented as seamlessly and straightforwardly as possible.

E-COMMERCE WEB APPLICATIONS

E-commerce represents a special case when considering transactional site posture. The use of e-commerce sites is definitely a transient activity for most users; they come to the site, do a widely variable amount of research (depending on the individual and context) on purchase items, and then either purchase or leave empty-handed, not returning for days. E-commerce sites are interesting because they combine the informational elements of a Web site (in the form of an online catalog) with the elements of a business transaction. In many cases, the Web site is also taking the place of a human sales clerk, with all the implications of brand identity and the value proposition surrounding customer service that this might entail. E-commerce transactions must be carefully designed because users can easily be dissuaded from an online purchase if the process is the least bit onerous or confusing.

E-commerce sites such as Amazon.com have incorporated many application-like features into their sites, while retaining a standard Web-page appearance. Some of these features include providing links to recently viewed items in a session and a semi-persistent shopping cart showing subtotals (but unfortunately, no estimated tax/shipping charges yet). These types of features, which capture and reflect the user's context, and thus ease and enrich the online-shopping experience, provide compelling reasons for users to return for future purchases.

The bottom line for an e-commerce site is its checkout process, which is (not coincidentally) the same part of the site that ends up frustrating and confusing the largest percentage of users. Designers should make use of principles of transient application posture when creating checkout interfaces. Simple input, clear affordances and instructions, clear visual feedback, an obvious flow from start to finish of the process, and a clear means for the user to correct mistakes are all critical to the success of e-commerce transactions and user satisfaction.

SOVEREIGN POSTURE WEB APPLICATIONS

Sovereign posture Web applications should and do strive to be nearly indistinguishable from their desktop cousins. A good example of such a Web application is the Microsoft's Outlook Web Access (OWA) client, which seeks to replicate as much as possible the look and feel of the desktop version, but from inside the browser. As Figure 37-1 shows, OWA replicates most of Outlook's interface within the constraints of browser technology and dial-up bandwidth constraints.

Unlike the design of page-oriented Web sites, the design of sovereign Web applications is best approached as if these applications are desktop applications. Designers also need a clear understanding of the technical limitations of the medium and what can reasonably be accomplished on time and budget by the development organization. Like sovereign desktop applications, sovereign Web applications should be full-screen applications, densely populated with controls and data objects, and they should make use of specialized panes or other screen regions to group-related functions and objects. Users should have the feeling that they are in an environment, not that they are navigating from page to page or place to place. Redrawing and re-rendering of information should be minimized (as opposed to the behavior on Web sites, where almost any action requires a full redraw).

The benefit of treating sovereign Web applications as desktop applications rather than as collections of Web pages is that it allows designers to break out of the constraints of page-oriented models of browser interaction to better address the complex behaviors that these client-server applications require. Web sites are effective places to get information you need, just as elevators are effective places to get to a particular floor in a building. But you don't try to do actual work in elevators; similarly, users are not served by forcing them to attempt to do real, transactional work using page-based Web sites accessed through a browser.

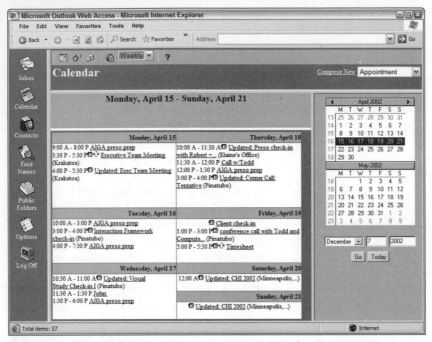

Figure 37-1: Microsoft Outlook Web Access, a good example of a sovereign Web application running in a browser. In the case of OWA, use of a browser as a container makes perfect sense because the purpose of the product is to allow access to Outlook from a computer with an Internet connection. Enterprise applications for which this need is not important or practical for users may consider using Internet-enabled technologies outside the browser. These might better support the rich interactivity and client-side processing and storage that are difficult or impossible to support with browser-based applications. Designers of browser-based sovereign Web applications should also consider hiding the standard browser controls. Use of the browser's Back and Forward buttons can produce unpredictable results in Web applications, and eliminating them from the user's view helps reinforce the mental model of an application versus a Web page. Creating a link on the user's desktop or the browser's Links toolbar can help solve the problem of initial access.

BROWSER-BASED VERSUS INTERNET-ENABLED APPLICATIONS

There are two possible approaches to creating sovereign Web applications. The first is to create a browser-based application that, in essence, takes over the browser window, hiding all browser controls and providing rich interaction within the browser-content area. The technologies used in the window can be a combination of HTML, DHTML, JavaScript, Flash, and Java applets, as best fits the circumstance. This approach gets you some layout and rendering for free, but also constrains the interaction to what is supported by the browser. It also creates compatibility headaches if multiple browser platforms need to be supported because each browser has its individual quirks that must be taken into account. This makes a lowest-common–denominator approach a tempting engineering solution, even if it isn't a good solution from the user's perspective. (This lowest-common–denominator approach is *not* always necessary, as we will discuss later.) Browser-based applications also encourage the idea of limiting the interface to a single primary window because browsers lack any real support for independent child windows (such as modeless dialogs).

The second approach for sovereign Web applications is to abandon the browser entirely and, instead, create a non-browser–based, *Internet-enabled* application. An Internet-enabled application is a desktop application that is Web-aware and makes use of technologies like Flash, Java, ActiveX, TCP/IP, or Microsoft .Net, along with or in place of traditional desktop GUI libraries. By taking the application outside the browser, you can provide rich, clean, sophisticated interactions without losing the ability to access data on the Web. You can improve interactions, not only by more robust GUI support and lack of collision with browser controls, but also because Internet-enabled applications are not restricted to the thin-client model of the browser. The client can save program state and data in volume, allowing the program to remember and react to user actions, store frequently used information, and provide all the other interaction benefits of sovereign desktop applications.

Not sure which approach to take? Here are some pointers:

✓ If access from any computer (with an Internet connection) is a feature required by your personas, a browser-based application is appropriate.

✓ If your customers are standardized on a specific browser (especially IE 5 or greater) and/or plug-in, it becomes much easier to create a rich experience with a browser-based application.

✓ Often the chief reason for considering a browser-based approach is ease of installation and maintenance. However, Internet-enabled applications (Microsoft Windows XP and RealNetworks' RealOne Player are two examples) are perfectly capable of updating themselves over the Web. The key is in designing this process to be as transparent as possible to the user.

✓ Browser-based applications are not easily capable of automatically saving data, or storing data on the client system. If your application's design demands these behaviors, an Internet-enabled desktop application is preferable. Supporting local data storage also means that servers are hit less often, improving application response time considerably.

✓ Personas and scenarios are key techniques that help push the boundaries of the constraints imposed by Web technology. By modeling your users and stepping them through their work contexts to determine their needs, you gain greater insight into which technical approach best suits your users' and your customers' situations.

INTRANETS, EXTRANETS, AND THE INTERNET

As discussed in Chapter 8, the appropriate behavior of Web sites and applications is heavily dependent on the context of their use. One primary factor that influences this context is whether the site is designed for consumer Internet use or for use within the enterprise.

As mentioned earlier in this chapter, informational and e-commerce sites need to maintain a design that balances sovereign and transient elements. These sites should display information at a density appropriate to a sovereign application. The primary navigational elements and transactional elements, however, should maintain the simplicity and clarity of a transient application that is infrequently used and whose behaviors and controls the user does not necessarily remember from session to session.

On the other hand, enterprise-oriented software that accesses corporate intranet or e-business information and transactions can take a more definitely sovereign posture. Users of these applications are likely to be frequent and long-term users who quickly become perpetual intermediates. Information and function density can be increased to better make use of full-screen real estate. If the enterprise in question standardizes on browser or other Internet-enabled application technologies, it can better take advantage of rich, visual, modeless feedback and other GUI idioms.

One exception to this rosy interaction picture is extranet design: Because it is more difficult to anticipate the configuration of your customers' customers, design of extranets must either resort to an Internet-style design approach or a full Internet-enabled application approach that skirts the issue of browser compatibility entirely. Because many customers have been taught that browser-based access is desirable (which, as we discussed, is true only in some circumstances), the latter can be, at least for now, a tough sell.

Here are a few further design tips that will help you to create satisfying Web applications for intranets, extranets, and the Internet:

✓ Internet Web sites and applications must almost always serve multiple primary personas, which typically fall into two categories: people who are regular visitors and people who are new or one-time visitors. Hence, there is always a tension between sovereign and transient posture in sites and applications created for broad Internet access. The balance depends on the precise domain and context of the service. It can be established through the research and modeling techniques outlined in Part I. Clear, consistent navigation and well-designed search help considerably.

✓ Because browser-based applications require hits to the server to load data, try to design your application to download related data in batch when the user selects some portion of it. You must be careful to balance the tension between optimizing the amount of data downloaded at a time and the response time of the system during the batch downloads. Testing will likely be required to determine the size of an acceptable (from a response-time standpoint) chunk of data.

✓ Be careful to use language on the site that matches user mental models, not implementation models or hackneyed language from the old days of the Web. Buttons with titles like Submit are not only demeaning, they are also not informative.

✓ When designing for browsers, be aware that users will often have multiple browser windows open at a time. Try to keep all the interaction limited to a single window.

✓ Because you can't guarantee (server side) automatic save of data in browser-based applications, you need to have users do so manually. The more your application resembles a desktop application, the more awkward this may seem to users. Therefore, you must try to smoothly integrate such manual saves into the flow of the application in a way that is not at odds with user mental models.

WEB APPLICATIONS AND VISUAL DESIGN

Because of the Web's history, in which many commercial Web sites began as marketing vehicles, a high value is placed on the messaging component of the Web. For Web applications, however, this market messaging needs to be executed primarily through the interaction and behavior of the system, which should reflect the brand value. There may be a temptation to use rich visuals in Web applications, but for the most part this results in slower load times and distraction from the real purpose of the application: to meet end goals of the users. Clean, simple color palettes and clear typography are much more important than visual sizzle in Web applications. Fancy graphics are not only distracting, but users have been well trained to ignore anything that seems like an advertisement or marketing ploy on the Web.

During the course of the design process, interaction designers and visual designers need to collaborate closely to effectively communicate the behavior and function of Web sites and Web applications using visual language that works within the context of the brand. Similarly, information architects and designers need to collaborate closely with interaction designers to match content with behavior.

IT TAKES BOTH DESIGN AND ENGINEERING EFFORT

One final caveat is in order before your organization embarks on a Web application: To successfully execute a sovereign Web application requires seasoned, professional programmers and software engineers — at both the front end and the back end — who can not only tackle the engineering issues with aplomb, but who also understand and support a rigorous design and engineering process. Web *sites* can be built quickly and relatively simply; Web and Internet-enabled *applications* require great attention to software architecture, as well as information architecture and interaction design. Be wary of any haphazard attempts to design or engineer a complex Web application. Doing so is asking for trouble, just as it would be for any other kind of software application.

Although Web applications are far more complex both interaction-wise and engineering-wise than page-oriented Web sites, the value they bring to users trying to do real work on the Web or through the Internet is worth the sweat. Web applications and Web services, powered by technologies like .NET, are the future of the Web. As with any complex software, the risks are considerable; but methods and principles of interaction design that are well planned and executed mitigate that risk and provide users with a higher level of online experience.

Chapter 38

Designing for Embedded Systems

The previous chapter dealt with issues concerning the Web as a design platform. **Embedded systems**, or software systems integrated into devices that we may not naturally think of as computers (such as cellular phones, TVs, microwave ovens, automobile dashboards, cameras, bank machines, and laboratory equipment), have their own sets of opportunities and limitations. You must be aware of these when you are designing embedded systems. Without careful design, adding digital smarts to devices and appliances results in products that behave more like desktop computers than the products that users expect and require them to be (Cooper, 1999).

This chapter discusses some common types of embedded systems and presents some useful principles for approaching these devices from the standpoint of goal-directed design.

General Design Principles

Embedded systems, although they may include software interactions, have some unique concerns that differentiate them from desktop systems. When designing any embedded system, be it smart appliance, kiosk system, or handheld device, keep in mind these basic principles:

- ✓ Don't think of your product as a computer.
- ✓ Integrate your hardware and software design.
- ✓ Context drives the design.
- ✓ Use modes judiciously.
- ✓ Limit the scope.
- ✓ Balance navigation with display density.
- ✓ Customize for your platform.

We discuss each of these principles in more detail in the following sections.

Don't think of your product as a computer

Perhaps the most critical principle to follow while designing an embedded system is that what you are designing is *not* a computer, even though its interface might be dominated by a computer-like bitmap display. Your users will approach your product with very specific expectations of what the product can do (if it is an appliance or familiar handheld device) or with very few expectations (if you are designing a public kiosk). The last thing that you want to do is bring all the baggage — the idioms and terminology — of the desktop computer world with you to a simple device like a camera or microwave oven. Similarly, users of scientific and other technical equipment expect to quickly and directly access data and controls within their domain, not wade through a computer operating system or file system to find what they need.

Programmers, especially those who have designed for desktop platforms, can easily forget that even though they are designing software, they are not always designing it for computers in the usual sense: devices with large color screens, desktop metaphors, lots of power and memory, full size keyboards, and mouse pointing devices. Few, if any, of these assumptions are valid for most embedded devices. Does it make sense, for instance, to include a Menu button on a TV remote control? Certainly you need to access functions, but Menu is a term from the world of computers, not TVs. Similarly, Cancel would not be an appropriate term for turning off an oven timer.

A much better approach than trying to squeeze a computer interface into the form factor of an embedded system is to see the device you're designing for what it is and to then figure out how digital technology can be applied to enhance the experience for its users. Microsoft could learn a lesson here with its PocketPC interface, although like all Microsoft products, it has improved gradually with each new version.

Integrate your hardware and software design

From an interaction standpoint, one defining characteristic of embedded systems is the often closely intertwined relationship of hardware and software components of the interface. Unlike desktop computers, where the focus of user attention is on a large, high-resolution, color screen, most embedded systems offer hardware controls that command greater user attention and that must integrate smoothly with user tasks. Due to cost, power, and form factor constraints, hardware-based navigation and input controls must often take the place of on-screen equivalents. Therefore, they need to be specifically tailored to the requirements of the software portion of the interface as to well as to the goals and ergonomic needs of the user.

It is therefore critical to design the hardware and software elements of the system's interface — and the interactions between them — simultaneously, and from a goal-directed and an ergonomic perspective. This seldom occurs in the standard development process, where hardware engineering teams regularly hand off completed mechanical and industrial designs to the software teams, who must then accommodate them, regardless of what is best from the user's perspective.

As a design practitioner, you need to lobby in your organization to begin the process of interaction design before the hardware platform has been completely specified. Many of the best, most innovative digital devices available today, such as the Handspring Treo and the Apple iPod, were designed from such a holistic perspective, where hardware and software combine seamlessly to create a compelling and effective experience for users (see Figure 38-1).

Figure 38-1: A Cooper design for a smart desktop phone, exhibiting strong integration of hardware and software controls. Users can easily adjust volume/speakerphone, dial new numbers, control playback of voicemail messages with hardware controls, and manage known contacts/numbers, incoming calls, call logs, voicemail, and conferencing features using the touch screen and thumbwheel. Rather than attempt to load too much functionality into the system, the design focuses on making the most frequent and important phone features much easier to use. Note the finger-sized regions devoted to touchable areas on the screen and use of text hints to reinforce the interactions.

Context drives the design

Another distinct difference between embedded systems and desktop applications is the importance of environmental context. Although there can sometimes be contextual concerns with desktop applications, designers can generally assume that most software running on the desktop will be used on a computer that is stationary, located in a relatively quiet and private location. Although this is becoming less true as laptops gain both the power of desktop systems and wireless capabilities, it remains the case that users will, by necessity of the form factor, be stationary and out of the hubbub even when using laptops.

Exactly the opposite is true for many embedded systems, which are either designed for on-the-go use (handhelds) or are stationary but in a location at the center of public activity (kiosks). Even embedded systems that are mostly stationary and secluded (like household appliances) have a strong contextual element: A host juggling plates of hot food for a dinner party is going to be distracted, not in a state of mind to navigate a cumbersome set of controls for a smart oven. Similarly, a technician on a manufacturing floor should not be required to focus on cumbersome test equipment controls — that kind of distraction could be life-threatening in some circumstances.

Thus the design of embedded systems must match very closely the context of use. For hand-helds, this context concerns how and where the device is physically handled. How is it held? Is it a one-handed or two-handed device? Where is it kept when not in immediate use? What other activities are users engaged in while using the device? In what environments is it being used? Is it loud, bright, or dark, there? How does the user feel about being seen and heard using the device if he is in public? We'll discuss some of these issues in detail a bit later.

For kiosks, the contextual concerns focus more on the environment in which the kiosk is being placed and also on social concerns: What role does the kiosk play in the environment? Is the kiosk in the main flow of public traffic? Does it provide ancillary information, or is it the main attraction itself? Does the architecture of the environment guide people to the kiosks when appropriate? How many people are likely to use the kiosk at a time? Are there sufficient numbers of kiosks to satisfy demand without a long wait? Is there sufficient room for the kiosk and kiosk traffic without impeding other user traffic? We touch on these and other questions shortly.

Use modes judiciously

Desktop computer applications are often rich in modes: The software can be in many different states in which input and other controls are mapped to different behaviors. Tool palettes are a good example: Choose a tool, and mouse and keyboard actions will be mapped to a set of functions defined by that particular tool; choose a new tool, and the behavior resulting from similar input changes.

Most embedded systems have difficulty supporting a large set of modes for these reasons:

✓ Screen real estate is limited, and therefore so is the ability to clearly convey mode changes.

✓ Embedded-systems users are most often (as in the case of many kiosks) beginners rather than intermediates and usually do not have time to familiarize themselves with modes and navigation between modes.

✓ Use of modes results in navigational excise when input mechanisms are constrained.

Embedded systems designs should in general avoid use of modes. If modes must be used, they should be limited in number; and mode switches should, ideally, result naturally from situational changes in context. For example, it makes sense for a PDA/phone convergence device to shift into telephone mode when an incoming call is received and to shift back to its previous mode when the call is terminated. (Permitting a call while other data is being accessed is a preferable alternative.) If modes are truly necessary, they should be clearly accessible in the interface, and the exit path should also be immediately clear. The four hardware application buttons on most Palm OS hand-helds are a good example of clearly marked modes.

In contrast, most cellular telephones offer extremely poor navigation of too many modes, which are usually organized in a hierarchical structure requiring multiple key presses to access. Most users of cell phones use only the dialing and address book functionality in their phones and quickly get lost if they try to access other functions. Even an important function such as silencing the ringer is often beyond the expertise of average phone users. Handspring has neatly addressed this problem by providing a clearly marked Ringer Mode switch next to the Power button on its Treo communicators, an interface feature that every cell phone should emulate.

The usability of a mode is completely dependent on input and display mechanisms. Both the input and display facilities of virtually every embedded system are significantly smaller and fewer than those found on a desktop computer. This means that modes implemented for embedded systems devices are, typically, difficult to perceive and navigate. Modes should, therefore, be reduced in number and in complexity.

Limit the scope

Most embedded systems are used in specific contexts and for specific purposes. Avoid the temptation to turn these systems into general-purpose computers. Users will be better served by devices that enable them to do a limited set of tasks more effectively, than by devices that attempt to address too many disparate tasks in one place. Devices such as Microsoft PocketPC handhelds, which of late have attempted to emulate full desktop systems, run the risk of alienating users with cumbersome interfaces saturated with functions whose only reason for inclusion is that they currently exist on desktop systems.

Many devices share information with desktop systems. It makes sense to approach the design of such systems from a desktop-centric point of view: The device is an extension or *satellite* of the desktop, providing key information and functions in contexts where the desktop system isn't available. Scenarios can help you determine what functions are truly useful for such satellite systems.

Balance navigation with display density

Most embedded systems (kiosks being the exception) are constrained by limited display real estate. Handheld devices are constrained by their form factor and power requirements. For appliances, cost is often the determining factor. Whatever the reasons, designers must create designs that make the best use of the display technology available, while meeting the information needs of users. Although it's possible to be a bit more lax with the layout of large displays, every pixel and every square millimeter of display counts for embedded systems. Such limitations in display real estate almost always result in a tradeoff between clarity of information displayed and complexity of navigation. By appropriately limiting the scope of functions, you can ameliorate this situation somewhat; but the tension between display and navigation almost always exists to some degree.

You must carefully map out embedded systems displays, developing a hierarchy of information. Determine what is the most important information to get across, and make that feature the most prominent. Then, look to see what ancillary information can still fit on the screen. Try to avoid flashing between different sets of information by blinking the screen. For example, an oven with a digital control might display both the temperature you set it to reach and how close it is to reaching that temperature by flashing between the two numerical values. However, this solution easily leads to confusion about which number is which. A better solution is to display the temperature that the oven has been set to reach and next to that, to show a small bar graph that registers how close to the desired temperature the oven currently is. You must also leave room in the display to show the state of associated hardware controls; or better yet, use controls that can display their own state, such as hardware buttons with lamps or that maintain a physical state (for example, toggles, switches, sliders, knobs).

Minimize input complexity

Almost all embedded systems share the quality of having a simplified input system rather than a keyboard or desktop-style pointing device. This means that any input to the system—especially textual input—is awkward, slow, and difficult for users. Even the most sophisticated of these input systems—touch screens, voice recognition, handwriting recognition, and thumboards among them—are cumbersome in comparison to full-sized keyboards and mice. Thus, it's important that input be limited and simplified as much as possible.

Devices such as RIM's Blackberry and the Danger Hiptop make effective use of a thumbwheel as their primary selection mechanism: Spinning the wheel very rapidly scrolls through possible choices, and pressing the wheel (or a nearby button) selects a given item. Both of these devices also make use of thumboards when textual data entry is necessary.

In contrast, the Handspring Treo makes use of a touch screen and a thumboard. This would be effective if you could adequately activate everything on the Treo screen by the touch of a finger. However, most Palm screen widgets are too small and require you to use a stylus to make accurate selections. This means that you must switch between stylus and thumboard, making input more awkward than it needs to be. Palm's Tungsten devices address a similar problem with the addition of a four-way directional pad and selection button, which allows stylus-free navigation of screen controls.

Kiosks, whose screens are usually larger, should nonetheless avoid textual input whenever possible. Touchscreens can display soft keyboards if they are large enough; each virtual key should be large enough to make it difficult for the user to accidentally mistype. Touchscreens should also avoid idioms that involve dragging; single-tap idioms are easier to control and more obvious (when given proper affordance) to novice users.

Customize for your platform

In the desktop world, software vendors sometimes try to develop interfaces across multiple platforms: The program looks and acts the same (or close to it) on MacOS, Windows, and Unix, for example. Not only does this create an enormous amount of programming overhead for the programmers, but it also usually ends up displeasing users, who would rather use an application native to their platforms, which takes advantage of the unique features, facilities, and interface idioms of their personal working environment.

This issue is compounded for embedded system software. It is almost impossible to port a desktop product to a device platform, and it is equally futile to try to develop cross-platform interfaces for devices with divergent operating systems and hardware profiles. In the embedded systems world, it is simply best to program and customize directly for each platform.

Designing for Handhelds

Handheld devices present special challenges for interaction designers. Because they are designed specifically for mobile use, these devices must be small, lightweight, economical in power consumption, ruggedly built, and easy to hold and manipulate in busy, distracting situations.

Especially for handhelds, close collaboration between interaction designers, industrial designers, programmers, and mechanical engineers is a real necessity. Of particular concern are size and clarity of display, ease of input and control, and sensitivity to context. This section discusses, in more detail, these concerns and useful approaches to address them. The following are the most useful interaction and interface principles for designing handheld devices:

✓ **Think about how the device will be held and carried.** Physical models are essential to understanding how a device will be manipulated. The models should at least reflect the size, shape, and articulation (flip covers and so on) of the device, and they are more effective when weight is also taken into account. These models should be employed by designers in context and key path scenarios to validate proposed form factors.

✓ **Determine early on whether the device will support one-handed or two-handed operation.** Again, scenarios should make it clear which modes are acceptable to users in various contexts. It's okay for a device that is intended primarily for one-handed use to support some advanced functions that require two-handed use, as long as they are needed infrequently. A handheld inventory tool, for example, that allows all counting to be done single-handedly, but then requires two hands to submit the entered data confers no advantage because the Submit function is part of a frequent-use scenario.

✓ **Consider whether the device will be a satellite or a standalone.** Most handheld data devices are best designed as *satellites* of desktop data systems. Palm and Symbian devices both succeed best as portable systems that communicate with desktop systems or servers. Rather than replicate all desktop functions, they are geared primarily towards accessing and viewing information and provide only lightweight input and edit features. (Full size, folding keyboards are available for these systems; but these, in essence, convert the device into a very compact desktop system while the keyboard is in use.) The latest handheld models extend the idea of a tethered satellite into the realm of wireless connectivity, making the idea of the satellite device even more powerful and appropriate.

On the other hand, some devices, such as standard cell phones, are truly designed to be standalone. It's possible to upload phone numbers from PCs to many cell phones, but most users never try to do so because of the interaction complexity. Such standalone devices are most successful when they focus on a narrow set of functions, but provide world-class behaviors for those functions. The RIM Blackberry is a great example of a narrowly focused, data-centric handheld; it excels at one function: real-time wireless reception, viewing, and sending of corporate e-mail. Blackberry devices include support for other PIM (personal information management) functions, but these are typically used infrequently. It is wireless e-mail that defines the product.

✓ **Avoid use of pluralized and pop-up windows.** On small, low-resolution screens, floating windows typically have no place. Interfaces, in this regard, should resemble sovereign posture applications (see Chapter 8), taking the full-screen real estate. Modeless dialogs should be avoided at all cost, and modal dialogs and errors should, whenever possible, be replaced using the techniques discussed in Chapters 33 and 34.

✓ **Strive for integration of functionality to minimize navigation.** Handheld devices are used in a variety of specific contexts. By exploring context scenarios, you can get a good idea of what functions need to be integrated to provide a seamless, goal-directed experience.

Most *convergence* devices run the risk of pleasing nobody by attempting to do too much. Communicators such as the Treo are at their best when they integrate functionality for a more seamless experience of communication-related functions. These devices, currently, do a reasonable job of integrating the phone and address book: When a call arrives, you can see the full name from the address book and, by tapping on a name in the address book, you can dial it. However, this integration could be taken a step further. Clicking on a name in an address book could show you *all* documents known to the communicator that are associated with that person: appointments, e-mails, phone calls from the log, memos including the caller's name, Web sites associated with him, and so on. Clicking on one of these documents could then take you to an interface to respond appropriately to that person. Some recent applications for communicators, such as iambic Inc.'s Agendus, are beginning to take this approach to integrating what were once different applications into a more seamless flow that matches user goals.

✓ **On-screen controls should be larger and brighter.** If you are using a touch screen on your device, controls should be large enough to be touchable by fingers. Styli can get lost and because of this (and the nerd factor), teenage users are often put off by the use of a stylus. Handheld screens are often low power and may have low brightness and contrast, so small icons and controls may also be difficult to see in some lighting conditions. Finally, because handheld interfaces must often be compartmentalized into several screens (only some of which may be used in any given context), handheld screens should resemble the transient posture applications (see Chapter 8) with large, high contrast, and colorful (if available) controls.

✓ **Use larger, sans-serif fonts.** Serif fonts are hard to read at low resolution; sans-serif fonts should be used for low-resolution handheld displays.

✓ **Don't require dragging.** Touch screens can support dragging, but it is difficult for users to perform, and risks accidental scratching of the screen. Ideally, a hardware control such as RIM's Blackberry thumbwheel or Palm's Up and Down buttons should provide the primary mechanism for scrolling. Drag-and-drop idioms should be avoided as well.

✓ **Don't require shifting input modes.** As mentioned earlier, input should remain as simple as possible. When the device sports a keypad or thumbboard, it should not also require a cumbersome switch from one-handed to two-handed use or a stylus to tap a screen. It is fine to allow both types of input independently, but requiring constant input mode switches in mid-use can lead to user frustration.

✓ **Clearly indicate when there is more data off screen.** Many people aren't used to the idea of a small screen with scrolling information. If there is more data than fits on a screen, make sure to boldly indicate that more data is available, ideally with a hint as to how to access it.

Designing for Kiosks

On the surface, kiosks may appear to have much in common with desktop interfaces: large, colorful screens and reasonably beefy processors behind them. But as far as user interactions are concerned, the similarity ends there. Kiosk users, in comparison with sovereign desktop application users, are at best infrequent users of kiosks and, most typically, use any given kiosk once. Furthermore, kiosk users will either have one very specific goal in mind when approaching a kiosk or no readily definable goal at all. Kiosk users typically don't have access to keyboards or pointing devices, and often wouldn't be able to use either effectively if they did. Finally, kiosk users are typically in a public environment, full of noise and distractions, and may be accompanied by others who will be using the kiosk in tandem with them. Each of these environmental issues has a bearing on kiosk design.

Kiosk posture and navigation

Because kiosks are used infrequently by any one user, and typically for a relatively brief span of time, kiosk interfaces should be weighted towards the transient posture described in Chapter 8. This means large, colorful, engaging interfaces with clear affordances for controls, clear mappings between hardware controls (if any) and their corresponding software functions, and minimal required navigation. As in the design of handhelds, floating windows and dialogs should be avoided; any such information or behavior is best integrated into a single, full screen (as in sovereign-posture applications). Kiosks thus tread an interesting middle ground between the two most common desktop postures.

Because kiosks often guide users through a process or a set of information screen by screen, contextual navigation takes on more importance than global navigation. The important navigational paradigm becomes "Where can/do I go from here?" rather than simply "Where can I go?" This said, it's important for kiosks whose primary purpose is transactional (see below) to provide escape hatches that allow users to cancel transactions and start over at any point.

Transaction versus exploration

Kiosks generally fall into two categorical types: transactional and explorational. Transactional kiosks are those that provide some tightly scoped transaction or service. These include bank machines (ATMs), ticketing machines such as those used in airports, train and bus depots, and some movie theaters. Even vending machines can be considered a simple type of transactional kiosk. Users of transactional kiosks have very specific goals in mind: to get cash, a ticket, a Tootsie Roll, or some specific piece of information. These users have no interest in anything but accomplishing their goals as quickly and painlessly as possible.

Explorational kiosks are most often found in museums. Educational and entertainment-oriented kiosks are typically not a main attraction, but provide additional information and a richer experience for users who have come to see other, possibly (but not necessarily) related exhibits. Explorational kiosks are somewhat different from transactional kiosks in that users typically have few expectations when approaching them. They may be curious, or have a vague desire to be entertained or enlightened, but have little in the way of end goals in mind. For explorational kiosks, it is the act of exploring that must engage the user. Therefore, the kiosk's interface must not only be clear and easy to master in terms of navigation, but it must also be aesthetically pleasing and visually (and possibly audibly) exciting to users. Each screen must be interesting in itself, but also encourage users to further explore the system.

Interaction in a public environment

Transactional kiosks, as a rule, require no special enticements to attract users. However, they do need to be placed in an optimal location to both be obviously visible and to handle the flow of user traffic they will generate. Use wayfinding and sign systems in conjunction with these kiosks for most effectiveness. Some transactional kiosks, especially ATMs, need to take into account security issues: If their location seems insecure (or is in actuality), users will avoid them or use them at their risk. Architectural planning for transactional kiosks should occur at the same time as the interaction and industrial design planning.

As with transactional kiosks, place explorational kiosks carefully and use wayfinding systems in conjunction with them. They must not obstruct any main attractions, and yet must be close enough to the attractions to be perceived as connected to them. There must be adequate room for people to gather: Exploration kiosks are more likely to be used by groups (such as family members). A particular challenge lies in choosing the right number of kiosks to install at a location — companies employing transactional kiosks often engage in user flow research at a site to determine optimum numbers. People don't linger long at transactional kiosks, and they are usually more willing to wait in line because they have a concrete end goal in mind. Explorational kiosks, on the other hand, encourage lingering, which makes them unattractive to onlookers. Because potential users have few expectations of the contents of an explorational kiosk, it becomes difficult for them to justify waiting in line to use one. It is safe to assume that most people will only approach an explorational kiosk when it is vacant.

When designing kiosk interfaces, carefully consider the use of sound. Explorational kiosks seem naturals for use of rich, audible feedback and content, but volume levels should be chosen so as not to encroach on the experience of the main attraction such kiosks often support. Audible feedback should be used sparingly for transactional kiosks; but it can be useful, for example, to help remind users to take back their bankcard or the change from their purchases.

Managing input

Most kiosks make use either of touch screens or hardware buttons and keypads that are mapped to objects and functions on the screen. In the case of touch screens, the same principles apply here as for other touch screen interfaces:

✓ Touchable objects should be large enough to be manipulated with a finger, high contrast, colorful, and well separated on the screen to avoid accidental selection.

✓ It may be tempting to make use of an on-screen keyboard for entering data on touch screen kiosks. However, this input mechanism should be used as a last resort — when, for example, an arbitrary code is required (a keypad may be more effective for this, too) or some other information that can't reasonably be chosen from a list.

✓ Drag and drop should be avoided as an idiom, and scrolling of any kind should be avoided on kiosks except when absolutely necessary.

Some kiosks make use of hardware buttons mapped to on-screen functions in lieu of touch screens, which are more expensive and more prone to malfunction. As in handheld systems, the key concern is that these mappings remain consistent, with similar functions mapped to the same buttons from screen to screen. These buttons also should not be placed so far from the screen or arranged spatially so that the mapping becomes unclear (see Chapter 11 for a more detailed discussion of mapping issues).

Designing for Audible Interfaces

Audible interfaces, such as those found in voice message systems and automated call centers, have some special challenges. Navigation is the most critical challenge because it is easy to get lost in a tree of functionality (which these systems almost always are) with no means of visualizing where one is in the hierarchy. The following are some simple principles for designing usable audible interfaces.

- ✓ **Organize and name functions according to user mental models.** This is important in any design, but doubly important when functions are described only verbally, and only in context of the current function. Be sure to examine context scenarios to determine what the most important functions are, and make them the most easily reachable.

- ✓ **Always signpost the currently available functions.** The system should, after every user action, restate the current available activities and how to invoke them.

- ✓ **Always provide a way to get back one step and to the top level.** The interface should, after every action, tell the user how to go back one step in the function structure (usually up one node in the tree) and how to get to the top level of the function tree.

- ✓ **Always provide a means to speak with a human.** If appropriate, the interface should give the user instructions on how to switch to a human assistant after every action, especially if the user seems to be having trouble.

- ✓ **Give the user enough time to respond.** Systems usually require verbal or telephone keypad entry of information. Testing should be done to determine an appropriate length of time to wait; keep in mind that phone keypads can be awkward and very slow for entering textual information.

Afterword: Dealing with the Inmates

Since *About Face* was first published in 1995, the world of digital products has certainly changed. The Web changed the way we think about information access, and the dotcoms have come and gone. As per Moore's Law, hardware has gotten an order of magnitude faster, and storage two orders of magnitude larger. Handheld data devices, then a cumbersome curiosity, are now everywhere and are beginning to merge with wireless telephones and digital cameras.

But for all the steaming piles of glorious technology around us, our lives are not significantly better. Computers are still hard to use. Cameras and phones sometimes crash and reboot instead of making calls and taking pictures when we'd like them to. And now our DVD players blink 12:00 after power loss along with our VCRs.

When will we learn that it isn't about the technology, but rather about the *behavior* of these products? Why should anything be different just because of hardware and bandwidth improvements? The old problem of stupid, rude, inappropriate software and software-enabled products still exists, same as ever.

Ultimately, we will make digital products better by examining and satisfying the user's goals. We will not make them better by moving to new platforms or by improving technology. Our technology is superb. What it lacked in 1995, and still lacks today, is better consideration of the human.

What is required is more than just great design. What we need are product development organizations that foster great design. Designers need to become not only advocates for the user, but also advocates for change within their organizations. Old thinking, based on old assumptions about technology constraints, permeates many development organizations. It is something that practitioners must actively take steps to overcome.

Scarcity Thinking

We now have a quarter-century of refinements to the PARC paradigm. We know how to create good error messages, confirmation dialog boxes, and alerts. But we still don't have much experience creating rich, visual, unified interfaces that work hard to support users. We have years of experience building systems with robust data integrity and sophisticated hierarchical file systems, but we don't yet have experience creating systems with data immunity and attribute-based storage systems.

The problem is simple: Everything we know about computers is wrong! Fifty years ago, there was less computing power on the entire planet than is in your wristwatch today. There is more computer power in your family car than there is in the space shuttle. Just twenty-five years ago, computers were precious commodities: extremely expensive, limited, and weak. In 1975, a state-of-the-art IBM 370/135 mainframe had *144K* of main memory. It had two 100 MB hard-disk drives, each the size of a refrigerator. It had a card reader, a punch, and a chain printer. It resided in its own room, nestled deep inside its own building.

Computing resources then were always very scarce. There was never enough memory, never enough storage, never enough cycles, and never enough bandwidth. If you wanted to be good at what you did, you worked hard to maximize the scarcest resource — you made sure that the CPU got all the breaks. You developed systems to maximize the use of disk, of RAM, even of punched cards.

The senior programmers and computer scientists in business and academia who lived through that era learned to think in terms of this rarified access to computing resources: **scarcity thinking**. And these same men and women, who know deep down in their guts that computer resources are scarce, are still setting the pace in the software industry today.

Abundance Thinking

We have, within a short score of years, left behind a world of scarcity and entered a world of abundance, with even greater realms of abundance just beyond the horizon. Our computers are as powerful as we want them to be. We have all the bits and bytes and cycles we need to design software that really serves humans.

The opposite of scarcity thinking is **abundance thinking**, and good interaction designers will have this sensibility. Abundance thinking frees designers from worrying about memory, storage, or cycles. They must worry, instead, about users, and they have the design talent and training to create interfaces and behaviors that make users more effective.

How to do you change people's minds about these issues? One method is to argue from authority. Being viewed as an expert is a possible starting step, and that step involves either in-depth experience or specialized training.

Training As a Designer

Interaction designers do not often come from the ranks of programmers, but are nonetheless technically savvy people. Non-technical people cannot imagine the wonderful new things that computers can do for us. Non-technical people do not understand the delicate balance between a CPU with time on its hands and one rushing to complete ten million instructions before the user's next keystroke. The non-technical people will have our computers treating us in the same lousy way they already do, but with prettier pictures. It is not obvious what computers can do for us. It takes natural talent, skill, training, and experience.

Pursuing academic training

In the last several years, programs across the country have begun offering courses in interaction design. Even so, interaction design is a new discipline that is still being defined in the academic setting. There are only a few institutions in the world offering graduate degree programs specifically in interaction design, and although their curricula share similarities, they are by no means standardized (which may very well be a good thing). Most of these and other computer-related, human-computer interaction (HCI), or new media design programs are outgrowths of either art schools or technical departments (often architecture or computer science departments) at larger institutions, each of which brings its own history, perspective, and preconceptions to its teaching approach.

There isn't yet agreement (although this is, happily, starting to change) in the academic community about what the core elements of an interaction design curriculum should be, or how to approach the teaching of that curriculum. Art schools tend to approach interaction design as a means of personal or brand expression rather than as an approach to solving product definition and usability problems; technical departments tend to teach interaction design from the perspective of exploring and implementing technologies rather than discovering and addressing human goals. Programs that emphasize HCI techniques tend to focus on cognitive theory and user research, with less emphasis on design methods and practices (the craft of design). Many design programs still focus on tools rather than methods, but that too is changing.

More universities still teach empirical usability engineering and empirical HCI than teach design. But this is changing, and more and more interaction designers are graduating from university programs every day.

Many academic institutions with new or established interaction design and HCI programs are beginning to develop an understanding of interaction design and the qualities and skills required of interaction designers. Some of the most forward-thinking of these institutions include:

- ✓ Carnegie Mellon University

- ✓ Institute of Design, Illinois Institute of Technology

- ✓ Interaction Design Institute Ivrea

- ✓ New York University, Interactive Telecommunications Program

- ✓ North Carolina State University

- ✓ University of Art and Design Helsinki

- ✓ University of California, Berkeley Institute of Design

- ✓ Virginia Commonwealth University

Other paths

Do you really need a Master's degree or Ph.D. to practice interaction design? There are advantages to rigorous studio training combined with adequate breadth of courses (in art, business, humanities, and science), to be sure. But some things, as in any discipline, can't easily be taught. Empathy with users and the ability to conceptualize working solutions (and then refine them ruthlessly) are difficult skills to teach. Some employers look for people with these talents, regardless of their formal education.

If you are considering interaction design as a possible career shift, here are a few things to keep in mind:

✓ Designers seldom code — if you are attached to programming, all power to you: The world needs more design-sensitive programmers. But unless you have complete control over your projects, you will be short-changing your users by trying to design and develop at the same time — it's a conflict of interest. So, if you can't stomach the thought of abandoning programming, interaction design may not be for you.

✓ Usability research is tremendously important, but it isn't design. It identifies problems, but doesn't (except at the most detailed level) suggest solutions. Can you envision and refine broad and detailed solutions, or are you more comfortable extracting facts from known situations? If the latter suits you better, usability may be a better focus for your interests.

✓ Temperament is important. The best interaction designers are interested in everything and willing (even eager) to immerse themselves in unfamiliar territories to learn and absorb. They are also very concerned about people as individuals and the human condition in general.

✓ Designers all need some basic skills; interaction designers should be able to draw or write well (doing both is rare and valued) and must be able to communicate superbly with both their colleagues and their clients. The toughest skill to acquire is that combination of creative insight and analytical thinking that is the hallmark of a great interaction designer.

No matter what the basis of your training is, as a design practitioner, you'll need to work closely with people in other roles within a larger development team. In all likelihood, *you* will need to be the agent of change in your organization to get people thinking in a goal-directed fashion. It's an uphill struggle, but one that offers great personal and organizational rewards. Getting recognition of your authority is key, but this means you'll need to deliver on several responsibilities.

Working with the Product Team

When designers synthesize a solution, programmers often have difficulty accepting their authority and tend to take matters into their own hands. Anyone who has worked for a while with programmers has had this experience: The team meets and everyone agrees on the course of action. Everyone acknowledges their tasks and what the program will look like. Two weeks later, when the group reconvenes, a programmer says — without any trace of irony — "Yeah, I decided to do it this way instead. I thought it was better," while the rest of the team gnashes their collective teeth. Even if it *is* better (which isn't often), it is still wrong to change things unilaterally when a team is depending on you.

A rigorous development process that incorporates design as an equal partner with engineering, marketing, and business management — and which includes well-defined responsibilities and authority for each group — can dramatically improve the situation. The following division of responsibilities, balanced by an equal division of authority, can dramatically improve design success and organizational support of the product throughout the development cycle and beyond (Korman, 2001). You should agitate for these in your own organization:

✓ **The design team** has responsibility for users' satisfaction with the product. Most organizations do not currently hold *anyone* responsible for this. To carry out this responsibility, designers must have the authority to decide how the product will behave. They also need access to information: They must observe and speak to potential users about their needs, to engineers about technological opportunities and constraints, to marketing about opportunities and requirements, and to management about the kind of product to which the organization will commit.

✓ **The engineering team** has authority over the system technology (the implementation details) that users do not see. For the design to deliver its benefit, engineering must have the responsibility for building, *as specified,* the behaviors that the designers define, while keeping on budget and on schedule. Engineers, therefore, need a clear description of the product's behaviors, which will guide what they build and drive their time and cost estimates. This description must come from the design team.

✓ **The marketing team** has responsibility for the product's appeal to customers, so they must have authority over all communications with the customer. (Remember that customers are not the same as users; customers purchase products, but don't necessarily use them as end users would.) In order to do this, the team members need access to information resources including the results of designers' research, as well as research of their own.

✓ **Management** has responsibility for the profitability of the resulting product and, therefore has the authority to make decisions about what the other groups will work on. To make those decisions, management needs to receive clear information from the other groups: design's product definitions, marketing's projections of sales, and engineering's projection of the time and cost to create the product.

Working with the Engineering Team

Design and engineering teams must have a healthy working relationship for a product to be a success (Korman, 2001). Many engineers have come to believe (from unfortunate past experiences) that designers are not entirely trustworthy. Software engineers may even call a design *impossible* in order to take control when they distrust designers' judgment. Therefore, the design team needs to make an extra effort to speak the language of the development team.

Designers have an obligation to understand the technology platform well enough that engineers can implement what they design. However, designers should concern themselves less with ease of implementation, than with *possibility*. Decisions based on the ease of implementation should be a management call that occurs only after engineering creates a time and cost estimate based on the design. This also implies that *management should not set an implementation deadline until they receive the time and cost estimate from engineering.*

During the design process, designers must draw on the domain knowledge of the engineers to understand the technological opportunities and constraints that will affect which behaviors the product can deploy. Designers must also create clear and appropriately detailed form and behavior specifications; a well-reasoned and meticulous design specification quells the fears of engineers because it leaves few interface questions unanswered. Thus, it reduces the likelihood of change requests or missteps that could disrupt engineering schedules.

After the designers hand off the design specifications to engineering, they remain as resources for the engineers. No specification can anticipate every possible behavior and situation, so the designers must support the specification with explanations, elaborations, and extemporaneous decisions on design details as the engineers proceed with the creation of the product. This also acts as a check on the designers, ensuring that they deliver as clear a specification as possible.

In effect, there is a reversal of relationship that happens at the handoff of the design specification: Before the handoff, engineers work in the service of designers, providing technology wisdom. After the handoff, designers work in the service of engineers, providing design wisdom throughout the implementation phase.

Back to the Future

Things *can* be different in the world of digital technology. There is endless potential for software and digital products that are designed from the outset to help users reach their goals, instead of being programmed for the convenience of the computer.

The rise and fall of the New Economy has been a sober wakeup call to high-tech markets. Technology sales are down. People realize that they have all the horsepower and more features than they could ever want from last year's PCs and cell phones. What they don't have — and aren't getting from anyone — are products that are truly a pleasure to use. The industry has received a vote of no confidence from consumers who are tired of useless add-on features, and looking, futile though the quest may be, for solutions that address their real problems. The design of products that meet user needs through appropriate behaviors is the future of the industry — the only future that makes sense. The New Economy must be about meeting the real needs of real people, not about the inexorable march of technology, crushing us all under its silicon-heeled boots.

We hope that this book has made a difference to you, and to the rest of the practitioners who have it on their shelves. It's been a hard, uphill struggle for us interaction designers to get where we are now, and the challenges aren't over yet. But as long as there are people who see, as we do, the importance of the *human* side of technology, and are not willing to let the technologists forget it, we have the hope of a brighter, more human future.

Appendix A

Axioms

CHAPTER 1

✓ Interaction design is not guesswork.

CHAPTER 2

✓ User interfaces should avoid implementation models in favor of user mental models.

✓ Goal-directed interactions reflect user mental models.

✓ Don't replicate mechanical age artifacts in interfaces without information-age enhancements.

✓ Significant change must be significantly better.

CHAPTER 3

✓ Nobody wants to remain a beginner.

✓ Optimize for intermediates.

✓ Imagine users as very intelligent but very busy.

CHAPTER 5

✓ Don't make the user feel stupid.

✓ Design each interface for a single, primary persona.

CHAPTER 8

✓ Users of sovereign applications are perpetual intermediates.

CHAPTER 9

✓ No matter how cool your interface is, less of it would be better.

✓ Well-orchestrated user interfaces are transparent.

✓ Design for the probable case; provide for the possible case.

✓ Ask forgiveness, not permission.

✓ Asking questions isn't the same as providing choices.

✓ Hide the ejector seat levers.

CHAPTER 10

✓ Eliminating excise makes the user more effective.

✓ Don't weld on training wheels.

✓ Don't stop the proceedings with idiocy.

✓ Never make the user ask permission.

✓ Allow input wherever you have output.

CHAPTER 11

✓ Inflect the interface for typical navigation.

✓ Users make commensurate effort if the rewards justify it.

CHAPTER 13

✓ Disks and files don't help users achieve their goals.

CHAPTER 14

✓ Software should behave like a considerate human.

CHAPTER 15

✓ The computer does the work, and the user does the thinking.

✓ If it's worth the user entering, it's worth the program remembering.

CHAPTER 17

✓ An error may not be your fault, but it's your responsibility.

✓ Audit, don't edit.

CHAPTER 19

✓ A visual interface is based on visual patterns.

✓ Visually distinguish elements that behave differently.

✓ Visually communicate function and behavior.

✓ Visually show what; textually show which.

✓ Obey standards unless there is a truly superior alternative.

✓ Consistency doesn't imply rigidity.

CHAPTER 20

✓ Users would rather be successful than knowledgeable.

✓ All idioms must be learned; good idioms need to be learned only once.

✓ Never bend your interface to fit a metaphor.

CHAPTER 21

✓ Rich visual interaction is the key to successful direct manipulation.

✓ Visually hint at pliancy.

CHAPTER 24

✓ Provide an escape from dragging and inform the user about it.

CHAPTER 25

✓ A dialog box is another room; have a good reason to go there.

✓ The utility of any interaction idiom is context-dependent.

CHAPTER 26

✓ A multitude of control-laden dialog boxes doth not a good user interface make.

✓ Never scroll text horizontally.

✓ Use bounded controls for bounded input.

CHAPTER 27

✓ Provide a pedagogic vector with menus and dialogs.

CHAPTER 29

✓ Use ToolTips with all toolbar and iconic controls.

CHAPTER 30

✓ Put primary interactions in the primary window.

✓ Dialogs break flow.

CHAPTER 31

✓ All idioms have practical limits.

CHAPTER 33

✓ User interface is not only skin deep.

✓ Make errors as impossible as possible.

✓ Users get humiliated when software tells them they failed.

✓ No crisis inside a computer is worth humiliating a human.

CHAPTER 34

✓ Do, don't ask.

✓ Make all actions reversible.

✓ Provide modeless feedback to help users avoid mistakes.

Appendix B

Design Tips

CHAPTER 2

✓ Users don't understand Boolean logic.

CHAPTER 6

✓ In early stage design, pretend the interface is magic.

CHAPTER 8

✓ Optimize sovereign applications for full-screen use.

✓ Sovereign interfaces should use conservative visual style.

✓ Sovereign applications can exploit rich input.

✓ Maximize document views within sovereign applications.

✓ Transient applications must be simple, clear, and to the point.

✓ Keep transient applications to a single window and view.

CHAPTER 9

✓ Don't use dialogs to report normalcy.

CHAPTER 13

✓ Save documents and settings automatically.

✓ Put files where users can find them.

✓ Disks are a hack, not a design feature.

CHAPTER 18

✓ Offer shortcuts from the Help menu.

✓ Offer the user a gallery of good-solution templates.

CHAPTER 21

✓ Support both mouse and keyboard use for motion and selection tasks.

✓ Single-click selects data or changes the control state.

✓ Double-click means single-click plus action.

✓ Mouse-down over data means select.

✓ Mouse-down over controls means propose action; mouse-up means commit to action.

✓ Indicating pliancy is the most important role of cursor hinting.

✓ Use cursor hinting to show the meanings of meta-keys.

CHAPTER 22

✓ Make selection visually bold and unambiguous.

✓ Use system highlight colors to show selection.

CHAPTER 23

✓ Drop candidates must visually indicate their receptivity.

✓ The drag cursor must visually indicate the source object.

✓ Any scrollable drag-and-drop target must auto-scroll.

✓ Debounce all drags.

✓ Any program that demands precise alignment must offer a vernier.

CHAPTER 24

✓ Cancel a drag on chord-click.

CHAPTER 25

✓ Build functions into the window where they are used.

CHAPTER 26

✓ Distinguish important text items in lists with graphic icons.

✓ Use non-editable (display) controls for output-only text.

CHAPTER 28

✓ Disable menu items when they are inapplicable.

✓ Use parallel visual symbols on parallel command vectors.

CHAPTER 29

✓ Toolbars provide experienced users fast access to frequently used functions.

CHAPTER 30

✓ Never create a system modal dialog.

✓ Visually differentiate modeless dialogs from modal dialogs.

✓ Give modeless dialog boxes consistent terminating commands.

✓ Never dynamically change the labels of terminating buttons.

✓ Programs must inform the user when they are about to become unresponsive.

✓ Never use transitory dialogs as error messages or confirmations.

CHAPTER 31

✓ All dialog boxes should have title bars.

✓ Use verbs in function dialog title bars.

✓ Use object names in property dialog title bars.

✓ Dialogs should be as small as possible, but no smaller.

✓ Offer OK and Cancel buttons on all modal dialog boxes.

✓ Never use terminating command words in dialog text.

✓ Don't put close boxes on modal dialogs.

✓ Put terminating buttons on the untabbed area of a tabbed dialog.

✓ Don't stack tabs.

CHAPTER 33

✓ Error message boxes stop the proceedings with idiocy.

CHAPTER 37

✓ Transient Web applications should clearly telegraph their functionality.

✓ Transient Web applications must be simple, direct, and to the point.

✓ Transient Web applications should fit into the user's mental models and flow in the context of the rest of the Web site.

✓ Carefully consider the problem of access to user data in Web applications.

CHAPTER 38

✓ Think about how a digital device will be held and carried.

✓ Determine early whether a device will support one-handed or two-handed use.

✓ Consider whether a device will be a satellite or a standalone.

✓ Avoid use of pluralized and pop-up windows on devices.

✓ Strive for integration of functionality to minimize navigation.

✓ Touch screen controls should be large and bright.

✓ Use large, sans-serif fonts on small, low-contrast screens.

✓ Don't require dragging on touch screen interfaces.

✓ Don't require shifting input modes on handheld devices.

✓ Clearly indicate when there is more data off screen in device interfaces.

Appendix C

Bibliography

Alexander, Christopher. 1964. *Notes on the Synthesis of Form*. Harvard University Press.

Alexander, Christopher. 1977. *A Pattern Language*. Oxford University Press.

Alexander, Christopher. 1979. *The Timeless Way of Building*. Oxford University Press.

Beyer, Hugh and Holtzblatt, Karen. 1998. *Contextual Design*. Morgan Kaufmann Publishers.

Borchers, Jan. 2001. *A Pattern Approach to Interaction Design*. John Wiley and Sons.

Borenstein, Nathaniel S. 1994. *Programming As If People Mattered*. Princeton University Press.

Buxton, Bill. 1990. "The 'Natural' Language of Interaction: A Perspective on Non-Verbal Dialogues." Laurel, Brenda, ed. *The Art of Human-Computer Interface Design*. Addison-Wesley.

Carroll, John M. ed. 1995. *Scenario-based Design*. John Wiley and Sons.

Carroll, John M. 2000. *Making Use: Scenario-based Design of Human-Computer Interactions*. The MIT Press.

Constantine, Larry L. and Lockwood, Lucy A. D. 1999. *Software for Use*. Addison-Wesley.

Constantine, Larry L. and Lockwood, Lucy A. D. 2002. forUse Newsletter #26, October. http://www.foruse.com/newsletter/foruse26.htm

Cooper, Alan. 1999. *The Inmates Are Running the Asylum*. SAMS/Macmillan.

Crampton Smith, Gillian and Tabor, Philip. 1996. "The Role of the Artist-Designer." Winograd, Terry, ed. *Bringing Design to Software*. Addison-Wesley.

Csikszentmihalyi, Mihaly. 1991. *Flow: The Psychology of Optimal Experience*. HarperCollins.

DeMarco, Tom and Lister, Timothy R. 1999. *Peopleware*. Dorset House.

Garrett, Jesse James. 2002. *The Elements of User Experience*. New Riders Press.

Gellerman, Saul W. 1963. *Motivation and Productivity*. Amacom Press.

Goodwin, Kim. 2001. "Perfecting Your Personas." Cooper Newsletter, July/August. `http://www.cooper.com/newsletters/2001_07/perfecting_your_personas.htm`

Goodwin, Kim. 2002. "Getting from Research to Personas: Harnessing the Power of Data." `http://www.uiconf.com/7west/goodwin_article_2.htm`

Goodwin, Kim. 2002a. Cooper U Interaction Design Practicum Notes. Cooper.

Grudin, J. and Pruitt, J. 2002. "Personas, Participatory Design and Product Development: An Infrastructure for Engagement." PDC'02: Proceedings of the Participatory Design Conference.

Heckel, Paul. 1994. *The Elements of Friendly Software Design*. Sybex.

Horn, Robert E. 1998. *Visual Language*. Macro Vu Press.

Johnson, Jeff. 2000. *GUI Bloopers*. Morgan Kaufman Publishers.

Kobara, Shiz. 1991. *Visual Design with OSF/Motif*. Addison-Wesley.

Korman, Jonathan. 2001. "Putting People Together to Create Good Products." Cooper Newsletter, September. `http://www.cooper.com/newsletters/2001_09/putting_people_together_to_create_new_ products.htm`

Krug, Steve. 2000. *Don't Make Me Think*! New Riders Press.

Kuutti, Kari. 1995. "Work Processes: Scenarios as a Preliminary Vocabulary." Carroll, John M., ed. *Scenario-based Design*. John Wiley and Sons, Inc.

Laurel, Brenda. 1991. *Computers as Theatre*. Addison-Wesley.

McCloud, Scott. 1994. *Understanding Comics*. Kitchen Sink Press.

Mikkelson, N. and Lee, W. O. 2000. "Incorporating user archetypes into scenario-based design." Proceedings of UPA 2000.

Mullet, Kevin and Sano, Darrell. 1995. *Designing Visual Interfaces*. Sunsoft Press.

Nelson, Theodor Holm. 1990. "The Right Way to Think about Software Design." Laurel, Brenda, ed. *The Art of Human-Computer Interface Design*. Addison-Wesley.

Newman, William M. and Lamming, Michael G. 1995. *Interactive System Design*. Addison-Wesley.

Nielsen, Jakob. 1993. *Usability Engineering*. Academic Press.

Nielsen, Jakob. 2000. *Designing Web Usability*. New Riders Press.

Nielsen, Jakob. 2002. http://www.useit.com

Norman, Donald. 1989. *The Design of Everyday Things*. Currency Doubleday.

Norman, Donald A. 1998. *The Invisible Computer*. The MIT Press.

Norman, Donald. 1994. *Things That Make Us Smart*. Perseus Publishing.

Papanek, Victor. 1984. *Design for the Real World*. Academy Chicago Publishers.

Pinker, Stephen. 1999. *How the Mind Works*. W. W. Norton & Company.

Reimann, Robert. 2002. "Perspectives: Learning Curves." edesign Magazine, Dec.

Reimann, Robert M. 2001. "So You Want to Be an Interaction Designer." Cooper Newsletter, June. http://www.cooper.com/newsletters/2001_06/so_you_want_to_be_an_interaction_designer.htm

Reimann, Robert M, and Forlizzi, Jodi. 2001. "Role: Interaction Designer." Presentation to AIGA Experience Design 2001. http://www.aiga.org/resources/content/5/5/6/documents/Artifact_Forlizzi_Reimann.ppt

Reimann, Robert M. 2002. "Bridging the Gap from Research to Design." Panel Presentation, IBM Make IT Easy Conference.

Rheinfrank, John and Evenson, Shelley. 1996. "Design Languages." Winograd, Terry, ed. *Bringing Design to Software*. Addison-Wesley.

Rosenfeld, Louis and Morville, Peter. 1998. *Information Architecture*. O'Reilly.

Rudolf, Frank. 1998. "Model-Based User Interface Design: Successive Transformations of a Task/Object Model.".Wood, Larry E., ed. *User Interface Design: Bridging the Gap from User Requirements to Design*. CRC Press.

Shneiderman, Ben. 1998. *Designing the User Interface*. Addison-Wesley.

Simon, Hebert. 1996. *The Sciences of the Artificial*. The MIT Press.

SRI Consulting Business Intelligence. 2002. http://www.sric-bi.com/VALS/

Tufte, Edward. 1983. *The Visual Display of Quantitative Information*. Graphic Press.

Veen, Jeffrey. 2000. *The Art and Science of Web Design*. New Riders Press

Verplank, B., Fulton, J., Black, A., and Moggridge, B. 1993. "Observation and Invention: Use of Scenarios in Interaction Design." Tutorial Notes, InterCHI'93, Amsterdam.

Weiss, Michael J. 2000. *The Clustered World: How We Live, What We Buy, and What It All Means About Who We Are*. Little Brown & Company.

Winograd, Terry, ed. 1996. *Bringing Design to Software*. Addison-Wesley.

Wirfs-Brock, Rebecca. 1993. "Designing Scenarios: Making the Case of a Use Case Framework." SmallTalk Report, Nov-Dec.

Wixon, Dennis and Ramey, Judith, eds. 1996. *Field Methods Casebook for Software Design*. John Wiley and Sons.

Wood, Larry E. 1996. "The Ethnographic Interview in User-Centered Task/Work Analysis." Wixon, Dennis and Ramey, Judith, eds. *Field Methods Casebook for Software Design*. John Wiley and Sons.

STYLE GUIDES

Apple Computer. 1992. *Macintosh Human Interface Guidelines*. Addison-Wesley.

Apple Computer. 2002. *Aqua Human Interface Guidelines*. `http://developer.apple.com/techpubs/macosx/Essentials/AquaHIGuidelines/`

Microsoft. 1995. *The Windows Interface Guidelines for Software Design*. Microsoft Press.

Sun MicroSystems. 1990. *Open Look Graphical User Interface Application Style Guidelines*. Addison-Wesley.

Index

Symbols and Numerics

continued

continued

continued

continued

W

www.cooper.com

→ **Sign up for the Cooper Newsletter**
to get our latest articles on personas, design,
research techniques, organizational change,
and more!